Building a Corporate Intranet

How to Order:

For information on quantity discounts contact the publisher: Prima Publishing, P.O. Box 1260BK, Rocklin, CA 95677-1260; (916) 632-4400. On your letterhead include information concerning the intended use of the books and the number of books you wish to purchase. For individual orders, turn to the back of this book for more information.

Building a
Corporate
Intranet

Steve Griswold

Prima Publishing

To my Mom and Dad, for their guidance and all the wonderful things that they have taught me over the years.

Acknowledgments

Behind the glitzy cover and slew of screen shots and text in this book is a large staff of hardworking professionals, without whose dedication and expertise this book would have not been possible. I would like to thank everyone who contributed to this book.

I need to start by thanking Prima Publishing. The entire staff at Prima was extremely helpful, and their guidance and knowledge helped greatly every step of the way.

I would like to thank Don Roche, Publisher, and Alan Harris, Acquisitions Manager, for giving me the opportunity to write this book.

Prima's fabulous three, Debbie Abshier, Susan Christophersen, and Angelique Brittingham, were by my side during the entire development of the book. All three put up with my rambling e-mails at 3:00 a.m. without a gripe.

Debbie Abshier, Acquisitions Editor, answered all my legal questions and always pointed me in the right direction when I needed help. Thanks! To Angelique Brittingham, Development Editor, thanks for keeping my ideas focused, and for your layout wizardry. Angelique kept the table of contents so organized that it is probably embedded in her mind for life. Susan Christophersen, Project Editor, kept my run-ons from running on and on and on, and also caught all my spellling errors—well, most of them. Susan also helped organize, and reminded me when I was getting off the subject <**Steve, get back on track, you are rambling again, SC**>. (Susan, Debbie told me you are up for a raise—hold out for the big bucks.) Thanks, Susan.

To Jill Byus, Assistant Acquisition Editor, I am sorry I did not get to spend more time with you one-on-one during the development of the book. Debbie tells me she was keeping you busy reviewing all my work as it came flooding in. I owe you thanks as well.

Hassan Schroeder, Technical Editor, did such a great job writing the foreword for the book that I kidnapped him as the technical editor. His experience from Sun Microsystems was very helpful and added a different perspective to my PC background. Thanks, Hassan.

Thanks to Tom Barich, we have an awesome CD-ROM in the back of this book. We almost set a record and were going to have to include six CD-ROMs, but Tom caught me when I tried to include the original beta version (from the '80s) of Pong and WordStar. What we have instead is one CD-ROM with some of the coolest applications. Thanks, Tom.

Two of the top-notch computer professionals from the Walt Disney Company helped contribute a great deal of content and their intranet experience to this book. Charlie Broschart and Tom Beaton were at my side developing content and examples to create the best intranet book on the market.

Charlie Broschart, the developer of the intranet at Disney's Grand Floridian Beach Resort, is a hard-core raw coder with first-hand intranet development experience. Charlie is the plug-in master and knows all 108 Netscape plug-ins like the back of his hand. He also authored the HTML appendixes and created HTML examples that you can follow on the CD-ROM. Thanks, Charlie.

Tom Beaton also works for the Walt Disney Company, for Disney's multimedia group. He is a master at multimedia and Web development. If it plugs into the wall, Tom can program it. From developing automated fireworks displays to writing custom programs for display telephones, Tom has done it all. Who better to write on CGI and graphic techniques than the best multimedia expert around. Tom, I'll miss the four-hour phone calls but not the bills; next time, use CoolTalk. Thanks, Tom.

I'd like to thank David Strom, who maintains a site called Webcompare, for the valuable information on Web server comparisons. This will help everyone who is trying to determine which Web server to run for an intranet. Thanks, David.

Thanks to Kevin Werbach, this book has the ultimate HTML reference guide in the back. If you ever need to look up a pesty little tag, it's here. Thanks, Kevin.

Many corporations and companies also were a tremendous help. I'd like to thank Chris Vandenberg and Tracy Van Hoof from Microsoft. The content and screen shots from Microsoft's Website were an enormous help in developing this book. Jeanette Gibson and Wendy McCarthy from PointCast kept me up-to-date on the latest happenings with their products, and provided valuable information for the book. Thanks to Nancy Blum and Adam Berrey from Allaire Corporation for helping to provide an easy-to-follow section that allows users to create dynamic Web pages without complex CGI scripts. Last but not least, Susan Anthony and Andrea Cook, along with the entire Netscape staff, deserve a round of applause for all their help, and for allowing leading-edge content and screen shots from their Web site to make this tome complete.

This is the paragraph that covers everyone I missed.☺ If I forgot you, it was not intentional. To the many individuals who worked behind the scenes to put this book together: Thank you.

I would have never started writing features for publications, not to mention this book, if not for Bonnie Joe Buck at Webster University. Thank you for giving me the drive to start writing—and thank you, Matilda, for explaining the dinosaur management techniques.

This is starting to sound like an Emmy acceptance speech, and lastly I would like to thank Mr. Coffee and the makers of Moon Pies for helping me get through all those sleepless nights of writing.

About the Author

Steve Griswold is a technical analyst for Vista United Telecommunications at Walt Disney World. He recently completed setting up an intranet for Disney's Grand Floridian Beach Resort with several partners. When he hasn't been staying late at work or squeezing in a few hours of sleep, he has been teaching Web development classes at Valencia Community College and writing articles for the likes of *LAN Magazine*, *Internet World*, and *BBS.net*. (And this book, of course.) In his spare time, Steve enjoys installing beta helper applications and "watching them kill each other."

Contents at a Glance

Introduction xxxi

Part I   **Intranet Basics**   **1**

   1   Introduction to Intranet 3

   2   Getting Your Intranet Started 29

   3   Project Design and Layout 61

   4   Setting up an Intranet Server 79

Part II   **Building Intranet Pages**   **131**

   5   Using Existing Files 133

   6   Graphics on an Intranet .159

   7   Accessing Information 183

Part III   **Advanced Intranet Programming**   **223**

   8   Forms 225

   9   Audio, Video, Animation, and More 251

  10   CGI Scripts and Image Maps 275

  11   Business Presentations 307

  12   Plug-Ins 333

  13   PCN: PointCast Network Intranet
        Opportunity 373

Part IV   **Finalizing Your Intranet**   **381**

    14   Creating a Secure Intranet 383

    15   Implementing and Selling your Intranet 405

Part V   **Appendixes**   **431**

    A   HTML Reference 433

    B   HTML 3.2 Features for Netscape
       and Microsoft 463

    C   Authoring for Your Intranet 499

    D   The Bare Bones Guide to HTML 511

    E   What's on the CD? 521

       Index 527

Contents

Part I   Intranet Basics   1

Chapter 1   Introduction to the Intranet   3

What is the World Wide Web? 4
    The Birth of the Web 4
    Graphical User Interface (GUI) 5
    URL—Uniform Resource Locator 8
    Hypertext and Hypermedia 8
    Multiplatform Support 9
    Netscape/Internet Explorer Analogy 11
The Intranet 12
The Difference Between an Intranet and Internet . . .13
    Services You Can Offer 15
    Everyday Tasks Are Easier 16
    Engineering 17
    Just-in-Time Information 18
    Interactivity 18
    Information Systems (IS) 19
Intranet Issues 20
    Are You Sure You Want an Intranet? 20
    What Is the Scope of the Intranet? 20
    What Should the Policies and Procedures
        Manual Contain? 21
    A Word About Policies and Procedures 21
    Can Each Department Have a Web Site on
        the Intranet? 22

After You Construct the Pages, Who
Should Approve Them? 22
How to Author Content 24
How Should You Store Content? 26
Theming 26
Links 26
File Size and Graphics 27
Helper Applications and Other Add-Ons 27
Summary 28
What's Next! 28

Chapter 2   Getting Your Intranet Started   29

Choosing Organizational Models 30
The Decentralized Approach 30
The Centralized Approach 30
A Little of Both .32
Planning Your Intranet 33
Generating Ideas for Your Intranet 33
Formulating Your Mission Statement 33
Defining Tasks 34
Coming Up with the Project Plan 36
Selling the Intranet 37
Defining the Audience 37
Determining Needed Equipment 38
Brainstorming 39
Conducting a Survey .40
Web Pages and Home Pages 42
Choosing a Presentation Method 43
Deciding on a Navigation Model 44
Hierarchical 44
Linear 47
A Mix of Hierarchical and Linear 48

Storyboarding 49
   Stages of the Storyboard 50
   Using Flow Diagrams 52
Testing the Basics 55
Developing the Prototype 57
Creating Killer Home Pages 59
Basic Navigating 59
Summary 60
What's Next! 60

Chapter 3   Project Design and Layout   61

Same Top; Different Look 63
Short Attention Spans 64
   Easy Navigation Using Frames 66
   White Space 68
Avoid Getting Lost 70
   Mastheadings 72
Other Ways to Make Documents
   Easy to Read 73
      Images 74
      Background Images and Colors 74
Summary 77
What's Next! 78

Chapter 4   Setting Up an Intranet Server   79

Choosing a Web Server .80
   Operating Systems .80
   Launching and Logging 81
   Protocol Support and Includes 83
   Security 85
   Other Features 86

Popular NT Web Servers 89
  Alibaba 89
  EMWAC Freeware HTTPS 93
  Microsoft Internet Information Server 96
  Netscape Enterprise Server 99
  Netscape FastTrack Server 103
  Purveyor WebServer 107
  Spinnaker Web Server 110
  WebSite Professional from O'Reilly &
    Associates 114
  Other Web Servers 117
Netscape Enterprise Server Introduction 118
  Netscape Server Selector 118
  The Configure Administration 122
Microsoft Internet Information Server 128
  Installation 128
  Features 129
  Creating Interactive Pages the Easy Way 130
Summary 130
What's Next! 130

Part II   **Building Intranet Pages**   **131**

Chapter 5   **Using Existing Files**   **133**

Miracle Toy Corporation 135
Dig It Up 135
Making a Page 135
  Word Processing Files 137
  Spreadsheet Files 150
Other Formats 156
Summary 157
What's Next! 157

Chapter 6   Graphics on an Intranet   159

Pros and Cons of Using Web Page Graphics 160
Starting with a Background 160
    Creating Your Backgrounds 160
    Giving Your Background an Image 162
Capturing Images 163
Human Resource Example 164
Different Types of Images 165
    Inline Images on Your Web Page 166
    Using Inline Images to Point to Other
        Web Pages 174
    Using External Images on Your Web Pages . . .175
Adding Icons to Your Web Page 177
Using Images with Transparent Backgrounds 178
Optimizing Your Web Pages for Quicker
    Loading 179
Summary 181
What's Next! 181

Chapter 7   Accessing Information   183

Linking to Other Pages in Your Intranet
    Structure 184
    Product Template 187
Human Resources 194
    Creating a Job Opportunities Web Area 194
    Listing by Job Title 195
    General Inquiries .196
    Personnel File 196
Cold Fusion 205
    System Requirements to Run Cold Fusion . . .206
    Getting Started 208
    Create a Template .212

Employee Database 214
Summary 221
What's Next! 221

Part III   Advanced Intranet Programming   223

Chapter 8   Forms   225

CGI Scripts 229
Building the Perfect Form—Tags Included 230
    <FORM> (The Form Tag) 230
    <INPUT> (The Input Tag) 231
Your Very First Simple Form 231
Using Radio Buttons and Check Boxes in
    Your Forms 233
    Radio Buttons 233
    Check Boxes 235
    <SELECT> (The Drop-Down Menu or
        Scrolling List Tag) 236
    The <TEXTAREA> Tag 240
The Netscape PowerStart 243
Summary 248
What's Next! 250

Chapter 9   Audio, Video, Animation, and More 251

Hypermedia 252
Audio 253
    The Different Audio Formats 253
    Embedding Audio in Your Intranet Pages . . .255
    Setting Up the Server 256
    Changing Your Tune 256
Video 258
    Creating Video Clips 258
    Popular Video Formats 259

Obtaining the Plug-Ins 260
Including an .AVI File in Your Pages 261
Links to Video and Audio Libraries 262
Animation 262
Macromedia AppletAce 264
Cool Talk and NetMeeting 268
Cool Talk by Netscape 269
NetMeeting by Microsoft 271
PowWow 272
Summary 273
What's Next! 273

Chapter 10   CGI Scripts and Image Maps   275

Creating Your Intranet Home Page 276
The Home Page Design 276
The Image Map 276
Using MapEdit 277
The Image 280
Creating Dynamic Intranet Pages 285
CGI Methods 286
The GET Method .286
The POST Method 287
First Things First 287
CGI Environment Variables 288
REQUEST_METHOD 288
QUERY_STRING 288
CONTENT_LENGTH 288
HTTP_USER_AGENT 289
HTTP_REFERER 289
REMOTE_ADDR 289
REMOTE_HOST 289
REMOTE_IDENT 289
REMOTE_USER 289
SERVER_NAME .290

SERVER_SOFTWARE 290
GATEWAY_INTERFACE 290
SERVER_ADMIN 290
CONTENT_TYPE 290
AUTH_TYPE 290
PATH_INFO 291
SCRIPT_NAME 291
SERVER_PORT 291
SERVER_PROTOCOL 291
Displaying Environment Variables 291
Explanation of Program to Display
    Environment Variables 292
Returning a Web Page Based on the
User's Browser 294
Explanation of Program to Return Web
    Page Based on the User's Browser 295
Sending E-Mail from an HTML Form Using
CGI/Perl 297
The Background 297
The CGI/Perl Solution 297
Summary 305
What's Next! 305

Chapter 11   Business Presentations   307

Time to Present 308
Presenting with a Browser 309
Choose Your Weapon 309
Creating Your Presentation 310
Microsoft PowerPoint 313
Other Applications 320
Automatic Slide Shows .321
Multimedia and Sound .322
ASAP Webshow by Software Publishing
    Corporation 323

Astound Web Player by Gold Disk Inc. 324
Formula Graphics Multimedia System by
    Harrow Software 324
HyperPage by LMSOFT 326
Mirage by Strata 326
PointPlus by Net-Scene 327
PowerMedia by RadMedia 327
PowerPoint Animation Player & Publisher
    by Microsoft .329
ActiveMovie by Microsoft 329
Setting Up Plug-Ins in Your Pages 330
Summary 332
What's Next! 332

Chapter 12   Plug-Ins   333

What Is a Plug-In? 334
    What Is MIME? 334
    Setting Up a Plug-In For Netscape 335
    Setting Up a Plug-In For Internet Explorer . .338
Installing Two Popular Plug-Ins 338
    Abobe Acrobat Reader 339
    RealAudio 341
Plug-Ins and Your Intranet 347
    Support Issues .348
    The Importance of Process 348
    Bob's Web Server 349
A Plethora of Plug-Ins 349
    Content Responsibility 350
    Technical Responsibility 350
    Information Ownership 351
    Accessibility and the Target Audience 351
Plug-Ins by Category 353
    Plug-Ins: Business and Utilities 354
    Plug-Ins: Presentations 361

Plug-Ins: 3-D and Animation 362
Plug-Ins: Audio and Video 368
Summary 371
What's Next! 372

**Chapter 13 PCN: PointCast Network Intranet
Opportunity   373**

PointCast I-Server 374
Company News 377
One-Step Web Creation 377
Security 377
Client Updating .378
Summary 379
What's Next! 380

Part IV   Finalizing Your Intranets   381

Chapter 14 Creating a Secure Intranet   383

Compromise for Security 384
Physical Placement of Your Server 385
Communication Security 385
What Goes on Your Web Server? 387
Security Basics 387
CGI Scripts 387
Stay in Contact with Your Vendors 388
Setting Usernames and Passwords 388
Browser Security 389
Setting Up the Administration Kit 390
Configuring Your Proxies 390
Security with Digital Certificates 391
Secure Socket Layers (SSL 3.0) 392
Security Challenges 392

Cryptography 393
   What Is Cryptography? 393
   Symmetric-Key and Public-Key
      Cryptography 394
   Public-Key Certificates 395
   How Can Encryption Help? 395
Secure Socket Layers 396
   Message Privacy .398
   SSL Handshake 398
   Message Integrity 398
   Mutual Authentication 398
   What Happens During the SSL
      Handshake? 399
   SSL 2 Versus SSL 3 400
Future Directions for Netscape Navigator 400
Netscape's SuiteSpot 401
SurfWatch ProServer from Spyglass 402
   Tailored Control .403
   Filtering Content .403
   Security on Your LAN 403
Net Nanny 404
Summary 404
What's Next! 404

Chapter 15 Implementing and Selling Your Intranet   405

Super Users 406
The Beta Test 407
   Okay, Now What? 408
Training 409
Screen Captures for Your Manuals 409
Make Your Manuals 415
Online Help 415
Creating a FAQ Web Page 416

Link Checkers 418
  Doctor HTML 419
  I Like the Little Guys 426
Content Ownership Issues 426
Selling and Marketing 427
  In the Beginning 427
  Promotions 428
  The Intranet Café 428
  Trade Show 428
  Flyers, Posters, Paycheck Attachments,
    and Other Junk Mail 429
  Free Stuff 429
  The Big Day 429
Summary 429
Book Wrap Up! 430

Part V   Appendixes   431

Appendix A Basic HTML   433

Raw Coding 435
Those Who Don't Remember the Past 435
Is All This Really Worth It? 438
The Browser Wars: Who Really Wins? 439
  Black-and-White versus Color TV 439
  To Converge or Diverge? That Is
    the Question 440
Just What Is HTML? 441
  Getting Under the Hood 441
  The Tags 443
Logical and Physical Character Styles 452
  Logical Style Tags .452
  Physical Styles 453

Lists 454
    <OL> (The Ordered List Tag) 455
    <UL> (The Unordered List) 455
    <TABLE> (The Table Tag) 456

Appendix B HTML 3.2 Features for Netscape and Microsoft   **463**

HTML 3.2: An Overview 465
    <!DOCTYPE> (Declaration Tag) 467
    <APPLET> (Tag and Attributes) 468
    <SMALL> and <BIG> Tags for Smaller
      and Bigger Text 470
    <BODY> 472

 with Clear Attributes 474
    <TABLE> 475
    The Table width Attribute 476
    The Column width Attribute 477
    Table Border Widths 477
    The cellspacing Attribute 478
    The cellpadding Attribute 478
    <DIV> (The Division Tag) 479
    The <TR> Tag with the bgcolor Attribute ...479
    <HR> (The Horizontal Rule Tag
      Attributes) 480
    The size Attribute 480
    The width Attribute 481
    The align Attribute 481
    <LI> (The List Item Tag and Its
      Attributes) 483
    Unordered List 483
    Ordered List 483
    <STRIKE> (The Strike-Through Text Tag) 485
    <SUB> (The Subscript Tag) 485

\<SUP\> (The Superscript Tag) 485
\<SCRIPT\> (The Inline Script Tag) 485
\<STYLE\> (The Style Markup Tag) 487
\<IMG\> (The Image Tag and Attributes) 488
The New Netscape Extensions 492
\<MULTICOL\> (The Multicolumn Tag and
Its Attributes) 492
\<SPACER\> (Horizontal and Vertical
Spacing Tag) 494
\<FONT\> (The `font face=fontname` Tag) 495
\<FRAMESET\> (The Frame Tag and Its
Attributes) 496

Appendix C Authoring for Your Intranet   499

Netscape Navigator Gold .500
Editing a Page 500
One-Button Publishing 501
Netscape Navigator Example 501
Other Authoring Tools .507
Microsoft FrontPage 97 507
Word Internet Assistant 508
NetObjects Fusion 508
What Should You Use? .509

Appendix D The Bare Bones Guide to HTML   511

The Bare Bones Guide to HTML 512
Formatting Of This Document 512
General 513
Structural Definition 513
Presentation Formatting 514
Links and Graphics .514
Dividers 515

Lists 515
Backgrounds and Colors 516
Special Characters 516
Forms 517
Tables 517
Frames 518
Java 518
Miscellaneous 519

Appendix E What's on the CD?   521

Running the CD 522
Windows 3.1 522
Windows 95 522
The Prima User Interface 523
Category Buttons 523
Options Buttons 523
The Software 524

Index   527

Introduction

So, you have been surfing the Web and the idea hit you, "Hey, what if I could utilize this easy-to-use, extremely powerful technology in my organization to disseminate information to my departments?" That is the daydream that everyone from CIOs to front-line employees have been having since the birth of the Internet. The good news is that it is no longer a daydream. You are holding in your hands "the bible" of intranet books. With a statement like that, you expect an amazing, informative book that you will reach for time and again—and that is what I hope to provide.

The Internet/World Wide Web (WWW) and, recently, the intranet have been the latest craze in the news, and for good reason. Now any organization can have the same communication, marketing, and just-in-time information as the top 100 companies. The Internet has leveled the playing field of businesses globally, just as the intranet is doing today. A recent 20-minute feature on CNN summed up the corporate race to be on the WWW and to develop internal webs (intranets). The feature highlighted how corporations are hiring college freshmen and sophomores, and even high school seniors before they graduate, to have them develop their WWW sites and intranets. Organizations are paying sometimes in excess of $60,000 dollars to these students, plus offering to pay for the rest of their education if they come and help them design their intranets and Web presence.

I can save you $59,950 today! This book contains all the tools that you will need to create your intranet. This book is not a "how to build an intranet in seven days" guide. Building an intranet is an continuing process; it never ceases. I will show you how to make a project plan and how to implement your intranet step-by-step to keep it evolving to meet your changing business needs. You will also be able to keep up-to-date with the latest developments in intranet and WWW technology by visiting Prima Publishing's WWW site for a comprehensive list of links to the latest Web technology:

(http://www.quicknet.com:80/primapub/home.html)

Why Buy This Book?

This book contains everything that you need to create a secure, professional, and successful, internal Web (intranet). Here in this one convenient book are all the tools that you need to create a successful intranet. You will read about:

◆ Infrastructure and communication issues

◆ Setting up your Web browser

◆ Creating internal web sites, using HTML, inline images, image maps, CGI

◆ Converting existing data "legacy systems" to be intranet ready

◆ Setting up your Web server and using it for your business needs

◆ Creating a dynamic and interactive presence

◆ Developing an attractive site that is responsive and quick

◆ Performing maintenance and support

◆ Using authoring tools to speed up development time

◆ Creating graphics and presentations for an intranet

◆ Setting up a secure server and intranet

◆ Keeping up with new technology and cool applications that can increase productivity on your intranet

You will learn that there is more to setting up an intranet than the coding, such as:

◆ Conveying your organization's vision

◆ Using navigation tips for easy access to just-in-time information

- ◆ Developing layout designs and planning (storyboarding) so that you do it right the first time

- ◆ Marketing, conducting brainstorming sessions, and creating a demonstration intranet

This book goes beyond the basic overview of other books and gives specific examples, tips, and hints that you can implement now. This "intranet bible" will not just show you how to create an intranet; it will show you how to create, manage, maintain, and implement a successful intranet.

Why an Intranet?

You have seen all the hype on television with the flashy commercials that almost always end with a Web address. On the way in to work, you drive by billboards that host the URLs of car manufactures, soft drink companies, and entertainment giants. In the past, you would need to be a UNIX propeller head and be able to program in a cryptic and complex language to establish any type of Web presence.

With the introduction of user-friendly graphical user interfaces (GUI), any size of organization can now set up an internal web with ease. Such a thing is no longer a luxury item for a handful of mammoth corporations with a staff of UNIX professionals working around the clock. The same principles that will allow an intranet to be set up at large organizations such as AT&T apply to everyone now. Now you can easily use the same World Wide Web (WWW) architecture internally to make your business run smoother and more productively. An intranet can be set up at a local pizza chain that has three or four locations and wants to communicate and disseminate information between locations.

Every business, every department, has something to communicate. Organizations are not charting their course into this new technology without some concerns, however. One such concern is that the average businessperson may turn into a late-night, red-eyed recreational surfer at home. Could an intranet or access to the external WWW turn productive employees into Web addicts? Fortunately, little evidence exists to support this view point.

Just as with the introduction of the telephone and all other communication technology, there is a fear of misuse and abuse. When the telephone, the fax machine, and e-mail entered the corporate scope, the same game was played. When the process was set in motion with these communication technologies, yes, there was an abuse factor. But the minimal abuse was far outweighed by the advantages: the increase in communication, sharing of best practices, and interactivity. No matter what restrictions you put in place, a small percentage of people will abuse any technology. This is an HR problem—not an information technology problem.

An intranet and external access to the WWW can be a valuable asset to your organization. The education and research that can be done surpasses any tool to date. Can you tailor this easy-to-use interface so that your employees can perform their daily business activities, learn more about the organization's goals, and research the competition with the click of a mouse? The answer is a resounding *Yes!*

Certain restrictions can and should be in place to protect sensitive material, and I discuss these issues with you, showing you ways to control access and offer alternatives later in this book.

What You Need Before You Start

To begin experiencing all the benefits of an intranet, you must, of course, have a computer. And, thankfully, that is about all this book assumes. All the information covered in this book just requires some time invested by you to read, digest, and implement what you have learned. I will be here every step of the way, to offer tips, hints, give examples, and offer guidance so that you can avoid all those first-time mistakes that businesses and corporations are making when entering into this new technology frontier: the intranet.

It is not required, but Windows NT Server and Netscape's Enterprise Server will be covered in Chapter 4. Graphics on an intranet is covered in Chapter 6, and a SVGA monitor is necessary to manipulate and work with images. The CD-ROM included with this book contains valuable shareware and freeware that provides stuff that may help you to set up an intranet. A CD-ROM drive is necessary, obviously, to access this software.

A dedicated connection to the Internet, or to your organization's internal Transmission Control Protocol/Internet Protocol (TCP/IP) network, is also required.

If you are interested in using the intranet's multimedia capabilities to its fullest, you will also need a sound card and speakers, or headphones to hear audio.

You will read books and hear people say that you can run a Web Server on a 386 PC if you just put enough memory in it and run a PC UNIX such as Linux, a freeware UNIX Operating System ported for the Intel based PC. It can be done, but this is not the route to take for a reliable, expandable intranet. I cover reasonably priced hardware and software that is powerful yet easy for an organization to implement.

When you complete this book, you will be able to design an intranet tailored to your business needs; author dynamic content by using Hypertext Markup Language (HTML); add helper applications that can expand the possibilities of your intranet; learn how to configure a Web server; and install Web browsers and helper applications on the client's workstations.

NOTE: HTML code is *not* case sensitive. You may enter your tags, attributes, and so on in upper- or lowercase, whichever you prefer.

PART

I

Intranet Basics

Chapter | 1

Introduction
to the Intranet

In this chapter, I cover some of the typical Internet, World Wide Web (WWW), and intranet basics. I start you out with the birth of the Web and quickly move into the key elements that have led to the WWW's success. I touch quickly on many topics to whet your appetite for more. The difference between an intranet and the Internet is covered in this chapter, as well as some main points for getting started. In case you are trying to think of new exciting applications that you can develop on your intranet, I offer you some examples of how Human Resources, Finance, Engineering, and other departments can implement an intranet in their areas. These examples should spark your imagination and start you imagining all the possible uses for your intranet. To top it off, I cover the "what ifs"—a handful of the top questions and concerns that will be raised repeatedly when you develop your intranet. Knowing at least some of the concerns that organizations have prior to creating your intranet is helpful so that your organization can set its own policies on these issues.

What is the World Wide Web?

Everybody is getting on the Web, and for good reason. The Web allows anyone, anywhere, to compete in business on a global scale. So, where did it all start? How was the Web born? If you have read any introduction to the Web books, you have most likely heard of Ted Nelson, who defined the term *hypertext*; Tim Berners-Lee, whose project at the European Laboratory for Particle Physics, commonly known as CERN, allowed fellow scientists to read research papers within CERN; the development of NCSA Mosaic Browser; and Marc Andreesen and the Netscape analogy.

The Birth of the Web

In late 1990, Tim Berners-Lee wrote the first Web browser for CERN, the European Particle Physics Laboratory near Geneva, Switzerland.

This first browser was designed to run on the NeXT workstation because CERN was mostly a NeXT shop. The browser enabled scientists at CERN to collaborate on ideas by browsing documents. The documents had a unique feature: they could be connected so that users could jump from document to document to drill down deeper into their research.

The links that allowed this connectivity are know as *hypertext* links. Hypertext, or *hypermedia*—the ability to link any media type to one another—enabled the necessary linkage between documents that could break the linear structure of traditional methods.

Hypertext allows the user to browse, or surf, information. Humans have a short attention span, and hypertext plays on this characteristic beautifully. If you are looking for information, you can jump to it instantly by clicking your mouse on a hyperlink.

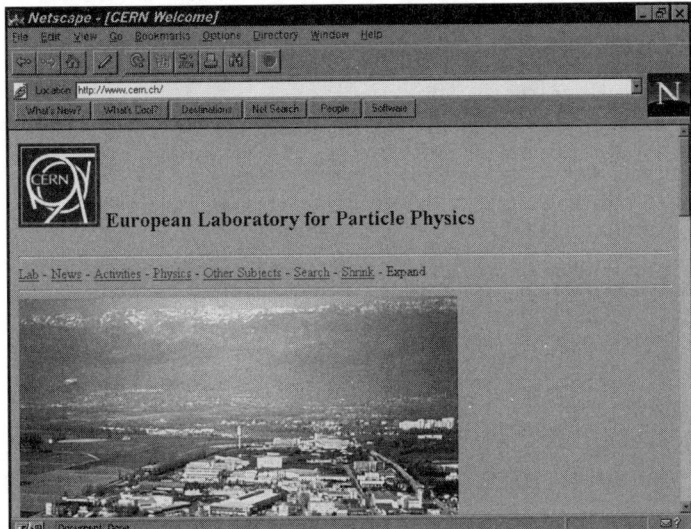

FIGURE 1-1

You can visit CERN's home page at http://www.cern.ch.

Taking this concept one step further, documents could be linked from computer to computer. Using the Internet and incorporating existing forms of information distribution such as FTP, Gopher, TELNET, Usenet newsgroups, and e-mail required a separate application for each. With the Web, all these applications have now been integrated into one easy-to-use browser, which allows you to view hypertext documents, look at inline images, download files with File Transfer Protocol from FTP sites, send e-mail, and read Usenet newsgroups. Tim Berners-Lee's browser created the foundation that he needed for global information sharing.

When Tim Berners-Lee invented the World Wide Web, he developed some key elements that have led to its continued success. These elements are also what is driving the intranet initiative.

Graphical User Interface (GUI)

The graphical nature of the Web is what started the general public's interest in "cyberspace." The first browsers, however, were not graphical in nature and were strictly text

based, because they ran on platforms such as UNIX that were strictly text only. Lynx was one of the first text-based browsers, developed at the University of Kansas. Lynx is an excellent browser for accessing information quickly. If you have been to a site several times and know what you are looking for, you can get what you need more quickly by using Lynx or by turning off graphic loading in your GUI browser. Lynx is used by universities for fast access to the WWW because it requires VT100 terminal emulation. A DOS version of Lynx is available for download at
`http://www.nyu.edu/pages/wsn/subir/lynx.html`.

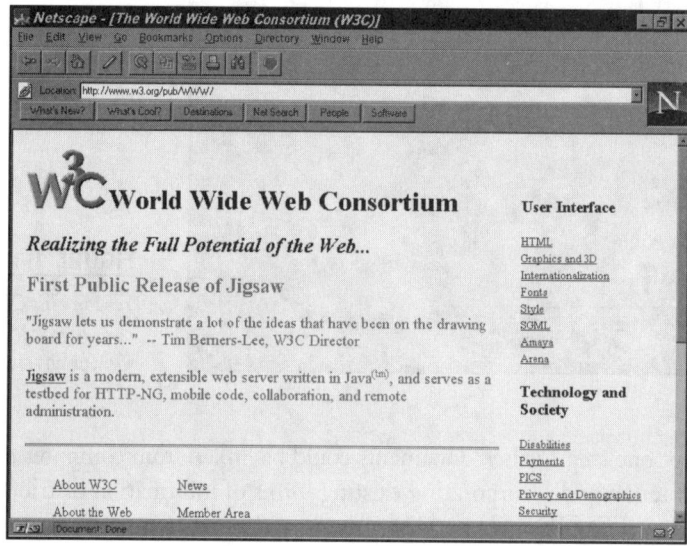

FIGURE 1-2

Keep up with the latest in WWW developments at the World Wide Web Consortium, also known as W3C (`http://www.w3.org/pub/WWW/`*).*

The graphical nature of the Web today calls for a GUI client—a graphical browser such as Microsoft's Internet Explorer (see Figure 1-3).

Another popular browser is Netscape Navigator from Netscape Communications Corporation (see Figure 1-4). As of this writing, Navigator accounts for 80 percent of the browser market, owing to its rich features and ease of use. Microsoft is already gaining ground with Internet Explorer 3.0, and should even the playing field and quickly gain the browser market share with its release of IE 4.0 by January 1997.

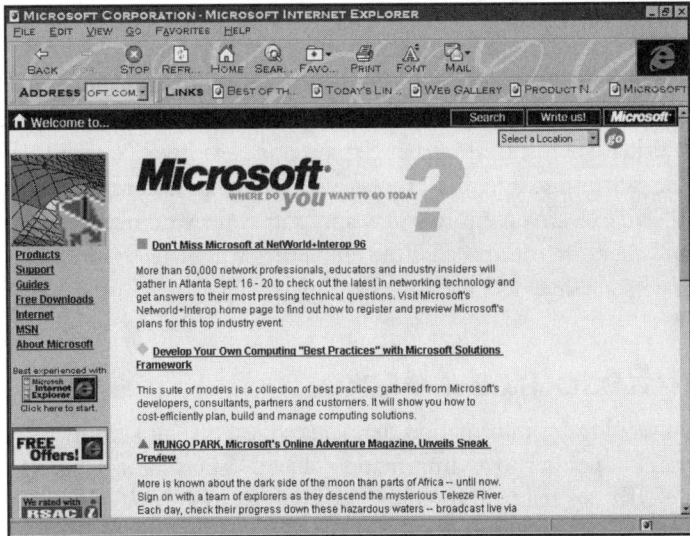

FIGURE 1-3

Microsoft's Internet Explorer allows you to easily navigate your intranet just by pointing and clicking on links and graphics.

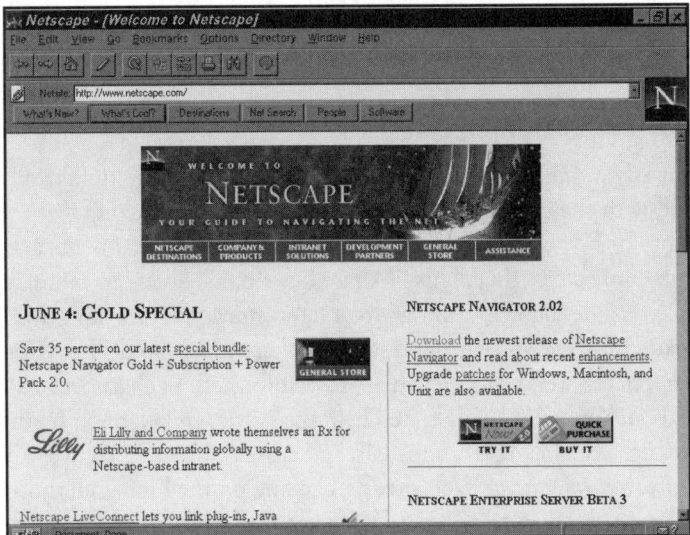

FIGURE 1-4

Netscape Navigator is another graphical browser that is very popular on the WWW.

With these browsers, you can take advantage of the graphical nature of the Web and also experience its full, rich multimedia environment. The Web's graphics and multimedia content has thrust its growth from minimal back when it was text based to an astonishing rate that everyone is frantically trying to measure. The GUI interface also sports the advantage of being fun and very user friendly. Because more and more of the working force has a computer at home, around 40 percent and even higher numbers of people have access to computers, including WWW access in schools, libraries, clubs, and so on. This fast-increasing use is a major reason to use Web technology in the work place. If your employees are using Microsoft's Internet Explorer or Netscape's Navigator at home, training them on the exact same interface at work will be a great deal easier . Your employees will not have to learn an entirely new application for your intranet. This saves on training and support costs, because the employees will be using the same technology in their personal lives as their business career.

URL—Uniform Resource Locator

The client/Web browser locates information that you request on the Web by using a specific URL. The URL is a pointer to an information object. When someone gives you a business card with a URL, or tells you to point your browser to a specific Web site, you can enter this information directly into the field labeled "Location" or "Go." On most browsers, doing so allows you to directly access the information at that URL. You can also access different URLs by clicking on hypertext links that take you from document to document on the Web.

Hypertext and Hypermedia

The ability to seamlessly jump from document to document across multiple platforms and across the world with the click of a mouse is one of the most amazing features of the WWW. With the use of Hypertext Markup Language (HTML), documents and pages of information can be linked together. This linking allows quick access to more detailed information. . While reading a quick summary of a news story, you can skim over it and then click on the parts of the story that interests you. These links can drill down to more detailed information related to the story, such as stock information, charts, related reports, photographs, and so on. You will be able to tell hyperlinks from regular text by the hyperlink's different color, usually blue. It is also usually underlined. Figure 1-5 gives an example of a *Wall Street Journal Interactive* Web site. By clicking on the blue underlined hypertext link Subscribe, you will taken to another Web page that explains several different ways to subscribe to the *Wall Street Journal Interactive Edition*.

Hypermedia is similar to hypertext, and you will hear the words used interchangeably by some in the field. Hypertext was originally derived from hypermedia. Hypermedia is the linking of text, music, graphics, video, sounds files, and other multimedia applications in a nondirect form. Similarly, *hypertext* can be defined as the linking of text documents with multimedia added for esthetics, and which does not follow any linear path. The most popular of the two terms is hypertext because that is the term that most users are accustomed to hearing and reading about.

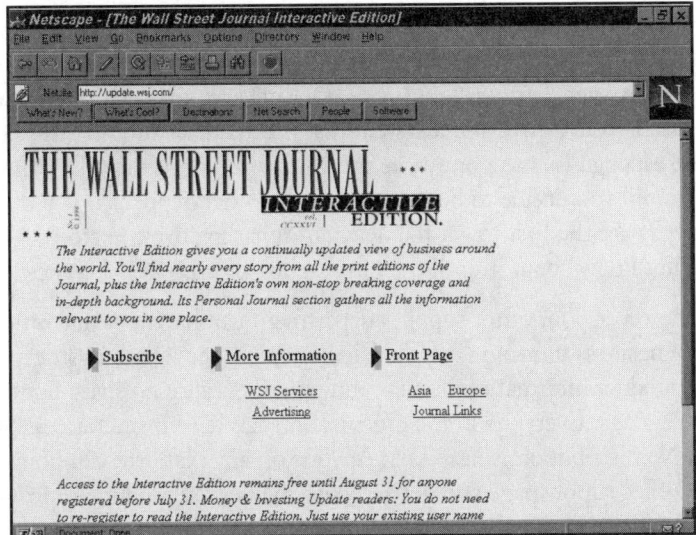

FIGURE 1-5

By clicking your pointer on any of the underlined text, you will be jump from page to page.

Multiplatform Support

Companies large and small more often than not have many platforms that they support. The norm is to have a Windows, UNIX, and Mac shop all under the same roof. Your business's intranet does not care about the wars between the software giants to see which operating system is the best. The intranet and WWW are cross platform, meaning that they will run on any of your systems. No more porting your applications from one system to another. If you have Microsoft's Internet Explorer, or Netscape's Navigator, or any browser, for that matter, you can view the same information on a Mac as you can on a PC. This advantage alone saves time and money on typical business practices. There are several alternatives to publishing electronic media on an intranet. For instance, you can publish information on CD-ROMs and distribute that information to individuals in the organization. An intranet can accomplish the same task with a significant reduction in time and cost.

Say, for example that you are distributing a catalog of office supplies. Rather than print the full-color, 300-page catalog every year and send one copy to each business unit, you decide to do a CD-ROM. Immediately, you save on the full-color printing cost. The

CD-ROM can be burned more cheaply than printing a full catalog, and it also allows for interactivity.

Now, say that you lose the CD-ROM or the dog-eared catalog. What do you do? Order another one and wait until it arrives?

There is a better way: An intranet. CD-ROMs as well as catalogs take a significant amount of time to produce. After they are produced, they must be distributed to each area, and someone always gets left out. With the CD-ROM, you are assuming that the recipient has a CD-ROM drive and a system that is capable of running it. The CD-ROM and the catalog also are a one-time shot. After you burn the CD-ROM, you're stuck with it until you decide to burn another one. What happens if you discontinue a product, or you are the first to get the new ten-dollar gig drive in stock? Your business units will not know about it until the next catalog or CD-ROM comes out.

With an intranet, however, your office supplies department can have a virtual office of the latest products. The business unit can view the latest supplies, see what's in stock, and even read pages of product information on new equipment because no space limitations exist as they do in catalogs. Everyone in the organization can have instant access to the same information. No distribution is necessary. Anyone on any platform can point his or her browser to the office supply page and get access to the newest product information. The office supply department can also inform departments of new products, out-of-stock items, specials, and any other information that might help those departments do their jobs more efficiently.

An intranet allows this type of information exchange this instantly, with the push of a button (well, a few buttons). The new information can be loaded onto the Web server and be available immediately to anyone in the organization with a computer.

So, am I suggesting that you should get rid of all your battered catalogs, as well as stop spending valuable time and money on creating CD-ROMs? Not exactly. An intranet could replace other communication devices in your organization, but it would be better to supplement these vehicles in the beginning until everyone gets used to the new system. Also, you will never be able to replace the look and feel of a quality book, magazine, or catalog. If you are trying to replace 100 percent of a communication piece with an intranet, consider the following:

- Remember that reading a magazine or catalog on a bus, in bed, on the beach, or in the employee's cafeteria is easier than reading a Web page.
- Some of your targeted readers won't have a computer, making some type of printed media available necessary.

◆ If you want to do a great deal of interactivity, video, audio, animation, using a CD-ROM to achieve large multimedia presentations is still better than a network such as an intranet. You can do video and sound over an intranet, but you are limited by file size and your LAN's infrastructure. A CD-ROM can hold a great deal of information and transfer it to the user's computer without taking up valuable bandwidth on the LAN with video and large sound files.

Browsers

When you start developing Web pages, one of the big challenges you will face is who to develop for. With so many browsers out there, developing pages for all of them is difficult. Netscape started the war of the browsers first by implementing its own HTML tags that only its browser could interpret. Microsoft and others soon followed and also developed proprietary tags. Later chapters devoted to HTML discuss specific tags for Netscape, but for now, bear in mind the following rule of thumb for developing content: If you are developing for the WWW at large, your task is much more difficult.

For the Web, you should develop for the least common denominator. This means having text-only pages for users who do not have graphical browsers such as Netscape's Navigator. You want to make sure that your page can be viewed by everyone on the WWW, so you need to offer the user several options.

For example, you might have an option on your opening screen that asks the user to choose a text-based Web site as opposed to a graphical site (sometimes you will be able to choose your connection speed to the Web on these Web pages, which in turn determines which pages will be sent to your browser). On your intranet, however, the task will be much easier. Because the intranet is like your own private Web, you can issue a standard browser with each new workstation, and install the browser that your organization decides to use on existing workstations as well.

Because you have control of what browser your company or business will use, you also control how your presentation will be displayed on the user's end. This control of the browser makes your task much easier than having to design two Web sites, a text-based site and a graphical site.

A word of advice: Netscape Navigator and Internet Explorer are the two largest browsers currently on the WWW. They both offer the widest range of features and are always introducing new HTML tags and helper applications. To date, a large amount of organizations are using NCSA Mosaic because this browser appeared early in 1993 and quickly became a standard. When Netscape came on the scene and based itself on the Mosaic code, it quickly grew in popularity. Netscape Navigator made a good browser great by adding all the features that the WWW had to offer into one easy-to-use interface. Giving it away for free evaluation with a very lenient usage policy also did not hurt its acceptance.

You are currently entering the realm of the intranet and WWW during a shift in the browser battle. The percentage of users on the Web today using Netscape is very high: 75 to 80 percent. This is due to the fact that Netscape always stays one step ahead of the competition by introducing new tags, applications, and features.

The Intranet

I define an intranet, in the simplest terms, as follows:

> An intranet is an organization's use of WWW technology inside that organization, to distribute information to employees through the organization's networks.

An intranet has the same look and feel as the WWW, in that it combines text, graphics, and multimedia into one interface. Just as the invention of the telephone, copy machine, and fax machine have produced great strides in communication, the intranet has and will continue to surpass expectations. Corporations and businesses are implementing intranets to combat the competitive pressures of everyday business. Business has shifted to a global market, and the firms that will survive are the ones that can communicate efficiently and effectively.

With the rapid growth of technology, organizations need to be quick to respond to change in order to collaborate on ideas in a timely manner. Employees need to have access to company information as well as information on the competition. Being wired is no longer a luxury but rather a necessity to compete and succeed in today's market. By implementing an intranet, employees can access a wealth of knowledge that will allow them to generate new products and services more effectively. Some of the most obvious benefits of an intranet to an organization's employees are as follows:

- ◆ **They won't have to reinvent the wheel.** An intranet helps employees avoid having to reinvent processes are already in place in remote, unknown parts of the organization. Employees can tap into services and information deposits that already exist within the organization.
- ◆ **They can access a global wealth of knowledge.** An intranet along with the Internet empowers all employees by enabling access to a wide variety and

depth of information. Internet access will allow employees to research products, services, and companies that are competitors.

♦ **They can keep up with the latest trends and strategies.** Employees will also be able to learn new techniques by reading about strategies that other organizations are implementing. These learning experiences can be pulled into the organization's intranet so that everyone can have access to and benefit from these resources.

An intranet is a truly amazing vehicle for communication. It allows immediate distribution and access to information, and it does this with an easy-to-use GUI interface that requires minimal training. Best of all, it is a very cost-effective means of communicating.

The Difference Between an Intranet and Internet

This book focuses on intranet technology and how to effectively design an organization's intranet. An intranet allows a business to effectively organize and distribute goods and information inside the organization. Most organizations are familiar with the Internet/WWW and are interested in developing a global Web presence in addition to developing an intranet. Keep in mind that the steps taken to develop an intranet are different from the ones you should take to construct a Web site for the Internet. Although doing so is difficult, try to keep focused on how the intranet can help your internal operation. You will undoubtedly come up with many good ideas that you would like your customers to have access to, so write them down on a separate piece of paper and keep them close by for when you decide to develop an external Web site.

When you are going through the storyboard and brainstorming phases of development for your intranet, remembering your audience is important. You will be designing a site for internal use, so keep the organization's goals, mission, and objectives in mind. Figure 1-6 shows the Webster University Web page. This page has been designed with internal use as a primary goal. Some information on the site is positioned for the general public; the majority of the content, however, is suited for the intranet reader. It is important to remember your audience, and develop for its needs. The Webster University site shows information that has been created to assist its audience, the staff, and the faculty. You can visit its site at http://www.websteruniv.edu/.

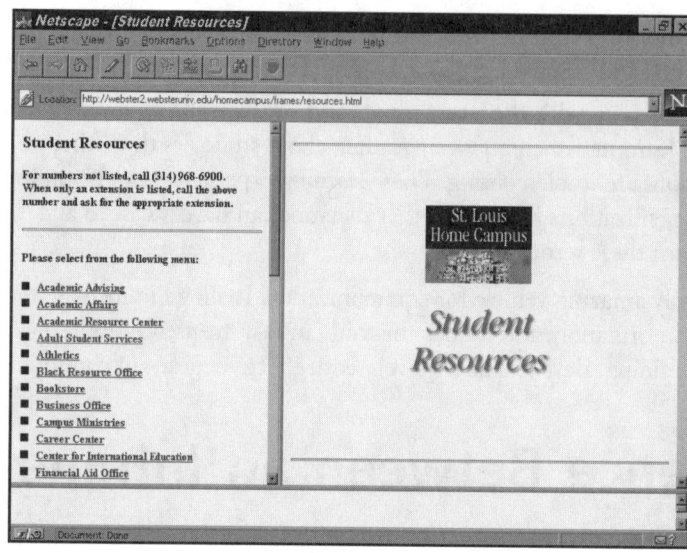

FIGURE 1-6

Webster University displays information that is pertinent to the staff and student body.

This Web page contains information that might be of interest to the general public, but its focus and worth is to the faculty and student body at this university. Others might be interested in some of the information that the Webster site contains, but the majority of the information is tailored toward the staff and student body at the university. Figure 1-7 shows the opposite.

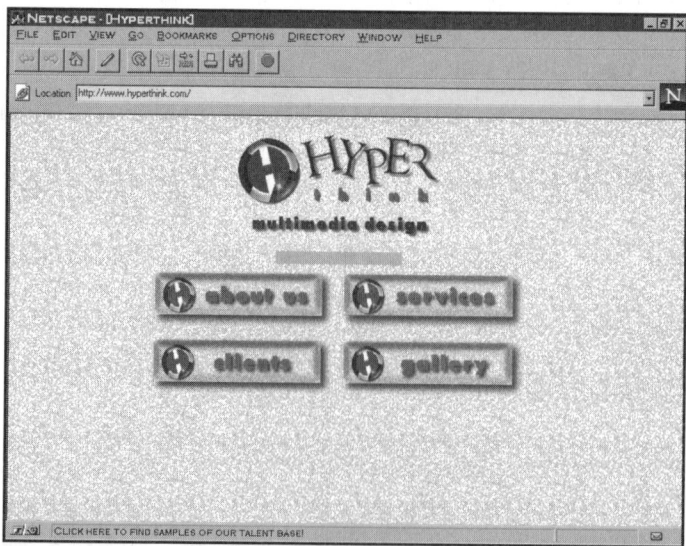

FIGURE 1-7

*External Web sites such as HyperThink (*http://www.hyper-think.com*) are tailored toward a general audience and are aimed at informing and advertising to their visitors.*

The HyperThink Web site aims at the Internet and WWW audience, not at the intranet. Sure, you can find information about the company, as well as the staff and press releases, but the major focus is to inform the general public about the company as a whole. The HyperThink Web site allows the user to learn more about the company in a fun and interactive way.

This type of external Web site is typically used for global advertising and PR. No better way exists to reach all corners of the globe than an external Web site that displays your product or service, describes your company's mission and vision, tells of public service and environmental participation, and communicates literally anything else that you want to communicate to the world. The key is to remember the difference between the strengths in an external Web and an internal web. Some overlap will occur in areas such as press releases, stock reports, and the like.

Your target audience for your intranet is different from your external global audience. You will need to define your audience and tailor your content and applications accordingly.

Services You Can Offer

As an organization, you provide a wide range of services inside your company to the employees and business units. These services cover a wide range and can be adapted to be more effective on an intranet. The possibilities are limited only by your imagination. The following sections provide a few general ideas of services that you can provide on your intranet.

Human Resources

This is probably the department that has the most to gain, in many organizations, from intranet technology. HR spends countless hours creating and distributing material to employees. An intranet can save HR a lot of time because that department can distribute its information to the entire organization through one vehicle. With the click of a mouse, employees can access the following:

- Benefit package information
- Up-to-date on-the-job training materials
- Policies and procedures handbooks
- Job postings
- Dress codes
- Procedures for reimbursement of expenses
- Company newsletters
- Phone directories
- Vacation information
- Stock purchase information

Employees can also access training and development materials online. They can examine work schedules, the latest bowling league scores, classified ads; they can even take a look at the current week's menu in the cafeteria. The information can be simply a text document that they can read online or print out to study at their leisure, or it can be exchanged through interactive forms and message forums.

Another use for the intranet is for training. Simple training can be accomplished with the appropriate use of text and graphics to draw the reader into training as a fun learning experience. More involved training can take place with the integration of sound and video into an intranet. Simple yet effective computer-based training can be accomplished on an intranet and save time and money over traditional training methods. Why keep files full of useful information when you can allow restricted or open access to this information throughout the entire organization via an intranet?

Just think about how much of Human Resources's time is used answering the same questions repeatedly. Employees who need to find out what holidays are paid by the company must search the office to try to find the memo that came out six months ago. When that search proves futile, they could look for their employee handbook or try to locate that colorful brochure that was floating around the break room. But with the intranet, employees could use their Web browser and access the Human Resources page in a matter of moments, obtaining the information on vacations and paid holidays with little effort.

Other employees might want to get a list of classes that are offered. Rather than call HR to request a catalog that may very well still be at the printer, they can access the same information on the intranet, right at their desk. Is preventive dental care covered in the new dental plan? The human resources Web page can answer that question and go into greater depth because the Web page is not limited on space as print media is. The savings in time alone for one department, Human Resources, is reason enough to implement an intranet.

Financial Information

Departments can have access to charts and graphs in a way that only an intranet can provide. Users can access the information by viewing the Web pages, or even by activating links to Excel spreadsheets and database applications that allow employees to view financial information easily. This information can be restricted to certain users or departments.

Everyday Tasks Are Easier

Every organization has a network of departments meant to accomplish specific tasks. Whether these tasks are engraving name plates for the door to your office, removing the trash from your trash can, packing up and shipping your proposal and report to a client, ordering office equipment, or repairing the copy machine in the hall, each department has information to share. By enabling fast access to this information, the entire organization can benefit.

For example, perhaps your department reorganized last year and you received all the new furniture that was ordered from your company's office supply catalog. Whatever happened to all the old workstations? Some of the chairs were still in very good condition. In fact, one entire workstation was never even occupied. If you're looking for some inexpensive or free office furniture and accessories (and who isn't?), then locating this warehouse of office supplies would be very worthwhile.

Traditional methods of locating that old office furniture make doing so nearly impossible. And, as time passes, finding the right people to assist in your search becomes increasingly difficult. An intranet page can be developed to tackle this task. Users can tap into a database of available office equipment, read about its characteristics, and find out about availability and price. Users can get the exact dimensions so that they know whether the furniture will fit before it is delivered. A photograph can even accompany each item to allow users to examine the item in detail before calling or filling out the online order form to obtain the item. Suddenly, a department whose existence was known by only a select few is now accessible to every employee right from a desktop personal computer.

Here are a few more examples to get you thinking of the possibilities.

Engineering

A hotel's engineering department has shelves of installation and technical manuals. These manuals sit on a shelf under a layer of dust, a handful of screws, and a couple of pieces of irregularly cut Plexiglas that, for some reason, has been saved for more than 10 years. Some of the manuals have not even been opened and are still wrapped in plastic, whereas a handful of others have made their way off the shelf and onto the plywood table. Of the many manuals sitting on the table, five are used daily.

The specs on the cooling system are among the most popular and, usually, hard to come by. With the company's new intranet, though, the cooling system manual was put into a digital format. This was easy to do because the manufacturer supplied a Microsoft Word 6.0 disk with the manual (in the past, that disk would have been used as a coaster in the engineering breakroom).

Even if the disk had not been supplied, the manual could have been scanned in easily with OCR software, or key parts could be entered by hand into the intranet. Now when a maintenance person goes on call to fix a cooling problem, that person can access all the information contained in that one manual from any computer in the company. The maintenance person can look at diagrams of the cooling system, take a look at blueprints, and even read about similar problems and solutions in the maintenance forum. This sure beats having to run back to the office to try to find that one manual, dig up a blueprint, or call a coworker at home who had a similar problem some time last year.

Just-in-Time Information

Bullets of just-in-time information allow employees to quickly access the facts and figures they need. Staying with the hotel example, you can easily see how just-in-time information can help the operation. Guest satisfaction in a resort is a major focus, and one of the main goals is getting guests quickly into their room of choice. With large resort hotels averaging easily over 1,000 rooms, it is difficult for the front desk staff, concierge, guest services, maintenance, and other service areas to keep track of which room have the best views, which rooms are close to the fire exits, which rooms have a connecting door, and what exactly is the square footage and decor of the suites. These are all very important issues to the guest who is checking into a resort for a dream vacation. An intranet can help the front desk cashier and support areas with this information.

You can design an easy-to-use graphical user interface (GUI) to show an aerial view of the resort. All the lodging buildings, restaurants, recreation areas, and adjoining areas can be browser sensitive so that, with the click of the mouse, the user can zoom in to more specific information. Users clicking on a lodge building will see the building floor plan, revealing hallways, fire exits, connecting rooms, laundry/vending and ice machine locations, as well as other important information. Users can click on the exact room number to see a drafted room diagram showing the exact room layout and dimensions, furniture and all. One step further will take users to actual color photographs of the rooms and the views from the balcony. Image maps like this can easily be constructed for organizations as a training tool and for daily operations.

Interactivity

Okay, here is where the intranet really gets exciting as two-way communication vehicle. If you have surfed the WWW, you have surely seen Web sites that ask you to fill out a survey or enter information with the hope of winning a vacation, Super Bowl tickets, or a new rodeo all-terrain vehicle. These forms are simple and effective. They are available to collect data 24 hours a day, 7 days a week and are set to deliver the response from the user to an e-mail account.

In Chapter 8, you'll see how to create a form with Hypertext Markup Language (HTML), and how to pass the information in the form to the server via a Common Gateway Interface (CGI) script, in Chapter 10. For now, Figure 1-8 shows a simple form that can be used by employees to update their employee identification card, or report it lost or stolen. After the employee fills out the form and submits it, the form is goes to the security department, which processes it. Forms like the one in the figure can be created for all departments to serve any purpose imaginable.

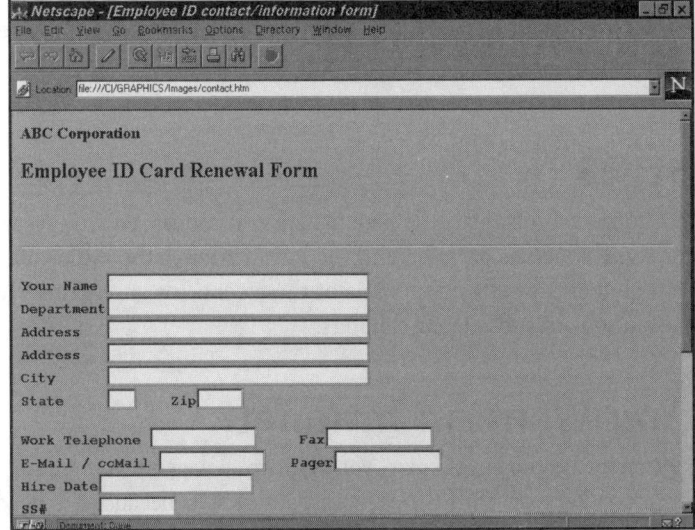

FIGURE 1-8

This form allows employees to directly interact with the security department and renew, change, or report a lost employee identification card.

Information Systems (IS)

Your Information Systems department will love the power that the intranet has to offer. If your organization has a help desk that takes questions on hardware, software, and PC/LAN issues, the intranet will help facilitate a quick response to the end user. Most help desks are overworked and understaffed because of the large amount of personal computers in organizations today.

With the introduction of new applications and new operating systems, managing information systems can be time consuming. Every help desk has a list of standard questions and problems that they are asked every single day. With an intranet in place, the users can pull up the Information Systems' help desk home page and choose from a variety of options. User can search under Printing Problems to find out why they can't print envelopes correctly. They can look under the Windows 95 directory for help on the newly installed Windows 95 operating system. All of the basic questions that users ask repeatedly can be stored and made accessible to the end user. Doing so would save time and allow the help desk to focus on more demanding challenges.

Message forums are also a fantastic way to disseminate information. Employees can access message areas on a variety of computer topics in search of help. The employee can read messages from others in the company who might have similar questions, and the employee can even drill down through the responses to gather answers. A message forum on Windows 95 is a perfect place to search and post questions that someone might have on the product. Experts from IS as well as superusers who have had the same questions in the past can answer just about anything anyone puts out there.

Intranet Issues

For corporations that construct intranets, the benefits are enormous. As with every new technology, however, some concerns do exist, and the intranet raises the same concerns as any communication tool does. I briefly cover some of these concerns and address them with more in-depth solutions in subsequent chapters.

Are You Sure You Want an Intranet?

Because corporate intranets are the latest craze, you want to make sure you are not implementing an intranet just to keep up with the corporate Joneses, or because the head of the department wants one because his buddy down the street has one in his organization. You should want and need an intranet to solve a problem. This problem is usually some type of communication challenge that you can overcome or do more productively with the use of an intranet.

You also need to consider your alternatives to intranet technology. Distributing a memo that needs to go to only three people is probably better to do on paper than to create a Web page for it. So, weigh your alternatives. Also consider this important note: An intranet's power lies in its ability to share information. It thrives on open communication and the sharing of ideas in Web sites, discussion groups and message bases, and links.

What Is the Scope of the Intranet?

Corporations need to write the mission statement for their intranet, and define the scope of the project from its inception. You need to define the issues as to what information will be allowed and what information will be prohibited on the intranet in the early planning stages. Establish the policies and procedures for your intranet. A mission statement should encompass the following: To disseminate information to the organization in a quick, usable format to improve overall communication.

What Should the Policies and Procedures Manual Contain?

This manual most likely already exists in your organization. It is sometimes called the employee handbook, or it might be concealed as policies and procedures. The policies that you already follow every day for work are the same policies that you should implement for your intranet.

Take a look at your telephone policies. The manual should state that the telephone is to be used for business purposes only. The same goes for the fax machine, the computer, and so on.

This business-use policy should apply to the intranet as well. An intranet should be used as a business tool, and nonbusiness material and material of a personal nature should not be disseminated on the intranet. The same rule applies for e-mail systems. (Recently, I was hit with a flood of chain letter e-mails asking to be signed and forwarded to help save Sesame Street from being taken off the air.) Moderating intranet message forums and checking content needs to be done to some extent to avoid these types of postings.

Common sense usually is enough to keep content on topic. All rules have exceptions, and most organizations publish a monthly newsletter containing birthdays, service awards, promotions, and the like. These types of HR recognition vehicles are perfect for employee moral and recognition. Information of a personal nature, when used appropriately in an HR context, can be very rewarding.

A Word About Policies and Procedures

An intranet is a virtual community and thus should be treated like a community. Creating a sense of community is difficult if you have to go through fences and locks to gain access to the intranet. Make it easy to create a sense of community and a rich environment of knowledge and information.

Can Each Department Have a Web Site on the Intranet?

Each department can and should have a Web presence on the intranet if those sites add value to the internal Web. What is considered valuable to one person or area might have no use to another, so determining value is a subjective. There are several ways to approach the design, maintenance, and support issues, and I cover these in more detail in the next chapter. The ultimate goal is to have each area or department constructing and maintaining its own Web site on the intranet. Because the department uses the information daily and knows its area and task better than anyone else, it should own its Web presence on the intranet.

After You Construct the Pages, Who Should Approve Them?

Guidelines used on the WWW and the Internet are appropriate for your intranet as well. Pay attention to copyright issues and the proper use of message forums and e-mail. Provide a basic layout and design reference for newcomers who are interested in learning more about design and presentation.

Just remember that guidelines are just that: guidelines. You don't need an intranet police department that counts every graphic byte or determines whether the content that people want to disseminate is valuable. A clearinghouse for Web content will bottleneck the process and kill the advantage that an intranet has to offer, which is to publish and disseminate information instantly.

The information should be written and approved at the department level or lower. Each department needs to decide what it wants to publish, and determine what value it adds to the community. It is then up to that department to review and edit its content. If you look to the WWW for examples, you will notice that poorly constructed Web pages with little content do not get as many hits as sites with soupier resources and content. The same evolution will develop in your intranet community. Sites with little value to the masses will get fewer hits than sites that go the extra mile and offer deep content.

To avoid duplication of information or inaccurate data, you should encourage content ownership in your intranet. Several ways to determine content ownership are available, and your organization's size plays a role in this decision. Small organizations might have a Webmaster who is responsible for the entire intranet. This responsibility would include the hardware and software side, as well as design, distribution, and ownership of all Web material. The typical setup for an organization would have three distinct roles: Webmaster, gatekeepers, and local authors. Each of these roles is described in the next few sections.

The Webmaster

Ideally, the Webmaster's role is to take charge of the technical aspects of the intranet. The Webmaster is responsible for the physical hardware and the software applications on that box. The Webmaster also keeps up with the latest developments in intranet technology, and is conscious of security issues.

The Gatekeepers

The gatekeepers are the designers and creators of the department Web sites. If a department has a fantastic idea for a Web site, but does not have the technical expertise or the time to design the site, then the gatekeeper does the storyboarding for the site, and helps the department with the site design and creation.

You will find that some departments have employees that are capable of design, authoring, and implementation of their Web site on the intranet. These departments don't need a full-blown site designed for them from scratch. All they require is a little guidance with style issues and a place to send their files.

The majority of your departments, however, will come to the gatekeeper with a cocktail-napkin sketch of their idea, and will need training and a great deal of guidance along the way. This is the case in almost all new intranets, especially in organizations that are just now entering into computer technology. Of course, organizations that are in the computer industry, as opposed to organizations in other fields, will have more individuals that are capable of designing their own sites,.

The goal of the gatekeeper is to train the department. This means getting the department involved in every step of the process. After the departments site is done and online, the real challenge is to teach a person or a team in that department how to maintain and create new content.

After the site is online, the gatekeeper needs to try to remove him- or herself from the process and just offer guidance and training when needed. Remember, an intranet is not like your typical application that you might be accustomed to creating. An intranet is a living application that will die if it is not maintained and updated. It is always evolving and changing.

I often compare an intranet to a newspaper. If you drive down to the corner store, buy a newspaper, and read it, and then drive back the next day and discover that this paper is an exact reprint of yesterday's, you'll stop buying the paper pretty quickly. If the content on your intranet is not fresh and up-to-date, your readers will not use the system and will stop coming back. This takes me to the last position in my content structure: local authors.

Local Authors

The local author is the person or staff in each department that creates the content for that department. Once again, each department should be responsible for its own content, and you will need to be able to offer the departments guidance and training as needed. The job of the local authors is to collect that department's "top stories" and turn them into Web pages for that department's site on the intranet.

Again, a newspaper comparison (or magazine) works here. There is a staff that collects and writes the stories, which can be press releases, catalogs, important meeting information, forms, on-the-job training, human resources materials, you name it. After the information is collected and a storyboard is drawn up, then the authors start creating the actual Web pages. The authors will need guidance when new graphics or new applications need to be added.

Depending on the complexity of the graphics or new applications, the author can be the sole creator, or the gatekeeper can step in and help with these new projects as they come along. The use of forums, online help, design tips, frequently asked questions (FAQs), and discussion groups will help provide the authors the support they need to develop an outstanding presence. You can set up a sample department Web site to allow users to explore your coding. Let your authors know that using the examples and graphics on these pages is all right, and explain to them that they will not learn how to create everything overnight. The learning takes time, and as their skills sharpen, they can always go back and add new things to their department Web sites.

How to Author Content

So, your business unit wants a Web and wants it yesterday. Before you take the plunge and move to the authoring stage, make sure that you've finished the proper planning and storyboarding. (I cover storyboarding in more detail in Chapter 2.)

When you are ready to author content, you basically have three choices.

The main choice is more like a requirement, and that is to learn HTML. I show you how to write beautiful, efficient, HTML later in the book and go through a bunch of examples that you can print and stick on your refrigerator for everyone to see. Why learn HTML? I know, you have this really cool editor that does it all for you. But what happens when Netscape Communication Corporation comes out with the new image layering tag? Do you want to have to wait six months for a new editor that supports the new tags? If you know HTML, you can just type the new tag yourself in your HTML code. Editors also do some funky things with your documents. What you create in your editor usually is not what displays the first time you plug it into your Netscape Navigator browser. You usually have to go into the code and edit some of the tags that the editor stuck in your page. So, why be wedded to your editor when you can have the latest tags available the day they are introduced to the world?

Learning the HTML coding is best so that you can understand what is taking place in the browser. After you get the coding down, you can then try out one the many editors available on the WWW. In Appendix C, I explain Netscape Gold and show you how to easily create documents in its easy-to-use WYSIWYG (What You See Is What You Get) interface. No cheating: you need to read the chapters on HTML and do all the examples before you go on to the Netscape Gold chapters.

I have already touched on the second choice you have when authoring content, which is to use an HTML editor. Editors make creating Web content a great deal quicker, and they are just to the point that they actually work pretty well. You will still run into bugs, or want to tweak your pages, and you will need to know HTML to do this. There are many editors available on the WWW that you can try out. Take a look at `http://tucows.com` and you will be able to find at least 50 editors at this site that will get you started. Microsoft also has a trial version of FrontPage 97 available at its Web site at `http://www.microsoft.com`. Netscape Gold is also a great editor, available at Netscape's Web site: `http://www.netscape.com`.

The third way to create Web content is to use a converter. This is a kind of filter that takes your regular documents, such as Microsoft Word, Excel, or PowerPoint, and converts them directly into HTML. This is an easy way to take your existing files and get them on your intranet. One disadvantage is that these converters don't offer the additional features and control that HTML editors do. So, your document might not look just the way you want it after it comes out of the converter. You can download Internet Assistants for your Microsoft Office products; this converts your existing files into HTML. Also Microsoft Office 97 has a built-in feature that allows you to save and publish your regular documents directly to your intranet server in HTML with a click of a button.

How Should You Store Content?

In the next two chapters, I discuss how to set up your directories and site navigation. These two items are separate and are not interconnected as most people think. Your directory structure should allow easy access to only privileged users (for security) and this also makes it easier to remember what is where. Your site navigation is the layout and structure of your intranet. You will want to make navigation easy and user friendly.

Theming

A common question that organizations ask concerns the site's theme. Some Webmasters like to have the entire intranet based on one theme. This requires more time and effort to try to keep every business unit using the same icons, bullets and buttons. Instead of focusing on a common theme, however, you should focus on superior content. Each business unit should be encouraged to develop its own theme, preferably reflecting its department's mission, function, and goals.

When each area has its own theme, users have an easier time determining which area of the intranet they are in. Place more of your time and effort on developing great content, instead of patrolling the intranet for guideline violations.

Links

This subject concerns navigation and layout. The main question here is, will the user get lost if you have links from one department to another department?

When you design your department's Web site, sooner or later you will want to connect to similar information and other materials that might not follow the standard hierarchical structure. You are probably scratching your head, saying "Of course I will want to link to other sites in the intranet. What's the big deal?" The concern here is a minimal one. Some areas might not want you to link your intranet site to another intranet site or department. The fear is that if one of the departments changes a page, you will have the famous 404 error, because of the broken link. Just recently, tools have been created, such as Microsoft's FrontPage, that will manage your Web site and keep all your links intact. As a result, this error is becoming less of an issue as applications are developed that address this concern.

When you start having your project development meetings for your intranet, you will come out with a notebook full of questions like the ones above. The easiest way to answer all these questions when you are starting up your intranet is to look at what is in place today, the WWW, and take what works from that and apply it to your situation. Don't try to reinvent the wheel. So, should you link from department to department? Yes! This is the strength of the Web.

When Tim Berners-Lee invented the World Wide Web, the reason he did it was so that he could globally share information. The strength of the Web lies in its ability to link documents and multimedia. Just like in the WWW, each Web site on the intranet will be responsible for maintaining its own links. Departments can send messages to the Webmaster, gatekeepers, and authors, if they are changing their directory structure to help avoid broken links. There are also tools available that will automatically check your links and let you know what is broken. This is the ideal way to monitor and maintain links.

File Size and Graphics

The Web currently supports two graphic file types: GIF and JPEG. Keeping these image files vibrant, colorful, and small is a challenge. You ultimately want your Web pages to load quickly, in 30 to 45 seconds or less. Graphics, sound files, and multimedia can add a new dimension and value to your site, but these elements exact a price in terms of loading time. I show you when to use GIF as opposed to JPEG formats, and how to reduce your file sizes to allow your pages to load quickly and smoothly while still displaying graphics and even animation.

When you are adding graphics that are large, make sure that they are adding value. Determine your Web page or site's objective from the beginning, and add the appropriate media. In other words, don't go whole hog and scan in the front page of the newspaper everyday, or design pages with a lot of animation and scrolling text just for the heck of it. In your style guide, you should give examples, screen shots, and drawings that show how to use graphics and multimedia in Web pages. The style guideline should be used only as a guideline, and the ultimate decision on each department's site should be left to that department.

Helper Applications and Other Add-Ons

With so many helper applications available, which ones should you use on your intranet? Standardizing on a browser and helper applications is difficult when you encounter, often available for free, a daily flood of new applications on the Web.

Choose the applications that will allow your departments to communicate more effectively, and that will allow them to be more effective on the intranet. With so much out there, the decision can be overwhelming, but you must make a decision to get started. It's just like shopping for a new personal computer for yourself. Each month, the *Computer Shopper* lists the system that you want for $200.00 less than it was last month, and each time it gets better. Last month's 8-speed CD-ROM is 10X this month. You're always waiting until next month to make the purchase.

You need to take the information that is available and make the best choice you can right now. If you're still waiting for the newest operating system to come out of beta and go through a few revisions before you seriously consider upgrading from DOS 1.0, you will never catch up to your competition.

Summary

By now, you have the basics out of the way and have covered the birth of the World Wide Web and the differences between the Internet and intranet. You should also now have some ideas of how an intranet can help your organization in its day-to-day operations, as well as in the future.

What's Next!

You can now move on to discussions of what you need to do to get your intranet started. I'll show you how to choose an organizational model, do some planning, determine the necessary skill sets, and develop your prototype.

Chapter | 2

Getting Your
Intranet Started

In the early days, Information Systems would have done everything needed in development, design, and maintenance of an intranet. Today, the power of the intranet is on everyone's desktop. The role of Information Systems is now more one of support, hardware, and connectivity. This new role gives more power to the areas and departments that ultimately create the content and use the system on a daily basis. Your organization needs to consider some important issues when designing and maintaining a Web site:

- What will be the overall design and look of your intranet?
- Will you need to set up a clearinghouse for each piece of information and every page to pass through before allowing it to be placed on the intranet? (With any luck, you won't, because instant publishing is the beauty of this system.)
- What policies and procedures will you have in place to handle inappropriate material and conduct that might occur in the intranet?
- How will you introduce new applications and features as they are released on the WWW?

Choosing Organizational Models

This section offers three organizational models to apply to the development of your intranet. You can choose the one best suited to your organization.

The Decentralized Approach

One method is a free-for-all. This works well in smaller organizations, whose size makes them easier to manage. This *decentralized* approach allows all the employees in the organization to set up a Web server on their desktop and publish their content. I see the hair rising on the back of the IS folks' necks. Yes, this is a support and training issue, and for larger organizations, this is probably not the way to go because you will run into different departments using different browsers and helper applications that might not be compatible.

The Centralized Approach

The other approach is to *centralize* everything. Information Systems houses the Web server(s) in one location, which increases physical security and improves maintenance. The centralization model provides a central shop for Web development. The key players in the Web development shop wear many hats. If your organization has a department that is responsible for communication, this area is the perfect place to set up your Web shop. With a Web shop, you instantly create a one-stop point of reference for all departments with Web and communication issues. The following describes how this model works.

A department, say Human Resources, wants to add a Web site to the corporate intranet. The members of the department discuss the issues and storyboard of the entire process with the gatekeeper. The Human Resources department has two sharp guys who are experts already in HTML and communication media. They have already started developing a Human Resources Web site demo for the head of the department. All this department needs is to dedicate some time and resources to these two gentlemen, and back them with support from the gatekeeper and the Web shop.

In case you don't remember, the gatekeeper is the person who works with the Web shop and helps the department get up and running. Gatekeepers share their intranet expertise, help train, explain style guidelines, and are available to give guidance. The gatekeepers also interact with the Web shop, and each keeps the other informed of new developments.

After Human Resources develops its Web site, all it really needs is space on the Web server. A 5- to 10-megabyte slot for each department should give adequate space for a new and growing site. The server and the space on the hard drive, as well as the connectivity, TCP/IP and IP addressing, and browser support all fall into Information Systems' hands. For departments that are capable of doing their own Web site, all that is needed is some guidance, a contact person who can help them avoid common mistakes (gatekeeper), and drive space and access privileges to their directory on the Web server.

 Another possibility is to have the exact opposite of the "two sharp guys" scenario. You might have departments full of people with fantastic ideas and uses for Web technology, but who have no idea how to begin. These areas need to be aware of your centralized Web shop and the services it offers. Otherwise, these areas might look outside and outsource a Web design and hosting Internet service provider (ISP) to do their site. You wouldn't want your company's valuable information sitting on someone else's server in some garage in Iowa.

Here's another example of the decentralized approach. Your office supply department hears about your Web shop and wants a Web site. The department currently produces a full-color catalog at $200 each, and sends these to each department in the company. Office supply department members realize that if they could have their own Web site, they could produce a full-color interactive presence instantly, for everyone in the company, at a tremendous cost savings.

But they don't know how to begin. They contact the Web shop and have a design team help them plan their site. The team works with the business unit to make a site that is tailored to their needs. After the team goes over the basics and draws up a storyboard of the site's main areas, it starts to design the site and develop a demo. The demo is shown to the office supply department for changes and modifications. When the office supply department likes the final product, it is placed on the intranet.

Now the office supply department has one of the following two options:

1. It can learn HTML and edit its own pages as new products are introduced and as needed.

2. The department can go back to the Web shop and have the shop make the changes.

The ultimate goal is to have the office supply department own and maintain its own site. If it does so, it can get the exact look and feel intended, and the department can update content instantly without having to wait for the Web shop to do the work. The office supply department would utilize the gatekeeper, online help, and the Web shop, as well as Information Systems for guidance and training.

Here is another example, with a different twist. The Web shop does everything for the department. The Web shop could charge each business unit for its development time to justify its existence. The disadvantage with having everything go through the Web shop is the amount of time this takes. Having a Web shop develop pages and set priorities concerning which site should be done first takes time. The department has to wait to have the information published and updated. If the information is time critical, this system will not work effectively. This is the ultimate in centralization: the Web shop is doing everything for the department. Here, everything is being done in one centralized location. The Web shop takes care of development and hosting, and the department just gives input on what it wants the shop to create. This is also comes with a price tag attached, and the department might have to wait longer to have the site and applications developed because the Web shop might have other jobs already in the queue.

A Little of Both

The final model takes pieces from both the centralized and decentralized models. This model has a main centralized intranet and enables different departments that want to do their own thing, to do so. Some departments in your organization will want to share some information with the rest of the organization and also keep some information secure in their own department. Security departments, for example, benefit from having an informational Web site explaining who they are, how to contact them, the latest Bolos, and so on, on the regular corporate intranet. They also want a secure intranet that is on their own server in their location, however.

Planning Your Intranet

Now that you have looked at all the different models, you are getting closer to the fun stuff: the design of your intranet. Previously, I discussed the different models for support and growth of your intranet. I also covered some of the basic challenges, and gave some examples of possible uses for intranet technology in your organization.

Each department has a different goal and mission in mind when deciding what it wants to convey and do on its intranet site. Make sure that you have an idea of what content you want to display and what features and services to offer on your site.

Generating Ideas for Your Intranet

You can look to the WWW to get ideas of external Web sites that work, and use these ideas in your corporate intranet. If you are new to the WWW and intranets, and the examples I gave earlier on uses for intranet technology did not spark your imagination, you can do several things to drum up some fantastic uses for intranet technology in your area. The best way to learn about the Web and to get an idea of its amazing capabilities and reach is to spend a few days surfing around the WWW. Another great way to generate ideas is to conduct brainstorm sessions with your department. If you still haven't determined a focus, keep reading this book. I go over a plethora of examples and display screen shots to get you thinking of the possibilities.

After you have put together these initial development steps as described so far, you will move on to developing your mission statement.

Formulating Your Mission Statement

When you put your ideas down in writing, you are well on your way to developing your intranet. The mission statement allows you to define your scope, purpose, and goals. A clearly defined mission statement should be 25 words or less. The first time I wrote down my mission statement, it was a page and a half long—about the length of a thesis title. That is okay for a start. Take your first version of your mission statement and tailor it again and again until you get to the heart of your scope. Doing so takes some time, and as I said, you can't always get it right the first time. When you are determining your department's mission, your Web shop's mission, or the Information Systems' mission, try to involve people who will be involved in the intranet effort. Eliciting input from everyone is a good general approach for all the decisions involved in your intranet development. The more minds you have working on the idea, the more user friendly and useful your end product will be.

Here are a few samples of mission statements for different areas:

- Human Resources: To provide an easy-to-access information system containing human-relations issues, including training and employee benefit programs.
- Web Shop: To provide Web authoring, graphics, and multimedia services to all business units in an efficient, timely manner. Train, support, and foster departments on intranet technology.
- Information Services: To provide the connectivity, support, and necessary hardware to allow current and future trends in the intranet arena.

After you define your mission statement, write down the specifics, policies, and procedures that fall under your defined scope. Start with a general mission, such as the ones in the preceding list, and then define more specifics later as your intranet develops.

Defining Tasks

Your mission statement gives you a broad view of what to offer and strive for. You need to take this broad view and define exactly what you plan to do. The Web shop's mission statement, "To provide Web authoring, graphics, and multimedia services to all business units in an efficient, timely manner. Train, support, and foster departments on intranet technology," explains the general scope of the Web shop.

But how, exactly, will you accomplish these goals and tasks? You must define these elements specifically. The Web shop obviously will want to offer training and guidance. It can do this through the gatekeepers. The gatekeepers can guide the business units that need that extra help to complete their intranet. They meet with all the areas in the Web shop to determine how to distribute the information effectively. They also help the business unit with each step, from layout, graphic design, and authoring, to implementation and upkeep. For the Web shop, the services need to be defined and assigned to the members of the team. The best possible team consists of four specific types of individuals, described in the following sections.

Marketing Dreamer

The marketing dreamer in the Web shop is the individual (or team) who sits down with the gatekeeper and the business unit and listens to what they are trying to accomplish with their internal Web site. The dreamer then takes all the information available about the department and the task at hand, and compiles it to get an overall idea of the content and feel for the site.

Dreamers suggest other innovative ways to display and convey the message and purpose of the site. This person is in touch with the latest developments in the industry, and doesn't necessarily know how to write CGI scripts, but knows enough about them and how they can be used to make the intranet more productive and interactive. Too often, intranets lack this dreamer and are constructed more by mainframe technical people. These people have skills on the technical side of an intranet, but are often not as creative and open as they need to be to play the role of the marketing dreamer.

Often, intranets that are created by just one entity, such as the technical Information Systems department, are created to complete a task. This is appropriate for applications such as a telephone directory, but not very effective for displaying a weekly newsletter or content that needs to draw users in and keep their interest. To create a successful intranet, you need a well-rounded team that can draw on each member's skills and expertise. Finding one individual with all these skills and traits is difficult.

The marketing dreamer is also in charge of—you guessed it—marketing. If you have a large organization, you need to advertise your services to the business units. Think of the business units as your customers. You need to inform them of your services via brochures, newsletters, phone calls, meetings, company trade shows, posters, and of course, on your Web site.

You will be amazed at the number of business units that are not aware of what an intranet is, or what it can offer. Educating business units on what an intranet is, and what it is not, is an important job. The marketing dreamer might also see, along with the gate-keeper, that the task the business unit is trying to accomplish simply cannot be done with Web technology. In this case, the marketing dreamer and gatekeeper guide the business unit toward the appropriate technology that can effectively handle the task.

Graphic Artist

After the marketing dreamer meets with the gatekeeper and the business unit, and they decide on what they want to accomplish with their Web site, the time has come to start making the actual graphic design and layout of the site. I discuss graphics in Chapter 6, and navigation techniques a bit later in this chapter and in more depth in Chapter 3. If you are not at all artistically inclined, leaving this work to the professionals is best. Smaller organizations may not have the luxury to hire a graphic artist and all the other positions that I describe. If that is the case, you need skills in all the aspects of implementing an intranet.

Although this implementation is not an easy task, you can accomplish it by starting small and growing gradually as you become more efficient in the different disciplines. If you can afford the luxury of having a graphic artist on your team, you will be adding a spark of professionalism that takes a certain eye and knack to achieve. The graphic artist is in charge of logos, designs, special effects, animation, sound, and other multimedia content that falls under this area. Creating quality graphics is time consuming, and having a professional who is skilled in Adobe Photoshop, Abode Illustrator, Adobe Page Maker, 3D Studio, various Corel programs, a list of utilities and special filters, as well as map and layout applications, can save you many sleepless nights trying to create that perfect logo.

The Author

Creating an intranet is much like creating a newspaper or magazine: You distribute information to the masses. Instead of paper, however, your canvas is electronic. This electronic distribution enables a greater reach, more interactivity, and significant cost reductions. Similar to a newspaper staff of writers, your intranet Web shop needs authors to write content and help areas convey their message in the most effective manner. These people should have a background in journalism, English, or a related field.

The Programmer

Every Web team needs a person who breathes life into the creation. The programmer is the person who takes the form and attaches it to a CGI script so that it can deliver responses to the business unit. The programmer works with Information Systems to develop databases and integrate existing systems with the intranet. Again, finding a great programmer who is also a terrific dreamer, marketer, graphic designer, and author is difficult. So, try to develop a team that has all these talents.

Coming Up with the Project Plan

Before you go out to the business units and offer your intranet services, or before you develop your department's own intranet Web site, have a plan of action. If you are an Information Systems department, a communication department, or any other department establishing an intranet services division (Web shop) for your organization, establish a team of players with the aforementioned skills, and start working on their individual roles and the Web shop's overall marketing role. Have your services listed. If you charge for these services, make sure that the charges are also stated. If you are a business unit, bring your organization into the technology age and establish an intranet starting with your area, and then find people in other areas who can become part of a team to develop your project plan. Bring Information Systems in at the start to help develop the intranet. People from Information Systems have the technical background and network expertise to answer your questions as you embark on this new venture.

After you have determined your plan of action, you need to start thinking about marketing and selling your intranet concept.

Selling the Intranet

So, you have made up your mind to conquer an intranet. Now you have to sell the idea to your boss, the department, and the organization.

The intranet is like the latest fashion craze. It's like a new line of American jeans that has just been introduced in Russia: people can't wait to get a pair. People don't even know what an intranet is or what it is capable of doing, in some cases, but they know they want a Web presence. Before you start setting up focus groups to discuss what an intranet can offer, you need to make a demonstration of some sort.

A meeting about the WWW and intranet is not effective if you just get up and talk. Remember that most of your audience probably has not seen or been on the WWW, and will have no idea what you are talking about unless you show it. Creating a demo site and doing a presentation in a browser such as Netscape Navigator are easy. The simplest Web site design with hyperlinks between documents and other Web sites impresses any crowd that is new to intranet technology. When you create your pages, use data and documents from your organization to show the audience a real example of what an intranet can do. (See Chapter 11, which covers making business presentations using your browser.) If you already have an idea of what you want to create and have a good storyboard drawn up, feel free to jump ahead and start discovering how to create your presentation.

Defining the Audience

Each department in your organization will have a different interest and different use for intranet technology. Don't overlook any department when you do your intranet demonstrations. Departments such as landscaping may surprise you with an interest that you didn't expect. Landscaping could post meeting minutes, set up focus groups, and even create a repository/photo dictionary of plants and flowers that are on the property. (Have you ever wondered why that plant in your office stays green year after and year while the plants you have at home have to be tossed out once a month? If the landscape department had a green thumb landscaping page, you could learn more than you ever imagined.)

The intranet brings every department together in a global environment that fosters information sharing and education. Also, remember that not every area in your organization has access to a computer. An intranet won't replace all forms of printed material immediately, and it probably won't ever completely replace paper documents.

You can allow access to the intranet for departments that do not have access to computers by turning your training facility into a career-development center. When you aren't using your training facility to teach computer classes, the facility can be open to the different departments to learn self-paced Windows programs, experiment on the intranet, and gain access to the WWW. With this facility, employees who lack access to a computer can educate themselves and learn what the other departments have to offer through the career development center. A department such as Concierge in a resort can access the WWW and print the top stories from a European newspaper for an international guest staying at the resort. Employees can use the facility during a break or before or after work to access company job listings. They also can use the facility to author their department's own Web content if they do not have access to a computer in their area.

Determining Needed Equipment

How you design your intranet is dictated by the equipment (workstations) on which you will be running it. To enjoy graphics, multimedia, and interactivity, strive for a Pentium 75 workstation in your departments. You can run an intranet on a 486, but the time it takes to process some of the tasks needed on your intranet will be excruciatingly slow. If your standard is a Pentium 75 box, you can use GUI interfaces, graphical Web browsers, and image maps. If you must design for the lowest common denominator for areas that cannot display graphics on their terminals, you have two options.

The first option entails the following:

- Create a graphically intense site for the users who have access to high-speed terminals with graphic capabilities
- Create a text-based virtual Web site

The disadvantage to this approach is that you have to maintain two sites with the same information. If you make a change to one site, you must do it again for the text-based site.

The second option entails the following:

- Use alternate text in place of images
- Use lists of hyperlinks along with image maps

The alternate text will display in place of the images for users who are graphically challenged. Image maps will not work for users who obviously cannot display images, so including a definition listing of the available hypertext links will allow your text-only users to access the information. When new equipment is ordered and installed in the areas, this is also a perfect time to stamp the computers with the Web browser and TCP/IP, set up IP addresses, and install and test all the helper applications standard to your organization. I hesitate to give specifics; when I give minimum equipment recommendations, I run the risk of someone picking up this book later and laughing at the words "Pentium 75" the way we laugh now at pictures of people in bellbottom jeans.

Brainstorming

You are very likely not the only one in your organization who has had the idea to build an intranet. When you do demonstrations, you will probably find individuals from diverse backgrounds who will be interested in your project.

Everyone in the organization can contribute to the success of the intranet. When you contact departments with similar expertise in Web technology, create a focus group that meets weekly or monthly to discuss ideas and interest. You should also include business units that are new to intranet technology, or that know nothing at all about it. After you introduce these individuals to a Web browser, they will immediately see a use for this technology in their area. The more people you can get to buy into the idea of an intranet, the better. Start early, so that business units can plan their budgets for computer upgrades if necessary.

> **NOTE:** You will be amazed at all the ideas that are generated from brainstorming intranet possibilities. Take your intranet demo even to the business units that you wouldn't expect to have a use for the tool. Have the front-line employees attend the demonstration, and then ask them to brainstorm ideas on how they could use this technology in their area.

Every area can use improved communication and instant access to up-to-date information. You are likely to walk away from your brainstorm sessions with a list of more than 100 uses for an intranet. Your job is then to reduce the list to a manageable size with the help of that department. Cut the list down to maybe 10 key applications. After you try out the first 10 applications on the intranet, you can start adding to the site as time permits.

Conducting a Survey

A great way to determine your user base is with a traditional survey. This helps determine your users' computer literacy, Internet and WWW experience, interest level in intranet technology, training requirements, current computer capabilities in the areas, and other valuable data. The following is a sample survey to use as a guide in developing your own survey.

To create the most effective and user-friendly intranet for Miracle Corporation, we would like to get your expertise and help from the start. The Miracle Corporation Intranet is a communication vehicle that you, the employee, will help to create and also maintain. So, please take the time to answer each question on the survey. If you are new to intranet technology, let me give a quick explanation. Think of an intranet as a type of electronic newsletter. It's sort of like e-mail with graphics and interactivity. It also allows you to link documents together. By clicking on hyper-links, you will be able to view the entire intranet at your leisure.

Over the next few months, we will be constructing our corporate intranet and we are interested in getting your ideas and assistance. We will be having department brainstorming sessions over the next month. Please attend the brainstorming session for your department on the attached sheet. If you have any questions, please feel free to give us a call.

Thank You for your time and support.

Intranet Survey

Name:_____

Department:_____

Work Status: ❏ Full Time ❏ Part-Time

Computer:

Do you have access to a computer at home?
❏ Yes ❏ No

(If Yes, what type of computer do you have access to?)
❏ IBM/PC ❏ MAC ❏ Other_____

Do you have access to a computer at work?
❏ Yes ❏ No

(If Yes, what type of computer do you have access to?)
❏ IBM/PC ❏ MAC ❏ Other_____

What do you use your computer for at home?

❏ Word Processing ❏ Desktop Publishing ❏ Finances
❏ Spreadsheets ❏ Internet ❏ E-mail ❏ Games
❏ BBSs ❏ Education ❏ Other _____

Do you have access to online services?

❏   AOL (America On-line)

❏   Prodigy

❏   CompuServe

❏   ISP - PPP/SLIP (Direct Connection)

❏   MSN

❏   Other_____

Have you ever been on the World Wide Web?
❏ Yes ❏ No

Do you have easy access to the computer in your department?
❏ Yes ❏ No

Are you interested in computer training at work?
❏ Yes ❏ No

Intranet Questions:

Read the following and choose as many as apply. What information and areas would you be interested in seeing on the Miracle Intranet?

❏   Training information

❏   Statistics and measurements

❏   Message forums

❏   Job postings

continues

continued

- ❑ Cafeteria menu
- ❑ Customer's comments
- ❑ HR information
- ❑ Management profiles
- ❑ Phone book
- ❑ Meeting notes
- ❑ Project team information
- ❑ Employee benefits
- ❑ Rumor mill answers
- ❑ Update memos

Your Ideas and Suggestions:

_____

_____

_____

Web Pages and Home Pages

Online publishing offers many features, such as the ability to use hypertext to link to documents and other sites. A poorly designed intranet does not take full advantage of hyperlinks and also makes navigation difficult. By drawing out a plan of how your intranet structure should flow, you can see any gaps in your layout and discover ways to make easier and more productive links between documents.

First, you need an understanding of what a Web page is (see Figure 2-1). If you have been on the WWW, you have already seen various Web pages on the different sites you visited. A Web page consists of a single document (in most cases, an .HTM or .HTML file) that is loaded and displayed by your Web browser.

The home page is the first page that loads when you visit a Web site (see Figure 2-2). The home page usually contains links and references to the main sections of your presentation, as well as to other Web sites on your intranet. The home page is the first page displayed when a coworker accesses your intranet's Web address.

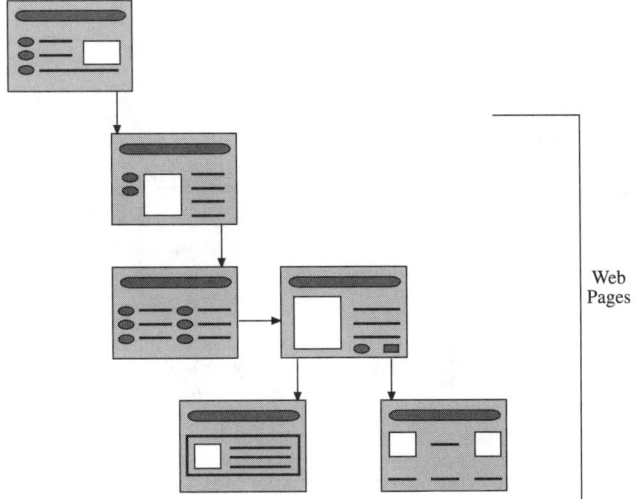

Web
Pages

FIGURE 2-1

The pages that follow the first (the home page) make up an intranet's Web pages.

Your address, also known as your *URL* (*Uniform Resource Locator*) is the address that is typed into the browser's address line and directly accesses your home page. An example is http://yourdomain.com/. Your Web server automatically loads the INDEX.HTM file (your home page) when you access your intranet. Each department can have its own home page and additional Web pages that branch off the main intranet home page.

Choosing a Presentation Method

Now it is time to decide on the best presentation method to convey your message and meet your site's goal. Do you want the user go in on the home page and just drill down through a numbered list of pages? Or, do you want the intranet site be set up like "eye candy" that invites users to surf around and explore areas as they happen across them?

If you were setting up an intranet site for an office supply catalog, you would have a few goals in mind. First, you would want users to have a way to pull up a specific item by name or category. After users find a category of similar products, you would probably want them to be able to compare price. You would also want them to be able to browse the entire selection at their leisure. Direct links to Web pages that tell how to order, give information on new products, and display this week's specials should be included on the home page. Direct links to these popular sections make access quick and easy.

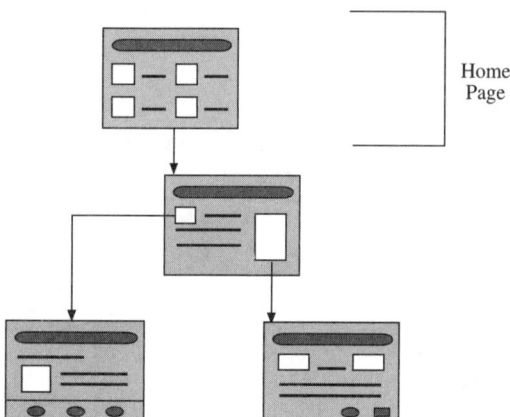

Home
Page

While you're storyboarding, you should break up your ideas into topics. The goal is to
determine how to divide your presentation into its main topics. Remember storyboarding
from Chapter 1? Or did you skip ahead? Making a storyboard is similar to drawing out
the key frames in an animated cartoon. This will allow you to get your key content and
ideas organized and to develop a flow from page to page. Try to maintain a similar size
for each of these topic areas, and create subtopics from the main topics, if necessary.
When you have gathered all your information, you can start determining how to turn
your topics into Web pages.

Deciding on a Navigation Model

I want to cover three main navigation models for intranet layout: hierarchical, linear, and
a mixture of both. These are discussed in the following sections.

Hierarchical

The easiest structure to navigate and understand is *hierarchical*. With hierarchical, the
guest enters from a main page with a broad listing or menu of topics. When the user
chooses a menu item, that selection takes them one page down in the structure to more
specific information. Hierarchical structure is easy to navigate, because users start at the
top and work their way down. When they want to return to the top, users go back up the
structure one page at a time or click on a home button that takes them directly back to
the beginning of the hierarchical structure. See Figure 2-3 for an example of a typical
hierarchical model.

Hierarchical

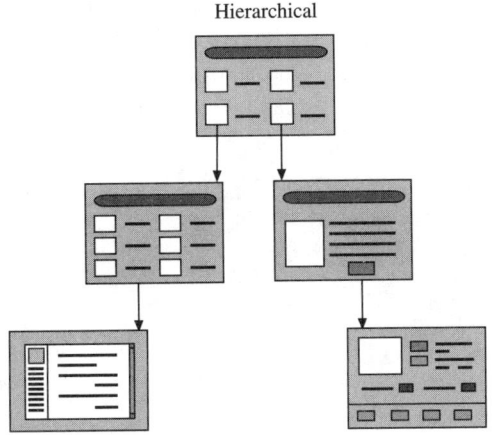

FIGURE 2-3

The hierarchical model starts from the top and moves down. This is similar to online help systems that you might have used in the past.

Most home pages in a hierarchical model will start with a listing of a table of contents. For example, a home page for an online office supply department might have a listing like the one in Figure 2-4.

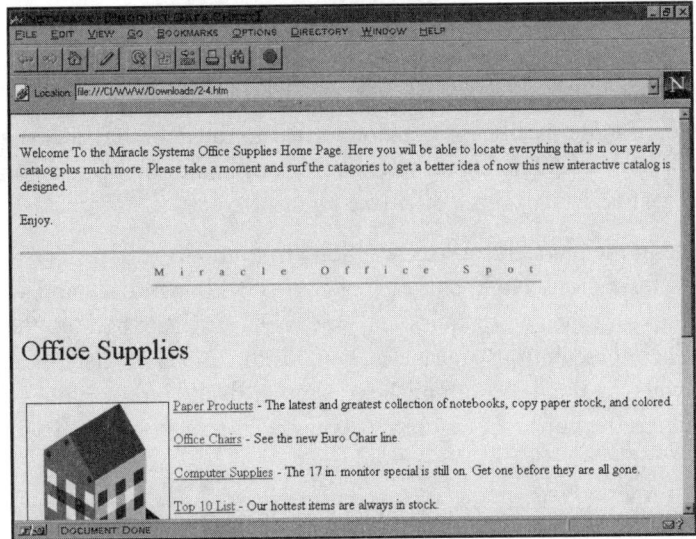

FIGURE 2-4

By selecting the category of interest (Paper Products), you can jump to another Web page in the Miracle intranet site.

The home page for the office supply department arranges the department's main topic areas in a definition listing that moves down one level when the user selects a product category.

This structure is similar to online help systems that have you start with a broad topic and narrow your search as you page through the menus. In the Miracle example site, when you select paper products, you are taken down one level to another menu that gives more specific information on the types of paper products available (see Figure 2-5).

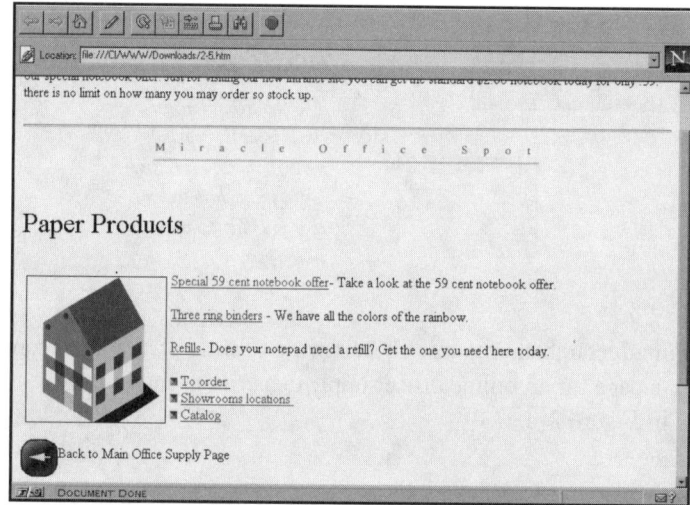

FIGURE 2-5

You are now linked deeper down in the hierarchical structure of the Miracle intranet site. You can continue down another layer by clicking on a hypertext link.

When you choose from this list of items, you again move one page down in the hierarchical structure to even more specific information related to the item in which you are interested. If you click on a $.59 notebook special offer, you link to the special notebook offer page and receive full details on the offer (see Figure 2-6).

Note that each page in the hierarchical structure flows from top to bottom. This makes getting lost unlikely for visitors. The top of each page also has both a Back and a Home button. These buttons give the guest a quick and easy way to navigate back up the hierarchical structure. When these buttons are labeled, your visitors can easily determine exactly where these icons will take them. A button labeled simply "Back," however, does not give as much information as the button in Figure 2-6, which tells the guest exactly where "Back" is (in this example, it's back to Paper Products).

One main disadvantage of a strict hierarchical model is the possibility of having to traverse many levels to reach the desired information. When you construct a hierarchy, try to keep the steps to get to information to a minimum. Three to four clicks down is a good gauge.

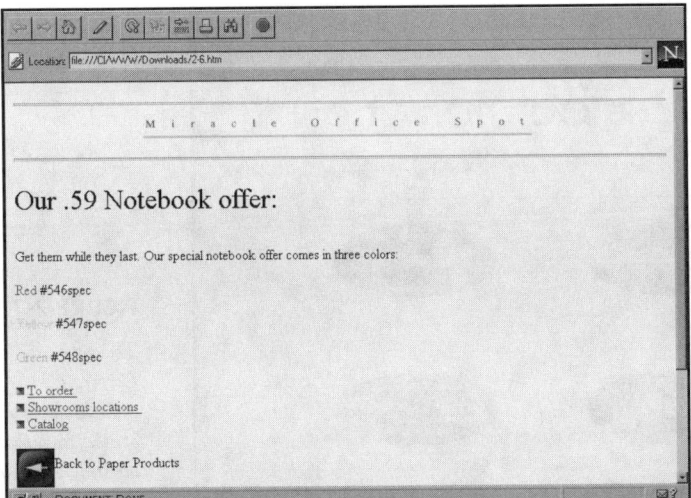

FIGURE 2-6

A graphic of the notebook and a full list of colors and styles available appear on this Web page. The user can even fill out an order online, or obtain information on ordering over the phone, by fax, or by mail.

Linear

Another popular model for Web presentations is a *linear* structure. Linear is the same structure that books use. You typically start reading a book at the beginning, and read page by page, one after the other until you reach the end. Linear is also easy for the user to understand, because users are restricted to the direction they can go in the presentation.

The linear model is great for on-the-job training, online books and manuals, directions, and material that is displayed in book format. Linear structure keeps your users on track, preventing them from surfing around the site and skipping over information. Because of its rigid structure, a linear site limits the users' ability to browse and explore the site freely. But, again, it is a perfect model for computer-based training sites.

Figure 2-7 shows an example of a site that uses linear modeling. The company tour, shown to all new hires in the organization, starts at the home page on the intranet site and moves from page to page in a book-like fashion. The user reads about the company's history on the first page, and then moves to the next page to see and hear a welcome announcement from the CEO of the company. By the end of the training tour, the user will have learned about the employee benefit package, vacation and sick days, where to park, what the company expects, and the overall company mission statement. Pages can be easily added and deleted from the linear structure when material needs to be changed or upgraded.

FIGURE 2-7

The home page for Miracle Corporation has four main links displayed and a list of other links that can be accessed by scrolling down the page.

By clicking on the Company Tour icon, the employee or new hire gets a guided tour of the organization. You can place hyperlinks in the linear structure to let the user skip ahead and avoid the strict linear design. Users working in the employee cafeteria, for example, might want to skip ahead to the production employee benefits pages and bypass the other benefit packages. This use of hyperlinks gives the reader a little more freedom in the linear structure (see Figure 2-8).

A Mix of Hierarchical and Linear

So, which model should you use for your intranet? Most of the time, you will use a mix of both hierarchical and linear. You need to be aware of some tricky maneuvers when you combine the two structures, however. Because users can now move backward and forward as well as side to side in the intranet site, becoming lost in your presentation is more likely. This can wreak havoc with a document such as an online book. While they're reading Chapter One, users might jump over to a related page in Chapter Three. When they click the Back button in the document, they go to the main introductory Web page for Chapter Three, which may not be what they expected. Returning to the page of several screens ago can be a confusing and difficult process.

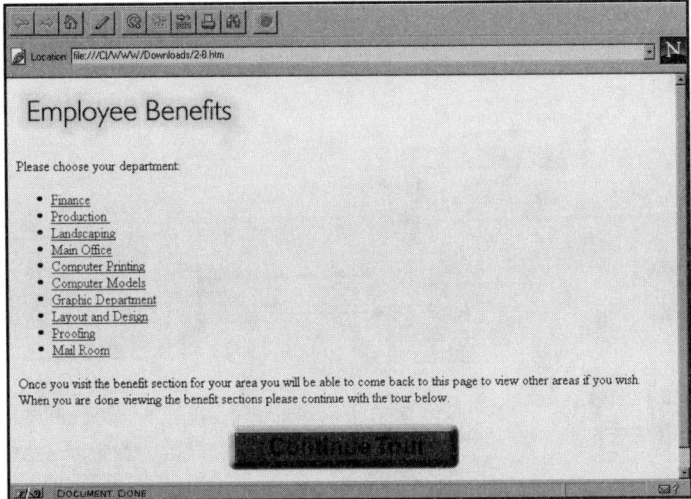

FIGURE 2-8

Users can pick their department and read information formatted for them without having to read all the other departments' information.

One way to minimize the confusion is to give complete descriptions in all your hypertext links. Let users know exactly where the link will take them. The mixture of hierarchical and linear structure in its most extreme form can also look like a Web, thus the name World Wide Web (see Figure 2-9). The Web structure is perfect for surfing around and gathering information as you happen across it. This type of Web model, however, does not work well with an intranet. Obtaining exact information is difficult if that information is not contained within a structure. In a Web model, pages are scattered around, and locating specific information is almost impossible.

Storyboarding

When you decide to build a Web presence, you'll find that doing so involves more than just putting up content. You need to understand design and navigation to create an effective, interactive intranet. The storyboard process is the first step in creating an easy-to-navigate intranet. When you start writing a report or a book, you don't start writing without first doing some planning, outlines, and creating a flow with a table of contents. This is similar to what you should do before you design your intranet. The best way to start designing your intranet is to write your ideas (keeping them on track with your mission statement), focus on the information you obtained from your brainstorming sessions, and apply this information to the goal that you want to accomplish with your intranet.

Web

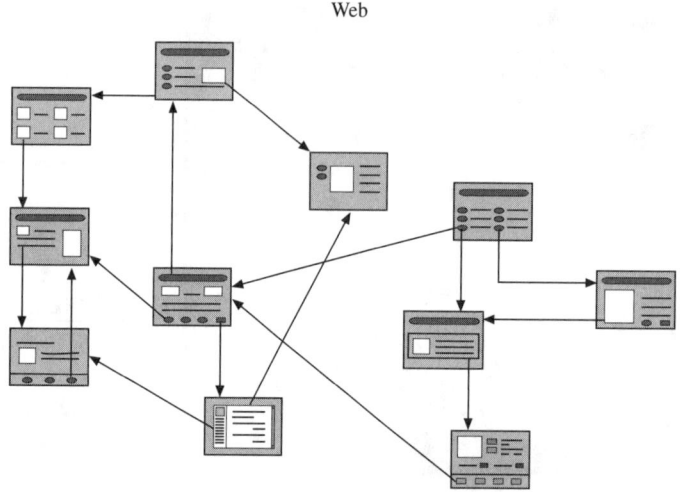

FIGURE 2-9

The directionless nature of a Web can make finding information difficult for users.

Stages of the Storyboard

This process physically lays out the theme, navigation, and sketches of page design for your intranet. In the storyboarding phase, you design rough sketches of your intranet pages. As a designer, you should make the complex undertaking of an intranet site easy to understand and to follow.

Material and content for your intranet arrives from many different sources, and you need to organize these components to create a layout and end design. Get your list of your Web page ideas. Taking the ideas from your brainstorming sessions, meetings, road shows, and individuals, create a main listing of what you want on your intranet. The listing for the fictitious Miracle Toys Corporation is displayed in Figure 2-10. You don't have to type the list. I typed it just to make sure that you could read it (my handwriting is terrible). The purpose of this listing is merely to get all the content you want on your intranet in written form.

When your list is done, take your Web page ideas and start putting them into logical groupings. Doing so allows you to organize your content and gives you ideas on the main sections that you need to create on your intranet (see Figure 2-11).

Certain content can be categorized into main groups. For example, some information and services will fit into human resources, sales, and company communications. By grouping your topics together into similar categories, you can start determining your home page categories and simplifying navigation for the user.

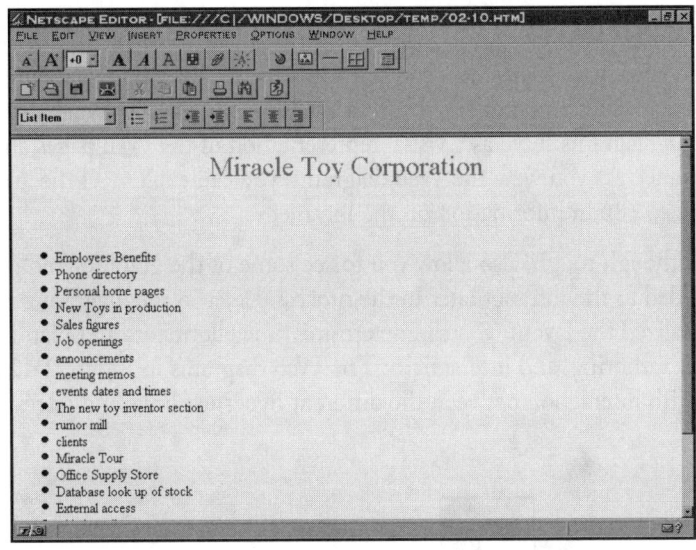

FIGURE 2-10

A listing puts your ideas and thoughts together about the services and content that you want to provide on your intranet.

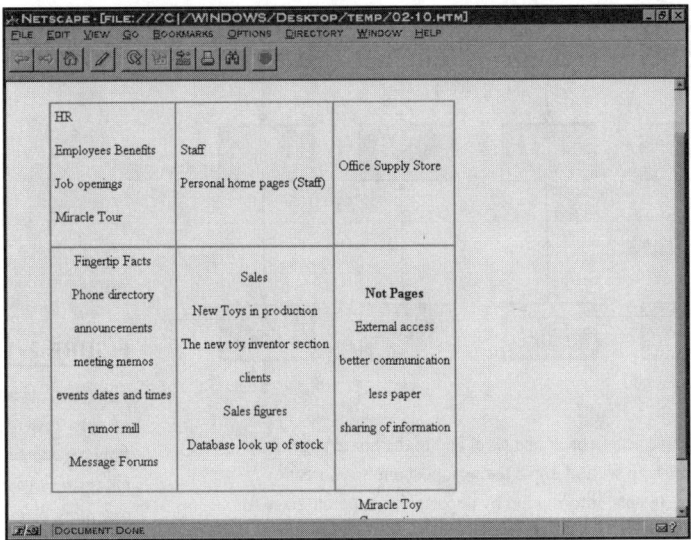

FIGURE 2-11

Grouping your ideas into main topic areas helps to establish categories for your intranet.

Using Flow Diagrams

After you establish your main topics, you can start drawing up Web flow diagrams. These diagrams are just rough sketches that allow you to establish the intranet's logic, structure, and navigation. The diagrams serve as a visual representation of the Web pages and the services in the intranet. As you view the Web diagrams, you can explore all the available links and pathways to obtain information on the intranet.

These diagrams, although rough, also allow you to see some of the graphics and page layout that will be added to the intranet later in the process. Later in the diagram process, when you have finalized the layout, you can determine time allotments and plan budgets for graphic design, authoring, and interactivity. The Web diagrams in Figure 2-12 show the rough layout with interaction between the different hypertext links and pages.

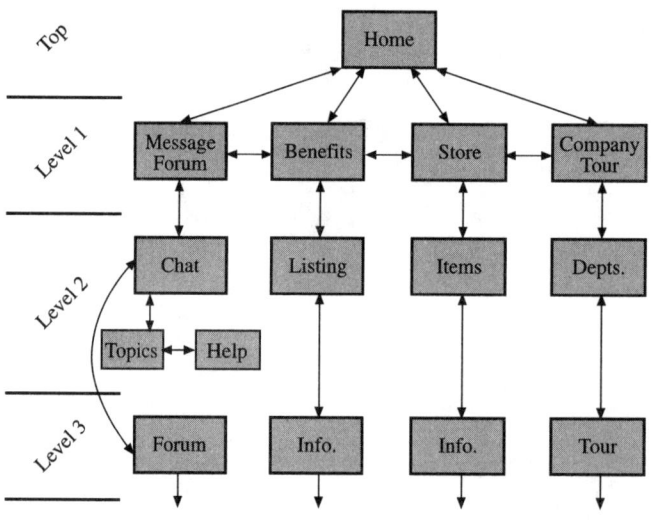

- Home: All pages have access back one level and to the home page
- Chat: Information, help section, topic listings, post and read areas
- Benefits: List of departments, information by department, separate page for 401K, medical, sick leave, vacation
- Store: Index by items, use search engine, sales page, contest, online ordering
- Company tour: Sound bites, video (break up by department)

FIGURE 2-12

The basic layout and your ideas on how to connect from page to page are conveyed in your Web diagrams, helping to visualize your project and make corrections before costly development.

NOTE: When you create your diagrams, you do not need to spend a great amount of time getting them to be 100 percent precise. The first diagrams that you create are to help you map out your ideas and navigation, and to allow you to catch mistakes before you create a final draft.

These Web diagrams draft the navigational model and help Web designers implement navigation elements in the pages. Remember, you will go through several sketches before you develop a final proposal. Don't spend large amounts of time trying to draw the perfect layout and graphics. These first drafts are to allow you to progress through the levels of your intranet design. Figure 2-13 takes the first rough draft to the next level. As the figure illustrates, you can start to see some links and graphic layout ideas. You can also add new pages and delete pages as you create more precise layouts. In this example, a help area is added that links off of the home page.

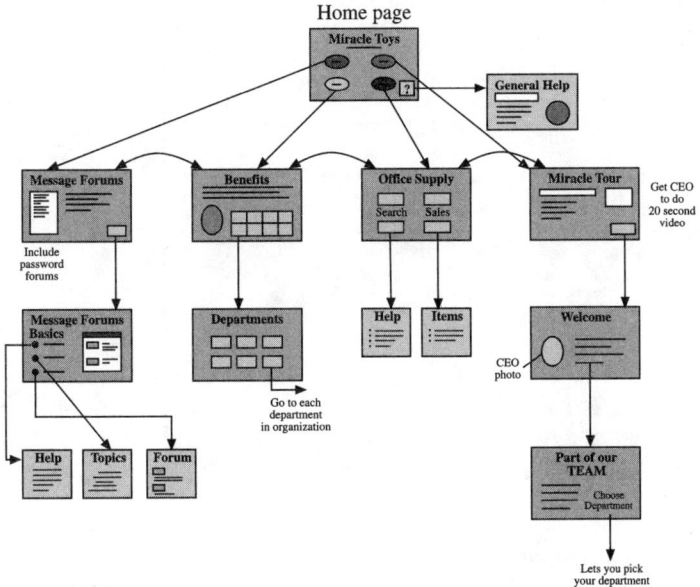

FIGURE 2-13

The next stage of your layout includes more detail.

As you can see in the figure, the layout includes more exact hyperlink paths and a more precisely detailed page layout. Information about content for the specific pages is indicated in the margins and next to the Web pages. At this stage in the process, all links to internal and external sites should be addressed. You should consider the site's mission and scope before haphazardly making hyperlinks just for the sake of making a link. Avoid the "here is a list of my favorite links" syndrome. Hypertext enables extremely open connectivity between documents. Just because you can make links to anything in the world does not mean that you should. Make sure that your links are relevant to your subject matter and won't confuse users or send them down a path of irrelevant information. Figure 2-14 displays an example of what to avoid when you design your intranet pages. In the figure, some links go to the same document and are in the Web page two or three times. Other hyperlinks have nothing to do with the topic of this Web page. This page also has "Click Here:" links; avoid these.

FIGURE 2-14

This page has too many links.

The next set of diagrams demonstrates the technical layout of your intranet presence. You can write brief notes to yourself next to the pages to keep track of your ideas for those pages and how to achieve the effects you require. These sketches show the interactive pages and also indicate how the pages will interact. This information is conveyed through image maps, client pull, Java, CGI, and numerous other ways. This is shown in Figure 2-15.

Probably the greatest challenge for you won't be in coming up with ideas for your diagrams, but rather in the project restraints that you face in the form of limits on time and money.

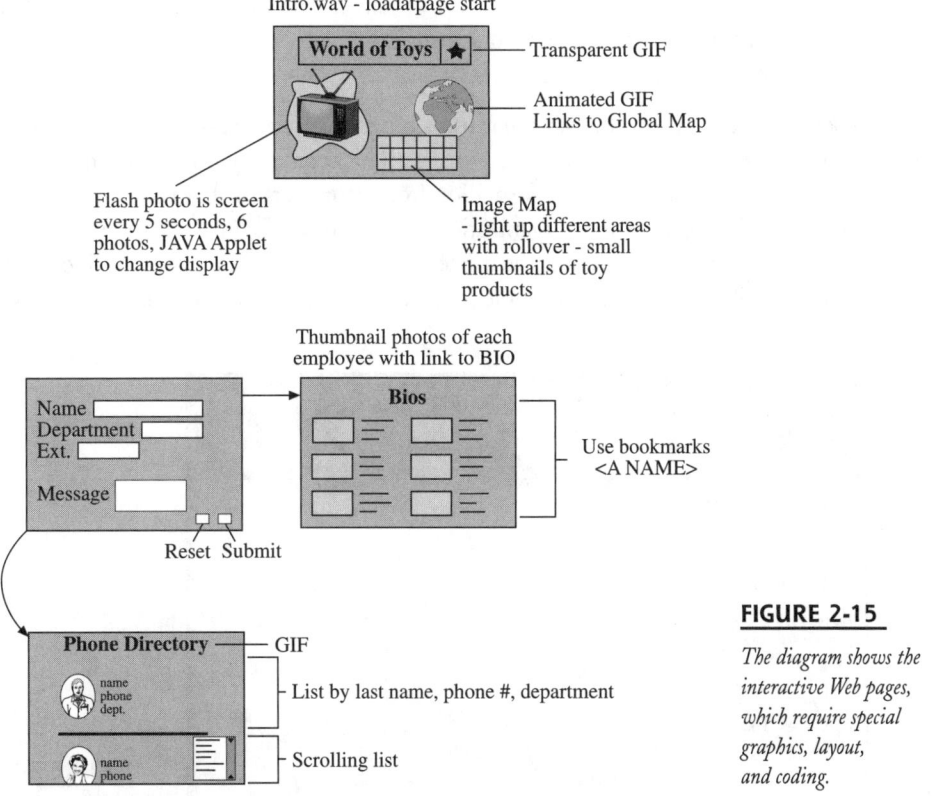

Intro.wav - loadatpage start

World of Toys ★ ── Transparent GIF

── Animated GIF
Links to Global Map

Flash photo is screen
every 5 seconds, 6
photos, JAVA Applet
to change display

Image Map
- light up different areas
with rollover - small
thumbnails of toy
products

Thumbnail photos of each
employee with link to BIO

Name
Department
Ext.

Message

Bios

Use bookmarks
<A NAME>

Reset Submit

Phone Directory ── GIF

name
phone
dept.

── List by last name, phone #, department

name
phone

── Scrolling list

FIGURE 2-15

*The diagram shows the
interactive Web pages,
which require special
graphics, layout,
and coding.*

Testing the Basics

Up to now, I have discussed creating the entire intranet Web site in a written, rough-draft
form. The next step is to check out your intranet's user-friendly interface. You can do so
by mapping out your pages as if they were being visited by a user on the intranet system.

Take a specific task, such as locating a new job opportunity, and follow the links from the
top of your intranet structure all the way to the bottom. Following the links allows you to
test the different navigation flow diagrams and determine the quickest and easiest route
for the user. By mapping out certain tasks, you discover ways to implement searches, hot
quick links, and ways to tailor pages more toward your users' personal preferences. You
also discover that a strong need exists to channel users based on their preferences or
memberships. Having your intranet channel users based on who they are is a bit more
advanced. But once set up, it allows your users to receive information tailored to their
preferences. The setup can be set based on the users' IP address or, in some cases, the

users can choose to customize their view, or join certain newsgroups as a member. You can also set this up with a password screen. Users who know the password would have access to certain areas on the intranet.

Take a look at some of the ways that users can join special areas, such as newsgroups, on your intranet, and gain access to other pages. The approach you're about to see can also be used just to study and collect information from your users so that you can continue to create a better intranet for your organization in the future. Figure 2-16 shows an example of a simple form. When users enter the office supply store, they are asked to fill out a simple form. This allows you to get valuable information directly from the users of the system.

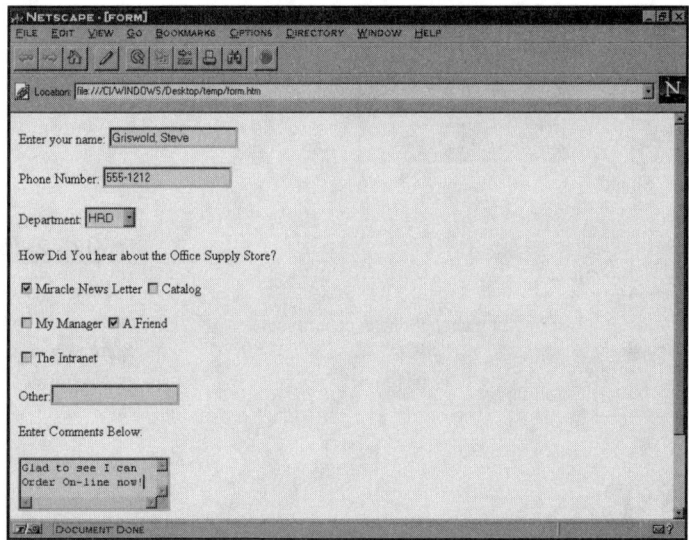

FIGURE 2-16

Forms like this can be generated quickly with raw HTML coding or by using an HTML editor.

Here, the access questionnaire is required only to allow the system to collect data that helps in evaluating the different areas and services on the intranet. Diagrams such as the ones in Figures 2-17 and 2-18 help you to design interactive sites quickly, without having to construct the Web pages in HTML, wasting valuable time.

In Figure 2-18, you can see the adjustments that make the structure more user friendly. The membership standings page could be left out, and the user name and password could be used to determine how many points the user has earned, and which Web page to display based on the points the user has received.

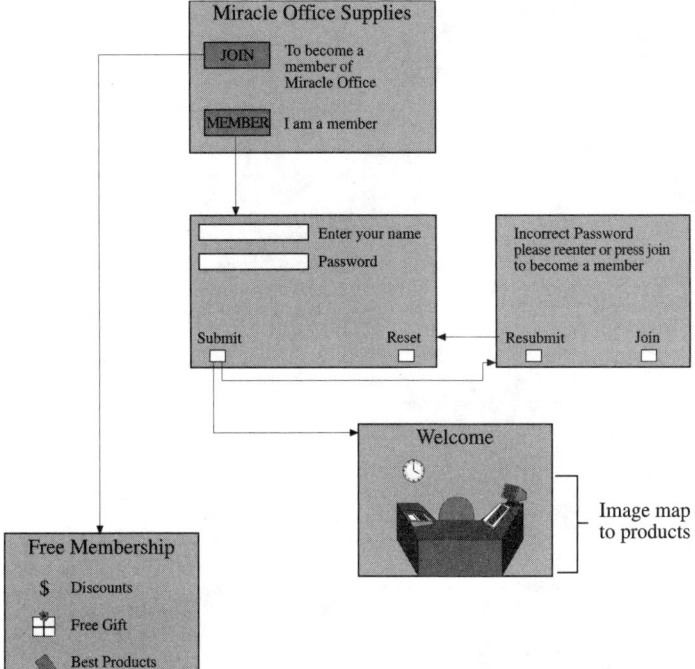

FIGURE 2-17

This diagram shows ways to route users who enter correct and incorrect information.

Don't jump in and start coding your intranet without doing these quick and basic sketches first. Changing your Web site on paper is much easier than redoing graphics and HTML pages. Your user, client, or project team will change the site's layout and design several times. By presenting the sketches to the client, you can avoid redevelopment work on the physical intranet. When you finish all your rough drafts, you can start developing some basic pages in HTML. I say *basic* because, at this point, you are developing only the basic layout; that is, a general layout that will serve as a placeholder for all the content on your intranet. With these basic Web pages, you are just trying to accomplish a general layout for all the content on your intranet.

Developing the Prototype

As you develop a prototype, you should focus on the interactivity and navigation issues of your intranet. Figure 2-18 illustrates a text-only prototype Web page. First, I made an HTML table, and then I placed the content for Miracle Toy Corporation into the appropriate sections of the table. A newcomer's first instinct is to start developing ideas with the use of graphics and a complete layout, without considering the goal and navigation

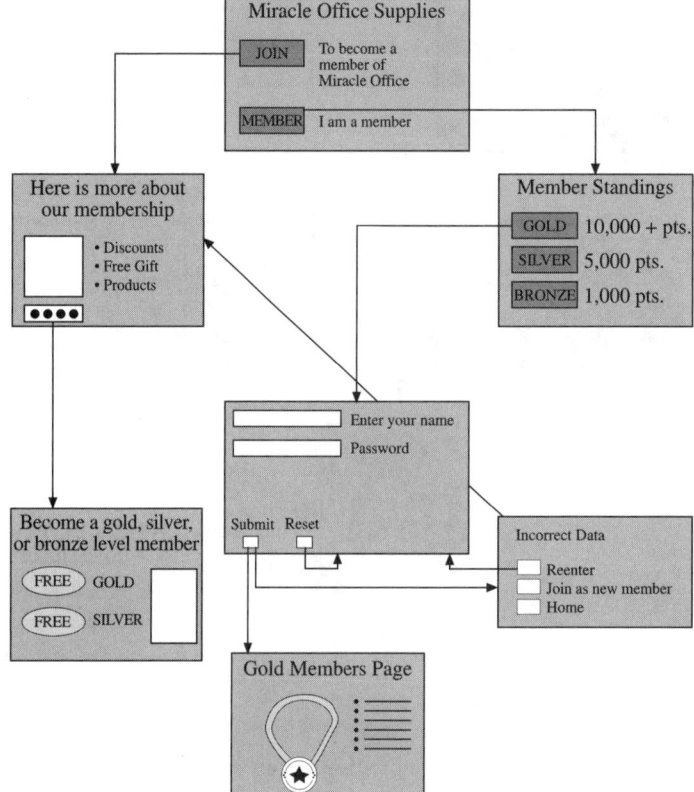

FIGURE 2-18

Here's another way to route users, based on their current membership standings and number of free points they have earned in the office supply store promotion.

associated with creating a user-friendly site. At this stage, you don't want to add many graphics to your layout, if any. You are just creating placeholders for your intranet site.

After you establish a basic page layout, you can use the same Web page, cutting and pasting the new content into it to create your other prototype pages. If you are unfamiliar with HTML (Hypertext Markup Language), don't fear. I walk you through the basics, along with the latest cool HTML tags and coding, in Appendixes A and B. You will also want to take a look at the CD-ROM in the back of this book, to read up on the Netscape Overview that I have provided there. After you learn the basics of HTML, you'll see how to create dynamic presentations by using Web editors. You have heard this before and you'll hear it again: Web editors are becoming easier to use for authoring content, but they still have a long way to go. So, you still need to be familiar with the tags and coding in HTML. I cover these editors in Appendix C, but don't jump ahead until you learn the basics for HTML (trust me on this one).

While you develop your prototype Web pages, keep them simple and to the point. After you have constructed a prototype, you can capitalize on one of the strengths of the intranet by placing your prototype on the Web server on your local area network. Doing so enables members of the project team to access your prototype and comment on it. This is also the perfect time to test out the prototype's basic functionality on the LAN with the different types of platforms in your shop. When you start to implement your interactive features such as ActiveX, Java, and CGI, place them on the LAN for the project team and client to evaluate.

Creating Killer Home Pages

I discussed home pages earlier in the chapter. Now I want to emphasize the importance of creating a stunning home page.

Your intranet site home page is a first impression. Making a positive and lasting first impression is very important, especially if yours is just one of many departments on your corporate intranet. For a medium- to large-scale Web site, your home page is usually a navigation page. Make sure that your navigation is easy to follow and contains links to all of your intranet's main topic areas. Establish your identity and broadcast this to the users on your home page. You can do this with company logos, custom graphics, and key phrases. Offering a link on your home page that connects to a help file for beginners, and for anyone interested in learning more about the intricacies of your intranet, is also a good idea.

Additionally, the home page is a fantastic page to place a search engine. Placing a search engine here enables users to do queries on keywords and phrases immediately. Clicking on the main topic categories on the home page takes users to a secondary page that displays either the sought-for content or another navigation page.

When you create navigation pages, make them easy to understand, and to the point. You can create top-level and lower-level navigation pages easily, but keeping your users from having to drill down through many levels of navigation to reach the desired content is difficult. A good rule of thumb is to keep all of your popular content three or fewer clicks away.

Basic Navigating

When you design your main topics pages and all of your content Web pages, you need to offer a way back to the previous page that the user just visited, and also a quick link back to the home page. Navigation buttons offer an easy way to return to the top of your intranet structure. The easier the site is to maneuver, the more time the user will spend surfing your intranet. By placing links to all your main topic areas—human resources, office supply store, and so on—on your navigation bar, you enable users to quickly access your main departments without having to traverse many Webs.

Summary

That covers it for getting your intranet started. I've discussed which organizational models you should consider, along with their advantages and disadvantages. I've also covered how to initially plan your intranet, formulate your mission statement, and put your plan in writing. I've defined the ultimate Web team as consisting of the Marketing Dreamer, Graphic Artist, Author, and Programmer. The chapter also discussed selling your intranet concept, and covering the areas of brainstorming, defining your audience, and using surveys to help you get started. I left off with the entry-level development of your intranet, with storyboarding, navigation, and issues to consider when you develop your home page.

What's Next!

This is a good time to take a 15-minute break and get a soda (or go back to the rest of your life for a while). When you get back, I'll move you on to the more advanced concepts as I cover project design and layout in the next chapter.

Chapter | 3

Project Design
and Layout

This chapter discusses project design and layout. In print media, you are limited by page size, color costs, and many other factors. Not so on the intranet. On your intranet, your entire site can be one page a mile long. I would not recommend it, but I mention this to emphasize that there are no page-length limits as you might be accustomed to in traditional media. With such freedom in design, layout, graphics, and color, you will encounter some amazing intranets out there, but also see your share of horrendously bad intranets. This freedom gives you the tools that designers have been dreaming about for years, but it also allows inexperienced developers a quick and easy way to shoot themselves in the foot. I cover the different design elements in depth so that you can be familiar with the many options available to you.

The prototype that you created in the previous chapter will become a functioning Web presentation. I don't cover HTML coding in this chapter, but I show how to effectively communicate and create navigation in your intranet. Never fear—I do cover HTML later in the book, in Appendixes A and B.

Your intranet site will most likely develop into a large-scale project. To communicate your site's mission and goals, you need to establish a working relationship with other departments and experts in your organization. The Web, just like your intranet, brings individuals and departments together that you probably never knew existed. By joining with other departments in your organization, you can communicate the entire corporation's views and goals instead of one department's view. You can communicate your content to the user in several ways.

In a large organization, the Web shop can set up guidelines and help coordinate the efforts of several departments in designing a cohesive site that flows when all the pieces are assembled. The Web shop helps the departments with design standards, and makes sure that navigation and the basic organization of the presentation are easy to follow.

Another avenue is to allow each department to develop its independent presentations with its own design, feel, themes, and focus on its own specific issues. This strategy works well because each department can determine its own design and communication method.

Either scenario can be successful if organized properly. The developers of the site need to come up with an easy-to-use graphical user interface. The user sees only the top layer of the intranet, which consists of the Web pages. Users will not and should not be concerned with the underlying code and database that make the Web site function.

Keeping the lingo to a minimum in your intranet is also important. If the departments are designing their own intranets that are pieced together by a centralized Web shop, stress to each department to keep the technical and business jargon out of the site. Users at a front desk in a resort would understand the terms *rack rate* and *NZBs*, but the rest of the users on your global intranet would be left behind. Make your content appeal to the organization as a whole, and develop special sections for individual areas that use jargon when necessary. Keep your target audience in mind when you develop your pages.

Same Top; Different Look

When you start to lay out your pages and work on themes, use your creativity to design a unique site for the department or organization. A site on an intranet for a Human Resources department would have a different objective and feel than a site for an accounting department. The accounting department would have certain items such as online reports and papers, memos, Excel spreadsheets, and facts and figures all displayed in a positive and formal manner. The HRD site would also want items such as memos, job postings, and important company content, but it would post in addition fun employee events and birthday information, and would have a fun and informal feel overall.

Each department develops its own feel and theme over time. Even similar areas have certain specializations that bring users back repeatedly. About 30 magazines cover the World Wide Web. They all focus on the same topic, but they all have a different layout, design, and theme. Figure 3-1 is a Web site that illustrates the way similar content can be displayed differently and still effectively on a site. The design works well and allows the user to see a thumbnail of the artwork available right from the home page.

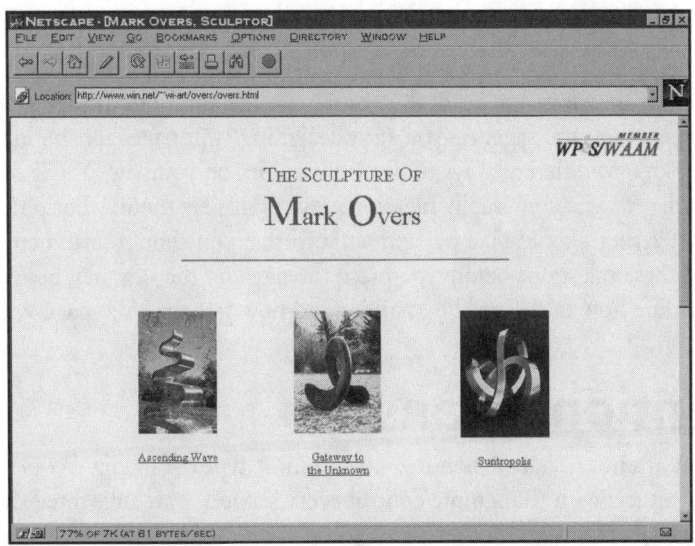

FIGURE 3-1

This Web site by Mark Overs is just one way of organizing and laying out the design for a sculpture art site.

Examine sites on the WWW that are classified under the same topic headings in one of the many search engines. Sites that focus on the exact same material use different, yet effective, ways of laying out their content. Figure 3-1 shows one of many ways that an art sculpture site can be designed and displayed. Figure 3-2 also gives you a different, but just as effective, view of a site that also displays sculptures. The site opens with more of a text information page, and offers links at the bottom of the site to get a more in-depth look at the actual pieces of work.

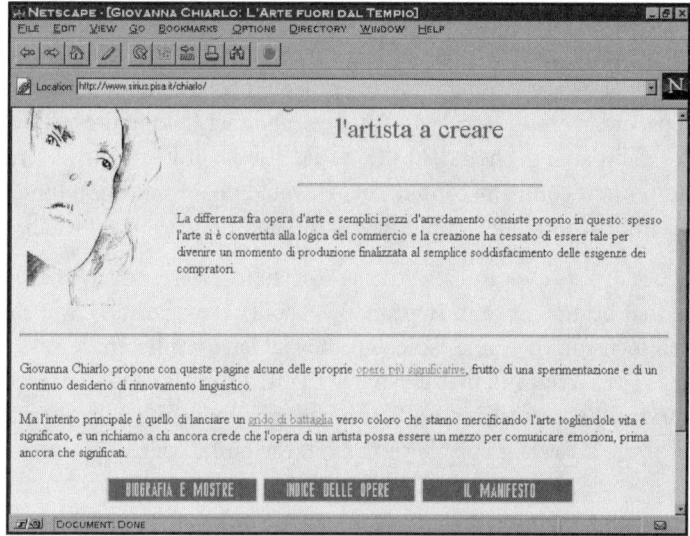

FIGURE 3-2

This site also focuses on sculptures, but with a totally different layout.

In the examples shown in these figures, both sites rely on the ability to display graphics on the Web to convey their message. As you start designing your pages for the intranet, you will also be looking at different ways to display graphics on your site. You'll consider issues such as which graphics are visually pleasing, how to display them, what physical size and memory size they should take up, and what format you should save them in. You need to answer all these questions before you place the page on the intranet, because the answers will determine how to design the graphics and how fast the Web page will load.

Short Attention Spans

Everyone has short attention spans when it comes to most types of media. People flip through the TV channels with the remote control every second, watching three shows at once while commercials play on the other two channels. The same is true for the Web and intranet sites. Users skim quickly over content to see whether they find anything interesting enough to click down another level for more in-depth information. So, making your pages so that users can scan them quickly is a must.

A good visual presentation allows users to instantly see the information they are looking for. You can create this perfect presentation by using effective layout, color, white space, graphics, and appropriate page elements. Don't crowd too many objects or options on a single page. Remember that there are no limits to the amount of pages you can have on your intranet, so space things out to make them easier to scan. When you place your navigation controls on your intranet pages, make sure that they are logical and follow the same design and placement on all of your pages. Doing so allows your users to easily scan forward, back, home, and to specific areas of interest.

If you keep the navigation controls the same in placement and design, your users can quickly learn how to navigate your site. Also, if you place your navigation controls on the top of all your pages, your users can navigate easier than if they have to scroll down to the bottom of the screen to the controls. Make sure that your links and buttons follow a pattern. If all the options on a page look the same, your users could become confused. Figure 3-3 shows an example of this confusing effect. All the buttons and all the text are the same. The user cannot easily scan the page and see which buttons are for the form and which are for navigation.

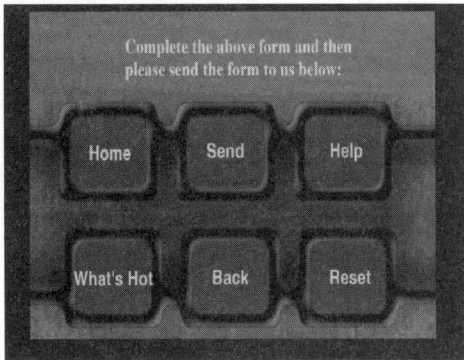

FIGURE 3-3

*Too many options are on
the screen.*

Notice that the page layout for Figure 3-3 looks cool and inviting, but it is almost impossible to scan quickly. Users must read the entire screen to find the button they need to send the form they just filled out. All the buttons look the same, and the layout is the same, so you can't tell the difference between the form and the navigation buttons. If the controls for the form and the controls for the global navigation are placed on different levels and have different features, it makes navigation much easier (see Figure 3-4). The local buttons (Send and Reset) complete the task at hand and thus are placed directly after the form. The navigation buttons in this example are now a different color, they have a different font and font color, and they have a different button shape than the form buttons. The navigation buttons are also separated by a yellow horizontal line.

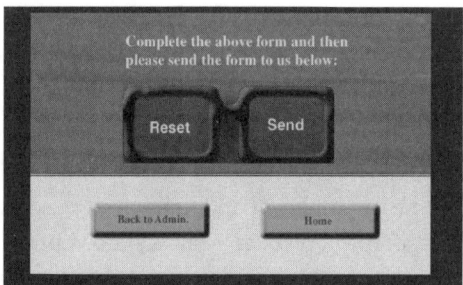

FIGURE 3-4

Scanning the page and finding the Send button for the form that the user just filled out is easier now.

This screen shot in Figure 3-4 is much easier to scan, and identifying the form buttons from the global navigation buttons is easier. It also helps if you tell users where the navigation buttons will take them. A button labeled Back to Administration tells the user much more than a button labeled simply Back.

Easy Navigation Using Frames

Netscape Navigator and other browsers such as Microsoft's Internet Explorer offer a feature known as frames. *Frames* enable the screen to be divided up into several different sections. In place of only one main Web page that scrolls up and down, frames enable several sections with scroll bars to be displayed side by side. The frame section at the top of the document in Figure 3-5 has main topic headings.

Rather than take you to a completely new Web page, these frames change the frame below. The red arrows are drawn in to show which frame changes when the topics are clicked. Using the frames allows users to keep all the navigation buttons on their screen and also to jump from page to page.

The mechanical.com Web site gives a great example of how to use frames. The site is uncluttered, and the frames do not take over the screen with a sea of scrolling boxes and text that rolls off the screen, as happens with so many sites that use frames. You can visit the site at http://www.mechanical.com/. When you click on the About Us icon, the frame below changes to the information about the company. The remaining navigation and icons on the left side of the Web page stay the same to allow for easy navigation. Figure 3-6 shows the new data for the About Us selection in the frame below the topic icons.

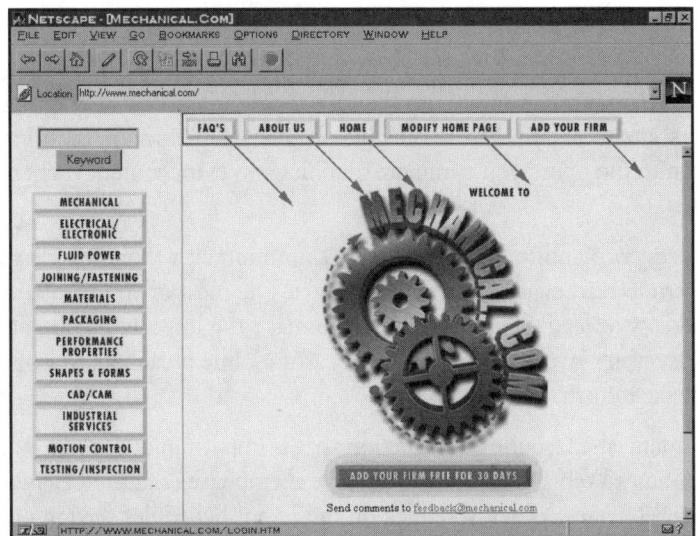

FIGURE 3-5

When you click on one of the main topics in the top frame, the lower frame displays that information, giving the user an easy way to navigate your intranet.

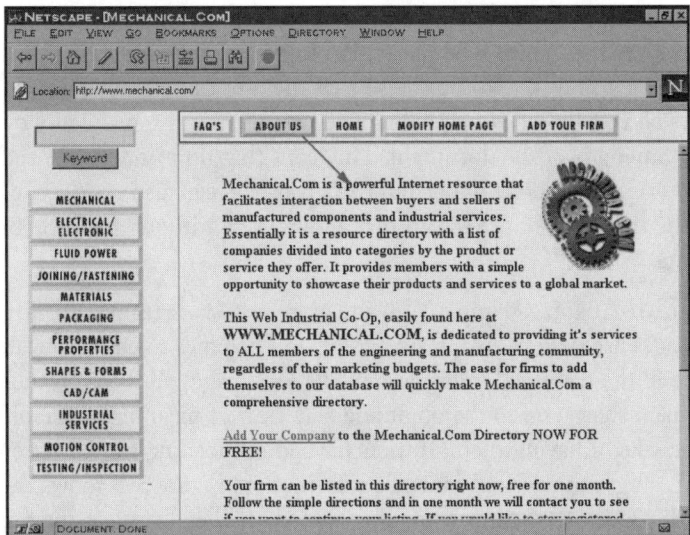

FIGURE 3-6

For this type of site, frames are a perfect match. The result of clicking on the About Us icon is that only one frame changes on the screen, which makes getting around easy.

Because its creators used the same type of icons, a precise layout in the top and left frame, and an overall attractive page design, this site accomplishes its task.

White Space

Although most of us have a burning desire to cover page after page entirely with graphics or text, the most effective intranets are those that use the right amount of graphics and text to get the users' attention and display valuable content in an easy-to-read format. By keeping your design to the point, you eliminate graphics and extra content that aren't necessary.

Keep your Web pages crisp and to the point. Make skimming over topics easy for users, without forcing them to read pages of meaningless text. The meat of your content should be easy to find and easy to read. Several ways exist to make the important content stand out on each page. By using layout, colors, different textures, line breaks, and just plain white space, you make information easy to find.

Figure 3-7 shows a fantastic layout of information that is important and to the point. The Atlanta Olympic Games Web site uses white space and emphasizes desired elements on the corresponding Web pages. When you click on the Event Schedules section on the Olympic Web site, you are immediately taken to the page of event schedules with no useless graphics and wasted space. Directly on the top of the screen is the IBM/Atlanta graphic that graces all the pages, and the word *Schedules* is displayed to let you know where you are in the Web structure. The navigation icons are small but easy to read, and they are placed near the top of the Web page so that the user can quickly move to other sections in the site. Next, a bold heading telling you that the event schedule follows is easy to see when scanning over the document. The icons that flow under the heading are easy to understand even if you don't understand English. You can also choose the events from a listing on the right side of the screen that allows users without graphical browsers to display the events.

You can visit the IBM/ Atlanta Olympic Web site at `http://www.atlanta.olympic.org`. All the Olympic pages use design, layout, size, color, and graphics to communicate the level of importance of the displayed information. The Web pages all focus on their objective. The pages remain sharp and to the point and stay clear of meaningless graphics and content just for the sake of having them. If users have image loading turned off on their browsers, they still can get the desired schedule information. Figure 3-8 shows the same event schedule Web page with the image loading turned off. The listing at the right is still displayed, allowing users to retrieve the schedule they desire. By using the Alt tag, the boxes that are now holding the places for the images contain a text message. This could have been added to make the site a bit easier to navigate in this mode. Alternate text can also be used in place of graphics that function as hypertext links. This allows the Alt text to be displayed and used as a link to the desired section.

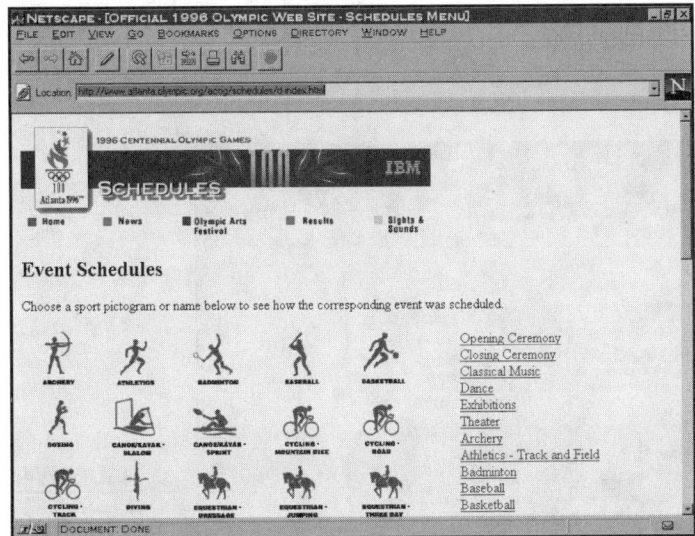

FIGURE 3-7

This page displays the information that the user requests(event schedules) directly at the top part of the Web page, making the information easy to locate and use.

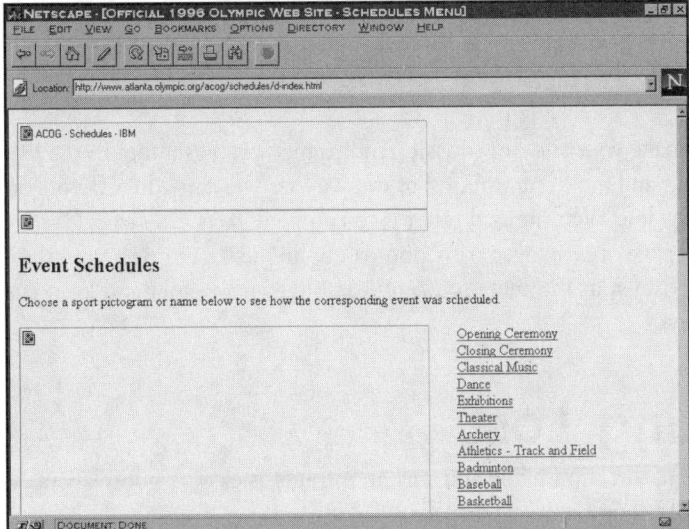

FIGURE 3-8

With image loading turned off, the Olympic site can still be navigated by using the text listing to the right of the image placeholders.

Each of the Olympic pages shows a factoid at the bottom that changes regularly (see Figure 3-9). This lets the user know that the information on the site is changing and not static. By adding colorful tables such as this to key pages, the user comes back regularly to get the latest factoid information. The entire IBM/Atlanta Olympic site has content that is constantly changing. You do not have to create an intranet that has changes updated every minute like the Olympic site to keep users coming back. You just need to have valuable and current content.

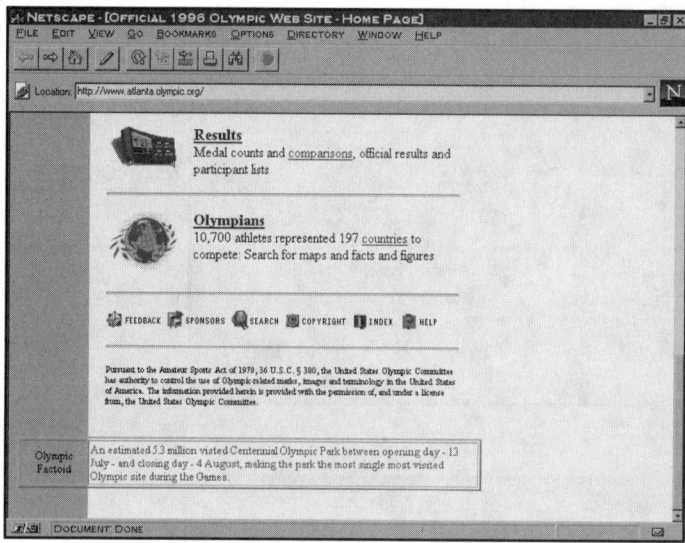

FIGURE 3-9

The Olympic factoid at the bottom of the Web page keeps users coming back, and also lets them know that the site is updated and not static.

You also want to make your site fun to visit. An intranet, even as a tool in the workplace, needs to be inviting and a bit entertaining to draw users. You can add a factoid similar to the one on the Olympic Web site and tailor it to company facts. You can do a page on company trivia. A page of employee baby photos inviting users to guess who they are can draw users deeper into your intranet. You can promote your intranet and keep it active in many different ways.

Avoid Getting Lost

Losing your sense of direction while you surf an intranet is easy. A good layout can minimize this feeling of being lost in cyberspace.

One of the objectives of your Web pages should be to clearly identify each page's content. Users should be able to jump to your page and know by a visual clue or text the exact location of where they have arrived. This helps keep your users from getting lost in the massive amount of information in your intranet.

If you place a matching graphic on the top title bar of all your main pages, your users will immediately know where they are. Figure 3-10 gives an example of this type of title bar. When users click on the lobster with the word "seafood" next to it on the Rusty Pelican home page, users instantly are reassured that they are at the correct Web page when they see the same lobster and "seafood" at the top of the Web page.

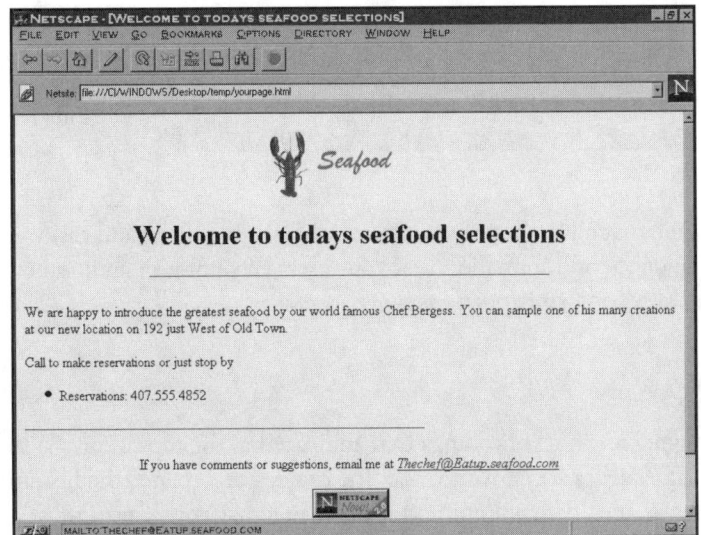

FIGURE 3-10

The same graphic on the home page and on the top of the department Web page lets users know exactly where they are in the intranet.

Figure 3-11 also displays the idea of headings to guide the user. The same familiar heading is used in the takeout Web page in Figure 3-11. Users again know that they are at the takeout page by looking at the familiar graphic that was also on the home page, and by seeing the same layout that's on all the main heading pages. If you use the same layout and design on your mastheadings, users know what level of the intranet structure they are on, and they also can scan the headings quickly to make sure they are in the correct area of interest.

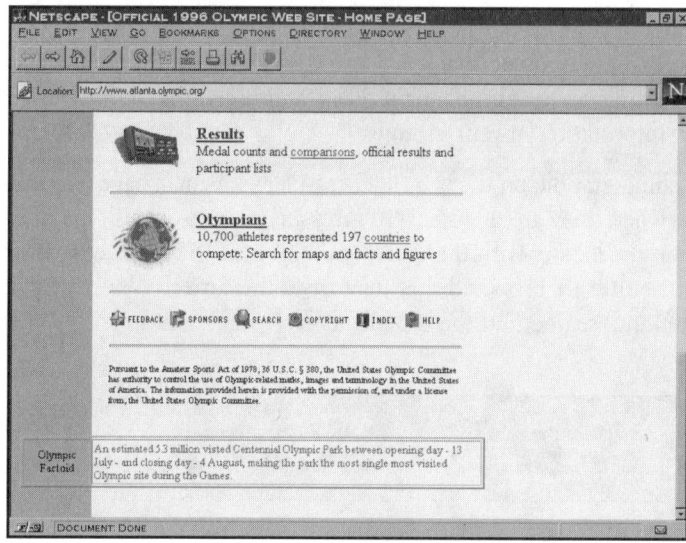

FIGURE 3-11

The graphic, text, and layout of this heading make it easy to read and scan.

Developing a scheme that allows your users to scan the pages quickly and easily is important. With the abundance of information that your users encounter in an intranet, a feeling of information overload can happen easily.

Mastheadings

Mastheadings are graphics or text headings that are placed at the top of each Web page in an intranet. Mastheadings are similar to the title of a research paper, the headings in the sections of a newspaper, the columns and features in a magazine, and almost all layout in today's print media. Many elements of layout and design in print also work wonderfully in an intranet, and the masthead is one of them. The masthead functions as a point of reference for users and helps them with direction in the intranet framework.

Users link into your documents from the top, bottom, and middle of your intranet structure. Search engines might place a user right in the middle of a document rather than at the top of your intranet structure, so it is important that each Web page can hold its own. If a user jumps in your intranet four levels down, he or she may not be aware that there is more information on the topic above that level. In case a user does jump into the middle of a document that cannot stand alone, you need to make sure that you've provided a hyperlink back to the previous level so that the user can get the needed information.

The masthead allows users to get their bearings so that they do not feel lost on the intranet. When you design your mastheads, keep them consistent. Place them in the same location on each Web page in the intranet. Use the same font and the same size. Also, keep a theme to your mastheads. You are creating a theme that should be used throughout your entire intranet. The user should see a consistent page design and masthead throughout the site.

Figure 3-12 shows just a handful of the mastheads on the main topic areas of the Olympic site. Each masthead is the same size and is placed at the top of the Web page in the same location. Users also can quickly identify the section they are in by looking at the themed graphic in the masthead. The same font size is used in each, making it easy to identify.

FIGURE 3-12

The mastheads on the IBM/Atlanta Olympic Web Site have a similar theme and enable easy recognition of the main topic areas.

The theme for another department or intranet on the LAN might be totally different. The theme in any given area should also be displayed on all the pages that are under that department or intranet. This way, users quickly know when they have left your intranet or department and have jumped to another. If you were to display restaurants on your intranet, you might have a gourmet menu with a romantic, exclusive type of theme relating to all of the pages. The local cafeteria would have a different theme and might post brightly colored graphics, with a design intended to conveying a feeling of quick, quality food.

Other Ways to Make Documents Easy to Read

Mastheads can be used as graphics or as text elements at the top of your documents, but you also want to include subheadings on pages further down in your structure. Using lists to display a group of items also makes content easier to follow. If you find yourself describing the steps necessary to complete a task or a group of related topics, you should use a listing. You can also make hyperlinks that allow quick access to other pages from your list items. Again, display only content that is appropriate for the particular section. Don't drown the important facts and figures in a sea of text; place them at the top of the document, or make them easy to see with color, placement, and layout.

Images

When you place images, avoid overcrowding your pages with graphics. Use graphics that go with your theme and complement your content. Consider what value the image brings to the page to help you decide whether to use the image or trash it. Large amounts of images not only clutter up an intranet Web page, but also slow down the response time that it takes for the page to load. Most intranets use a graphical browser such as Netscape Navigator and are capable of attractively displaying your artwork. You may have users on your intranet who do not have access to a graphical browser, however. They also need to have access to the same information. Two ways can accomplish this. Using an HTML tag known as the <ALT> tag, you can tell the browser to display the alternate text rather than the image. Doing so enables users of text-only browsers to display a description or a hyperlink in place of the image.

The other option is to provide an intense graphical site and a separate text-based site. At the home page, users choose whether they want to display the graphical site or the text-only site. The disadvantage to this method is that you must create and maintain two separate sites whose content is basically the same. This might be a perfect solution if you have a large mix of text and graphical browsers on your intranet, but keep the maintenance time in mind while you set up your intranet in this format.

Background Images and Colors

In an effort to always stay one step ahead of the competition, Netscape introduced the background tag a while back. All the main browsers on the market support it now. The background tag allows the designer to change the color of the Web document. Similar to adding wallpaper to your desktop in Windows, you can choose from a grand selection of solid colors or even use images for your document's background. Once again, doing so can enhance your intranet greatly, or it can destroy it.

When you choose a background, make sure that the text in the document is readable on the background. Black text on a dark blue background is almost impossible to read. Try different color combinations of backgrounds and text. You can set your document's solid background color in two different ways: You can use what is known as a hexadecimal number, or you can use one of the allowed words, such as red, orange, yellow, green, blue, or violet. The easiest way is to stick with the hexadecimal numbers. Here's a quick introduction to changing background colors. I cover the topic in depth in Chapter 6, "Graphics on an Intranet."

The tag looks like this:

```
<BODY BGCOLOR="rrggbb">
```

First, the < lets the browser know that this is an HTML tag. The code between the opening and closing brackets (< and >) is read by the browser. The word BODY tells the browser that this is the main body of the HTML document. Next comes the background color tag. The BGCOLOR="rrggbb" tells the browser that the background color equals the code in between the quote marks. The ending bracket, >, closes the tag. Simple enough.

The rrggbb is the color values. They stand for red, green, and blue. The color values can represent a hexadecimal value between 0 and F. So, if you set all the color values to 0, what do you think you'll get? Zero represents negative color, or depletion of color, so you'll get the color black. Here is the HTML tag displayed that gives you the color black:

```
<BODY BGCOLOR="000000">
```

The first two zeros take away the red; the next two affect the level of green; and the last two zeros affect the level of blue. So, by entering different hexadecimal values in place of the "rrggbb", you can change the color of the document's background. Because zero is the absence of color, it makes sense that F is the presence of a maximum color level. If you type the following:

```
<BODY BGCOLOR="FF0000">
```

the result is a true red. Remembering a few hexadecimal numbers in your head is easy, but when you create colors such as dark salmon, it gets a bit more complex. Dark salmon is as follows:

```
<BODY BGCOLOR="E9967A">
```

No, you don't have to memorize all these hexadecimal codes. Many WWW sites have created applications that define colors for you. These sites range from color listings and their hexidecimal values to color palettes that allow you to see what your final product will look like. You can also use the words the same way as the hexidecimal codes. For example, the following:

```
<BODY BGCOLOR="RED">
```

is the same as typing:

```
<BODY BGCOLOR="FF0000">
```

You can also visit a Web site to get instant hex codes. There are many to choose from, but the one that follows is easy to use and has a palette that allows you to select your colors. Figure 3-13 shows some of the standard colors from which to choose. By clicking on the color swatch, you are given the hex equivalent for your intranet.

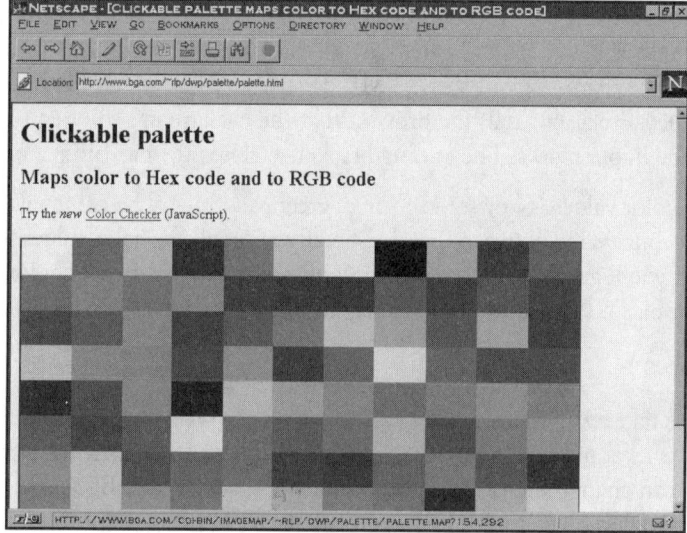

FIGURE 3-13

The color palette at `http://www.bga.com/~rlp/dwp/palette/palette.html` *allows you to use basic colors quickly and easily in your documents.*

This Web site is easy to save in your bookmarks and refer to as needed. Picking and choosing basic colors is made simple. You can also type the RGB numeric values from one of your favorite graphics programs, and the color and hexadecimal code are then displayed (see Figure 3-14).

Several sites on the WWW make color layout easy. You can try different color schemes at:

```
http://www.schnoggo.com/rgb2hex.html
```

Here you will get a color rainbow color palette that allows you to choose any color you want by simply clicking on it. You will get a the hexadecimal value and a sample color swatch showing you the exact color you chose.

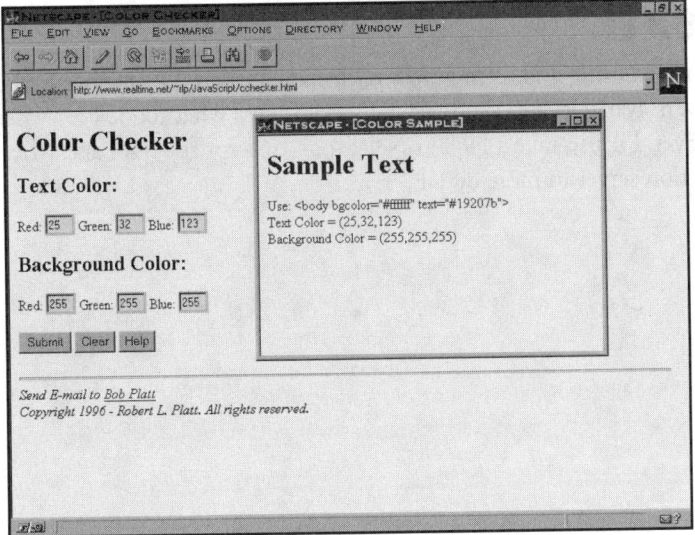

FIGURE 3-14

By using a JavaScript-enabled browser such as Netscape, you can get the hexadecimal code and a sample of the text color. Just type the RGB values from your favorite graphics program.

Changing the text color also emphasizes content and makes it easier to read. Dark text on a light background is the easiest to read. With so much new freedom in intranet design, you can also change the colors of hyperlinks. An unfollowed hyperlink, one that has not been clicked on, usually has a default color of bright blue. After you visit the link, the color changes to a default of dark purple. Some HTML tags allow you to change the unfollowed and visited links' color. If you decide to change the color of your hypertext links, make sure that you are consistent. You can confuse the user if one page has red and green links and the next page has totally different colors. Also, make sure that the new link colors are readable on your document.

Summary

Using mastheads, different layouts, graphics, and color schemes, can make your pages easy to navigate. When you start coding HTML, you will learn ways to use different tags to structure your layouts to make perfect graphical user interfaces. Keep the ideas in this chapter in the back of your mind for when you start coding the intranet Web pages.

What's Next!

Now I move on to choosing and setting up your intranet server. I'll cover several of the current Web servers available for Windows NT, and discuss what to look for when choosing your Web server. I'll also take a look at Netscape's Enterprise server and Microsoft's Internet Information server in more detail.

Chapter |4

Setting Up an
Intranet Server

In this chapter, I discuss several Windows NT Web servers that are currently available on the market. After I show you some of the most popular Web servers for intranets, I focus on Netscape's Enterprise Web Server and walk you through the setup and features of this top-notch Web server.

Choosing a Web Server

All the servers discussed in this chapter run on Windows NT. Several of the servers also have versions available for UNIX, Macintosh, and the other Windows platforms. So, if you are not running NT, this information is still useful because the server software that you are considering is likely to also run on other platforms. Several of the servers discussed here are also included on the CD-ROM that comes with this book. So, please install them and test them out on your system before you make your decision and spend a bunch of money. Some of the servers are also free. You can't beat that price!

Operating Systems

In the list that follows, all the Web servers run on Windows NT as well as several other platforms. Each Web server has been dissected to make it easy to compare features between all of them. The layout for each Web server covers which operating system it can run on, information concerning include statements, launching and logging issues, protocol support, security, and other features. To help you better understand how the features of the different Web servers are categorized, a description of the different categories follows.

- ◆ UNIX: Runs on at least one variant of UNIX
- ◆ Windows NT: Runs on Windows NT 3.5 / 4.0 on Intel
- ◆ Windows 95: Windows 95
- ◆ Windows 3.1: Windows 3.1
- ◆ OS/2: OS/2 Warp
- ◆ Macintosh OS: Macintosh OS
- ◆ Novell Netware: Novell's Netware
- ◆ VMS: DEC's VMS
- ◆ Amiga OS: AmigaOS
- ◆ AS/400: IBM's AS/400 for minicomputers
- ◆ VM/CMS: IBM's VM/CMS for mainframes
- ◆ MVS: IBM's MVS for mainframes

- MS-DOS: Runs under plain MS-DOS
- Be OS: Be OS for the BeBox

UNIX Variants

The information that you will find in the server comparisons for UNIX-based servers covers the UNIX variants on which the server is known to run. This list should be as specific as possible. For example, "Solaris" is not specific enough if the server runs on Solaris for SPARC but not Solaris for Intel.

Windows NT CPUs

This is for NT-based servers, the CPUs on which the server is available. The choices are Intel, MIPS, PowerPC, and Alpha.

Launching and Logging

If you want to find out exactly what each heading is about when you're checking out the NT servers in the following section, take a moment to read over the criteria that was used to separate the men from the boys, the women from the girls, the Timex Sinclairs from the Cray. I cover each measuring point and feature that these servers offer on these pages.

- **Can run from inetd (UNIX and OS/2 systems only):** Many UNIX-based and OS/2-based servers must be run as daemons (that is, all the time). Others can be started each time a request comes in, using the inetd daemon. Running from inetd is slower, because the entire server process must be started for each request. Some servers that have a "Yes" for this feature allow you to run from inetd, but doing so is not recommended.

- **Can serve different directory roots for different IP addresses:** If the operating system allows a single CPU to have more than one IP address, a Web server can use different IP addresses and hostnames to indicate different Web sites. The easiest way to do this is to say that each IP address gets a different directory tree from which to serve.

- **Runs as Windows NT service and/or application:** On NT-based systems, the server can run as an application, a service, or both. The values here must be application, service, or both, logging with syslog (UNIX) or Event Log (Windows NT). These two logging systems allow many servers to keep consistent logs regardless of load.

- **CERN/NCSA common log format:** HTTP access logs are kept in the same format as the CERN and NCSA servers. The format is as follows:

  `remote_host ident authuser [date-time] "Request-Line" Status-Code bytes`

  `remote_host`: Client DNS hostname, or IP address if not available

  `ident`: The identity check token or "-" if not given

  `authuser`: The Authorization username or "-" if not given

  `data-time`: dd/mmm/yyyy:hh:mm:ss zone zone: +dddd or -dddd

  `Request-Line`: Exactly as received from client

  `Status-Code`: Result from server or "-" if unknown

  `bytes`: Size of Entity-Body transmitted or "-" if unknown

- **Log files can be automatically cycled or archived:** The Web administrator can specify that new logs are started regularly (normally, each day) and that old logs are kept for later review.

- **Normal (hit) log entries can be customized:** The format of the log can be changed to be in a different order or to include different fields.

- **Can write to multiple logs:** Some servers keep many logs, such as error logs. Others allow the same information to be written to different logs in different formats, with the formats often defined by the administrator. Others allow different logs for different kinds of actions (GET vs. POST, for example).

- **Server can generate non-hit log entries (such as comments):** Particular events (time passing, server load over a certain limit) can generate entries in the log.

- **CGI scripts can create their own log entries:** CGI scripts can enter information in the log, such as security alerts or abnormal user requests.

- **Performance measurement logs:** These can be logs of items such as server load, number of hits per minute, number of requests refused because the server was too busy, and number of requests aborted in mid-transmission.

- **Can generate referer log entries:** It is important for many Web administrators to know how people found out about their site. This referer log can be integrated with the standard log, be its own log, or just be a field that an administrator can add to custom logs.

- **Can generate browser log entries:** Determining which browsers (more properly called *user agents*) are being used to view a site can help determine which features to use. This log can be integrated with the standard log, be its own log, or just be a field that an administrator can add to custom logs.

- **Can track individual users in log:** Some servers can track users as they move around a Web site using automatic cookie generation, allowing you to store information about a user's behavior, and other techniques. In order to qualify for this feature, the server must do user tracking automatically, without requiring the Web administrator to make changes to the HTML source of the content.

Protocol Support and Includes

This section covers the support for the protocols and includes of Web servers described in this chapter. When you read about each individual server, you can refer back to this section to get more information about the items listed.

- **Automatic response to If-Modified-Since:** The server responds to all GET requests that have If-Modified-Since headers without using CGI scripts.
- **Select documents based on Accept header:** The server will allow the administrator of the Web site to send back information to the browser that all may be returned for the same URL, and the rules for how the server chooses between them based on the Accept, Accept-Charset, Accept-Encoding, and Accept-Language headers. These rules must be implemented without CGI scripts. Note that the Accept headers are no longer part of the HTTP/1.0 specification.
- **Select documents based on User-Agent header:** The server allows the Web administrator to specify a set of responses that all may be returned for the same URL depending on the value in the User-Agent header. This must be implemented without CGI scripts.
- **Includes based on HTML comments:** Document authors can include HTML comments that the server expands into standard information before the document is sent out.
- **Includes can be based on request headers:** Server-side includes can be triggered by values of request headers. For example, the include might be a construct such as "if-User-Agent-is Netscape" or "if-Referer-is."
- **Server can force includes:** The server can force information to appear at the beginning or end of all documents, of certain document types, or of documents in a particular directory.
- **Automatically include any HTTP headers in responses:** Without using CGI, the server can include any administrator-defined headers in responses for all document types.

- **Access to server state variables from CGI or other scripting:** Scripts or programs written by the Web administrator can include non-CGI values such as date, time, server load, number of accesses in a particular time frame, and so on.

- **Has built-in scripting language:** Servers with built-in scripting languages usually let Web administrators do more to customize their site using fewer programming skills. These scripting languages also often allow greater access to the state variables than plain CGI interfaces. So far, only a few scripting languages are implemented in more than one server.

- **Has built-in image-map handling:** Built-in image map handling means that the description of the hot spots of an image map can be entered using something other than CGI scripts. Some servers implement this feature with HTML comments; others, as server directives that are usually easier to enter than CGI script commands.

- **Supports HTTP/1.1 PUT:** The PUT method was poorly defined in HTTP/1.0. PUT is commonly used to allow a remote user to add material to a Web site. In HTTP/1.1, the PUT method is more clearly defined in section 9.1.2 of draft -03 of the HTTP/1.1 specification.

- **Nonsupported methods can invoke a script:** If a client sends a nonsupported method, the server may automatically start a script or program rather than just send back a 501 error. This feature allows Web administrators to deal with methods not anticipated by the vendor.

- **Supports the Windows CGI interface:** The server supports the Windows CGI protocol, defined at `http://www.city.net/win-httpd/httpddoc/wincgi.htm`. This is an extended CGI mostly of use to Windows-based servers.

- **Comes with SNMP agent:** The Simple Network Management Protocol lets network administrators watch and change remote services. To qualify for this feature, HTTP servers must have their own SNMP agents (and the accompanying MIB) because there is no standard agent and MIB for HTTP servers. For more information on HTTP MIBs, see `http://http-mib.onramp.net/`.

- **Supports HTTP/1.1 byte ranges:** HTTP/1.1 clients can request part of the content of an item using byte ranges, as described in section 7.14 of draft 03 of the HTTP/1.1 specification. Byte ranges are optional for HTTP/1.1 clients and servers, but servers that support it will be able to restart aborted transmissions more easily.

♦ Supports HTTP/1.1 persistent connections: The server can keep a connection with an HTTP/1.1 client open for more than a single request. This is described in section 17 of draft 03 of the HTTP/1.1 specification.

♦ **Understands full URLs in HTTP/1.1 requests:** HTTP/1.1 specifies that servers must be able to understand two types of requests: those with absolute paths (old-style locators), and those with full URLs. The latter is new to HTTP/1.1. This is described in section 9.1.2 of draft -03 of the HTTP/1.1 specification.

♦ The name that is shown in the Server: response header: Each server software should respond with its name in the Server: response header, as described in section 10.14 of the HTTP/1.0 specification. Note that a few servers reply with names that contain spaces; doing so violates the HTTP/1.0 specification.

Security

This section covers the type of security provided for the Web servers described in this chapter. When you read about each individual server, you can refer back to this section to get more information about the items listed.

♦ **Can require password (Authorization: user):** The server can require realm-based passwords, as described in section 11 of the HTTP/1.0 spec.

♦ **Supports SSL v. 2:** The server can communicate using the SSL version 2 protocol.

♦ **Supports SSL v. 3:** The server can communicate using the SSL version 3 protocol.

♦ **Supports S-HTTP:** The server can communicate using the S-HTTP protocol.

♦ **Supports PCT:** The server can communicate using the PCT protocol.

♦ **Prohibit by domain name:** The Web administrator can deny access to some or all documents based on the requester's domain name. The domain name is determined by a reverse-lookup on the requester's IP address (not using the From header field).

♦ **Prohibit by IP address:** The Web administrator can deny access to some or all documents based on the requester's IP address.

♦ **Configurable user groups (not just a single user list):** The Web administrator can create multiple user groups based on domain name, IP address, or authenticated user name of requesters. The user groups then determine access to documents.

- **Can change user access control list without restarting server:** Changes to the access control list(s) take effect without the Web administrator having to restart the server software.

- **Can hide part of a document based on security rules:** Within a single document, you may want to display certain parts to certain users only. Servers that allow this have security rules that hide those parts except for users in particular user groups, or those coming from certain domain names or IP addresses.

- **Security rules can be based on URLs:** Security rules can be set for resources based on the URL requested rather than the file to which the URL might refer.

- **Default security model for file-based documents:** All Web servers allow the Web administrator to specify the top of the served hierarchy. This option is the model that describes the basic security for files below that top, if no other security is specified. The four choices are as follows:

  - Deny access to all files unless listed in an access file

  - Allow access to all files unless listed in an access file

  - Allow access to all files (no access file)

  - Has no access to file system at all (pure database)

- **Hierarchical permissions for directory-based documents:** If a file comes from a directory that has no access file, the server checks each successively higher level of the directory tree and uses the permissions of the first access file found.

- **Additional security features:** Many servers have security features other than those listed here. Few are standardized, and many have not been extensively tested on the Web.

Other Features

This section covers miscellanous propietary features of Web servers described in this chapter. When you read about each individual server, you can refer back to this section if you need more information of the items listed.

- **GUI-based setup:** The server is configured using a GUI program (instead of editing a text file).

- ◆ **GUI-based maintenance:** The server's running information (hit counts, load, performance) is displayed using a GUI (instead of as a text file).

- ◆ **Remote maintenance:** The server software can have its configuration changed using a terminal or client program running on a computer different than the server. The remote connection must be able to be established using software that comes as part of the operating system or the server software (no extra expense for the remote software).

- ◆ **Real-time performance measurement tools:** The server has real-time indicators for turnaround time for requests and/or number of requests refused because the server was too busy.

- ◆ **Script or action based on output media type:** The Web administrator can specify a program to be run automatically or an action to be taken automatically if the outgoing document has a particular media type (such as image/gif). This is useful for repackaging documents as multipart/alternative, or for adding additional headers for certain media types.

- ◆ **Also serves other TCP protocols:** A few Web server packages also serve other TCP protocols, such as Gopher and FTP.

- ◆ **Automatic directory tree:** If the URL is for a file directory (not a specific file), the server can respond with a listing of all the readable files in that directory.

- ◆ **User directories:** The server can remap file directories from outside its normal directory hierarchy to within the hierarchy without using file system aliases. This is normally done with regard to all users to make part of their home directory space available on a central Web site.

- ◆ **Search engine:** The server includes a built-in search engine.

- ◆ **Has direct (non-CGI) link to a DBMS:** The server has a direct link to a DBMS package that does not require a CGI script to use. Such servers usually create an active link to the DBMS when they start up and keep the link open the entire time they run. Thus, DBMS requests through such a server is inherently faster than through a CGI that must start up the DBMS link each time it is run.

- ◆ **Includes user interaction tools:** The server software includes software that helps users of the Web site communicate with each other, and that interaction software is supported to the same level as the core server software is.

- **Type of server-side imagemaps:** Two different ways exist to do image maps: the CERN way, which is used by servers with CERN legacies (or who prefer the CERN method); and the NCSA way. The difference lies in the formatting of the map file. The two types of map files are described at:

  CERN:

  ```
  http://www.w3.org/hypertext/WWW/Daemon/User/CGI/HTImageDoc.html
  ```

  NCSA:

  ```
  http://hoohoo.ncsa.uiuc.edu/docs/setup/admin/Imagemap.html
  ```

  Most servers support one or the other, and a few support both.

- **Allows nonblocking DNS:** When a Web server accepts a new request, the operating system provides the server with the IP address of the client making the request. Some server access control policies are based on the Internet host name rather than on the numeric IP address, and some CGI requests require a host name. To reliably obtain the Internet host name takes two DNS lookups: first to "reverse map" the IP address to the host name, then to "forward map" the host name back to the IP address as a validity check. In some cases, these lookups take several seconds even when all the computers involved are functioning normally. Nonblocking DNS lookup means that after accepting a request from a client, the server reads and parses the request in parallel with it looking up the DNS record (possibly using a local DNS cache). The server blocks sending the response only if the DNS information is required for security, for passing to a CGI script, for logging, and so on.

- **Has a support mailing list:** The vendor supporting the server has a tech support mailing list. Some server buyers want to browse such a mailing list before using the software to be sure that the vendor provides adequate support, or at least that good support comes from other users of the software.

- **Also acts as an HTTP proxy server:** The server software can also be used as an HTTP proxy.

- **Proxy server also caches:** If the server software can be used as an HTTP proxy, that proxy also acts as a caching proxy.

- **Includes full source code for server:** The server comes with full source code for compiling it from scratch. This gives the Web administrator great assurance that the code is secure, and allows a programmer to change the way the server works if that is desired. The possible responses are as follows:

- ◆ Always included
- ◆ Extra fee
- ◆ None available

- ◆ **Pricing:** The choices concerning the cost of the software are as follows:
  - ◆ Commercial
  - ◆ Free
  - ◆ Free with fee for support
  - ◆ Shareware

    Note: Please be aware that prices may have changed since this book went to press. Check the URL for current pricing information.

- ◆ **Pricing (more info):** This is a description of the pricing given by the vendor.

- ◆ **Best features (as described by the vendor):** Every vendor has opinions about why its server is better than others. This is a short (25 words or fewer) description of what each vendor considers the best features of its product.

- ◆ **URL for more information:** Visit the server's home site maintained by the vendor for more information.

Popular NT Web Servers

In the following sections, I have listed the popular NT Web servers for your browsing pleasure. The list of categories will help in determining which server to choose when you consider which server will best fit the needs of your intranet.

Okay, now that you know what criteria was used to rate each Web server, take a look at the different servers available and see how they rank among each other.

Alibaba

Alibaba is a intermediate Web server that offers an amazing amount of features and security for an unbelievably low price. Alibaba has built-in performance measurement logs that allow you to check on the server's performance. You can monitor the number of hits and other statistics that are important in determining server load and bandwidth concerns on an intranet. Alibaba also supports ISAPI and CGIDLL. It comes with built-in image-map handling, and is easy to administrate with its GUI-based setup and maintenance. Maintenance can even be done remotely. Alibaba comes with a search engine included; the entire product ships for only $99.00.

Version described: 2.0.

Operating Systems

Windows NT: Yes

Windows 95: Yes

Windows 3.1: No

Windows NT CPUs: Intel

Launching and Logging

Can run from inetd (UNIX and OS/2 systems only): No

Can serve different directory roots for different IP addresses: Yes

Runs as Windows NT service and/or application: Both

Logging with syslog (UNIX) or Event Log (Windows NT): Yes

CERN/NCSA common log format: Yes

Log files can be automatically cycled or archived: Yes

Normal (hit) log entries can be customized: Yes

Can write to multiple logs: Yes

Server can generate non-hit log entries (such as comments): Yes

CGI scripts can create their own log entries: Yes

Performance measurement logs: Yes

Can generate referer log entries: Yes

Can generate browser log entries: Yes

Can track individual users in log: Yes

Protocol Support and Includes

Automatic response to If-Modified-Since: Yes

Select documents based on Accept header: Yes

Select documents based on User-Agent header: Yes

Includes based on HTML comments: Yes

Includes can be based on request headers: Yes

Server can force includes: Yes

Automatically include any HTTP headers in responses: Yes

Access to server state variables from CGI or other scripting: Yes

Has built-in scripting language: ISAPI, CGIDLL

Has built-in image-map handling: Yes

Supports HTTP/1.1 PUT: No

Nonsupported methods can invoke a script: No

Supports the Windows CGI interface: Yes

Comes with SNMP agent: No

Supports HTTP/1.1 byte ranges: No

Supports HTTP/1.1 persistent connections: Information not available

Understands full URLs in HTTP/1.1 requests: Information not available

The name that is shown in the "Server:" response header: Alibaba

Security

Can require password (Authorization: user): Yes

Supports SSL v. 2: Yes

Supports SSL v. 3: No

Supports S-HTTP: No

Supports PCT: No

Prohibit user access by domain name: Yes

Prohibit user access by IP address: Yes

Configurable user groups (not just a single-user list): Yes

Can change user access control list without restarting server: Yes

Can hide part of a document based on security rules: No

Security rules can be based on URLs: Yes

Default security model for file-based documents: Allow access to all files unless listed in an access file

Hierarchical permissions for directory-based documents: Yes

Additional security features: None

Other Features

GUI-based setup: Yes

GUI-based maintenance: Yes

Remote maintenance: Yes

Real-time performance measurement tools: No

Script or action based on output media type: Yes

Also serves other TCP protocols: No

Automatic directory tree: Yes

User directories: Yes

Search engine: Yes

Has direct (non-CGI) link to a DBMS: No

Includes user interaction tools: No

Type of server-side imagemaps: Information not available

Allows nonblocking DNS: Information not available

Has a support mailing list: No

Also acts as an HTTP proxy server: Yes

Proxy server also caches: Yes

Includes full source code for server: None available

Pricing: $99

Best features (as described by server author): Alibaba SSL is a high-performance WWW server for conducting secure electronic commerce and communications on the Internet and intranet, with the ability of easy administration.

URL for more information: http://alibaba.austria.eu.net/

EMWAC Freeware HTTPS

EMWAC is a no-frills server. It does not offer all the features that the other NT servers in this list do; however, it is perfect if all you really want to do is serve up some Web documents for others to see in an intranet setting. Also, EMWAC can fit in any department's tight budget because it is free.

Version described: 0.99

Operating Systems

Windows NT: Yes

Windows 95: No

Windows 3.1: No

Windows NT CPUs: Intel, Alpha, MIPS, PowerPC

Launching and Logging

Can run from inetd (UNIX and OS/2 systems only): Not applicable

Can serve different directory roots for different IP addresses: No

Runs as Windows NT service and/or application: Service

Logging with syslog (UNIX) or Event Log (Windows NT): Yes

CERN/NCSA common log format: No

Log files can be automatically cycled or archived: Yes

Normal (hit) log entries can be customized: No

Can write to multiple logs: No

Server can generate non-hit log entries (such as comments): No

CGI scripts can create their own log entries: No

Performance measurement logs: No

Can generate referer log entries: No

Can generate browser log entries: No

Can track individual users in log: No

Protocol Support and Includes

Automatic response to If-Modified-Since: Yes

Select documents based on Accept header: No

Select documents based on User-Agent header: No

Includes based on HTML comments: No

Includes can be based on request headers: No

Server can force includes: No

Automatically include any HTTP headers in responses: No

Has access to server state variables from CGI or other scripting: No

Has built-in scripting language: No

Has built-in image-map handling: Yes

Supports HTTP/1.1 PUT: No

Nonsupported methods can invoke a script: No

Supports the Windows CGI interface: No

Comes with SNMP agent: No

Supports HTTP/1.1 byte ranges: No

Supports HTTP/1.1 persistent connections: Information not available

Understands full URLs in HTTP/1.1 requests: Information not available

The name that is shown in the Server: response header: HTTPS

Security

Can require password (Authorization: user): No

Supports SSL v. 2: No

Supports SSL v. 3: No

Supports S-HTTP: No

Supports PCT: No

Prohibit by domain name: No

Prohibit by IP address: No

Configurable user groups (not just a single-user list): No

Can change user access control list without restarting server: No

Can hide part of a document based on security rules: No

Security rules can be based on URLs: No

Default security model for file-based documents: Allow access to all files (no access file)

Hierarchical permissions for directory-based documents: No

Has additional security features: No

Other Features

GUI-based setup: No

GUI-based maintenance: Yes

Remote maintenance: No

Real-time performance measurement tools: No

Script or action based on output media type: No

Also serves other TCP protocols: No

Automatic directory tree: Yes

User directories: No

Search engine: WAIS Toolkit for Windows NT

Has direct (non-CGI) link to a DBMS: No

Includes user interaction tools: No

Type of server-side imagemaps: Information not available

Allows nonblocking DNS: Information not available

Has a support mailing list: Yes

Also acts as an HTTP proxy server: No

Proxy server also caches: Not applicable

Includes full source code for server: None available

Pricing: Free

Pricing (more info): Information not available

Best features (as described by server author): The price

URL for more information: `http://emwac.ed.ac.uk/html/internet_toolchest/https/`

`contents.htm`

Microsoft Internet Information Server

Microsoft IIS is a high-end Web server that is integrated with Windows NT server. It is easy to use, provides high-level security, and it's free. You can download it from `http://www.microsoft.com/iis`.

Version described: 2.0

Operating Systems

Windows NT: Yes (server only)

Windows 95: No

Windows 3.1: No

Windows NT CPUs: Intel, Alpha, MIPS, PowerPC

Launching and Logging

Can run from inetd (UNIX and OS/2 systems only): Not applicable

Can serve different directory roots for different IP addresses: Yes

Runs as Windows NT service and/or application: Service

Logging with syslog (UNIX) or Event Log (Windows NT): Yes

CERN/NCSA common log format: No

Log files can be automatically cycled or archived: Yes

Normal (hit) log entries can be customized: Yes

Can write to multiple logs: No

Server can generate non-hit log entries (such as comments): Yes

CGI scripts can create their own log entries: Yes

Performance measurement logs: Yes

Can generate referer log entries: No

Can generate browser log entries: No

Can track individual users in log: No

Protocol Support and Includes

Automatic response to If-Modified-Since: Yes

Select documents based on Accept header: No

Select documents based on User-Agent header: No

Includes based on HTML comments: Yes

Includes can be based on request headers: No

Server can force includes: Yes

Automatically include any HTTP headers in responses: No

Access to server state variables from CGI or other scripting: Yes

Has built-in scripting language: Yes

Has built-in image-map handling: Yes

Supports HTTP/1.1 PUT: No

Nonsupported methods can invoke a script: No

Supports the Windows CGI interface: Yes

Comes with SNMP agent: Yes

Supports HTTP/1.1 byte ranges:

Supports HTTP/1.1 persistent connections:

Understands full URLs in HTTP/1.1 requests:

The name that is shown in the "Server:" response header: Microsoft-Internet-Information-Server

Security

Can require password (Authorization: user): Yes

Supports SSL v. 2: Yes

Supports SSL v. 3: No

Supports S-HTTP: No

Supports PCT:

Prohibit by domain name: No

Prohibit by IP address: Yes

Configurable user groups (not just a single user list): Yes

Can change user access control list without restarting server: Yes

Can hide part of a document based on security rules: Yes

Security rules can be based on URLs: Yes

Default security model for file-based documents: Allow access to all files unless listed in an access file

Hierarchical permissions for directory-based documents: Yes

Additional security features: Read or execute permissions for virtual directories, script mapping for hiding application executables, administrator control for password length, password uniqueness, minimum/maximum password aging, automatic account lock-out with manual or automatic reset

Other Features

GUI-based setup: Yes

GUI-based maintenance: Yes

Remote maintenance: Yes

Real-time performance measurement tools: Yes

Script or action based on output media type: No

Also serves other TCP protocols: HTTP, FTP, Gopher

Automatic directory tree: Yes

User directories: Yes

Search engine: No

Has direct (non-CGI) link to a DBMS: Information not available

Includes user interaction tools: No

Type of server-side imagemaps: Information not available

Allows nonblocking DNS: Information not available

Has a support mailing list: Information not available

Also acts as an HTTP proxy server: No

Proxy server also caches: Not applicable

Includes full source code for server: None available

Pricing: Free with fee for support

Pricing (more info): Information not available

Best features: Easy to set up and manage, great platform for Internet/intranet application development with the Internet Database Connector and the Internet Server API.

URLs for more information: Information not available

Please note: Microsoft has three Web servers. Version 1.0 of IIS runs on NT Servers 3.51 with Service Pack 3 or better installed. It will not run on NT Workstations. It is freely downloadable from:

```
http://www.microsoft.com/Infoserv/iisinfo2.htm
```

Version 2.0 of IIS is included as part of the NT Server 4.0 software package. It will not run on earlier versions of NT, nor will it run on NT Workstation. You can get more information at:

```
http://www.microsoft.com/windows/common/contentNTSIAC02.htm
```

Netscape Enterprise Server

Netscape Enterprise Server 2.0 is a high-performance, secure, World Wide Web platform for creating, managing, and intelligently distributing information and live, online applications. It provides advanced capabilities for content creation and management, including WYSIWYG editing, full text search, and revision control. Netscape Enterprise Server extends the development platform to include open, server-side applications. Enterprise has increased security and network management capabilities, including SSL

3.0, client-side certificates, and advanced access control. It also has support for secure, remote, cross-platform administration, SNMP, and reporting. If you are seriously looking for the ultimate intranet solution, take a close look at Netscape's Web Servers. Check out the SuiteSpot Servers at Netscape's home page. The SuiteSpot package is being implemented by many organizations because it offers a complete solution and has all the necessary components, including the Enterprise Server.

Version described: 2.0

Operating Systems

UNIX: Yes

Windows NT: Yes

Windows 95: No

Windows 3.1: No

UNIX variants: Solaris (for Intel and Sparc); SunOS; HP-UX; AIX; IRIX; Digital UNIX; SCO UNIX; NEC UNIX; SINIX; Sony UNIX

Windows NT CPUs: Intel, Alpha, MIPS

Launching and Logging

Can run from inetd (UNIX and OS/2 systems only): No

Can serve different directory roots for different IP addresses: Yes

Runs as Windows NT service and/or application: Service

Logging with syslog (UNIX) or Event Log (Windows NT): Yes

CERN/NCSA common log format: Yes

Log files can be automatically cycled or archived: Yes

Normal (hit) log entries can be customized: Yes

Can write to multiple logs: Yes

Server can generate non-hit log entries (such as comments): Yes

CGI scripts can create their own log entries: Yes

Performance measurement logs: Yes

Can generate referer log entries: Yes

Can generate browser log entries: Yes

Can track individual users in log: Yes

Protocol Support and Includes

Automatic response to If-Modified-Since: Yes

Select documents based on Accept header: No

Select documents based on User-Agent header: Yes

Includes based on HTML comments: Yes

Includes can be based on request headers: Yes

Server can force includes: Yes

Automatically include any HTTP headers in responses: Yes

Access to server state variables from CGI or other scripting: Yes

Has built-in scripting language: NSAPI and Java applet API

Has built-in image-map handling: Yes

Supports HTTP/1.1 PUT: Yes

Nonsupported methods can invoke a script: No

Supports the Windows CGI interface: Yes

Comes with SNMP agent: Yes

Supports HTTP/1.1 byte ranges: Yes

Supports HTTP/1.1 persistent connections: Yes

Understands full URLs in HTTP/1.1 requests: Yes

The name that is shown in the Server: response header: Netscape-Enterprise

Security

Can require password (Authorization: user): Yes

Supports SSL v. 2: Yes

Supports SSL v. 3: Yes

Supports S-HTTP: No

Supports PCT: No

Prohibit user access by domain name: Yes

Prohibit user access by IP address: Yes

Configurable user groups (not just a single user list): Yes

Can change user access control list without restarting server: Yes

Can hide part of a document based on security rules: Yes

Security rules can be based on URLs: Yes

Default security model for file-based documents: Allow access to all files unless listed in an access file

Hierarchical permissions for directory-based documents: Yes

Additional security features: Chroot (UNIX); multiple user information directories; client-side certificates; access control for HTTP-Put

Other Features

GUI-based setup: Yes

GUI-based maintenance: Yes

Remote maintenance: Yes

Real-time performance measurement tools: Yes

Script or action based on output media type: Yes

Also serves other TCP protocols: No

Automatic directory tree: Yes

User directories: Yes

Search engine: Yes

Has direct (non-CGI) link to a DBMS: Yes

Includes user interaction tools: Yes

Type of server-side imagemaps: NCSA

Allows nonblocking DNS: Yes

Has a support mailing list: No

Also acts as an HTTP proxy server: No

Proxy server also caches: Not applicable

Includes full source code for server: None available

Pricing: $0 - $995

Best features (as described by server author): An easy-to-use, programmable, high-performance Web server; includes text search, revision control, configuration rollback, SNMP, high-performance API, and a simple forms-based UI

URL for more information: `http://home.netscape.com/`

Netscape FastTrack Server

For those who want to publish on the Internet but fear the complexity and cost of Web server software, Netscape has more of an entry-level server, the FastTrack Server. The FastTrack Server is an easy-to-use, entry-level Web server designed to enable novices create and manage a Web or intranet site. It is a complete solution for creating and managing Web sites on the Internet or intranet. It is easily upgradable to Netscape Enterprise Server.

FastTrack is an open platform for publishing traditional Internet documents as well as developing and deploying live network-centric and media-rich applications. This server is very easy to install. Businesses and individuals can quickly establish a presence on the Internet and deploy intranet solutions. FastTrack also includes Netscape Navigator Gold for creating and editing rich documents. I cover Netscape Gold in Appendix C, "Authoring for Your Intranet," at the end of this book.

Version described: 2.0

Operating Systems

UNIX: Yes

Windows NT: Yes

Windows 95: No

Windows 3.1: No

UNIX variants: Solaris (for Intel and Sparc); SunOS; HP-UX; AIX; IRIX; Digital UNIX; SCO UNIX; NEC UNIX; SINIX; Sony UNIX

Windows NT CPUs: Intel, Alpha, MIPS

Launching and Logging

Can run from inetd (UNIX and OS/2 systems only): No

Can serve different directory roots for different IP addresses: Yes

Runs as Windows NT service and/or application: Service

Logging with syslog (UNIX) or Event Log (Windows NT): Yes

CERN/NCSA common log format: Yes

Log files can be automatically cycled or archived: Yes

Normal (hit) log entries can be customized: Yes

Can write to multiple logs: Yes

Server can generate non-hit log entries (such as comments): Yes

CGI scripts can create their own log entries: Yes

Performance measurement logs: Yes

Can generate referer log entries: Yes

Can generate browser log entries: Yes

Can track individual users in log: Yes

Protocol Support and Includes

Automatic response to If-Modified-Since: Yes

Select documents based on Accept header: No

Select documents based on User-Agent header: Yes

Includes based on HTML comments: Yes

Includes can be based on request headers: Yes

Server can force includes: Yes

Automatically include any HTTP headers in responses: Yes

Access to server state variables from CGI or other scripting: Yes

Has built-in scripting language: NSAPI and Java applet API

Has built-in image-map handling: Yes

Supports HTTP/1.1 PUT: Yes

Nonsupported methods can invoke a script: No

Supports the Windows CGI interface: Yes

Comes with SNMP agent: No

Supports HTTP/1.1 byte ranges: Yes

Supports HTTP/1.1 persistent connections:

Understands full URIs in HTTP/1.1 requests: Yes

The name that is shown in the Server: response header: Netscape-FastTrack

Security

Can require password (Authorization: user): Yes

Supports SSL v. 2: Yes

Supports SSL v. 3: Yes

Supports S-HTTP: No

Supports PCT: No

Prohibit by domain name: Yes

Prohibit by IP address: Yes

Configurable user groups (not just a single-user list): Yes

Can change user access control list without restarting server: Yes

Can hide part of a document based on security rules: Yes

Security rules can be based on URLs: Yes

Default security model for file-based documents: Allow access to all files unless listed in an access file

Hierarchical permissions for directory-based documents: Yes

Additional security features: Chroot (UNIX); multiple user information directories client-side certificates; access control for HTTP-Put

Other Features

GUI-based setup: Yes

GUI-based maintenance: Yes

Remote maintenance: Yes

Real-time performance measurement tools: Yes

Script or action based on output media type: Yes

Also serves other TCP protocols: No

Automatic directory tree: Yes

User directories: Yes

Search engine: No

Has direct (non-CGI) link to a DBMS: Yes

Includes user interaction tools: Yes

Type of server-side imagemaps: NCSA

Allows nonblocking DNS: Yes

Has a support mailing list: No

Also acts as an HTTP proxy server: No

Proxy server also caches: Not applicable

Includes full source code for server: None available

Pricing: With Netscape Gold: $295; Add Live Wire: $495 for all three

Pricing (more info): FastTrack with Navigator Gold is $295; FastTrack with Navigator Gold and LiveWire is $495

Best features (as described by server author): An easy-to-use, programmable, high-performance Web server; features include text search, revision control, configuration rollback, high-performance API, and a simple forms-based UI

URL for more information: http://home.netscape.com/

Purveyor WebServer

Purveyor offers an advanced, easy-to-use Web Server software. Purveyor was developed by Process Software Corporation. The Web server has been developed to make the process of developing an intranet or Web presence very simple and fast. It does so while still delivering a wide range of features to complement the most complex intranet sites.

Its introduction to the WWW community in April, 1995 made Purveyor the first commercial Web server for Windows NT. Now Purveyor is also available for users of Windows 95, OpenVMS, and Netware.

Purveyor is not available for UNIX, but many other platforms are under development.

Purveyor makes communicating and publishing content for intranet via a LAN a simple task.

The security features allow confidential information to be shared and delivery across departments in an intranet. Purveyor WebServer for Windows NT (version 1.2) is powerful enough to allow you to attach multimedia content and connect to databases. This allows corporations to use Purveyor to disseminate intellectual content, share information, and update confidential corporate and departmental information, greatly enhancing efficiency and productivity.

Version described: 1.2

Operating Systems

Windows NT: Yes

Windows 95: Yes

Windows 3.1: No

Novell Netware: Yes

VMS: Yes

Windows NT CPUs: Intel, Alpha

Launching and Logging

Can run from inetd (UNIX and OS/2 systems only): Not applicable

Can serve different directory roots for different IP addresses: Yes

Runs as Windows NT service and/or application: Service

Logging with syslog (UNIX) or Event Log (Windows NT): Yes

CERN/NCSA common log format: Yes

Log files can be automatically cycled or archived: Yes

Normal (hit) log entries can be customized: Yes

Can write to multiple logs: Yes

Server can generate non-hit log entries (such as comments): Yes

CGI scripts can create their own log entries: Yes

Performance measurement logs: Yes

Can generate referer log entries: Yes

Can generate browser log entries: Yes

Can track individual users in log: Yes

Protocol Support and Includes

Automatic response to If-Modified-Since: Yes

Select documents based on Accept header: Yes

Select documents based on User-Agent header: No

Includes based on HTML comments: Yes

Includes can be based on request headers: Yes

Server can force includes: No

Automatically include any HTTP headers in responses: Yes

Access to server state variables from CGI or other scripting: Yes

Has built-in scripting language: ISAPI

Has built-in image-map handling: Yes

Supports HTTP/1.1 PUT: No

Nonsupported methods can invoke a script: No

Supports the Windows CGI interface: No

Comes with SNMP agent: No

Supports HTTP/1.1 byte ranges: No

Supports HTTP/1.1 persistent connections:

Understands full URIs in HTTP/1.1 requests:

The name that is shown in the Server: response header: Purveyor

Security

Can require password (Authorization: user): Yes

Supports SSL v. 2: Yes

Supports SSL v. 3: No

Supports S-HTTP: No

Supports PCT: No

Prohibit user access by domain name: Yes

Prohibit user access by IP address: Yes

Configurable user groups (not just a single-user list): Yes

Can change user access control list without restarting server: Yes

Can hide part of a document based on security rules: Yes

Security rules can be based on URLs: Yes

Default security model for file-based documents: Allow access to all files unless listed in an access file

Hierarchical permissions for directory-based documents: Yes

Additional security features: External authentication (usernames/passwords can reside in external database or NT registry username database)

Other Features

GUI-based setup: Yes

GUI-based maintenance: Yes

Remote maintenance: Yes

Real-time performance measurement tools: Yes

Script or action based on output media type: Yes

Also serves other TCP protocols: No

Automatic directory tree: Yes

User directories: Yes

Search engine: Verity and WAIS

Has direct (non-CGI) link to a DBMS: No

Includes user interaction tools: No

Type of server-side imagemaps: Information not available

Allows nonblocking DNS: Information not available

Has a support mailing list: Yes

Also acts as an HTTP proxy server: Yes

Proxy server also caches: Yes

Includes full source code for server: Extra fee

Pricing: $295 - $495

Pricing (more info): Varies by platform, with lower prices for North America

Best features (as described by server author): Purveyor is loaded with administrative features and is extremely easy to use; all features are GUI based and tightly integrated into the operating system

URL for more information: http://www.process.com/

Spinnaker Web Server

Searchlight Software has developed a Web server called Spinnaker. This new Web host product combines the functions of a traditional Web server with conferencing, file libraries, user profiles and security, an application interface, and a server-side script language. Spinnaker is ideal for small and midsized businesses because it gives them the ability to run highly interactive Web sites on a low-cost Windows NT or Windows 95 platform.

Spinnaker has arrived from a different viewpoint onto the Web Scene. Searchlight Software is known for its BBS software and has developed Spinnaker to take advantage of many of the traditional BBS features. Spinnaker also introduces a feature called

Dynamic HTML, which enables you to put two or more versions of an HTML statement in one document and dynamically choose between them based on the browser type. Spinnaker autodetects the browser type, making your Web pages foolproof: users get the right HTML code for their browser every time.

> **NOTE:** These extra features that Spinnaker offers can be nice, but there is something to be said for standards. If Dynamic HTML is something your organization must have, then go for it. Just be aware that all these extras might not be supported later on when the Web starts to buckle down on set standards.

Version described: 2.0

Operating Systems

Windows NT: Yes

Windows 95: Yes

Windows 3.1: No

Windows NT CPUs: Intel

Launching and Logging

Can run from inetd (UNIX and OS/2 systems only): Not applicable

Can serve different directory roots for different IP addresses: No

Runs as Windows NT service and/or application: Application

Logging with syslog (UNIX) or Event Log (Windows NT): Yes

CERN/NCSA common log format: Yes

Log files can be automatically cycled or archived: No

Normal (hit) log entries can be customized: No

Can write to multiple logs: No

Server can generate non-hit log entries (such as comments): No

CGI scripts can create their own log entries: Yes

Performance measurement logs: Yes

Can generate referer log entries: No

Can generate browser log entries: No

Can track individual users in log: No

Protocol Support and Includes

Automatic response to If-Modified-Since: Yes

Select documents based on Accept header: Yes

Select documents based on User-Agent header: Yes

Includes based on HTML comments: Yes

Includes can be based on request headers: Yes

Server can force includes: Yes

Automatically include any HTTP headers in responses: Yes

Access to server state variables from CGI or other scripting: Yes

Has built-in scripting language: Dynamic HTML

Has built-in image-map handling: Yes

Supports HTTP/1.1 PUT: Yes

Nonsupported methods can invoke a script: Yes

Supports the Windows CGI interface: Yes

Comes with SNMP agent: No

Supports HTTP/1.1 byte ranges: No

Supports HTTP/1.1 persistent connections: No

Understands full URIs in HTTP/1.1 requests: No

The name that is shown in the Server: response header: Spinnaker

Security

Can require password (Authorization: user): Yes

Supports SSL v. 2: No

Supports SSL v. 3: No

Supports S-HTTP: No

Supports PCT: No

Prohibit user access by domain name: No

Prohibit user access by IP address: Yes

Configurable user groups (not just a single-user list): Yes

Can change user access control list without restarting server: Yes

Can hide part of a document based on security rules: Yes

Security rules can be based on URLs: Yes

Default security model for file-based documents: Deny access to all files unless listed in an access file

Hierarchical permissions for directory-based documents: No

Additional security features: Workgroups

Other Features

GUI-based setup: Yes

GUI-based maintenance: Yes

Remote maintenance: No

Real-time performance measurement tools: Yes

Script or action based on output media type: Yes

Also serves other TCP protocols: No

Automatic directory tree: No

User directories: No

Search engine: No

Has direct (non-CGI) link to a DBMS: Yes

Includes user interaction tools: User profiles, conferencing, file submissions

Type of server-side imagemaps: NCSA

Allows nonblocking DNS: No

Has a support mailing list: No

Also acts as an HTTP proxy server: No

Proxy server also caches: Not applicable

Includes full source code for server: None available

Pricing: $0 - $495

Best features (as described by server author): Interactive conferencing, user profiles, file submissions

URL for more information: http://www.searchlight.com

WebSite Professional from O'Reilly & Associates

WebSite runs perfectly on a LAN running TCP/IP. This makes it a perfect fit for all users, ranging from those within corporations, businesses, and organizations to individuals. The power and performance of the software, its intuitive graphical user interface, and the comprehensive, easy instructions in the book make WebSite a natural choice for a wide variety of users. In a corporate LAN environment, you can use WebSite to publish project information, online training material, corporate policies, and company news. WebSite's powerful server engine allows you to publish large sets of corporate data, including sophisticated CGI forms, with excellent performance and reliability. With WebSite's access control features, you can restrict access so that confidential information, such as sales reports and employee records, is accessible only to people in a specific group or department. WebSite runs on Windows NT and Windows 95.

Version described: 1.1F

Operating Systems

Windows NT: Yes

Windows 95: Yes

Windows 3.1: No

Windows NT CPUs: Intel

Launching and Logging

Can run from inetd (UNIX and OS/2 systems only): Not applicable

Can serve different directory roots for different IP addresses: Yes

Runs as Windows NT service and/or application: Both

Logging with syslog (UNIX) or Event Log (Windows NT): No

CERN/NCSA common log format: Yes

Log files can be automatically cycled or archived: Yes

Normal (hit) log entries can be customized: Yes, with .DLL programming.

Can write to multiple logs: Yes

Server can generate non-hit log entries (such as comments): No

CGI scripts can create their own log entries: No

Performance measurement logs: Yes

Can generate referer log entries: Yes

Can generate browser log entries: Yes

Can track individual users in log: No

Protocol Support and Includes

Automatic response to If-Modified-Since: Yes

Select documents based on Accept header: No

Select documents based on User-Agent header: No

Includes based on HTML comments: Yes

Includes can be based on request headers: No

Server can force includes: No

Automatically include any HTTP headers in responses: No

Access to server state variables from CGI or other scripting: Yes

Has built-in scripting language: No

Has built-in image-map handling: Yes

Supports HTTP/1.1 PUT: Yes

Nonsupported methods can invoke a script: No

Supports the Windows CGI interface: Yes

Comes with SNMP agent: No

Supports HTTP/1.1 byte ranges: Yes

Supports HTTP/1.1 persistent connections: Yes

Understands full URIs in HTTP/1.1 requests: Yes

The name that is shown in the Server: response header: WebSite

Security

Can require password (Authorization: user): Yes

Supports SSL v. 2: Yes

Supports SSL v. 3: No

Supports S-HTTP: Yes

Supports PCT: No

Prohibit user access by domain name: Yes

Prohibit user access by IP address: Yes

Configurable user groups (not just a single-user list): Yes

Can change user access control list without restarting server: Yes

Can hide part of a document based on security rules: No

Security rules can be based on URLs: Yes

Default security model for file-based documents: Allow access to all files (no access file)

Hierarchical permissions for directory-based documents: Yes

Additional security features: None

Other Features

GUI-based setup: Yes

GUI-based maintenance: Yes

Remote maintenance: Yes

Real-time performance measurement tools: Yes

Script or action based on output media type: No

Also serves other TCP protocols: No

Automatic directory tree: Yes

User directories: No

Search engine: Built-in indexer and search engine

Has direct (non-CGI) link to a DBMS: No

Includes user interaction tools: No

Type of server-side imagemaps: Both

Allows nonblocking DNS: No

Has a support mailing list: Yes

Also acts as an HTTP proxy server: No

Proxy server also caches: Not applicable

Includes full source code for server: None available

Pricing: $499

Best features (as described by server author): The software's power and performance, its intuitive graphical user interface, the comprehensive information in the enclosed books, and the suite of included support applications

URL for more information: http://software.ora.com/

Other Web Servers

Every day, someone is out in a garage working on the next Web server that will surely change the way we view and think of traditional Web servers. There are many platforms and many approaches that companies are using when they develop Web servers in this new and changing environment. The best advice is to choose a company that has great technical support, is constantly improving its product, and is familiar with the WWW.

Standards are also very important. Many companies are developing their own proprietary systems for the WWW and intranets, but getting proprietary systems to talk to other systems that are based on standards is difficult. You might need a special browser, or thin client, to even use these proprietary systems. Stick with a system that offers standards but also is constantly pushing ahead to develop better products and standards. Please take a look at the hundreds of Web servers available on the market before you make your choice. Thanks to David Strom, all the latest Web server information is right here in this book. To keep up-to-date on new servers, you can visit the site he maintains at:

http://Webcompare.iworld.com/

David keeps statistics on all the top Web servers up-to-date in formats that are easy to follow. So, check out this site to get other server information.

Netscape Enterprise Server Introduction

Here, I take a more in-depth look at Netscape's Enterprise Server, and go over some of Enterprise's features and configuration options.

Netscape Server Selector

When you install and launch Netscape Enterprise Server, you enter the Administration Server (see Figure 4-1).

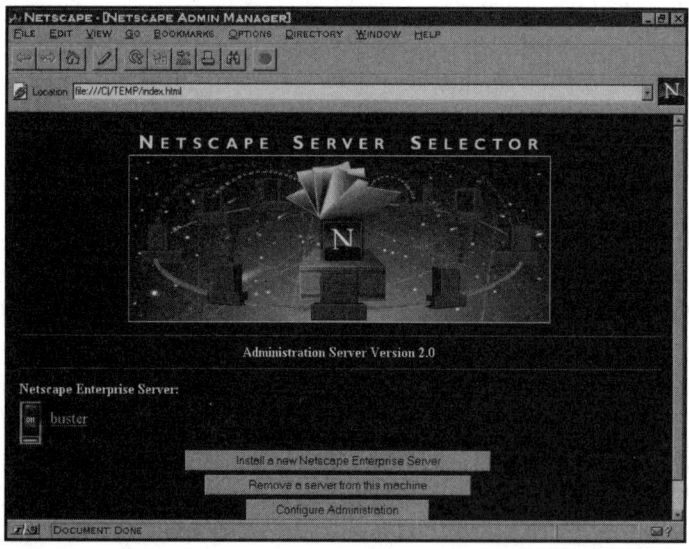

FIGURE 4-1

The Netscape Sever Selector is an easy-to-use GUI that allows you to select servers and set your preferences for your intranet Web server.

This is the gateway to where you activate your Web server, configure options, and set all your preferences for the Enterprise Web Server. The first button that you see on the Administration index page is Install a New Netscape Enterprise Server.

When you click on the New Netscape Enterprise Server button, you receive an HTML page that gives you a form with several options to set up a new server. Figure 4-2 shows the top half of the Server Installation window.

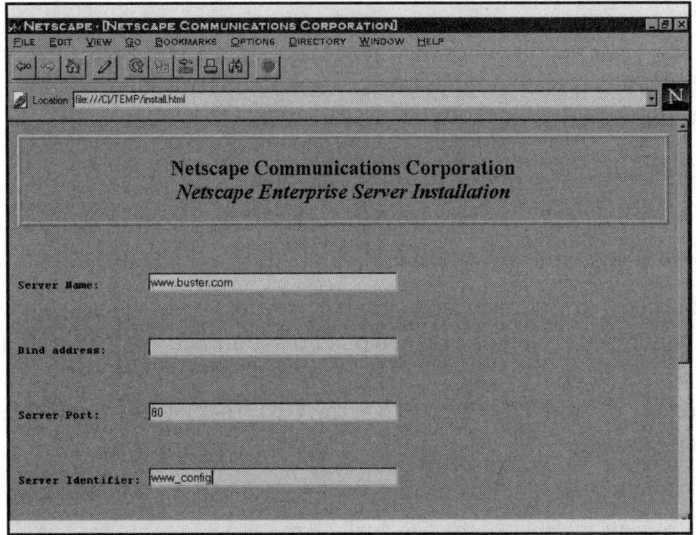

FIGURE 4-2

By accessing the Netscape Enterprise Server Installation window, you can set up additional Web servers.

Before you try to install a server, make sure that you shut down any servers that might already be running on the same port.

Server Name

The server name is the first host name, the part of the Uniform Resource Locator (URL) that defines your pages. (Of course, the protocol designator—http://, ftp://, and so on—precedes the server name.) You may want to have your network administrator(s) alias your server name—say, antipodes—to www so that accesses to www.internal.you.com are processed and returned without the user having to know the actual server name. This makes system upgrades and migration easier, as well as giving the end user a consistent system to look for.

Bind Address

As you develop and expand your intranet, you might find that it would be beneficial to have your server answer to different URLs. That way, you could serve different URLs, such as `http://retail.you.com` and `http://wholesale.you.com`, from the same machine. If you have set your Web server to already accept multiple IP addresses and you would like to try this out, you need to tell this current install which IP address it belongs to.

Server Port

Your Web server box has a number of ports. These ports are used by your computer to tell what type of request it is seeing. It does this by using different protocols. The standard port addresses are as follows:

- Telnet 23
- HTTP 80
- HTTPS 443

You are allowed to choose any number from 1–65535 when you are choosing a port address. Make sure that you do not choose a number of a port address that is already in use. If for some reason you decide to change your port to something other than the standard setting, remember that doing so will change the URL that people use to access your home page on your intranet.

If you have a machine name that is `www.buster.com` and you are using a default setting of 80, then the URL to your intranet home page will be the usual `http://www.buster.com`. If you change your port settings to, say, 44, however, then the URL to your home page will not be the standard HTTP/WWW default, and your user must type `http://www.buster.com:44/` to reach your home page.

Previously, when you saw the standard port settings that I listed, you may have noticed that HTTPS, for security on your server, has a default port setting of 443, not 80. Before you activate security, you should run on the standard port 80. After you activate security, you will want to change this to the default of 443. If you get confused about the port setting and just don't know what to run on, it is safe to use the standard defaults for all your port settings.

Server Identifier

To help in your Web server administration, you should give your server a name. This identifier will be used by Netscape to create a directory name just under your server root. Netscape will store your configuration files in this directory. When you decide on a name, remember to stay clear of spaces and slashes. Take a look at this in Figure 4-3.

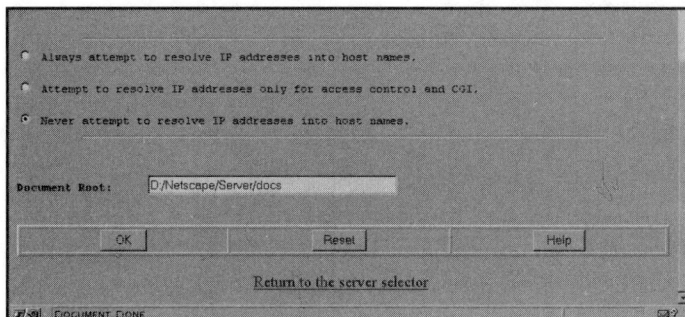

FIGURE 4-3

The rest of the Netscape Enterprise Server Administration screen allows you to set IP/Host Resolving and your document root directory.

Resolve IP Addresses

When a user first connects to the Web server, the server can identify the user only by the user's IP address. This is the address that looks like 198.24.6.34, with periods in it. Sometimes the server needs to know that the IP address is someone like the system administrator who has access to operations such as access control, CGI scripts, and other important reports. By telling the server to always resolve IP addresses into host names, the server can then discern that the IP address actually is www1.netscape.com, or some other address. It will turn a standard IP address into a host name that is easier for you to identify.

If you have a very busy Web server that is taking many hits every day, you will want to tell the server not to try to resolve all of these users' IP address. By selecting the second option on the form, you can reduce the load on your domain name server and speed up your response time.

The last radio button should be turned on if you do not have access to a DNS server.

Document Root

You must create a root directory for your documents. The installer creates this directory if it does not already exist.

The Configure Administration

The Configure Administration page is a doorway to several other options in the Netscape Enterprise Server. You can see the page layout in Figure 4-4. This heading has three main areas branching off to several other HTML pages of options that can be set. The first is Daemon Configuration.

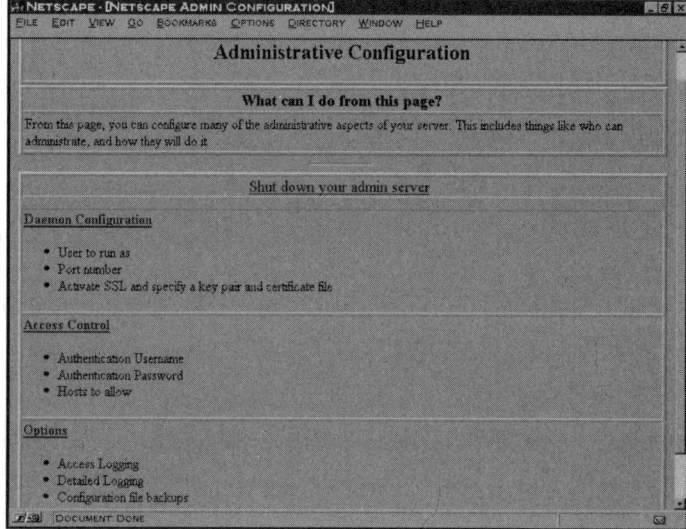

FIGURE 4-4

The Administrative Configuration page allows you to set the daemon configuration, access control, and options.

Daemon Configuration

On this Web page (see Figure 4-5), you can change:

- ◆ Which user the administration server runs as
- ◆ Which port the administration server runs on
- ◆ You can activate SSL on the administration server
- ◆ You can set a key and certificate file
- ◆ You can tell the administration server where your server is located

Administration Server User

The default of the Netscape Administration server is to run in the LocalSystem account (see Figure 4-5, shown previously). If you want to change this setting, you can choose to have the server run in another account.

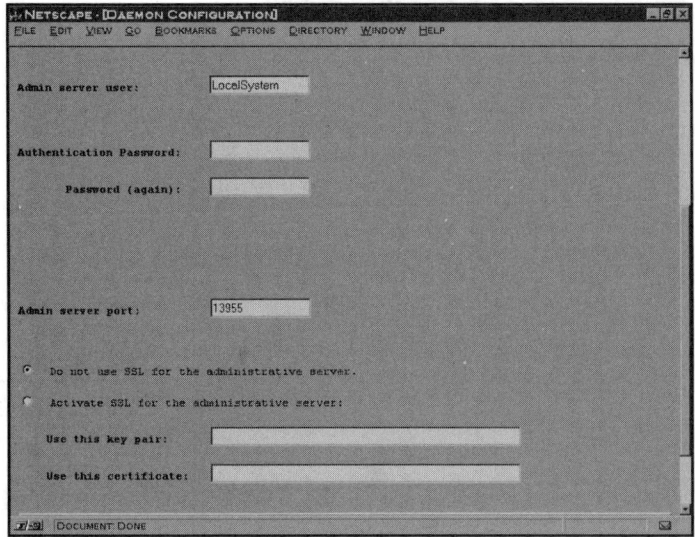

Administration Server Port Number

This is where you choose a port number to use for server administration. Make sure that the port number is different from the port you used for your HTTP server. This port is used to connect to the administrative server only. In Figure 4-5, shown previously, the port has been set to 13955.

SSL Radio Buttons

Here you can activate SSL for the administrative server. To do this, check the lower radio button. After you've checked this, you will need to already have a certificate file and a key pair file. If you have a Netscape Commerce server running in secure mode on this same machine, you can use this key pair file for your administrative server also.

Access Control

From here, you can allow or deny access to the server several different ways. The Access Control allows you to do the following:

- Restrict which hosts are allowed to administrate your server
- Change the authentication username
- Change the authentication password

In Figure 4-6, all of these options are displayed.

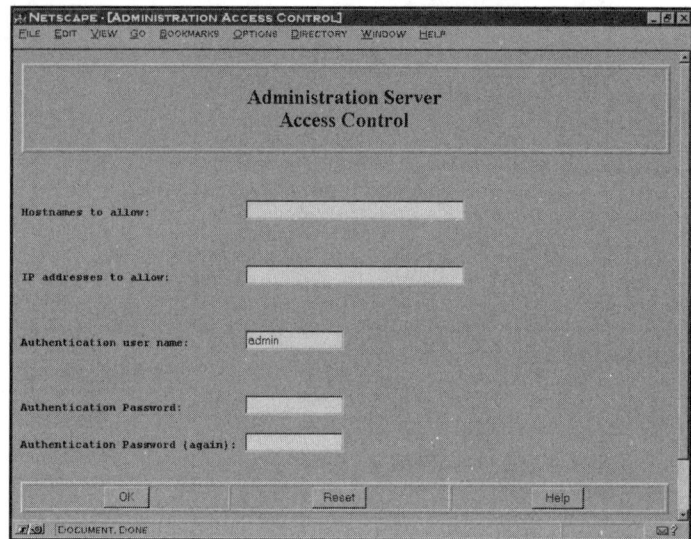

FIGURE 4-6

The Access Control page is where you set permissions for which hosts you will allow to publish to your server.

Hostnames to Allow

For security reasons, you may want to restrict which hosts are allowed to administrate your server. However, host access restrictions are only as secure as the identified systems. In the case of operating systems that have no user authentication (like DOS/Windows 3.1), that's no security at all. Other systems with native networking capabilities may, as a default, allow unlimited remote access to a given system, which also means "no security" using IP address restriction. And the downside of using a host restriction is that you can't, in an emergency, use an arbitrary machine to access the system.

You can also enter a wildcard pattern of hosts that you wish to allow. If you want to restrict access, you have two options from which to choose: by host name or by IP address. Restricting by host name is the better choice because it is more flexible—you will not have to do any updates as a machine's IP address changes. The other option, restricting by IP address, also has its advantages. If for some reason a DNS lookup fails for a connected client, then the host name restriction cannot be used.

Authentication User Name

From here, you can change your user name. This is the name that your server uses to allow access the server administrator. You should already have a user name in this field because this is the name you gave when you accessed the server manager for the very first time.

This came from the first time that you logged in and chose a name and a password for your identity. This name is an HTTP user name, so it is usable only within the server. By choosing a name and entering it here, you will cause the server to create the user for you.

Authentication Password

The authentication password is the password you give the server after you enter the authentication username.

Note that if you leave this password blank, the administration password will remain unchanged (as opposed to being removed).

Options

This Web page allows you to configure some of the options on your administration server. It allows you to do the following:

♦ Activate/deactivate access logging
♦ Activate/deactivate detailed logs of changes
♦ Enable configuration file backups

This is displayed in Figure 4-7.

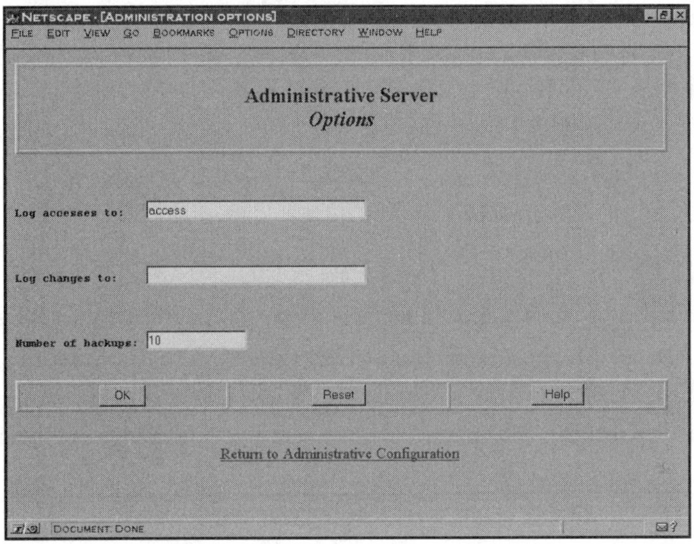

FIGURE 4-7

The Access Control page is where you will want to set permissions for which hosts you will allow to publish to your server.

Access Logging

The administrative server can keep access logs in the Common Logfile Format (the same format that the HTTP server normally uses). Each logfile entry will look like this:

```
hostname.incoming.com - admin. [04/Oct/1996:22:29:00 -0500]
➥"POST /admin.-serv/bin/confopt HTTP/1.0" 200 842
```

which contains the following fields:

- ◆ `hostname.incoming.com`—The hostname of the incoming connection
- ◆ `admin.`—The username given for authentication
- ◆ `[04/Oct/1996:22:29:00 -0500]`—The current time
- ◆ `"POST /admin.-serv/bin/confopt HTTP/1.0"`—The document that the client accessed
- ◆ `200`—The HTTP response code given
- ◆ `842`—The number of bytes returned to the client

You can deactivate access logging by leaving the text box, Log Accesses, under Administration Server Options, blank. You can also type a relative path from your administrative server root. Or, you can type a full path to the place where you want to keep the access logs.

Detailed Logs of Changes

In addition to access logging, you can also have the server keep a log of all the configuration changes that you make to your servers. Each entry in the log file will look something like this:

```
admin@host.acme.com: www.acme.com-secure [09/Sep/1995:00:23:44] system
➥magnus.conf: 'User' set to 'wiley'
```

which contains the following fields:

- ◆ `admin.`—The user name the administrator used to authenticate the change
- ◆ `host.acme.com`—The host name from which the administrator made the change
- ◆ `www.acme.com-secure`—The name of the server to which changes are being made
- ◆ `[09/Sep/1995:00:23:44]`—The time that the change was made

- ◆ system—The name of the program making the change
- ◆ magnus.conf—The type of change made; includes magnus.conf, obj.conf, userdb, and so on

The remainder of the entry is a description of what change was made. You can deactivate detailed logging by leaving this field blank. You can also type a relative path from your administrative server root. Alternately, you can type a full path to the place where you want to keep the detailed logs.

Backup Files

The administrative server can also keep backups of configuration files, which get made every time a change is made to the file. These backups are stored in the server root, in the directory ADMSERV/HTTPS-SERVER-NAME.

Type the number of backups that you want to keep here. If you don't want to keep any backups, leave the field blank.

Other Configurations

By clicking your mouse on your server name (next to the on/off switch on the main index page), you will enter Enterprise's main control area. From here, you can tweak all of Netscape Enterprise's settings, and set CGI, security, access controls, and logs. Enterprise is a very powerful server for intranet hosting and development. Take the time to try different settings and test it out.

Microsoft Internet Information Server

I know that a bunch of you who will be using Microsoft Windows NT 4.0 Server are also going to be interested in Microsoft Internet Information Server 3.0 (IIS). This latest version of IIS was just recently released, and it's a winner.

So, take a look at it now while I point out the sites as you tour the IIS.

Microsoft IIS comes along with Windows NT 4.0 Server. At the present time, you still need to visit Microsoft's Web site to get the new IIS version 3.0, because NT ships with an older version. Windows NT is the up-and-coming operating system, although UNIX isn't going anyplace soon. IIS 3.0 is designed to use NT's operating system to the fullest. Microsoft makes both NT and IIS, and together, these two sing. This is a high-performance server that covers all the bases in security and is wrapped in a friendly GUI.

IIS offers native support for the following:

- JAVA
- JavaScript
- Visual Basic
- VB Script
- Visual C++
- CGI
- WINCGI

Before I forget, another bonus with the IIS 3.0 version is its built-in search engine (Index Server 1.1), and also the management tools. Microsoft FrontPage also comes packaged with NT now, and the WYSIWYG operation along with the templates and wizards get you up and running with a very powerful intranet solution.

Installation

Installation is a snap. Because IIS comes with Windows NT Server, you just install NT Server and IIS is installed during the process. That is just one of the advantages with having a product that is integrated with the operating system. The Windows NT Server install is also very easy because there are wizards to help you along the way.

Features

The IIS 3.0 comes packed with goodies, including the following:

- NetShow —Does streaming media on your IIS
- Index Server 1.1—A search engine
- Crystal Reports 4.5—For reporting, graphs, and analysis, and support of all FrontPage's latest server features

In the next sections, I go over these in a bit more detail.

NetShow

NetShow allows you to send live media over your intranet. Its streaming feature allows users to receive the media as it covers over the network. This way, users do not have to wait to receive the entire file before they can view it. NetShow was also created taking in the concerns of IS administrators over bandwidth issues on corporate LANs and WANs.

NetShow changes the way intranets will deliver content in the future. Does your organization need video conference calls, training with rich video and audio content, audio and video presentations? Does your organization need to receive the latest updates, or see an important meeting that happened last week? NetShow can deliver them to your users on demand. Training is enhanced with the addition of audio and video to demonstrate tasks and procedures, and Human Resources documents can come alive now with audio and video explanations of benefit packages.

Index Server 1.1

This search engine allows your users to search HTML, text, Microsoft Word, Excel, and PowerPoint documents. As your documents change and are updated on your intranet, the Index Server will automatically do incremental updates to look for these changes. Index Server also talks to your NT security, ensuring that users who don't have permission to certain sections, or documents, do not get hits back when they search for documents that result in a match based on their search criteria.

Crystal Reports

A copy of Crystal Reports is now included with NT 4.0. This allows you to analyze your log files and create meaningful results.

FrontPage

FrontPage, Microsoft's Web creation and management tool, now comes with NT 4.0. It allows you to create Web content for your intranet and publish to IIS with the click of just one button. The site map feature allows you to inspect and fix your broken links, and move files around your intranet without breaking links.

Administration

You can use the Internet Service Manager or any Web browser for administration. With the Web browser, Microsoft's IE 3.1, or Netscape Navigator 3.1, you can manage your Web from anywhere on the network.

Creating Interactive Pages the Easy Way

Microsoft introduces Active Server Pages. This is a relief to those who have been developing for intranets since back in the days when people thought the word *intranet* was just a typo. CGI scripts can still be used, but Active Server Pages offers you much more.

Microsoft offers a new way of creating interactivity, Active Server Pages, which now allow you to add in script in your Web pages along with your regular HTML tags. Also, you can use any tool you like. IIS supports VBScript as well as JavaScript. It also supports other scripting languages through the use of plug-ins. Connecting to databases is also made easy with Active Data Object (ADO). This allows you to connect to ODBC databases so that you can access your existing legacy data for use on your intranet.

Summary

Boy, was that a long chapter! You now know about some of the top Web servers available that you can use for your intranet. I ranked several top-notch Web servers, and discussed configuration of Netscape's Enterprise Server. I also took a look at all the awesome features that are in Microsoft's IIS Server.

What's Next!

Now it's time to move on to ways to use your existing files on your intranet. I'm going to have you dig up all those valuable files you have around your office, and look at several different ways of getting the content on your intranet. So, grab your word processing files and spreadsheets, and meet me next door.

PART

II

Building Intranet
Pages

Chapter | 5

Using Existing Files

So far, I have covered a great deal of preliminary design, concept, and layout. I hope I've also coaxed you into doing some blue-sky sketches and idea tossing. Now it's time to take some of these concepts and start designing your intranet. Keep in mind that this chapter is just a starting point. It should help you to quickly move some of your important content up onto the intranet with few bells and whistles.

This chapter is much like the quick-start inserts that come with most of your new software applications. Those inserts always seem to come with a 500-page, in-depth book that nobody reads, and a quick-start pamphlet. After you spend hours trying to cut and paste some simple text, you finally reach into the box for some help. Of course, you grab the quick-start pamphlet and feverishly look for that quick fix.

This chapter is that pamphlet. I want you to look through your desk drawers, on the cafeteria walls, in the filing cabinets, and in that box that you have not opened in three years. What are you looking for? Anything and everything that contains information about your organization. If you find it on an employee bulletin board, in a file cabinet, or in a corporate publication, it is information that is important to your employees.

> **NOTE:** This chapter does not go into the how-to part of HTML, but shows you how to get information up on your intranet quickly. This is kind of a plug-n-play intranet chapter that allows you to get content on your intranet now, and then you can see how to dress it up later.
>
> I go into the HTML coding in Appendices A and B. Make sure that you take the time to read these sections after you have the basics from this chapter down pat.

> **NOTE:** You'll dive in and get started on your intranet quickly in this chapter. I know the boss wants the intranet up and running yesterday, and if you could just get a photo of him on the intranet with a little bit of text welcoming everyone to your department, you could surely buy some time. So, I cover some quick ways to get your existing content up on your intranet. If you don't know HTML, you can still follow along and try your hand at this chapter. I suggest that you do take a look back at Appendix A and B and the HTML authoring tools references in this book to get yourself up to speed. Starting with Appendix A, I cover HTML basics, walk you through examples, and explain the code each step of the way. Then, I cover more advanced HTML and tags meant specifically for Netscape Navigator in Appendix B. I wrap it up with some authoring tools that make your HTML creation easy and smooth in Appendix C.

Miracle Toy Corporation

If you have been reading this book from the beginning and have not skipped ahead, you have been following the saga of the Miracle Toy Corporation. Miracle Toys is a make-believe organization that is implementing an intranet. The organization is going through the same situations as the rest of corporate America, and is getting its intranet up and running with some basic content as soon as possible. So, you'll take a look at Miracle and see what it's doing to get some content on its intranet in record time.

Dig It Up

I told you that you would be doing this, and I bet you didn't believe me. Yes, it's time for you to get out of your chair and start looking around the office. You need to hunt down files, notes pasted on cork boards, company publications, white papers, meeting notes, catalogs, on-the-job training material, newsletters, phone books, this week's lunch menu, and anything that is of importance in your organization. Stop by your human resources office and make sure you bring a shopping cart to haul off all the valuable information you find there. Make sure that you get information on job postings, employee benefits, special events, and employee handbooks, just to name a few. Even more information needs to be rooted out of your departments. Look for any information used by your organization that is already in an electronic format. This is like gold. If you can find hard drives full of information, boxes of tape backups and floppy disks, you will save countless hours of re-typing and organizing company content.

Making a Page

You are about to create the world's easiest Web page. It's no beauty to look at, but it gets the job done. A simple yet effective way exists to get your existing word processing documents up on the intranet. I don't care whether you are using Ami Pro, Microsoft Word, WordPerfect, or your three-year-old's first attempt at a word processing application. As long as it gives you an option to save the file as a plain-text file (no special character formatting, please), you are set. Try this. Open Netscape Navigator or Internet Explorer 3.0, and then open a word processing file in your browser. Try doing this with a file that's not an .HTM file. I show a Microsoft Word file in Netscape Navigator in Figure 5-1. You get strange character formatting commands in the document, so this is why you want to open them in Netscape as plain-text files.

Now you'll see something really cool. Open the same page in Microsoft's Internet Explorer. Take a look at Figure 5-2.

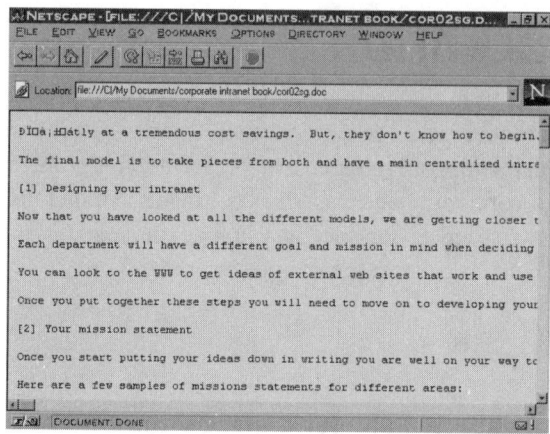

FIGURE 5-1

See how the document opens up in Netscape as plain text. It's that easy.

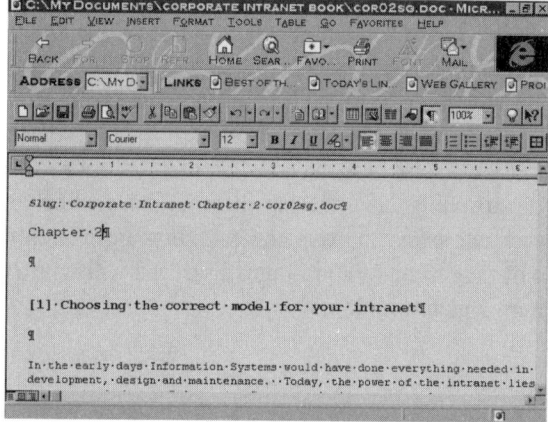

FIGURE 5-2

In Microsoft Internet Explorer, the browser automatically launches a window inside the browser that gives the user the Word document exactly as it is meant to be seen.

If users have the Microsoft Office products, they can use all of the features in that package with documents in that file format in Internet Explorer. They can edit and make any changes they want to Microsoft Word documents, just as they do in Word, right in the Internet Explorer browser.

If users do not have Microsoft's Office products, users can download a view to go in their browser that will allow them to view the documents that are in Word, Excel, or PowerPoint. They can also format and print those documents, but they will not be able to edit the documents unless they already have the full version of these applications.

NOTE: This is a great way to get content up on your intranet. If you have Microsoft Word, Excel, or PowerPoint documents, you can place them on your intranet as is, in their regular format, and view them in Internet Explorer. For users who have the full versions of these products, they can edit these documents and have all the same features that they have in the full versions inside the Internet Explorer browser window. In case you are wondering, users who have the ability to edit these documents cannot edit and repost these documents on your intranet unless you have granted them security access to do so.

Word Processing Files

When a department's representative comes up to you and says "We have this 300-page catalog that we really need on the company intranet. Here is the hard copy," you need to casually ask that person whether the catalog exists in a Microsoft Word file or some other word processing file format. Usually the answer is yes, and finding the file is just a matter of tracking down the person with the floppy disk. When you have obtained the disk, you have just saved yourself a good week or two of re-entering the entire catalog from scratch. By opening the file in the appropriate word processor and resaving the document as a plain ASCII file (just a plain, ordinary text file), you can dump it on your intranet as is. It's that simple. Of course, you don't want to tell the department that.

So, now what do you do with the other two weeks you have just banked? Just dumping a 300-page catalog on your intranet is a start, but not necessarily the correct solution. Use the rest of your time to go over the content, and create an index that lets users jump right to the page that has the information they are looking for. Add graphics, character formatting, and spell-check the content. Just dumping in text is not very valuable. Sure, all employees now have access to the document, they know that it will always be there, and they don't have to worry whether that one employee who has everything stored in his head will leave the company. But, the intranet allows you to do so much more than just store information in a paperless filing cabinet.

Human Resource Example

It's time to create your first simple intranet page. From your scavenger hunt that you did in the "Dig It Up" section of this chapter, choose a piece of information that is already in electronic format. Use the Save As function from your word processing application, and save the file as an ASCII file or a plain-text file (.TXT). Now, launch Netscape Navigator and use File | Open File In Browser to locate the file you just created. When you open it in

Netscape Navigator, you will see the entire file displayed as is in your browser window. This is exciting and keeps you entertained for about a day as you call up all of your buddies in the office to show them what you have done. After the initial excitement has worn off, you may want to add links, formatting, color, and interactivity to the page.

> **NOTE:** Before you place these new files on your intranet, make sure they work. That sounds pretty basic, but sometimes you get caught up in the whole process and forget to check your work. If you are placing some uncommon word processing files up on your intranet as plain-text files, be sure to test them in your official company standard browser to make sure that they contain no surprises.

So, now I show you how to do just that, in the form of adding HTML and dressing up the memo in the next example. Take a look at a memo from the Human Resources department at Miracle Toys. While I was digging through Miracle's HR department, I found the following memo in a Microsoft Word 7.0 format:

Debbie Summer

12/15/96

Human Resources Follow Up

At the December 8 Human Resources meeting, the following issues, questions, and concerns were brought to my attention. There seems to be some confusion on the price for non-Miracle employees for this year's Christmas party, as well as some issues with the proper dress. I made a list of some of the questions that I did not have the answers to at the meeting, and I believe this memo should answer most of your questions. We will try to send memos like this to the six leaders in the head departments via inter-office mail. Due to the nature of inter-office mail around here, please be patient while the memo is in transit to your area's mailbox. Please share this information with your department managers and staff. If you still have further questions, you can contact our office at X1245 between the hours of 10 a.m. and 4 p.m., Monday through Thursday. We are constantly in and out of the office, so please try again if we are not available to take your call.

Thanks,

Debbie Summer

What is the location of this year's Staff Christmas party?

This year's staff Christmas Party will be held at the Grand Floridian Beach Resort at Walt Disney World. The Convention Center at the Grand Floridian will host our 25th Christmas celebration here at Miracle Toys. For a map to the facility, please stop by HR at the hours listed above. The party is from 6 p.m. to 10 p.m. December 23 in the Grand Ballroom. Valet Parking is available at the main entrance to the resort. Although there is no parking fee, please be sure to tip the valets for their gracious service. After your car is parked, the convention center is just down the path to your left.

Can I bring my spouse?

Yes. Just like last year, you can bring your spouse and there is no additional charge. If you bring an additional guest, the fee is $25.00 to help us cover the guest's dinner and expenses.

Who do I call to be added to the Miracle HR newsletter?

The Miracle newsletter is sent out every month to each department supervisor. Every department should receive a minimum of 25 copies. If you are not receiving your copies, please call us at the HR office.

What is the Miracle HR newsletter?

What, is nobody getting this thing? Our monthly newsletter is done skillfully by the HR staff and showcases all special events and employee issues here at Miracle. We have a monthly trivia question that offers a $50.00 prize. If you have not seen the newsletter, please contact us and we will try to find out why you're not receiving it.

What is the dress for the Christmas party?

This year's party is not formal, but please dress nicely for the event. If you are coming directly from your work shift, you can come in your work attire and still be admitted to the party.

I heard we are now having casual Fridays for all business units. Is this true?

This issue was addressed last month, and an e-mail was sent to all the department heads at Miracle. There seems to still be some confusion, so I will address the issue one last time. If you are in the Miracle Toy Team 1 assembly crew, casual attire is allowed for Fridays. Please get a copy of the handbook for guidelines and regulations on this. If you are in a front-office area, there is NO casual attire.

continues

continued

> I did not pick up my T-shirt at this year's Miracle Toys Summer Bash. Do we have any left?
>
> We stated to the management that there would be no T-shirts given out after the Summer Bash. We ordered only a limited amount and distributed them only at the Summer Bash event.
>
> Is there a way to find out about job openings at Miracle?
>
> We have a job listing in my office that you are welcome to look at. Please come by my office anytime to see the listing. I have only one copy, so please make sure you do not walk away with it.

That's quite a memo. So, placing this memo on Miracle Toys' new intranet is a good idea. Because the memo is already a Word file, all I have to do is save the existing file as a different document name and make sure that I save it as a .TXT file (see Figure 5-3).

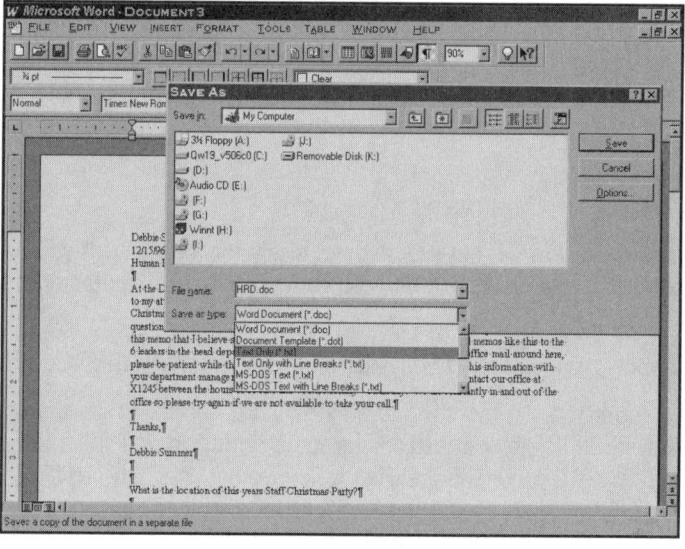

FIGURE 5-3

In Microsoft Word, you can use File | Save As and then choose a plain-text file output to easily save files that can be placed right on your intranet.

After you save the file in your word processing program, you can look at it in your browser to see how it will appear on your intranet. Figure 5-4 shows the memo that you just saved as a text file, displayed on the intranet in the Netscape Navigator browser.

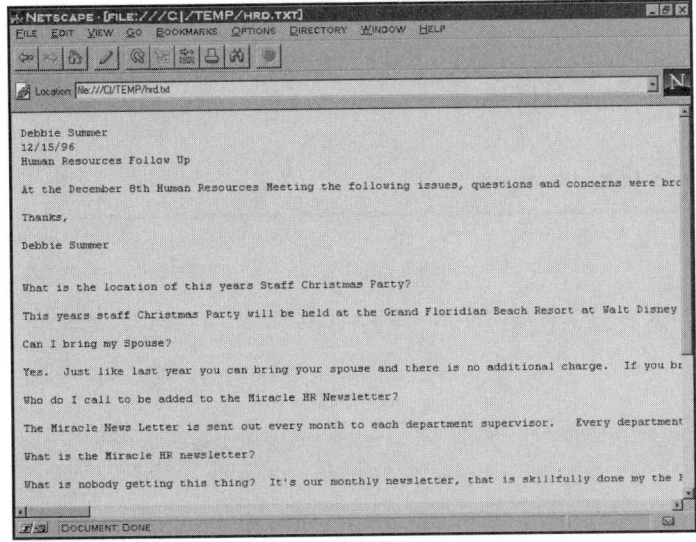

FIGURE 5-4

Here is the memo just seconds later on your intranet.

Your users now do not have to have access to Microsoft Word or any other word processing application to file this document. All they need is Netscape Navigator or another quality browser, and they can view a variety of documents that used to be in countless other formats. Another big advantage to quickly adding content to your intranet in this fashion is that now users can save copies of the file on their local hard drive if necessary, and they can also print out a copy if needed.

Notice that if you had formatting in your word processing document, such as tables or graphics, the conversion to a plain-text file has destroyed those tables and has probably deleted your images. Coding needs to be added back into the document. Conversion tools save more of the original formatting. These tools take your word processing document and turn it into HTML. To learn more about conversion software, look at Appendix C.

So, the formatting is not that great. You have to scroll across the page to read some of the lines of text. After you bring several pages of quick content up on your intranet, you can start formatting and massaging it to make it more user friendly. Now I take the original memo in the Microsoft Word format and add HTML formatting to it. The following code is some simple HTML coding. I don't discuss the HTML tags in this chapter, so if you are not familiar with HTML, please start with Appendix A in the back of this book and work through some of the HTML exercises before you read on in this chapter.

Formatting

Lisitng 5.1 shows the same memo from the floppy disk, with some HTML tags added in to make it easier for the user to read. This is the next step if you are converting text or word processing files over to HTML.

Listing 5.1   Miracle Toys HR memo.

```
<HTML>
<HEAD>
<title>Human Resources FAQ</title>
</HEAD>

<BODY>

<P ALIGN=CENTER>Human Resources On Going FAQ </P>

<P> At the December 8 Human Resources meeting, the following issues, questions, and
➥concerns were brought to my attention. There seems to be some confusion on the price
➥for non-Miracle employees for this year's Christmas party, as well as some issues with
➥the proper dress. I made a list of some of the questions that I did not have the
➥answers to at the meeting, and I believe this memo should answer most of your
➥questions. We will try to send memos like this to the six leaders in the head
➥departments via inter-office mail. Due to the nature of inter-office mail around here,
➥please be patient while the memo is in transit to your area's mailbox. Please share
➥this information with your department managers and staff. If you still have further
➥questions, you can contact our office at X1245 between the hours of 10 a.m. and 4
➥p.m., Monday through Thursday. We are constantly in and out of the office, so please
➥try again if we are not available to take your call. </P>

<P>Thanks, </P>
```

<P>Debbie Summer </P>

<P><STRONG>What is the location of this year's staff Christmas party?</STRONG> </P>

<P> This year's staff Christmas party will be held at the Grand Floridian Beach Resort
➥at Walt Disney World. The Convention Center at the Grand Floridian will host our 25th
➥Christmas celebration here at Miracle Toys. For a map to the facility, please stop by
➥HR at the hours listed above. The party is from 6 p.m. to 10 p.m. December 23 in the
➥Grand Ballroom. Valet parking is available at the main entrance to the resort.
➥Although there is no parking fee, please be sure to tip the valets for their gracious
➥service. After your car is parked, the convention center is just down the path to your
➥left. </P>

<P><STRONG>Can I bring my spouse? </STRONG></P>

<P> Yes. Just like last year, you can bring your spouse and there is no additional
➥charge. If you bring an additional guest, the fee is $25 to help us cover the guest's
➥dinner and expenses. </P>

<P><STRONG>Who do I call to be added to the Miracle HR newsletter? </STRONG></P>

<P> The Miracle newsletter is sent out every month to each department supervisor. Every
➥department should receive a minimum of 25 copies. If you are not receiving your
➥copies, please call us at the HR office. </P>

<P><STRONG>What is the Miracle HR newsletter? </STRONG></P>

<P> What, is nobody getting this thing? Our monthly newsletter is done skillfully by the
➥HR staff and showcases all special events and employee issues here at Miracle. We have
➥a monthly trivia question that offers a $50 prize. If you have not seen the newslet
➥ter, please contact us and we will try to find out why you're not receiving it. </P>

<P><STRONG>What is the dress for the Christmas party? </STRONG></P>

```
<P> This year's party is not formal, but please dress nicely for the event. If you are
➥coming directly from your work shift, you can come in your work attire and still be
➥admitted to the party. </P>

<P><STRONG>I heard we are now having casual Fridays for all business units. Is this
➥true? </STRONG></P>

<P> This issue was addressed last month, and an e-mail was sent to all the department
➥heads at Miracle. There still seems to be some confusion, so I will address the issue
➥one last time. If you are in the Miracle Toys Team 1 assembly crew, casual attire is
➥allowed for Fridays. Please get a copy of the handbook for guidelines and regulations
➥on this. If you are in a front-office area, there is NO casual attire. </P>

<P><STRONG>I did not pick up my T-shirt at this year's Miracle Toys Summer Bash. Do we
➥have any left? </STRONG></P>

<P>We stated to the management that there would be no T-shirts given out after the
➥Summer Bash. We ordered only a limited amount and distributed them only at the Summer
➥Bash event. </P>

<P><STRONG> Is there a way to find out about job openings at Miracle? </STRONG></P>

<P> We have a job listing in my office that you are welcome to look at. Please come by
➥my office anytime to see the listing. I only have one copy, so please make sure you do
➥not walk away with it. </P>

</BODY>

</HTML>
```

Adding a few basic formatting tags changes the appearance of the original text file to a more functional Web page. Remember to save your new intranet Web page as an .HTM file now instead of a .TXT file. Figure 5-5 shows the new document in the Web browser.

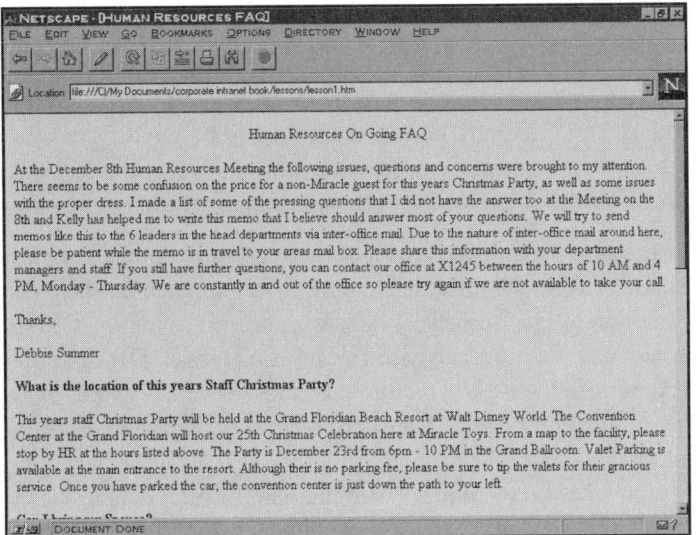

FIGURE 5-5

The text now fits nicely on the screen and is formatted into paragraphs with bold headings for each question asked at the meeting.

NOTE: If you are using DOS or Windows 3.x, you will have to save it as an .HTM file, because these operating systems allow only three-character file extensions. You're also limited to eight characters for the file name before the dot, and can't mix upper- and lowercase. If your desktop operating system allows, however, use longer, more descriptive filenames and make the suffix HTML; it's *highly* unlikely that your server will be using DOS/Win 3.x. On the other hand, if you must use the shorter .HTM suffix, make sure that your server includes both forms in the MIME types configuration file, or your CONTENT.HTM file may be delivered as raw text!

Mixing cases in URLs can improve readability, but makes user error (through mistyping) more likely.

Other Examples

This formatting is a step in the right direction, but it still does not allow you to do all the cool things that make an intranet powerful in a corporate environment. When you read the memo, you surely noticed some of the current communication problems that HR has with the rest of the Miracle Corporation. The first problem is in delivering information in a timely manner. This memo had to be typed and then sent to the heads of each department. Doing so can take several days, which brings up another significant problem. Some of the memos aren't read and then passed on to the staff in these areas. So, if your manager is not proactive 100 percent of the time, you might never even hear about these HR issues.

This problem is solved in the next re-creation of this Web page. If you place this information on your intranet, you give every person in the organization with access to it. You are no longer dependent on a few individuals to pass information on to everyone in the organization. Each staff member can look up HR information quickly and easily.

Contacting HR at Miracle is another problem. The department has limited office hours and is not always available. With the information now on the intranet, this helps ease some of HR's communication problems. Employees can always access the information from their desktop. Employees also can communicate with HR by using e-mail. HR can now send one message to everyone with the push of a button. If employees want to find out about the Christmas party, the information is there. They don't have to try locating a hand-drawn map to the party, either. They can now click on a link and see a map in full color right on their screen. If they want a hard copy to bring with them in the car, a simple click will print it. No more getting directions wrong by asking a friend how to get there.

Another problem in HR concerns distribution of the Miracle HR newsletter. Apparently, some of the copies are not getting to the employees, copies are limited, and the information is outdated almost as soon as it is printed. Now the newsletter is in a full-color version on the intranet. Everyone can access it, and it is updated when needed rather than just once a month. A hard-copy newsletter is still printed, so employees can take it home or read it in the break room. But, the full-color version on the intranet has saved on printing costs and is much more up-to-date.

The next issue also addresses poor communication. The e-mail messages sent out to certain employees about the dress code for Fridays were not received by all of the necessary individuals. It never fails: When you send an e-mail, you always leave out someone who needs to know about your message, and you always send a bunch of junk to people who have no need for your message. If you place this information on the intranet in a whitepaper (a kind of digital report), however, everyone can access it. The people who don't need the information don't get bombed with junk mail, and everyone is much happier and better informed. Employees can also look at the Employee Handbook online on the intranet. An employee with a question does not have to hunt down an HR representative to get a copy of the handbook.

More Examples

What about jobs? Human Resources gets a listing once a week in a hard copy. Right now, only one person in the company can read this document at a time, You can compare this to a library, which may have only one copy of a book on the shelf. When someone checks the book out, you have to wait until it comes back in, travel to the library to get the book, and then return it before the due date.

If you place the jobs listing on the intranet, everyone can view the same document. No trees are killed, no late fees are incurred, and no traveling is involved. The employees can now view all the jobs on the intranet. They can even print out a company resume form, or fill one out online. Of course, HR is still there to help them in their career growth, but now HR has more time because it is not wasting efforts on tasks that have been eliminated.

Now, you can continue to see how to make the HR memo easier to navigate. Take a look at the new HTML code. I added some of the ideas discussed in the preceding paragraphs to this new HR Web page.

Listing 5.2   Miracle Toys HR memo made easier to navigate.

```
<HTML>

<HEAD>

<TITLE>HR FAQ</TITLE>

</HEAD>

<BODY>

<H3 ALIGN=CENTER><FONT COLOR="#004000">Human Resources Ongoing FAQ </FONT></H3>

<P>Welcome to the Human Resources Frequently Asked Questions Page. We will continue to
➥add answers to the most common questions we get here at Human Resources. You can also
➥always contact us in our office at X1245 between the hours of 10 a.m. and 4 p.m.,
➥Monday - Thursday. We are aware that we are not always available in person in our
➥office so you can also leave us an e-mail message here at: HR@miracle.com</P>

<P><STRONG>Questions:</STRONG></P>

<P><STRONG>Special Events:</STRONG></P>
```

```
<BLOCKQUOTE>
<STRONG>What is the location of this year's <A HREF="#special1">Staff Christmas
➥party</A>?</STRONG> <BR>

<STRONG>Can I <A HREF="#special2">bring my spouse</A>? </STRONG><BR>

<STRONG>What is the <A HREF="#special3">dress</A> for the Christmas party?</STRONG><BR>

<STRONG>I did not <A HREF="#special4">pick up my T-shirt</A> at this year's Miracle
➥Toy's Summer Bash. Do we have any left?</STRONG><BR>
</BLOCKQUOTE>

<P><STRONG>Miracle Publications:</STRONG></P>

<BLOCKQUOTE>
<STRONG>Who do I call to <A HREF="#news1">be added to the Miracle HR
➥newsletter</A>?<BR></STRONG>

<STRONG><A HREF="#news2">What is the Miracle HR newsletter?</A> </STRONG><BR>
</BLOCKQUOTE>

<P><STRONG>Dress Guidelines:</STRONG></P>

<BLOCKQUOTE>
<STRONG>I heard we are now having <A HREF="#dress1">casual Fridays</A> for all business
➥units. Is this true? </STRONG><BR>
</BLOCKQUOTE>

<P><STRONG>Job Postings:</STRONG></P>

<BLOCKQUOTE>
<STRONG>Is there a way to find out about <A HREF="#job1">jobs that Miracle has
➥available</A>? </STRONG><BR>
</BLOCKQUOTE>
```

<P><A NAME="special1"></A><STRONG>What is the location of this year's Staff Christmas
➥party?</STRONG> </P>

<P>This year's staff Christmas Party will be held at the Grand Floridian Beach Resort at
➥Walt Disney World. The Convention Center at the Grand Floridian will host our 25th
➥Christmas Celebration here at Miracle Toys. The <A HREF="lesson3.htm">map is available
➥right here</A>. So please print up a copy. The Party is December 23rd from 6pm - 10 PM
➥in the Grand Ballroom. Valet Parking is available at the main entrance to the resort.
➥Although there is no parking fee, please be sure to tip the valets for their gracious
➥service. Once you have parked the car, the Convention CCer is just down the path to
➥your left. </P>

<P><A NAME="special2"></A><STRONG>Can I bring my Spouse? </STRONG></P>

<P>Yes. Just like last year,you can bring your spouse and there is no additional charge.
➥ If you bring an additional guest you will need to pay the $25.00 guest fee to help us
➥cover the guests's dinner and expenses. </P>

<P><A NAME="special3"></A><STRONG>What is the dress for the Christmas
➥party?</STRONG></P>

<P>This year's party is not formal, but please dress nicely for the event. If you are
➥coming directly from your work shift, you can come in your work attire and still be
➥admitted to the party. </P>

<P><A NAME="special4"></A><STRONG>I did not pick up my T-shirt at this year's Miracle
➥Toys Summer Bash. Do we have any left? </STRONG></P>

<P>We stated to the management that there would be no T-shirts given out after the
➥Summer Bash. We ordered only a limited amount and distributed them only at the Summer
➥Bash Bash event. </P>

<P><A NAME="news1"></A><STRONG>Who do I call to be added to the Miracle HR newsletter?
➥</STRONG></P>

<P>The Miracle newsletter used to be sent out every month to each department supervisor.
➥ Every department used to receive a minimum of 25 copies. But now we have a virtual
➥newsletter in FULL COLOR that is updated as needed instead of just monthly. You
➥can check out the full color content packed addition of the <A HREF="miracle.htm">
➥Miracle HR Newsletter</A>now on-line.</P>

<P><A NAME="news2"></A><STRONG>What is the Miracle HR newsletter? </STRONG></P>

<P>Our monthly newsletter is skillfully done by the HR staff and showcases all special
➥events and employee issues here at Miracle. We have a monthly trivia question that
➥offers a $50.00 prize. If you have not seen the new newsletter, please take a moment
➥and check it out. We are also interested in your comments. So please e-mail us or call
➥us at X1245.</P>

<P><A NAME="dress1"></A><STRONG>I heard we are now having casual Fridays for all
➥business units. Is this true? </STRONG></P>

<P>If you are in the Miracle Toy Team 1 assembly crew, casual attire is allowed for
➥Fridays. If you are in a front-office area, there is NO casual attire. For more detail
➥on this issue see our <A HREF="dress.htm">whitepaper</A>, and also look at the
➥<A HREF="handbook.htm">employee dress code handbook</A>.</P>

<P><A NAME="job1"></A><STRONG>Is there a way to find out about jobs that Miracle has
➥available? </STRONG></P>

<P>The JOB POSTINGS are now on-line on our intranet. Please feel free to view all
➥the jobs at your leisure and you can even get a copy of the resume form in the Jobs
➥Web page. We are still here for counseling and guidance so if you have any questions
➥about the jobs listed here on the intranet please come on by.</P>

<BODY>

</HTML>

Notice the changes in the new HR Web page shown in Figure 5-6. Type the preceding example to see how the new HR Web page works and how it enables linking navigation on the same page when a user selects a question. The links that go to other Web pages are not operational because the code for the other Web pages is not displayed here.

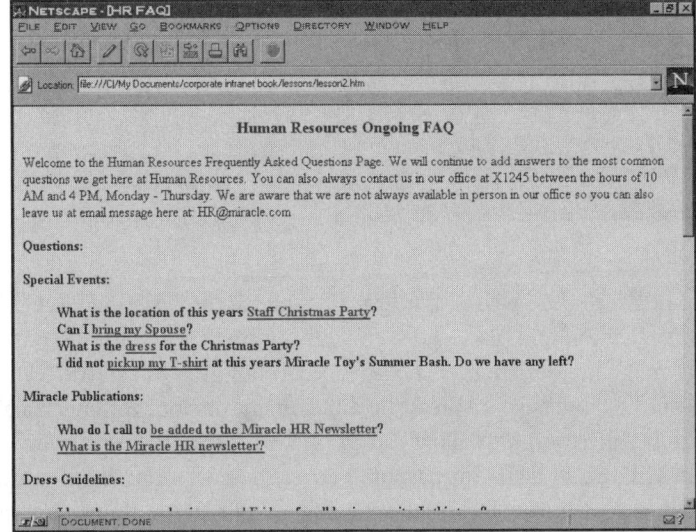

FIGURE 5-6

Now users can quickly navigate the page and link to the information that they need instantly.

Spreadsheet Files

This process is not just limited to word processing documents. You can quickly get most of your existing files up on your intranet in one form or another. If you have a great deal of legacy data in your systems, this also can be converted for use on your intranet. Start with spreadsheet data. Like all of your other files, if you can save it as plain text (ASCII), you have something you can instantly use on your intranet. This means you can use Microsoft Excel files and Lotus 123 files in your intranet with little effort. Start with an Excel file.

Excel Example

You can pull Excel files right into Microsoft's Internet Explorer as is. The file is just as it appears in Excel. You can also do some basic Excel functions and save the changes to your hard drive. Then you can e-mail it to someone in your organization. Look at Figure 5-7 to see an Excel file in Internet Explorer.

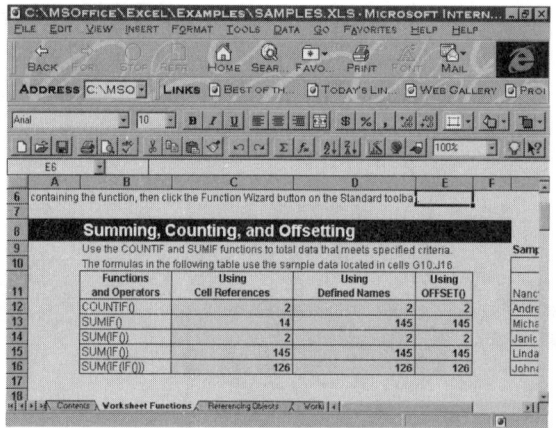

FIGURE 5-7

Microsoft's Internet Explorer enables you to pull all Microsoft Office Applications directly into the Explorer Browser with no HTML required.

I also created a file in Excel and saved it as a text file. You can use existing Excel files that you have in your organization and place them on your intranet today, even if you are not using Internet Explorer. The files are not as fancy and do not give you all the features as Internet Explorer, but Excel gets your spreadsheet document on your intranet quickly. Viewers available from Microsoft also allow you to view your spreadsheet documents in Netscape Navigator with no HTML formatting. I cover these in more depth in examples that follow. For now, look at how you can take existing Excel files, or almost any spreedsheet file for that matter, and make it into a document that can display on your intranet. Figure 5-8 shows the file I made in Microsoft Excel.

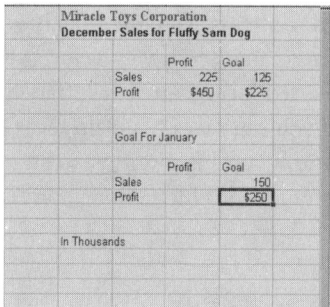

FIGURE 5-8

By saving your existing spreadsheet files as text files, you can instantly use them in your intranet. You need to go back and add formatting to them when you get the time.

If you are using Netscape and don't have a fancy add-on viewer to make this Excel file look the same as it does in Microsoft Excel, then the file will just display as a bunch of garbage if you try to pull it in as an .XLS file right into Netscape Navigator. But if you use Save As in Excel and save the file as a text file, you now have a file you can now work with in Netscape. Now look at the text file in Netscape Navigator. The same data in Netscape Navigator, as shown in Figure 5-9, is in Excel. Now, even those who don't have Excel on their workstation can view your Excel work.

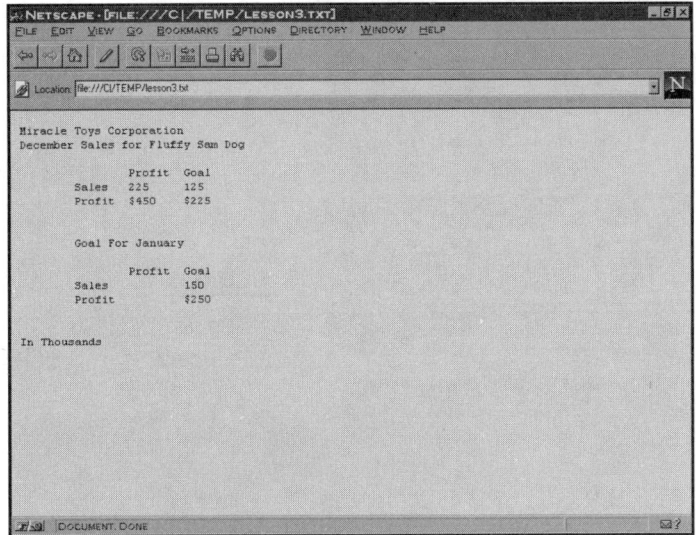

FIGURE 5-9

The Excel file in Netscape Navigator looks almost identical to the original file that I created in Excel. Bringing this information up on the intranet took only a few minutes

Excel Files on Miracle Toys' Intranet

Miracle Toys has some Excel files to place on its intranet. After doing some research, Miracle discovers an application that it can add on to Netscape Navigator, its standard company browser. That application will allow it to pull Excel files right into its browser. This add-on plug-in is available at http://www.microsoft.com/msdownload/. You can also get PowerPoint and Word Viewers at that address, which allow you to pull and display Word and PowerPoint files into your Netscape Browser. Your job of coding is much easier now, and your users can publish documents in these formats without having to learn a thing. You don't have to be a computer expert to begin making all types of content available on an intranet.

Microsoft Excel Viewer is a small, no-charge program that lets people view and print Microsoft Excel for Windows (version 2.0 and greater) and Microsoft Excel for the Macintosh (versions 2.2a and greater) spreadsheet files. Microsoft Excel Viewer also gives users the ability to view page layout, copy, zoom, AutoFilter, and control cell sizes. The Microsoft Excel Viewer can view any Microsoft Excel or Lotus 1-2-3 file.

I installed the Microsoft Excel Viewer, and the Miracle Toys Excel spreadsheet that I made in Excel and saved as a regular .XLS file is shown in Figure 5-10. I then opened the file in Netscape, with the viewer installed.

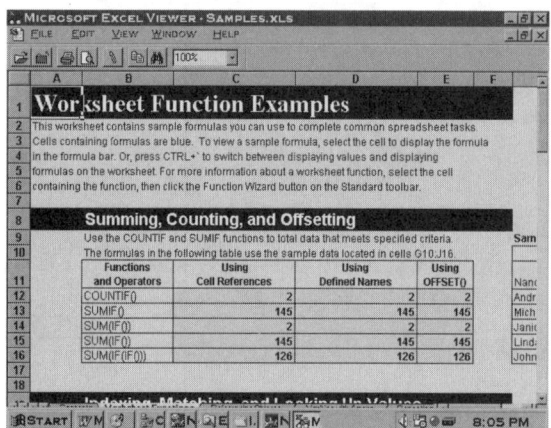

FIGURE 5-10

Now you can pull regular Excel files up from Netscape Navigator with no HTML coding.

As you can see, the Excel Viewer used with Netscape Navigator pulls up the viewer as a separate application. Netscape is still running as an application under the viewer screen, and you can toggle between the two of them using Alt-Tab. Unlike Internet Explorer, it does not pull up the file directly into the browser. But it beats having to type up HTML code, and it gives you spreadsheet files instantly on your intranet.

> **NOTE:** All of these viewers and helper applications are great. The problem is supporting all of them. If you have a large organization, keeping everyone up-to-date with the latest applications is hard. This also might bring up more training issues because users will now have to learn how to use all of these helper applications. I believe that the benefits of some of these applications such as Excel, Word, and PowerPoint Viewer, outweigh the training issues. Just choose wisely. Internet Explorer and Java applications can inform you of when a new version of an application is available, so the user automatically receives updates when a new version is introduced in your intranet, which makes administration easier on your part. Before long, you will overcome these issues on administration and training as the WWW continues to develop.

Well, I think you get the idea. You can take almost all of your existing data and convert it quickly to get it up and running on your intranet. The intranet may not look pretty, but if you are pressed for time, at least you can get content up fast, and then work on presentation later.

Now you'll see how to do the same with another plain-text file. I take plain text and make an HTML table out of it so that it can display in a table format on your intranet. Here is the plain-text file in Netscape Navigator:

```
              Miracle Toys Corporation
         December Sales for Fluffy Sam Dog
                        Profit              Goal
Sales                   $225               $125
Profit                  $450               $225
Goal For January:
                        Profit              Goal
Sales                   $150
Profit                                     $250
In Thousands
```

The file is nothing but text. No HTML tags, no fancy headings, just straight text. You can dress it up like the Microsoft Word file you did earlier to make it look a bit more appealing. I added some HTML tags to the Excel File to give it a spreadsheet look. Try out the following code:

Listing 5.3   Making an HTML table out of a plain-text file.

```
<HTML>
<HEAD>
<TITLE>Miracle Figures</TITLE>
</HEAD>
<BODY>
<TABLE BORDER=2 WIDTH=100%>
<TR><TD WIDTH=33%></TD><TD ALIGN=CENTER WIDTH=33%><FONT COLOR="#800040"><FONT SIZE=4>
➥Miracle Toys
Corporation  </FONT></FONT></TD><TD ALIGN=CENTER WIDTH=34%></TD></TR>
<TR><TD WIDTH=33%></TD><TD ALIGN=CENTER WIDTH=33%><EM><STRONG>December Sales for Fluffy
Sam Dog  </STRONG></EM></TD><TD ALIGN=CENTER WIDTH=34%></TD></TR>
```

```
<TR><TD WIDTH=33%></TD><TD ALIGN=CENTER WIDTH=33%></TD><TD ALIGN=CENTER WIDTH=34%>
➥</TD></TR>
<TR><TD WIDTH=33%></TD><TD ALIGN=CENTER WIDTH=33%><FONT COLOR="#FF0000">Profit
➥</FONT></TD><TD ALIGN=CENTER WIDTH=34%><FONT COLOR="#0000FF">Goal</FONT></TD></TR>
<TR><TD WIDTH=33%>Sales</TD><TD ALIGN=CENTER WIDTH=33%>225</TD><TD ALIGN=CENTER
➥WIDTH=34%>125</TD></TR>
<TR><TD WIDTH=33%>Profit</TD><TD ALIGN=CENTER WIDTH=33%>$450</TD><TD ALIGN=CENTER
➥WIDTH=34%>$225</TD></TR>
<TR><TD WIDTH=33%></TD><TD ALIGN=CENTER WIDTH=33%></TD><TD ALIGN=CENTER WIDTH=34%>
➥</TD></TR>
<TR><TD WIDTH=33%><STRONG>Goal For January:</STRONG></TD><TD ALIGN=CENTER WIDTH=33%>
➥</TD><TD ALIGN=CENTER WIDTH=34%></TD></TR>
<TR><TD WIDTH=33%></TD><TD ALIGN=CENTER WIDTH=33%><FONT COLOR="#FF0000">Profit
➥</FONT></TD><TD ALIGN=CENTER WIDTH=34%><FONT COLOR="#0000FF">Goal</FONT></TD></TR>
<TR><TD WIDTH=33%>Sales    </TD><TD ALIGN=CENTER WIDTH=33%></TD><TD ALIGN=CENTER
➥WIDTH=34%>150</TD></TR>
<TR><TD WIDTH=33%>Profit</TD><TD ALIGN=CENTER WIDTH=33%></TD><TD ALIGN=CENTER
➥WIDTH=34%>$250</TD></TR>
<TR><TD WIDTH=33%>In Thousands    /TD><TD ALIGN=CENTER WIDTH=33%></TD><TD ALIGN=CENTER
➥WIDTH=34%></TD></TR>
</TABLE>
</BODY>
</HTML>
```

This listing produces a nice table with the data for Miracle Toys in an easy-to-follow format. Figure 5-11 shows the table in Netscape Navigator. The table was created in a matter of minutes in NotePad. By taking the regular text file and adding color, increasing some font sizes, adding bold, and the table tags, you can make a regular text file into a nice presentation with little effort.

Other Formats

I realize that not everyone is working in the same environment; some of you have MACs and UNIX, so not everything is going to convert over to a plain-text file so easily.

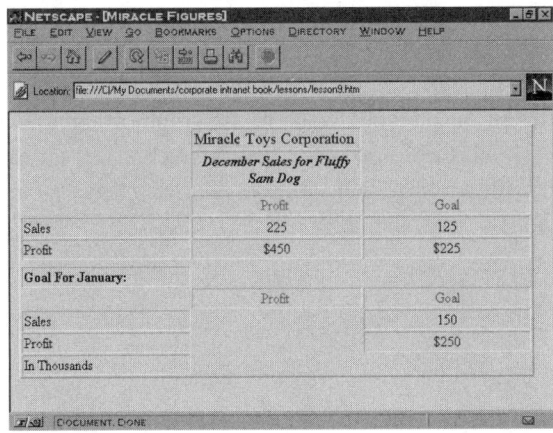

FIGURE 5-11

The Excel text file has been formatted with some HTML tags to make it appear as a table.

Adobe Acrobat is a the fast and easy-to-use solution for publishing on your intranet. It allows you to display the document without losing any of the column formatting, fonts, and layout. With Adobe Acrobat, you create what is called a Personal Document Format, or .PDF, file. This file keeps all your original formatting and layout intact. This is the perfect way to display products and catalogs on your intranet. You can create Adobe Acrobat files in Adode Acrobat or Adobe PageMaker. You can convert your existing PageMaker files to .PDF format by running them through the Adobe Distiller that comes with both products. After you have created your .PDF, your users can view it either with an Adobe plug-in or helper application. The plug-in allows users to launch the .PDF file inside their browser window, and the helper application launches the Abobe Acrobat Reader. The Adobe Acrobat is available in Windows, MAC, and UNIX versions at:

```
http://www.adobe.com/prodindex/acrobat/main.html
```

Summary

I have covered some of the quick and easy ways to get content up on your intranet. Mountains of valuable information sit in file cabinets and on disks all over your organization. Tracking down all of this information takes longer than converting it and placing it on your intranet by using the quick methods discussed in this chapter. Just displaying plain-text files is not what the intranet is all about, however. You added hyperlinks and a few easy-to-do tables to your pages in this chapter, and this leads you into the next chapter, which takes you a step closer to a full-blown intranet. You also have seen viewers that you can download for free and use in Netscape Navigator, or use the built-in applications in Internet Explorer to display business documents. What a great way to share information across the LAN.

What's Next!

Chapter 6 covers how to create graphics and all you ever wanted to know about images on your intranet. I cover the different image types, when to use graphics, and how to keep them small in file size for quick downloads. I also look at several techniques for making your images transparent, how to capture images, and ways to control image spacing and height and width parameters.

Chapter | 6

Graphics on an Intranet

Lists, tables, and text formatting allow you to convey most types of information on your intranet Web pages, but many types of information can be better conveyed with a graphic, or image. Images on a Web page consist of page backgrounds, icons, illustrations, and photographs.

Pros and Cons of Using Web Page Graphics

Although graphics are used to spice up personal and commercial sites on the Internet with flashy color backgrounds, pictures, and icons, more discretion should be used on intranet pages. Unless your company is involved in graphic arts, it will probably use intranet Web pages to convey company information. Your employees don't want to wait long periods of time for graphics to load just to make the pages look pretty. Large image files, or many images on one page, should be avoided.

Take care when you are selecting images for your Web pages. You can design or scan images yourself, using commercial clip art or photographic collections, or you can download them from the Internet. Be aware that many graphics not designed by you are copyrighted and owned by someone else. Others may not be happy that you are using their work without paying royalties. If you plan to use commercial, or downloaded, graphics, make sure that the licensing agreement for the graphic permits your usage.

Starting with a Background

Originally, most Web pages were limited to either white or gray backgrounds, because browsers did not give you the option of specifying a background. Now, many browsers give you the option of changing the "standard" background color to a customized color or image.

Creating Your Backgrounds

The BGCOLOR attribute is added to the standard HTML <BODY> tag to specify a custom background color for your Web page. The format for the <BODY> tag with the BGCOLOR attribute is as follows:

```
<BODY BGCOLOR=#rrggbb>
```

To use this tag, you must substitute hexadecimal codes for the rrggbb portion of the tag, where each pair of letters, rr, gg, and bb, represents a value from 00 to FF in hex, or 0 to 255 in decimal. A total of 16,777,216 colors can be used for your background.

The following table demonstrates some sample hex codes for use with the BGCOLOR keyword:

Hexadecimal Code	Color
000000	Black
FF0000	Red
00FF00	Green
0000FF	Blue
FFFF00	Yellow
FF00FF	Magenta
00FFFF	Cyan
FFFFFF	White

Depending on which camp they're in, some Web designers insist on light backgrounds with dark content (text and graphics), whereas others want dark backgrounds with light content. Fortunately, both are correct. The deciding factor is not the lightness or darkness, but the contrast and complement of the chosen colors. Make sure that the colors complement each other, and offer a large contrast in brightness. For example, dark-brown text on a black background is not a wise color combination. In the same sense, a lime-green background doesn't work with a bright-pink graphic in most cases.

> **NOTE:** Choose your color scheme carefully, and, whenever possible, check your scheme on as many different browsers as possible. Hundreds of browsers are available for people to download, therefore your content will be displayed differently on each one of them. Luckily, the browser market has only two big players to date, Netscape and Microsoft, and content displayed in these browsers looks almost identical. So, when you design your intranet pages, at least view them in both these browsers to make sure that your text is still readable with the background you have chosen.

It is also important to note that some browsers, such as Netscape Navigator, have a particular color palette that they are happy with. In Netscape Navigator, this palette has 216 colors. Colors that are not in this palette get dithered to an approximation. Designing with colors that do not fit this palette can cause some pages to be hard to read.

This is also a good time to bring up the a point on text color and hyperlink colors. When you start changing the backgrounds on your pages, you need to make sure that the text still is easy to read. This may mean changing the text color and size. Changing the color of the text can, however, confuse as to what text is a hyperlink and what text has been changed to a different color just to make it readable.

Giving Your Background an Image

Solid colors are generally preferred for Web page backgrounds, but when you must use a picture, the BACKGROUND attribute is available.

Images placed onto a Web page as a background are automatically tiled. This tiling can be used to your advantage when you create a repetitive background, such as a piece of cloth or parchment paper. By creating a small graphic, you enable the image to be downloaded to the viewer quickly.

By contrast, you also can use large, low-color depth images as backgrounds on Web pages to convey the appearance of a watermark. The key to making this type of background work is to keep the file size as close to the pixel height and width of the viewer's browser as possible, and to keep the color depth as low as possible. Large background files take too long to download to the viewer. Remember, the large background image tiles, if necessary, which is why you need to keep it as close to the browser's size as possible.

You add backgrounds to the browser in much the same way as you add solid colors: by attaching the BACKGROUND attribute to the HTML <BODY> tag. The format for the <BODY> tag with the BACKGROUND attribute is as follows:

```
<BODY BACKGROUND="image.gif">
```

Substitute the name of your image file for image.gif in the preceding example.

To be sure that you have all browsers covered, you should include both BGCOLOR and BACKGROUND attributes in the HTML <BODY> tag. Adding these attributes gives your viewers an opportunity to view a solid background color, rather than the standard gray or white, if the browser doesn't support the image background, or if viewers have their images turned off.

Capturing Images

I want to cover a quick way to get graphics up on your intranet so that you can show charts, graphs, and maps that are important to your organization while you work on more elaborate graphics. The fastest way to place graphics on your intranet is to use ones that already exist. Make sure that your organization owns the images before you use them on your pages. After ensuring ownership, you can capture graphics for your pages by using a screen-capture program. Paint Shop Pro, Collage Capture, and Hi Jaak are just a few that are available and easy to use. I cover the basics of using Collage Capture.

The simplest way to add images to your intranet while you're still just trying to get it off the ground is by using a screen-capture program. With a program such as Collage Capture, you can take a screen shot of the image, and then convert it into the appropriate format so that it can be displayed on the intranet. Figure 6-1 is a graphic of Florida that shows all of the sales offices in Florida for Miracle Toys. The original file here is a PSD file (a Photoshop file). On the WWW and thus on your intranet, two formats are currently supported by browsers: GIF and JPEG. Both have advantages and disadvantages, because both use different methods of compression when you save files. Because everyone does not have a copy of Adobe Photoshop to pull in this image and convert it to another format, I had to take a screen shot of the image and tell Collage Capture, my screen-capture software, to save the screen shot as a .GIF file.

FIGURE 6-1

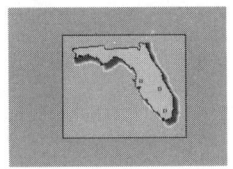

The original image file was captured as a .PSD file, and then saved in .GIF format so that it could be used instantly on the intranet.

Now you can view the image directly in Netscape Navigator. By going to File | Open File and choosing a file type of All Files, you can open the .GIF file and display your image. With a little HTML coding, you can quickly make a link from one of your intranet documents to this file. Figure 6-2 shows the new .GIF file displayed in the browser.

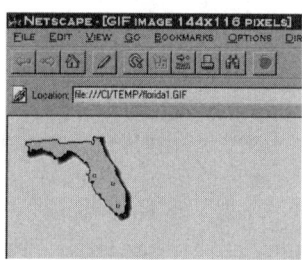

FIGURE 6-2

Maps, charts, and diagrams can be screen-captured and turned into .GIF and .JPEG files so that you can quickly display them on your intranet with little time and effort.

Human Resource Example

This example adds to the link on the Human Resources intranet page built in Chapter 5. Adding the link enables the user to click on a hyperlink to display a road map to the Christmas party.

The <A HREF="lesson3.htm">map is available right here</A>

The HTML code that tells the browser to jump to an intranet page is called lesson3.htm. The lesson3.htm file follows:

Listing 6.1 LESSION3.HTM

```
<HTML>

<HEAD>

<TITLE>Map to XMAS Party</TITLE>

</HEAD>

<BODY BGCOLOR="FFFFFF">

<CENTER>

<P>Press Print to get a hard copy of these directions to this year's Miracle Toys
➡Christmas party. Directions follow under the map graphic.<BR><BR>
```

```
<IMG SRC="map.gif">

</CENTER>

</BODY>

</HTML>
```

This code makes up the intranet page that Human Resources is using to give directions to the Christmas party. By clicking on the Human Resources Frequently Asked Questions Web Page, the user can link to the directions and print out a copy before leaving for the event. This is an example of a good use for images on an intranet. Users can even print a copy of the directions by selecting the print icon from their Web browser.

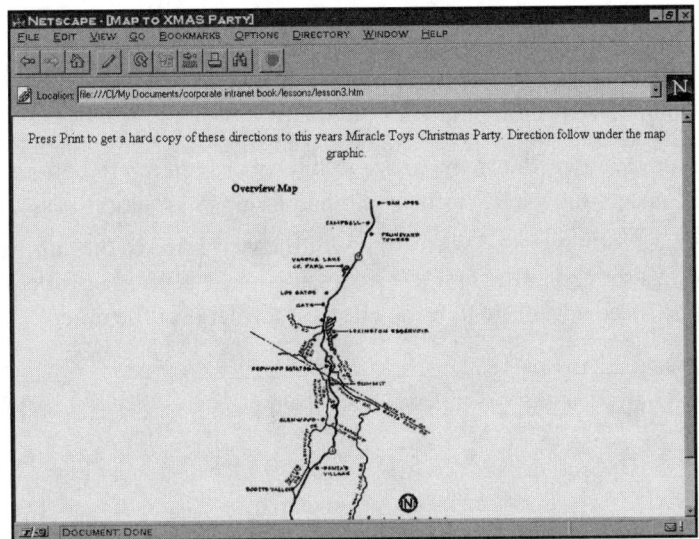

FIGURE 6-3

Here a .GIF is combined with content to give directions to the users.

Different Types of Images

Two types of images can be displayed on your Web pages, as follows:

◆ *Inline* images appear on your Web page. They are loaded when the page loads into your browser, assuming, of course, that you have a graphical browser.

♦ *External* images are loaded only when the user specifically requests the image by clicking on a link. This link is usually either a small thumbnail of the larger image, which has been included as an inline image, or a simple text reference of the underlying external image.

Images can be saved in many different formats, but two types are generally accepted and displayed by most browsers without additional plug-ins or helper applications. To maintain compatibility with most browsers, stick with either GIF or JPEG formats.

Inline Images on Your Web Page

Images that appear automatically when you load a Web page, assuming that you have a graphical browser and the graphics are turned on, are inline images.

With today's browsers, many different formats of graphics are usually supported, but to be sure that your inline images are displayed on all browsers, stick with GIF images.

Line art, or illustrations, is best displayed with the GIF format. GIF files for Web pages come in two flavors: GIF87 (also known as CompuServe GIF, or just GIF) and GIF89a (a format that enables transparent backgrounds). GIF files can be further split into two different types: noninterlaced and interlaced.

♦ The *noninterlaced* type draws the image in full detail from top to bottom. Interlaced images draw in a "horizontal" blind fashion in multiple passes.

♦ The *interlaced* format is used when you want the viewer to see the entire picture rapidly, although in the first few passes, the image is not clearly defined. There is no speed advantage to using one GIF format over the other.

> **NOTE:** I cover transparent backgrounds in more depth later, near the end of this chapter.

The second most common graphic file format for images is JPEG, although not all browsers support this file type. The JPEG file format is best suited for photographic images, which do not contain a lot of solid color areas in the picture. JPEG's compression techniques tend to mess up solid color areas.

Most image editing, or paint, packages on the market today support these file formats. Adobe Photoshop, Corel Paint, and Paint Shop Pro are excellent choices for image editing. If you already have image files that are not GIF or JPEG, you can use the aforementioned packages to convert your images, or use programs such as DeBabelizer or LView Pro to convert your files to GIF or JPEG.

Inline images are added to your Web page using the <IMG> tag. The <IMG> tag has many different attributes: SRC, ALT, WIDTH, HEIGHT, ALIGN, LOWRES, HSPACE, VSPACE, and BORDER. Descriptions of these attributes follow.

The SRC Attribute

The SRC attribute is the only attribute required to display an image. SRC is used to indicate the filename, in quotation marks, which should be included on the Web page. In its simplest form, as shown in Figure 6-4, this is the <IMG> tag with only the SRC attribute:

```
<IMG SRC="gears.gif">
```

Here you would substitute the name of your image file for gears.gif.

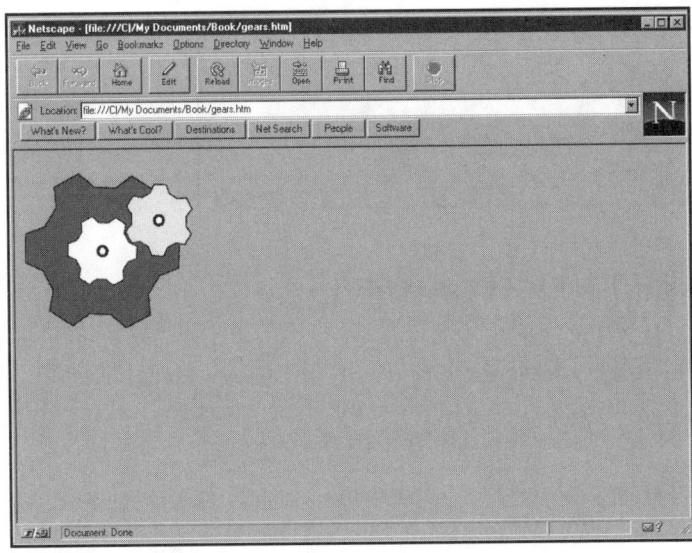

FIGURE 6-4

Inserting an image into your intranet requires only the <IMG> tag plus the SRC attribute.

The ALT Attribute

Because not all browsers are capable of displaying graphics, or some users may have graphics turned off to speed up the load time of pages, supplying an "alternate" text name of the associated graphic is a good idea. In newer versions of Netscape and other browsers, the alternate text appears before the graphic loads.

When you use the ALT attribute with the <IMG> tag, your HTML line looks like this:

```
<IMG SRC="gears.gif" ALT="Gear Diagram">
```

In this example, as shown in Figure 6-5, the text, "Gear Diagram," appears to users whose browsers can't display graphics, or who have graphics turned off.

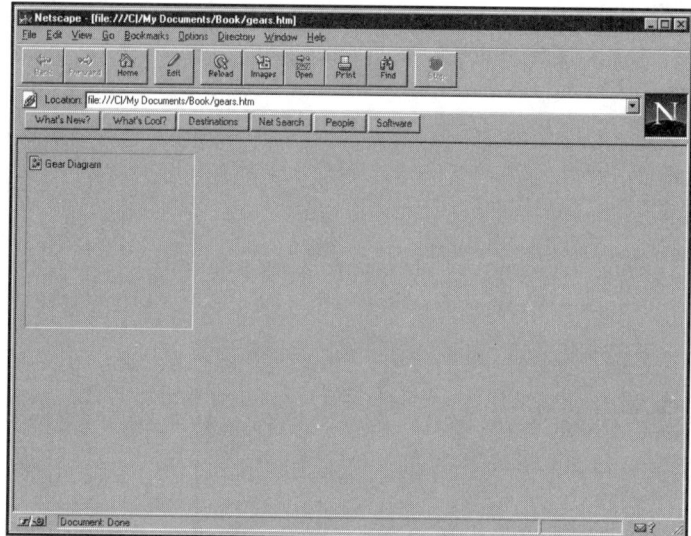

FIGURE 6-5

The <IMG ALT=> tag with images turned off in the browser.

The WIDTH and HEIGHT Attribute

The WIDTH and HEIGHT attributes can be used to specify the size of an image to the browser. Most Web browsers display an image in its original size, unless the WIDTH and/or HEIGHT attributes are specified. If you use these attributes, you can also shrink or expand the size of an image as it is displayed by the browser.

By using the WIDTH and HEIGHT attributes in all images on your page, you enable the browser to show the entire text content of the page before it loads and displays any of the images on your page.

> **NOTE:** Make sure that you use the HEIGHT and WIDTH attributes in all your Web pages. The bonus you get is a faster load time. Normally, your browser must figure out the images size before displaying it in the browser. It takes time for the browser to calculate how much space to allow for the image. If you tell the browser up-front the size of the image, HEIGHT and WIDTH, then you are saving precious seconds in download time.

After you add the WIDTH and HEIGHT attributes to the <IMG> tag, the HTML looks like this:

```
<IMG SRC="gears.gif" ALT="Gear Diagram" WIDTH=200 HEIGHT=200>
```

Take a look at Figure 6-6. Here is the image, and I have pointed out that the HEIGHT and WIDTH attributes have been added to allow this image to load quickly and to give it the correct dimensions.

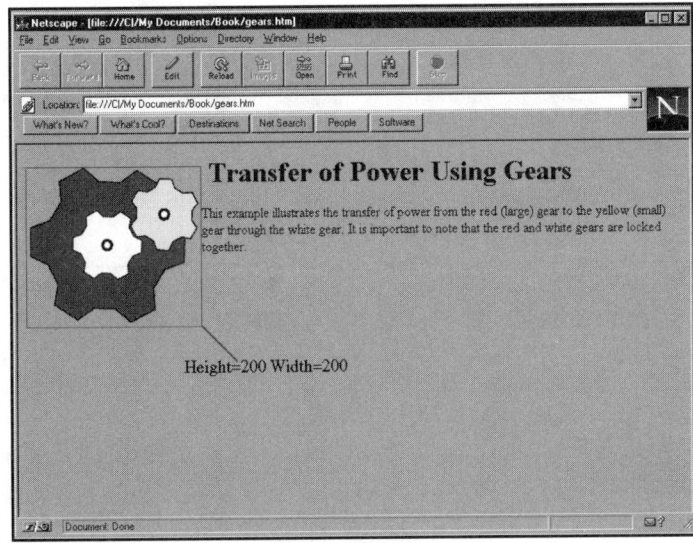

FIGURE 6-6

Using the WIDTH and HEIGHT attributes.

The ALIGN Attribute

Images can be aligned on the page with respect to the surrounding text using the ALIGN attribute of the <IMG> tag. If the ALIGN attribute is not specified, ALIGN=BOTTOM is assumed.

Eight different ALIGN options are available, as described in Table 6-1.

Table 6-1   Alignment Options for the Image <IMG> Tag

Option	Description
LEFT	Aligns the object with the left side of the browser window with multiple lines of text wrapping on the right side of the image
RIGHT	Aligns the object with the right side of the browser window with multiple lines of text wrapping on the left side of the image
TOP	Aligns the image with the top of the line (tallest item in the line)
TEXTTOP	Aligns the image with the top of the text items on the line
MIDDLE	Aligns the middle of the image with the bottom of the line of text beside the image
ABSMIDDLE	Aligns the middle of the image with the middle of the line of text beside the image
BOTTOM	Aligns the bottom of the image with the bottom of the line of text beside the image (assumed if no ALIGN attribute is specified)
BASELINE	Essentially the same as BOTTOM

Figure 6-7 demonstrates how the following HTML document is displayed by the browser:

```
<HTML>
<HEAD>
<TITLE>Gear Diagram</TITLE>
</HEAD>
<BODY>

<H1>
<IMG SRC="gears.gif" ALT="Gear Diagram" HEIGHT=200 WIDTH=200>Transfer of Power Using
➥Gears
</H1>

<P>This example illustrates the transfer of power from the red (large) gear to the
➥yellow (small) gear through the white gear. It is important to note that the red and
➥white gears are locked together.</P>

</BODY>
</HTML>
```

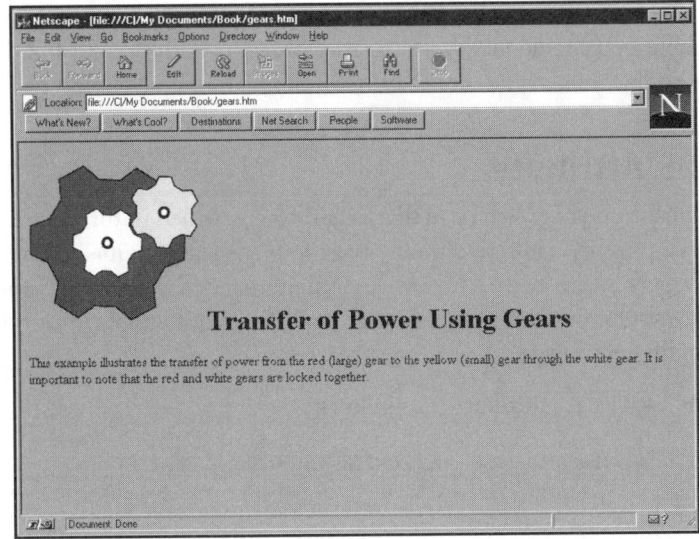

FIGURE 6-7

The effect of an <IMG> tag without an ALIGN attribute.

The same page is shown in Figure 6-8 using the ALIGN=LEFT attribute in the image tag:

```
<IMG SRC="gears.gif" ALT="Gear Diagram" HEIGHT=200 WIDTH=200 ALIGN=LEFT>
```

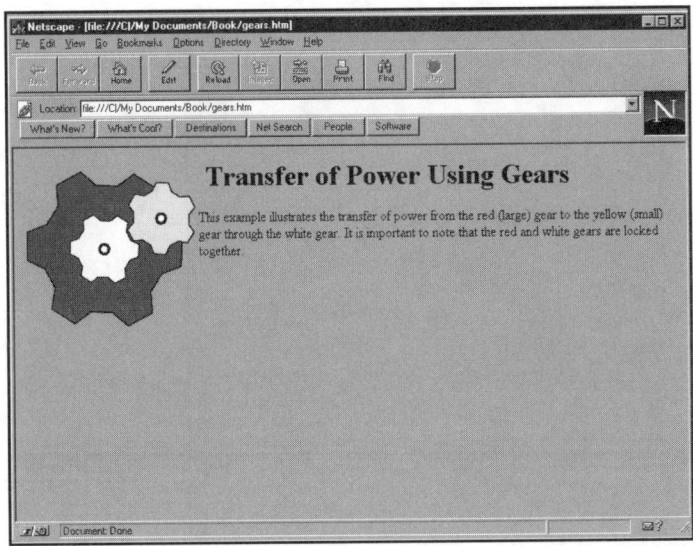

FIGURE 6-8

The effect of an <IMG> tag with an ALIGN=LEFT attribute.

Use the ALIGN attribute with caution, because not all browsers recognize it. If you use the ALIGN attribute, you should view your pages in browsers both that do and do not recognize the tag, so that you can be sure that the content is still acceptable.

The LOWRES Attribute

If you display an image on your Web page that is fairly large, which in turn causes a long loading time, you can specify a low-resolution image to be displayed initially, while the high-resolution (larger) image loads. The low-resolution image may be a black-and-white version of the high-resolution image, a version of the high-resolution image with fewer colors, or a totally different image.

The format for the LOWRES attribute is as follows:

```
<IMG SRC="gears.gif" ALT="Gear Diagram" HEIGHT=200 WIDTH=200 ALIGN=LEFT
➥LOWRES="gears2.gif">
```

In this example, `gears2.gif` represents the low-resolution image, and `gears.gif` represents the high-resolution image.

When you use the LOWRES attribute, be sure to use JPEG or noninterlaced GIF image types for the SRC attribute, because interlaced GIFs almost immediately write over the entire LOWRES image.

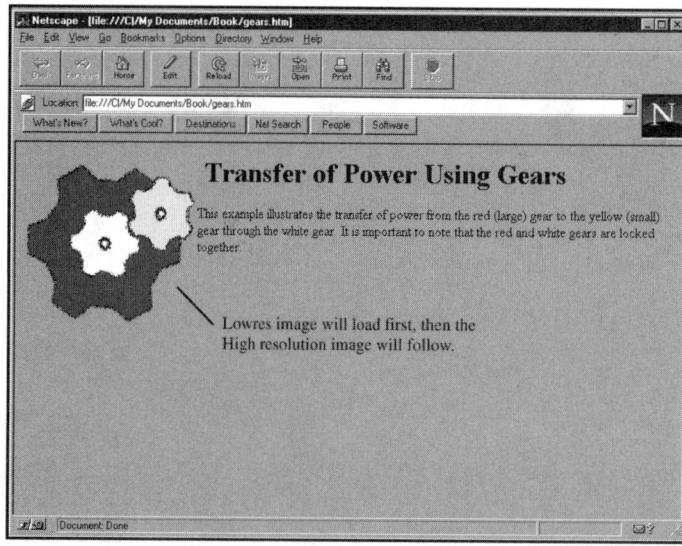

FIGURE 6-9

Using the LOWRES attribute.

The HSPACE and VSPACE Attributes

The HSPACE and VSPACE attributes enable you to separate the images and text on your page by a specified number of pixels. The HSPACE attribute affects both the left and right spacing of the image by the same distance, whereas the VSPACE attribute affects both the top and bottom spacing.

To specify a 20-pixel left and right separation, and a 30-pixel top and bottom separation, the <IMG> tag would be written as follows:

```
<IMG SRC="gears.gif" ALT="Gear Diagram" HEIGHT=200 WIDTH=200 ALIGN=LEFT
➡LOWRES="gears2.gif" HSPACE=20 VSPACE=30>
```

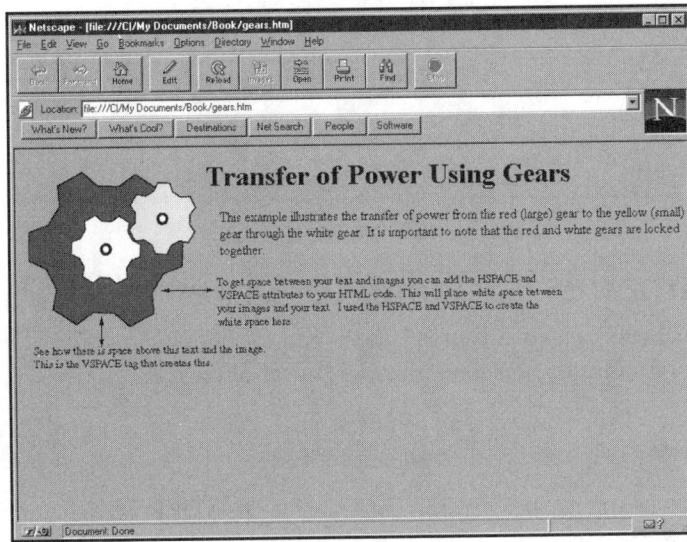

FIGURE 6-10

HSPACE and VSPACE attributes.

The BORDER Attribute

This attribute gives you the means to place a frame around your image with a variable line width. The line width is specified in pixels. If you are not making this image into a "clickable" item on your page, this is the only way to place a border around the image, other than to incorporate the border into the image itself.

To place a -5-pixel border around the image, the HTML code looks like this:

```
<IMG SRC="gears.gif" ALT="Gear Diagram" HEIGHT=200 WIDTH=200 ALIGN=LEFT
➡LOWRES="gears2.gif" HSPACE=20 VSPACE=30 BORDER=5>
```

The result of this HTML line is shown in Figure 6-11.

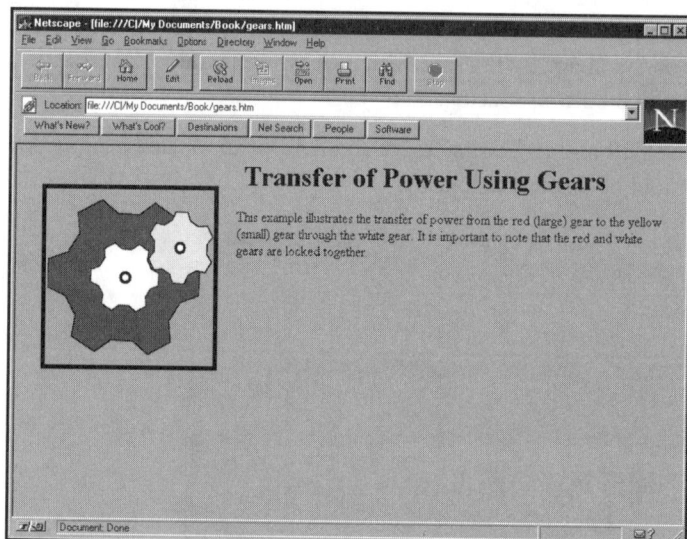

FIGURE 6-11

*The effect of an <IMG>
tag with ALIGN,
HSPACE, VSPACE, and
BORDER attributes.*

Using Inline Images to Point to Other Web Pages

In some cases, small images used as thumbnails are best for pointing to other Web pages that contain additional information about the topic under discussion.

By surrounding your <IMG> tag with an anchor tag, you can use the image displayed on your Web page as a hyperlink to another page in your site.

Typically, when you use the anchor tag, you don't use the BORDER attribute of the <IMG> tag, because the anchor tag provides its own border (unless it is set to zero).

In the following example, I have reduced the gears.gif image to 30 by 30 pixels and saved it as sm_gears.gif. I have added more instructions to the text to let the user know what additional information is available by clicking on the small icon of the gears image. The HTML code for Figure 6-12 is as follows:

```
<HTML>
<HEAD>
<TITLE>Gear Diagram</TITLE>
</HEAD>
<BODY>
```

```
<H1>
<A HREF="detail.htm"><IMG SRC="sm_gears.gif" ALT="Gear Diagram" HEIGHT=30 WIDTH=30
➥ALIGN=LEFT></A>Transfer of Power Using Gears
</H1>

<P>This example illustrates the transfer of power from the red (large) gear to the
➥yellow (small) gear through the white gear. It is important to note that the red and
➥white gears are locked together. You may click on the small gear icon to see a larger
➥view with a more detailed description of the process.</P>

</BODY>
</HTML>
```

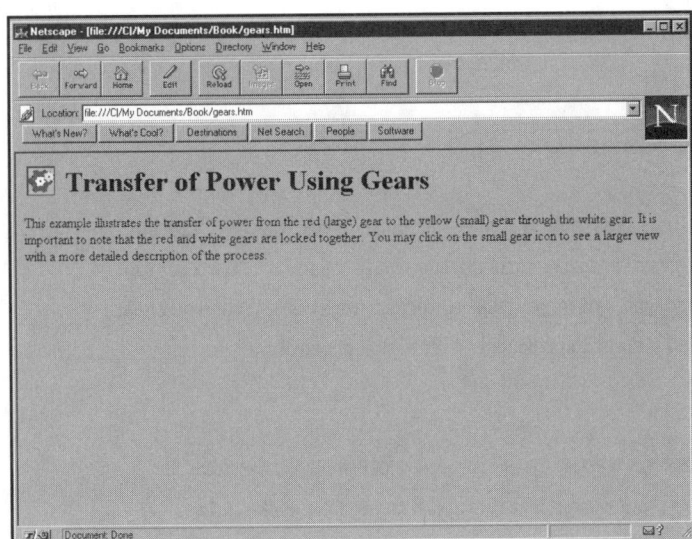

FIGURE 6-12

Using an anchor tag along with an image tag to link to another HTML page.

Using External Images on Your Web Pages

In general, external images are any images that do not load with a Web page, but are accessed by the user clicking on a hyperlink to the image. By definition, the external images are not limited to graphic files, but may also be sounds or video clips, although this chapter concentrates on the graphic forms of external images.

All graphic browsers accept and display GIF files. Therefore, displaying a small GIF thumbnail of a graphic and then providing a larger or higher resolution of the file as a hyperlink from the loaded Web page is standard practice. If you specify files on your Web page as external images, you give your users optional ways to view the external images, such as allowing different sizes or graphic types.

When you use external images, the anchor tag on your Web page provides hyperlinks to actual image files as opposed to a hyperlink to another Web page.

You can create external images in the same way as inline images, except that external images are usually much larger files than inline images.

The following HTML code, with the results illustrated in Figure 6-13, demonstrates how you can give your users a choice of different images based on their selection:

```
<HTML>
<HEAD>
    <TITLE>Power Transfer</TITLE>
</HEAD>
<BODY>

<H1>Transfer of Power Using Gears</H1>

<P>This example illustrates the transfer of power from the red (large)
gear to the yellow (small) gear through the white gear. It is important
to note that the red and white gears are locked together. You may choose
one of the following selections below to see the process.</P>

<UL>
   <LI><A HREF="gears.gif">Power Transfer (20K GIF file)</A></LI>
   <LI><A HREF="gears.jpg">Power Transfer (7K JPEG file)</A></LI>
</UL>

</BODY>
</HTML>
```

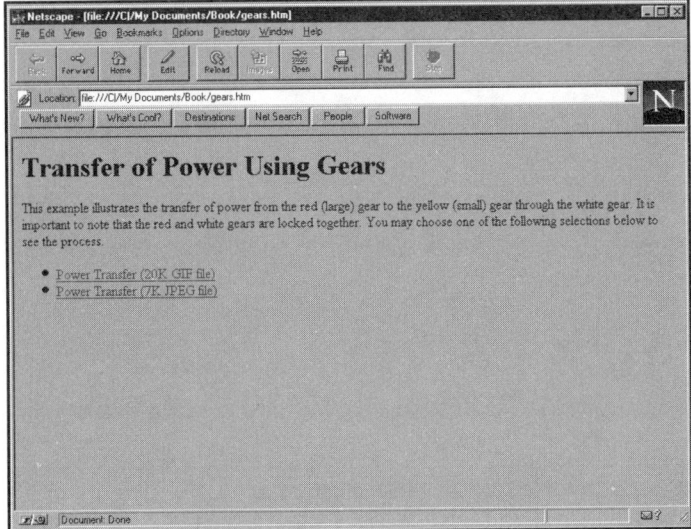

FIGURE 6-13

This gives the user a choice to load an external GIF or JPEG image.

Adding Icons to Your Web Page

Icons are small graphics added to accent the information on a Web page. Accent lines, bullets, and small graphic animations are just a few samples of how you can use icons on Web pages.

Although the standard bulleted list (as shown earlier in the chapter, in Figure 6-13) is acceptable in most cases, you will at times want to deliver a custom bullet icon to your users. This icon can be a descriptive thumbnail of the item that it bullets, or simply a stylish bullet. As an example of custom bullet icons, see Figure 6-14 for an example of how custom bullet icons may be used. The HTML code for Figure 6-14 looks like this:

```
<HTML>
<HEAD>
<TITLE>Power Transfer</TITLE>
</HEAD>
<BODY>

<H1>Transfer of Power Using Gears</H1>

<P>This example illustrates the transfer of power from the red (large) gear to the
➥yellow (small) gear through the white gear. It is important to note that the red and
```

```
➥white gears are locked together. You may choose one of the following selections below
➥to see the process.</P>

<P><IMG SRC="sm_gears.gif" ALT="Gear Bullet" HEIGHT=30 WIDTH=30><A HREF="gears.gif">Power
Transfer (20K GIF file)</A></P>

<P><IMG SRC="sm_gears.gif" ALT="Gear Bullet" HEIGHT=30 WIDTH=30><A HREF="gears.jpg">Power
Transfer (7K JPEG file)</A></P>

</BODY>
</HTML>
```

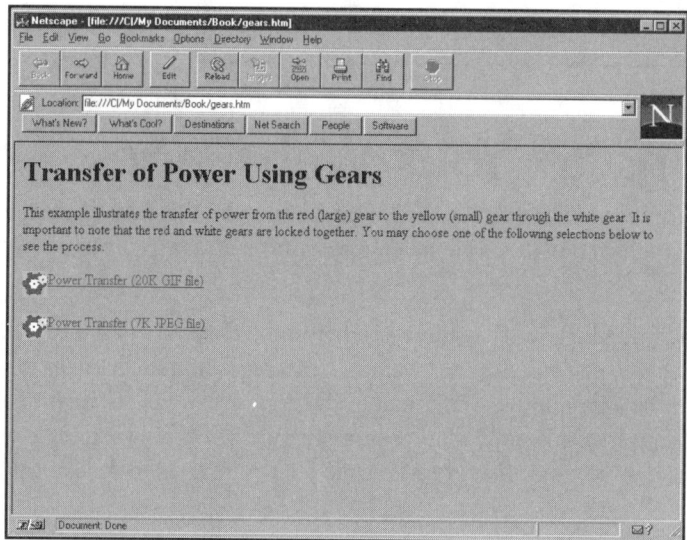

FIGURE 6-14

Using images as icons for a bulleted list.

Using Images with Transparent Backgrounds

Within the past year, many Web browsers have included the ability to display GIF files with transparent backgrounds. By using images with transparent backgrounds, you can make your graphics appear to as an integral part of your Web page.

Traditional GIF images are stored using the GIF87 image format, and do not support transparency. By creating your image in, or converting your image to, the GIF89a format, you can select a color that becomes transparent when the image is displayed in the browser.

Line art and graphics with a single color background are the best types of images to save with transparency. Photographs generally do not have a single background color, and, therefore, do not have an entirely transparent background.

The gear graphic shown in the previous examples has a transparent background. In Figure 6-15, the gear graphic is shown with and without a transparent background.

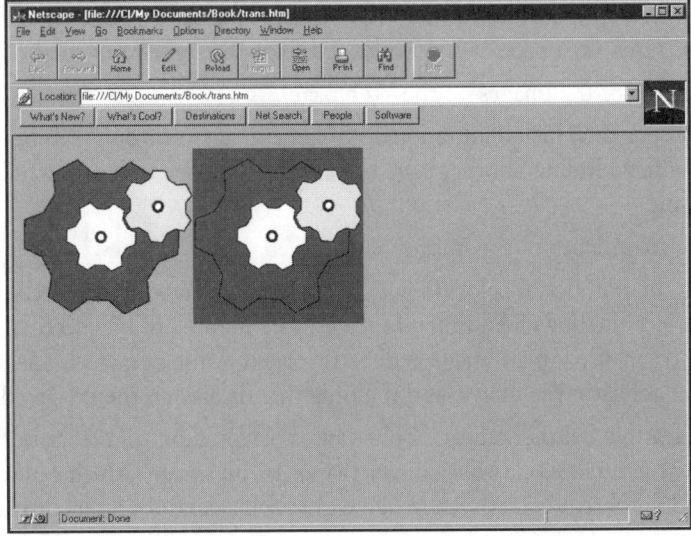

FIGURE 6-15

Comparison of transparent and nontransparent backgrounds.

The actual color you choose for the background of your image is not of particular importance, except for situations in which you do not have control over the browser used to view your pages. If the browser doesn't support backgrounds and transparent GIFs, your choice of color should be very close to the background color of the target browser.

Optimizing Your Web Pages for Quicker Loading

The total time that downloading a Web page to a browser takes is directly related to the total size of all text (HTML) files and all graphic files necessary to compose that page.

Obviously, the smaller the file, the quicker it loads.

Although you can optimize your Web pages in a variety of ways, I concentrate on the ones that give you the most savings.

- Limit the number of images on the Web page.

  Limiting the total number of unique images on your Web page decreases the time that downloading the page from the Web server takes. Having fewer images results in less information necessary to display the page.

- Make use repeatedly of images on the Web page.

  Because of how the Internet works, each unique image on a Web page also represents a new connection to the Web server. If the same image appears numerous times on a page, it is downloaded from the server only once.

- Limit the size of the images on the Web page.

  Whenever possible, include thumbnails of large images on your Web page, offering either a link to another page or an external image link to the full-size image.

- Limit the color depth of the images on the Web page.

  Reducing the number of colors (color depth) in your images is an excellent way to reduce the download time of images. The number of bits necessary to store the colors used in an image is directly related to the size of the file, the number of colors in the image, and the time that displaying the image takes.

  An image with a color depth of 24 bits can display millions of colors, but displaying them takes one-third longer than a 16-bit image (which can display 65,536 different colors). An image with a color depth of 8 bits displays twice as fast as a 16-bit image, but can display only 256 different colors.

  As an extreme example, if you have a black-and-white line-art image, you can store this image as a 1-bit color depth image. A 1-bit has two states: on (white) and off (black).

The default color depth for most computer systems is still only 256 colors, so you need use only 256 colors in most cases.

Software packages such as Adobe Photoshop, LView Pro, and Fast Eddie are available to assist you in reducing the color depth of images for your Web pages.

Summary

I have discussed the advantages and strategies for adding graphics to your intranet. I covered everything from backgrounds, capture applications, and image formats to ways to optimize your images to make your pages load quicker. The key is to keep them small and use images when they enhance your presentation.

What's Next!

You can now move on to look at several different ways to access valuable information and use it on your intranet. You'll take a look at Alliare's Cold Fusion, which allows you to access information from your databases and generate live HTML pages on the client's browser. You'll also see other ways to display and access information, including client-side image maps and the use of bookmarks to drill down your Web pages.

Chapter | 7

Accessing Information

In the last chapter, I discussed ways to add graphics to your intranet without compromising bandwidth. I covered all the layout tricks that allow you to place graphics where you want them in your page layouts. In this chapter, I move on to more of the meat of your intranet: the ability to access information from databases, and the use of other methods to get at information that you want to include on your intranet.

Linking to Other Pages in Your Intranet Structure

With the home page constructed, it is now time to move on to the other main Web pages on the Miracle Toy Corporation intranet. I start from the left and move to the right. First, I cover the New Baby Toy Line. Most organizations have a product or service that they want to make sure all employees are aware of. Employees can find information that they need to make their daily job easier, and can locate information for a customer who might be on the phone line wanting to know more about certain products or services. The New Baby Toy Line is an example that you can customize to your specific organization. Look at the Web page for the New Baby Toy Line (Figure 7-1) and then read on to examine its construction.

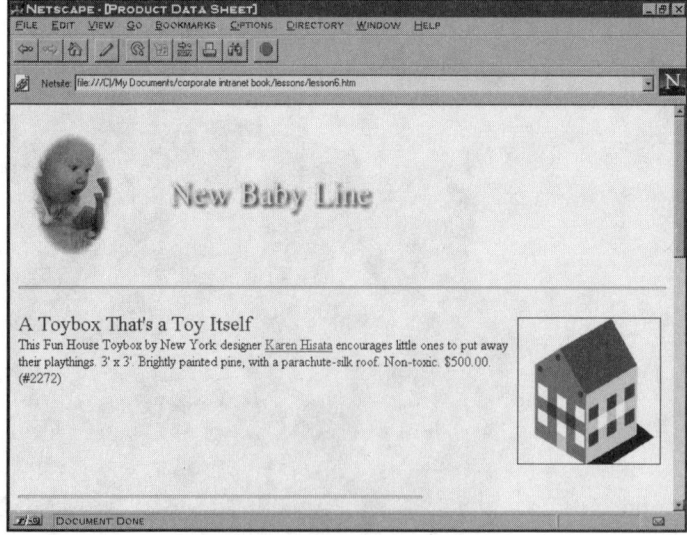

FIGURE 7-1

The first hyperlink off of the Miracle Home Page takes you to a product description page that gives employees all the necessary information about a new product line.

When you are on the product description area, you can create a high-level menu that allows the users to choose new products from a definition list as they are added to the new product line. Currently, the Baby Toy Line is brand new, so there is only one product in the line and no need for a Web page with a listing of the available products. I therefore start with the one new product that is available. The Fun House ToyBox that is now displayed when a user enters this page is set on a template. You can create and use a standard template for all of your products. After you create the general outline in HTML, you can cut and paste new products (content and images) in as they become available. This saves a great deal of time when you are adding deleting and updating your product listings. Take a look at the HTML that created this page so that you can use it for product information on your intranet.

> **NOTE:** Because your users can set their personal preferences for background colors, links, and text, it is good practice to specify all of these color settings in your Web pages, to avoid instances when users might have their text color set to white and you set the background color to white in your Web page.

Listing 7.1   New Baby Toy Line.

```
<html>
<head>
<title>Product Listing</title>
</head>
<body bgcolor="#FFFFFF">
<p><img src="baby1.jpg" align=bottom width=125 height=175 alt="baby image">
➥<img src="les6.gif" align=bottom width=265 height=52 alt="lesson 6 image"> </p>
<hr>
<p><img src="tybx.gif" align=right hspace=5 vspace=5 width=167 height=167 alt="toy box
➥image"><font color="#800040"><font size=5>A Toybox That's a Toy Itself</font></font>
➥<br>
This Fun House Toybox by New York designer <a href="mailto:info@hisata.com">Karen
➥Hisata</a> encourages little ones to put away
their playthings. 3' x 3'. Brightly painted pine, with a parachute-silk roof. 
➥Non-toxic. $500.00.
(#2272) </p>
```

```
<hr>

<h2>Contents:</h2>

<ul>

<li><a href="#summary"><strong>Product Summary</strong></a></li>

<li><a href="#features"><strong>Key Features</strong></a></li>

<li><a href="#specs"><strong>Specifications</strong></a></li>

</ul>

<hr>

<h2><a name="summary">Product Summary</a></h2>

<p>Our New Fun House ToyBox is now shipping. We have targeted the release for this years
➥Christmas Season and are anticipating a marvelous response. The ToyBox is 3' x 3' so
➥it will hold all kinds of toys, and it is constructed of a hard pine.
We will be shipping four color options to see how they do in the market and will add
➥new colors after our initial test. (See the
color Options below)</p>

<p><a href="#top">Back to Top</a></p>

<hr>

<h2><a name="features">Key Features</a></h2>

<p><font color="#800040"><font size=5>Specifications <br>

<img src="bullet2.gif" align=bottom width=9 height=9></font></font> <a
➥href="http://home.netscape.com/assist/net_sites/starter/nowhere.html">Latched pole</a>
➥prevents collapse <br>

<img src="bullet2.gif" align=bottom width=9 height=9> Soft edges <br>

<img src="bullet2.gif" align=bottom width=9 height=9> Portable <br>

<img src="bullet2.gif" align=bottom width=9 height=9> 

<a href="http://home.netscape.com/assist/net_sites/starter/nowhere.html">Quick
➥assembly</a> and tear-down <br>

<img src="bullet2.gif" align=bottom width=9 height=9> Stores easily in its own
➥<a href="http://home.netscape.com/assist/net_sites/starter/nowhere.html">carrying
➥case</a> </p>

<p><font color="#800040"><font size=5>Color Options</font></font><font size=5> <br>

<img src="bullet2.gif" align=bottom width=9 height=9></font> Purple, Teal, and
➥Yellow (#2272) <br>

<img src="bullet2.gif" align=bottom width=9 height=9> Pink, Teal, and Purple
➥(#2273) <br>
```

```
<img src="bullet2.gif" align=bottom width=9 height=9> Red, Teal, and Purple (#2274)
➥<br>
<img src="bullet2.gif" align=bottom width=9 height=9> Burgundy, Green, and Gold
➥(#2275) <br>
</p>
<p><a href="#top">Back to Top</a></p>
<hr>
<h2><a name="specs">Specifications</a></h2>
<ul>
<li>3' x 3' overall size.</li>
<li>Shipping:    4' x 4' in box</li>
<li>Weight: 36 lb. in box</li>
<li>Fully assembled</li>
</ul>
<p><a href="#top">Back to Top</a></p>
<hr>
<h5>Steve Griswold.<br>
Copyright &#169; 1995 [Miracle Toys]. All rights reserved.<br>
Information in this document is subject to change without notice.<br>
Other products and companies referred to herein are trademarks or registered trademarks
➥of their respective companies or mark holders.<br>
</h5>
</body>
</html>
```

This looks pretty complex. But trust me—it's not, if you take it piece by piece.

Product Template

I start with the basic HTML structure tags:

```
<html>
<head>
<title>Product Listing</title>
</head>
```

Here I have defined the basic HTML structure and told the browser to display the title of the document as "Product Listing." You will be using this same layout, with a title, of course, for all your HTML documents. Next, I move into the beginning of the body of the page.

```
<body bgcolor="#FFFFFF">
<p><img src="baby1.jpg" align=bottom width=125 height=175 alt="baby image">
➥<img src="les6.gif" align=bottom width=265 height=52 alt="lesson 6 image"> </p>
<hr>
<p><img src="tybx.gif" align=right hspace=5 vspace=5 width=167 height=167 alt="toy box
➥image"><font color="#800040"><font size=5>A Toybox That's a Toy Itself</font>
➥</font><br>
This Fun House Toybox by New York designer <a href="mailto:info@hisata.com">Karen
➥Hisata</a> encourages little ones to put away
their playthings. 3' x 3'. Brightly painted pine, with a parachute-silk
➥roof. Non-toxic. $500.00.
(#2272) </p>
```

You start with the <BODY> tag. This tells the browser that you are starting the body of this document and to format accordingly. You add an attribute to the <BODY> tag, which tells the Web browser to change the background color to white. This is the <body bgcolor="#FFFFFF"> tag. The hexadecimal value for white is FFFFFF (see Chapter 6, "Graphics on an Intranet," for more on changing font and background colors). After you change the background to white, you'll start a new paragraph. You do this with the <P> tag. The first thing in this paragraph is an image of a baby. You must tell the browser where the image is, so include the following line:

```
<p><img src="baby1.jpg" align=bottom width=125 height=175><img src="les6.gif"
➥align=bottom width=265 height=52> </p>
```

The <img src="baby1.jpg"> lets the browser know that the image source is a JPEG file named BABY1.JPG. You go on to tell the browser more detailed information to align the image and to allow it to load quicker. You do this in the rest of the line:

```
align=bottom width=125 height=175>
```

Here, you tell the browser that you want the image aligned to the bottom, and that the width and the height of the image is expressed in pixels so that the browser doesn't have to take the extra time to figure out the image dimensions while it is loading. You do the same thing with the next image file on this line to get the New Baby Line graphic to come in, and then you end it all with a closing </P> tag.

```
<hr>

<p><img src="tybx.gif" align=right hspace=5 vspace=5 width=167 height=167>
```

The next line of code tells the browser to first insert a horizontal rule (a dividing line) across the page. You then insert another image, but this time align it to the right side of the screen. This is the ToyBox graphic. Now you want to have a descriptive paragraph of text next to the graphic. You will find that the next butts up right next to the graphic and does not allow any white space at all if you start typing in your paragraph from this point. To avoid this problem, you should tell the browser to leave some space (in pixels) around the image. The use of hspace=5 vspace=5 accomplishes this. The hspace tells the browser to leave a horizontal border of space between the text and image (in this case, 5 pixels). The vspace does the same. It tells the browser to leave 5 pixels of space vertically next to the image. Experiment with the pixel amounts until you get the amount of space you like when creating templates for your intranet. Again, you tell the browser the height and width of the image, and then you close the image tag.

```
<font color="#800040"><font size=5>A Toybox That's a Toy Itself</font></font><br>
```

Now you'll put in the purple title that is larger than the rest of the text. First, you'll tell the browser to make the font purple by inserting the hexadecimal value for that color into the <FONT> tag. Next, tell the browser that you want the font to be bigger. To do this, insert a font size of 5. You can also use plus and minus signs; for example, you might increase the font by +1, +2, and so on. This way, if users have their default font sizes already increased in their browser settings, your heading will still be bigger than the standard text because you have told the browser to increase so much over the standard font size setting.

Now you'll insert the text that you want to have affected, and then you'll close the font size tag and the font color tag with the two </FONT> tags. You want to jump down to the next line directly below the title that you just created, so place one <BR> break tag in the code.

The rest of the code is mostly just the text description of the product until you get to the link that allows you to send mail to the New York designer Karen Hisata.

```
This Fun House Toybox by New York designer <a href="mailto:info@hisata.com">Karen
➡Hisata</a> encourages little ones to put away
their playthings. 3' x 3'. Brightly painted pine, with a parachute-silk
➡roof. Non-toxic. $500.00.
(#2272) </p>
```

To create a hyperlink that will invoke the mail client, you need to insert a tag and the e-mail address that you want the mail sent to. You must first let the browser know that you want to create a hyperlink, so you start with the <a href="name"> part of the tag. The <a href> lets the browser know that this is a hyperlink. In turn, the hyperlink sends `mailto:` the e-mail address `info@hisata.com`. Now you need to tell the browser what text to insert between the opening and closing anchor <a> tags that will act as your hyperlink. So, insert the name `Karen Hisata`, and then close the link with the </a> tag. Any text between the opening and closing </a> tag will be part of the hyperlink.

Now you can move on to the next part of the code:

```
<h2>Contents:</h2>

<ul>

<li><a href="#summary"><strong>Product Summary</strong></a></li>

<li><a href="#features"><strong>Key Features</strong></a></li>

<li><a href="#specs"><strong>Specifications</strong></a></li>

</ul>
```

Because I wanted Contents: in a larger font, I used a heading tag. The <h2> gives me with a fairly large heading, and I close the tag with the </h2>.

To create a nice presentation, I now add a list of items to the document. It is also time to take a look at the next screen shot of the document so that you can see the rest of the product page (Figure 7-2).

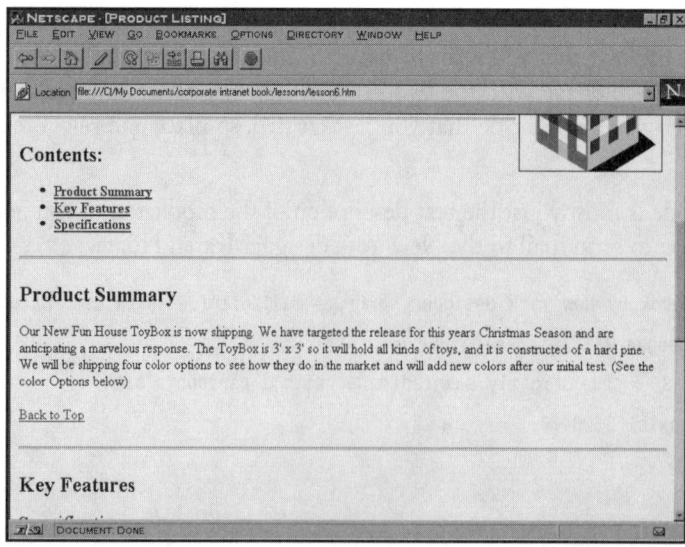

FIGURE 7-2

You start to get into the content of the product page; it is divided into several sections that are linked together to make navigation easier for the user.

To make the list with product summary, key features, and specifications, I first start with an unordered list tag. The `<ul>` tag lets the browser know that an unordered list will follow. The browser will generate the bullets automatically. I now need to start with the first item in the list. So, I insert an `<li>` list item tag. I'll also be making this item a link, so I insert the `<a href="name">` tag. This time, the tag looks a little different. The name of the file has a number sign in front of it. That happens because I plan to link to another section of the current Web page I'm in, rather than link to another Web page. The `"#summary"` tells the browser to look for a spot in the document that has been named "summary," and to jump to that spot in the document when a user clicks on this link.

```
<li><a href="#summary"><strong>Product Summary</strong></a></li>
```

The rest of the line formats the text that I'm using for the link with a strong emphasis, and then I close all my tags. I repeat this procedure for all the items in my unordered list, and close the unordered list with the `</ul>` tag.

Just after this section, I enter the Summary content for my product:

```
<h2><a name="summary">Product Summary</a></h2>
```

The `<a name="summary">` tag is the destination anchor for the hyperlink that I defined previously. Users will be transported here when they click on the hyperlink labeled `Product Summary`.

I've used the same tagging method to define other areas that I want to link to in the same document.

I add my descriptive text and place a horizontal rule in to visual separate this section from the rest. I follow this for the three main areas in this document. The next section looks like this:

```
<hr>

<h2><a name="features">Key Features</a></h2>

<p><font color="#800040"><font size=5>Specifications <br>

<img src="bullet2.gif" align=bottom width=9 height=9></font></font> 
➥<a href="http://home.netscape.com/assist/net_sites/starter/nowhere.html">Latched
➥pole</a> prevents collapse <br>

<img src="bullet2.gif" align=bottom width=9 height=9> Soft edges <br>

<img src="bullet2.gif" align=bottom width=9 height=9> Portable <br>
```

```
<img src="bullet2.gif" align=bottom width=9 height=9> 

<a href="http://home.netscape.com/assist/net_sites/starter/nowhere.html">Quick
➥assembly</a> and tear-down <br>

<img src="bullet2.gif" align=bottom width=9 height=9> Stores easily in its own
➥<a href="http://home.netscape.com/assist/net_sites/starter/nowhere.html">carrying
➥case</a> </p>

<p><font color="#800040"><font size=5>Color Options</font></font><font size=5> <br>

<img src="bullet2.gif" align=bottom width=9 height=9></font> Purple, Teal, and
➥Yellow (#2272) <br>

<img src="bullet2.gif" align=bottom width=9 height=9> Pink, Teal, and Purple
➥(#2273) <br>

<img src="bullet2.gif" align=bottom width=9 height=9> Red, Teal, and Purple (#2274)
➥<br>

<img src="bullet2.gif" align=bottom width=9 height=9> Burgundy, Green, and Gold
➥(#2275) <br>

</p>

<p><a href="#top">Back to Top</a></p>

<hr>
```

This section of code is the same as the last, but has a little different formatting. Rather than use an unordered list as I did earlier, here I want to create a list with those cool fancy icons that you see all over the WWW. I do this by inserting an image (bullet2.gif) in front of each line in the list. I make the text jump down to the next line by placing a simple <br> tag at the end of each item in the list.

To see this list, take a look at Figure 7-3.

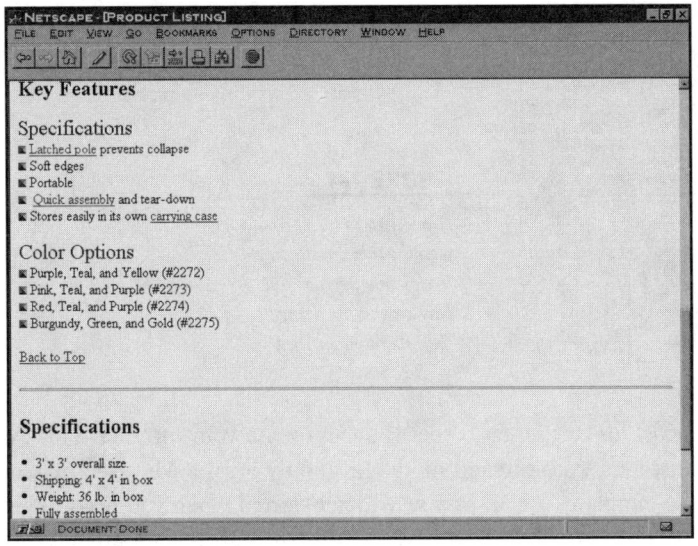

FIGURE 7-3

*The document continues
with several sections that
define the product description even further. You can
easily add your own con-
tent in these sections to
jump-start your own
intranet.*

I'm going to jump to the end of the document because I have covered the tags that keep
repeating themselves up to this point. I end the document with some descriptive text, and
with the closing structure tags:

```
<hr>

<h5>Steve Griswold.<br>

Copyright &#169; 1995 [Miracle Toys]. All rights reserved.<br>

Information in this document is subject to change without notice.<br>

Other products and companies referred to herein are trademarks or registered trademarks

➥of their respective companies or mark holders.<br>

</h5>

</body>

</html>
```

To make the copyright symbol, I've used the &#169 character entity. Take a look at Figure
7-4 to see some of the other ISO-Latin-1 character sets.

```
8-bit ISO 8859-1 Latin 1 characters
160        176 °   192 À   208 Ð   224 à   240 ð
161 ¡      177 ±   193 Á   209 Ñ   225 á   241 ñ
162 ¢      178 ²   194 Â   210 Ò   226 â   242 ò
163 £      179 ³   195 Ã   211 Ó   227 ã   243 ó
164 ¤      180 ´   196 Ä   212 Ô   228 ä   244 ô
165 ¥      181 µ   197 Å   213 Õ   229 å   245 õ
166 ¦      182 ¶   198 Æ   214 Ö   230 æ   246 ö
167 §      183 ·   199 Ç   215 ×   231 ç   247 ÷
168 ¨      184 ¸   200 È   216 Ø   232 è   248 ø
169 ©      185 ¹   201 É   217 Ù   233 é   249 ù
170 ª      186 º   202 Ê   218 Ú   234 ê   250 ú
171 «      187 »   203 Ë   219 Û   235 ë   251 û
172 ¬      188 ¼   204 Ì   220 Ü   236 ì   252 ü
173 -      189 ½   205 Í   221 Ý   237 í   253 ý
174 ®      190 ¾   206 Î   222 Þ   238 î   254 þ
175 ¯      191 ¿   207 Ï   223 ß   239 ï   255 ÿ
```

FIGURE 7-4

If you need to insert a special symbol, write in a foreign language, or just play around, try using these character entities.

Templates already exist for certain tasks that you can use on your intranet. This example was taken from Netscape's Web site and modified slightly for the Miracle Toy Company example here. These templates are an easy way to get started when you need to get some structure to your intranet pages but don't have the time to start from scratch.

Human Resources

Under the human resources link from the intranet main page, you should drop down to a navigation page that gives a wide range of services that human resources offers. I show you how to make a job opportunities section that enables users to look at all the available jobs in your organization, and also lets them fill out a form, an online questionnaire, and submit it to you on your intranet if they have questions, or if they want to put their name in a bank for future jobs that are not posted. After I show you that, I introduce a product by Allaire called Cold Fusion that makes it easy to create live HTML documents on the fly.

Creating a Job Opportunities Web Area

This is a long one. Feel free to take the code, change it around, and add to it. With the previous example, I walked you through step by step practically every line of the HTML code. In this example, I basically show you the screen shots in sections and show you the code that generated that section. I display some forms, but I won't explain each tag here. Instead, please take a look at the HTML sections in Appendixes A and B to get the basics under your belt, and then everything here should be crystal clear.

Take a look at the first screen shot, shown in Figure 7-5.

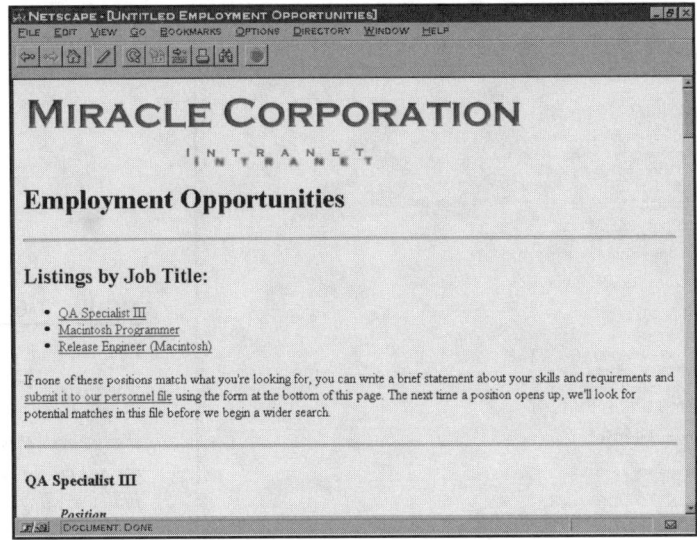

FIGURE 7-5

*An Employment
Opportunities page in the
Human Resources Section
enables current employees
to look for other positions
in the organization.*

By looking at Figure 7-5, you can get a good idea how to structure an employment
opportunities area on your intranet. The page starts off with a graphic of the company,
Miracle, and then has a heading that stands out to let everyone know they are on the
Employment Opportunities page. I am using horizontal rules to separate the page
into sections.

Listing by Job Title

The first section can house all of your current job openings. If you have a large amount
of jobs, make a higher level menu that drills down to more specific individual jobs. In
the example, I listed three jobs in a bulleted list. I also left a link that allows individuals
to submit their personal information to Human Resources if they don't see any jobs that
interest them at present. After they submit their information in the form at the bottom
of this page, they will be kept in a database and considered for future jobs that become
available.

The First Listing (QA Specialist III)

By clicking on the job titles, the user is taken down the current page to the information
sheet on the job requested. Figure 7-6 shows the qualifications needed for the QA
Specialist III.

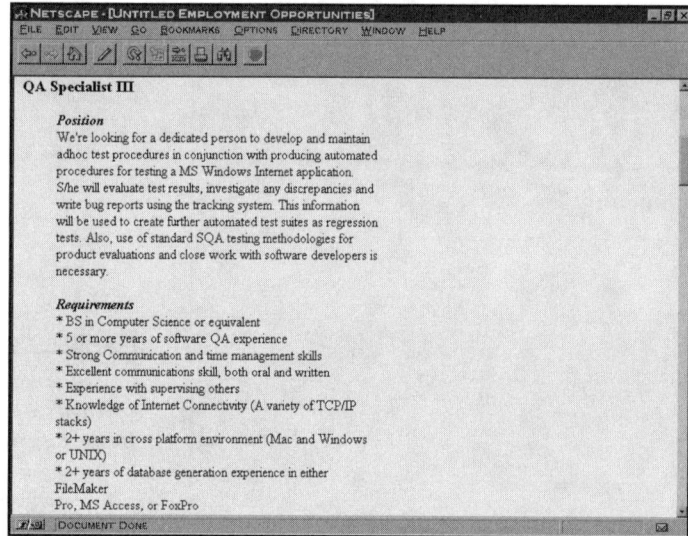

FIGURE 7-6

By clicking on the job listing, users are brought directly to the specific job that interests them. Users can also browse all the jobs just by scrolling down the page.

The other two jobs in this example are also listed in the same fashion.

General Inquiries

The page also contains contact information. Users can mail or fax a resume to the Human Resources Department if they wish. There is also an online form that the user can fill out to be considered for future jobs. The form can also be modified easily so that users can apply for jobs that are listed currently on the site. Figure 7-7 is the part of the intranet page that lets the users know how to contact Human Resources.

Personnel File

The personnel file is fairly large, so it is displayed here in two figures (see Figures 7-8 and 7-9). This form allows employees to enter information about themselves and also about what jobs and areas they might want to work in. Human Resources can then try to match them up with jobs in the company that fit both parties' needs. For people who lack the necessary skill set for a particular job, Human Resources can keep these files, contact these employees, and help them with training and guidance so that they can meet their professional goals.

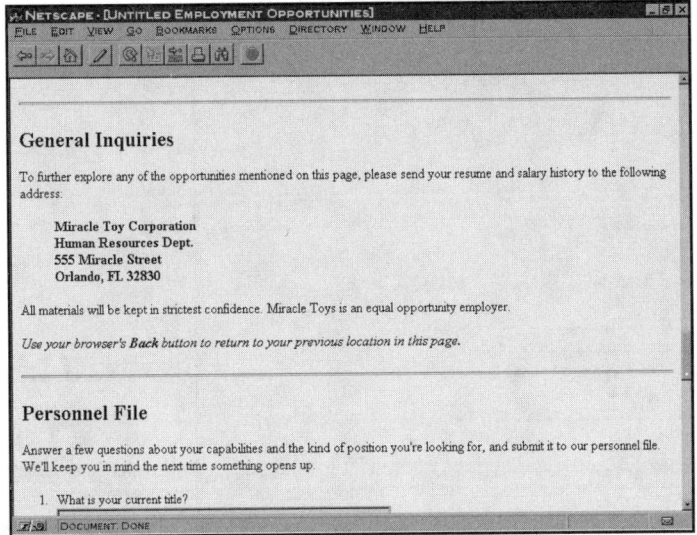

FIGURE 7-7

Users can get general information on how to submit resumes and to contact Human Resources while they're on the same page as the job opportunities.

An area like this on your intranet is a win-win situation. The company gets positions filled with qualified individuals, saving time and money with this new process, and the individuals in the organization get to see new jobs the second they are available, and can now interact with Human Resources more frequently to help build their skills.

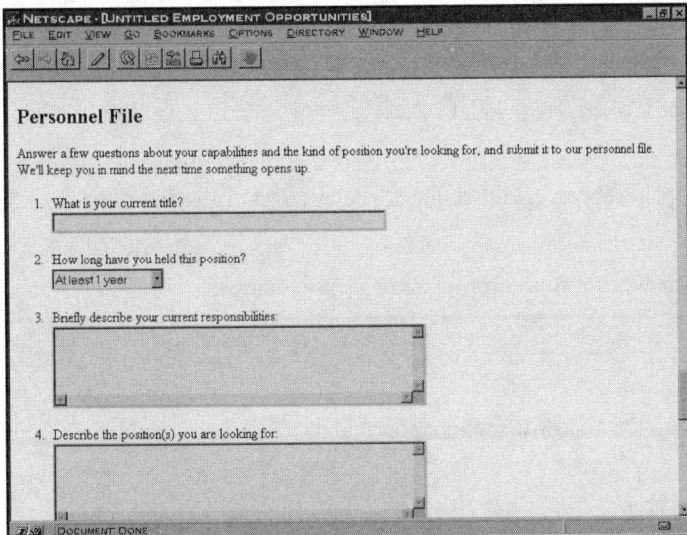

FIGURE 7-8

The first half of the form lets employees enter information on their current position and also on what position they are striving for.

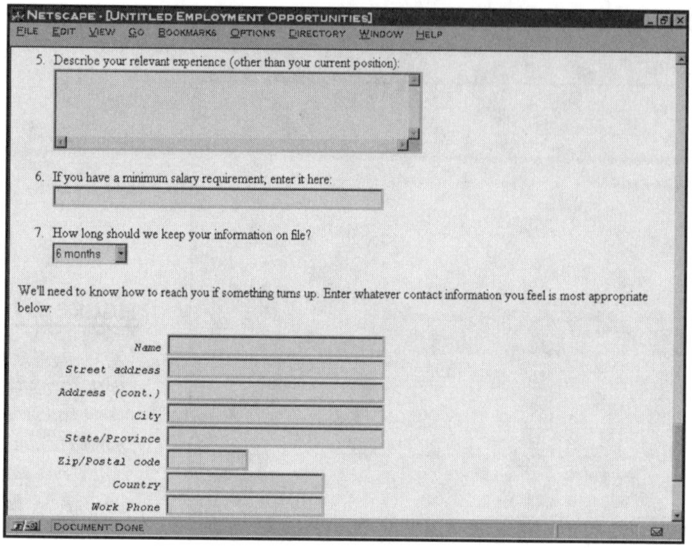

FIGURE 7-9

The next half of the form lets users enter their contact information so that HR can reach them for training or job openings.

So that you can create this template and change it around for your intranet, I have included the code that follows. You can also get a handful of great business templates for your intranet from Netscape's Web site at:

(http://home.netscape.com/home/gold2.0_templates.html)

If you are using Netscape Gold, you can customize the templates right in Gold and get them running in no time. Microsoft also has some great templates that come with FrontPage. You can get more information on FrontPage from Microsoft's Web site at:

(http://www.microsoft.com/frontpage/)

FrontPage is also shipping with Windows NT Server 4.0. I used a FrontPage template to get me started on this Web page, and changed the elements I needed to fit my needs.

Listing 7.2   Miracle Corporation employment opportunities.

```html
<html>
<head>
<title>Miracle Employment Opportunities</title>
</head>
<body bgcolor="#FFFFFF">
<h1><img src="../../../GRAPHICS/Images/miracle.gif" align=bottom width=591 height=96>
```

```
Employment Opportunities</h1>
<hr>
<h2><a name="top">Listings by Job Title:</a></h2>
<ul>
<li><a href="#qa">QA Specialist III</a></li>
<li><a href="#mac">Macintosh Programmer</a></li>
<li><a href="#rel">Release Engineer (Macintosh)</a></li>
</ul>
<p>If none of these positions match what you're looking for, you can write a brief
➡statement about your skills and requirements and <a href="#form">submit it to our
➡personnel file</a> using the form at the bottom of this page. The next time a position
➡opens up, we'll look for potential matches in this file before we begin a wider
➡search. </p>
<hr>
<h3><a name="qa">QA Specialist III</a></h3>
<blockquote>
<p><font size=3><em><strong>Position</strong></em></font><br>
We're looking for a dedicated person to develop and maintain<br>
adhoc test procedures in conjunction with producing automated<br>
procedures for testing a MS Windows Internet application.<br>
S/he will evaluate test results, investigate any discrepancies and<br>
write bug reports using the tracking system. This information<br>
will be used to create further automated test suites as regression<br>
tests. Also, use of standard SQA testing methodologies for<br>
product evaluations and close work with software developers is<br>
necessary. </p>
<p><em><strong>Requirements</strong></em><br>
* BS in Computer Science or equivalent <br>
* 5 or more years of software QA experience <br>
* Strong Communication and time management skills <br>
* Excellent communications skill, both oral and written <br>
* Experience with supervising others <br>
* Knowledge of Internet Connectivity (A variety of TCP/IP<br>
stacks) <br>
```

```
* 2+ years in cross platform environment (Mac and Windows<br>
or UNIX) <br>
* 2+ years of database generation experience in either<br>
FileMaker <br>
Pro, MS Access, or FoxPro <br>
* 2+ years experience with generation of Automated Test<br>
scripts. <br>
(QAPartner, MSTest, VU, or other). <br>
* Extensive knowledge of QA process and methodologies <br>
* Familiarity with process flow for fixture of from beta/defect <br>
feedback -regression testing </p>
<p><br>
<em><strong>For more information</strong></em><br>
You may send a short e-mail message describing your relevant experience to
➥<a href="mailto:eng-jobs@company.com">eng-jobs@company.com</a>, or
send your resume to <a href="#hr">Human Resources</a>.</p>
</blockquote>
<h5><a href="#top">Back to Top</a></h5>
<hr>
<h3><a name="mac">Macintosch Programmer</a></h3>
<blockquote>
<p><em><strong>Position</strong></em><br>
We're looking for experienced, self-motivated programmers to<br>
join our team of engineers to complete the development of an<br>
Internet-enabled Macintosh application. <br>
<br>
<em><strong>Requirements</strong></em><br>
Individual must have 3+ years Macintosh experience with solid<br>
working knowledge of C and C++. Preferred skills include the<br>
following: <br>
* TCP/IP networking <br>
* Graphics/Animation <br>
* PowerPlant/Codewarrior <br>
* Power PC development <br>
```

```
* OpenDoc <br>
* AppleEvent object model <br>
<br>
Mail or fax resume care of Jobs/Macintosh Programmer<br></p>
<p><br>
<em><strong>For more information</strong></em><br>
To further explore this opportunity, please contact our <a href="#hr">Human
➥Resources</a> office.</p>
</blockquote>
<h5><a href="#top">Back to Top</a></h5>
<hr>
<h3><a name="rel">Release Engineer </a></h3>
<blockquote>
<p><em><strong>Position<br>
</strong></em>The successful candidate will perform release engineering<br>
functions for all internet products on the Apple Macintosh<br>
platform. This role also involves development and maintenance<br>
of product installation software. <br>
<br>
<em><strong>Requirements<br>
</strong></em>* Maintain/improve software development and integration<br>
process <br>
* Maintain source code trees, makefiles, and utilities <br>
* Develop automated build and test tools <br>
* Develop and maintain installation/startup scripts for client<br>
products <br>
* Coordinate alpha and beta testing <br>
* Work closely with the developers and the Quality Assurance<br>
group <br>
* BS in Computer Science (preferred) or equivalent <br>
* 2-4 years experience in software engineering, QA,or release<br>
engineering <br>
* Experience with the Apple Macintosh development<br>
environment <br>
```

```
* At least 1 year experience writing C/C++ programs <br>

* Experience in using source control systems <br>

* Experience in Cross platform development issues <br>

* Strong scripting skills (batch files, makefile, etc.) <br>

* Excellent communications skills </p>

<p><br>

<em><strong>For more information</strong></em><br>

To further explore this opportunity, please contact our <a href="#hr">Human
➡Resources</a> office.</p>

</blockquote>

<h5><a href="#top">Back to Top</a></h5>

<hr>

<h2><a name="hr">General Inquiries</a></h2>

<p>To further explore any of the opportunities mentioned on this page, please send your
➡resume and salary history to the following address:</p>

<blockquote>

<p><strong>Miracle Toy Corporation<br>

Human Resources Dept.<br>

555 Miracle Street<br>

Orlando, FL 32830</strong></p>

</blockquote>

<p>All materials will be kept in strictest confidence. Miracle Toys is an equal
➡opportunity employer.</p>

<p><em>Use your browser's </em><em><strong>Back</strong></em><em> button to return to
➡your previous location in this page.</em></p>

<hr>

<h2><a name="form">Personnel File</a></h2>

<p>Answer a few questions about your capabilities and the kind of position you're
➡looking for, and submit it to our personnel file. We'll keep you in mind the next time
➡something opens up.</p>

<form action="/cgi-bin/contact" method="POST">

<ol>

<li>What is your current title? <br>

<input type=text size=54 maxlength=256 name="CurrentTitle"><br>
```

```
<br>
</li>
<li>How long have you held this position? <br>
<select name="CurrentTime" size=1>
<option>Less than 1 year</option>
<option selected>At least 1 year</option>
<option>At least 2 years</option>
<option>3 to 5 years</option>
<option>More than 5 years</option>
</select><br>
<br>
</li>
<li>Briefly describe your current responsibilities:<br>
<textarea name="Responsibilities" rows=4 cols=52></textarea><br>
<br>
</li>
<li>Describe the position(s) you are looking for:<br>
<textarea name="DesiredPosition" rows=4 cols=52></textarea><br>
<br>
</li>
<li>Describe your relevant experience (other than your current position):<br>
<textarea name="RelevantExperience" rows=4 cols=52></textarea><br>
<br>
</li>
<li>If you have a minimum salary requirement, enter it here:<br>
<input type=text size=54 maxlength=256 name="MinimumSalary"><br>
<br>
</li>
<li>How long should we keep your information on file?<br>
<select name="Expiration" size=1>
<option>3 months</option>
<option selected>6 months</option>
<option>9 months</option>
<option>1 year</option>
```

```
<option>indefinitely</option>
</select></li>
</ol>
<p>We'll need to know how to reach you if something turns up. Enter whatever
➥contact information you feel is most appropriate
below:</p>
<blockquote>
<pre><em>              Name </em><input type=text size=35 maxlength=256
➥name="Contact_FullName">
<em>   Street address </em><input type=text size=35 maxlength=256
➥name="Contact_StreetAddress">
<em> Address (cont.) </em><input type=text size=35 maxlength=256 name="Contact_Address2">
<em>              City </em><input type=text size=35 maxlength=256 name="Contact_City">
<em>   State/Province </em><input type=text size=35 maxlength=256 name="Contact_State">
<em> Zip/Postal code </em><input type=text size=12 maxlength=12 name="Contact_ZipCode">
<em>           Country </em><input type=text size=25 maxlength=256 name="Contact_Country">
<em>        Work Phone </em><input type=text size=25 maxlength=25
➥name="Contact_WorkPhone">
<em>        Home Phone </em><input type=text size=25 maxlength=25
➥name="Contact_HomePhone">
<em>               FAX </em><input type=text size=25 maxlength=25 name="Contact_FAX">
<em>            E-mail </em><input type=text size=25 maxlength=256 name="Contact_Email">
</pre>
</blockquote>
<p><input type=submit value="Submit Information"><input type=reset value="Clear
➥Form"></p>
</form>
<h5><a href="#top">Back to Top</a></h5>
<hr>
<h5>Miracle Toys<br>
Last Updated:</h5>
</body>
</html>
```

Static pages are good for many areas on your intranet that don't change, or change very seldom. But the real power comes in when you can connect to databases, and create live HTML pages from your query information. There are several products on the market that make sending and retrieving information to your database fairly easy. Allaire makes a product called Cold Fusion that allows you to develop intranet applications that integrate relational databases. The pages are dynamic and are generated on the fly from information that is stored in databases that has been input by your users. You can download a trial version of Cold Fusion from Allaire's Web site at:

```
http://www.allaire.com.
```

Cold Fusion

The quickest and often most effective way to introduce connectivity to databases is with the use of a rapid development tool. You can write intense CGI scripts in Perl, and I cover this in an entire chapter dedicated to CGI. But I have discovered at numerous conferences that the attendees at these conferences are no longer just hard-core Web heads. Average computer-literate company employees are being assigned the task to develop intranet applications and to get more done with less in half the time.

Sound familiar? Intranets are now arriving at a turning point. No longer is it necessary to have a huge information systems staff to create and maintain an intranet. A small-sized intranet can be created and maintained by a department with the right hardware, software, and some basic computer knowledge. Tools such as Allaire's Cold Fusion makes creating dynamic intranet applications quickly much easier, and with literally no traditional programming such as Perl, C++, Visual Basic, or Delphi.

Cold Fusion lets you create applications for your intranet such as the following:

- ◆ Customer feedback
- ◆ Online order entry
- ◆ Event registration
- ◆ Searches of catalogs
- ◆ Directories and calendars
- ◆ Bulletin-board style conferencing
- ◆ Online technical support
- ◆ Interactive training
- ◆ Many other content publishing applications

Now individuals can create these dynamic intranet applications much faster and without the headaches of the traditional, code-intensive techniques. Information System departments can also benefit from Cold Fusion and development tools like it because those tools allow them to work faster and smarter.

Cold Fusion allows you to develop applications faster because there is no code, except for simple HTML-type tags, making up what is called the Cold Fusion Markup Language (CFML).

All database transactions are encapsulated in a single, rock-hard database processing engine, making Cold Fusion applications very robust.

The Cold Fusion Application Server handles all connections and manages multiple user requests against one database. The engine runs as a 32-bit multithreaded system service, which means that Cold Fusion can scale across multiple processors, allowing it to perform as fast as NT will allow.

Cold Fusion applications are also very flexible. Because Cold Fusion uses standard HTML files to create its presentations and do its formatting, you can modify and view the files easily, whenever you want. This beats having to edit and recompile source code.

System Requirements to Run Cold Fusion

Cold Fusion uses the standard Common Gateway Interface (CGI) to communicate with your Web server. Because CGI is a standard interface, any Windows 95 or NT Web server that supports CGI will run Cold Fusion. The upcoming release of Cold Fusion (version 2.0, which is probably shipping as this book goes to print), includes tight integration with Web servers via their native APIs. For those that support only CGI, there are several servers that have been tested with Cold Fusion. These are as follows:

- O'Reilly WebSite
- Microsoft IIS
- EMWAC HTTPS
- Process Software Purveyor
- Netscape Communications / Commerce Server
- Netscape Enterprise and FastTrack Servers
- Internet Factory Communications / Commerce Builder
- Spry Safety Web Server
- CSM Alibaba

All these Web servers have been tested with Cold Fusion, and they are fully supported. If you are using a different server, you can check the Cold Fusion Support Forum to make sure that your server supports Cold Fusion. Check http://www.allaire.com/support to see whether your server has been tested by the Cold Fusion team. All top-notch servers are supported.

To add an element of interactivity to your intranet, you need to add a database. Cold Fusion uses 32-bit ODBC drivers to communicate with a variety of relational databases. Cold Fusion has been tested to make sure that it is compatible with the Microsoft ODBC desktop drivers. You get these drivers with the product, and they support the following databases:

- Microsoft SQL Server
- Microsoft Access 1.0, 2.0, and 7.0
- Oracle 7
- Microsoft FoxPro 2.0, 2.5, and 2.6
- Borland Paradox 3.x, and 4.x
- Borland dBase III and dBase IV
- Microsoft Excel 3.0, 4.0, 5.0, and 7.0
- Plain Text Files

Cold Fusion has also been tested with several of the drivers in the Intersolv DataDirect ODBC pack. The drivers that have been tested are the following:

- All versions of dBase, FoxPro, and Clipper
- Microsoft Excel
- Plain Text Files

If you don't see the driver that you are looking for here, don't fear. Cold Fusion is still very likely to work, even with a different driver. As long as it is an ODBC driver and it meets the following requirements, you should be ready to go:

- Must be a 32-bit driver
- Must meet the Level 1 standard of the ODBC API
- Must also support the Core SQL Grammar
- Must have support for date and time data types in order for Cold Fusion to use the date/time entry functions

About every ODBC driver covers these requirements, but you should still take a look at the Cold Fusion On-Line support forum just to keep up-to-date on the latest drivers, and to make sure that your driver has been tested and has passed the formal compatibility test.

You must also make sure that your hardware is up to some basic standards to be able to run Cold Fusion. To run your corporate intranet, you should have hardware well above these basic standards, so these requirements should not hold you back:

- You must have Microsoft Windows, NT 3.51 or greater, or Windows 95.
- A Pentium processor is best, but Cold Fusion will even run on a 80386.
- You will need 10MB of hard drive space to load Cold Fusion.
- If you are running NT, you will need to have 24MB of RAM, or 16MB of RAM for Windows 95.
- You need to have TCP/IP software installed and running.
- You need to have your Web server installed and running on a Windows NT or 95 platform.

Getting Started

You will need to download a trial version of Cold Fusion from `http://www.allaire.com`. After you download a copy, take a minute to install it on your intranet server. After you get Cold Fusion installed, you'll see how to build a simple Cold Fusion application so that you can see how Cold Fusion operates.

To install Cold Fusion, you will need to run the Cold Fusion SETUP.EXE file. When Cold Fusion is installed, you can access a test application, an online tutorial, and Cold Fusion example applications, by making an HTTP connection to the page called GET-START.HTM. This page will be located in the CFPRO directory that Cold Fusion created. You must make an HTTP connection to the GETSTART.HTM file (merely opening it in a browser locally will not allow the tutorial and Cold Fusion examples to work properly).

After you have Cold Fusion installed, you should be able to display the Cold Fusion Getting Started home page in your Web browser. Figure 7-10 shows this screen.

From this Getting Started home page, you can test your Cold Fusion installation. To do this, click on the first hypertext link to verify installation and configuration. This will take you to another Web page that has a simple form. The form will try to submit a query to make sure that Cold Fusion is set up correctly. Figure 7-11 takes you to the form where you can perform this test.

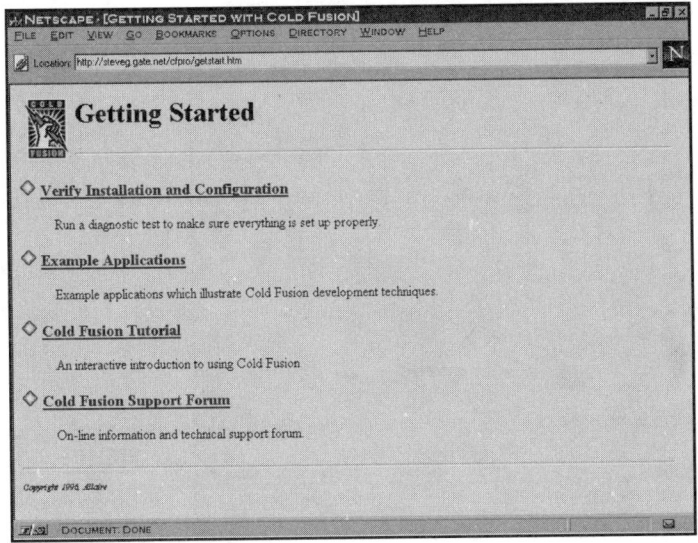

FIGURE 7-10

After Cold Fusion is installed on your Web server, you can display the opening Getting Started home page in your Web browser. From here, you can test your install, take a tutorial, or look at sample applications.

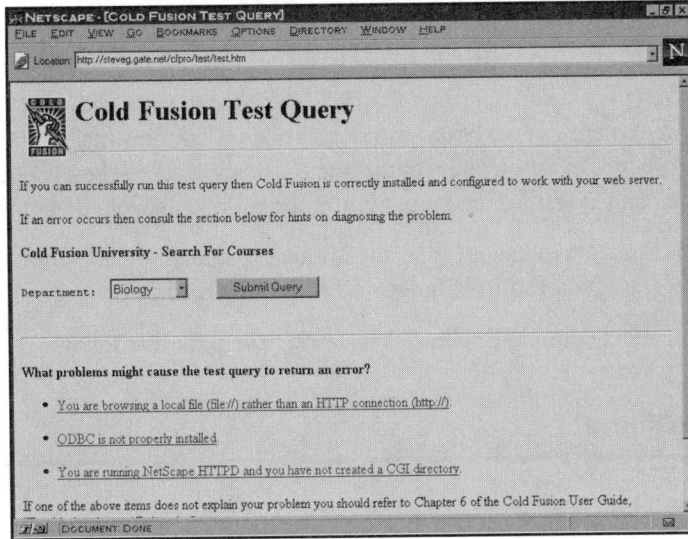

FIGURE 7-11

Click on the Submit button on the Web page to make sure that you have set up Cold Fusion correctly.

Next, you should get a test query results page displayed in your browser window, along with a message that Cold Fusion has been correctly installed and configured. This looks like the screen shot in Figure 7-12. If you did not get this Web page returned to you, then read the help files on the Cold Fusion test query page; you should then be able to make the correct configurations.

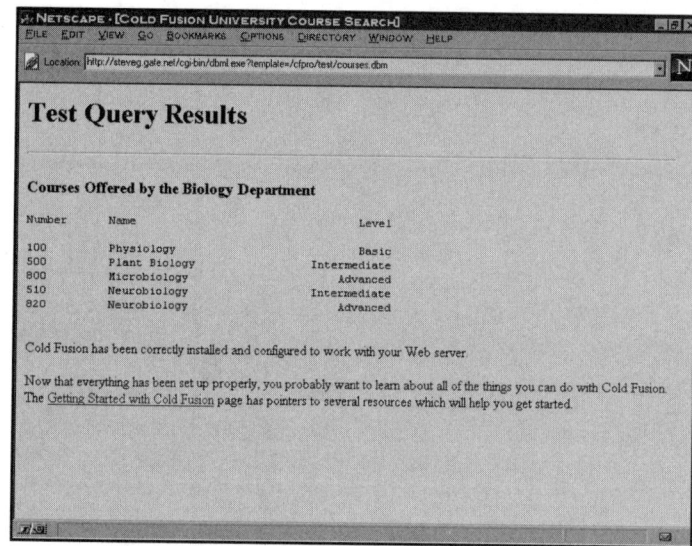

FIGURE 7-12

You have successfully set up Cold Fusion.

Now I want you to make a quick application in Cold Fusion to see how Cold Fusion works.

First, you create a Web page. The Web pages that will be created to work with Cold Fusion need to contain form elements. These basic form elements are what allow the user to enter information into text boxes, to choose radio buttons, and to click on check boxes. I have covered an entire chapter on forms, Chapter 8, to give you the basics on how to design them.

To create the HTML form to allow users on the intranet to query, you'll open a text editor. For example, I use NotePad in Windows 95 to create my form.

Go ahead and open a text editor and follow along. Enter the code that follows.

Listing 7.3   SEARCH.HTM

```
<html>
<head>
<title>Cold Fusion Sample</title>
</head>
</body>
<form action="/cgi-shi/dbml.exe?template=results.dbm" method=post>
<h4> Human Resources Classes available</h4>
```

```
<hr>

Departments: <select name="Department">

<option value="biol" selected> Biology

<option value="chem">Chemistry

<option value="econ">Economics

<option value="math"> Math

</select>

<p>

<center><input  type="submit" value="Submit Query"></center>

</form>

<hr>

</body>

</html>
```

NOTE: The cgi-shi that I have placed in the first form action line of the preceding code is the path to your Web server's CGI directory. Your Web server's CGI path might be different than the one in the example, so please change it to the correct path.

Okay, now that you have re-created the preceding code example in a text editor, you need to save your file. When you save your file, make sure that you save it in the root directory of your Web server HTML document directory. Save this file as SEARCH.HTM.

Now you can take a look at the HTML form that you just created. To do so, open up your Web browser and enter:

http://127.0.0.1/search.htm

The page should display in your Web browser and look like the example in Figure 7-13.

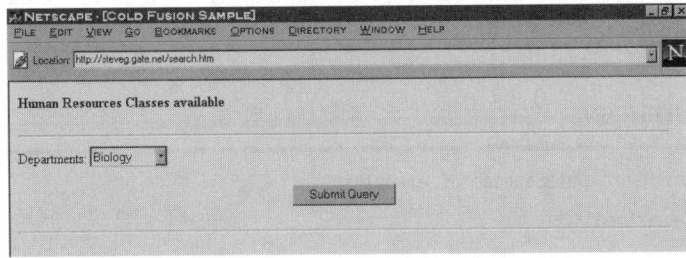

FIGURE 7-13

Your first Cold Fusion Web Page.

Don't click on the Submit Query button just yet. You still need to create the template file that will process the form for you, which is what you'll do next.

The template file is similar to an HTML file, but there are significant differences that allow template files to be more dynamic.

The Cold Fusion template files are not stored in the HTML Web server document directory. Template files have their own directory (CFUSION\TEMPLATE).

> **NOTE:** With Cold Fusion 2.0, all template files are stored in the same directories as HTML files, making development that much more easy and integrated.

The main difference between HTML files and template files is that template files also contain DBML tags. These database markup language tags tell Cold Fusion how to interact with your database. Template files also contain regular HTML tags, and these are used to format live pages that Cold Fusion generates.

The templates are also processed by the Cold Fusion Engine, and then are returned to the users' Web browser.

Template files are very similar to HTML files, but they also include to new DBML tags. These DBML tags in the template tell Cold Fusion what to do. These files let Cold Fusion know what database to use, which table it needs to get information from, and what to retrieve. The template also has all the information it needs on how the retrieved data should be displayed on the users Web browser. This allows Cold Fusion to generate HTML pages that are dynamic.

Create a Template

Templates are created and viewed the same way as HTML files. All you need to create a template is a text editor, such as NotePad, and a Web browser, such as Netscape Navigator. I am going to create a template that will process the query that I created a while back in my HTML file. Please open your text editor and enter the following code to create your template file:

Listing 7.4   RESULTS.DBM

```
<dbquery Name="Department" DataSource="cf examples"
    sql="select DepartmentName
```

```
            FROM Departments
            WHERE Department_id = '#Form.Department#' ">


<dbquery Name="Courses" DataSource="CF Examples"
    SQL="SELECT *
            FROM CourseList
            WHERE Department_ID = '#Form.Department#' ">


<html>
<head>
<title>Cold Fusion University Course Search</title>
</head>
<body>


<h1>Test Query Results</h1>
<hr>


<dboutput Query="Department">
<h3>Courses Offered by the #DepartmentName# Department</h3>
</dboutput>


<dboutput Query="Courses">
#CourseNumber# - #CourseName# (#CourseLevel#) <br>
</dboutput>


<p>
<hr>
</body>
</html>
```

Okay, now save this code as RESULTS.DBM. Make sure that you save this file in the template subdirectory. This will be under the Cold Fusion main directory: C:\CFUSION\TEMPLATE.

Now you need to view your SEARCH.HTM file that you created earlier. Enter the following URL:

http://127.0.0.1/search.htm

in your Web browser. Doing so will bring up your original HTML file that allows you to search. Now click on the Submit Query button, and you should get a live HTML document returned to you (see Figure 7-14). This live HTML document was generated by Cold Fusion, based on your search.

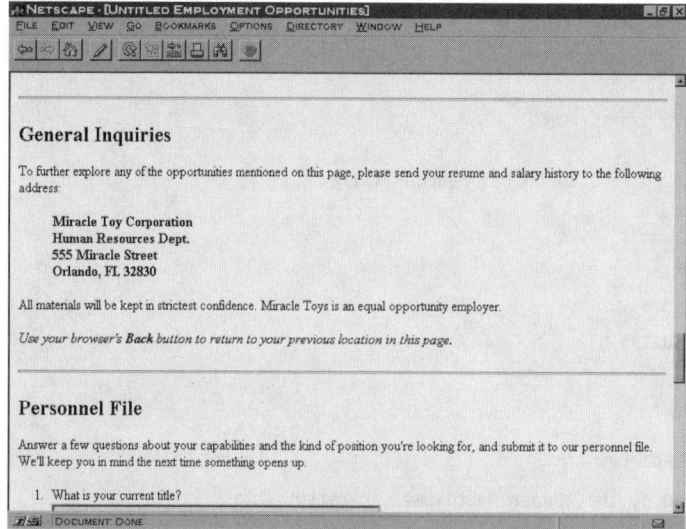

FIGURE 7-14

You did it. This is the live HTML Web page generated by Cold Fusion.

The live HTML document displays the fields that you set up in the template file. Each page is retrieved from the database, generated by the template file, and displayed back in your Web browser. This is just one of many cool applications that you can develop in Cold Fusion.

Employee Database

The following example demonstrates how users who have access privileges can edit and add users to a database from an intranet Web page.

Figure 7-15 shows the intranet page that allows the user to add or edit users in the database.

The screen shown in Figure 7-15 was generated by a file called MAIN.DBM. MAIN.DBM is a template that allows the user to specify a record that is to be edited or to add a record to the database. Cold Fusion reads specific tags in the code that allow it to interact with the database. You will need Cold Fusion to try out this example for yourself. You can download a trial version from `http://www.allaire.com/`. You can also see many demos on how to create dynamic Web pages at this URL. On with the first file:

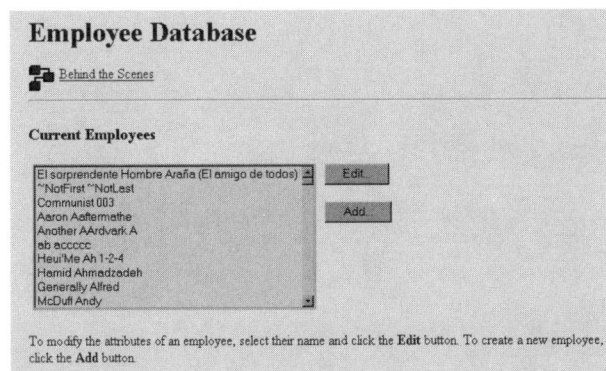

FIGURE 7-15

This example demonstrates how applications can be deployed quickly and with little maintenance to allow rapid development of new applications for users.

Listing 7.5   MAIN.DBM

```
<!-- This template is the main template that displays a list of  employees in the
database -->


<!-- If the update parameter is sent then run this update -->
<DBIF #ParameterExists(Employee_ID)# is "yes">


<DBUPDATE DATASOURCE="CF Examples" TABLENAME="Employees">


<DBELSE>


<!-- If the insert parameter is sent then run this insert -->
<DBIF #ParameterExists(Email)# is "Yes">
<DBINSERT DATASOURCE="CF Examples" TABLENAME="Employees">
</DBIF>
```

```
</DBIF>

<!-- Use DBQUERY to retrieve all information from the table 'Employees' in the Data
➥Source 'CF Examples'. -->

<DBQUERY NAME="Employees" DATASOURCE="CF Examples" SQL="SELECT * FROM Employees ORDER BY
➥LastName">

<HTML>

<HEAD><TITLE>Employee Database Example</TITLE></HEAD>

<BODY>

<H1>Employee Database</H1>
<P>
<a href="/cfpro/examples/employee/detail.htm"><img src="/cfpro/examples/how.gif" border=0
➥align=middle></a>
<a href="/cfpro/examples/employee/detail.htm">Behind the Scenes</a>
<HR>
<P>


<H3>Current Employees</H3>

<!-- This DBOUTPUT takes all records from the Employees table (selected above) and
➥displays the Name Values as hyperlinks. Note that the Employee ID is passed in the URL
➥which will allow the next template to use the ID to gather more detailed information
➥about that employee -->

<TABLE><TR>

<FORM ACTION="/cgi-
shl/dbml.exe?action=query&template=/cfpro/examples/employee/update.dbm" METHOD="POST">
```

```
<INPUT TYPE="hidden" NAME="Employee_ID_required" VALUE="You must select an employee to
➥edit.">

<TD>

<SELECT NAME="Employee_ID" SIZE=10>
<DBOUTPUT QUERY="Employees">
<OPTION VALUE="#Employee_ID#">#FirstName# #LastName#
</DBOUTPUT>
</SELECT>

</TD>

<TD VALIGN=TOP>

<INPUT TYPE="Submit" VALUE="   Edit...  "> <BR>

</FORM>

<FORM ACTION="/cgi-shl/dbml.exe?action=query&template=/cfpro/examples/employee/new.dbm"
➥METHOD="POST">

<INPUT TYPE="Submit" VALUE="   Add...  ">

</FORM>

</TD>

</TR></TABLE>

<P>To modify the attributes of an employee, select their name and click the <B>Edit</B>
➥button. To create a new employee, click the <B>Add</B> button.
<P>
<HR>
```

```
[ <a href="/cfpro/examples/examples.htm">Example Applications</a> ]
[ <a href="/cfpro/getstart.htm">Getting Started with Cold Fusion</a> ]
</BODY>
</HTML>
```

The next file displays the information about the employee that you select, and allows you to edit the record. This is the UPDATE.DBM file that follows:

Listing 7.6   UPDATE.DBM

```
<!—- This template allows a user to update data about an employee in the database —->

<!—- This query retrieves the employee information from the Employee database using the
➥employee ID to search —->

<DBQUERY NAME="GetEmployee" DATASOURCE="CF Examples" SQL="SELECT * FROM Employees WHERE
➥Employee_ID=#Employee_ID#">

  <HTML>
<HEAD><TITLE>Employee Database Example</TITLE></HEAD>
<BODY>
<H2>Edit Employee Record</H2>
<HR>
<DBOUTPUT QUERY="GetEmployee">
<H3>#FirstName# #LastName#</H3>
<FORM ACTION="/cgi-shl/dbml.exe?template=/cfpro/examples/employee/main.dbm" METHOD=POST>
<!—- Primary Key Fields —->
<INPUT TYPE="Hidden" NAME="Employee_ID" VALUE="#Employee_ID#">
<!—- The 'DBIFs' below are used to determine which value should be selected as the
➥default when the information is displayed —->
<pre>
Dept:<SELECT NAME="Department">
<OPTION VALUE="Sales" <DBIF #Department# is "Sales">selected</DBIF>>Sales
<OPTION VALUE="Accounting" <DBIF #Department# is "Accounting">selected</DBIF>>Accounting
```

```
<OPTION VALUE="Engineering"  <DBIF #Department# is
➥Engineering">selected</DBIF>>Engineering
<OPTION VALUE="Administration"  <DBIF #Department# is
➥Administration">selected</DBIF>>Administration
</SELECT>
Name:<INPUT TYPE="Text" NAME="FirstName" VALUE="#FirstName#" SIZE=12> <INPUT TYPE="Text"
➥NAME="LastName" VALUE="#LastName#">
Email:<INPUT TYPE="Text" NAME="Email" VALUE="#Email#">
Phone:<INPUT TYPE="Text" NAME="Phone" VALUE="#Phone#">

</pre>
<INPUT TYPE="Submit" VALUE=" Update Record ">
</FORM>
</DBOUTPUT>
<HR>
[ <a href="/cfpro/examples/examples.htm">Example Applications</a> ]
[ <a href="/cfpro/getstart.htm">Getting Started with Cold Fusion</a> ]
</BODY>
</HTML>
```

Take a look at Figure 7-16 to see what this looks like when it's read by your browser.

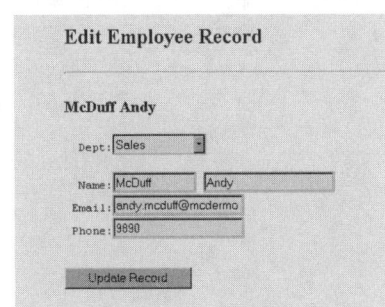

FIGURE 7-16

By selecting the Edit option, you can now edit employees in the database.

The UPDATE.DBM file allows you to edit any employee record. In the example in Figure 7-16, I am editing Andy McDuff's record. By just clicking in the text fields, I can change any of the items and then finish the update by hitting the update record button.

The last file is the NEW.DBM file. This allows you to add new records to the database. It displays a blank template into which you can enter information. Figure 7-17 shows the template with some new information that I have started to enter into it.

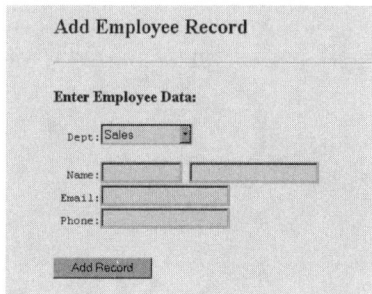

FIGURE 7-17

Here you can enter new employee data into your intranet database.

Listing 7.7   NEW.DBM

```
<!—- This template allows a user to insert a new employee record into the database —->
<HTML>
<HEAD><TITLE>Employee Database Example</TITLE></HEAD>
<BODY>
<H2>Add Employee Record</H2>
<HR>
<H3>Enter Employee Data:</H3>
<FORM ACTION="/cgi-shl/dbml.exe?template=/cfpro/examples/employee/main.dbm" METHOD=POST>
<INPUT TYPE="Hidden" NAME="FirstName_required">
<INPUT TYPE="Hidden" NAME="LastName_required">
<INPUT TYPE="Hidden" NAME="EMail_required">
<INPUT TYPE="Hidden" NAME="Phone_required">
<pre>
Dept:<SELECT NAME="Department">
<OPTION VALUE="Sales">Sales
<OPTION VALUE="Accounting">Accounting
<OPTION VALUE="Engineering">Engineering
<OPTION VALUE="Administration">Administration
</SELECT>
```

```
Name:<INPUT TYPE="Text" NAME="FirstName" SIZE=12> <INPUT TYPE="Text" NAME="LastName">
Email:<INPUT TYPE="Text" NAME="Email">
Phone:<INPUT TYPE="Text" NAME="Phone">
</pre>
<INPUT TYPE="Submit" VALUE=" Add Record ">
</FORM>
 </DBOUTPUT>
<HR>
[ <a href="/cfpro/examples/examples.htm">Example Applications</a> ]
[ <a href="/cfpro/getstart.htm">Getting Started with Cold Fusion</a> ]
</BODY>
</HTML>
```

Summary

I have covered ways to set up your intranet home page, develop templates that can be used for different department functions, and do simple interaction with a database to allow interaction with a product called Cold Fusion.

What's Next!

Now it's on to forms. I'll examine how you can use forms in your organization to collect content from users, make password interfaces, and more. I'll look at the different form tags used in HTML, and provide plenty of code examples as well.

PART III

Advanced Intranet
Programming

Chapter | 8

Forms

A good friend of mine recently returned from one of those humungous Web conferences where they have about 10,000 sessions telling you how everyone is getting, or is going to get, rich on the Web. You know the ones: You don't sleep for three (or four) days and the "geek factor" is off the scale. Later, you're on the plane looking out the window and wishing that the darn plane could go a lot faster because you see that you *need* to land right now because you *must* get in front of your PC, and when you finally crank it up your Web page starts to load and you start to feel dizzy and sick to your stomach at the sheer petrified and uninteractive look of your static Web pages. Ugh! How could you have let this happen? You thought you knew every HTML trick and workaround there was.

Thought is the operative word here. Remember that geek at the conference (who couldn't have been more than 17—don't get me started) who said, with a trace of a smirk, that "static Web pages and sites" were "dead"; "interactive" and "dynamically-generated" Web pages and sites were the future of the Web. Remember how you snickered and thought to yourself, "As if I need to hear this. Wonder if the buffet is still open?" But now, sitting here staring at your pages, you realize . . . the geek was right! Interactive or database-driven Web pages and Web sites are the next wave, and one of the main doorways or tickets of admission will be *forms*—and interactive ones, at that.

Is this description based on a true story? Most of it. A friend did actually come back from one such conference and, yes, he did make the statement that "static Web pages and sites" were soon to be a thing of the past. If you need proof, then head right on over to the following sites:

```
http://corteza.acns.nwu.edu/prh/videograb/VideoGrabber.acgi
```

When you select the link to go to the preceding site, a CGI script is run on the NWU server that loads an image (.JPG, in this case), taken by a "webcam" showing what looks to be some sort of Computer Learning Lab. Check back every so often and this image changes; you might even see an actual person in the frame. This is a very simple example of how a Web page can be made more "interactive." You are asked only to select the link—no form is required, but this page does utilize a CGI script, which is the critical component that is also used in a Web form.

If you would like to see a site for which nearly all (if not all) of the information transmitted is generated by scripts, then head over to `http://www.pathfinder.com`. This site is very interactive and gives you the choice of having one of the following: a text-based site, Java site, and non-Java site.

Up until the past few months or so (actually, longer back then that, but who's counting?), the majority of Web pages and sites were created by someone or a group of someones, and then the content was posted to a Web server. There it would sit until either you or I would fire up our browser and stumble onto the humble hyperlink or hotlist entry that would lead us to their site. Once there, we were treated to the dreaded "static Web pages." This was, and still is to some degree, cool for quite some time, because everyone seemed to be on a more or less equal footing as far as Web page and site creation went. But, all good things must pass (as Mr. G. Harrison once said, or sang), and people started clamoring and clicking for more interaction on their pages and their sites. Animated GIFS (once touted as the "poor man's Java") were becoming passé and downright annoying. Even the dreaded "blink tag" (or <BLINK>—hey, try it yourself and see if you aren't annoyed!) was starting to look like a long-lost friend.

Using fill-in forms on your Web pages was a step in the right direction, because the user was in a very real sense "interacting" with your Web page. A typical fill-in form would have the user entering information into text boxes, clicking on radio buttons, and making selections from drop-down boxes, after which the Submit button would be pressed and the completed form would be whisked away to a server, where our old friend the CGI script would process the form. After the form was processed by the CGI script, the resultant information would most likely be sent to the owner of the form. Figure 8-1 and the following HTML code show an example of a typical form that you might see on a Web page.

```
<HTML>
<HEAD>
<TITLE>Miracle Toys Annual Christmas Survey</TITLE>
</HEAD>
<BODY>
<H1>Miracle Toys Wants Your Opinion!</H1>
<FORM ACTION="/cgi-bin/toys.cgi/work/survey.template" METHOD=POST>
Your name: <INPUT TYPE="TEXT" NAME="name" SIZE=30><BR>
Your e-mail address: <INPUT TYPE="TEXT" NAME="FROM" SIZE=25>
<INPUT TYPE="HIDDEN" NAME="SUBJECT" VALUE="Survey Results">
<P>
<B>What's your favorite toy?</B>
<INPUT TYPE="RADIO" NAME="toy" VALUE="teddybear"> TeddyBear
<INPUT TYPE="RADIO" NAME="toy" VALUE="barbiedoll"> Barbie Doll
<INPUT TYPE="RADIO" NAME="toy" VALUE="horse">A Horse
<INPUT TYPE="RADIO" NAME="snack" VALUE="kite"> A Kite
<P>
<B>How much money do your parents make?</B>
<SELECT NAME="money" SIZE=3 MULTIPLE>
```

```
<OPTION>20-40K
<OPTION SELECTED>50-80K
<OPTION>Not Much
<OPTION>A Whole Lot
</SELECT>
<P>
<B>Tell us about your investment portfolio</B><BR>
<INPUT TYPE="CHECKBOX" NAME="stocks" VALUE="Yes">Stocks<BR>
<INPUT TYPE="CHECKBOX" NAME="bonds" VALUE="Yes">Bonds<BR>
<INPUT TYPE="CHECKBOX" NAME="coins" VALUE="Yes">Coins
<P>
<TEXTAREA NAME="comments" ROWS=4 COLS=30>
Any other comments?
</TEXTAREA>
<HR>
<CENTER>
<INPUT TYPE="SUBMIT" VALUE="Submit Survey">
<INPUT TYPE="RESET" VALUE="Clear Form">
<H2>Miracle Toys says——Thank You!</H2>
</CENTER>
</FORM>
</BODY>
</HTML>
```

The form in Figure 8-1 is typical of the type that you will find strewn throughout the Web. Notice that, in the preceding code, I have boldfaced the line of HTML code that tells the browser where to send the form—in this case, to the cgi-bin where the information will be processed and then sent on to the owner of the form. The form simply won't do anything without the needed CGI script to help it on its way.

My intention in this chapter is not to delve too deeply into CGI (if at all). I cover CGI in a later chapter; my goal at this juncture is to explore exactly how the front-end or the Web form itself is created and put together *before* it goes to the server to be processed. I take you through a somewhat painful if necessary forms tutorial, which I enliven with a sprinkling of examples of useful and cool forms that I have found on the Web.

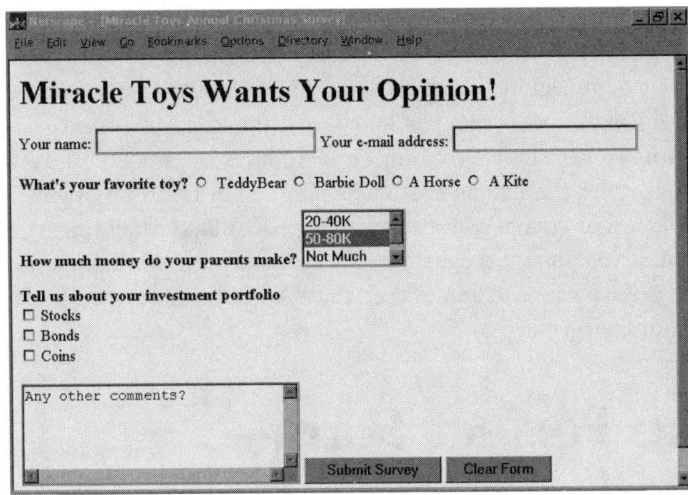

FIGURE 8-1

*A typical Web form
showing all sorts of user
input options.*

Oh, and if you just have to know more about CGI scripts and would also like to see a
bunch of useful examples showing how wonderful CGI scripts can be to your Web life,
then I highly recommend that you head over to the following URL:

`http://worldwidemart.com/scripts`

This is the address for *the* source (also known as "Matt's Script Archives") on the Web for
CGI scripts and other script-related subjects. Don't miss it. The important place to go for
ideas on this site is to the gallery of real-world examples showing actual, living and
breathing people who have used Matt's CGI scripts on their very own Web pages.

CGI Scripts

Although I have just mentioned that I will not dig too deeply into CGI, I couldn't pass
up an opportunity to set the stage for what happens with your form after you create it.
Please keep in mind that a much more detailed exploration of CGI takes place in
Chapter 10.

Say that you have created a Web page and built some nice survey forms that will gather
data from all those who take the time to fill out and submit the form back to you. This is
what happens when they click on the ol' Submit button: The information that they submitted is sent to a program on your server. This program is called a CGI script (and can
be in Perl, C, or a variety of other languages). The CGI script takes the submitted information, processes it, and then shoots it back to the server and back out to the owner of
the data—who is probably you.

The place where the CGI script resides is called the cgi-bin, which, for security reasons, is usually located in a directory on the server. Because a CGI script is what is called an *executable*, your system administrator won't be too keen on giving you much access to the cgi-bin (at least until you can prove that you know what the heck you're doing!). This, then, is why the cgi-bin is kept in its own directory—to limit the amount of damage that could be done to the system through an executable program of nefarious origins. So, don't take it personally when your system administrator laughs out loud when you ask for access to the cgi-bin. If you go visit the system administrator, or send that person some scripts that actually make sense (and work), then the SA will be more open to allowing you to poke around in the cgi-bin.

Building the Perfect Form—Tags Included

Before you actually build your form, you must make a decision concerning the method that you would like to use for sending the form's data to the server for processing. You can choose from two methods: POST and GET. Without getting into a long discussion of which is better than the other, let me go out on a limb and say that you should probably choose POST for the majority of your forms. Why? Just do it—just POST that form! Okay, the problem with the GET method is that if you have a form with a lot of data to process, the server may "choke" on the form and some of your data may end up on the proverbial cutting floor. POST does not suffer from this choke factor and is therefore the better choice.

<FORM> (The Form Tag)

This tag has both opening and closing attributes. You can have as many forms on a page as you like, or can fit, but you can't "nest" them as you can with ordered and unordered lists, for example. The <FORM> tag has the following attributes:

- ◆ method: This is how the form will be submitted. Remember that you can choose from either GET or POST, but also remember that you are going to choose POST, right? I thought you would.

- ◆ action: This attribute is used to indicate what script will be used by the server to process the form when it arrives.

<INPUT> (The Input Tag)

This tag indicates that some sort of input is on its way. The attributes for the <INPUT> tag are as follows:

- ◆ type: This is the type or kind of form element that will appear within the <INPUT> tag.

- ◆ name: This is literally the name of the element within the <INPUT> tag. You can choose any name that you want for the name attribute, but picking one that is a good description of your element makes sense, obviously; doing so helps others who may look at your code.

- ◆ hidden: This attribute is used when the form needs to send information to the server but the user doesn't need to see what is happening. For example, a user might submit information on a form, and then that information is used to create or invoke a second form, which would then be processed and sent back to the owner of the form. A hidden field is used because the user does not need to know how all this is happening, and probably doesn't care. (P.S. Just because the field is "hidden" doesn't mean that people can't see it— just view the source code and you quickly find the hidden fields.

- ◆ size: This attribute allows you to create a larger text box in your form. Please try to keep your size attribute at 50 or under so that your text box will not roll off the side of the screen.

Your Very First Simple Form

Don't panic. Building a form is pretty much the same as building a Web page: you are just using plain old HTML. Sure, there are a few new tags, but nothing to really worry about. You'll try a real simple one to see what I mean. Take a look at this code and Figure 8-2.

```
<html>
<head><title>Your First Form!</title></head>
<FORM METHOD="POST" ACTION="http://hoohoo.ncsa.uiuc.edu/htbin-post/post-query">
<INPUT type="text" name="text"><big>Your Name?</big><P>
<P>
<INPUT TYPE="submit" VALUE="Submit Query"><br><br>
<input type="reset"  value="Start Over">
</form>
```

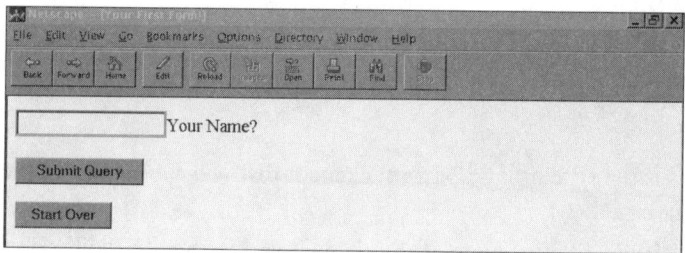

FIGURE 8-2

Your very first simple form.

Was that easy, or what? Try this form out for yourself; it will actually work. Just type your name or any other text entry and then press the Submit button. The form will be sent to the URL listed in the action attribute of the preceding <FORM> tag. Try it, you'll like it. Invite some friends over and sit back and smile as you while away the hours typing your name, then Bill's name, then Jane's name, then Bill's name again—submit, submit, submit.

I want to fool with this form just a bit so that you can explore some neat things that you can do with the text field in the preceding example. No matter how small your text box is on the screen, users will be able to type as much or as little text into it as they choose. You can still make the text box larger on screen, if you like, by inserting the size attribute that I mentioned previously in the <INPUT> tag description. Figure 8-3 shows the effect of using the size attribute, allowing you to enlarge your text box.

But first, a look at the relevant code:

```
<INPUT type="text" name="yourname" size=50><big>Your Name?</big><P>
```

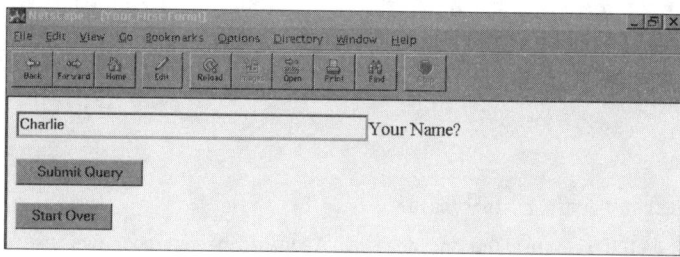

FIGURE 8-3

Your very first form with a wider textbox.

Can you see the difference? I sure hope so. Does it really bother you that your users might have the audacity to type an unlimited number of characters into your text box—maybe just to spite you? Well, then, just insert the maxlength attribute, and bingo: they are now limited in the number of characters that they can put there.

What about inserting a password capability? Sure, just add the password attribute to the <INPUT> tag. This is *not* a truly secure password; that is, it could be intercepted after being sent, because it is not encrypted. The password attribute simply inserts asterisks (*) in place of any text that you type (to preclude anyone who might be looking over your shoulder from reading what you type). Figure 8-4 shows the result of inserting the password attribute.

The relevant code follows:

```
<input type="password" name="secret">
```

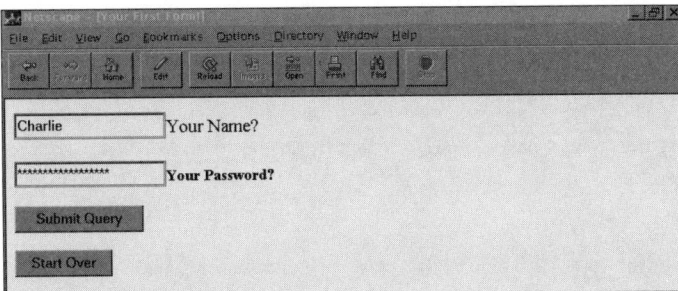

FIGURE 8-4

Your very first form using the password *attribute to create a* password *field.*

Using Radio Buttons and Check Boxes in Your Forms

So far, the forms that you have created have been "interactive" to some degree, but what if you wanted to make your form truly interactive (and even fun, to boot)? Should you sprinkle it with cool graphics? Maybe, but would that help you sell more Miracle toys to unsuspecting consumers? No. What you need is a way to allow visitors to your site to be able to pick and choose items that they might like to purchase. You want your customers to be able to virtually shop on your site. How? You will accomplish this feat through the use of radio buttons and check boxes.

Radio Buttons

In a list of radio buttons, you can select only one item. After you select one item, the other items become deselected. (Trying to select more than one can help you pass the time if you are, for instance, waiting for plane or even a train: just select one item and then try to select another, all the while seeing whether you can select more than one item at a time . . . bet'cha can't). Anyway, please make sure that all of your name attributes are the same, assuming that you are creating a group of radio buttons. Each value attribute must be unique so that the server script knows which value it is receiving.

Now, put your very first form aside and build something completely different (see Figure 8-5).

```html
<html>
<title>Radio Buttons</title>
<FORM METHOD="POST" ACTION="http://hoohoo.ncsa.uiuc.edu/htbin-post/post-query">
Type in your street address: <INPUT NAME="address"><br>
Type in your phone number: <INPUT NAME="phone"> <p>
Yes, we want your money.  Choose a method of payment: <p>
<ol>
<liI> <INPUT TYPE="radio" NAME="payus" VALUE="cash" checked>Cash
<li> <INPUT TYPE="radio" NAME="payus" VALUE="check"> Check
<li> <I>Credit card:</I>
<ul>
<li> <INPUT TYPE="radio" NAME="payus" VALUE="mastercard"> Mastercard
<li> <INPUT TYPE="radio" NAME="payus" VALUE="visa"> Visa
<li> <INPUT TYPE="radio" NAME="payus" VALUE="americanexpress">
     American Express
</ul>
</ol>
<table width=50%>
<tr align=right valign=top>
<td valign=top><input type="submit" value="SENDMONEY">
</tr>
</table>
</form>
</html>
```

Notice that I slipped a small table into this form with radio buttons; check out the code. This allowed me to place my Submit button where I wanted it, which made *me* happy, anyway.

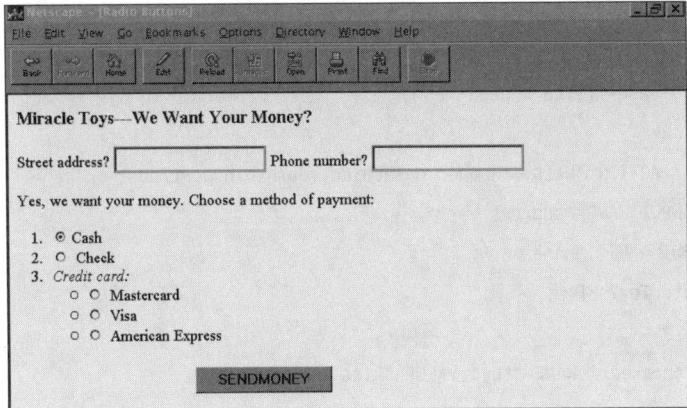

FIGURE 8-5

"Please send us money"—a form with radio buttons.

Check Boxes

Unlike radio buttons, check boxes allow you to select multiple or more than one item at a time from a list of items. In the following form example shown in Figure 8-6, you can select either the kite, the bicycle, the teddy bear, or any combination of the three, including all three simultaneously.

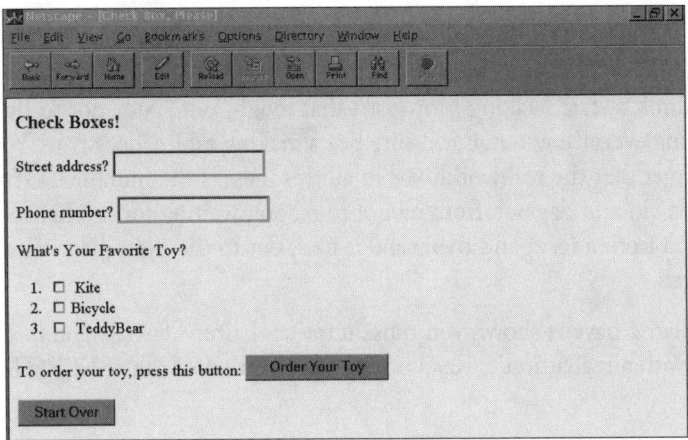

FIGURE 8-6

A simple form with some check boxes included.

```
<html>
<head>
<TITLE>Check Box, Please</TITLE></head>
<h3>Check Boxes!</h3>
<FORM METHOD="POST" ACTION="http://hoohoo.ncsa.uiuc.edu/htbin-post/post-query">
Street address? <INPUT NAME="address"> <P>
Phone number? <INPUT NAME="phone"> <P>
What's Your Favorite Toy? <P>
<OL>
<LI> <INPUT TYPE="checkbox" NAME="toy" VALUE="kite">
     Kite
<LI> <INPUT TYPE="checkbox" NAME="toy" VALUE="bicycle">Bicycle
<LI> <INPUT TYPE="checkbox" NAME="toy" VALUE="teddybear">
     TeddyBear
</OL>
To order your toy, press this button: <INPUT TYPE="submit"
VALUE="Order Your Toy"> <P>
<input type=reset   value="Start Over">
</FORM>
</html>
```

So, what do you think so far? Making forms isn't that tough, is it? Nah, not really. It's kind of a pain laying everything out, but it sure beats making tables, doesn't it? You bet it does. Just don't forget that the real workhorse in all this mess is the humble CGI script, just sitting there day in and day out, from reboot to reboot, waiting for its chance to process information from a form and then send it back out to the right place with all the data neatly arranged.

Hey, you know what? I haven't shown you those ultra-cool, drop-down menu boxes that you see on forms with a real attitude. Read on for a description of the <SELECT>, or selection, tag.

Two guys on the future of the Web

Recently, I was speaking with a colleague from our IS department; we were once again sitting back and conjecturing about the state of the Web and how the management of our current Web pages and sites would have to change as things continued to grow. And, yet again, the subject of using "dynamic HTML" and "database-driven content" was brought up. We agreed that the database was going to be one of the next important evolutions in Web design and development. We also agreed that one important method for getting to those databases was the interactive, or fill-in, form.

Most important, we agreed on a particularly critical point: Databases would eventually become the means to "serve" Web pages to our users.

\<SELECT\> (The Drop-Down Menu or Scrolling List Tag)

The \<SELECT\>, or selection, tag is useful when you might have a rather long list of selections for your users to choose from when they are inputting data. For example, you might want your users to select a particular month or even day of the week as part of their form input. Putting all 12 months or even days of the week wouldn't make sense because that would take up unnecessary space on your form and make it look very cluttered. So, using the \<SELECT\> tag, you could put in all those months but they would not show up on-screen until and unless the user chose to click on that particular option.

The \<SELECT\> tag has both opening and closing attributes. The \<OPTION\> tag is used to indicate the individual options that will appear as a result of the \<SELECT\> tag being used. Ever wonder where you want to go on the Web (or in your life?) and how you might get there? Take a look at Figure 8-7 to add some direction to your Web-life; there you will find an excellent example of the use of the \<SELECT\> and \<OPTION\> tags.

```
<html>
<title>Drop Down Menus</title>
Where Do You Want To Go Today?
<HR>
<FORM METHOD="POST" ACTION="http://hoohoo.ncsa.uiuc.edu/htbin-post/post-query">
Where do you want to go today?
<SELECT NAME="what-to-do">
<OPTION>yahoo.com
```

```
<OPTION SELECTED>word.com

<OPTION>catz.com

<OPTION>dogz.com

<OPTION>hyperthink.com

</SELECT> <P>

How would you like to get there?<P>

<DL>

<DD>

<SELECT NAME="how-to-do-it">

<OPTION>Mosaic

<OPTION>Arena

<OPTION>Explorer

<OPTION SELECTED>Netscape

<OPTION>Internetworks

<OPTION>Lynx

</SELECT>

</DL>

To submit your choices, press this button: <INPUT TYPE="submit"

VALUE="Submit Choices"> <P>

To reset the form, press this button: <INPUT TYPE="reset" VALUE="Reset">

</FORM>

</html>
```

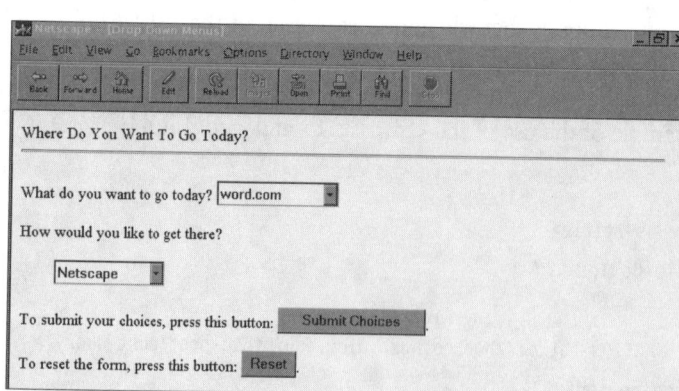

FIGURE 8-7

Drop-down menus allow you to organize your content and make your intranet forms more user friendly.

NOTE: Notice the <HR> tag that I inserted at the top of the screen. The <HR> tag is a definite friend of the family when it comes to laying out and designing fill-out forms. A well-placed <HR> tag can create a nice, clean, crisp layout for your form, as well as prevent your form elements from crashing into one another. Try it. Also, please notice that when you pull the page up in your browser, you will see the options `netscape` and `word.com` already selected (so to speak). Why? Check the preceding code a bit closer and you will see the `selected` attribute inside the <OPTION> tag for both `netscape` and `word.com`. You can change which option will come up as the selected one by moving the `selected` attribute to one of the other options listed in your code.

Remember back when I discussed radio buttons? The <SELECT> tag works similarly in that you can typically choose only one option; the others become deselected. There is a way around this if you wish to allow your users to have "multiple input" capability. How? Just insert the `multiple` attribute into the <SELECT> tag, as shown in Figure 8-8. I also add a `size` attribute of 3. The code looks like this:

```
<SELECT NAME="what-to-do" multiple size=3>
<OPTION>yahoo.com
<OPTION SELECTED>word.com
<OPTION>catz.com
<OPTION>dogz.com
<OPTION>hyperthink.com
</SELECT> <P>
```

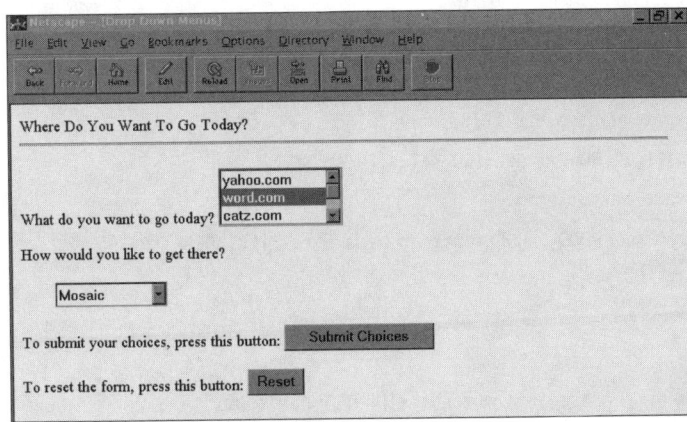

FIGURE 8-8

Drop-down menu with a `multiple` *attribute of* `size=3`.

If you loaded this code into your browser (as you should be doing in all examples), then you may have noticed a "bug" in the form. Did you? Go ahead, I'll wait while you start your computer and open your browser. :>... Okay, ready now? Good. The bug I speak of occurs when you try to make a `multiple` selection from your Options menu and you find that you still can't pick more than one. Did that happen? If so, try holding down the Ctrl key as you make your `multiple` selections. This will work 99 percent of time; I'm not responsible for the other 1 percent.

The <TEXTAREA> Tag

The <TEXTAREA> tag is pretty cool in that it will let you put gobs and gobs of text into a form field and still allow your users to see most of what they are typing in. This capability is very useful for e-mail or comment/suggestion forms that require more than one line of text entry. This tag requires an opening <TEXTAREA> and a closing </TEXTAREA> tag. The <TEXTAREA> tag has the following useful attributes assigned to it:

- ◆ `name`: Identifier of what is being sent to the CGI script
- ◆ `rows`: Height of the text area; that is, number of rows of text
- ◆ `cols`: Width of the text area in columns

A helpful example, and one that you will probably use again and again, is the "comment or feedback" form. Figure 8-9 is an example of a typical comment or feedback form.

```
<html>
<title>Your Comments And Feedback</title>
<FORM METHOD="POST" ACTION="http://hoohoo.ncsa.uiuc.edu/htbin-post/post-query">
Please enter any positive comments below:<br>
<TEXTAREA NAME="positive" ROWS=3 COLS=40></TEXTAREA>
<P>
Please enter any negative comments below:<br>
<TEXTAREA NAME="negative" ROWS=1 COLS=20></TEXTAREA> <P>
Please enter your name below:<br>
<TEXTAREA NAME="username" ROWS=1 COLS=40>Your Name Here</TEXTAREA> <P>
<table width=100%>
<tr align=middle>
<td>
To submit your comments, press this button: <INPUT TYPE="submit"
```

```
VALUE="Submit Comments"> <P>

<td valign=top>

To clear the form, press this button: <INPUT TYPE="reset"

VALUE="Clear Form">

</tr>

</table>

</FORM>

</html>
```

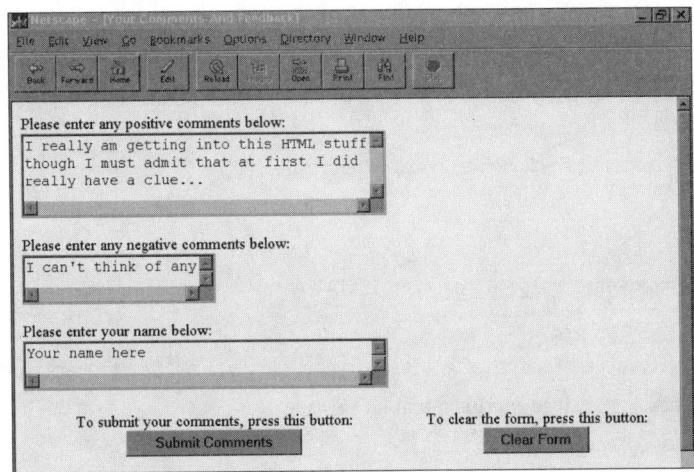

FIGURE 8-9

*Comment and feedback
form with multiline
<TEXTAREA> tags.*

Another form that you will use quite often is the e-mail form (not to be confused with the "mailto"). Take a look at Figure 8-10 to see how a typical e-mail form is constructed:

```
<HTML>

<HEAD>

<title>Your Very First email Form</title>

</HEAD>

<body bgcolor=#b4b2b4 text="#841111" link="#5c0000" vlink="#5f3030">

<BODY>

<center><H2>Your Very First Email Form</H2>

</center><p>

<form method=POST action="http://gandhi.cs.luorc.edu/cgi-bin/FormMail.pl">

<input type=hidden name="recipient" value="info@hyperthink.com">
```

```
<dl>
<dt><i>Subject :
    <dd><SELECT name="subject">
        <OPTION>My suggestions
        <OPTION>My comments
        <OPTION>Add my email address
        <OPTION>Others
        </SELECT>
<dt>Your Name :
    <dd><input type=text name="realname" size=30>
<dt>Your Email Address :
    <dd><input type=text name="email" size=30>
<dt>Your Phone :
    <dd><input type=text name="phone" size=30> (not required)
<p>
<dt>Message :
<dt><TEXTAREA name="comments" cols=40 rows=2></TEXTAREA><p>
</dl></i>
<dt><input type=submit value="Send this"> <input type=reset value="Start Over"><p>
<input type=hidden name="required" value="email,realname">
<input type=hidden name="env_report"
value="REMOTE_HOST,REMOTE_ADDR,REMOTE_USER,HTTP_USER_AGENT">
<input type=hidden name="print_config" value="realname,email">
<input type=hidden name="sort" value="order:phone,comments">
<input type=hidden name="title" value="Thank You for Your Suggestion">
<input type=hidden name="bgcolor" value="#FFFFFF">
<input type=hidden name="text_color" value="#000000">
<input type=hidden name="link_color" value="#FF0000">
<input type=hidden name="vlink_color" value="#0000FF">
<input type=hidden name="return_link_url" value="http://www.lamar.edu/">
</form>
</BODY>
</HTML>
```

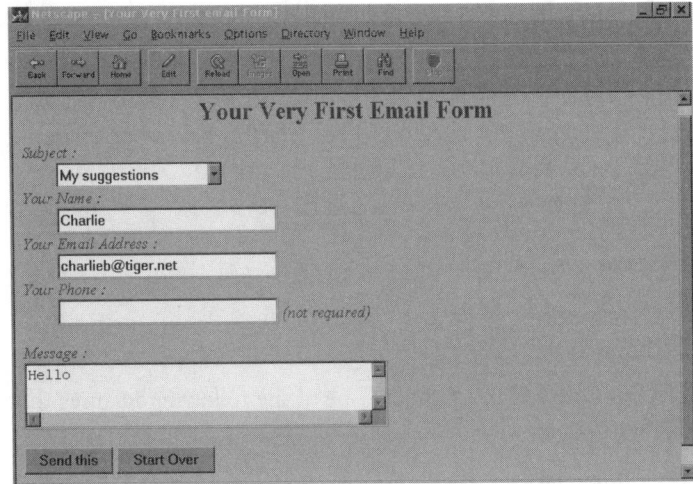

FIGURE 8-10

Your very first e-mail form.

This is a typical layout for an e-mail form. Notice the line of code that looks exactly like this:

```
<form method=POST action="http://gandhi.cs.luorc.edu/cgi-bin/FormMail.pl">
```

This as, you know, is the <FORM> tag with the POST method being used to send the form data to the script on the server at the address shown (which is where the CGI script called "FormMail.pl", meaning "perl," resides). For this example, I'm using this script to show you how an e-mail form works. You should contact your Internet Service Provider (ISP) or the System Administrator in your company to set up your form to access your own cgi-bin; in other words, don't send your e-mail (or other) forms through other people's servers unless you have their permission. This is, at the least, a courtesy on your part, and something you should seriously consider as part of being a good netizen. Hey, and most times, if you ask them they will probably let you.

The Netscape PowerStart

I've talked a bit about how dynamically-generated Web pages, or pages that are created based on a user's input, are going to be the next evolution of the Web and the corporate intranet. I haven't really shown you an example of one, however. Therefore, I want to take you to the one of the coolest (IMHO) sites that I have seen. Users must use their own input to create their own personal home page. Here is the address of the Netscape PowerStart page:

```
http://personal.netscape.com/custom/index.html
```

Go and check it out for yourself, and in the meantime, I'll show you some screen shots to whet your appetite.

This is just the beginning (see Figures 8-11 and 8-12). Netscape gives you an example of what you might like; now you can just click on Quick Start to have your entire page built, or you can build it piece by piece from the following selections:

- General
- Business and Finance
- Sports & Entertainment
- Technology

You are getting closer, but now you must choose one of the following features that will appear on your PowerStart page:

- Netscape Headline News
- Notepad
- Stock Ticker

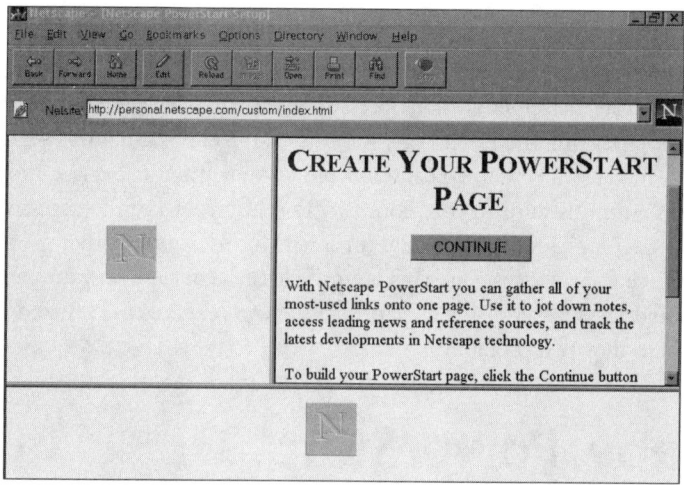

FIGURE 8-11

Creating your own personal Netscape home page with PowerStart.

I chose the Notepad and the Stock Ticker (see Figure 8-13)—I get too much news already.

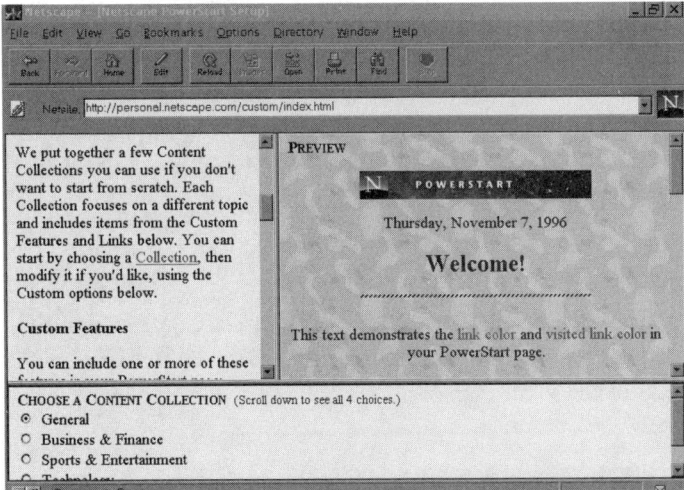

FIGURE 8-12

Selecting your personal collection of content information.

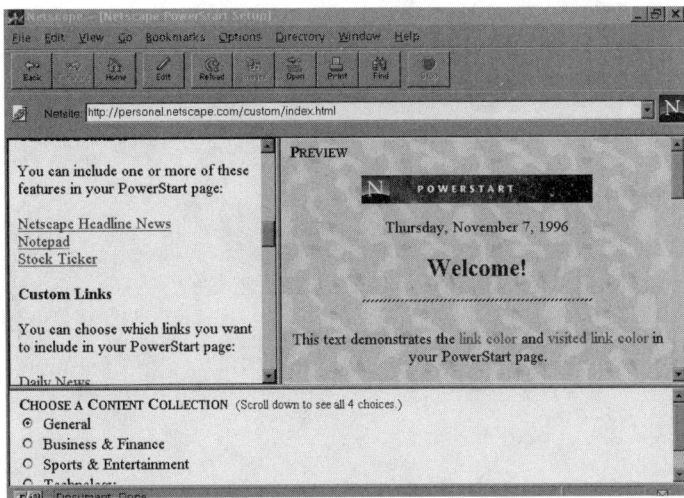

FIGURE 8-13

Selecting features.

Now you have the opportunity to put in some custom links that you would like to see appear on your page, along with any personal links. You can choose from the following suggested list:

◆ Daily News, Business & Finance, Sports, Technology News, Internet Search, Reference

◆ Entertainment, Shopping, Netscape, Cool Sites

◆ Personal Links

I chose Technology News, Internet Search, and Cool Sites. The following are my choices under each of those categories (see Figure 8-14):

◆ Technology News: @ Computerworld; CMP's TechWeb; c|net; IDG; InfoWorld Electric; Macworld Online; Netscape World Online; NetworkWorld Fusion; The New York Times CyberTimes; PC Week Online; Red Herring; ZDNet

◆ Internet Search: A2Z; AltaVista; Excite; Infoseek; Lycos; Magellan; search.com; shareware.com; Yahoo

◆ Cool Sites: Cool Site of the Day; Interesting Devices Connected to the Net; Netscape What's Cool; Point Communication's Best; Project Cool Sighting; Yahoo's Picks of the Week

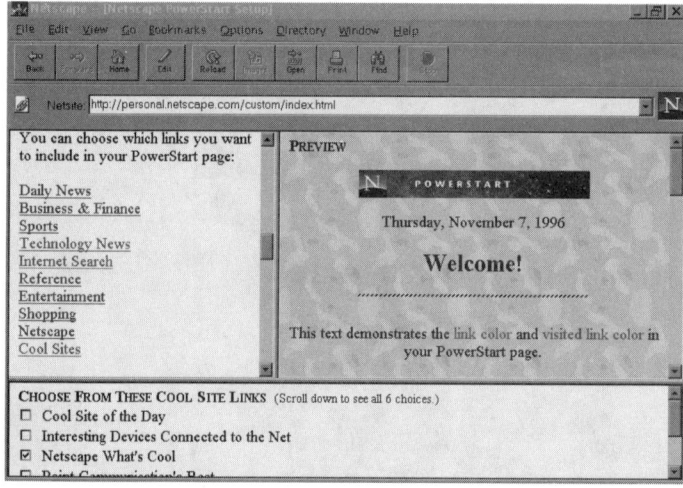

FIGURE 8-14

I'm adding some custom links.

Note: Keep in mind that you can build your page totally from scratch if you have a lot of time on your hands. I'm just picking from some subtle suggestions that Netscape has provided us right before our very eyes.

Now it's page layout time. You can pick from about 17 different page layouts, or style sheets. You click on the one that you like and it will appear in the main frame of the page so that you can see whether you like it. I have chosen a sort of watery-looking blue background for no particular reason (see Figure 8-15).

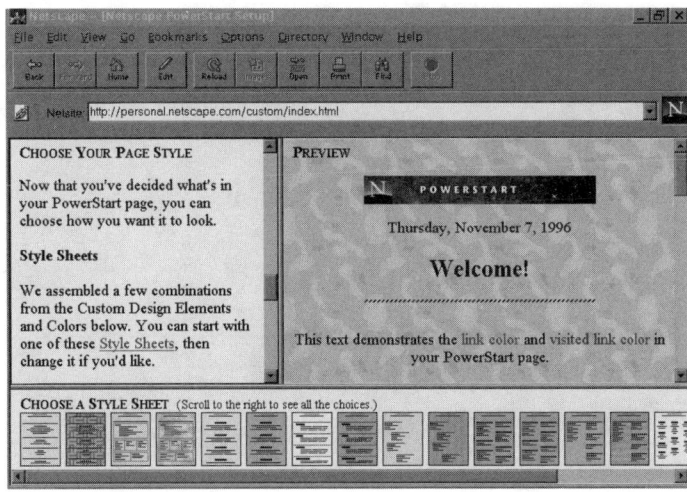

FIGURE 8-15

Choosing my page layout.

Now I can choose from the following elements:

◆ Layout

◆ Personal greeting or headline

◆ Headline image

◆ Horizontal lines

◆ Custom colors

First, I look at my layout choices (see Figure 8-16). I have about nine from which to choose.

I am not going to choose a personal greeting or headline. I will choose a headline image because these look good to me (see Figure 8-17).

I've just decided to click on Build, which brings a message up reminding me to bookmark my personal page so that I can find it again (see Figure 8-18).

As you can see in Figure 8-19, my little notepad is just floating in a pool of water with a message for me already— "Don't forget to bookmark this page, bunky!" I am not sure I am too hot on the layout that I chose, however; it seems a bit long and drawn out.

If you decide to change any of the features or options that you choose in your own personal home page, you can click on Change PowerStart, located on the Netscape toolbar.

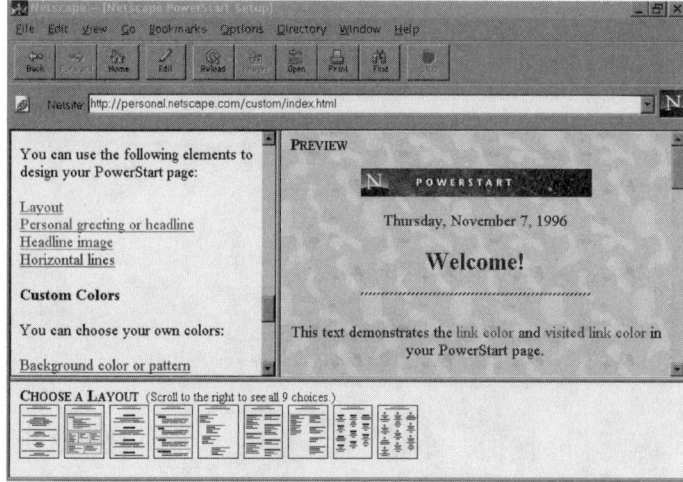

FIGURE 8-16

Choosing my actual page layout for elements.

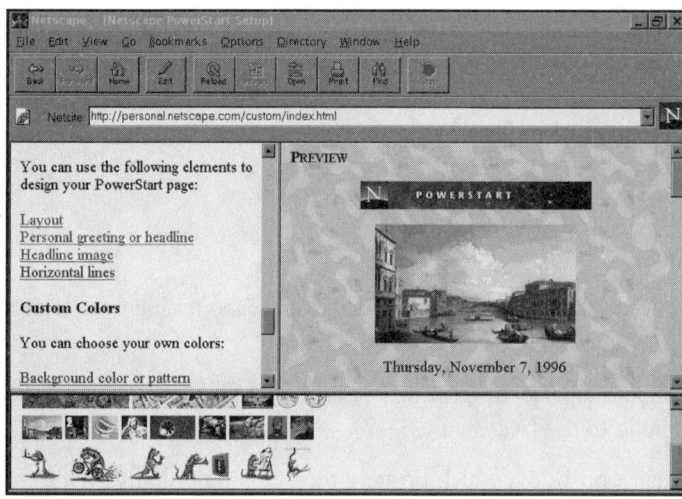

FIGURE 8-17

My own personal headline image.

Summary

Forms are the gateway to exciting, dynamically created Web pages. Gone are the days of static Web sites. In this chapter, you've seen how a very simple form is laid out; you've also seen an interactive form full of radio buttons and check boxes. I discussed the use of the password field, and pointed out the advantages of using POST rather than GET

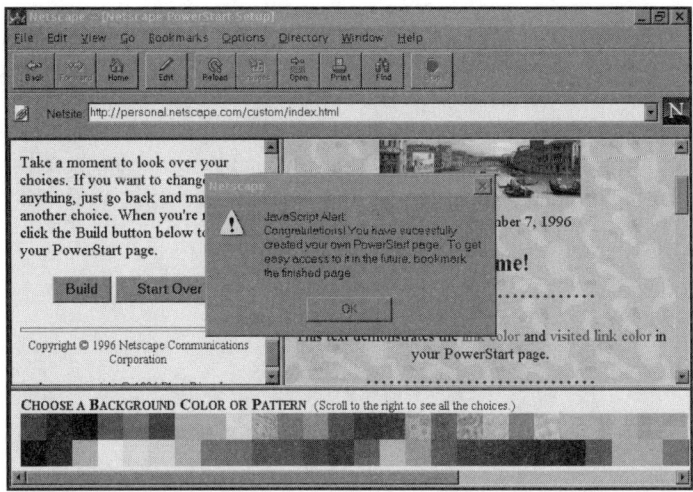

FIGURE 8-18

Clicking on Build brings up the bookmark reminder message.

FIGURE 8-19

My completed Netscape PowerStart personal home page.

when defining your form's input method. Finally, you have found that creating a form consists of using some new HTML tags—anybody can do it. Bear in mind, though, that even the most well-designed form will just sit there without our good friend, CGI, which is covered in Chapter 10.

What's Next!

I continue with the theme of interactivity and move on to Chapter 9 to take a look at adding value to your intranet with the use of audio, video, and animation. You'll see how to use these elements to enhance your intranet while also conserving bandwidth.

Chapter | 9

Audio, Video, Animation, and More

It's time to add some audio, video, and dancing bologna (animation) to your intranet, and I do just that in this chapter. I cover the different audio and video formats, and ways to embed audio and video in your pages. You'll see how to make some java applets with an easy-to-use tool called AppletAce. Then, it's on to voice and video over the intranet. You'll see several applications that allow you to talk and send video over the Internet and intranet.

Hypermedia

Static pages get the job done for certain tasks, but the ability to create pages with sound, animation, and video brings your intranet to the next level. Hypermedia encompasses all of this interactive content that can be created and displayed on your intranet. With the ability to add audio and video into your hypertext, you can now create intranet pages that do more than just display your corporate information. With audio, you can add small sound bites to Web pages, and users can listen to parts of a presentation, hear a sound bite from the CEO on the current quarter's earnings, or just hear a phone ring when they connect to the phone repair department. Longer audio files can be downloaded over the intranet and player with plug-ins, such as Real Audio, directly in your Web browser.

Video can also be sent over the intranet. Video clips can be played inline in your Web presentation, or downloaded and played with a video plug-in player. While I'm on the subject of audio and video over the intranet, I should mention that you need to keep your eye on your LAN/WAN infrastructure issues and make sure that you are not sending 20MB video clips over your intranet and slowing down mission-critical applications. Make sure to keep your files small, and when you use applications such as audio and video, do so to enhance your application, not just because it is the latest cool thing to do.

I often find myself learning the latest cool application that has come out for the intranet about once a week. The danger here is that there are new applications coming out every minute. The next one on the line does everything better and faster than the last one— and does it in 3D, even, with dancing bologna.

Resist the lure of "the latest and coolest," and focus instead on the task that you're trying to perform. Choose applications that fit that task. After you decide on applications, close your eyes to the other ones and finish your project. If you don't, you will always be finding other applications that you want to learn and try out, and you'll never get anything accomplished. When you get your project done, you can go back in your free time and look for other applications to try. Trust me, though: you won't have much free time.

Audio

Now you can get started on your journey into HyperMedia, beginning with audio. Of course, you need a microphone and a sound card in your computer in order to record and play back audio. Your users on your intranet will also need a sound card and speakers, or, better yet, headphones, so that they can hear the audio clips that you are sending on the intranet. You also need to make sure that your users have the correct helper application and/or plug-in to play audio clips. Most browsers are now coming with the popular plug-ins included when you download them.

Whatever sound recorder you use, it needs to be able to allow you to define the sampling rates, so that you have control over the quality of the sound that will be produced. The typical sample rate can range from 5.5 kHz on up to 44kHz. You can also select from mono or stereo output.

The other value to be aware of when you create sound files is the resolution. This is the number of bits. You will see files on intranets with 8 or 16 bits. The trick here is to get great sound quality while still keeping your sound files small. You also have the ability to record in mono or stereo. Stereo gives you the sound that you are used to from your home entertainment system, but it also gives you tremendous overhead.

Consider the business reason, or purpose, for using sound files on your intranet. If it is a simple voice-over broadcasting information over the intranet, which is a good business application, then you need to consider sampling rates, resolution, and stereo or mono output. File size and bandwidth are your main enemies and need to be examined before you install audio on your intranet. Audio files can grow in size rapidly, so experiment with low sampling rates and mono output.

The Different Audio Formats

Many audio file formats are popular on the WWW and on intranets. This section discusses five of them that are good for intranets because they have great compression and are widely used on the WWW today.

AU

This is the most common file format used on the Internet today, and for good reason. The files are small, and many audio players are available to play .AU files, which explains their popularity. The trade-off with .AU files is the sound quality. The quality, close to what you get from an old clock radio, is not the best available, but if you are just sending voice files at 8 kHz over your intranet, .AU files are just right.

MPEG

MPEG is also one of the more common file formats on the WWW today, because MPEG files can be compressed very easily and they don't lose much sound or video quality. MPEG files are used in both audio and video to compress files down to a manageable size for the WWW. MPEG is also a good choice for intranets. You can offer .AU files for users who want to hear information quickly, and you can also offer the larger MPEG files for the users who do not mind waiting a bit longer to get a higher-quality sound.

Streaming Audio

The newest form of sending audio over the WWW is a method called streaming audio. The most popular audio type used to transmit streaming audio over the WWW today is RealAudio. RealAudio and other audio compression types like it use a special server to send audio streams to a helper application that is on the user's computer. As soon as enough of the file has been received, the audio will begin playing on the user's computer. Streaming audio relies on good bandwidth rates.

RealAudio is one of the most popular streaming audio players. It can be downloaded from the WWW at:

```
http://www.realaudio.com
```

You can also get pricing information and find out about the RealAudio Intranet Server. With a RealAudio Intranet Server, your organization can deliver messages in the form of audio rather than just standard text-based Web pages. This type of message can enhance your computer-based training applications and also enhances time-sensitive information on your intranet. With the RealAudio server, you can offer your intranet users on-demand streaming audio right from within your intranet. The server also allows you to monitor the RealAudio traffic that is traveling over your intranet.

Streaming audio does not come without a price, however. It starts around $4,000 for the RealAudio Intranet System 100. Reductions in training costs and the improvement in communication in an organization, however, justifies the cost very quickly.

WAV

The WAV format comes from Microsoft and is a standard for Window systems. The sound quality that you get in .WAV files is a very high-quality sound—CD quality; however, the file size of these files is very large. You can cut down file size by using a mono channel output rather than multichannel. You also have a choice of sampling rates that allow you to cut down the file size. The average file on the Web and your intranet is a single-channel, 8-bit, 8kHz sample. This type of file cuts down on the quality of the audio, but allows you to sleep at night not worrying about bandwidth.

MIDI

MIDI files are the most popular format to send electronic, synthesized music over the WWW. They are popular because they are much smaller than regular digital audio files, and can be created and edited fairly easily. If you want to play a quick tune on your intranet site, say as an introduction to a presentation or a training Web page, then take a look at http://www.headspace.com. There you can listen to a sample of catchy tunes that you can use on your intranet. You can also purchase the collection for around $25, and use the music on your intranet.

This takes me into a few basic HTML tags and an introduction to Java Script, to use for including these MIDI files in your Web pages. So, take a look at some ways to embed audio files in your intranet pages.

Embedding Audio in Your Intranet Pages

You can include audio files in your intranet pages with the use of a new Netscape HTML tag. The <EMBED> tag is used to incorporate plug-ins for your Web pages.

To include a sound file, such as a MIDI file in a Web page, you need to include a line of code to your page that looks like this:

```
<EMBED SRC="file.extension" WIDTH="number" HEIGHT="number">
```

The EMBED SRC= tells the browser where to find the correct plug-in, and the WIDTH and HEIGHT numbers tell the browser how much room to allow for the plug-in. You can also add other attributes that will allow features such as looping of the audio file, and automatic start, which has the file start when the Web page loads. The code for this would look like:

```
<EMBED SRC="file.extension" WIDTH="number" HEIGHT="number" AUTOSTART=TRUE LOOP=TRUE>
```

> **NOTE:** When you include MIDI files in your pages, always make sure to set your WIDTH and HEIGHT equal to 2, as follows:
>
> WIDTH="2" HEIGHT="2"
>
> Netscape may crash if you set either of these settings to a 0.

If you are having difficulty getting your MIDI file to play, make sure that you have the correct path set in your HTML code. It is easiest to place your sound files in the same directory as your HTML and image files. You can make a special folder for them, but just make sure that the path to them is correct.

Setting Up the Server

So, your MIDI file plays fine on your computer, but when you load it up to the intranet server, it doesn't work anymore. This can happen with many new applications. In such a case, your server needs to be set to handle .MID files. To set your server so that it sends the correct MIME type for .MID files, add in the following:

MIME Type	Description	Suffix/File Extension
audio/x-midi	MIDI	.mid
audio/midi	MIDI	.mid

Changing Your Tune

Before I move on to the section on video, I want to show you some tricks to gain more control over your music. Right now, you can play an audio file when a user hits a page, but when the user travels to another Web page, the audio file stops, or you have to embed another audio file on that page as well. The audio on the second page also starts from the beginning. A way exists, though, to have the audio file play continuously across Web pages. You can do this with the help of frames. Netscape introduced frames to help divide the browser surface and allow greater control. Frames can also be made invisible by setting the frame dimensions to 0. Doing this enables you to have a hidden frame on all of your Web pages that contains the audio file, while your user navigates in the large content frame from page to page. Now your audio will travel with you from page to page, uninterrupted.

Now go a step further and make your audio file selection a bit more interesting. To do this, you'll take a quick step into JavaScript. JavaScript is a scripting language that allows you to do some interactive content on the client's end. Using JavaScript, you can write a few lines of code that will allow you to change the audio file each time a user hits your Web page. This way, users can be greeted with a different audio file each time they hit a particular Web page. Another nice thing about JavaScript, owing to its being a scripting language, is that you just add it in to your HTML file and you're done.

To come up with a new audio file each time the user visits your Web page, you'll use the numbered file approach. In this approach, you use JavaScript to generate a random number to choose the audio file that will be played. The number will be set in the range that you select. So, if you have 10 audio files, you could name them FILE1.MID, FILE2.MID, FILE3.MID, and on up to FILE10.MID. After you have named your audio files, you need to place them in the same folder as the HTML file that is going to play these files.

Here's how it works. The JavaScript will create a random number between 1 and 10, and then create a file using the filename plus the random number.

Here is the JavaScript:

```
<SCRIPT>


    total_files = 15;
    files_name = "your-files-prefix";


with (Math) {document.writeln ('<EMBED SRC="' + files_name + (round (random () *
(total_files - 1)) + 1) + '.mid" AUTOSTART=TRUE WIDTH=2 HEIGHT=2 VOLUME=100
LOOP=TRUE>')}


</SCRIPT>
```

> **NOTE:** There are quite a few tags out there that are not following the HTML standards. < EMBED> is one of them. Because it's a Netscape tag, it should eventually be added to the latest HTML specifications. You do take a risk, however, that might come back to haunt you when you use these new tags before they are widely accepted.

You should place this script in your HTML page. Also, make sure that you place it near the bottom of the HTML page. This script will run almost as is. You just need to replace two areas with your own information. In the line that says:

```
total_files = number
```

enter the total number of MIDI files that you will be playing.

In the following line that says:

```
files_name = "your files prefix";
```

enter the prefix for your MIDI files between the quotation marks. As an example, say that you have 10 MIDI files called FILE1.MID, FILE2.MID, and on up to FILE10.MID. You should enter:

```
files_name = "file";
```

This script tells the user's computer to use the filename that you just told it, and to add a random number to the end of that filename, plus the extension .MID. The file that is found in the same directory as the Web page then starts to play.

Video

The first thing you need to know is that video presently has some challenges and limitations if you are expecting the high quality video to which you are accustomed from other mediums. To deliver broadcast quality video to your desktop, you would require either a large amount of local storage space—RAM and disk—for downloading video files, or a high-bandwidth LAN connection for real-time (streaming) video.

So, for now I focus on how you can send lower-quality video clips over an intranet and still get the message across. You can do this by sending fewer frames per second, using smaller screen sizes, and using compression techniques. All these methods are widely used on the WWW and can be adapted for intranets.

Creating Video Clips

There are several basic ways to make video clips for your intranet applications. The first way produces the most professional, best quality video clips for your intranet, but it comes at a price. This setup includes owning a high-end system that has been made to do video production and editing, or at least buying and assembling the necessary hardware and software for a Windows 95 or NT machine. UNIX machines such as SGI Web Force come with everything you need to jump into video clip production and editing.

If you can't afford a box like that, then your next alternative is to get your hands on a video capture card for your machine. This card enables you to hook up a video camera, VCR, or other type of video device to your computer. With it, you can import your video frame by frame and edit it in one of your favorite software packages. You will most likely wind up with one of Adobe's products, such as Premiere. You should also get some basic software with your video capture board that you can use to start creating your video clips.

Video clips on the WWW are not like traditional video and are created by using the old-fashioned flip book, animation techniques. You are creating your video by rapidly changing images from one to another, which creates the illusion of movement. Your video input, when run through a video editing package, will allow you to see the video frame by frame. You can take short video clips, or remove frames to bring your video file size down.

Another way to obtain video clips for your intranet is by buying them or finding them on the WWW. You'll find lists of sites on the WWW that have piles of video clips in different formats. Finding video clips on the WWW that are useful and fit your particular need is almost impossible, however, for the following reasons:

1. You need to make sure that they are free and that you can use them on your intranet.

2. You have to find them in the correct format, and they need to contain useful information.

3. When you search for videos that are in, say, .AVI format, Yahoo! is not going to bring up a nice list of video clips that discuss training issues in Corporate America. You are more likely to get a list of cyber-smut in .AVI format.

If you are seriously considering adding video clips to your intranet, then your best route is to make an investment in hardware and software and some quick training to bring you up to speed.

For those of you who don't have the bandwidth or pocket cash just quite yet, several other ways exist to deliver animation and video on your intranet. I am going to cover animation with an application called GIF construction set, which will enable you to create some basic animations. Then, I show you MacroMedia's AppletAce that allows you to create Java Applets with ease for doing animated bullets, rollovers, and billboard type displays. But first, I want to show you how to include an .AVI video clip directly in your Web page. I also want to explain a few of the more popular video formats.

Popular Video Formats

Many different video formats are available on the WWW and in use on intranets, but I discuss only two of the more common ones so that I can move on.

MPEG

I discussed MPEG previously in the section on audio formats. MPEG is popular because of its ability to compress audio and video down to small files that still keep the quality of the original file. This compression lets you send quality multimedia over your intranet without taxing your bandwidth too much. A great number of applications also allow you to create MPEG files, and there are players that allow you to view MPEG along with other popular formats.

AVI

AVI format was created by Microsoft. You will also hear it called video for Windows. If you have Microsoft Windows, then you get a copy of the media player that plays .AVI files. You'll also find several players out on the WWW that you can try out if you are looking for more features and performance. One to check out is QuickTime by Apple. It runs on both PC and MAC platforms, and can be downloaded from:

```
http://www.quicktime.apple.com/
```

Obtaining the Plug-Ins

Some popular plug-ins that you can find to display video clips are widely available on the WWW as shareware, for purchase, or even free. I describe these in the following sections.

CineWeb by Digigami

CineWeb allows you to view real-time, streaming audio-video using standard file formats (AVI, MOV, and MPG) and audio (WAV, MID, and MP2) files. No special server software is needed, so now we can all afford to put independent TV and radio-style content on our intranet. With CineWeb, it does not matter what video format you prefer. QuickTime MOV, AVI, MPG and FLC files can be viewed right inside your Netscape Navigator HTML documents using the <EMBED> tag. CineWeb also has a suite of authoring tools for creating video clips and adding them to your HTML documents. These authoring tools consist of Digigami's Weblisher and MegaPEG. Give it a try. You can download CineWeb at:

```
http://www.digigami.com/CineWebPress.html
```

ClearFusion by Iterated Systems

ClearFusion is a streaming Video for Windows AVI plug-in that you can test from its Web site. It enables any Video for Windows AVI file to be viewed inline as it's received. I already discussed how to include .AVI files within your HTML documents. Now you can include small and simple animations in AVI format to enliven a Web page. Because this player uses streaming video, larger .AVI files present no more "download downers," because film clips are seen as soon as they begin to arrive and can be replayed at full speed. ClearFusion also does not choke on corporate firewalls; .AVI files are streamed over standard HTTP connections, and no special servers are needed. You can download a copy to try at:

```
http://www.iterated.com/clrvideo/decoder/info/cp_fswin.htm
```

Including an .AVI File in Your Pages

Now that you have looked at a few of the video formats available for the Web and intranets, you can see how to add a video flip to one of your intranet pages. I add an .AVI file to an intranet page in the example that follows shortly.

Including an .AVI file is exactly like adding an image file to your Web pages. I cover adding HTML tags in Appendix A and B. You should also note that as of this writing, this is an Internet Explorer tag only. Other browsers that do not support this tag will display just a static image rather than the video clip. Netscape and Microsoft both introduce their own proprietary tags, and it takes a while for them to adopt each other's tags. So, you run into the same standard issues as with the audio tags. Multimedia embedded directly into Web pages is fairly new to the Web and intranets, so putting standards in place for these elements will take some time yet.

The attribute that you need to add to your <IMG> tag is the DYNSRC (Dynamic Source) tag.

The HTML used to insert the video clip is as follows:

```
<IMG DYNSRC="myfile.avi" SRC="myfile.gif" WIDTH=50 HEIGHT=50 LOOP=INFINITE ALIGN=CENTER>
```

What does this HTML code do?

It tells the Web browser to play the dynamic source, the .AVI file if the browser supports it. If not, then it will display the .GIF file instead. You can also set attributes such as the height and width of the .AVI or .GIF; and here, I've set the LOOP attribute to run repeatedly. In this example, I also align the image to the center of my Web page.

Microsoft's Site Builders Workshop is a place to spend the rest of your life if you want to learn about all the latest happenings in the world of intranets, WWW, and development tools. The site also has a hard-to-find but very useful page with some .AVI files that are free to download. These are not full-feature videos, but they are nice, simple .AVI files that you can add to a page here and there.

Check the site out at:

```
http://www.microsoft.com/workshop/design/mmgallry/
```

Links to Video and Audio Libraries

Another way to offer video and audio is by offering links to files that can be downloaded. This way, the files are not going to pop up and start loading when a user hits a page. Users can see an icon or read some descriptive text telling them about the files, and then they decide whether to download them and view or listen to them. You add links by making a list or catalog of files using the <A HREF> tag. Here is an example:

```
<A HREF="videos/train.avi">How to install a 7 digit line</a>(.AVI format 1200 K)
```

This HTML code creates a hyperlink to the AVI file so that users can read the description, and see the file format and file size to help them decide whether they want to take the time, and determine whether they have a player to view the file.

Animation

The use of animation enhances your intranet with an endless variety of dazzling images to prevent the catatonic trance so common in today's employees. A great many tools are available to create animation, and I go over the most popular ones that will get your icons dancing in no time.

You can use animation to emphasize an area. You can indicate to your users that an area is new, or updated, by using a flashing icon. You can also use animation to demonstrate activities and procedures that focus around training. In this section, I show you how to link several photographs together to create an animated frame that can be placed in a story about your organization, on a training page to show a user how to complete a task, or used just to add spice to your pages. These files are small in comparison to video files, but still give a nice effect and a different way to demonstrate tasks and procedures.

To create an animated GIF, you first need to have some .GIF files. These are image files that you can create in Paint Shop Pro, Adobe Photoshop, or any image-editing software.

First, you need to decide what you want to demonstrate. Here, I want to demonstrate, in a computer-based training section on the intranet, how to clear a hotel room for a guest. I need to create the content for the Web page, and I can do so in a text editor or an HTML editor. After I put in the text and format it as HTML, I can add a single animation on the page, or multiple animations, to demonstrate the training material the user is reading. I don't like millions of flashing, dancing icons on my pages (they can be distracting), so I want create just one animated GIF for the page, and make it demonstrate the four steps to cleaning a hotel room.

I have several options at this point:

◆ Create drawings to demonstrate the tasks

◆ Use stock photographs or clip art

◆ Use a digital camera

◆ Take regular photographs and scan them in on a scanner

I've chosen to take four photographs, scan them into Photoshop, and work with them there. After I have the four shots and have created four .GIF images that are the exact same height and width, I can stitch them together into an animated GIF with the GIF construction set.

Here I have launched the GIF construction set and am starting to join my four images together into an animation frame by frame. Take a look at Figure 9-1.

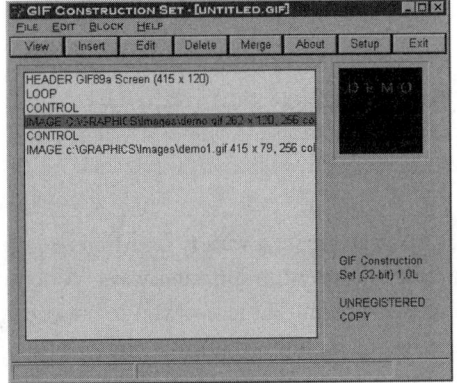

FIGURE 9-1

A GIF construction set. This enables you to link images together and then save the image as a .GIF file that you can place into an HTML page.

The GIF construction can be downloaded from the WWW at:

`http://www.mindworkshop.com`

You can use a wizard that will walk you through the entire process, as follows:

◆ It will help you create image for use on a Web page or other applications.

◆ You can choose to have the animation run once and stop, or continuously loop.

◆ If you have photographs or line art, the GIF construction set will make them come out perfectly when you choose which one you will be using.

◆ You can also select the delay between each image. Do you want the animation to move fast or at a slower pace?

♦ The last step is choosing your GIF files. You will need to tell the GIF construction set where to locate your images.

That's it. GIF construction will combine all your images into one GIF file; all you need to do is save it and then reference that .GIF file in one of your HTML pages. When the GIF is displayed, it will run through all the .GIF files at the delay option you choose. You can also preview your creations in the GIF construction set. You will have to take the same steps on your own if you forgo the wizard, but this also allows you greater control over your final .GIF image output.

> **NOTE:** The more images that you use and larger they are, the larger your final animated GIF will be. You want to try to keep these small so that the user does not have to wait to see the animated demo.

Macromedia AppletAce

AppletAce by Macromedia allows you to create animated display type Java applets quickly and easily. You'll find the program at:

```
http://www.macromedia.com/software
```

After you install AppletAce and launch it, you can create a variety of different Java applets that will allow you to display and link to content in different ways. When you launch AppletAce, you initially receive a tabbed screen that allows you to choose a Java applet to create from a drop-down menu. On this menu, you also set the size (height and width) of the applet you are creating. After you choose the applet that you want to create, and have set its height and width attributes, you are prompted with more options (see Figure 9-2).

Now I'll show you how to create a banner. It is similar to a video file in appearance, and you can add a background and a message, and you can set transitions and timing. From the applet drop-down box on this first page, choose "banner," which brings up all your other tabbed pages with additional options. The next screen that you will come across is the "text" page. On this page, enter your text message that you want to convey. Figure 9-3 shows several text boxes and drop-down boxes here that enable you to enter your message(s) and then choose the typeface, size, color, style, and effects.

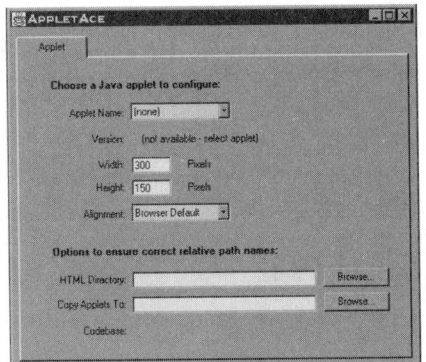

FIGURE 9-2

The opening screen for Macromedia's AppletAce is where you choose what type of applet you are interested in creating.

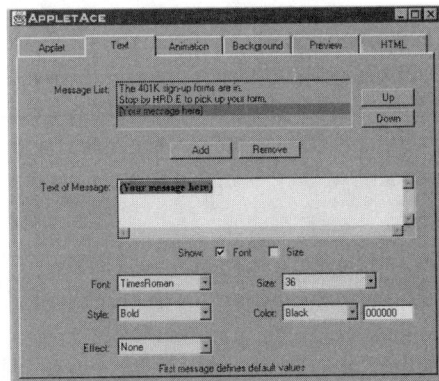

FIGURE 9-3

The second tabbed page has you type the message(s) that you want displayed in your banner.

After you have entered your message, you move on to the animation tab. Here you choose the effect that you want to create. This is the transitions, or entrance and exit effects, for your messages. You can also tell the applet text to pause in between the entrance and exit effects for a certain amount of time.

I am creating a banner that is going to go on the home page advertising the new 401K forms at HRD. I have two messages to switch back and forth between, and I've set the first message to scroll on the screen from left to left, and the second message to zoom out, pause for one second, and then zoom in. You can see these settings in Figure 9-4.

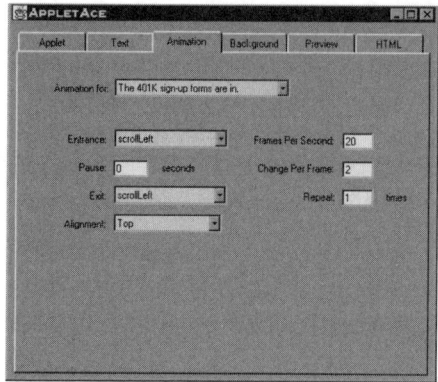

FIGURE 9-4

The animation tab lets you set the animation effects for your applet.

The next tabbed page is for setting your background for your banner. You can have a solid background or use an image file for your background. Each message that you want to display can have a different background, and you can also set hyperlinks to other Web pages or frames. This enables users to read different advertisements on your changing banner. Users can then click on the advertisement while it is up, and be transported to a Web page with more information.

I am displaying an ad for Human Resources and have the banner linked to the HRD.HTM page. I also use an image rather than a solid color for the background. This ability to use an image is a nice feature, enabling you to show an image of a product, service, or whatever you like, and then have the text describe the item. Take a look at Figure 9-5 to see how I set my background up.

The preview tab is the last step in creating your Java applet. Here you get to see your creation before you go and place it in a Web page. In the preview window, your Java applet runs so that you can see how it will look on your intranet site. You can then go back to the previous tabbed pages and make corrections and changes. Figure 9-6 shows one of the screens on my banner.

The last tabbed page is the HTML code that was created to configure this Java applet. You can save this code as a text file and place it in one of your intranet pages, or just copy and paste the text from here into your intranet page. After you place the HTML code in your Web page, you only need to copy the Java Class files that come with AppletAce into that same directory as well.

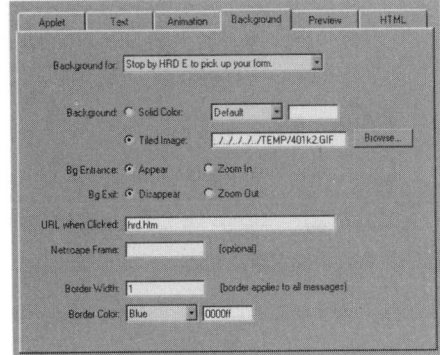

FIGURE 9-5

Here you can choose a solid background color or use an image for your banner's background.

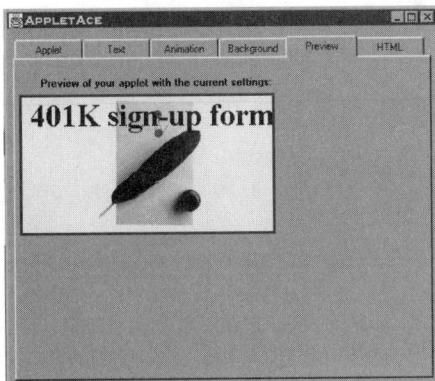

FIGURE 9-6

Preview allows you to check out your Java applet before placing it on your intranet.

NOTE: You cannot rename the Class files. They must keep their original names in order to work.

Figure 9-7 shows the HTML tabbed page in AppletAce.

You can also create other Java applets with AppletAce. Bullets, Banners, Charts, and Image Maps are currently available. Figure 9-8 shows a sales graph created on the fly with AppletAce.

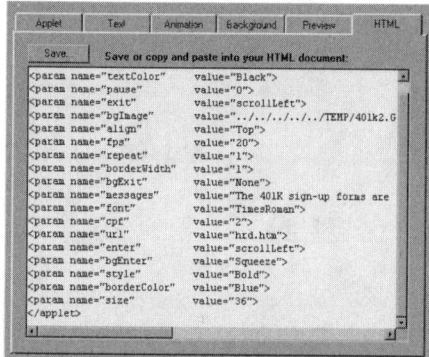

FIGURE 9-7

Copy and paste this generated Java code into your HTML intranet page, and place a copy of the Class files that come with AppletAce in the same directory—then you're set!

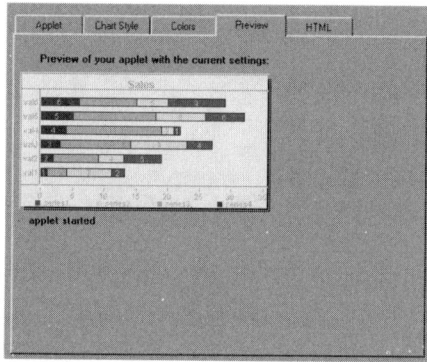

FIGURE 9-8

A chart created in a matter of seconds as a Java applet using AppletAce.

It's time to move on to some new communication tools that allow you to send and receive audio as well as collaborate on ideas with others in your organization and even worldwide.

Cool Talk and NetMeeting

Cool Talk is Netscape's Internet Phone and NetMeeting is Microsoft's Internet Phone product as well. Both of these applications do far more than the first entries into the Internet phone arena. In addition to allowing you to send voice over the Internet to anywhere in the world with no long distance charges, both of these applications have some cool collaboration tools that allow you to do *whiteboarding* (the ability to share and edit documents with other users over the Internet or your intranet) and other useful tricks. I begin with Cool Talk.

Cool Talk by Netscape

Cool Talk is available for download at Netscape's Web site. Cool Talk comes packaged with the Netscape Navigator 3.0 release. During Netscape Navigator installation, you are asked whether you want to install and have Cool Talk running in the background to answer calls. You can also launch it from your Netscape Navigator folder by clicking on the Cool Talk icon or the COOLTALK.EXE file. Figure 9-9 shows you the Cool Talk application.

FIGURE 9-9

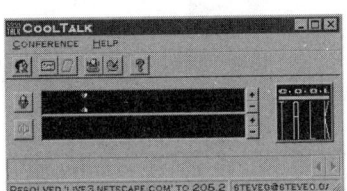

Cool Talk by Netscape allows you to use the Internet/intranet as a telephone. It also gives you a whiteboard feature and more.

If you have a high-speed connection as well as a good sound card and microphone, then Cool Talk lives up to its name (it's very cool). If you are running on a standard 14.4 modem, your sound card is only 16 bit as opposed to 32 bit, and your dial-up connection is not that great. In this case, Cool Talk is more of a fun toy than a tool.

Here is how it works. If you have a static IP address, you can run Cool Talk, and others on your Internet/intranet can call you on your computer. You have all the settings for screen calls, collect business cards from callers, and an answering machine that will take a message while you are away from your computer. For local office intranet applications, picking up the phone is still easier, but for collaboration and long-distance calls, you might want to give Cool Talk a try. These programs still are not very reliable, and both parties need to have adequate equipment so that you don't spend the first ten minutes of your call yelling at each other, "Can you hear me?"

Cool Talk has an address book that you use to store your friends' IP addresses; or, you can connect to a Cool Talk server and surf the massive listing of users who don't have static IP addresses. If you have a dynamic IP address, one that is assigned every time to log in, then you must connect to a Cool Talk server on the WWW at Netscape and tell people your login name so that they can look for you in the phone listing and then call you. The static IP address is definitely the way to go for internal intranet use. After you reach the other party, you can share ideas on the whiteboard, or send text messages back and forth in the chat area. See Figure 9-10 for a look at the whiteboard feature.

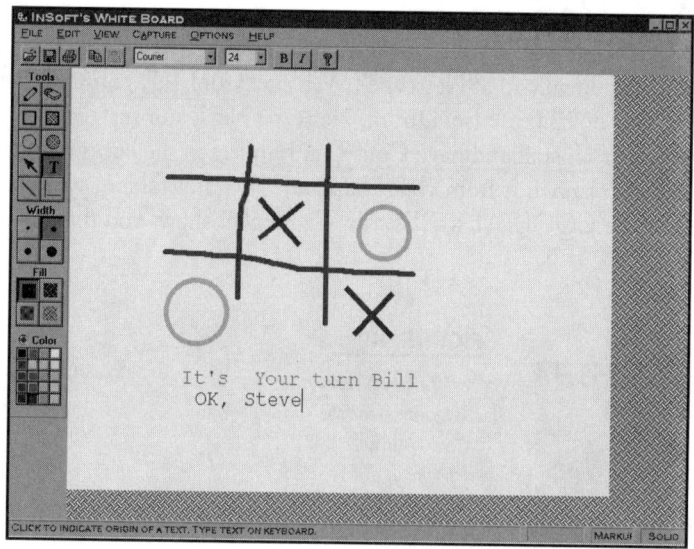

The business card feature is nice in Cool Talk. When someone calls you, a caller ID screen pops up and tells you who is calling. If you accept the call, you can view the caller's business card and save it so that you can read it at a later date. The card contains the caller's photograph and address information on it. Your answering machine will also collect business cards as well as voice messages from callers while you are away from your computer (see Figure 9-11). Neat idea.

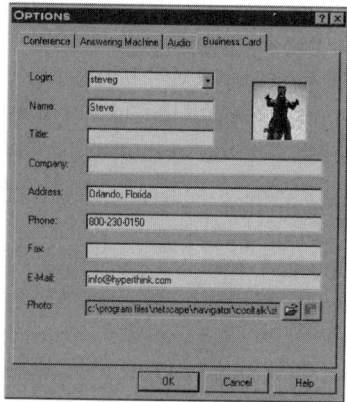

FIGURE 9-11

Cool Talk's business card information.

NetMeeting by Microsoft

NetMeeting is as cool as Cool Talk, and even offers more features that fit the business needs of an intranet.

NetMeeting also comes with Microsoft's Internet Explorer browser, and you install it during your Internet Explorer 3.0 installation. You can also learn more about NetMeeting from Microsoft's Web site at:

```
http://www.microsoft.com/netmeeting/
```

Some possible scenarios in which NetMeeting can be used to improve the effectiveness of communication between two or more people include Internet phone calls, virtual meetings, document collaboration, customer service, telecommuting, distance learning, and technical support. NetMeeting has an Internet Phone that enables conference calls involving more than one user; it also comes with a chat feature and a whiteboard (see Figure 9-12).

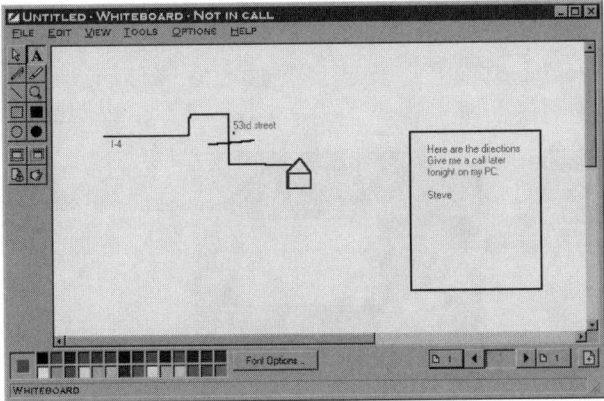

FIGURE 9-12

NetMeeting's whiteboard enables you to exchange ideas while talking in a conference call.

Multipoint Application Sharing enables you to share a program running on your computer with other people in a conference, allowing them to see the same data or information that you have on your PC. NetMeeting works with existing Windows-based programs, allowing applications to be shared transparently without requiring any special knowledge of conferencing capabilities. When an application has been shared, the other people in the conference see the actions that are performed as the person sharing the application works on the program (for example, editing content, scrolling through information, and so on). In addition, the person sharing the application can choose to collaborate, allowing other people in the conference to take turns editing or controlling the application. Each member of the conference does not need to have the given application on his or her system; this is required only of the person sharing the application. This way you can share and edit Microsoft Word documents while conferencing with several other individuals, all of whom may be in different locations.

Again, this application requires everyone to have a sound card, microphone, and a fast connection, but it is worth a beta test in your area.

PowWow

PowWow is an Internet/intranet program for Microsoft Windows that allows up to seven people to chat together, as well as transfer files and cruise the World-Wide Web as one big group. PowWow also has conferencing, and the latest version—3.0—has text-to-speech capabilities. You can host your own private conferences, use the whiteboard, and chat with up to seven others. Take a look at the Personal Communicator, whiteboard, and sound effects windows in Figure 9-13.

You can download PowWow at:

```
http://www.tribal.com/powwow/download/
```

FIGURE 9-13

PowWow, by Tribal Voice, is a chat program that is packed full of useful groupware tools.

Summary

Wow. This chapter covered a bunch. To recap: I discussed what hypermedia is and how it can be used for business purposes in your intranet. I covered several audio and video file formats, listing the advantages and disadvantages of each. I then discussed embedding audio and video files into Web pages using several different methods. There are many audio players and video players available on the WWW, and I touched on a few. I ended the chapter with some voice programs and collaboration tools.

What's Next!

Next, I discuss CGI scripts and go over examples that allow you to get those forms to work—the ones that you created in Chapter 8.

Chapter | 10

CGI Scripts
and Image Maps

Remember what you learned from the forms section in Chapter 8? It's time to create the CGI backend for those forms. I also make an image map in this chapter.

Creating Your Intranet Home Page

By far one of the more complex tasks is creating your intranet home page. The design phase should have helped you along this path so that you know what links, navigation structure, and layout you are aiming for on this page.

> **NOTE:** In this section, I again assume that you know how to design graphics and do some HTML coding. For HTML guidance, read up on Appendices A and B.

The Home Page Design

I start by looking at the sketches I made for Miracle Toy Corporation. I made notes of the areas that they wanted immediate access to from the home page, and looked at my overall design to make sure that it was clean and easy to navigate. I then fired up Adobe Photoshop and started to design the page. I decided, in the layout phase, to make the home page an image map. I could easily have made the home page a bunch of separate images and just used HTML tables to control their layout. But I did an image map instead, for two reasons:

♦ To show you how to do an image map, because there seems to be a feeling among designers that image maps are some difficult, mysterious entity

♦ Image maps allow you greater flexibility in your layout and design

The Image Map

To make an image map, you first need to create your graphic that you'll use for your Web page. I want to explain image maps a little more before I dive in. An image map allows you to take any image—a map of the United States, for example—and, with mapping tools, select certain regions and make them clickable. When I say *clickable*, I mean that you can assign a URL to that area. When the image is placed in a Web page, the user can click on different areas of the image and be taken instantly to another Web page. In the following section, I show you how this works with a map of the United States and a tool called MapEdit.

Using MapEdit

First, look at Figure 10-1. Using MapEdit, I browsed to locate the HTML page that I created in Netscape Gold. MapEdit then let me select the image I wanted to edit (MAPUSA.GIF) in the Image Filename box.

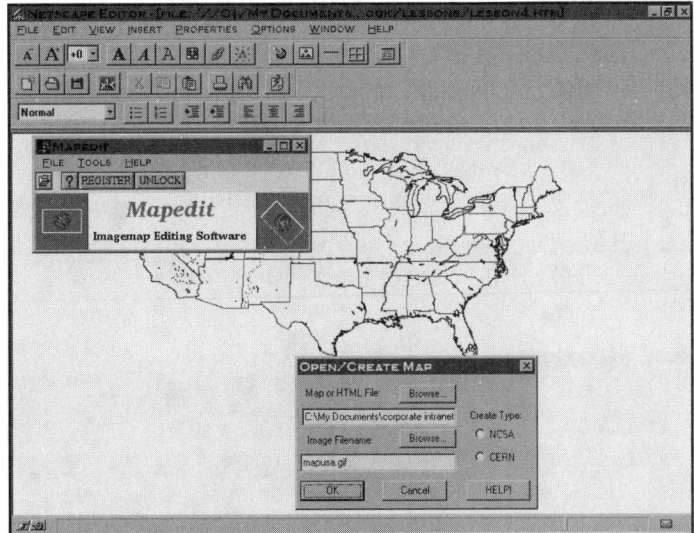

FIGURE 10-1

Using MapEdit to select an image.

That was easy enough. I just created a simple graphic of the United States and saved it as a .GIF image by using Adobe Photoshop. I then launched Netscape Navigator Gold and told it to place the image that I created in Photoshop in the center of the HTML Web page. I then saved the Web page in Netscape Navigator Gold. Then, I launched MapEdit. I told map edit the HTML file and image that I wanted to edit, and it displayed the pop-up menu that you see in Figure 10-2.

Now I have the U.S.A. map that I want to turn into an image map. I have chosen to make this a client-side image map. This means that no CGI script exists to run on the server. The advantage to this is that your server does not get bogged down trying to calculate where the user clicked on the image so that it can send back the correct Web page or result. This saves time and allows users to process everything on their end. Now I simply need to outline the state that I want to be a hot link.

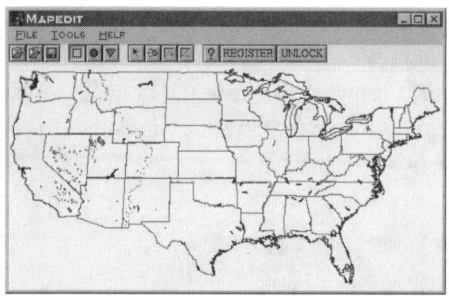

FIGURE 10-2

From here, you can create circles, rectangles, and polygons on your image. After you outline an area, you can then tell MapEdit to attach a URL to that hot area.

I chose Florida because I live there. Using the polygon tool, I outlined the border of Florida, line by line. This is the part that takes a while. When I finished outlining the hot area (Florida), I right-clicked with my mouse to tell MapEdit that I was done. MapEdit popped up the URL window that allowed me to enter the URL for this area and any alternative text that I would like to display (see Figure 10-3).

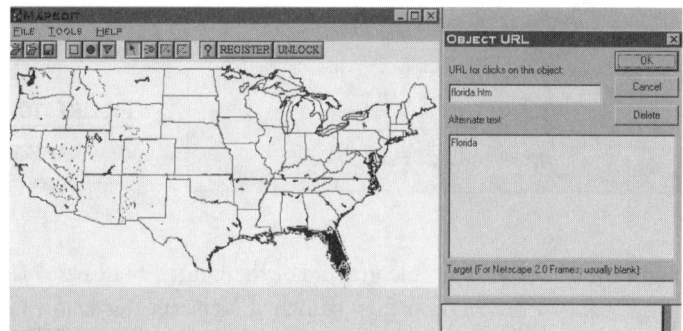

FIGURE 10-3

You can test your hot areas in MapEdit to make sure they work. Here, you can see the hot area and the URL to which it points.

If you want to outline more than one area, you need to do this for all of the states. Each object that you want to define needs to have its x and y coordinates mapped. You are mapping these points when you are tracing around the object, which in this case is the states on the map. For this example, I used only Florida. I then saved the file in MapEdit. Now, when I look at the new Web page in Netscape Navigator Gold and refresh the page, I have an image map. When I roll over the state of Florida, my mouse pointer turns into a hand that lets me know that this is a link. The bottom of Netscape's browser window also tells me that this link takes me to the FLORIDA.HTM page (see Figure 10-4). When users click on the image map on Florida, the link will take them to a HTML page called FLORIDA.HTM. I must now create the Web page FLORIDA.HTM to make the link complete.

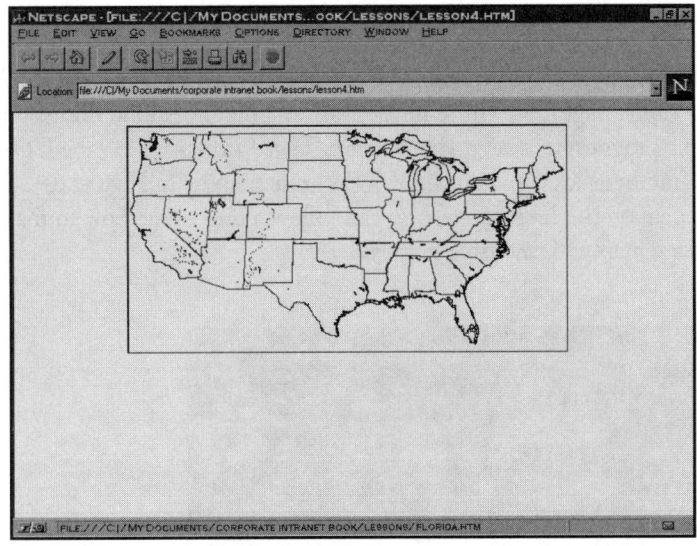

FIGURE 10-4

In Netscape Navigator, the new Web page now has the image map on it and is fully functional.

Here is the HTML code generated in Netscape Navigator Gold for this page:

```
<HTML>
<HEAD>
<TITLE>USA Image Map</TITLE>
<META NAME="Author" CONTENT="Steve Griswold">
<META NAME="GENERATOR" CONTENT="Mozilla/3.0Gold (Win95; I) [Netscape]">
</HEAD>
<BODY TEXT="#000000" BGCOLOR="#FFFFFF" LINK="#0000EE" VLINK="#551A8B" ALINK="#FF0000">
<CENTER><P><IMG USEMAP="#mapusa" SRC="mapusa.gif" HEIGHT=256 WIDTH=512></P></CENTER>
<P><MAP name="mapusa"><AREA shape="polygon" alt="Florida" coords="334,186,335,195,356,
➥197,356,201,368,197,382,208,385,232,398,243,404,249,411,229,393,191,357,188,335,188"
➥href="florida.htm"><AREA shape="default" nohref></MAP></P>
</BODY>
</HTML>
```

Try this exercise for yourself. It will take some time, and you will quickly learn that no single application exists yet that can do everything you need when it comes to creating your intranet.

When you finish here, here join me in the following section as I start to map the home page for Miracle Toys.

The Image

If you take a look at Figure 10-5, you will see the graphic that I designed for the Miracle Toys Corporation home page. The entire image was designed in Adobe Photoshop. You can use any graphic program to design your images. There are several on the CD-ROM in this book, and hundreds available on the WWW. The graphic in Figure 10-5 will be used as an image map on the home page. You can follow along to see how to make a more complex image map with multiple hot areas.

FIGURE 10-5

This image will work well for Miracle Toys as its opening to its intranet site.

I start by making the home page in Netscape Navigator Gold. By inserting the image and centering it on the home page, the effect that I want is almost accomplished. I just added some background color to make the image blend in a little better, which gives me the effect I need for a responsive intranet home page, as shown in Figure 10-6. I saved the file as an .HTM file so that I can create hot areas on the page with MapEdit.

Now I open MapEdit. I need to tell MapEdit what HTML file I want to work on and what image I want to edit. After I do so, MapEdit pulls up the image file so that I can work on it. Now I have pulled up the Miracle Toys Corporation home page. By selecting the rectangle tool, I can trace over the four hot areas that I want to define so that the user can hyperlink to other Web pages on the Miracle Toy Corporation intranet. I do this by outlining the hot areas, right-clicking on the mouse, and telling MapEdit what file to open when the user selects a point in the defined area. Figure 10-7 shows the defined areas.

FIGURE 10-6

I placed the Photoshop image in Netscape Navigator Gold and touched up to make it presentable on the page.

FIGURE 10-7

I selected the four areas on the home page and told MapEdit where to hyperlink these points to.

When you view the figure in Netscape Navigator, it still looks like a normal page with an image. Now, however, the image is an image map, so when users roll their mouse over one of the four hot areas, they will be told at the bottom of the Netscape Navigator screen where the link goes. Where the links will travel is obvious because they can see a graphic and a text description for each of these main topic areas.

Not much code is needed to generate this page. Less than one screen full of code generates this entire home page.

```
<HTML>
<HEAD>
<TITLE>Miracle Corporation Home Page</TITLE>
<META NAME="Author" CONTENT="Steve Griswold">
<META NAME="GENERATOR" CONTENT="Mozilla/3.0Gold (Win95; I) [Netscape]">
</HEAD>
<BODY TEXT="#000000" BGCOLOR="#8080C0" LINK="#0000EE" VLINK="#551A8B" ALINK="#FF0000">
<map name="miracle">
<area shape="rect" alt="The New Baby Toy Line Is Here!" coords="37,177,168,402"
➥href="babyline.htm">
<area shape="rect" alt="Visit Human Resources Anytime Day or Night"
➥coords="183,180,313,403" href="humanr.htm">
<area shape="rect" alt="Join in one of the many message forums today"
➥coords="326,180,457,403" href="messages.htm">
<area shape="rect" alt="About Miracle Toys" coords="470,180,600,402" href="aboutus.htm">
<area shape="default" nohref>
</map>
<CENTER><P><IMG SRC="miracle.jpg" HEIGHT="480" WIDTH="640" usemap="#miracle"></P></CEN-
TER>
</BODY>
</HTML>
```

I made a brief mention of server-side image maps a while back. When someone clicks on a server-side image map on your intranet, the x and y coordinates of the cursor is sent to the server. The location that was activated is then looked up on the server side, and the corresponding object is sent back to the user. Server-side image maps have several advantages and disadvantages, and, as with most things on the Web, there are alternatives.

Client-side image maps can decrease the amount of activity on your Web server, therefore increasing performance and response time for your users. Client-side image maps address the problem of getting access to your server's CGI directory. With security being such a hot topic, obtaining access to this directory is often difficult. With client-side image maps, all the files reside on the client's (browser) end, so there is no need to beg for access to parts of the server.

I now show you the HTML code from the Miracle Toys Corporation home page, and then dissect it.

```
<HTML>
<HEAD>
<TITLE>Miracle Corporation Home Page</TITLE>
<META NAME="Author" CONTENT="Steve Griswold">
<META NAME="GENERATOR" CONTENT="Mozilla/3.0Gold (Win95; I) [Netscape]">
</HEAD>
<BODY TEXT="#000000" BGCOLOR="#8080C0" LINK="#0000EE" VLINK="#551A8B" ALINK="#FF0000">
<map name="miracle">
<area shape="rect" alt="The New Baby Toy Line Is Here!" coords="37,177,168,402"
➥href="babyline.htm">
<area shape="rect" alt="Visit Human Resources Anytime Day or Night"
➥coords="183,180,313,403" href="humanr.htm">
<area shape="rect" alt="Join in one of the many message forums today"
➥coords="326,180,457,403" href="messages.htm">
<area shape="rect" alt="About Miracle Toys" coords="470,180,600,402" href="aboutus.htm">
<area shape="default" nohref>
</map>
<CENTER><P><IMG SRC="miracle.jpg" HEIGHT="480" WIDTH="640" usemap="#miracle"></P>
➥</CENTER>
</BODY>
</HTML>
```

The beginning of the code consists of general structure tags. These tags tell the browser that this is a HTML document. The head of the document contains a title that will be displayed as "Miracle Corporation Home Page." Following this heading are some meta tags that tell the browser who the author of the document is and what the document was created in.

The code then goes into the body of the document. Here you are setting the colors of the different elements for this page. I set the body text color, the background color, unvisited links, visited links, and active link colors.

Now you start to get into the meat of the file.

```
<map name="miracle">
```

The first element in this tag tells you that you will create a map and give it a name. In this example, the name is miracle. The <IMG> tag at the bottom of the code example will use this map information later (see the word usemap; this is where the magic happens— more on that later). On to the next line:

```
<area shape="rect" alt="The New Baby Toy Line Is Here!" coords="37,177,168,402"
➥href="babyline.htm">
```

The code first tells the browser that you want to select an area, and the shape of this area, in this case, is going to be a rectangle. The coordinates (coords) are 37,177,168,402. The use of these coordinates creates an invisible rectangle around the first navigation box for the New Baby Toy Line. When the user clicks on the rectangle, a request goes to hyper reference (href), and sends the user to the requested Web page, the URL—which is babyline.htm.

Other shapes can be used to create hot areas on your image. In addition to rectangles (rect), you can use circles (cir) and polygons (pol). You can also place any legal URL after the href, such as mailto, ftp, http, and more. How do you determine the x and y coordinates? The simplest way is with the use of a tool like MapEdit. You can download MapEdit at:

```
(http://www.boutell.com)
```

Continuing with the preceding code example, I define the other three boxes on the home page the same way:

```
<area shape="default" nohref>
```

After defining all the hot areas on the image map, you need to tell the browser what to do if the user clicks on an area that does not have a URL assigned to it. The AREA SHAPE="DEFAULT" tells the browser not to respond if someone clicks outside of a hot area. The nohref means do not send the user to a hyper reference (href).

Next, you need to tell the browser that this is the end of the map information, so you close the map tag with the </MAP>.

```
<CENTER><P><IMG SRC="miracle.jpg" HEIGHT="480" WIDTH="640" usemap="#miracle"></P></CENTER>
```

Finally, you tell the browser to load an image `<IMG>` and the source being `miracle.jpg`. The `usemap="#miracle` is the slick part that tells the browser to look up the coordinates if a user clicks on the image, and to use the `MAP NAME` "miracle" information.

Netscape's Navigator, and Microsoft's Internet Explorer both support client-side image maps, but what happens if someone is using a browser that does not support client-side image maps? All good browsers will ignore tags that they do not understand, so the `<MAP>` and `<AREA>` tags will be ignored, and the browser will just display the image. This is why it is important to include the code for a server-side image map, and this will be read by the browser, if it is not familiar with the client-side image map tags. The code to run both client-side, if available, and to drop to server-side, if needed, looks like this:

```
<A HREF="/cgi-bin/images/theimage.map">

<IMG SRC="miracle.jpg" USEMAP="#miracle"  ISMAP></A>
```

Client-side image maps offer great interactivity without having to program CGI scripts and you even don't have to have a server. This allows you to use client-side image maps in presentations, demos, and other non-Web applications with ease.

Creating Dynamic Intranet Pages

HTML documents, unlike their more traditional print-based counterparts, lead a much more dynamic life. An HTML document is not bound by the same constraints often associated with printed documents, because they can be modified on the fly by simply rewriting the HTML coding. After the document has been modified and resaved to the Web server, the results can be seen immediately by anyone loading the document.

At some point, you will want to add an even more dynamic twist to your Web site by allowing your viewers to affect the content of the Web page they are requesting. Through the use of Common Gateway Interface (CGI) programs, forms, and server-based databases, you can customize the Web pages being sent to your viewers.

The Common Gateway Interface (CGI) is a mechanism built into Web servers. CGI allows clients (your viewers) to execute programs directly on the Web server. The CGI application is referenced with a URL, similar to the URL used to access an HTML document. If your CGI application, myprog.cgi, were stored in a directory named cgi-bin under the domainname root directory, the URL for this application would be:

```
http://www.domainname.com/cgi-bin/myprog.cgi
```

The output of the CGI application is an HTML page that can be displayed by your viewer's Web browser.

CGI applications can be written in just about any language (C, C++, Microsoft Visual Basic, and Perl, just to name a few), as long as the application will run on your Web server. Some CGI applications are compiled, and some are interpreted. A *compiled* application is usually written in an upper-level language, such as C or C++. The source code is run through a program (or compiled) into native machine code, which will run on the Web server. An *interpreted* application does not run through a compiler. Instead, it is interpreted by a program that runs on the Web server when it is executed.

If an application gets a high amount of usage, or if the application is very "calculation" intensive, using a compiled application is better. For most routine applications, an interpreted language is fine. Perl is one of the most popular CGI application languages, and is the one highlighted in this chapter, because it is relatively easy to learn and use.

In this chapter, you will learn:

- What CGI methods are available and when they are used
- What necessary permissions and privileges are required to run CGI scripts
- Why CGI environment variables exist and what they are
- How to determine the values of the CGI environment variable
- How to deliver a Web page depending upon which browser your viewers are using

CGI Methods

CGI applications, as mentioned previously, are called by sending a URL to the Web server. Two different methods call a CGI program: the GET method and the POST method. The method used determines how data is sent to the CGI application.

The GET Method

The GET method is used when requesting information from the Web server. This method is used to request HTML documents from the server, as well as being able to request the execution of a CGI application. When you use the GET method, the CGI application receives its data through the QUERY_STRING environment variable.

Because most Web servers truncate the length of a URL and its associated query string to 1,024 characters, this method of passing data to a CGI application should be limited to short messages. Because of this limitation, the GET method is well suited for sending keywords to a CGI search application, but it is much less well suited for sending an entire form.

The POST Method

The POST method is the preferred method of receiving data from a client when information needs to be added or updated, such as filling out a form. Although the GET method is limited in the number of characters it may receive, the POST method reads its data using standard input (STDIN) routines of the application to receive its data.

The POST method essentially returns an entire document from the client to the Web server, and therefore is well suited for larger amounts of data. After the data from the client arrives at the Web server, it is up to the CGI application to query the CONTENT_LENGTH environment variable to determine how much information has been sent from the client.

First Things First

Before you actually get into CGI application development, you need to make sure that a few things are in place:

1. To execute CGI applications, you need to have rights to create and run executable applications on your Web server. This privilege must be given, or assigned, to you by the system administrator, and should be regarded with care.

2. After you have written your CGI application, and compiled it if necessary, you must make sure that the file permissions for your application are set so that the Web server is allowed to execute the file.

    File permissions tell the Web server who has access to the files in your directories and whether they are simple text files or executable files. Because you will be using Perl as your CGI application language, and it is an interpreted language, the files that you create will be both text and executable files. The commands used to change the file permissions will differ depending on which Web server you are using.

3. Because Perl is an interpreted language, you also need to know where the Perl executable is located. Once again, this is a question for your system administrator.

    It is very important that you test and re-test your CGI scripts. Security is the name of the game when it comes to allowing access to important information on your server, so make sure that you examine *all* CGI scripts that you might happen to download from archives on the Web. There are many archives that have pre-made CGI scripts that you can use on your intranets. But you should make sure that you get the source code so that you can be absolutely sure what this script is going to do.

CGI Environment Variables

CGI applications almost always receive their input from environment variables, which are reserved words within the Web server used to relay information from the client, through the Web server, to the CGI application. In a CGI application started with the GET method, the environment variables are the only way to get user input from the client to the application. Using the POST method requires that you read the standard input device to get information from the client. In either case, you can learn a lot of information about the client, its host server, and your Web server through the CGI environment variables.

REQUEST_METHOD

REQUEST_METHOD returns the name of the method used to invoke the CGI application. The most common return values are GET and POST.

QUERY_STRING

When using the GET method, the QUERY_STRING environment variable contains everything following the question mark on the URL being sent to the Web server. For example, if you request a search for the words *red cat*, the string sent to the Web server by the browser might look something like this:

```
http://www.yourdomain.com/cgi-bin/searchapp.cgi?keywords=red+cat
```

Note how the client browser has replaced the space between *red* and *cat* with a plus sign.

The two biggest downfalls with the GET method are as follows:

- The information being sent back by the client can be viewed on the URL line of the client's browser
- There is a limit of 1,024 characters for the total URL line length

If the request method is POST, this variable will be empty.

CONTENT_LENGTH

If the request method for your CGI application is POST, this environment variable specifies the length of the data, in bytes, attached after the request headers. This data is read by the CGI application through the standard input device. For a GET method request, this variable will be empty.

HTTP_USER_AGENT

The HTTP_USER_AGENT environment variable contains the name of the Web browser making the request. If you use Netscape version 1.1 to request the Web server to run your CGI application, the HTTP_USER_AGENT environment variable will contain Mozilla/1.1N (Windows; I; 16bit). When a user's browser sends information back to the server, this is what will be displayed. Windows is the operating system, and 16bit is the version of Windows software.

HTTP_REFERER

The HTTP_REFERER environment variable contains the URL of the form or document that contained the link to the current URL.

REMOTE_ADDR

The REMOTE_ADDR environment variable contains the numeric Internet Protocol (IP) address of the browser or remote computer calling your CGI application.

REMOTE_HOST

The REMOTE_HOST environment variable contains the domain name of the client requesting the CGI application. If the REMOTE_HOST environment variable is blank, the only information available about the client's remote computer is in REMOTE_ADDR. This information can be used to help figure out who is calling your scripts.

REMOTE_IDENT

The REMOTE_IDENT environment variable contains the user name, as given by the Web server identification daemon (IDENTD), requesting execution of your CGI application. This environment variable is available only if both the requesting server and your Web server are running the identification daemon.

REMOTE_USER

The REMOTE_USER environment variable returns the authenticated user name of the client making the request in response to the user name/password response to a response status of Unauthorized Access (401) or Authorization Refused (411). Server authentication must be turned on to use REMOTE_USER.

SERVER_NAME

The SERVER_NAME environment variable contains the host and domain name (if applicable) of the server you are using to execute your CGI application. If the name is not available, the IP address of the Web server will be returned.

SERVER_SOFTWARE

The SERVER_SOFTWARE environment variable contains the type of server under which your CGI application is running.

GATEWAY_INTERFACE

The GATEWAY_INTERFACE environment variable is the name and version of the gateway interface that is being used on your server.

SERVER_ADMIN

The SERVER_ADMIN environment variable, if available, contains the e-mail address of the Web master on your Web server. As a courtesy to your server administrator, this address should not necessarily be distributed to your viewers/clients. This is so that the server administrator does not get a million e-mail messages, because that person is in charge of maintaining the box, as opposed to the Webmaster, who maintains the site.

CONTENT_TYPE

The CONTENT_TYPE environment variable contains the MIME type of the data sent to your CGI application using the POST method. If the GET method is used, or if no data is being sent, the CONTENT_TYPE environment variable will be blank. For standard information posted from a form, the CONTENT_TYPE environment variable will contain application/x-www-form-urlencoded.

AUTH_TYPE

The AUTH_TYPE environment variable defines the authentication method used to access your CGI application. The AUTH_TYPE is usually basic, but is beyond the scope of this book to discuss in further detail.

PATH_INFO

The PATH_INFO environment variable is used when data follows the CGI application name, and before the beginning of a QUERY_STRING environment variable. The PATH_INFO environment variable can be used to pass any type of data to your CGI application. The data is URL decoded before it's placed into the PATH_INFO environment variable.

SCRIPT_NAME

The SCRIPT_NAME environment variable contains the name of the CGI application that is currently running. For example, /cgi-bin/myapp.cgi.

SERVER_PORT

The SERVER_PORT environment variable contains the TCP port number on the Web server running your CGI application. The default port for HTTP requests is 80.

SERVER_PROTOCOL

The SERVER_PROTOCOL environment variable contains the protocol and version number being used on the Web server. The protocol and version number are separated by the forward slash, and it is currently almost always HTTP/1.0.

Displaying Environment Variables

One of the first things that you should do is become familiar with the environment variables available to you on your Web server. To do this, a simple CGI application (see the following example) can be written to display all available environment variables. Figure 10-8 shows the sample output from this application.

```
[A]     #!/usr/bin/perl


[B]     # CGI script to display all env. vars. on a Web server.
        # The output of the program is returned as an HTML document.


[C]     print "Content-type: text/html\n\n";
[D]     print "<html>\n";
        print "<head>\n";
```

```
         print "<title>Environment Variables</title>\n";
         print "</head>\n";
[E]      print "<body>\n";
         print "<h1>Environment Variables</h1>\n";
         print "<center>\n";
         print "<table>\n";
         print "<th align=center><bold>Environment<br>";
         print "Variable</bold>\n";
         print "<th align=center><bold>Contents</bold><tr>\n";
[F]      foreach $envvar (sort keys(%ENV)) # Step through env. vars.
         {
[G]         print "<td> $envvar <td> $ENV{$envvar} <tr>\n";
         }
[H]      print "</table>\n";
         print "</body>\n";
         print "</html>\n";
```

Explanation of Program to Display Environment Variables

[A]   This line should appear as the first line of every Perl script. No lines (even blank lines) should be above it. The purpose of this line is to instruct the Web server shell where it can find the Perl interpreter, and what it is called. The contents of this line are based on a default installation, and may be different than that used in this example, based on where the Perl interpreter is located on your system. For UNIX-based Web servers, the Whereis Perl or Which Perl commands can be used.

[B]   Any text following a # until the end of the line is recognized by the Perl interpreter as a comment. Always include comments in your scripts.

Information that makes perfect sense today may be obscure in six months when you need to update your application.

[C]   This line is the first line printed by the Perl application to the user's Web browser. The information, HTTP `Content-type: text/html`, tells your Web browser that the information being sent from the Web server is a dynamically generated HTML document. Note that the characters `\n\n` are also included within the print line. The first indicates the end of the Content-type line, and the second sends a blank line letting your browser know that it has reached the end of the header, and the rest of the information it receives will be document data.

[D]   With the exception of the Print commands surrounding the text on these lines, you should recognize the text as being standard HTML commands to build a Web page. This group of lines sets up the HTML page and defines the document head and title.

NOTE: Every print line in the CGI script is followed by `\n`. This makes the resulting HTML code easier to read when it displays. These characters are included only to make the resulting HTML document easier to read in your browser if you choose to view the HTML document source.

[E]   Within the body of the HTML document, "Environment Variables" appears as the heading above a centered table with two columns.

[F]   The `foreach` loop iterates (steps) through each element in the `%ENV` array, sorted by the environment variable names. The variable `$envvar` takes on each successive value of `%ENV`.

[G]   This line, within the `foreach` loop, prints the name of the current environment variable `$envvar` and its contents `$ENV{$envvar}` within the context of the HTML table.

[H]   The remainder of the lines close out the table, body, and HTML document.

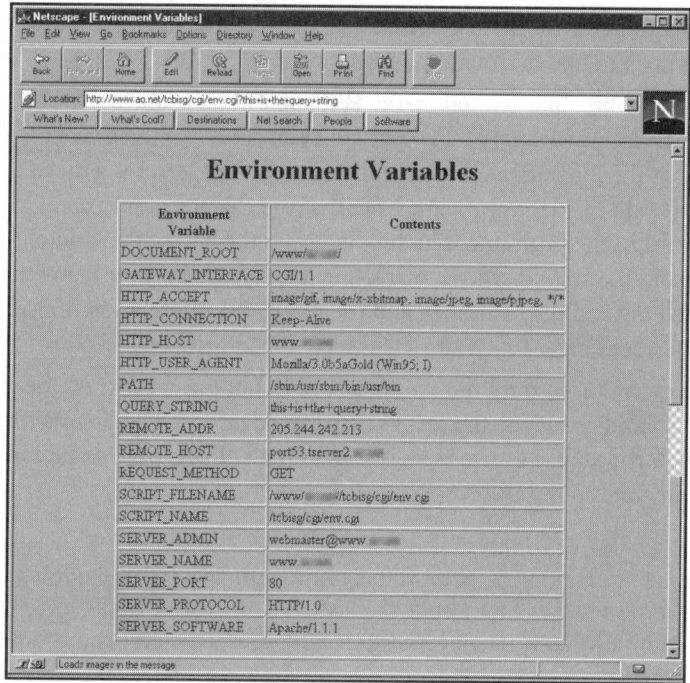

FIGURE 10-8

The browser output of the CGI/Perl Program to display environment variables.

Returning a Web Page Based on the User's Browser

This CGI/Perl application is an example of how to use the environment variables to influence what a user sees. The HTTP_USER_AGENT environment variable contains the name and version of the Web browser that your user is using to access your CGI application.

```perl
[A]     #!/usr/bin/perl


        # CGI script to return one of two Web pages to a user based
        # on the Web browser they are using. Users with Netscape
        # browsers version 1.1 or later will see page1.html, all
        # other users will see page2.html.


[B]     @user_agent = split(/\//,$ENV{'HTTP_USER_AGENT'});
[C]     if (($user_agent[0] eq "Mozilla")
```

```
         {
[D]          $version_number = substr($user_agent[1],0,3);
[E]          if ($version_number >= 1.1))
             {
[F]             print "Location: http://www.domain.com/page1.html\n\n";
             }
             else
             {
[G]             print "Location: http://www.domain.com/page2.html\n\n";
             }
         }
         else
         {
[H]          print "Location: http://www.domain.com/page2.html\n\n";
         }
```

Explanation of Program to Return Web Page Based on the User's Browser

[A]   This line should appear as the first line of every Perl script. No lines (even blank lines) should be above it. The purpose of this line is to instruct the Web server shell where it can find the Perl interpreter, and what the interpreter is called. The contents of this line are based on a default installation, and may be different than that used in this example, based on where the Perl interpreter is located on your system. For UNIX-based Web servers, the Whereis Perl or Which Perl commands can be used.

[B]   This line of the CGI/Perl script stores the contents of the HTTP_USER_AGENT environment variable in an array variable called @user_agent, after splitting it in half at the first forward slash (/). The Perl split function has the following syntax: split(/pattern/,expression). The pattern, in your case, is the forward slash, and the expression is $ENV{'HTTP_USER_AGENT'}. Because the forward slash is used to delineate the pattern string, and the pattern for which you're searching for is also a forward slash, you must "escape" the slash with a backslash, making the pattern / \/ /.

In the case of a Netscape browser, the HTTP_USER_AGENT environment variable might look like Mozilla/1.1N (Windows; I; 16bit). For this example, the two elements of the @user_agent array would be:

```
$user_agent[0] = "Mozilla"

$user_agent[1] = "1.1N (Windows; I; 16bit)"
```

> **NOTE:** The array is referred to as @user_agent, but the elements in the array are referenced as $user_agent[0] and $user_agent[1].

[C] This line makes a decision to execute the code beginning at [D] if the contents of $user_agent[0] equal "Mozilla". If the condition is not met, execution of the script continues at [H]. The letters eq are used to test for equality. If the equal sign (=) is used, the Perl interpreter stores the text "Mozilla" in $user_agent[0], rather than test for the equality condition.

[D] The substr function has the syntax substr(expression, offset, length). Because you are dealing with a Netscape browser (based on the decision at [C]), this line stores three characters from $user_agent[1], beginning with the first character (the first character in the string is at character position zero). At this point, $version_number contains "1.1", the first three characters of $user_agent[1].

[E] Another decision is made at this point to see whether the $version_number variable is equal to or greater than 1.1. If this condition is met, the Perl script continues at [F]. Otherwise, the script continues at [G].

[F] At this point, you are processing a request from a Netscape 1.1 or later browser, so you send a location response header to the viewer's Web browser directing them to http://www.domain.com/page1.html. The Web server steps in before sending the location response header text back to the Web browser, and sends a status header similar to HTTP/1.0 302 Redirection. The combination of the status header and location response header causes the Web browser to look for the requested Web page at a different location—in this case, http://www.domain.com/page1.html.

[G] Now you have a Netscape browser, but the version is prior to 1.1, so you send a location response header to the viewer directing it to http://www.domain.com/page2.html.

[H] The CGI/Perl script is sent to this point if the user's Web browser is not a Netscape browser, so you send a location response header to the viewer, directing it to http://www.domain.com/page2.html.

Sending E-Mail from an HTML Form Using CGI/Perl

One of the most common uses of CGI is to create a form that can be filled in by your viewers. This form can be used to solicit ideas, feedback, orders, and many other types of information.

The Background

The simplest way to get information from the viewer is to include a `mailto` URL on your Web page. The mailto URL is best suited for use in Web pages in which you simply ask your viewers to send you a message. The mailto URL can be implemented as follows:

```
<A HREF="mailto:myaddress@domain.com">myaddress@domain.com</A>
```

Unfortunately, this technique has a few drawbacks:

- Not all browsers support the mailto URL link.
- Rather than present a custom-made form to viewers for their comments, this technique uses the standard e-mail window within the user's browser.
- You can't control what types of information the user can enter.

The CGI/Perl Solution

Because the mailto URL is not the best way to proceed, the method you will use to allow controlled user feedback is a combination of an HTML form and a CGI/Perl script.

The HTML Document to Send Comment Form to Viewer

The first thing you will create is the HTML form used to allow the input from the viewer. The HTML form serves two purposes:

- It gives the viewer guidelines for information you wish to receive from the viewer.
- It executes the CGI/Perl script using the POST method.

The following is the code that shows the HTML document to deliver the form to the viewer. Figure 10-9 shows the sample output of the HTML document.

[A]
```
<html>

<head>
  <title>Feedback from You</title>
</head>

<body>

<h1>We Want Your Feedback!</h1>

<p>
We need your help to improve our service. Please take a few
minutes of your time to fill-out our short feedback form.
</p>

<hr>
```

[B]
```
<form method=POST
  action="http://www.domain.com/cgi-bin/feedback.cgi">
```

```
<pre>
```

[C]
```
Name:   <input type="text" name="name" size="30"
            maxlength="30"><br>
E-Mail: <input type="text" name="email" size="30"
            maxlength="30"><br>
<br>
How did you hear about our service?
```

[D]
```
<input type="radio" name="how" value="radio">Radio
<input type="radio" name="how" value="tv">Television
<input type="radio" name="how" value="paper">Newspaper
<input type="radio" name="how" value="other">Other
<br>
```

```
           Please tell us what you like and dislike about our service:
[E]        <textarea name="comments" rows="10" cols="50">

           </textarea>

           </pre>


[F]        <input type="submit" value="submit"


           </form>


           </body>

           </html>
```

This HTML document sends a comment form to the viewer.

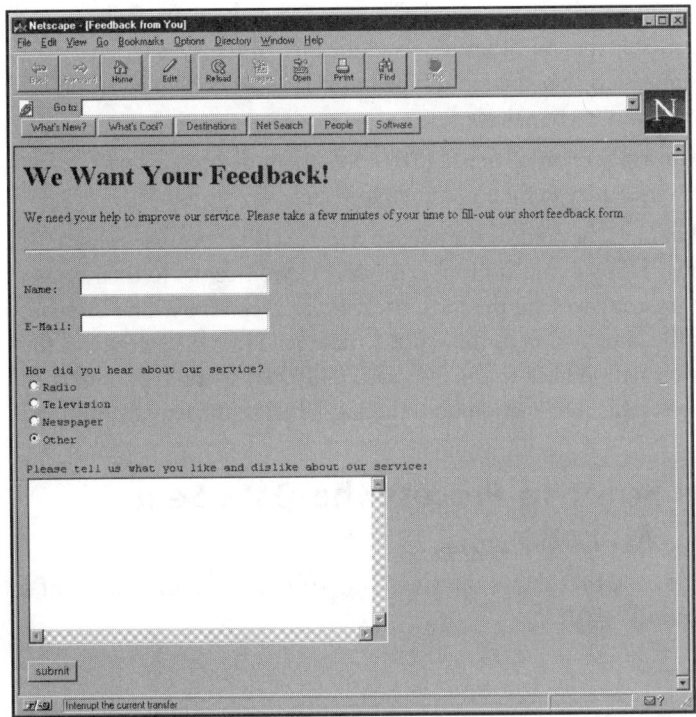

FIGURE 10-9

Here is the browser output of the HTML feedback form.

Explanation of HTML Document to Send Comment Form to Viewer

[A] The first section of this code is standard HTML, setting up the title of the document and instructions to the viewer.

[B] The form portion of the document is enclosed within the `<form method=POST action="http://www.domain.com/cgi-bin/feedback.cgi">` and `</form>`, where `www.domain.com/cgi-bin` is the domain name of your Web server and the location of your CGI scripts. Feedback.cgi is the name of the CGI/Perl script that will be processed when the viewer clicks the Submit button.

[C] This section of the HTML form presents the viewer with two text boxes, one called Name and the other called E-mail. These two boxes have a size of 30 characters and a maximum length of 30 characters. These two boxes have a width of 30 characters and maximum length of 30 characters.

[D] Because you are interested in learning how viewers heard about your service, you give them a series of four "radio" buttons to make their choice of radio, television, newspaper, or other. The significance of the `type="radio"` over `type="checkbox"` is that the radio type buttons allow only one button in the `name="how"` group to be selected.

[E] The `<textarea>` section of the HTML document displays a text box in which viewers can type their comments.

[F] The final item in the form is the `<input type="submit" value="submit">` HTML tag. This submit "button" is the way viewers signal to their browser that they are ready to send the form back to the Web server. The Web browser then uses the information in the `<form … action>` HTML tag to send the viewer's information back to the indicated CGI/Perl script. Not until the Web server receives this information does the CGI/Perl script actually execute.

The CGI/Perl Script to Process the Data Sent from the HTML Form

The following is the code that shows the CGI/Perl script to send the comment form to the viewer (see Figure 10-10).

```
#!/usr/bin/perl


# This CGI/Perl script accepts input from an HTML form and
# emails the information to a predetermined email address.
```

```
       # Define some variables

[A]    $mailto = '/usr/lib/sendmail';
[B]    $emailto = "youraddress\@domain.com";


       # Get the user input from the Web server

[C]    read(stdin, $temp, $ENV{'CONTENT_LENGTH'});


       # Split the name-value pairs into an array called @nvpairs

[D]    @nvpairs = split(/&/, $temp);


       # Split each pair into separate arrays @name and @value

[E]    foreach $nvp (@nvpairs)
       {
          ($name, $value) = split(/=/, $nvp);


          # Translate '+' symbols into spaces

[F]       $name =~ tr/+/ /;
          $value =~ tr/+/ /;


      # Translate 'escaped' hex codes into their actual chars.

[G]          $name =~ s/%([a-fA-F0-9][a-fA-F0-9])/pack("C", hex($1))/eg;
             $value =~ s/%([a-fA-F0-9][a-fA-F0-9])/pack("C", hex($1))/eg;


          # Add the trans. name and value pairs to an array %TNVP

[H]          $TNVP{$name} = $value;
       }


          # Build HTML document which will be returned to the viewer
```

```perl
[I]    print "Content-type: text/html\n\n";
       print "<html>\n";
       print "<head>\n";
       print "   <title>Form Response</title>\n";
       print "</head>\n";
       print "<body>\n";
       print "<h1>Thank you for your information!</h1>\n";
       print "Thank you for taking the time to give us your ";
       print "feedback. Your responses will allow us to ";
       print "customize our future service to you.<br>\n";
       print "Below is a recap of the information you have ";
       print "submitted:<br>\n";
       print "<br>\n";


       # Start the sendmail program and open a pipe for output


[J]    open(MAIL, "|$mailto -t") || die "Can't open $mailto!\n";
       print MAIL "To: $emailto\n";
       print MAIL "From: $TNVP{'email'} ($TNVP{'name'})\n";
       print MAIL "Subject: Email response from Feedback Form\n\n";


       # Step through each element in the name-value pairs array &
       # print them to the mail 'pipe' and to the users as HTML


[K]    foreach $nvp (@nvpairs)
       {
           ($name, $value) = split(/=/, $nvp);


           # Translate '+' symbols into spaces


           $name =~ tr/+/ /;
           $value =~ tr/+/ /;


           # Translate 'escaped' hex codes into their actual chars.
```

```
$name =~ s/%([a-fA-F0-9][a-fA-F0-9])/pack("C", hex($1))/eg;
$value =~ s/%([a-fA-F0-9][a-fA-F0-9])/pack("C", hex($1))/eg;


# Send name-value pair to MAIL pipe
```

[L]
```
print MAIL "$name:  $value\n";


# Send name-value pair to user as HTML


print "$name:  $value<br>\n";
}


# Close the MAIL pipe to send the email message
```

[M]
```
close(MAIL);


# Send remainder of HTML document


print "</body></html>";
```

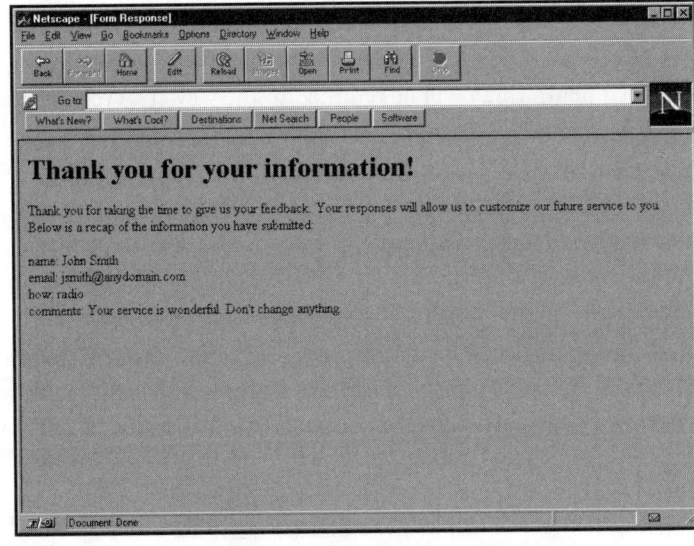

FIGURE 10-10

Here is the browser output of the HTML Feedback Response from the CGI/Perl script.

Explanation of CGI/Perl Script to Send Comment Form to Viewer

[A]   The $mailto variable contains the Web server path and name of the send-mail application used by your CGI/Perl script to send an e-mail message containing the viewer's comments.

[B]   The $emailto variable contains the e-mail address that receives the comments from the viewer. Note the backslash \ before the @ symbol is required, because the @ symbol is a reserved symbol in the Perl language. The backslash is used to "escape" the @ symbol.

[C]   This line of the CGI/Perl script reads the entire contents of the data being sent from the viewer's browser into a variable called $temp. The length of the data is contained in an environment variable called CONTENT_LENGTH. The syntax of the data stored in $temp is as follows:

```
name1=value1&name2=value2&etc…
```

[D]   Because the name-value pairs are separated by the ampersand (&) character, this line splits all of the name-value pairs in $temp into the @nvpairs array.

[E]   The foreach loop is now used to further split all of the name-value pairs in @nvpairs into separate $name and $value variables.

[F]   The two lines in this section are used to translate the plus signs into spaces.

[G]   These two lines convert "escaped" hex codes into their actual characters.

[H]   This line stores the $name and $value variables into an associative array called $TNVP.

[I]   This section of the CGI/Perl script prints out the header and top portion of the HTML document, which will be returned to the viewer's Web browser.

[J]   To send a response by e-mail, you need to open a *pipe*, or output stream, to the sendmail program that you defined previously in section [A]. If the sendmail program cannot be run for any reason, the Die command prints a message stating that the pipe could not be opened. The next three lines specify who the message is to (from section [B]), who the message is from (retrieved from the viewer's form), and the subject of the message.

[K]   This section, once again, splits the original @nvpairs array into the $name and $value variables, and then it translates the plus symbols into spaces and the "escaped" hex codes into their actual characters. Performing this translation a second time is easier than extracting the data from the associative array, $TNVP.

[L]   The line print MAIL "$name: $value\n" sends the name and value of each
      form variable to the sendmail program. The next line, print "$name:
      $value
\n", prints the same information back to the viewer as part of the
      HTML document.

[M]   At the conclusion of the foreach loop, the Close(MAIL) command closes the
      pipe to the sendmail program, which actually sends the e-mail message. The
      final Print command ends the HTML document being returned to the
      viewer.

Summary

In this chapter, I created dynamic Web pages throughout the use of CGI programs.
Programs can process information from users' Web browsers using GET or POST methods. The CGI program interacts with the Web server to retrieve information by using
environment variables.

Three applications were presented in this chapter. The first displays the available environment variables; the second demonstrates how a CGI program can deliver a Web page,
depending upon which browser the user is using; and the third program is used to return
form data from an HTML form by way of e-mail.

What's Next!

Now I'll move on to Business Presentations. The overhead projector will soon be a thing
of the past. Doing your presentations in a Web browser allows your audience to experience multimedia presentations while in a meeting and then again later, back at the desktop. There are many plug-ins and programming tricks that allow you to create amazing
professional presentations, and I'll cover them in the next chapter.

Chapter | 11

Business
Presentations

Time to Present

Overhead transparencies are a thing of the past. With the introduction of laptop computers and the Web browser, audiences no longer have to sit through presentations conducted on overhead projectors with transparencies that are impossible to read. Better yet, participants can view the same presentation at their desktop on the corporate intranet. They can now receive training and view presentations without having to attend the traditional conference room setting with a large group of students.

Gone are the days of your traditional overhead transparencies that were impossible to read and extremely boring in black and white.

Now, the days of the slide show are numbered as well. Clicking from slide to slide, only to get a question on slide number 32 when you are only on slide 4 makes for poor presentations. And don't forget the slide that displays like this:

upside down

Another fantastic use for Web and intranet technology that you do not see discussed much, or at all, is for company, convention, and personal presentations. HTML is basically a structure language that allows you to structure content and layout, with a certain degree of control, in a Web browser. It has not developed to the standards of desktop publishing quite yet, so you will have some difficulty getting an advertisement to display exactly the way you want it to. Because the power is in the browser, it will interpret the content as it sees fit. But, you still can develop some great presentations that will get the point across at your next meeting or convention, and you will have some fun doing it.

HTML is also moving ahead rapidly. The new 3.2 specification addresses layout issues, and vendors are developing their own tags for the language that will no doubt be added in as the norm if everyone likes them. Microsoft has some new layout tags that allow you to develop borderless frames, and that do style sheets. The layout tags are great because they allow more control over how the page will look in the browser. Right now these tags are supported only by Microsoft's Internet Explorer 3.0, but if they become popular, Netscape should soon follow.

In this chapter, I show you how to impress your boss and your friends. I show you how to do presentations with a Web browser, and the advantages that come with it. I also write some HTML that makes a self-running slide show that you can use at conventions and trade shows. After you do a basic presentation, you will add sound, music, and other multimedia to your presentation.

Presenting with a Browser

Presenting with a Web browser gives you several advantages. First of all, if you are doing a presentation on the World Wide Web, the Internet, intranet, or any technology subject, you should be using a Web browser to do your presentation. It is easier to explain Netscape Navigator and all of its uses to an audience if you are using it for the presentation itself. And, it's easy to do.

Just some of the advantages that you gain by using a Web browser for presentations are the following:

- ◆ If your users can't see the text because it is too small, or if the background you choose makes your content hard to read, just click to change these preferences, and the problem is solved. Try doing this with a transparency.

- ◆ You just flew in to Orlando to do your presentation and your slides are lost on another flight to Texas. You are dead in the water. If you have your presentation up on your Web site, you can use your laptop—or anyone's laptop—with a Web browser and show your presentation anywhere in the world.

- ◆ The audience wants more information on the slide you are showing. With a slide show, you have to click several slides ahead to get to that information, and then back again to where you left off. With your presentation on the Web, however, all you have to do is give out your Web address and anyone in the conference or meeting can get a copy right at his or her desk.

NOTE: For a quick Netscape tour, go to Prima's Web site for the "Netscape Overview" document at:

`www.primapub.com/cpd/76150849.html`

I have sat through many presentations about the Internet and about Web browser software, never to see the Internet or a Web browser. Why not show the audience what it is you are doing your speech on?

Choose Your Weapon

You need to decide what browser you are going to use. I suggest you use Microsoft's Internet Explorer version 3 or higher, or Netscape Communication's Navigator version 3 or higher. These browsers are the most popular in the market, and they have the most features. You need to choose a browser so that you can create your presentation the way you want to for that particular browser. If you are making your presentation in HTML and do not know what browser you are going to be giving it in when you arrive to give the presentation, try to use standard HTML tags. Test your presentation in Navigator and IE 3 to make sure it works and looks good in both. To get your hands on some raw HTML coding examples, turn to Appendix A and B. When you're done there, you can also learn about authoring tools in Appendix C.

I will show you some of the pages I designed in both Netscape and Microsoft's browsers.

> **NOTE:** It is important to try out your presentation in at least Netscape and Microsoft's Web browsers if you are traveling to a location to give a presentation, and are not bringing your own equipment and Web browser. One advantage to doing your presentation in a Web browser is that you can save all of your presentations on your Web site and just pull up the URL when you speak at a conference. This way you can let people in the audience view your presentation later at their leisure, and they can also print it when they pull up your presentation later at home. But, you need to make sure your presentation works and looks good in several browsers so that you don't give a presentation that does not work, or you cannot read.

Creating Your Presentation

After you organize your notes and have your presentation mapped out, you can start to design your Web pages to display your ideas. I designed this presentation quickly by just using raw HTML code and adding some images that I made.

My splash screen just welcomes everyone to Miracle Toys, and lets them know what I am going to be covering in the presentation. After I begin the presentation, I just click on the alpha block in the center of my browser screen, and this is a hyperlink to my first slide. Take a look at Figure 11-1. Here you can see the opening slide. You will also notice that the toolbar and most of the other control bars are minimized to allow for more viewing area. The presentation also is designed for a 640 x 480 LCD panel. If you have your own projection unit that you will be using for your presentation, and if it can handle 800 x 600, take advantage of it. Most LCD panels handle only 640 x 480, and won't display anything if you have your settings higher than this.

Alternatively, you may have a projection TV system attached to a workstation that gives you much higher resolution; if so, a presentation that's constrained to a 640 x 480 image will probably look cartoonish. For best results, find out what's available where you'll be presenting; for minimal work, design for the lowest common denominator.

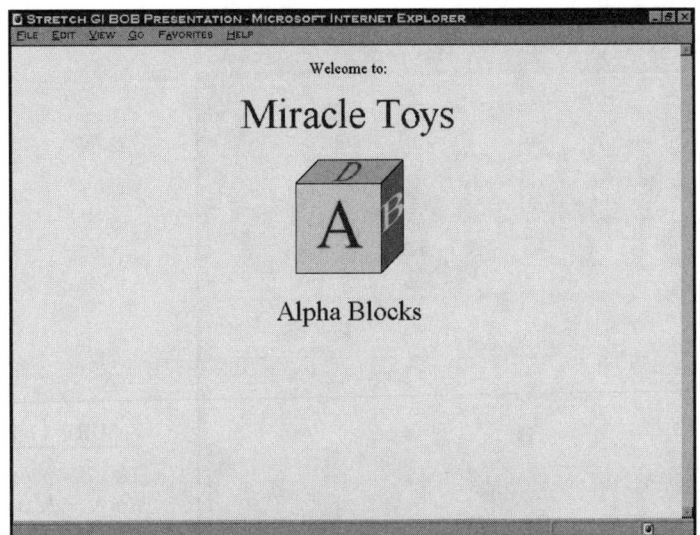

FIGURE 11-1

The opening screen of the presentation is running in Microsoft's Internet Explorer. Most toolbars are minimized to allow for a greater screen size.

NOTE: Consider the display device(s) that you'll be using to give your presentation. Test out your screen resolution on one of these units if you have time. Also, check to make sure the colors are easy to see and that the size of your content is big enough for people to see and read.

Move on to the next slide in the presentation. By clicking on my link to the next slide, I arrive at the first content slide in the presentation. You can design your slides as you wish. I have taken this same basic layout for most of the slides in the presentation. This way, I can use this slide as a template and change the basic content inside. Figure 11-2 shows you the first real slide in the presentation. Each slide has a Back and Next hyperlink at the bottom so that you can navigate around the presentation.

One of the nice things about doing your presentation in a browser is that you can quickly adjust the font size if people in the back rows cannot see it. You can do this in both Netscape Navigator and in Internet Explorer. Let me show you how to do this in Internet Explorer, because I am using it for this presentation. It's very simple. By selecting View | Fonts, and then the font size, you can change the text size in all your slides. I changed the font size to the largest setting in Internet Explorer; instantly, my slides changed. Take a look at Figure 11-3. You can also change the font size in Internet Explorer by pressing the font icon on the toolbar. Each time you press the icon, your font size increases one interval until it cycles to the beginning.

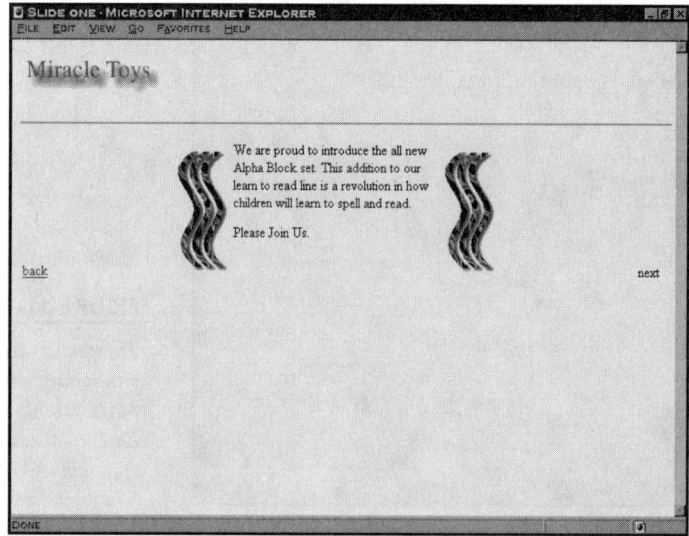

FIGURE 11-2

The slides in the presentation have the same layout, so creating new ones is easy.

> **CAUTION:** You should try your presentation at all possible font settings *before* you're in front of an audience. Choosing a large font setting can have unexpected impact on your layout, and may actually diminish readability.

Netscape Navigator gives you even more flexibility by allowing you to choose a font point size. From the menu bar choose: Options | General Preferences | Fonts. From here, you can set the font and point size.

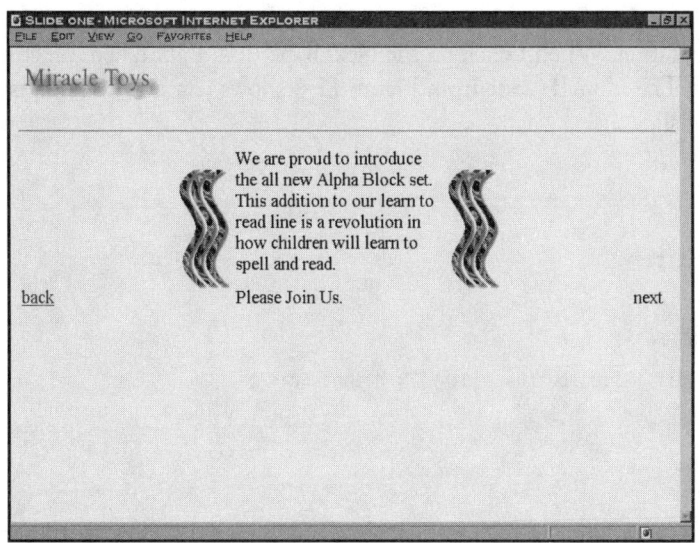

FIGURE 11-3

Need to make that font a bit bigger? Just change your font size in the browser settings, and you are done.

Microsoft PowerPoint

PowerPoint is a fabulous presentation tool. You can make slides quickly and easily with all of the wizards and clip art that comes with the package. After you see the same old guy with a hammer smashing the computer for the tenth time, you start to get sick of the same old thing. Presenting in a browser lets you be as creative as you want to be, and you can create as many confusing graphs and charts as you like to hide last month's sales figures.

So, you are worried about losing all of those PowerPoint files you made if you switch over to doing presentations in a Web browser. Don't fear, you can still use them and can keep using PowerPoint to your heart's content. Let me show you how to pull PowerPoint files into your presentation, right into your Web browser, with no conversions. First you will look at Microsoft's Internet Explorer, and then I tell you how to accomplish the same thing in Netscape's Navigator.

I don't show you how to create presentations in PowerPoint. It's pretty easy, and you should be able to get around the program with just a slight learning curve. Just like all programs, you can quickly learn the basics, or you can spend the rest of your life learning every trick that PowerPoint can perform. If you are searching for a degree in PowerPointism, then I suggest getting one of the many books that cover the topic (such as *Essential Office '97* by Bill Bruck, ISBN 0-7615-0969-0, published by Prima).

From my presentation in Microsoft's Internet Explorer, I made a hyperlink to my PowerPoint Presentation. When I click on the Next hyperlink, I am taken directly to my PowerPoint slides. The HTML code from Figure 11-3 shows you how the link is made to the PowerPoint slides.

```
<html>
<head>
<title>Slide one</title>
</head>
<body bgcolor="#FFFFFF">
<p><img src="logo.gif" align=bottom width=173 height=50></p>
<hr>
<table width=100%>
<tr>
<td colspan=2 width=33%></td>
<td width=33%></td>
<td colspan=2 width=34%></td>
</tr>
<tr>
<td valign=bottom width=17%><a href="gibob1.htm">back</a></td>
<td align=right width=16%><img src="squig.gif" align=bottom width=64 height=157></td>
<td valign=top width=33%>We are proud to introduce the all new Alpha Block set. This
addition to our learn to read line is a revolution in how children will learn to
➥spell and read.
<p>Please Join Us.</p></td>
<td width=17%><img src="squig.gif" align=bottom width=64 height=157></td>
<td align=right valign=bottom width=17%><a href="gi-bob.ppt">next</a></td>
<td valign=bottom></td>
</tr>
</table>
</body>
</html>
```

This code generated the Web page presentation. The line that allows you to link to your PowerPoint Presentation is near the end:

```
<a href="gi-bob.ppt">next</a>
```

Here, you are just setting up a normal hyperlink. Instead of linking to a Web page, you are telling the browser to link to a PowerPoint file named GI-BOB.PPT when the user clicks on Next. This opens the PowerPoint Presentation.

Figure 11-4 shows the first slide in the PowerPoint Presentation. The downside, of course, is that a lot of your on-screen real estate is wasted by all the application's control objects.

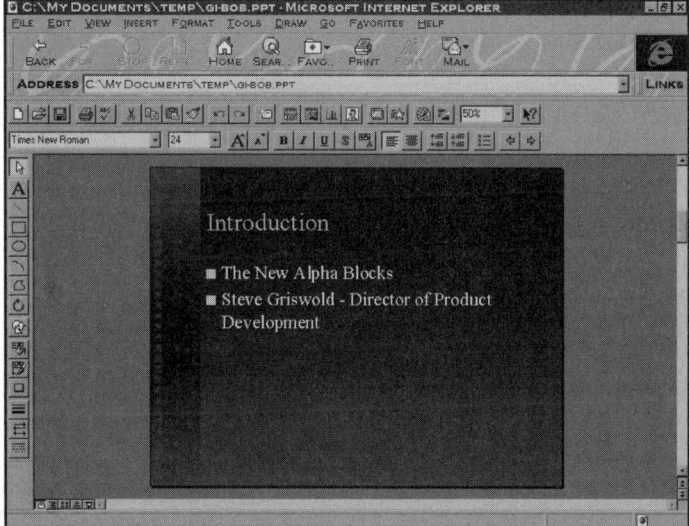

FIGURE 11-4

PowerPoint opens up inside Microsoft's Internet Explorer. You are still in the browser and can move around your PowerPoint presentation, and also navigate in the browser.

So, now you have the best of both worlds. You can use PowerPoint and your browser to stun your audience. After they're stunned, you can conveniently attach the ear tags with the miniaturized radio transmitters so that they can be tracked after being returned to the wilds.

You can use Netscape Navigator, and with the help of a viewer, you can open PowerPoint files while doing your presentation. Unlike Internet Explorer, the viewer that you need to get for Netscape Navigator launches a separate application, so the presentation does not run directly in the browser. You can download the viewer for free from Microsoft's Web site at http://www.microsoft.com. After you install the viewer, you can make links to PowerPoint files in your presentation, and Netscape Navigator will launch the viewer when it encounters a .PPT file.

If you have the Microsoft Windows 95 version of PowerPoint, you also have another option when doing presentations in a Web browser. Again, from Microsoft's Web site you can download a free application that automatically converts your PowerPoint presentations into HTML. The converter does all the work. I took a PowerPoint presentation that I made in PowerPoint for Windows 95, and after downloading and installing the converter, I saved it as an HTML file. From the menu bar in PowerPoint, choose File, Export as HTML, and that is all there is to it. When you launch your Web browser (I use Netscape Navigator in this example), you can open the PowerPoint file directly in the browser. I open the PowerPoint file that I just exported as an HTML file. In Figure 11-5, you can see the first HTML file that the converter made. Obviously, once converted, you can fine-tune the visual elements based on your knowledge of HTML.

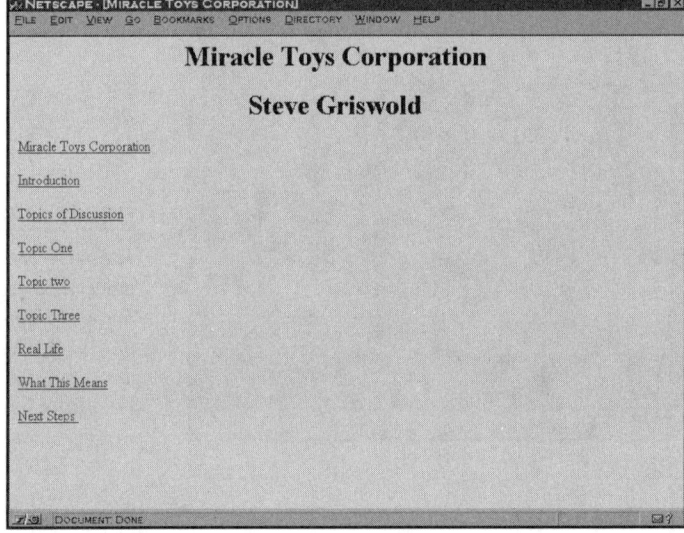

FIGURE 11-5

Microsoft's PowerPoint converter takes your PowerPoint files and turns them into HTML files. This page was generated 100 percent by the converter.

When you export your presentation as an HTML file, you will get a pop-up menu that gives you a few options to choose from. This option pop-up box allows you to set the presentation output style. You can choose from gray scale or color, which makes your PowerPoint files appear in shades of gray or in color when they are converted into HTML. Choose color for most exports. This displays your files using the same colors as your original presentation in PowerPoint.

Now you get to choose your file format for your slides. You can choose from JPEG or GIF. This is the file format that your slides use to display in your browser. There are advantages and disadvantages to these two file formats. GIF files are slightly bigger in size, but on basic solid color images, you get a better quality image. JPEG images are smaller in size, but have a blur effect on text and solid color images. If you save your files as JPEGs, you can select the compression rate by using the slider control in the option pop-up box. A low setting on the slider makes your image size smaller and faster to load, but the image quality also goes down.

After you choose your image type, select the location to save your files. You can type in the folder name or choose Browse to pick a location for your presentation files. It's safest to create a new directory for this, because the default action of the program is to create an INDEX.HTM file, which you may already have in an existing directory.

After you click the OK button, your presentation starts to convert to HTML. While this conversion is taking place, make sure that you do not move your mouse over the slide show. If you do this, your presentation might display the slide show pop-up menu button. You can go to the menu bar and select Tools | Options | View Tab, and uncheck the pop-up menu button box to avoid displaying the button.

While your presentation is being converted, a new window appears. Your slides appear in this window as they are converted. The longer your presentation, the longer it takes to convert.

After your files have been converted, you will notice several files in your new directory. These are the HTML files and the image files for your slides. The file labeled INDEX.HTM is your beginning file for your presentation. When you open this file, you get your presentation's title, your name, and your company name printed on the top of your browser screen. Also, all of your slides are listed on the left side, which allows you to link directly to any slide in your presentation.

SLD001.HTM is the first slide from my PowerPoint presentation. This HTML file takes my image file of slide SLD001.JPG and inserts it into the HTML page SLD001.HTM. The navigation buttons at the bottom of the page are generated by the other .GIF files that you see in the folder.

You also see TSLD001.HTM files that are numbered in ascending order. These are similar to the SLD001.HTM files, but are the text versions of these files. You can choose to display the graphical version of your presentation or a text version that loads faster and works on nongraphical browsers.

If the images of your slides are too small or too large, you can change the size. The resolution of these images is controlled by your monitor screen resolution setting. If you save your presentation while your monitor settings are 640 x 480, your images will be smaller than if you do the same when your settings are at 1024 x 768. By experimenting with your display resolution, you can adjust your .JPG and .GIF image size.

After you have finished your presentation, you can move it to your intranet. Now you can show your presentation from your intranet, and your employees can access the same presentation back at their desk. When you upload your files to your intranet, make sure you keep all the files in the same folder. This keeps all of your links and images intact.

The Web allows you to create the ultimate presentation. You are not limited by one means to display your information. You can use HTML pages and images, you can add in PowerPoint and other presentation applications, and you can add sound and multimedia directly into your presentation. With PowerPoint's Internet Assistant, you can do some creative and useful tricks.

You can make images and objects in your slides hyperlink to other slides, and even to pages on the World Wide Web. The next paragraph describes how to make an object link to another slide.

Insert your image in the slide using PowerPoint. This can be done by selecting Insert from the menu bar in PowerPoint. Then you can choose to insert an image, a movie, clip art, and even sounds. I insert a standard clip art image. After I have the image on my slide, I now want to link this image to the next slide in my presentation. To do this, I select my clip art by clicking on it, and then going to the menu bar and choosing Tools | Interactive Settings. This brings up the pop-up window shown in Figure 11-6.

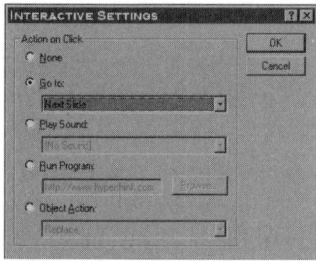

FIGURE 11-6

In PowerPoint, you can make your Web presentation images link to other slides, or even Web pages, by using the interactive settings and then exporting to an HTML file.

In the Interactive Settings window, choose the Go To radio button. Then you can use the drop-down menu to pick which slide you want your image to link to. When you export your presentation, you have a link to the slide you selected when you click on the image in your slide.

You can also link to URLs on the WWW. You do this the same way as in the preceding paragraph, but rather than choose Go To on the Interactive Settings, choose Run Program. After you select Run Program, type the URL to any page on the WWW.

When you convert the file by exporting it to HTML, you have a link from your presentation to the WWW.

NOTE: You might find it interesting to know that each of your HTML files is supported by a template file. The IMAGE.TPL file is used to create the graphic versions of your slides, and the TEXT.TPL is used to create the text versions. If you are daring, you can edit these files. They are just normal text files, and you can edit them in a regular text editor such as NotePad. Modifying these templates allows you to customize your presentations.

Notice that these files are basically standard HTML files. There are <BODY> tags and the like. Placeholders are in these files for your slide images, the control buttons that appear on your pages, and an area to insert notes in your presentations.

You can do several things to customize these screens. You can use a <META> tag to do Client Pull, which allows you to set time intervals that will change the slides automatically for you. I show you how to do this in the section that follows on self-running slide shows. You can change the graphic files so that the navigation buttons are your own custom creation, and you can experiment with alignment and left align, right align, or center your presentations.

NOTE: Make sure that you make backup copies of your .TPL files before modifying them so that you can always return to the original if you toast your files while playing with them.

In Figure 11-7, the slides are displayed in the browser, now that they have been converted into HTML. At the bottom of each of the slides are navigation controls that are also done in HTML. You can navigate back one slide by pressing the back arrow on the far left of the screen. You can move to the next slide by pressing the Next button, the second from the left. The third button, with the double arrows, takes you back to the main menu, the table of contents. The last button, with a capital letter A, changes the display from a graphical slide show to a text-based slide show. All the navigation buttons and slides are generated automatically when you save them in PowerPoint as HTML format.

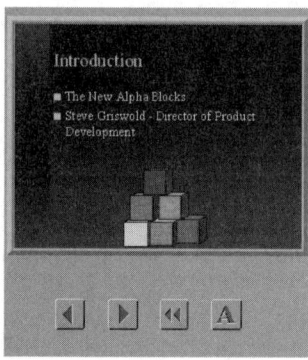

FIGURE 11-7

*The PowerPoint presenta-
tion has been converted
into HTML and now can
be viewed as an HTML
file.*

Even the clip art object of the blocks is a hyperlink to a page on the Web. Using a Web browser along with an application such as PowerPoint, adds great flexibility for presentations and computer-based training.

Other Applications

Another advantage of doing training and presentations in a Web browser is that you can use many helper applications to accomplish different tasks. I showed you one: PowerPoint. Another useful application for corporations, when it comes to training, is Lotus ScreenCam.

Lotus ScreenCam Player acts just like a regular video player. You can play, rewind, pause, and fast-forward movies just as you can with a VCR. The Lotus ScreenCam Player is also free. You can download it from Lotus's Web site at:

`http://www.lotus.com/screencam/211a.htm`

To record your own training videos and presentations, you need to purchase the Lotus ScreenCam Recorder. But it costs only around $100.

For class-type demonstrations, presentations, and training, the Lotus ScreenCam Player works great. You can play quick movies that show how to work applications, and you can incorporate sound or text to narrate your videos. The ScreenCam Player is easy to use and can be run as a stand-alone application, or it can be launched from your Web browser.

If you are using Netscape Navigator, you can download ScreenCam movies and launch the ScreenCam as a helper application. To do this, follow these steps:

1. Go to Preferences in the Options menu.
2. In the Preferences dialog box, choose Helper Applications in the pull-down menu.
3. Click on the New... button, and enter **application** as the MIME type, and **x-screencam** as the MIME subtype. Click on OK.
4. Enter **scm** in the Extensions box.
5. Click on the Browse button and locate your installed copy of the Lotus ScreenCam Player (SCPLAYER.EXE). Click on Open.
6. Select your preferred action (Save or Launch).
7. Click on OK.

Lotus ScreenCam, the player, and the recorder are easy to use and can aid your training and conference presentations.

Automatic Slide Shows

If you are doing an open house or a trade show booth for your project, or you want to set part of your presentation to run by itself, you can use the Web to accomplish this task. With a self-run slide show, you can make your Web presentation change automatically.

The coding for this is simple and consists of only one line. First, you need to make your presentation. You can do this in raw HTML or use an editor to develop your presentation.

The tag that performs the client pull, which causes your Web pages to change automatically, is the <META> tag.

```
<META http-equiv="refresh" content="n;
```

```
URL=http://www.somewhere.com/file.html">
```

Place this line in your HTML page, in the <HEAD> element.

Take a look at the two attributes in this line:

```
http-equiv="refresh"
```

You must use `"refresh"` as a value here. This tells the Web browser to refresh the screen.

```
Content="n"
```

The number of seconds that you want the browser to wait until the <META> tag requests the next Web page is represented by "n". Then, the <META> tag requests the URL that follows in this line of code.

Try using the URL to request something other than another Web page. You can request sounds, or animations. You also can have the browser spawn an external application.

Here is the <META> line with some real values and a URL in place.

```
<META http-equiv="refresh" content="5;URL=http://www.hyperthink.com/product.htm">
```

Here, I am telling the browser to go from the Web page that is currently displayed on the screen, wait five seconds, and then load the product Web page from Hyperthink's Web site. If I wanted to do an automated tour of the products at this Web site, I could continue to add META tags at the top of each of theses pages of code and jump from page to page.

> **NOTE:** When you make an automated slide show, judging how long to wait in between slides before moving on to the next page or special effect can be difficult. Sometimes, downloading a Web page takes so long that the page changes to the next Web page before the user has a chance to see the entire screen. Some users also read faster than others, and they will not want to wait for the slides to change on their own. To solve some of these issues, you can add navigation buttons on each of your Web pages. With these buttons, a user can go at a faster pace or jump back to a previous slide. You can also make self-paced training tours and automated training tours, allowing users to choose which one they would like to do right from the beginning.

Multimedia and Sound

Everyone is adding plug-ins to expand the capabilities of the Web and intranets. Some amazing plug-ins are out there that can help you complete your tasks, and they are all easy to install and set up.

First of all, what is a plug-in?

A *plug-in* enables you to launch an application inside the browser. If you have been using Netscape Navigator, two types of applications can be launched when you click on a link to another application: a helper application or a plug-in. When you activate a helper application by clicking on it on your intranet or on the WWW, the Web browser then looks for that application on your computer. When the browser finds that application, it opens the application and displays the graphic, sound, or document in that application. You still have your Web browser running, but it is on the desktop under the application that you just launched. You therefore have two separate applications running, and you have to switch between the two. Plug-ins do one better. When you activate a plug-in, you launch an application, but the plug-in launches inside the browser window instead of launching a totally new application. This way the user does not have to switch between two applications, and they are always in a familiar environment.

I go over some of the plug-ins available that will aid you in creating presentations in this chapter, and I show you how to set them up. Literally hundreds of plug-ins are available for free from the WWW; you can use these plug-ins on your intranet. I've dedicated Chapter 12 in this book to plug-ins, where I cover some of my favorites for intranets. While I am thinking about it, the following is a good place to find all the plug ins you could ever want:

```
http://home.netscape.com/comprod/mirror/navcomponents_download.html
```

From here, you can read up on the different plug-ins, download them, and try them out. You'll even find a special link for plug-ins that are just for presentations. Let's take a minute and go over some plug-ins that can help you deliver more dynamic presentations.

ASAP Webshow by Software Publishing Corporation

ASAP WebShow is a Netscape Navigator 2.0 plug in presentation viewer for viewing, downloading, and printing graphically rich reports and presentations from the Web. Download a beta version to see how transmission times for presentation files — estimated at a rate of three pages per second — are significantly faster than standard streaming rates. ASAP WebShow lets anyone view any document created by Software Publishing Corporation's award-winning ASAP WordPower report and presentation software package. Take a look at Figure 11-8.

```
http://www.spco.com/
```

Available for Windows 3.X and Windows 95

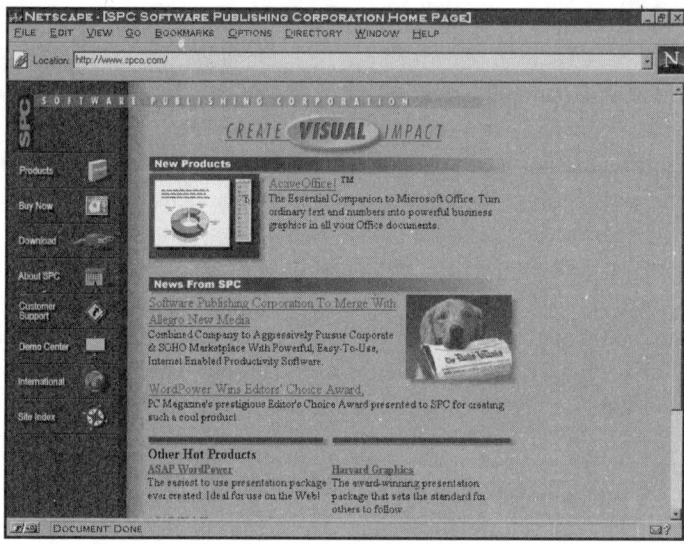

FIGURE 11-8

ASAP Webshow is perfect for viewing and printing graphical reports.

Astound Web Player by Gold Disk Inc.

The Astound Web Player is a Netscape plug-in that plays dynamic multimedia documents created with Gold Disk's award-winning Astound or Studio M software. These documents can include sound, animation, graphics, video, and interactivity. The Astound Web Player features dynamic streaming; each slide is downloaded in the background while you view the current slide. It is shown in Figure 11-9.

http://www.astoundinc.com/

Available for Windows 3.X and Windows 95

Formula Graphics Multimedia System by Harrow Software

There are no limits to the animation and interactivity that Formula Graphics can add to a Web page. It has an easy-to-use graphical interface and a powerful multimedia language that is suitable for both business applications and animated, arcade-quality action games. Figure 11-10 shows a snapshot that I made quickly. The Formula Graphics multimedia system and the plug-in for Netscape Navigator are free to download and use. Install the plug-in and try out a demo.

http://203.22.232.3:80/formula/

Available for Windows 95 and Windows NT

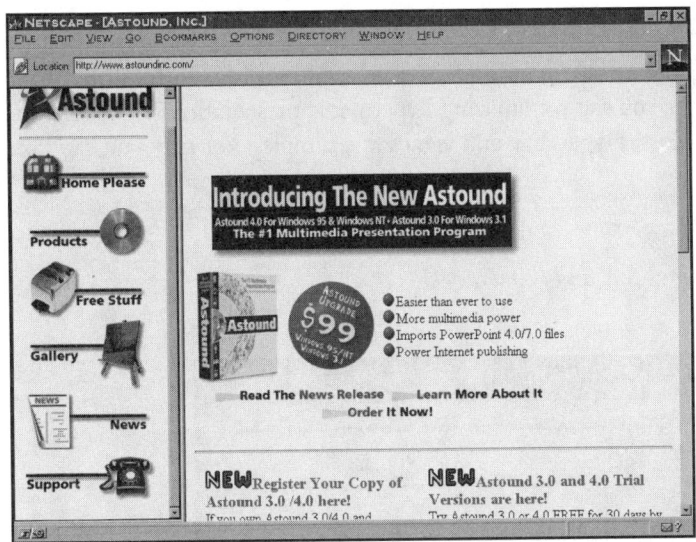

FIGURE 11-9

The Astound Web Player lets you display slides and multimedia content in presentations and on your intranet.

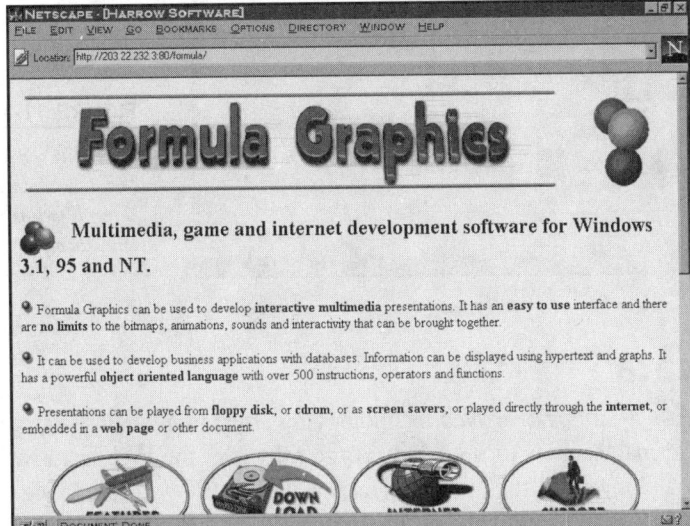

FIGURE 11-10

For interactive Web presentations, screen savers, and multimedia, check out Formula Graphics.

HyperPage by LMSOFT

HyperPage is a hypermedia authoring tool developed by LMSOFT. With the HyperPage plug-in, you can see amazing hypermedia presentations embedded in HTML documents. Download HyperPage and view some samples. For now, you can take a peek in Figure 11-11.

```
http://www.lmsoft.ca/index.html
```

Available for Windows 3.X and Windows 95

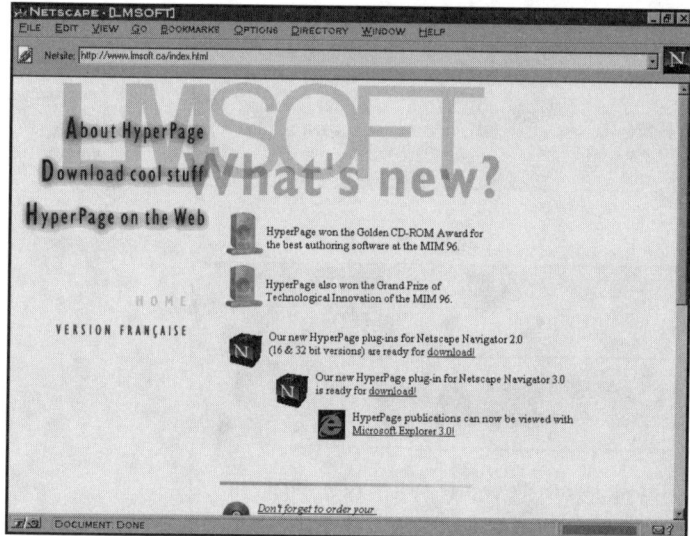

FIGURE 11-11

HyperPage is a software that assembles multimedia elements such as videos, animations, hypertexts, images, and sounds.

Mirage by Strata

Strata's Mirage uses new, innovative Web technology for streaming MediaForge titles over the Internet. It enables users to run MediaForge titles over the Web from within Netscape Navigator. Conversely, the Mirage Netscape plug-in allows users to view and interact with MediaForge titles virtually anywhere in the world. By downloading Mirage, users can use the plug-in to play their favorite MediaForge titles, games, presentations, or kiosks. The Mirage plug-in is great for learning, training, interactive media, and presentation building. See Figure 11-12.

```
http://www.strata3d.com/products/MForge/~mirage/~mirageMain.html
```

Available for Windows 95 and Windows NT

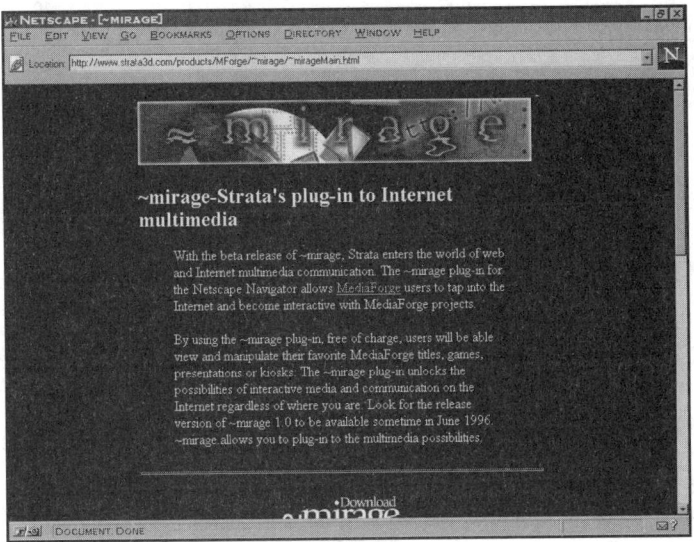

FIGURE 11-12

By using the Mirage plug-in, free of charge, users will be able view and manipulate their favorite MediaForge titles, games, presentations or kiosks.

PointPlus by Net-Scene

The PointPlus plug-in allows you to view dynamic and colorful presentations embedded in HTML pages. It is especially useful for viewing corporate PowerPoint presentations on a Web page. You can see it here in Figure 11-13. Because it uses sophisticated compression and streaming technologies, it plays presentations with no delays and at fast rates, even on slower dial-up lines. Download PointPlus and view some demos.

http://www.net-scene.com/

Available for Windows 3.X, Windows 95, and Windows NT

PowerMedia by RadMedia

You can see PowerMedia by RadMedia in Figure 11-14. This is the first visual multimedia authoring software for business communications on the World Wide Web. Designed for corporate communicators and Web designers, PowerMedia provides authoring and viewing of interactive content, presentations, training, kiosks, and demos with seamless playback in Netscape Navigator 2.0.

http://www.radmedia.com/

Available for Windows 95 and Windows NT

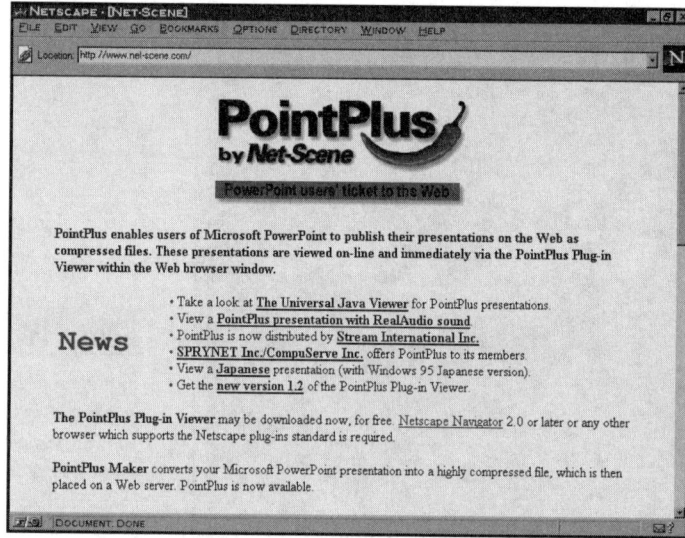

FIGURE 11-13

For compressing PowerPoint Files on your intranet, try PointPlus.

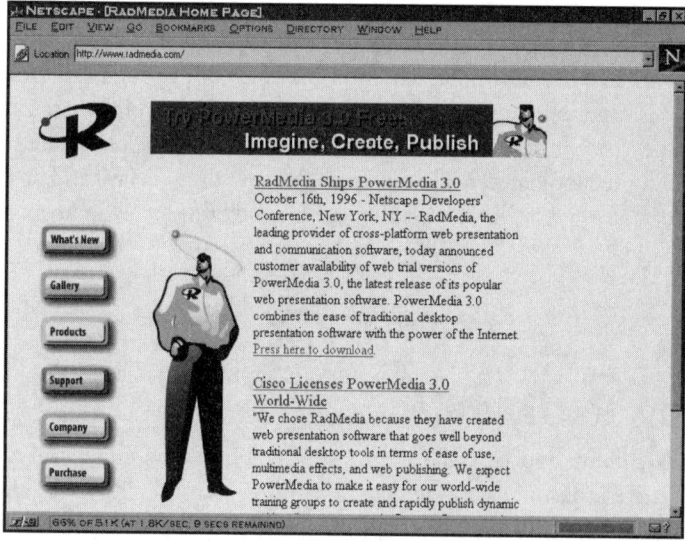

FIGURE 11-14

PowerMedia is designed for developing and playing interactive presentations, and for training in Netscape Navigator.

PowerPoint Animation Player & Publisher by Microsoft

The new Microsoft PowerPoint Animation Player & Publisher provides users with the fastest, easiest way to view and publish PowerPoint animation and presentations in your browser window. Millions of PowerPoint users can now take advantage of the enhanced animation, hyperlinks, sound, and special effects with which they are familiar in PowerPoint for Windows 95, to create dynamic, animated Web pages. Download the Animation Player to see some samples of PowerPoint used in Web pages (see Figure 11-15).

```
http://www.microsoft.com/mspowerpoint/internet/player/default.htm
```

Available for Windows 95 and Windows NT

FIGURE 11-15

An easy way to add sound and animation to your PowerPoint presentations on the intranet.

ActiveMovie by Microsoft

What is ActiveMovie? ActiveMovie is the next level on intranet and Internet digital video for your desktop.

Want to create awesome special effects, and clear audio and video? ActiveMovie is your ticket. As a developer, you will be able to play back MPEG television-quality video, and even play back MPEG at full screen. ActiveMovie has been designed with intranets and the Internet in mind, and allows video streaming to allow for a faster playback. Enough chat: here it is in Figure 11-16.

```
http://www.microsoft.com/intdev/controls/ctrlref-f.htm
```

Available for Windows 95 and Windows NT

Setting Up Plug-Ins in Your Pages

Because I am discussing presentations and training, I want to touch on some of the ways to add multimedia and sound to your presentations and training tools. To include this type of media in a Web presentation, I cover a newer tag in the HTML language, the <EMBED> tag. This tag follows a basic structure for all of its appearances in your HTML code:

```
<EMBED SRC="file.extension" WIDTH="number" HEIGHT="number">
```

> **NOTE:** This is currently a Netscape proprietary tag, so it could change in the future. Just wanted to make you aware of certain HTML tags that are on the cutting edge, but might also change as time passes.

In this code, the source SRC is the filename that works with a particular plug-in. The WIDTH and HEIGHT attributes let the browser know how much room to set aside in the browser for this plug-in. Each plug-in also has attributes that you can add to your code.

A test that Honeywell created is a good example of how you can use a plug-in (in this case, Shockwave by Macromedia, at http://www.macromedia.com), and a Web browser to distribute an interactive test to employees. You can view this demo at:

```
http://www.macromedia.com/shockwave/epicenter/shockedsites/honeywell/index.html
```

You need to download and install the Shockwave plug-in to get the presentation to work. You can also see just a quick screen shot of the opening screen in Figure 11-17.

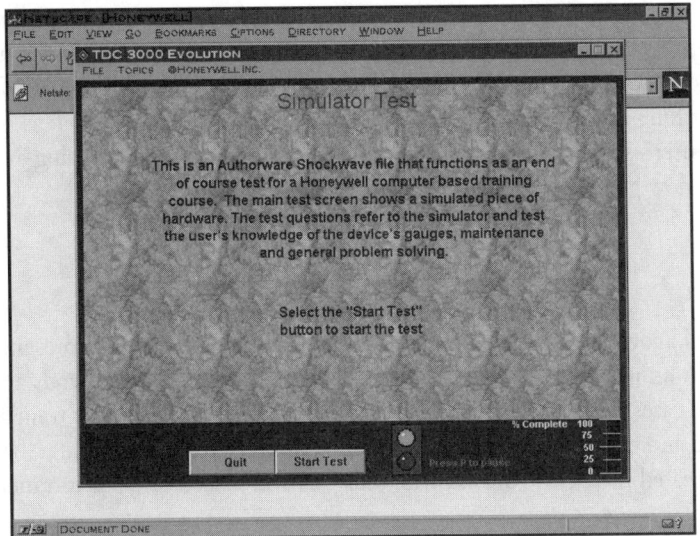

FIGURE 11-17

Visit Honeywell's Web site to see a demo of an intranet training tool being used with Shockwave.

To place this plug-in into the HTML code, the following HTML code was used:

```
<EMBED SRC="test.aam" width=100 height =72 window=ontop>
```

This will activate this plug-in. The `window=ontop` opens a separate window with the `height` and `width` dimensions, and launches the `test.aam` file in this window.

But what happens if someone hits this Web page and does not have the correct plug-in?

A way to solve this problem exists: a <NOEMBED> tag. The <NOEMBED> tag takes care of this problem if the user does not have the correct browser or plug-in. This way, the user does not just get a blank screen.

Here is how it works:

```
<EMBED SRC="test.aam" width=100 height =72 window=ontop>
<NOEMBED>
<H1>Please Note:</H1>
In order to run this intranet training course you will need to have
➥<a href="http://www.netscape.com>" Netscape Navigator 3.0 </a>or higher, and the
➥<a href="http://www.macromedia.com>"Macromedia Shockwave</a> Plug in.
</NOEMBED>
```

This blob of code first tells the browser what to do if users have the correct version and the correct plug-in on their system. This is done with the <EMBED> tag. If the user does not have the correct plug in, the <EMBED> tag is ignored and the <NOEMBED> tag is read. Everything in between the opening and closing <NOEMBED> tags is then displayed on the user's screen. This area has links to the sites that have the plug-ins so that the user can now go and download the needed plug-in.

Summary

Until now, no tool allows has enabled you to conduct training and produce presentations of the quality that an intranet provides. Some people may argue that overheads are just fine, and, in some cases they are, but with a corporate intranet, you can now train and present to anyone and everyone. Presentations can be interactive, and computer-based training can be created in one of your favorite plug-ins and placed on your intranet instantly.

What's Next!

It's time for Chapter 12, which is one of my favorites because I get to play with all the latest and greatest new toys: plug-ins! I'll also discuss how to install plug-ins, what the difference is between helper applications and plug-ins, and how you can get copies to try them out yourself.

Chapter | 12

Plug-Ins

Got plug-in fever yet? No? You must not even be on the Net then, are you? Don't answer that, because if you are reading this book, you'd better be surfing the Web quite regularly; how else could you think that you'll be able keep up on the latest, the greatest, the most cutting-edge stuff that's out there?

What Is a Plug-In?

A plug-in is basically a *helper application* that runs within the Netscape Navigator browser (but that is integrated in a much closer or tighter fashion). What is a helper application? It's a program that the browser will call upon when it encounters a file type that it does not understand or is not set up to handle. Typically, the browser is already set up to handle file types such as HTML and even image-types such as GIF, JPEG, and XBM. When it runs into other MIME-types/files, though, the browser may stop and say, "Hey, what the heck kind of MIME-type file is this?" This is when the helper application or plug-in steps in and takes over. Helper applications, when called upon, will start a window that is "outside" of the Netscape viewing area.

What Is MIME?

MIME stands for Multipurpose Internet Mail Extensions. MIME is a standardized method for organizing different file formats. Each file has what is called a "MIME type." When a browser requests a file, the browser looks at the MIME type and then consults its internal tables to see whether it has the capability to interpret the file properly, and whether a helper application or plug-in is loaded that can do the processing work. If no helper application or plug-in is available to handle the MIME type in question, then a window opens, indicating that you are trying to open a file requiring a plug-in that is not loaded in your browser. Typically, you are then given the opportunity to either obtain the necessary plug-in or save the file to disk.

The preceding process used to be terribly confusing and, in fact, downright annoying. Downloading and configuring plug-ins and helper apps was often a real pain, and after much frustration (and searching for instructions on how to actually set these things up), most people would just give up. But it sounds more complicated than it actually was: After you went to the Netscape Handbook and printed the instructions for setting up helper applications/plug-ins, 10 minutes was about all it took to figure everything out.

Nowadays, things are a bit easier. Most plug-ins will download nice and easy, and, after you click on their "self-extracting" setup file, they very politely install themselves into the Netscape Plug-ins directory snug as a bug. This is a good thing for you, me, and every other user (and for your corporate intranet), and, more important, for the wide and wonderful world of plug-ins that are just waiting for you to click on them. About 108 plug-ins are available for download on the Netscape site. Feel lucky? Then click away!

Setting Up a Plug-In For Netscape

Take a look at how you can configure your own helper application in Netscape.

First, click on the Options drop-down menu at the top of your browser window. Then select General Preferences. Click on Helpers and you will see the window shown in Figure 12-1 appear.

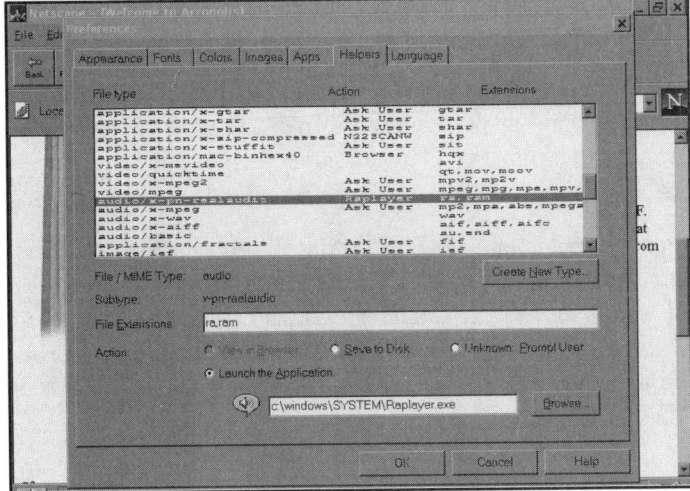

FIGURE 12-1

Configuring your helper applications—the place to do it in Netscape.

You will see a list of the different MIME/file-types that are available to be configured by the user. Take a look at the three column headings:

◆ MIME/file-type: These are the various types of files that the browser might encounter.

◆ Action: What do you want the browser to do when it encounters a MIME/file-type? Take note of the typical actions that the browser might undertake:

◆ ask user: You will see a window pop up that will ask you how you want to handle the encountered MIME/file-type.

- ◆ browser: The browser will invoke or take advantage of its built-in functionality and will just go ahead and do the required processing—such as opening a JPEG or GIF image.
- ◆ actual application name: An example of this is raplayer (for RealAudio Player). This is an actual plug-in that will be invoked by the browser to handle the MIME/file-type.
  - ◆ Extension: A listing of the different file extensions that will be appended to a MIME/file-type.

As I mentioned previously, you won't need to be digging around much in the helper application window, because most of the plug-ins available today will download and put themselves into the correct place(s) all by themselves (or with minimal interaction from you). Or, you will (usually) be given very clear instructions concerning how to go into the helper's window and go about setting things up properly. Progress; what a wonderful thing.

Another way of saying all this is that helper applications and plug-ins expand Netscape's abilities by letting you automatically decompress downloaded applications, listen to sounds, play movies, and display images. Here are some thoughts about the types of files that a helper application or plug-in will encounter and how they will be processed:

- ◆ Compression: You might encounter or download programs on the Web that are in formats your computer doesn't understand. In this case, you would want to put a program like PKUNZIP or WinZip (or Stuffit Expander for the Mac) into your helper application's window; in this way, one of these programs would be automatically launched when the browser encounters the entered MIME/file type.
- ◆ Sounds: Sound files are typically not in a format that your computer can automatically play. Install and configure a helper application and you will be humming right along.
- ◆ Pictures/movies: Netscape can handle GIF, JPEG, or XBM file formats in terms of displaying them, but you may wish to have another viewer launched in order to view your image files. If so, then configure one in your helper application's window.

The following sections, coming directly from the Netscape site, provide the actual instructions for configuring your helper applications for both Windows and Macintosh.

How to Configure Helper Applications for Windows

Under Options|Preferences|Helper Applications, you will see a box with the following headings: File Format (Mimetype/subtype), Action, and Extensions. It might, for example, look like this:

> Mimetype: video
>
> Subtype: x-msvideo
>
> Action: launch
>
> Extension: avi

Mimetype is the type: video, basic, multipart. For more detailed information about helper applications, please open Netscape Navigator, pull down the help drop-down menu, and select Handbook. When the Handbook opens, scroll down a bit until you see an alphabetical listing. Select H (for helper applications).

Subtype is the application name.

Action is what you want Netscape to do when it encounters a file or link with the extension given.

Extension is where you put the file type extension.

Click on New and enter the MIME type and application name, as well as the extension. Then, choose an action for when Netscape Navigator encounters a link matching the extension. Action choices are as follows:

- ◆ Use browser as viewer
- ◆ Save
- ◆ Launch application
- ◆ Unknown: prompt user

How to Configure Helper Applications for the Mac

Under Options/Preferences/Helper Applications, you will see a box with the following headings:

MIME type (mimetype), Application (subtype), Action, and Extension. For example:

> Mimetype: image
>
> Subtype: jpegview

Action: launch

Extension: tif, tiff

Mimetype is the type: video, basic, multipart. Take a look in the Handbook in Netscape Navigator for more detailed information on helper applications.

Subtype is the application name.

Application is the name of the application.

Action is what you want Netscape to do when it encounters a file or link with the extension given.

Extension is where you put the file type extension.

Click New, enter the Mimetype (image link to media.types) and application name (subtype), as well as the extension. Then, choose an action for when Netscape Navigator encounters a link matching the extension. Choices are as follows:

♦ Save

♦ Launch Application

♦ Use Netscape as Viewer

♦ Unknown: prompt user

Setting Up a Plug-In For Internet Explorer

Here's a look at how you configure helpers and plug-ins using Explorer from Microsoft.

Call me crazy, but I am really thinking that Microsoft has actually made this process much less of a hassle compared with Netscape's handling of plug-ins. Take a look at Figure 12-2 for a quick look at how Microsoft handles downloading and installation of helper applications and plug-ins. I strongly encourage you to go to www.microsoft.com, get Internet Explorer 3.0, and decide for yourself.

Installing Two Popular Plug-Ins

Now that I've covered some of the basics on how to obtain and install plug-ins on both Netscape Navigator and Internet Explorer, take a look at some of the plug-ins available that will enhance your intranet.

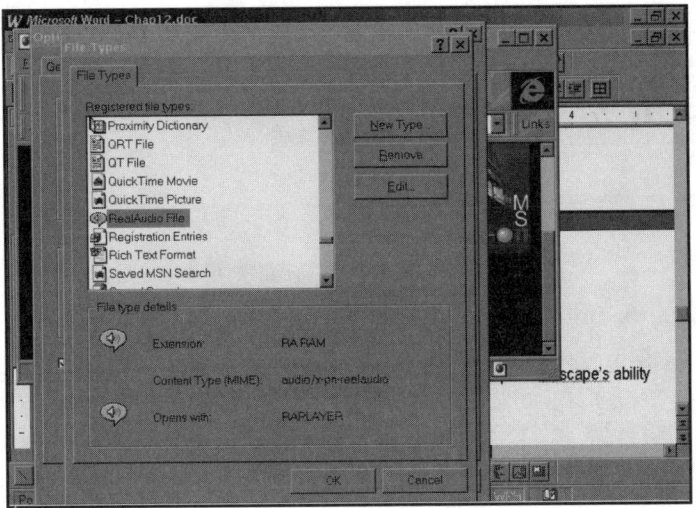

FIGURE 12-2

*Configuring helpers
and plug-ins the
Explorer way.*

Abobe Acrobat Reader

Adobe Acrobat Reader 3.0 will allow you to view, navigate, and even print PDF (Portable Document Format) files right inside your Netscape Navigator window. If you haven't worked with PDFs before, now is a very good time to start. PDFs offer design control, print-ready documents, and extensive authoring control. Just a short while back, the PDF was one of the few ways to have total control over the design and layout of a document that you wished to load on to a Web page. The PDF was not restricted by the layout limitations imposed by HTML; with a PDF, you could use any font, page layout, or image placement that you wanted because the PDF worked as a plug-in through your browser (thereby allowing the PDF to open in a type of "shell" within your browser window).

An example of a PDF file appears in Figure 12-3, followed by a short discussion of what a PDF is and how it will work for you and your users.

But what if you don't have the Adobe Acrobat Reader 3.0 plug-in? Well, now is a good time to go and get it. The Acrobat Reader is free, and you should download it ASAP—you will find many uses for it, especially in a corporate intranet. Fire up your browser of choice and go to the Adobe Web site to pick up the Acrobat Reader (and bunches of other great software) at:

```
http://www.adobe.com
```

FIGURE 12-3

An example of a cool PDF! The Acropolis magazine.

When you arrive at the Adobe site, take a look around and see whether you notice any links for Acrobat 3.0. If you cannot locate one right away, just select Products from the image map menu. On the Products page, you will find a link to the Acrobat Reader 3.0, as well as some other good Adobe products. Click on that link and you will be taken to a series of screens and steps for downloading this useful and necessary plug-in. Notice that the Acrobat Reader 3.0 is available for Windows, Macintosh, and even UNIX boxes (and a few others as well).

So, go ahead and download and install the Acrobat Reader 3.0 plug-in. I'll wait for you to finish and then you will get to go to one of the best sites on the Web for anything and everything having to do with PDFs:

```
http://plaza.interport.net/acropolis/
```

There you will find the Acropolis Magazine, where you will be greeted by this message: "You have reached Acropolis, the Web site dedicated to electronic publishing using Adobe."

Spend some time scrolling around this document. Click on some of the toolbar selections, such as the hand icon, for instance. Use this hand to literally move the page around (kind of like the hand icon in Photoshop). Now, click on the magnifying glass icon and use this to zoom in or out on sections of the document—kind of neat, huh? Also, take a look at the left side of the screen. See those small items that look like pages? Those are links to the other pages in your PDF document: you can click on any given page, and that page will be loaded in the main viewing area.

You can also use the hand icon to maneuver around the main viewing area. Contrast this with what you can typically do with a standard Web page, and you can see the beauty of using a PDF. Probably the most important aspect of the PDF and its power as a publishing tool is that all formatting and layout from the original document is retained when viewed in the Netscape Navigator or Microsoft Internet Explorer 3.0 browser window. Retaining these elements is accomplished through the Acrobat Reader. The Acrobat Reader is an indispensable tool that should be on every one of your corporate desktops. PDF files tend to be a bit larger than traditional Web pages, but there are ways to reduce this drawback and make your PDFs a bit slimmer and trimmer. You can also break your PDFs into "chunks" that are then reassembled by the Acrobat Reader upon receipt.

Keep in mind that the Acrobat Reader allows you only to read, print, and move around in a given PDF; if you want to create your own PDFs, then you must use another Adobe product called Adobe Acrobat 3.0. Get this product and you can create PDFs of all your documents (Word, Excel, and so on).

RealAudio

RealAudio 3.0 is an indispensable audio program that brings broadcast-quality audio to the Internet, delivering stereo sound to 28.8 modems and near-CD quality to ISDN and LAN connections. RealAudio is fast becoming the industry standard for delivering high-quality audio to a Web page near you.

I keep mentioning how easy it is today to download and configure helper apps and plug-ins, so you ought to actually see this in action. I now go to the RealAudio Web site (www.realaudio.com) and attempt to download and configure its very popular RealAudio Player. Figure 12-4 shows what happens.

I'm at the site and I say, "Hmmmm. . . sure would like to have that new RealAudio Player v3.0 beta that all my friends are talking about." So, I click on the download link and, after reading all the legal and disclaimers, I start to download the program, as you can see by the download window that has popped up in my browser window. This particular download is going to my program files directory, where it will then open my Norton AntiVirus Scanner (NW.EXE). There it will be scanned for any viruses before it goes onto my hard drive for good. I recommend that you use either the Norton program or something similar. I like it because it gives me the opportunity to decide where I want the file to go before completing the download. (Sometimes I have a problem locating the program that I've just downloaded.)

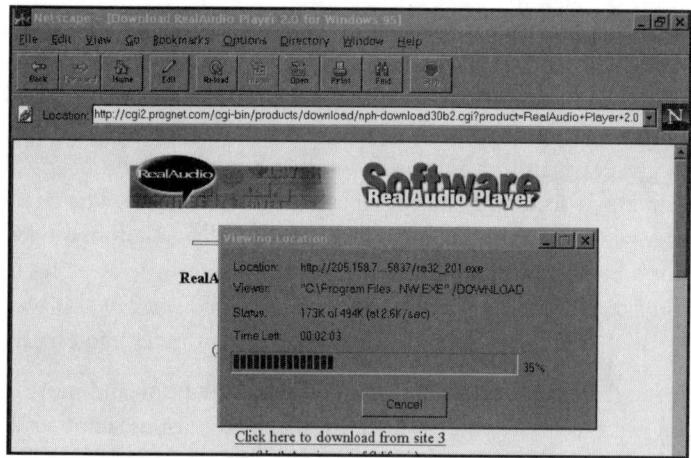

FIGURE 12-4

Downloading the RealAudio Player.

After I download the plug-in (which will typically head for the correct Netscape directory), I go back to my file manager and find the plug-in file with the .EXE extension, which I then click on. The file will explode, expand, unzip, or self-extract itself (usually) and I am then presented with a SETUP.EXE file. I click on that file to complete installation of the plug-in.

Keep in mind that this is just one of the ways that this process happens (though it is probably the most common); some plug-ins will download, extract themselves, and then proceed to install themselves in the Netscape plug-in directory (I wish all would do this, but they don't). Still others will require you to actually unzip the files by invoking PKUNZIP or WinZip (this is a pain). Regardless of which method you employ, instructions are almost always given at the site from which you retrieve the plug-in. Make sure to either print (recommended) or read and memorize these steps; doing so will save you trouble later on. I usually will go back and read the instructions over a few times while the plug-in is downloading. What else is there to do? Isometric exercises? Crossword puzzles?

Figure 12-5 shows what the RealAudio Player looks like when it pops up in the Netscape window.

Once in a while (okay, often) I switch over to Microsoft Internet Explorer to see how that browser is coming along. If you have not done this, I strongly suggest that you do, because Microsoft is definitely doing some cool stuff. I went over to the Microsoft site and attempted to download the RealAudio Player plug-in as I had done from Netscape Navigator. I'll get to what I found in a moment.

But first, take a look at something interesting that happened (see Figure 12-6) when I first went to the Microsoft site (actually, I went to the www.msn.com site):

FIGURE 12-5

The RealAudio Player in the Navigator window.

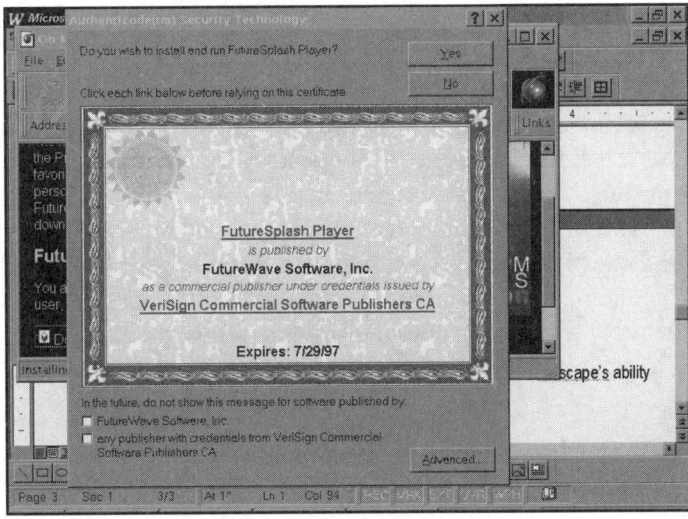

FIGURE 12-6

Automatic download of a plug-in and a security certificate!

Wow! As soon as I arrived at the MSN site, this window popped up and asked me whether I wanted to download (and install!) the new FutureSplash Player from FutureWave software (get this program if you have the chance—it's a vector-based animation program, it's small, and it has cool graphics for your Web pages). The security certificate that pops up supposedly assures you that this plug-in is what it says it is. So, I clicked, and then, to my amazement, the plug-in was downloaded and installed just like that. Now that's pretty cool.

Anyway, back to downloading RealAudio using Microsoft Internet Explorer.

I open the Microsoft Internet Explorer (they should really shorten this name), go to the RealAudio site, and start the download of the RealAudio Player 3.0 beta. Figure 12-7 shows what is displayed.

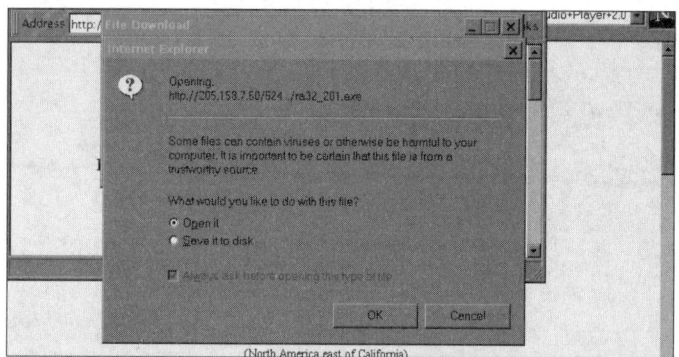

FIGURE 12-7

Downloading the RealAudio Player in Internet Explorer 3.0.

Take a closer look at this window and contrast it with the Netscape download window shown previously in Figure 12-4. You should see a slight difference: I have a choice of either saving the file to disk or opening it. Now, keep in mind that I also have somewhat similar options in Netscape: If I do *not* have a viewer designated in my helper apps, then Netscape will give me the choice of saving the file to disk (or looking for a viewer or helper app). But the big difference in the Internet Explorer window is the "open it" choice with which I am now presented. This option allows me to download the plug-in, after which it will be automatically extracted and installed in the proper places. To me, this is easy and extremely user friendly. In fact, this seamless integration is exactly what Microsoft is trying to pull off as it heads toward making everything happen from its browser.

When the plug-in is finished downloading, I see the Authenticode Security screen pop up before the plug-in has completed the download (see Figure 12-8).

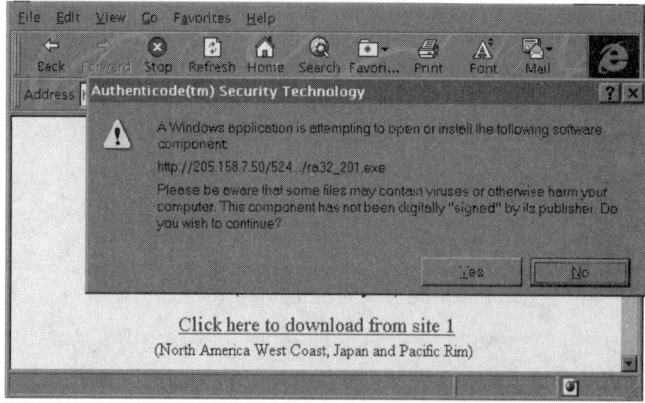

FIGURE 12-8

A bit of caution before installing the plug-in; a warning about possible viruses and digital authenticity of the file.

The Authenticode screen pops up before the download actually is completed. Clicking on Yes starts the installation of the RealAudio Player plug-in (and this is where the cool part really begins). The plug-in begins loading, showing the screen in Figure 12-9.

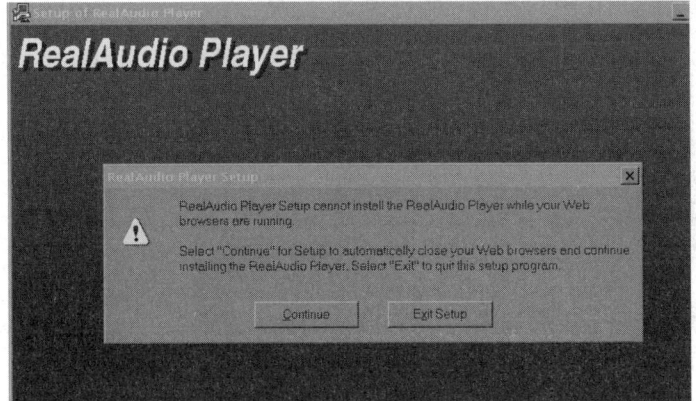

FIGURE 12-9

The RealAudio plug-in starts to load and asks you to close down browsers.

What is Authenticode Security Technology? According to Microsoft:

> Microsoft and many software publishers are proposing a new standard that uses digital signatures to provide accountability for code downloaded from the Internet. This is an open standard—it will be used to sign all forms of executable code, and is designed to run on all platforms. Supported in Microsoft Internet Explorer 3.0, Authenticode is Microsoft's implementation of this widely supported code signing proposal. Through Authenticode, end users know who published a piece of software and whether the software has been tampered with, before downloading the software to their PCs.

Want more info? Point your browser at www.microsoft.com. Do a search on *authenticode* and you will find several articles that discuss this innovative new security technology.

I'm asked to close any open browsers that I might have running, so that the plug-in can begin loading. After I close my browsers, I click on Continue and the plug-in finally starts to load. I am then presented with a screen that just about changed my life; take a look at Figure 12-10 and you'll see why.

Do you see what is happening on this screen? I'm being given the opportunity to install my plug-in for use with *both* Microsoft Internet Explorer and Netscape Navigator. Unbelievable. Read the sidebar, which shows text taken from the Microsoft site, to see Microsoft's approach to plug-ins, and you will see why the company has done it this way (it's very clever).

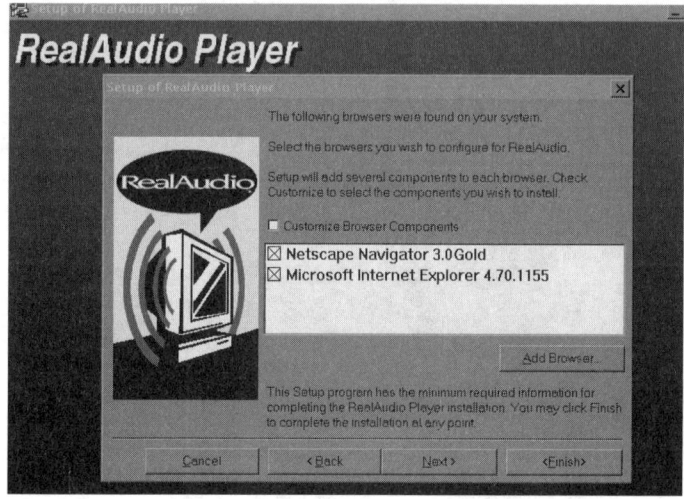

FIGURE 12-10

Your chance to choose installation options for each of your browsers.

Use Your Existing Plug-ins

There's really nothing to it. Internet Explorer uses the plug-ins you're already using: Go to any Web page you've viewed before that contains plug-ins. Internet Explorer detects the plug-ins needed, locates the plug-ins on your computer, runs them, and you're ready to go!

Add New Plug-Ins

Whether you've been using another Web browser and are just switching to Internet Explorer 3.0, or this is this your first browser on this computer, plug-ins and ActiveX controls are easy to install.

1. When you go to a page that requires plug-ins, Internet Explorer checks to see if you have the needed plug-in(s) installed.

2. If you don't have a plug-in installed, then you can install either the plug-in or an ActiveX control, if available.

3. Install the plug-in to the Netscape Navigator folder (if you've been using Netscape Navigator), such as "C:\program files\netscape\navigator\program\plugins," or to the Internet Explorer folder: "C:\program files\plus!\microsoft internet\plugins."

4. When you've installed the ActiveX controls or plug-ins you need, then you're ready to go!

This approach makes it very easy for you to download plug-ins for Netscape and still make them available for Internet Explorer as well. Sounds good to me. After the plug-in has been successfully installed in both Netscape Navigator and Microsoft Internet Explorer, you can see the screen shown in Figure 12-11, which gives a recap of what has just occurred.

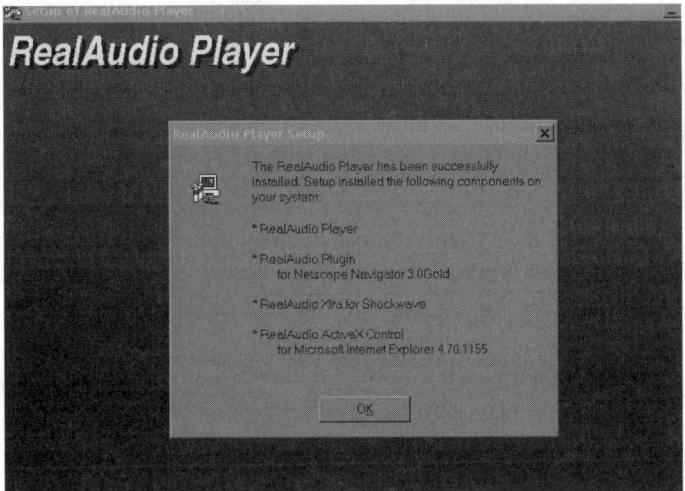

FIGURE 12-11

Everything is coming up roses! Our RealAudio plug-in is installed.

Plug-Ins and Your Intranet

Plug-ins and helper applications sound as if they would be very useful tools to implement and take advantage of in your corporate intranet, right? You'd better believe it, but—as with anything that tastes good and that you really enjoy—you have to use them in moderation, especially in a corporate intranet.

Imagine, if you will, users who are downloading helper apps and plug-ins willy-nilly and then (shudder!), they start creating applications with these plug-ins. A good example of what could happen is with Adobe Acrobat. Say that one of your users is very savvy when it comes to desktop publishing, and he wakes up one morning feeling that his mission in life is to put every paper document in the area into a PDF (this is, by the way, a very good idea). Okay so far? Yes, but here's where the touchy part (from an IT perspective) comes in: After our user has created all of his PDFs, he feels this incredible urge to make them available on his area's Web pages so that *everybody* can have access to them. This would be wonderful, wouldn't it? Now, everyone throughout the company can have instant access to a wealth of documents whose words were formerly "stuck" inside a paper medium. This is good! Or is it?

Support Issues

There are some support issues to consider before you let everyone plug-in in such a big way. Say, for example, that Tony over in Accounting is making vector animations with the FutureSplash program. Who will be able to see Tony's great works of art? The answer: No one. Why? Because no one has the FutureSplash plug-in viewer installed on his or her PC. This can be a major problem for Tony (who spent all that time creating cool content that no one can see) and for Tony's colleagues, who think that Tony is a bit clueless. You can be sure that they won't be returning to his page anytime soon—and why should they, when they could just as easily go over to Mickey's Hall of Fame of Static Web Pages, where they can be assured of a consistent, if not terribly exciting, display of very static and mostly text-based Web pages. I think that you are starting to get the point, yes?

It is a very important issue for a Webmaster of a corporate intranet to consider: what plug-ins and helper applications will the IT (Information Technology) department recommend, and, more important, be able to support? Is it terribly important for your users to have a plug-in that tells them the time in Lagos, Nigeria? Or one that brings them the latest stock reports? Maybe both are very important, depending on what your company is involved in; or, maybe both are an absolute waste of time and could become an intractable support issue.

The Importance of Process

I want to emphasize the importance of a having a sensible Web development process, either on its way or in place as you begin rolling out your Web. Your Web development team, group, klatch, gathering, or whatever you name it, should be taking a long, hard look at the issue of plug-ins, in terms of which ones, how many, and who should have them. Be proactive (if I can get by with that terribly overused word) and have a person on your team who is responsible for seeking out new and exciting technologies and plug-ins, to boldly go where no Webmaster has gone before!

What is your reaction to my suggestion that you have a Web development process on the way? Does it go against the way you usually plan major rollouts of projects? You may well be thinking that it's better to have a plan in place before rolling out something substantial? Yes, it usually is, but take heed: By the time you have a plan in place and you are ready to roll out your Web development process, there will be three to five areas that will have done one of the following:

- Built their own Web site and are now busily shopping around for server space to post their new Web
- Installed their own Web server, which they have also attached to your network

Bob's Web Server

I have a friend who works in another area of our company. My friend called me recently and said, "Hey, type in this URL." Which I did, and up popped a screen that said, "Bob's Web Server—Under Construction." Well the "under construction" part certainly didn't surprise me :>, but the first part was a bit of a shocker. Bob's Web Server? Bob's Web Server was on the corporate network, and guess what? Bob set up his server using the Web server included with Microsoft FrontPage 97, and he said he did it in about an hour! Bob also did all this without consulting with or even opening a work order through the IT department (oops!). This is a bit scary, but don't jump off any mainframes just yet; not everyone will be as sharp as Bob (though it seems to be getting easier and easier to set these Web servers up, and Bob set the server up on a Pentium machine). But it's something to think about when your Web development team meets.

My point is that all this Web stuff is moving so quickly that your process document or Web development strategy will, and should be, a living, breathing, and, I hope, growing thing: hit the ground, develop a framework, create content, roll it out, hit the ground again, get back up, and then tweak your framework as the needs of the areas become more obvious and apparent. Can you lose? Sure, but you'll have a great time getting there.

What's the flip side? You'll spend time in endless meetings trying to determine the difference between the Internet and the intranet while your areas are growing impatient and exploring the possibility of getting an ISP to post their Web site, or even of putting up their own server. When you finally get out of those meetings, it won't matter what the difference between the Internet and an intranet is, because by then, you probably won't be able to tell one from the other.

A Plethora of Plug-Ins

Way back, when browsers choked and pundits spoke of what no one was really sure, the whole issue of plug-ins and helper applications was a very touchy one. But it was also a bit easier in that there were not a whole lot of plug-ins to worry about. Now, of course, there are a very large number out there, at least 108 on the Netscape site the last time I checked, and many, many more coming down the pike. If you go to the Netscape site, you can even find instructions and an SDK (Software Development Kit) for making your very own plug-ins! All this might make you long for the good ol' days when there were only a handful of plug-ins for an IT professional to worry about, and they were easily administered and monitored.

Those days are gone for sure. Then, how to deal with this abundance of plug-ins? I discussed this bit in the preceding sections of this chapter, but here are some other issues to consider regarding the use of plug-ins on your corporate intranet:

- Who is responsible for the content piece of your intranet?
- Who is responsible for the technical piece of your intranet?
- Who "owns" the information that resides on Web servers throughout your company?
- Who can access the information contained on your Web servers (what is your target audience)?

The following sections cover each of these issues.

Content Responsibility

This is a very important, and controversial, part of your Web development process, and one that must be as clearly defined as possible. Why? If you don't solve this piece of the Web development puzzle near the beginning, then there will always be a lingering doubt as to who or what entity, or what part of the corporation, is really the ultimate gatekeeper of this aspect of your company's Web development effort. This would seem to be an obvious concept to define and work with, but the Web is a strange animal in that it is both an artistic or creative endeavor and a technical one.

Technical Responsibility

Of course, Information Services (IS) takes charge of this aspect, and not just in terms of the "box" or the network. As Web pages move from static to dynamic implementation schemes, the IS department again becomes a critical player who provides the programming expertise necessary to link the front-end that the content types create to existing (as well as new) databases. These, in turn, provide that dynamic element to an area's Web pages. In this sense, the "content types" become inextricably linked to the IS or "technical types," and they end up becoming information partners in the truest sense of the word. What a concept!

So, after the content and technical pieces have been defined and agreed upon, you can start taking a hard look at plug-ins and how they might facilitate and enhance the delivery of information through your company's intranet. The content types can list those plug-ins that might help them publish and view documents (Adobe Acrobat, Envoy, and so on), whereas the technical folks might be more interested in a plug-in that would automate software distribution from Web pages (Net-Install). The trick is to strike a balance between content needs and technical realities.

Information Ownership

Determining who "owns" the information is also an important piece of your Web development and in determining your plug-in deployment strategy. Because the Web has such a low point-of-entry cost (that is, it is very easy to write and even post your department's very own Web pages), you will run into many instances of duplication of information. In other words, you will have two departments on opposite sides of the company (or even the other side of the same room) who will be working on creating exactly the same information.

This is obviously a waste of someone's time and effort. It is up to your Web development group, in conjunction with the affected areas, to determine who will create (and maintain) and eventually "own" the information on their Web pages. The owner, in this case, is the area that has created content relevant to their operating area. The area should continue to create, update, and otherwise maintain this information and make it available, through linking, to any other areas of the company that might want to access it. So, in this sense, ownership of information denotes having "information repositories" spread throughout the company that are accessible to everyone, but the content on those servers is the responsibility of a specific or particular area or department in order to avoid duplication.

A good example of ownership of information is Tony's accounting Web page that I mentioned earlier. Tony's Web site contains a wealth of accounting-related information that is now accessible, in one central place, to all who might need it. Now, if Kim in Payroll decided to also put up a Web site, and she decided to include some accounting information, she can create a link from her site to the existing information contained in Tony's Web site.

After you have determined the owners of any given information, you can decide how and where to implement your plug-in deployment strategy. When you have a better handle on the types of information that is out on your Web server, you can better determine which areas really need which plug-ins.

Accessibility and the Target Audience

You can create the greatest Web site in the world, but it won't really matter unless someone can see it. Access to the information that you are creating on your Web site is a critical aspect of your evolving Web development strategy. What kind of information do you want delivered, and in what kinds of places or venues? Would you want to have a graphically rich Web site accessible in a mission-critical area where customers were waiting for information? Or, in this instance, would a more text-based Web site be quicker and more reliable?

There is obviously a place for a site rich in graphics, sound, and video, but the realities of the network infrastructure must be taken into account when you determine Web access points—especially in terms of where and how plug-ins are to be utilized and delivered. Although a PDF is a very useful electronic publishing tool, you don't want your users to be loading PDFs in a high-intensity customer interaction area such as a credit desk at a department store.

When you have a handle on the access question, you should consider the following implementation questions:

- How will you deliver the plug-ins to your users? How will they install them?
- Who will users call for plug-in support questions?
- Will the company determine a list of approved plug-ins?
- Can users have the ability to download and install plug-ins not supported by the IS department?
- What types of plug-ins will you approve for widespread usage?

The preceding are all very important issues that should be worked out as democratically as possible by those creating and maintaining Web pages and the IS department. Of course, in any successful business, the integrity of the network is paramount and should not be put in jeopardy by a reckless (or even sometimes well-meaning) use of plug-ins. Although those creating the content for the company's intranet may see a need for certain types of plug-ins, this perceived need should be balanced by a realistic technical assessment done by the IS department.

As for what types of plug-ins to approve for widespread use, you might take a cue from the Netscape site (one of the best for obtaining the latest and greatest plug-ins), which groups plug-ins into the following categories:

- Business and Utilities
- Audio/Video
- 3-D and Animation
- Presentations

In terms of planning for your corporate intranet, the types of plug-ins to watch closely are those in the Audio/Video and the 3-D and Animation categories. Why? Because the plug-ins listed in these areas will typically be the ones that are bringing in content that is very intensive on your network. Audio/video streams and files are not things that you want flying across your network wires on an unrestricted basis. Until most company's networks become more robust and able to handle large volumes of traffic on a continuing basis, it is a good idea to try to localize access to network-intensive applications.

A good example of localizing content delivery is in a Learning Center that you have available for employee development. In this Learning Center, you might have a number of PCs that are connected to the network and take advantage of Web content that is basically accessible to everyone on the corporate network. Simultaneously, you may have some video, or sound files, or even a training program that is delivered from a CD-ROM that you also want your employees to be able to access while in the Learning Center.

How would you arrange this access? One way would be to have all of this potentially bandwidth-intensive stuff loaded on a type of server that could be housed in your Learning Center and be used for local access only of your video, sound, and CD-ROM materials. You could also have similar types of video and audio servers located at various points throughout your network, in order to take the weight off the network to a significant degree.

Localizing delivery of bandwidth-intensive content is one way to allow your users to take advantage of plug-in technologies that you might not wish to ride on the mission-critical corporate network wires. As technologies such as ATM and Fast Ethernet become more widespread, you will find that you can more easily send bandwidth-intensive sound, video, and 3D files.

Plug-Ins by Category

This section looks at some very popular and useful plug-ins that you might consider for use in your own corporate intranet. I have gone to the Netscape site and chosen a few that would fit well in my own particular work situation. By the time you read this, though, there will probably be 20 or 30 more plug-ins available for your downloading pleasure. I go to each site where you can download the plug-in, and then I show you some cool things (also useful) that you can do with each. I encourage you to go to the following URL to download and try some of these exciting new "extensions" to Netscape Navigator (also accessible to Microsoft Internet Explorer):

`http://home.netscape.com`

When you're there, scroll down until you see a link to netscape plug-ins (or something close to that).

Now I describe some plug-ins from each of the four categories of plug-ins that I listed previously.

Plug-Ins: Business and Utilities

These are the plug-ins that will help you get your work done in the most efficient manner possible. Business and utilities plug-ins enhance and extend the already powerful information-sharing capabilities of your corporate intranet's Web browser. The next sections look at a few of the more popular and particularly useful business and utilities plug-ins; you should keep in mind that there are many more where these came from. You will need to determine your own specific business requirements and needs.

Adobe Acrobat Reader 3.0 Beta

I wanted to mention this one again even though I already did at the beginning of this chapter. You simply must get this plug-in. End of discussion. This plug-in is available for the following applications (at the time of this writing):

♦ Windows 95
♦ Windows NT
♦ Windows 3.X
♦ Macintosh 68K
♦ Power Mac
♦ Sun OS
♦ Solaris
♦ HP-UX
♦ Irix

Go get it at http://www.adobe.com.

ActiveX by Ncompass

ActiveX is Microsoft's answer to Java applets. It also offers the capability to view what are called Active Documents (such as Word, Excel, PowerPoint) in Web pages. Ncompass has created a plug-in that allows Netscape Navigator users to take advantage of Microsoft's ActiveX technology. I guess this is sort of like a compromise on Netscape's part; it would prefer that ActiveX did not exist (IMHO, of course). So, if you are wedded to Netscape but you still feel the occasional urge to utilize an ActiveX control, then start downloading.

ActiveX is available for the following platforms:

♦ Windows 95
♦ Windows NT

NOTE: It is estimated that there are around 10,000 Java applets on the Gamelan site (www.gamelan.com) whereas another estimate puts the number of ActiveX controls created to date at only a couple of thousand.

Go get it at http://www.ncompasslabs.com.

The opening or splash screen of Ncompass Labs, which is the home of the ActiveX plug-in suite for Netscape Navigator, is shown in Figure 12-2.

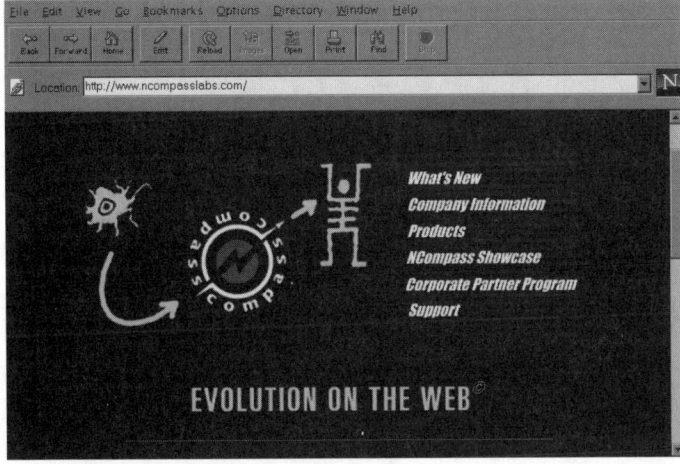

FIGURE 12-12

The Ncompass home page is where you obtain the ActiveX plug-in for Netscape.

Something interesting happened on my way to load this plug-in. When I tried to click on one of the examples, I was met with the following dialog screen, informing me that the application I was trying to load required a plug-in that I did not have loaded (see Figure 12-13).

After I clicked on Get the plug-in, I was sent to the page shown in Figure 12-14, which is called, appropriately enough, the Netscape Plug-in Finder page. This page instructed me to scroll down a bit for a listing of the plug-in that I needed. I did so and found the ActiveX plug-in I had been seeking. The only drawback was that I when I clicked on the Download button, I was taken back to the NCompass site, where I then proceeded to download the plug-in (I would have liked to have just retrieved it from the Netscape site—hey, I'm lazy).

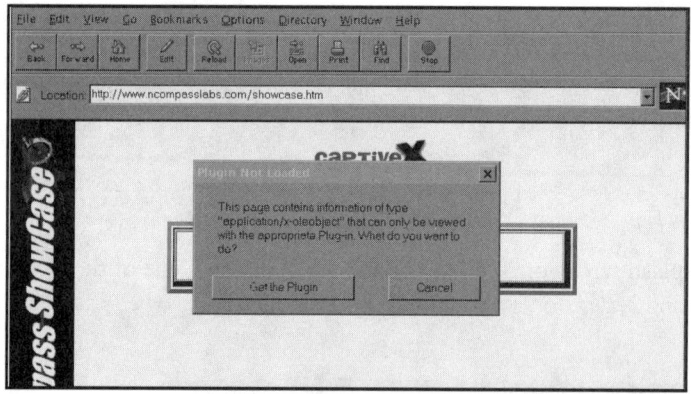

FIGURE 12-13

Oops! Don't have that plug-in loaded yet—I think I'll go get it.

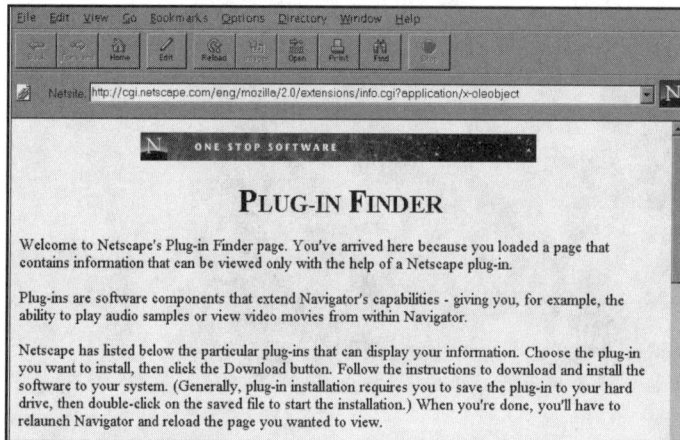

FIGURE 12-14

The Netscape Plug-in Finder Page—help for the plug-in challenged surfer.

After downloading and installing the ActiveX plug-in, I went back to the NCompass site to check out a sample of an ActiveX control called CaptiveX. This ActiveX control allows you to put interactive advertising on your Web site. CaptiveX allows the use of multiple images that change, thereby enabling you to send multiple-part messages or even have more than one advertiser appear. Figure 12-15 shows what it looks like.

Carbon Copy/Net by Microcom

This plug-in allows you to remotely control another PC over the Internet (see Figure 12-16). You can run applications, and access and view files, just as if you were sitting in front of the remote PC. It's also excellent for collaboration on projects, remote support, and even remote software demos. Carbon Coby/Net is available for the following platforms:

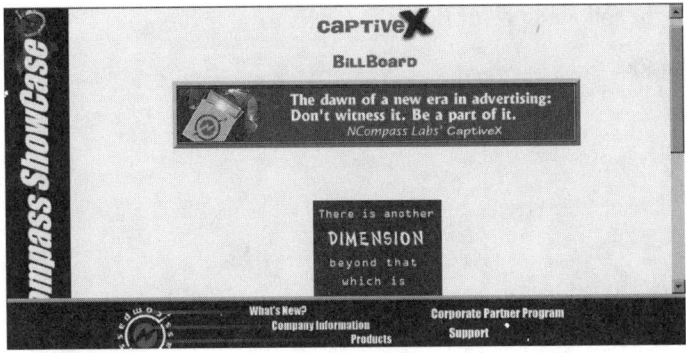

- ◆ Windows95
- ◆ Windows 3.X

Go get it at http://www.microcom.com.

FIGURE 12-16

Connecting to a remote PC through Carbon Copy/Net.

Ichat by Ichat

This is the first plug-in to integrate the ability to "chat" directly into Netscape Navigator (and Microsoft Internet Explorer through an ActiveX control). When you encounter or link to another Ichat-enabled Web site, you will see a window (or frame) that opens in the lower part of the browser window; there you will become involved in a real-time (live), ongoing chat session between all the visitors to that Web page. There is a unique "Web-tours" capability that allows you to take your friends or colleagues on a tour of the Web. Ichat has also just released ROOMS version 2.2, which takes chat one step further by allowing users to represent themselves through avatars and enhance chat communications with images and graphical navigation. In addition to enhancing the Ichat Plug-in, ActiveX, Java and HTML clients, ROOMS 2.2 allows connections from standard IRC clients.

Ichat is available on the following platforms:

- ◆ Macintosh 68K
- ◆ Power Mac
- ◆ Windows 3.X
- ◆ Windows95
- ◆ Windows NT

Go get it at http://www.ichat.com.

Ichat is fast becoming the "chat of choice" among knowledgeable Webmasters and is considered to be on the cutting edge of Web chat technology. Figure 12-17 shows the Ichat log-in screen.

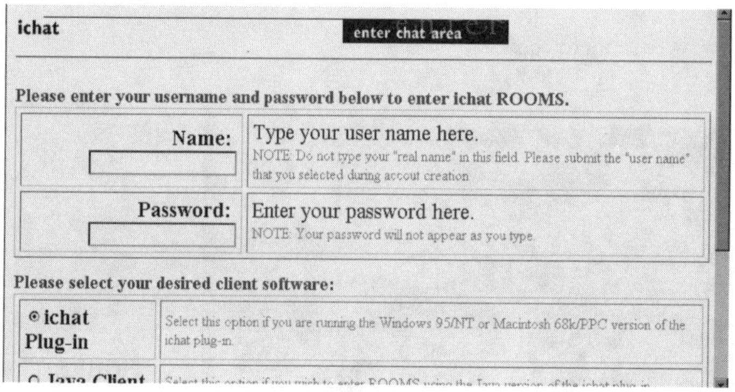

FIGURE 12-17

Logging on to Ichat.

Downloading this plug-in went smoothly. I installed it and immediately went to an Ichat-enabled site—in this case, the Capitol Speakers Bureau (see Figure 12-18). Tonight was a scheduled "chat" with Eleanor Clift and Fred Barnes, two political pundits. But, alas, although I was able to log in, that night's chat had been cancelled. Oh, well. Notice the Ichat frame that opens up at the bottom of the screen shown in Figure 12-18.

Jetform Webfiller by Jetform Corporation

Already popular as a stand-alone application, Jetform brings new functionality to your Web site by enabling you to seamlessly integrate JetForm forms onto your Web pages. When you access the JetForm plug-in, the form will be displayed in the Netscape window, as opposed to invoking a separate helper application. Jetform is available on the following platforms:

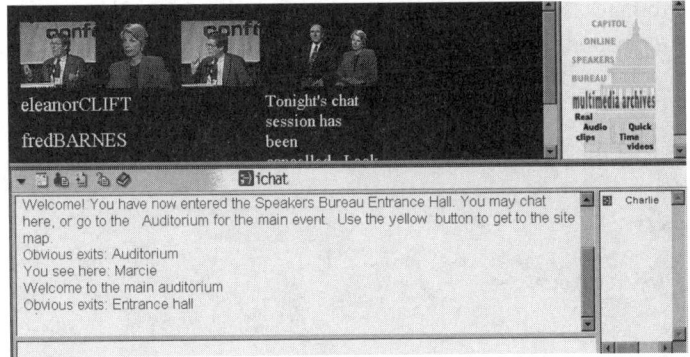

FIGURE 12-18

Connected to an Ichat session at the Capitol Speakers Bureau.

◆ Windows 3.X

◆ Windows95

◆ Windows NT

Go get it at http://www.jetform.com.

The Jetform plug-in can be an invaluable business tool. This plug-in can make the often tedious (and time consuming) task of filling out forms seem like a walk in the park. Figure 12-19 shows an example of a form near and dear to most successful companies: the purchase order form.

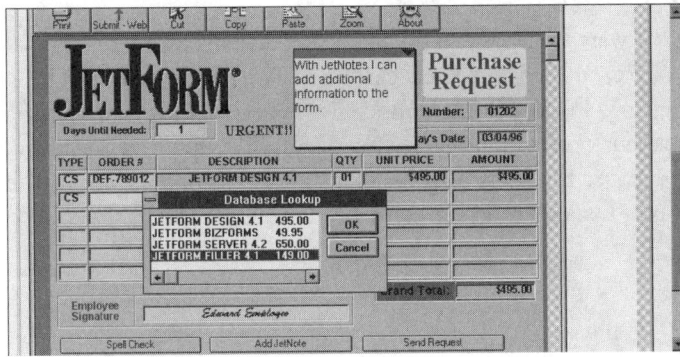

FIGURE 12-19

A purchase order Web form in JetForm Webfiller.

KeyView by FTP Software, Inc.

This plug-in enables you to view, print, convert, and manage almost 200 different file formats from inside Netscape (see Figure 12-20). You can also copy, paste, and convert formats such as Microsoft Word, WordPerfect, Microsoft Excel, EPS, PCX, and nearly 200 more. KeyView Eliminates the need to configure different viewers in Netscape's preferences list. Sounds good to me!

KeyView is available on the following platforms:

◆ Windows 3.X

◆ Windows95

◆ Windows NT

Go get it at http://www.ftp.com.

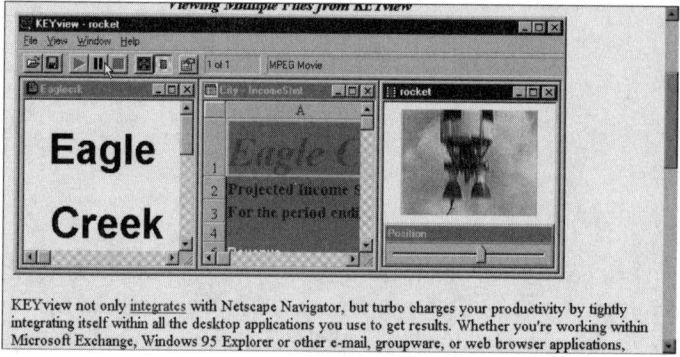

FIGURE 12-20

KeyView has the ability to process more than 200 file formats.

Net-Install by 20/20 Software, Inc.

Want to distribute software from your Web pages? Net-Install is your answer. Just by clicking on a link, Netscape Navigator users can download, decompress, and install software in one easy step (see Figure 12-21). This could be one solution to the distribution of plug-ins throughout your corporate intranet. Imagine having a plug-in download area where users could go to see the latest plug-ins that have been approved for use on the corporate intranet. Net-Install is available for the following platforms:

◆ Windows 95

◆ Windows NT

◆ Windows 3.X

Go get it at http://www.twenty.com.

These are just some of the many plug-ins available for the Business and Utilities category. Please go to the Netscape site to check for any new ones that are coming out regularly.

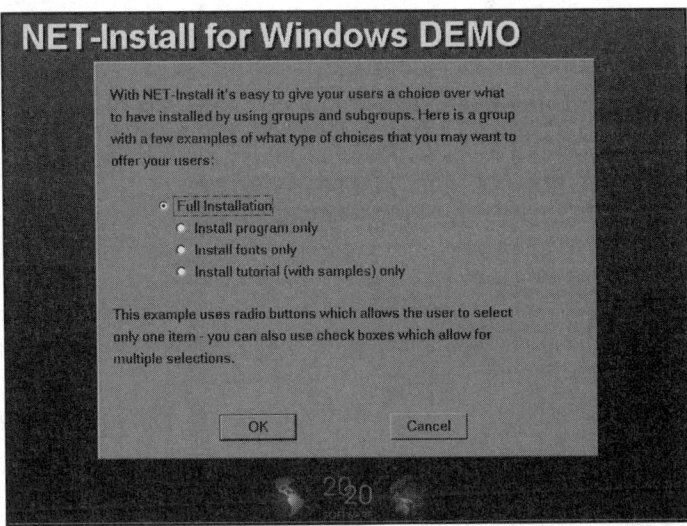

FIGURE 12-21

*Downloading
software from a Web
page with Net-Install—
it's automatic!*

Plug-Ins: Presentations

Presentations, and successful ones at that, are the lifeblood of any corporation that plans on being around for any significant length of time. Microsoft PowerPoint has probably been the tool of choice for many corporations, and its PowerPoint Viewer software is freely available for distribution. The viewer makes it easy for John in Seattle to see the presentation that Steve in Orlando put together, even though John didn't have PowerPoint on his PC. The Viewer allowed him to fire it up. Now, all of PowerPoint's capabilities are available for viewing through your friendly neighborhood Web browser. Though I have focused on the PowerPoint plug-ins, please keep in mind that there are many other excellent presentations plug-ins available. Go to the Netscape site to check some of them out.

PointPlus by Net-Scene

This plug-in allows you to view dynamic and colorful presentations embedded in your Web pages. It is very useful for viewing PowerPoint presentations from within your browser. Use of sophisticated compression and streaming technologies allows presentations to be played with no delays. PointPlus is available on the following platforms:

♦ Windows 3.X

♦ Windows 95

♦ Windows NT

Go get it at http://www.net-scene.com.

Figure 12-22 shows an example of a PointPlus presentation. Though you can't see it here, this presentation has animation and sound..

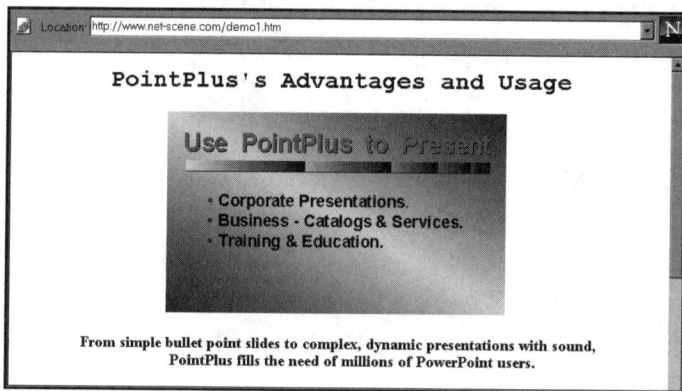

FIGURE 12-22

Caught in the middle of an animated PowerPoint presentation with sound included!

PowerPoint Animation Player and Publisher by Microsoft

This plug-in provides you with the fastest, easiest way to view and publish PowerPoint animations and presentations from within your browser window. Take advantage of enhanced animation, hyperlinks, sound, and other special effects. PowerPoint is available for the following platforms:

◆ Windows 95
◆ Windows NT

Go get it at http://www.microsoft.com.

Put all your PowerPoint presentations into your Web pages; amaze your friends by inviting them to dine at the Coyote Café (shown in Figure 12-23). Make the coyote howl!

Plug-Ins: 3-D and Animation

Down with static Web pages, up with animation! This is the battle cry of Webmasters throughout the world, and corporate America is no exception. Animation, if used in the right way, is an attraction that will draw users to your site again and again. 3-D is becoming increasingly popular as online merchants search for a way to allow visitors to virtually touch and feel their product line. 3-D is also finding much use in the training and development arena.

FIGURE 12-23

The PowerPoint Animation Player—hear and feel the wind!

FutureSplash by FutureWave

FutureSplash enables you to view vector-based animations in your Web browser. FutureSplash files are extremely small, and include interactive buttons, antialiased graphics, outline fonts, and zooming control. FutureSplash is available on the following platforms:

♦ Macintosh 68K

♦ Power Mac

♦ Windows 3.X

♦ Windows 95

♦ Windows NT

Go get it at http://www.futurespace.com.

Vector animations are becoming very popular as a means of putting professional-looking images that are small and actually move on your Web pages. Figure 12-24 is a good example of a fun (and small) vector animation.

Live3D by Netscape

Experience this 3-D VRML platform that lets you fly through VRML worlds through your Web browser. Netscape Live3D features 3-D text, background images, texture animation, morphing, viewpoints, collision detection, gravity, and RealAudio streaming sound. Live3D is available for the following platforms:

♦ Windows 3.X

♦ Windows 95

♦ Windows NT

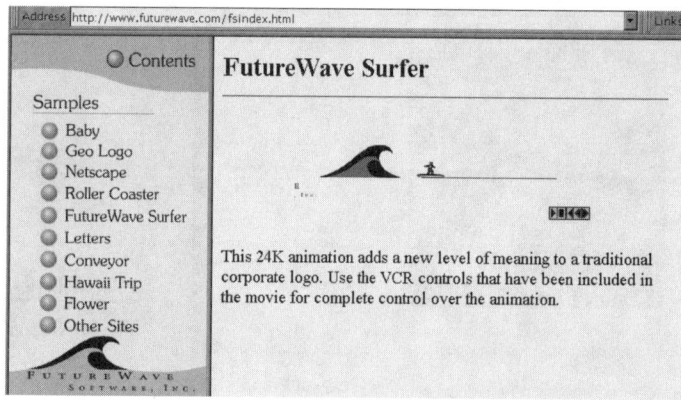

FIGURE 12-24

The FutureWave Surfer vector animation, with "vcr" controls included.

Go get it at `http://home.netscape.com/comprod/products/navigator/live3d/download_live3d.html`.

Here's a cool example of something that everyone is always worried about but no one can ever correctly predict: the weather. Figure 12-25 presents an interesting 3-D perspective on the world's weather.

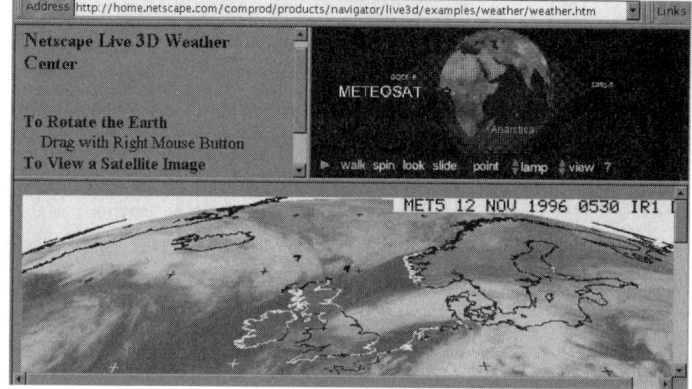

FIGURE 12-25

Live3D VRML Weather Map.

Notice the controls in the upper-right frame of Figure 12-25; use these to manipulate images in window.

Figure 12-26 is an example of one of the many 3-D worlds—in this case a space station—that you will find on the Web. You can visit sites such as `www.paragraph.com`, where you can download the beta version of Internet Space Builder. This program has many ready-to-use 3-D worlds that you can customize for placement on your Web site.

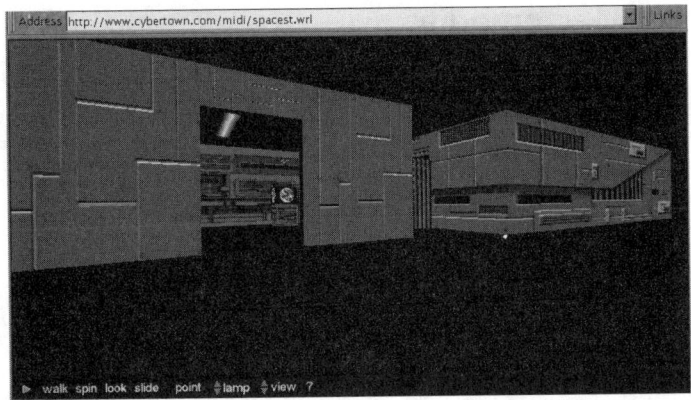

FIGURE 12-26

The VR Space Station. Controls allow you to walk through the scene.

ProtoPlay by Altia

This plug-in allows you to run electronic prototypes on your Web pages that help manu-facturers sell products by allowing your customers to see and try them before buying. Unlike pictures, multimedia presentations, or video, electronic prototypes take advantage of interactivity, as shown in Figure 12-27, to educate consumers about product benefits. ProtoPlay is available on the following platforms:

* Windows 3.X
* Windows 95
* Windows NT

Go get it at http://www.altia.com.

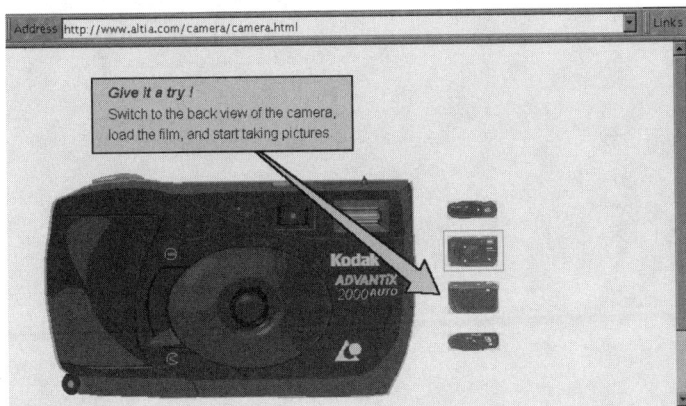

FIGURE 12-27

The interactive camera tutorial from within your Web browser.

Shockwave by Macromedia

This plug-in is the industry standard for delivering and experiencing quality interactive multimedia, graphics, and streaming audio on the Web. Companies such as CNN, Capitol Records, Warner Brothers Records, Sony, Paramount, and Virgin utilize Shockwave as an integral part of their Web sites. Shockwave is available for the following platforms:

- Macintosh 68K
- Windows 3.X
- Windows 95

Get shocked at `http://www.macromedia.com`.

When you click on a Shockwave link the first time, you will see a screen similar to the one in Figure 12.28. Subsequent clicks on the same link will cause the Shockwave file to be drawn from your cache (provided that you have not flushed or dumped it), thereby drastically reducing load time.

Just looking at these Shockwave screenshots does a severe injustice to what you would see live on a Shocked site on the Web—go out and find one. Start at the Macromedia site (see address listed previously). I was able to fully manipulate every part of the "Deep Forest" image that you see in the preceding pictures; I could select songs, change the "mix," and even raise and lower the volume (using the leaf on the right side of the image).

FIGURE 12-28

This is the first screen that you see after you click on a Shockwave link.

FIGURE 12-29

This is what you see after the image loads. Sorry— you can't hear the music.

Viscape by SuperScape

This plug-in brings you true interactive 3D experiences to your Web pages. It takes the Web from interactive to hyperactive by letting you grab objects, do walkthroughs, and hear sounds. This is an excellent plug-in that your corporate intranet could use for training and marketing efforts. Viscape is available for the following platforms:

♦ Windows 95
♦ Windows NT

Go get it at http://www.superscape.com.

Take a look at the SuperCity in the browser right frame shown in Figure 12-30. Note the navigation controls. If you click on corporate items in city, then you will be taken to that company's Web site.

FIGURE 12-30

The SuperCity viewed with the Viscape plug-in.

Plug-Ins: Audio and Video

Bandwidth, bandwidth, bandwidth, or lack of it: this is the constant refrain that you hear in the real world and in regards to the corporate intranet. The bandwidth question is extremely critical in the corporate environment because the amount of bandwidth can greatly affect mission-critical systems within the organization. For example, say that you are working at a rather large and luxurious resort. Is it a good idea to have Web pages full of sound and graphics (or video) streaming to a workstation at the check-in area? Probably not, and this is where bandwidth becomes very critical.

Plug-ins can help. The following sections list a few. I also encourage you to visit the Netscape site to see the latest.

MacZilla by Knowledge Engineering

This plug-in is available only for the Macintosh, and it claims to be able to do almost everything in terms of audio/video that you would ever want a plug-in to do. It uses QuickTime; ambient MIDI background sounds; WAV, AU, AIFF audio, MPEG, and AVI video. MacZilla can update itself over the Net with just the click of a button. It's available for Macintosh. Go get it at http://www.maczilla.com.

RealAudio by Progressive Networks

In an earlier section of this chapter, "Installing Two Popular Plug-Ins," I showed you how to download this plug-in. RealAudio is available for the following platforms:

- ◆ Macintosh 68K
- ◆ Windows 3.X
- ◆ Windows 95
- ◆ Windows NT

Go get it at http://www.realaudio.com.

VDOLive by VDOnet

VDOLive compresses video images without compromising quality on the receiving end. The speed of your connection determines the delivery rate. With a 28.8 Kbps modem, VDOLive runs in real time at 10 to 15 frames per second. VDOLive is available for the following platforms:

- ◆ Windows 95
- ◆ Windows NT
- ◆ Windows 3.X

Go get it at http://www.vdo.net.

After you click on a link to a video clip, the VDOLive player plug-in is activated and a window pops up inside your browser window (see Figure 12-31).

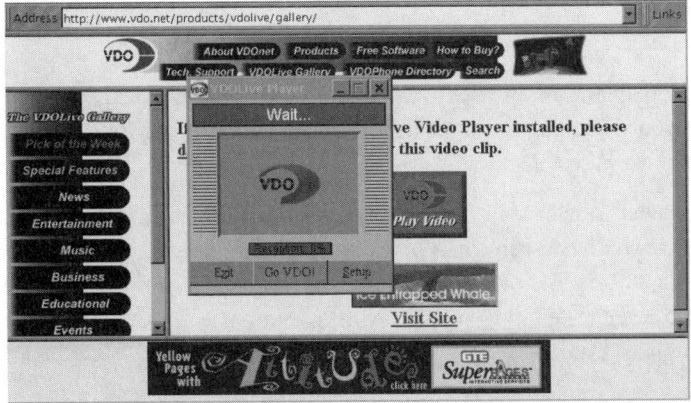

FIGURE 12-31

The VDOLive Player starts loading or streaming a video clip.

After a short time (depending on your connection speed), the video clip starts playing in the pop-up window, as shown in Figure 12-32.

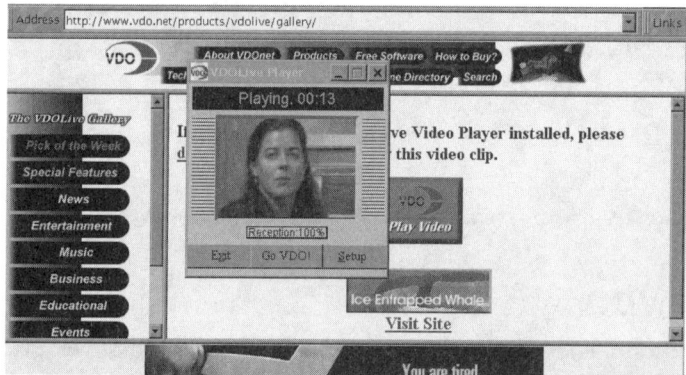

FIGURE 12-32

Seconds later, the video clip starts playing with sound.

ViVoActive Player by Vivo Software

The VivoActive Player is a streaming video plug-in for Netscape Navigator. It is the simplest and fastest way to get video clips to your Web page. VivoActive videos are transmitted using HTTP, so anyone who can view your Web pages can see your video. It's available for the following platforms:

♦ Power Mac

♦ Windows 3.X

♦ Windows 95

♦ Windows NT

Go get it at `http://www.vivo.com`.

Like the VDOLive plug-in, the VivoActive plug-in allows you to quickly download and play video clips in your Web pages. Figure 12-33 shows a unique way of having a video clip appear inside of a TV screen.

I am sure that I have left one of your favorite plug-ins out, and for this I humbly apologize. My hope is that you have seen some new ones here that you might have missed before. I am also hopeful that you went to each of the sites listed in this chapter and downloaded all of the suggested plug-ins. Did you? I thought you would. Thanks for listening. Now, go on and start writing your own plug-ins.

FIGURE 12-33

A VivoActivated Web site.

Summary

In this chapter, you learned what plug-ins and helper applications are and how they can make your browsing life much more pleasant. You learned how to set-up your helper applications in both Netscape Navigator and Microsoft Internet Explorer. You also learned how to look for and download the needed plug-in, and how the process, though it is getting easier, is at times a bit cumbersome. You now know that Microsoft might actually be on to something useful with its method of handling plug-in downloads, and you might feel inclined to call or write Netscape to ask that company to at least attempt to follow Microsoft's lead in this one area.

I've explored the implications of using plug-ins in your corporate intranet, as well as some of the steps that you might wish to consider when formulating your plug-in strategy. Finally, I took a look at some of the most popular plug-ins that are currently available for downloading.

Plug-ins and helper applications are your friends; they are there to help you through the quagmire of the various file formats, and jump into action when you need them (and only when you need them). The rest of the time, they just sit quietly by waiting for the next upgrade.

Will plug-ins even be around in the next year or so? Maybe—and maybe not. At a recent Netscape Developer's Conference, Mark Andreeson (Netscape's vice president of technology), casually mentioned that plug-ins (at least as we know them now) could disappear in the very near future. Andreeson indicated that the same functionality that a plug-in currently offers could be delivered through Java applets. You would think that this would cause much consternation among the many developers who are up late at night hacking out the latest plug-in, but not so, according to industry sources who say that they have already been working on the Java applets that Andreeson spoke about in anticipation of the impending death (or evolution) of the plug-in.

My guess would be that plug-ins and helper applications are here to stay, at least for the next few years (computer years, that is).

What's Next!

Now I move on to another way to broadcast information to the users in a company. It's a unique twist to the corporate intranet, and it is called PointCast. PointCast allows you to broadcast content to your users computer. Your users won't have to worry about missing new content and important information when it is updated in your intranet. PointCast allows news flashes to be sent to a smart screen saver and a viewer application that keeps users informed.

Chapter | 13

PCN: PointCast Network Intranet Opportunity

So far, I have focused on intranets from one viewpoint. Several other packages are available for organizations that allow collaboration and dissemination of information to users in the organization. The standard intranet model of a Web server and a thin client (Web browser) is very popular, but I want to open your eyes also to a new way of broadcasting information throughout your organization. When I say *broadcast*, I mean to emphasize the ability to display information in the same way as traditional television broadcasting. The advantage to this method of information sharing is that users get information displayed at their desktop immediately, without having to surf through the corporation's Web pages and look to see whether anything has changed. By broadcasting information, a message can be displayed on the user's desktop instantly. A few products are going in this direction, and I want to share with you information on the one that I believe is leading the pack. It is known as PointCast, or you may also have heard it referred to as "PCN."

PointCast I-Server

PointCast has recently released a new product called the PointCast I-Server. This lets your organization broadcast information to your users' desktop. This is perfect for sending announcements, sales, employee benefits information, and all types of company information.

With the PointCast I-Server, you can broadcast internal news on your own channel via the PointCast Network.

You may be familiar with the PointCast Network (the free service that broadcasts news and information via the Internet directly to a viewer's computer screen whenever it is idle). This is available for download at:

`http://www.pointcast.com`

Currently, the PointCast Network consists of two components:

- ◆ A central broadcast facility at PointCast's headquarters in Cupertino, California
- ◆ The PointCast Network client software, which displays news, stock, services, weather, sports, and more on each viewer's computer screen

You can now have your own corporate broadcast facility right at the workplace. PointCast I-Server is a new part of the PointCast Network that resides behind a corporate firewall and acts as a local broadcast facility for the PointCast Network. It extends the capabilities of the PointCast Network to enable companies to broadcast internal news alongside of the PointCast public channels, including news, industries, weather, and more.

Rather than explore company Web sites or shift through e-mail messages to read company news and updates, employees can now view up-to-the minute company news broadcasts throughout the day directly on their individual computer screens. This ensures that important company information, such as employee benefits announcements, sales updates, or upcoming events, is widely seen and read.

PointCast uses a technology of its own invention, called SmartScreen, which automatically begins running content from a company's private intranet channel and the network's public channels when an employee's computer is not in use. (Of course, this assumes that an individual employee will have a computer "not in use," and simultaneously be looking at it.) Employees can read the full-text story by simply clicking on a headline in the SmartScreen. This screen replaces uninformative screensavers with breaking news. Your company news can now be displayed via moving headlines, a scrolling ticker, and animated graphics (see Figure 13-1).

On the public PointCast Network channels, advertisements are displayed in the upper right corner of the SmartScreen. On your company's private PointCast I-Server channel, you can now communicate news and announcements with colorful moving images in this window for your intranet.

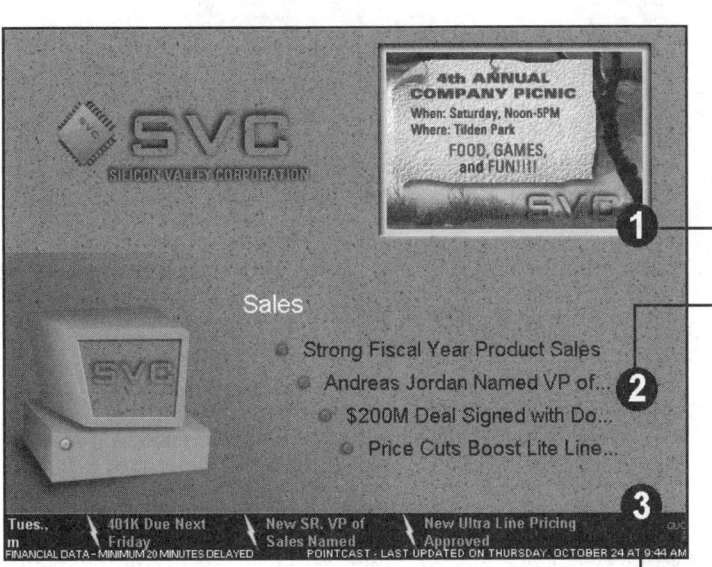

Display any headlines you want. The SmartScreen allows you to attract attention to the top news and stories in your organization.

FIGURE 13-1

The SmartScreen can be customized for your corporate broadcast channel.

You have a cool scrolling newsflash ticker which you can display late-breaking news on for employees.

Take a look at the figure and I will go over the SmartScreen with you.

Employees can also view the full story. By just clicking on the headline in the SmartScreen, the employee is taken to the PointCast channel viewer. The channel viewer can also be activated when the employee clicks on the PointCast Client desktop icon.

You create articles for the Channel Viewer in HTML. The articles and news in the channel viewer can be complex and creative, or they can appear as simple text. You can broadcast simple text documents or get into layouts that include tables, charts, and images. The PointCast I-Server also has support for URLs. This support means that you can embed URLs in your articles and news stories. So, you can broadcast short stories and include a URL to the full feature on your intranet.

Figure 13-2 shows the PointCast channel viewer.

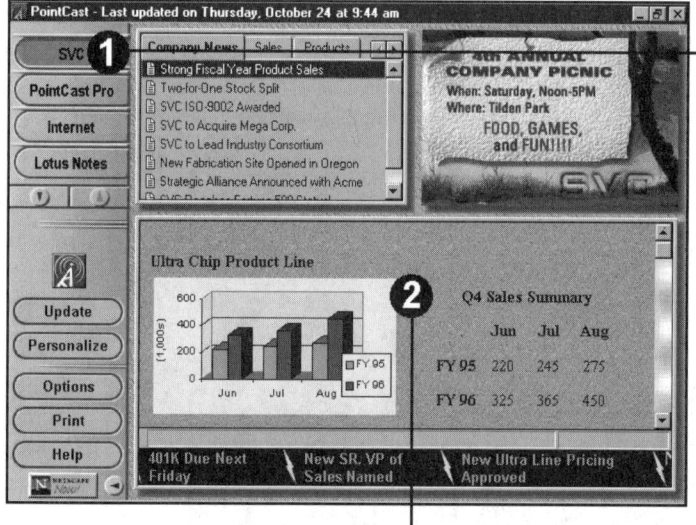

This is where your corporate channel appears with the other public channels.

FIGURE 13-2

The PointCast channel viewer allows you to list another channel for your corporation's channel along with the regular PointCast Network public channels.

Place your intranet and Internet URLs in your content to let employees get the full story and more information if they wish.

PointCast I-Server is also optimized for delivering information over the network. Installed on any Windows NT machine, it minimizes local network traffic to enable companies to broadcast news to hundreds or even thousands of employees instantly.

Because it resides behind the corporation's firewall, PointCast I-Server makes corporate intranets operate more efficiently by reducing the flow of local network traffic through the firewall by up to 80 percent. This efficiency is in contrast to traditional Web-based proxy servers, which are not optimized for managing dynamic, real-time delivery of information directly to the desktop monitor.

The PointCast I-Server works in conjunction with PointCast's central broadcast facility in Cupertino, California, as well as with the PointCast Network client software that is installed on employees' computers. Therefore, employees can now view the regular PointCast news feed as well as your own corporate channel news.

Your company can broadcast announcements, news, and reminders directly to employees' computer screens, ensuring that important information is seen throughout the organization. This broadcasting ability enables employees to receive instant updates on news that your organization needs to communicate. The following sections break down the key benefits that capability delivers to your organization.

Company News

This is your personal channel where authorized administrators can broadcast corporate content on the PointCast Network. You can also create and display custom SmartScreens to show company messages and ideas.

One-Step Web Creation

On your intranet, administrators can create Web pages on the fly right from their favorite Web browser. They can do this by filling out PointCast-supplied Web forms. PointCast then takes these Web forms and automatically converts the information into dynamic SmartScreens, which in turn are broadcast throughout your corporation.

The PointCast I-Server content manager tools enable you to set up each department so that it can create and maintain its own content. This ability means you don't have to spend the time gathering information and creating Web content. Each department can create and display its own information, allowing direct communications with their employees.

Create and maintaining your corporate channel is easy with the I-Server Administration Utility (see Figure 13-3).

Security

The PointCast I-Server resides within the corporate firewall, giving it the same security options as other corporate servers. Only authorized administrators can create and broadcast corporate news and information. The PointCast Network clients within your corporation's intranet will have access to this content.

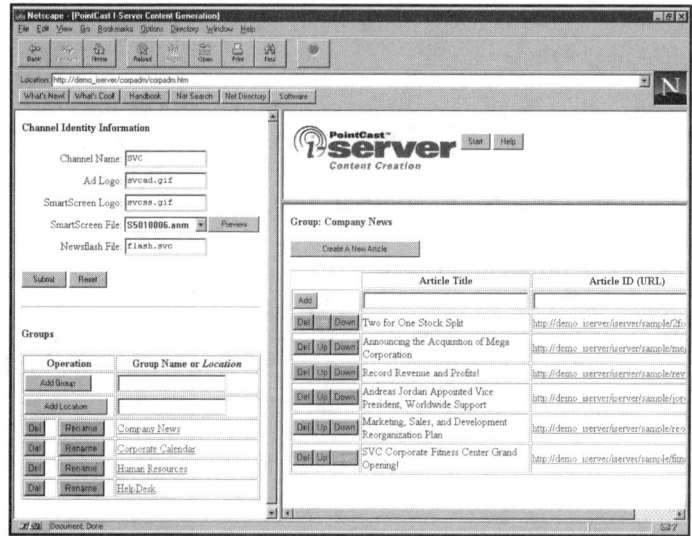

Client Updating

As new clients are added, the corporate channel is automatically configured on each additional client. This mean that no additional support or time is needed to set up clients.

PointCast I-Server leverages the same client/server technology as the Pointcast Network for optimal performance. New Smartcache technology minimizes network traffic by updating news, sports, weather, and more from the central broadcast facility and caching it internally on PointCast I-Server. This enables companies to quickly and efficiently broadcast news and information to its employees.

The PointCast I-Server is very easy to use. It provides administrators with time-saving forms and templates to make installing and setting up a corporate intranet quick and easy. A unique one-button installation program guides administrators through set-up and configuration.

The hardware requirements are also minimal.

Requirements for the server are as follows:

- ◆ Intel-based computer - Pentium 75 minimum
- ◆ 32MB RAM
- ◆ 500MB of hard drive space, minimum, and more space for your content

- ◆ Microsoft Windows NT 3.51 server with the service pack level 4 or higher, or NT 4.0, server or workstation
- ◆ Microsoft Internet Information Server (IIS)

Another requirement beyond the server requirements is to be using Netscape Navigator 2.0 or later.

Client requirements are as follows:

- ◆ 486/33 or faster PC
- ◆ Windows 95, Windows 3.1, or Windows for Workgroups
- ◆ 8MB of RAM, and 10MB of hard drive space
- ◆ 256 color monitor
- ◆ Connection to the Internet to receive news feed

NOTE: Each server supports approximately 500 clients.

After the PointCast I-Server is installed within a corporation, existing clients using the PointCast Network are automatically configured and redirected to the local server. This enables easy scalability for corporations installing PointCast I-Server in large networks with many PointCast Network viewers.

Authorized administrators can instantly create HTML content for their channel using the prepackaged forms. Templates are also available for creating company SmartScreens.

The Pointcast Network software is, as of this writing, free, and can be used in corporations with or without PointCast I-Server, although, without a server, you can't offer company-specific content. Another good point is the price of the server software. As of now, the PointCast I-Server software costs $995 per server CPU. Not bad for all the bells and whistles you get.

Summary

PointCast is another way to communicate your organization's events throughout your company. It's very simple to set up and is also user friendly. The templates make it easy to create your content and get up and running quickly. PointCast can be used as a stand-alone piece but gives you even greater communication and information sharing when it is combined with your intranet.

What's Next!

Next, I move on to the topic of security for your intranet. I'll discuss the physical location of your box, as well as communication security. I also discuss security issues with CGI scripts, and look at Secure Socket Layers (SSL). There are easier ways to set up your clients' Netscape Web browsers than having to visit each workstation, so I look at an administration kit that allows you to set preferences and lock down your settings. Finally, the next chapter looks at digital certificates and cryptography.

PART IV

Finalizing Your Intranets

Chapter | 14

Creating a
Secure Intranet

You can't go a single day without seeing a column, television show, or newspaper with a feature on the Internet, the World Wide Web, intranets, and, of course, security on the WWW. You've probably heard the story many times about the eight-year-old computer hacker who stole a Fortune 500 company's password list, broke into the corporate finance department, and funneled a million dollars into his Swiss bank account in a matter of 30 seconds. Well, maybe the story was not that shocking, but you get the idea. Oh, I almost forgot: he also installed a virus that brought the entire corporate WAN to its knees, put the company out of business, and then was hired in a week as a security consultant making a gazillion dollars an hour with the previous company's competitor.

Where does this stuff come from? A great deal of it is on the covers of magazines, on television talk shows, and in local newspapers. Most of it is overly hyped. But the problem is one of the public's perception: Now, people don't want to send any information over the Internet because this eight-year-old kid is out there waiting for them.

The public perceives that credit card transactions over the Internet are unbelievably unsafe. People aren't stopping to think how many times a day they give out their credit card number to complete strangers. Recently, I bought a dinner at TGIF (Friday's). When the bill came, I handed the waiter (a complete stranger) my credit card. I've also ordered a magazine over the telephone and given the person on the phone information about me and my credit card number. It would be so much easier for someone to go in the back of a restaurant and write down my credit card number than it is to try to grab packets of data speeding over the Internet all mixed together.

But, again, we have to implement security to ease this perception and to protect the organization in case an attempt is made to hack the server. There are several ways to implement security; I discuss several of them in this chapter.

Compromise for Security

When it comes to intranet security, we are battling a different beast altogether. On an intranet that does not have an entrance from the Internet, you are concerned with security internally—that is, security that is related to your organization's users, who already have access to your LAN in one form or another.

When you implement a very secure system, you need to realize that you will be losing something in return. You will lose, to some degree, the user-friendly interface that allows honest users to access your intranet. Your users will have to go through more steps and procedures to access your system.

Because you are setting up an intranet in your organization, you will have a known user base accessing your intranet with a standard Web browser. This will be housed inside a corporate firewall, so your intranet will be protected from outsiders on the Internet.

Security for an Internet Web server is very different from security issues for an intranet. In this chapter, I focus on intranet security issues because these are the issues that will affect your organization.

By placing appropriate security in your intranet, you can offer even greater services to your organization. This approach allows you to add even greater functionality to your intranet instead of looking at your security in a negative light. By implementing the appropriate security, you can now add important documents to your intranet that you may not have considered before; therefore, you may be adding even greater value to your intranet content. Certain departments will want to place information on your intranet that they want only people in that department to have access to. Without some sort of security in place, value-added content like this will not be placed on your intranet, because the entire organization will have access to it. So, by adding a simple password-protected area, users who need the information can now obtain that information 24 hours a day, 7 days a week on the intranet.

Physical Placement of Your Server

When mainframes were the norm, a great deal of money went into constructing secure rooms with climate controls, security cameras, and restricted access. Nowadays, an intranet server could be sitting under your desk. Because these servers can run on almost any kind of box, they are popping up everywhere in organizations.

There are three approaches to physical security for your intranet. The first is to lock your server into some hi-tech secure room somewhere and not let anyone near it. The second approach is to have the server on your desktop in plain sight, creating the impression that nothing is on the server that you don't want people to be able to access. The best approach is, of course, in the middle between these two. You should have some sort of physical security to keep the box from walking out the door late one night. By placing the box in a secure room, you will greatly reduce your risk, because most of your worries for an intranet will come from inside your organization.

Communication Security

The greater risk lies with communication security. You must protect your intranet from intruders who will access it from modems and your LAN. Several ways exist to do this.

By far the most common is a firewall. A firewall enables you to put up a wall between your intranet and the outside Internet. You can then control traffic that comes in and goes out of your intranet. A firewall is simply a box that sits on your LAN. When a packet of data is sent from or to your intranet, the firewall intercepts the packets and examines it to make sure that it is allowed access to or from your intranet.

I describe two types of firewalls in this chapter. One type can be as simple as a screening router that has a set of simple instructions on how to filter information on up to dedicated computers. The screening router can be used to protect your intranet from outside intruders. The router can be configured to allow certain information to pass, and it can also stop information that is not authorized to enter the system.

When you configure a screening router there are many settings that can be tailored to your security needs. Please note that the more secure you make your screening router, the fewer will be the data types that are allowed to pass through—which limits the type of information that can be passed over your intranet. So, high security comes at a price.

If you implement high security, you are limiting the usability of your system by honest users. The limitations of the screening router needs to also be taken into consideration when you set up your intranet security. A screen router works well in certain situations, but a screening router is not blessed with the knowledge that it needs to understand high-level protocols that will be traveling on your network. To best solve this issue, you need to look into the second firewall solution, the application gateway.

The other type of firewall consists of an application gateway that can also allow and deny access based on set configurations. The application gateway gives each packet of data a more thorough interrogation when it travels over the network. You may be familiar with application gateways already if you have Internet access in your organization. This type of gateway is also known as a proxy server, or a caching proxy server. This box gathers information for you rather than allow your client browser to access the Internet directly.

Here's how it works. When you request a Web page on the Internet from your browser, your browser sends the request to the proxy server. The proxy server stores, or caches, all the requested pages it can handle in its memory. So, when you ask to get a certain Web page, the proxy server first looks in its cache to see whether it already has the information you are requesting. If it does, it will send you that page. If not, it will access the Internet for you and return the requested Web page to your browser while caching a copy for the next user who makes the same request. Limitations can be set on the proxy server to allow or deny access to certain information. If you want users to be able to access only, say, Federal Express, then the proxy server can cache that information, and the user who does not have access to the Internet (only access to the corporate intranet) can now view Federal Express on the proxy server.

What Goes on Your Web Server?

Computers are getting so inexpensive these days that it is very feasible to have a dedicated intranet Web server. When I say *dedicated*, I mean a Web server that has only your Web content housed on it and nothing else. This will reduce security risks from the start. The simpler you keep your Web server, the less chance you will have of security holes caused by other applications. Also, if you keep only Web-related information on your Web server, intruders can't access anything except your Web content.

Think about this for a moment. Why are you putting this information on a Web server in the first place? So that users can access and use it. Therefore, a good general rule of thumb is to place only information on your Web server that you want users to be able to access. All other information does not belong on this box. You will, of course, have some Web information that you will want only certain departments to have access to, and this can reside on the same box and be protected by user passwords.

Security Basics

There are many ways to limit access to your intranet server. I have touched on screening routers, application gateways, and physical security. One of the best and easiest ways is by setting up some general guidelines, and by informing your users of security issues and how to avoid common mistakes.

CGI Scripts

Common Gateway Interfaces are easily written to send password information over the network to an intruder who is trying to gain access to your system. So, before you download any free CGI scripts that you might find on the Internet, make sure that you get the source code and verify that the CGI script has not been written to do any harm to your system. If you have departments that are doing their own pages for your intranet, help them by writing CGI scripts for their forms. If they write their own CGI scripts, make sure that they are solid and will not tax the Web server when they are run.

You can also avoid some of the CGI script dilemma by purchasing a third-party software package such as Cold Fusion. These packages allow Web pages to search and access databases without having to write complex CGI scripts. I look at these solutions in Chapter 7.

Stay in Contact with Your Vendors

When security holes are found in Web products, a patch is issued almost instantly. The Web allows you to quickly download a patch for a security hole in a matter of minutes. You don't have to call up the vendor, wait a week to get a floppy disk in the mail, and then install the patch. So, it is very important to keep up with the latest security news in newsgroups and from your vendors. All the patches in the world will not help make your system more secure if you don't keep up with the news and install them.

This also leads me to another point. When you are installing all of your services on your intranet, make sure that you limit yourself to services that you are going to use. If you don't plan to use services such as WAIS and Gopher, don't install them. The more complex your setup is, the greater the risk for security holes.

Setting Usernames and Passwords

Netscape Communication's server line, and all top-notch Web servers, enable you to easily set usernames and passwords for your intranet. In a server management Web page, you can set up new users with identification and passwords. You can give new users access to different areas and files by setting access controls. By doing so, you can keep track of which users have access to specific groups and file areas, and allow and deny access accordingly.

There are some drawbacks. Unfortunately, you have to do this manually for each user. So, you've got 15,000 employees? Sorry to hear it, but you've got a lot of typing to do. Oh, and you need to let all employees know what user ID and password you've assigned them—for every Web server with information they'll need. And you need to create a process by which each of them can change his or her password if it's compromised (preferably not by calling you!) and a process to insure that people who leave the company are deleted from the password files, and so on. It's too bad that none of the existing server implementations interface directly to any existing directory services. If nothing else, at this point it's a good argument for having any content provider group (Human Resources, Tech Support, whatever) take responsibility for administering Access Control Lists for their restricted content that they keep on their own group Web server. And no, it's not perfect, but distributed responsibility scales reasonably well. :-)

Each server will go about addressing how to set user rights slightly differently, but they are fairly straightforward and easy to use.

Browser Security

Now organizations can customize Netscape Navigator 3.0 to their exact needs before distributing Navigator to end users. Netscape has an Administration Kit that makes it easy for corporations to specify a wide range of Navigator settings. This way, you can adjust the browser setting the way you like and then permanently lock them in place to increase security and provide better administrative control for both the Internet and intranet. This allows you more control and makes it easy to update and customize your organization's browsers from one central location, thus saving you precious time and money.

The Netscape Administration Kit is a separate product from Netscape Navigator 3.0. If you are using Netscape Navigator for your organization's intranet, you should purchase one or more copies of the toolkit for IS people to use in managing the distribution of software. Netscape allows you to use one copy of the toolkit multiple times to configure Netscape Navigator for use throughout your organization.

There is technology already in Netscape Navigator 3.0 that allows the Administration Kit to create an enterprise data file. This enterprise data file is then distributed with Netscape Navigator and installed onto the user's system. After this is done you can do the following:

♦ You are able to override either the default value or user-specified preference for certain parameters in Netscape Navigator.

♦ You can now redefine directory button labels and the underlying URLs attached to these buttons.

♦ You can also redefine the description and underlying URLs for the nonrequired entries in the Directory and Help menus. So, you can change the description for items such as registration information, software, and about plug-ins, to name a few, and also change the URL for any items in this area. (The About Netscape entry on the Help menu is the only required entry.)

♦ Believe it or not, you can now modify the browser animation (the animated Netscape logo in the upper right). You can replace this image with your own corporate logo.

With the Netscape Administration Kit, the job of distributing and managing the Netscape Navigator Web browser in your organization has become a whole lot easier. Users are prevented from editing application preferences, and firewall access is regulated through the redirection of URLs pointed to by Navigator's directory buttons and menus. Application preferences that can be specified and locked include:

- Home page (if any) to load at start-up of Navigator
- Proxy server configurations
- Outgoing SMTP mail server
- Incoming POP mail server
- E-mail preference for leaving mail on server or removing on download
- News NNTP server
- Toggle to enable/disable Java and JavaScript execution

Setting Up the Administration Kit

The Administration Kit includes:

- Netscape Navigator Configuration Utilities for all supported platforms (Windows, Mac, and UNIX)
- Sample configuration files
- Online HTML documentation

It is easy to make changes to Netscape Navigator's configuration by using a text editor such as NotePad to edit the sample configuration files included with the kit. International versions of Netscape Navigator can also be configured in this way by using a text editor that supports the corresponding language. These configuration files are very similar in nature to Windows .INI files, and changes can be made by adding or changing TAG=VALUE pairs within the file.

After you have created your configuration input file, you simply process it with the included configuration wizards and make a Netscape .LCK file. This file is added to the Netscape Navigator distribution disk set. This allows you to conduct your installations with your custom configuration in place.

Configuring Your Proxies

Netscape Navigator 3.0 now offers automatic proxy configuration, making it much easier to specify complicated proxy configurations for an entire site (including specifying a large number of hosts that should not be using a proxy).

This allows you to tell Navigator to use different proxies, depending on the URL or host being contacted. Rather than be limited to one proxy per protocol, it is now possible to allow different proxies based on URL wildcard pattern matching. You can also designate multiple proxies to provide support if the primary proxy becomes unavailable or unresponsive.

The proxy configuration is specified in a script and stored at a particular URL on a server. Because the proxy configuration is stored in a central location, the system administrator can easily update the proxy configuration for a number of users without having to reconfigure each individual user's Netscape Navigator.

You can still manually configure your proxies if you wish. Just check the appropriate radio button in the Proxy Preferences panel and enter your proxy or SOCKS host. Netscape Navigator's default setting is set to not use proxies.

With manual proxy configuration, each individual user's system must be reconfigured every time a change is made to a proxy server. But with automatic proxy configuration, this headache is gone because the configuration is stored at a central site and accessed by each system upon start-up. It is therefore easily updated at any time by the system administrator.

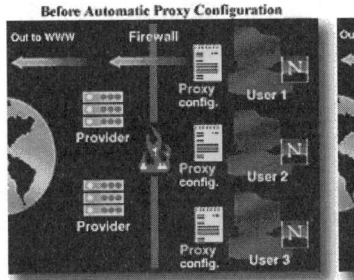 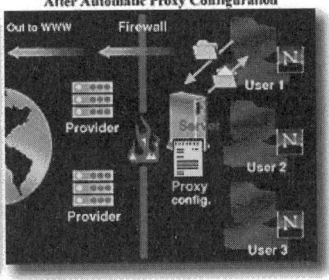

FIGURE 14-1

With automatic proxy configuration, it is much easier for the system administrator to update this information in one place when necessary.

To use the Automatic Proxy Configuration, go to the Options Menu | Network Preferences| Proxies panel in Netscape Navigator. Now check the Auto Proxy Configuration box, and enter the URL of the proxy configuration file on the server. The configuration file has the MIME content-type of application/x-ns-proxy-auto-config and is written completely in JavaScript (not HTML).

Security with Digital Certificates

The latest security feature to come around is something called digital certificates. When you enter a secure server site, a digital certificate authenticates your identity in a more secure manner than passing an unencrypted password over the network, and can be used to allow you to access secure information and purchase goods. In the future, digital certificates will replace the need for multiple passwords and usernames because authentication is automatic.

You can obtain a digital certificate from a variety of Certifying Authorities, such as VeriSign (http://www.verisign.com). After you contact one of these authorities, you can obtain a digital certificate for a specific payment method such as Visa or MasterCard. You can also use certificates for practical uses on your intranet to control access to sensitive information.

> **NOTE:** In case others can physically access your computer, or if they can access it over the network, you can set Netscape Navigator with password protection. This will allow you to protect your digital certificates.

Secure Socket Layers (SSL 3.0)

Secure Socket Layers SSL 3.0 offers better certificate management, as well as more encryption mechanisms and broader support for hardware devices. SSL 3.0 is also very efficient, thereby strengthening the protocol itself. This gives you a very secure connection between Netscape Navigator and the secure Web server to which you are connecting. You can verify the security of a document by examining the security icon in the bottom-left corner of the Netscape Navigator window and the color bar across the top of the content area. The icon consists of a door key on a blue background to show secure documents, and a broken doorkey on a gray background to show insecure documents. The color bar across the top of the content area is blue for secure and gray for insecure documents.

I describe SSL in more depth later in this chapter.

Security Challenges

There are many challenges you will face when building a full-service intranet that provides safe communications and collaboration. As the exponential growth of the public Internet demonstrates, TCP/IP solves many problems in a remarkably scaleable way. TCP/IP was not designed to offer secure communication services, however.

Because TCP/IP was not designed with security in mind, additional technology and policies needed to be implemented to solve typical security problems, such as the following:

- ♦ How do you authenticate users to make sure that they are who they claim to be? Standard Web protocols such as TCP/IP and HTTP make impersonating a person or an organization relatively simple. For example, if Alice connects to http://www.well-known-retailer.com, how does she know that this site is actually operated by the well-known retailer?

- How can I perform authentication without sending usernames and passwords across the network in the clear?

- How can I provide single-user login services to avoid costly username and account maintenance for all the servers (Web, proxy, directory, mail, news, and so on) across the enterprise? Can I provide single-user login without compromising security or incurring high administrative costs?

- How can I ensure that these services not only work on my intranet but also scale to the Internet? In other words, how can I avoid managing a separate security scheme for inside my firewall, and a completely different scheme for outside the firewall?

- How can I protect the privacy of my communications, both those in real time (such as the data flowing between a Web client and a Web server) and those with store-and-forward applications such as e-mail?

- How can I can ensure that messages have not been tampered with between the sender and the recipient?

- How can I safeguard confidential documents to ensure that only authorized individuals have access to them?

Remarkably, there is a single technology that provides the foundation for solving all of these challenges: *cryptography*.

Cryptographic technology is embodied in industry-standard protocols such as SSL (Secure Sockets Layer), SET (Secure Electronic Transactions), and S/MIME (Secure Multipart Internet Mail Encoding). These standards provide the foundation for a wide variety of security services, including encryption, message integrity verification, authentication, and digital signatures.

Cryptography

Cryptography is a surprisingly general technology that provides the foundation for each of the security challenges listed previously. The next sections describe how public-key technology works, explaining its role in industry-standard protocols such as SSL and S/MIME.

What Is Cryptography?

Cryptography comprises a family of technologies that include the following:

- Encryption transforms data into some unreadable form to ensure privacy. Internet communication is like sending postcards, in that anyone who is interested can read a particular message. Encryption offers the digital equivalent of a sealed envelope.

- Decryption is the reverse of encryption; it transforms encrypted data back into the original, intelligible form.

- Authentication identifies an entity such as an individual, a machine on the network, or an organization.

- Digital signatures bind a document to the possessor of a particular key and are the digital equivalent of paper signatures.

- Signature verification is the inverse of a digital signature; it verifies that a particular signature is valid.

All of these technologies make use of sophisticated mathematical techniques.

Symmetric-Key and Public-Key Cryptography

Symmetric-key or secret-key cryptography uses the same key to encrypt and decrypt messages. This is a familiar real-world phenomenon: We use the same key to unlock and lock our car doors, for instance. The problem with symmetric-key cryptography is having the sender and receiver agree on a secret key without anyone else finding out. How can they do this? Over the phone, on a floppy disk, using a courier? All of these are cumbersome, slow, and error-prone techniques. In addition, the number of keys tends to be much larger than the number of nodes; that is, people may have multiple keys that they use for different purposes.

Public-key cryptography was invented in 1976 by Whitfield Diffie and Martin Hellman to solve precisely this problem. With public-key cryptography, each person gets a pair of keys: a public key and a private key. Each person's public key is published, whereas the private key is kept secret. When Alice wants to send Bob a secure message, she encrypts it using Bob's public key. When Bob gets the message, he decrypts it using his private key. The sender and receiver no longer have to share secret information before they can communicate securely.

In practice, both symmetric-key and public-key techniques are used in popular security protocols such as SSL and S/MIME because symmetric-key algorithms tend to be much faster than public-key algorithms. Going back to Alice and Bob again, they want to communicate securely, but they also want to communicate quickly. Here's what they do:

1. Alice generates a random number (key) that will be used for actually encrypting her message to Bob.
2. Alice encrypts the random number with Bob's public key.
3. Bob decrypts the random number with his private key. Now Bob has a secret shared with only Alice that they can use to encrypt and decrypt messages to each other.

In reality, most security protocols are much more complicated than this, but this three-step process gives you an idea of the fundamentals. SSL is an excellent example of a security protocol that uses these techniques to safeguard communications.

Public-Key Certificates

Digital certificates, also called digital IDs, digital passports, or public-key certificates, are defined by an ITU standard called X.509. A certificate is the digital equivalent of an employee badge, passport, or driver's license.

The certificate and corresponding private key identify you to someone who needs proof of your identity. If you are pulled over by the highway patrol, you need to show your driver's license to prove that you are legally licensed to drive a car. If you want to get into a secure workplace, you might have to show a badge to prove that you are an employee of the company. If you want to make a credit card purchase, you typically have to show a credit card and demonstrate that you can produce a signature like the one on the back of your card. All of these forms of identification allow you to establish your identity with someone.

Over a network, a certificate serves the same role as a driver's license, employee badge, or credit card: It establishes your identity. Servers may be configured to grant access only to people with particular certificates; similarly, clients may be configured to trust servers that present certain certificates.

What's in a certificate? An X.509 certificate is typically a small file that contains the information shown in the Table 14-1.

How Can Encryption Help?

With this overview of public-key technology in mind, I'll review the challenges described previously and see how public-key technology embodied in industry-standard protocols such as SSL and S/MIME offers solutions for those challenges. Table 14-2 gives some examples of how public-key technology can be used.

Table 14-1   **Information in an X.509 Certificate**

Field	Description	Examples
Subject's distinguished name (DN)	A name uniquely identifying the owner of the certificate	C=US, O=Netscape Communications, OU=Technology, CN=Marc Andreessen
Issuer's distinguished name (DN)	A name uniquely identifying the certificate authority that signed the certificate	C=US, O=VeriSign, CN=VeriSign Class 1 root
Subject's public key	The owner's public key	512-bit RSA key
Issuer's signature	The certificate authority's digital signature from which the certificate derives its authenticity	RSA encryption with MD5 hash (signature itself is not human readable)
Validity period	Dates between which the certificate is valid	Not before Wed, Nov 9, 1995, 15:54:17 Not after Fri, Dec 31, 1997, 15:54:17
Serial number	A unique number generated by the certificate authority for administrative purposes	02:41:00:00:01

Table 14-2   **Public-Key Technology**

Requirement	Public-Key Technology	Example of Typical Use
Authentication of users without username and password in the clear	Digital certificates (X.509)	SSL handshake includes exchange of client and server certificates and corresponding signatures
Single-user login	Digital certificates (X.509)	Servers may be configured to demand digital certificates rather than username/ password pairs

Requirement	Public-Key Technology	Example of Typical Use
Scalability to the Internet	Standards-based encryption and message digest algorithms (for example, RSA, DES) negotiated using industry-standard protocols (for example, SSL)	Unlike most proprietary security systems, SSL works both inside and outside the firewall
Message privacy (real-time as well as store-and-forward applications)	Public-key encryption and RSA decryption (for example, RSA); often used in conjunction with symmetric-key technology (for example, RC2, RC4, and DES) for higher performance	SSL protects the session key used to encrypt and decrypt a data stream with public-key encryption. S/MIME uses a similar technique for encrypting and signing e-mail messages in a store-and-forward paradigm
Message integrity	Message authentication codes calculated using message digest algorithms (MD5, SHA1)	SSL calculates message authentication codes (MACs) using a message digest algorithm and a key negotiated during the SSL handshake.
Protection of confidential documents from unauthorized access	Digital certificates (X.509) and signatures	Binds users listed in access control lists (ACLs) to certificates or requires that users present a particular certificate (for example, signed by the Netscape Marketing Certificate Authority) for access

Secure Socket Layers

Secure Socket Layers (SSL) is an industry-standard protocol that makes substantial use of public-key technology. SSL is widely deployed on the intranet as well as over the public Internet in the form of SSL-capable servers and clients from leading vendors including Netscape, Microsoft, IBM, Spyglass, and Open Market as well as public-domain products such as Apache-SSL. All Netscape products—clients, servers, and applications—incorporate SSL to provide advanced security services. The features in each product are described in detail in the following sections.

SSL provides three fundamental security services, all of which use public-key techniques. Examples of its use appear in Table 14-3.

Table 14-3   SSL Security with Public-Key Technology

Service	Underlying Technology	Protection Against
Message privacy	Encryption	Eavesdroppers
Message integrity	Message authentication codes (keyed hash functions)	Vandals
Mutual authentication	X.509 certificates	Impostors

Message Privacy

Message privacy is achieved through a combination of public-key and symmetric key encryption, as described previously. All traffic between an SSL server and SSL client is encrypted using a key and an encryption algorithm negotiated during the SSL handshake. Encryption thwarts eavesdroppers who can capture a TCP/IP session using devices such as IP packet sniffers. Even though packet sniffers can still capture the traffic between a server and client, the encryption makes it impractical for them to actually read the message.

SSL Handshake

SSL has been designed to make the security side transparent to the user. This allows the user to just press the button marked Visa, for example, and the security aspect is all hidden. When this button is pressed, the user is connected to a different port, not the normal HTTP port 80, and the SSL Handshake takes place. After this handshake has been performed, the information is encrypted and checked until the session is ended.

Message Integrity

The message integrity service ensures that SSL session traffic does not change en route to its final destination. If the Internet is going to be a viable platform for electronic commerce, we must ensure that vandals do not tamper with message contents as they travel between clients and servers. SSL uses a combination of a shared secret and special mathematical functions called *hash* functions to provide the message integrity service.

Mutual Authentication

Mutual authentication is the process whereby the server convinces the client of its identity and (optionally) the client convinces the server of its identity. These identities are coded in the form of public-key certificates, and the certificates are exchanged during the SSL handshake.

To demonstrate that the entity presenting the certificate is the legitimate certificate owner (rather than some impostor), SSL requires that the certificate presenter must digitally sign data exchanged during the handshake. The exchanged handshake data includes the entire certificate. The entities sign protocol data (which includes their certificates) to prove they are the legitimate owner of the certificate. This prevents someone from masquerading as you by presenting your certificate. The certificate itself does not authenticate; the combination of the certificate and the correct private key does.

What Happens During the SSL Handshake?

SSL is designed to make its security services as transparent as possible to the end user. Typically, users click a link or a button on a page that connects to an SSL-capable server. A typical SSL-capable Web server accepts SSL connection requests on a different port (port 443 by default) than standard HTTP requests (port 80 by default).

When the client connects to this port, it initiates a handshake that establishes the SSL session. After the handshake finishes, communication is encrypted and message integrity checks are performed until the SSL session expires. SSL creates a session during which the handshake needs to happen only once. Performing an SSL handshake for every HTTP connection would result in poor performance.

The following high-level events take place during an SSL handshake:

1. The client and server exchange X.509 certificates to prove their identity. This exchange may optionally include an entire certificate chain, up to some root certificate. Certificates are verified by checking validity dates and verifying that the certificate bears the signature of a trusted certificate authority.

2. The client randomly generates a set of keys that will be used for encryption and calculating MACs. The keys are encrypted using the server's public key and securely communicated to the server. Separate keys are used for client-to-server and server-to-client communications for a total of four keys.

3. A message encryption algorithm (for encryption) and hash function (for integrity) are negotiated. In Netscape's SSL implementation, the client presents a list of all the algorithms it supports, and the server selects the strongest cipher available. Server administrators may turn particular ciphers on and off.

SSL 2 Versus SSL 3

The first generations of Netscape products (including, for example, Netscape Navigator 2.0, Netscape Commerce Server 1.0, and Netscape News Server 1.0) implement SSL version 2.

The current generation of Netscape products (including Netscape Navigator 3.0 and the Netscape SuiteSpot server products) implement version 3 of the SSL protocol. The SSL 3 protocol incorporates feedback on SSL 2 from a wide variety of companies. The basic services that SSL provides (message integrity, message privacy, and mutual authentication) are the same in both versions 2 and 3 of the protocol. SSL 3 boasts a number of protocol enhancements, however, such as the following:

- Fewer handshake messages for faster handshakes.
- Support for more key-exchange and encryption algorithms (for example, Diffie-Hellman, Fortezza). With Diffie-Hellman or Fortezza, the server's public parameters are contained in the server key exchange message, and the client's are sent in the client key exchange message. Eavesdroppers who do not know the private values should not be able to find the Diffie-Hellman result (that is, the premaster_secret) or the Fortezza token encryption key.
- Support for hardware tokens in the form of Fortezza cards. This is the first step toward more general support for cryptography-capable smart cards.
- An improvement to the client certificate request protocol that allows a server to specify a list of certificate authorities that it trusts to issue client certificates. Navigator returns a certificate signed by one of those certificate authorities. If it does not have such a certificate, the handshake fails. This frees the user from having to choose a certificate for each connection.

Future Directions for Netscape Navigator

Future releases of Navigator will support features such as the following:

- Secure e-mail using S/MIME, which requires X.509 certificates. This open secure mail standard, spearheaded by RSA, enables Navigator to exchange secure e-mail with any S/MIME capable client. In general, no changes to existing Internet mail servers that support POP3, SMTP, or IMAP4 are necessary.

- Smart cards and other hardware tokens. These devices range from simple "stored value" cards that can be used for simple digital cash transactions to full-featured devices that generate key pairs, manage certificates, and implement full cryptographic suites.

- Certificates and key pair migration. Users will want to move their key pairs and corresponding certificates between machines (for example, between their home and office machines) using floppy disks or other storage devices.

- Improved checks for certificate status and certificate revocation lists. Netscape has defined a X.509v3 extension that lists URLs where client applications can check on certificate status, download certificate revocation lists, renew a certificate, and so on.

Netscape's SuiteSpot

The complete Netscape SuiteSpot server family implements (or will implement) SSL 3, although the exact use of SSL varies from server to server. All servers are capable of the following:

- Communicate privately using an encryption algorithm negotiated with an SSL client such as Netscape Navigator. The traffic that is carried depends on the server. For example, Netscape Enterprise Server 2.0 carries HyperText Transfer Protocol (HTTP) data; Netscape News Server 2.0 carries Network News Transport Protocol (NNTP) data; and Netscape Mail Server 2.0 uses SSL to encrypt communication between Navigator and the Mail Administration Server, enabling administrators to manage the server securely from any network node.

- Use a message digest function, also negotiated with the client during the SSL handshake, to perform message integrity checks on data coming from the client.

- Authenticate itself to clients using a digital certificate (server authentication).

The first Netscape server to support client authentication is Netscape Enterprise Server 2.0, which has the following unique features:

- Allows administrators to map client certificates to entries in the access control database. In this scenario, users present a certificate rather than a username and password to gain access to access-controlled documents. Presents certificates to server-side applications via NSAPI and as CGI environment variables.

- All SuiteSpot Servers will eventually support client authentication. Client authentication based on certificates has the following advantages over authentication based on username and password combinations, IP addresses, or DNS names:

  - No passwords flow across the network. Certificates are public information, so users may be authenticated without sending sensitive information such as a password over the network.

  - Improved user experience. Users do not have to remember separate username and password pairs for every Web server they visit. They simply log in to Navigator, and Navigator sends the necessary certificate to establish the user's identity.

  - Strong authentication. Certificates are a stronger form of authentication because they are based on what the user has (the certificate) as well as what the user knows (the password that protects the private key corresponding to the certificate).

  - Lower administration cost. Certificate-based authentication can lower the cost of server administration. Rather than manage separate access control lists (ACLs) at every server, servers may simply be configured to grant access to users who present certificates signed by an approved list of certificate authorities.

SurfWatch ProServer from Spyglass

Everyone in your organization is going to want access to the WWW. When users have an intranet, the benefits of having Internet access available to your users is an issue that will soon appear. Although Internet access allows a research tool that reveals the greatest libraries, organizations are worried about what users will be viewing, and whether it is appropriate content. This has sparked a high demand for products that can filter content, based on preferences set by the IS department, or the controlling area.

Spyglass has developed the SurfWatch ProServer, a high-speed proxy server that filters and caches content.

In addition to filtering content, this server also acts as a proxy server so that it can cache pages that are accessed frequently. This allows users to quickly access necessary information without having to travel out to the Internet for every click of the mouse. Wrapped in the same package in SurfWatch ProServer is a filter that filters out inappropriate or unwanted content.

This package is very scaleable, so it can grow with your organization.

By maintaining better control, you will be able to ease the worries of upper management, which has been reading all those checkout-counter trade rags that talk about making pipe bombs, X-rated content, and drugs on the Internet. This will allow you to focus on your task and your users to focus on theirs. Productivity will rise and liability will fall when a product like this is used to help manage Internet content. You can get more information on SurfWatch at:

```
http://www.surfwatch.com
```

Tailored Control

There are several packages available that can limit access and content. SurfWatch is one of the better ones; it has been around for a while and is moving in the right direction. Net Nanny is another new start-up company that is also starting to move into developing a product for organizations. When you look at different products, it is important to remember that different Web users have different content viewing needs. So, it is important to find a product that addresses your organization's needs and allows you to customize what is blocked and what is not. SurfWatch ProServer features the unique ability to block requests for documents based on predefined lists that can be customized to meet any need.

Filtering Content

SurfWatch uses a filtering technology that blocks searches, queries, and URLs containing prohibited words and derivatives of them. It comes with a listing of 10,000 URLs that contain inappropriate content for organizations, and it also allows you to write custom lists to filter any type of content you choose. If the user tries to search a search engine for undesirable words, SurfWatch will block the search before the search engine returns results. You can also set SurfWatch to allow access to only certain URLs. By doing so, you can allow users to access only sites that are on a preapproved list.

Security on Your LAN

With SurfWatch, all of your Internet traffic has to go through the proxy server, enabling you to control access to the Net. It also allows you to create reports on Internet traffic to show how the Internet is being used productively.

Net Nanny

Net Nanny is another software package available on the WWW that allows you to block certain content and information from the viewer. These packages started out to allow parents to control what their children could view while surfing the WWW. Net Nanny is one of the popular packages that can keep kids from venturing into inappropriate areas of the Web. Net Nanny is in the process of developing a product for corporate LANs. A package like this can be tailored to limit access to users in your organization when they are out surfing the Internet. Keep an eye on their Web site at:

```
http://www.netnanny.com
```

Summary

Many ways exist to implement security on your intranet. Most of your security issues will arise from internal, company employees, if you are just planning on developing your intranet for internal use. When you venture outward into the Internet, then you have to add more protection to allow access to only privileged users and to keep unwanted visitors away. Certificates, SSL, browser locks, and firewalls are some of the effective ways to restrict access and communication.

What's Next!

Now I'll shift from security issues and move into implementation of your intranet. The next chapter covers setting up training, all the new intranet technologies out there, and maintenance issues. See you there.

Chapter | 15

Implementing and Selling Your Intranet

It's time to implement your intranet. In this chapter, I discuss user training, maintenance issues, and cool new intranet technologies that will help you maintain your intranet and allow you to check your work.

Training is one of those very important items that needs to be done right to have a successful rollout, but it is often overlooked because of lack of funding or lack of time. After you spend 16 hours a day developing your intranet, the last thing you usually want to do is write up lengthy training material and think about training the users. But to make the entire project a success, this needs to be done with the same amount of energy as the development of your intranet.

Maintaining your intranet is also going to be a bear. After you get most of your content up on the intranet, you will go into a maintenance mode. Of course, you will still be adding new areas, applications, and departments, but you will be spending a great deal of time doing Web maintenance. Anything you can do to cut down maintenance time means more free time for you. So, I'll show you the latest new applications that will help you create the intranet pages right the first time, check your links, and do all kinds of cool stuff to help you save time.

Super Users

Every organization has them. These are the users like myself who can drive an IS department crazy at times with all the request tickets they put into a help desk. These are also some of your best resources for an enthusiastic group to conduct your training. In most large organizations, lack of time and money makes giving each user individual training impossible. If you are in a small organization and can take this route, go for it. But for large organizations, there is a better, more productive way to train the masses.

First, you do not want to do a global rollout. This is a giant Windows 95-type ordeal. After the system has been tested and all the bugs are squashed, then you can do a big publicity campaign to get all the areas excited and using the system. But first, you want to teach your super users how to use the system and get their opinions, ideas, and have them be your beta testers.

> **NOTE:** Don't do your big Windows 95 promo before you beta test your intranet and train your users. You don't want the kind of publicity that New Coke got years ago. Remember how the New Coke product was not received very well by consumers? So, do your homework, make sure that the thing works from end to end, and then roll out the red carpet.

The Beta Test

So, you need to get super users. First, you need to find out who they are. This is fairly simple. If you are starting with a fairly small department intranet, you can just ask around and you should be able to get to know the department fairly quickly. If you are dealing with a user base of around, say, 1,500, then you need to do some more work. I met a gentlemen a few months back at an intranet conference who was trying to build an intranet for a major hotel chain. So I'll take his situation and start with one hotel, and get the intranet up and running in all the major departments of that hotel. (Oh, what hotel chain was it? Well, it rhymes with bread, and the second word is what's on top of your house. You can rule out "dead leaves" from your choices.)

To get a group of users together to help with the training of this type of project, here is what I would look at doing. First, when you started the dream phase of your project way back when, you should have run into individuals who took an interest in your project. Bingo! These are some of your best sales people and trainers. Remember that lady in your brainstorming sessions who had all those great ideas about putting the cafeteria menu online, adding a job posting section, and the rumor mill? Give her a call. The more people you can get to help you with the implementation, the better.

Make sure that you also use the tools you have available to recruit trainers and supporters for your intranet. This would be things such as e-mail, company newsletters, paycheck memos, posters, meetings, special events.

Send an e-mail to all mail boxes, in just your department or local areas, to see whether anyone is interested in helping beta test your intranet and help with the training. You should get a response right away.

Make posters and flyers and post them in backstage areas where employees will read them—hallways, breakrooms, by the time clocks. A simple flyer asking for volunteers to call or stop by to get more information on the intranet beta test can generate some good leads.

You can also attach a memo to your employee paychecks, if your organization will allow you to do this. Attaching a memo can help you be certain that everyone in your organization will be notified about the beta test.

Go to the department meetings and ask for five minutes of time before the meeting to explain your intranet beta test and that you are interested in getting volunteers and trainers for the rollout.

There are many ways to get a staff together to help with your project. Food is one popular bribe. If you provide food, especially donuts, then you can attract all the super users that you can possibly handle for your beta.

> **NOTE:** Stay away from the lemon-filled donuts. Yuck! Glazed will attract the hard-core super users to your project better than lemon-filled any day.

Okay, Now What?

Now you have a list of all the people in your organization who are interested in helping with your beta test as well as with training. If you have a large organization that is going to be using the system, make sure that you have at least one person from each department. You don't want to create a lost-and-found system for the hotel and not have someone from lost and found tell you the challenges in that department. Get my drift?

You will need to have your intranet loaded on several PCs so that you can have the users run through the site and make notes. If you have access to three or four PCs, then you can set up a week on beta testing right in your area. If your organization has a training facility with computers, then reserve that room and conduct your beta test in there. You can also go and install the intranet application on the user's PC. To do so, you will need to purchase and install TCP/IP stacks and a browser such as Netscape Navigator or Microsoft's Internet Explorer. You will also need to pester the users more if you do the beta testing only on their personal PC. The users will tend to forget about the application and become bogged down in their daily routines, making your beta test less successful than you had hoped. If you can get the users to dedicate 30 minutes in a lab or in your development area to test the intranet, then do it.

In 30 minutes, you will want to cover as much as possible, so make sure that you plan out your time beforehand. Try to make sure that your class size is manageable. It is important, too, to have a PC available for everyone. After a brief introduction, you can cover your project in as much detail as time allows. Make sure to allow each user time to play and test out the system after you give the users basic instructions on how the system works. With a pen in hand and a pad of paper at each station, have the users write down anything that they have questions about, as well as incorrect information, misspellings, broken links, applications that don't work, and anything that they don't understand.

Keep a master listing of all the comments and suggestions, and make sure that you address each one individually so that the users know that their input is being used to better the project. After several beta tests and all the bugs and content issues are addressed, it is time to start training.

Training

For training, you should make sure that you have input from at least one user per department. The concept here for a large organization is to train one or two super users in each department so that they can field questions and help users in their area, instead of having to train every single user and answer every possible question.

Set up a day or week when you can sit down with groups of your trainers and cover the basics of your intranet. Make sure that you try to cover everything; these trainers will be getting questions that might seem very basic to you, but to a new user who has never used a PC, the questions might be very valid. Luckily, Web browsers are easy to use and require only a little practice with a mouse and a short learning curve to get even the beginner of beginners up and running.

A training manual and quick reference cards are sure to help your trainers when they are back in their departments. Your training manual does not need to be a work of art, but should cover the basic operation of your Web browser, as well as the navigation and structure of your intranet application.

Screen shots do amazing things for any informative manual. It is much easier to understand what is being explained if there is a screen shot showing it to accompany the text. Screen shots are not mysterious, either. They can be taken quickly and easily and added to your text manual in your favorite word processing software. The next section takes a look at a few screen capture applications that can help you construct your training material.

Screen Captures for Your Manuals

One of the easiest and most popular screen capture applications on the Web is Paint Shop Pro. It does so much more than screen captures, but that's what I use it for in this section. Paint Shop Pro is shareware: you can download it from the WWW from many locations, such as http://www.jasc.com. If you like Paint Shop Pro, make sure that you register it before your trial period expires.

After you install and launch Paint Shop Pro, you will be taken to the main application screen. At the top of the screen, you will see a menu bar with the option called Capture. By clicking on Capture, you will get a drop-down menu with the Setup option. Choosing Setup will give you the information displayed in Figure 15-1.

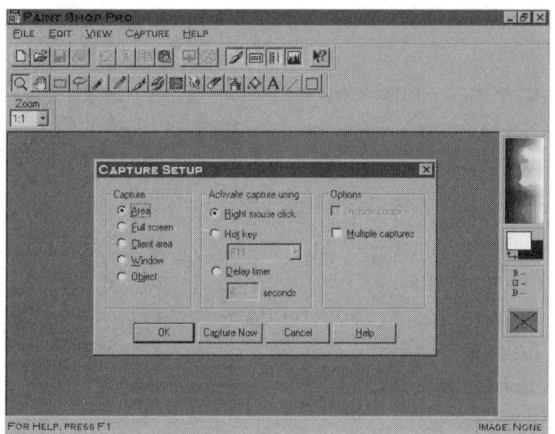

FIGURE 15-1

Paint Shop Pro allows you to customize your screen captures here in the Capture Setup window. You can choose what you want to capture, what will activate the capture, and other options from this window.

I set my options to capture the entire screen (full screen) and I choose the hot key to be F11. Then, I just click on Capture Now and go to the application that I want to take a screen shot of. In this case, I went back to Netscape Navigator and took two screen shots of the Jasc home page. When I was in Netscape and had the part of the page I wanted to capture on my screen, I simply pressed the hot key that I had set (F11) and the screen shot was done. Now, in Paint Shop Pro, you can see that screen shot in Figure 15-2.

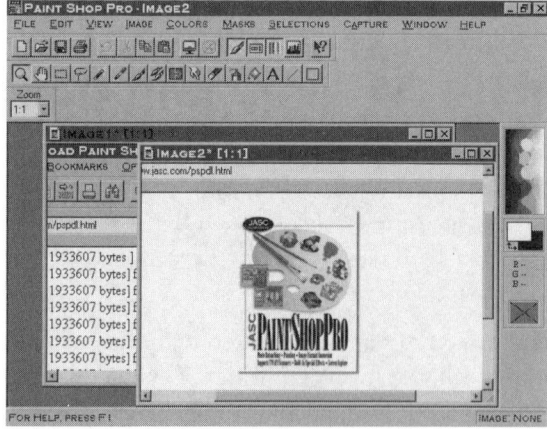

FIGURE 15-2

Paint Shop Pro will surface after you take the screen shot, and it will open it in its own window. From here, you can edit the image and then save it in the file format that you need.

But this gives you the entire screen. Everything. You have to go and edit it in Paint Shop Pro, or some other application, to get just the part of the page that you want. So, go back to the Paint Shop Pro and change the capture settings to get only an area. Do this by choosing Area and then launching the capture. You can now go back into Netscape or any other application and press the hot key (F11) to start the capture.

This time, when you press F11, you get a set of crosshairs. You need to line up the crosshairs by the outer limits of the area that you want to capture. When you have them in place, just click on the left mouse button once and start drawing the box that appears around the object you want to capture. One more click and you should have the image (see Figure 15-3).

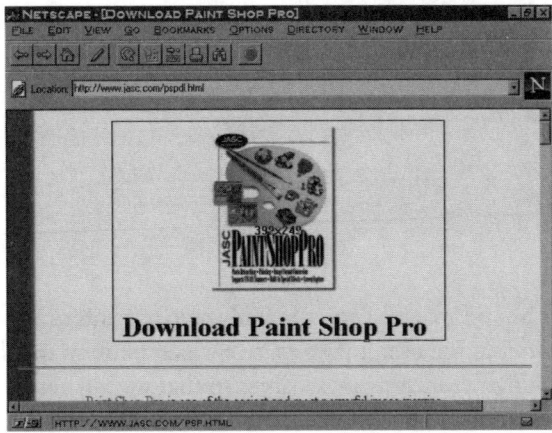

FIGURE 15-3

Here I outlined just the heading and the image from the Web site, and now I have a nice crisp image that I can edit and use in training materials.

These are just a few of the options for taking screen shots, and just one of many applications that can take screen shots for you. After you have laid out your manual, you can start to take and add screen shots. Screen shots of the browser toolbar, and information explaining the different buttons and their functions such as Home, Back, and Reload, will help out the first-time user tremendously.

After you've had some practice with screen shots, you can start adding lines and descriptive text directly in the image with some simple image tools. Looking at Paint Shop Pro again, I show you how to add an arrow pointing to Netscape's Toolbar and put a figure number under the arrow for your users.

I start by capturing an area in Netscape Navigator. From Paint Shop Pro, I choose Capture | Start. Then I go into Netscape and make sure that I have the toolbar displayed the way I want it for the screen shot. I then press the hot key to start the screen capture (F11), and click once on the corner of the toolbar that I am capturing. I now drag my mouse over the area I want to capture, and then click one more time to save this area as a screen shot in Paint Shop Pro. Figure 15-4 shows the image I captured. But it would be nice to show the user exactly what icon you are talking about. So, adding more information to the image in Paint Shop Pro is the next step.

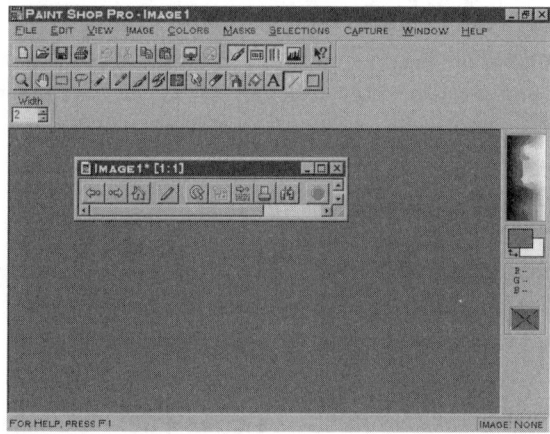

FIGURE 15-4

Here is just a plain, ordinary toolbar that you can place in your training material.

Now I have the image in Paint Shop Pro, and I want to add some text information and a line pointing to the Back icon so that the user knows exactly which button I'm talking about. My first challenge is making the image canvas larger so that we can get more room to work with, and add out line and descriptive text.

I need to change the Image Canvas size. I do this by choosing Image from the toolbar, and then choosing Enlarge Canvas. A pop-up window will allow me to change the width and height of the canvas (see Figure 15-5).

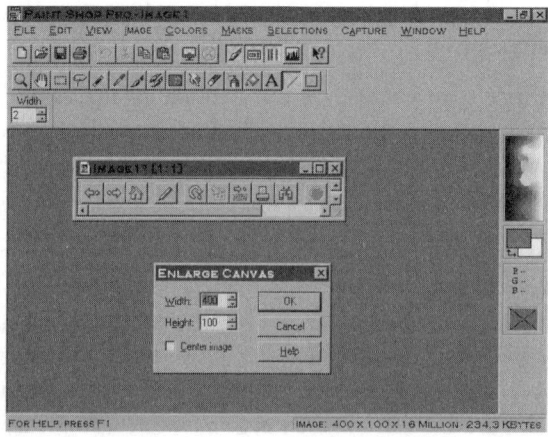

FIGURE 15-5

To change the canvas size, simply choose Image | Enlarge Canvas from the toolbar. Then choose a larger width and height so that you have some room to work with the image.

NOTE: If you do not change the background color to white, then you will get the default canvas color, which is set to black. To change your canvas color to white, click on the horizontal and vertical arrows under the color swatches to get the white color swatch in the bottom square.

Now I have a nice amount of room around my image to work with. I also have a white canvas because I chose white from the color pickers on the right of my screen. Now I'm adding to the image in Figure 15-6. I am going to add a red line to the screen shot and add some text to tell the users that this icon in the upper left of the Netscape toolbar is the Back button.

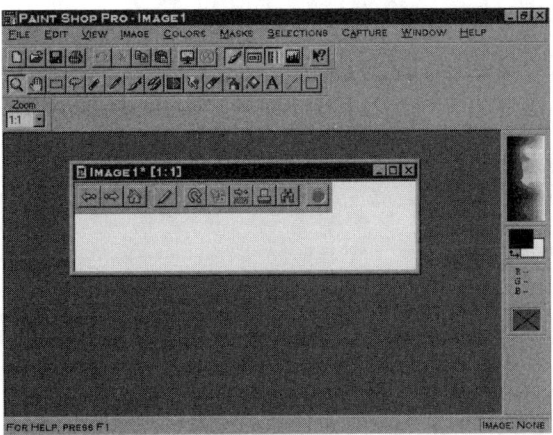

FIGURE 15-6

Give yourself enough room to work with on your canvas. You can always crop the image later if there is too much room.

In Paint Shop Pro, I click on the top color swatch (the black one in my screen) and a color palette of all the colors in the rainbow appears. From here I can click on any color I want. I choose a nice red from the basic colors, and then select OK. I now have a red color for my foreground color. I am now going to select the line tool from the Paint Shop Pro toolbar. You can't miss it; it looks like a line. Now I draw a red line at an angle, but I hold down the Shift key as I draw. (You can also change the line width in the width box at the top left of your screen.) I choose a width of two.

If you are going to be printing out a color manual, or doing a color presentation on an overhead, then you can have fun with colors. If you are going to be printing black-and-white manuals, then colors will show up as 256 colors of gray and are not as important when you are editing your screen shots.

I am now going to add some descriptive text to my image. I do this in Paint Shop Pro by selecting the Text Tool, which looks like a capital A on the toolbar. I now click on the crosshairs that I get for a mouse pointer, in the location that I want to type my text. I get a pop-up menu that allows me to choose a font, font size, and some other options for formatting. You can see all these options in Figure 15-7.

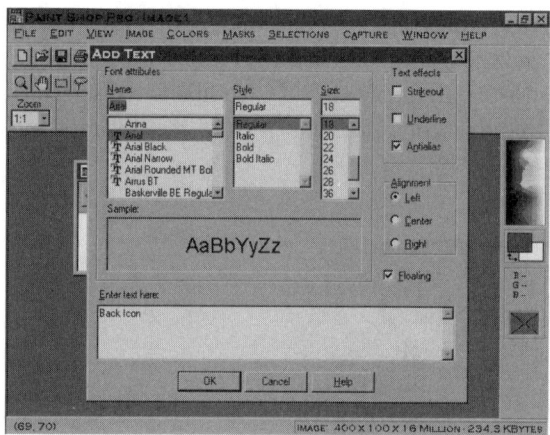

FIGURE 15-7

Paint Shop Pro allows you to choose a font and font size for your descriptive text. From here you can test different looks by trying different font styles.

I choose a simple Arial font with a point size of 18. The words "Back Icon" now display on my image; they have a row of marching ants around them. This lets me know that the text is selected, and from here I can move it into the exact location I want it on the screen. By just placing my mouse cursor over the text, I get a four-way directional arrow cursor that allows me to move the text any place I want on the canvas. I move the text right under the line and the finished product, which I've saved as a GIF in this example, is displayed for you in Figure 15-8. This can be done easily with tables, icons, images, and anything you want to add emphasis to in your training materials.

FIGURE 15-8

The finished screen shot is now ready to be placed in a manual to help train your staff.

Make Your Manuals

With all your screen shots done, it is time to put together your training manuals. Try to cover Windows basics if you have a user base that is going from a DOS environment to Windows, or new users. Also, make sure that you cover the browser software you are using. Let users know how to get around and what to do in case they get lost. Explain what a 404 error is, and let the user know that pages on the Internet, if they have outside access, can sometimes come up as broken links. Explaining these possibilities will help stop the flood of calls to your help desk by newbies. Go over some of the manual with your trainers and answer their questions so that they can answer the questions in the field. The more they know, the quicker your users will grasp your new intranet.

After your super users have played on your intranet and you are ready to roll it out, you can also use your super users to help promote the event.

Online Help

You can not be available around the clock to answer questions and help users out of situations that might arise on your new intranet, but a help file on the intranet itself can be there for some guidance. One of the greatest tools an intranet brings is the ability to distribute information 24 hours a day.

> **TIP:** A very smart thing to incorporate into your home page of your intranet is a help button.

When the help desk is closed down and you are the only one around on the graveyard shift, you can still get information on the employee benefit package, help files, and the breakfast menu from the breakroom. Use this to your advantage and set up a Frequently Asked Questions (FAQ) page. A simple listing of the top 20 questions can keep you from having to tell all your users to set their colors to 256 for the 1 millionth time. Other areas with technical support should be set up to allow users to leave messages concerning challenges they are having. In the next section, I discuss setting up a quick Web page that can address FAQs.

Creating a FAQ Web Page

You can create a fairly simple FAQ page and move on up to a more complex page with diagrams and images to help illustrate your points. I made a simple FAQ page that you can use and add to as your get more complex areas to address. Take a look at Figure 15-9 to see the FAQ page in all its glory. Luckily, this book is in black and white, sparing you the awful yellow background that I chose. You can, however, see the page by running the code that follows shortly.

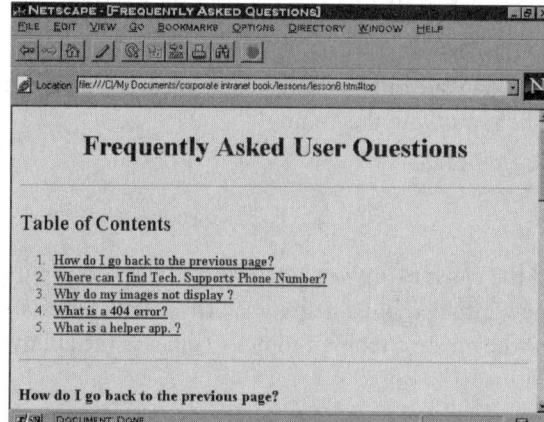

FIGURE 15-9

This is a very simple FAQ page, but it gets the job done.

This FAQ page allows you to make a numbered list of questions, and hyperlink them to answers that are anchored later down the page. Designing your Web page in this manner is similar to a table of contents in a book, with the relevant content located in the pages that follow. Please take out the questions I have and place your own content in to start a FAQ page of your own. Here is the HTML code that made the FAQ page. Run this code to see how all the links work. Enjoy.

```
<html>

<head>

<title>Frequently Asked Questions</title>

</head>


<body bgcolor="#FFFF80" text="#800040">

<p> </p>

<h1 align=center>Frequently Asked User Questions</h1>
```

```
<hr>
<h2><a name="top">Table of Contents</a></h2>
<ol>
<li><a href="#how"><strong>How do I go back to the previous page?</strong></a></li>
<li><a href="#where"><strong>Where can I find Tech. Supports Phone
Number?</strong></a></li>
<li><a href="#why"><strong>Why do my images not display ?</strong></a></li>
<li><a href="#what1"><strong>What is a 404 error?</strong></a></li>
<li><a href="#what"><strong>What is a helper app. ?</strong></a></li>
</ol>
<hr>
<h3><a name="how">How do I go back to the previous page?</a></h3>
<p>In Netscape you can use the back icon located at the top left of your browser screen.
You can also
use the back icons at the bottom of each of the web pages to navigate around the
intranet.</p>
<h5><a href="#top">Back to Top</a></h5>
<hr>
<h3><a name="where">Where can I find Tech. Support Phone Numbers?</a></h3>
<p>You can contact Tech. Support at 555-1212. Or better yet you can leave a message in
Net Forum
under the Tech. Support Newsgroup. You can also send us an email at
➡Techsupport@miracle.com.</p>
<h5><a href="#top">Back to Top</a></h5>
<hr>
<h3><a name="why">Why do my images not display?</a></h3>
<p>There can be several reason's for this. If this were a real tech. support file I
would list them out. But
since this is an example your out of luck bud.</p>
<h5><a href="#top">Back to Top</a></h5>
<hr>
<h3><a name="what1">Who is a 404 error?</a></h3>
<p>This is an error you get when you try to connect to a web page on the World Wide Web
that can
```

```
not be located. &quot;404, URL Not Found&quot;. This is also slang for someone who's

clueless. &quot;Don't ask Dan, he's 404, man.&quot;</p>

<h5><a href="#top">Back to Top</a></h5>

<hr>

<h3><a name="what">What is a helper app.?</a></h3>

<p>A helper application is a program that can be launched by Netscape to allow you to

display other

applications that the browser does not support. We have Adobe Acrobat Reader on our

intranet,

which allows you to view pages the way they were met to be displayed with fonts, and

true page

layout. When you click on an Adobe link in the intranet the reader will automatically

launch. More

helper apps. will be added as we add more to our intranet and we will distribute the

apps. to your

desktops as they become available.</p>

<h5><a href="#top">Back to Top</a></h5>

<hr>

</body>

</html>
```

Link Checkers

After you have your intranet in place, you will have created a virtual Web of information. As more and more departments come online, their will be links to all kinds of information on your intranet. And, just like the World Wide Web, there will be broken links. The dreaded 404 error will raise its ugly head, always seeming to do so when you really, *really* need to see a certain page. When a page can't be located on the Web or on your intranet, you will get a 404 error, just like the one shown in Figure 15-10.

To avoid errors like these, you need to look at ways to manage your intranet content. These link validation services and programs allow you to check all of your hyperlinks to make sure that they are all intact and working properly. These programs follow each link and check to make sure that the documents they connect to exist. These are the most basic services you will find when you look for tools that will help you keep your Web or intranet in tip-top shape. There are a bunch of services and programs on the WWW that you can test for yourself. The next sections cover a handful that I found and like.

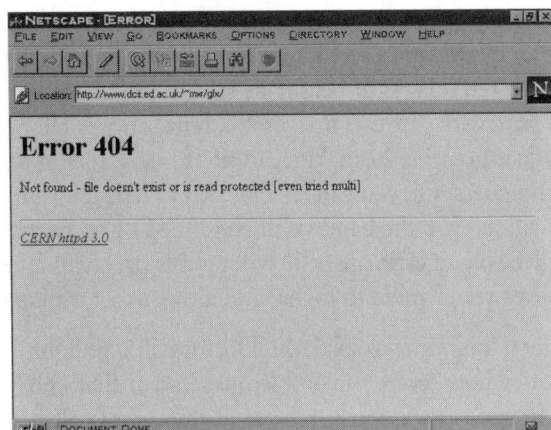

FIGURE 15-10

This is the dreaded 404 "file not found" error. As your intranet grows, so will these unless you use a management tool.

Doctor HTML

The first link verification application/service that I want to cover is Doctor HTML. It is much more than just an application that verifies hyperlinks. You can get to Doctor HTML on the WWW at:

www2.imagiware.com/RxHTML/

Doctor HTML will check your HTML documents for spelling errors. This is a must before you place anything on the intranet. You can spend weeks developing a fantastic intranet presentation, and one spelling error is what will stand out in the user's mind. There are Web authoring tools on the market that already offer spell checking, but some of the popular ones, such as Netscape Navigator Gold, do not come standard with a spell checker built in. If you look long and hard, you can sometimes find add-on packs that will do this task.

It is also important to find a spell checker that does not choke on HTML tags. Nothing is more frustrating than having a spell checker pull up every tag in your document. I am proud to say that Doctor HTML does a magnificent job of catching spelling errors and passing over tags.

The Doctor also gives all of your images a check-up. It takes all of your image files and looks for some important properties in all of your images. I can't tell you how many times I have heard individuals voice their concerns about network bandwidth. When you look at a page that has ten images on it, and then look at a page with two images on it, you might assume that the page with ten images takes up tons of valuable bandwidth. You can hear the screams now: the network is going to crash if you send that page over the LAN.

Bandwidth is a concern, which is why proper graphic techniques need to be used. By using compression, changing color depth, and preempting the browser by adding height and width tags, the Web page with ten images can easily be smaller and a quicker load than a poorly constructed Web page with just two images. So, how can you tell how fast that Web page that you just made is going to load? You can sit at home, dial in to your LAN with your 14.4 modem, and guess. Or, you can let Doctor HTML tell you. This is a cool feature. Doctor HTML will tell you the bandwidth consumed by each image in your intranet page. It will also give you an estimate of how long this page will take to load over a 14.4 modem. This gives you a guide to follow and a way to set standards.

If an image in your page is taking a long time to load, the Doctor will highlight it in different shades of red to let you know how severe the problem is. And, if that's not enough, the application will tell you the image's size as well as the total amount of colors in the image. This way, you can go back redesign images that don't measure up to your intranet standards.

Doctor HTML also looks for HTML code disasters waiting to happen. It will check your HTML code and look for HTML tags that are not closed. It will also look for HTML tags that you placed in the document that are extras. Both of these features can help you avoid disaster with browsers that are not so lenient about improperly structured pages.

You always make sure that you have the height, width, and alternate text tags in all of your image tags, don't you? I know I do, or should. But, when it gets late and I'm sick of working on the same intranet page for countless hours, I start to cut corners. Everyone does this. And the first thing to go is the height, width, and alternate text tags in your image tags. What good are they, anyway?

They make your documents load slightly faster, and more important, appear to load much faster. When your browser sees an image tag, it first looks to see whether you were nice enough to put in the height and width tags to help it out. If you didn't, then the browser must figure out the image's height, and width. This takes time, so make sure that you use them.

Doctor HTML has another neat feature that looks at your image tags to make sure that you have provided this height, width, and alternate text information. If you haven't, it will let you know.

Of course, Doctor HTML checks hyperlinks. It will check the hyperlinks on your pages to make sure that they connect to another document. This makes broken links a thing of the past.

These are just some of the features of Doctor HTML that make it great. I've set up an appointment with the Doctor so that you can take a look for yourself.

The Doctor has a very affordable price structure, and I am not going to cover it, but please take a look at www2.imagiware.com/RxHTML/. You will also need to point your browser to this site if you want to follow along with me as I walk you through some of the features of this application.

FIGURE 15-11

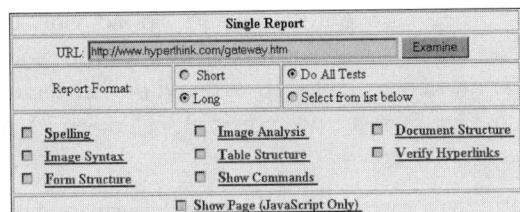

This form allows you to enter a single report. By entering a URL in the form, and choosing between a long and a short report, you can choose your report formats.

Okay, I entered my URL and chose "Do All Test." This way, I did not have to check all the boxes for the individual tests. That's it. When I click on Examine, Doctor HTML does the rest.

I then get a report, shown in Figure 15-12.

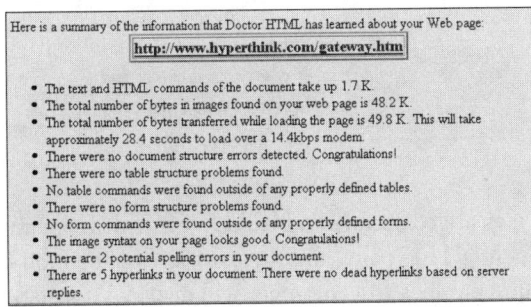

FIGURE 15-12

A report is generated that tells me everything I need to know about my Web page. This is perfect for testing your Web pages.

First, the report tells me that the text and HTML tags in the page I am checking take up 1.7K. Not much at all. It then tells me the total for all the images I have on this page. This is important because images take up more bandwidth, and a total can give you a quick idea of how long it will take a user to download the Web page. I came up with a total of 48.2K for all the images on this page. That's a bit more than I would like, but not bad.

So, how long will this take over the LAN? Doctor HTML can't tell you that, but it will give you some idea by telling you about how long it will take over a 14.4 modem. I rank

28.4 seconds to load at 14.4. Around 30–40 seconds maximum is about as long as a user is going to wait for a page to load. (Although this may not seem important initially, because you're using a relatively high-speed LAN, you may well have field locations that are using dedicated, but slower, lines to access that LAN. In addition, as telecommuting becomes more common, you'll have users remotely accessing your intranet using dial-up modem connections.)

I received an A+ in document structure errors, because the report showed none. There were also no problems with my tables on this page. Nor were there any form problems or table tags hanging around outside of my defined tables. Also, I used the height and width tags, so my image syntax looks good. Hey, there are two potential spelling errors, but all of my hyperlinks are working perfectly.

All this information helps out greatly, but I can do more. I can drill down and take a look at these reports. Take a look at the document structure report in Figure 15-13.

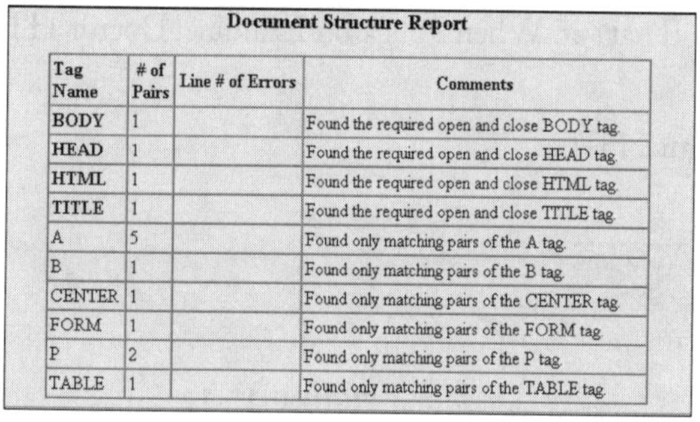

Document Structure Report			
Tag Name	**# of Pairs**	**Line # of Errors**	**Comments**
BODY	1		Found the required open and close BODY tag
HEAD	1		Found the required open and close HEAD tag
HTML	1		Found the required open and close HTML tag
TITLE	1		Found the required open and close TITLE tag
A	5		Found only matching pairs of the A tag
B	1		Found only matching pairs of the B tag
CENTER	1		Found only matching pairs of the CENTER tag
FORM	1		Found only matching pairs of the FORM tag
P	2		Found only matching pairs of the P tag
TABLE	1		Found only matching pairs of the TABLE tag

FIGURE 15-13

The document structure report tells me whether all of my structure tags and other common tags are correct.

I can see that all of my structure tags are correct. My <HEAD> tag has an opening and closing tag. My A tag has all of its matching pairs, and there are five of them on this Web page. If there are any errors, the line number and comment will display information that helps you fix potential problems.

In the next test, I pull up a Web site that has an error in it so that you can see how nicely Doctor HTML tells you about problems that might be in your documents. Figure 15-14 shows the table structure analysis. In this Web page, Doctor HTML found one error.

The table that Doctor HTML examined covers lines 9 through 13. In line 11, it found an error. There are some extra table data <TD> tags in this document, which might cause some browsers to choke on them. Doctor HTML also does reports on forms and lets you know whether your form structure has any problems.

FIGURE 15-14

By examining another Web page, I came across some mistakes. Can't tell you the site; you will have to find that out on your own. See how easy it is to find mistakes in your pages.

Table Structure Analysis

Table 1 Structure (lines 9 - 13):

Tag Name	# of Pairs	Line # of Errors	Comments
TD	0	11	Found extra open TD tags in this document. Please remove them.
TR	1		Found only matching pairs of the TR tag.

Now I'm going to jump down to the Image Analysis (see Figure 15-15). This is great. I get a list of all the images on my page in a nice, easy-to-read table. It tells me the name of each image, the file type, the file size, how many seconds each image takes to load, the exact width and height of each image in pixels, and the number of colors in each image. It also tells me what line number the image is on in my HTML code so that I can go back and find it if I want to work on it. Under the size column, the number that tells me the image size in bytes is also color coded in different shades of red. These color codes let you know at a glance whether you have images that have a large file size.

Image Analysis

Name	Type	Size (bytes)	Time (sec)	Width (pixels)	Height (pixels)	Colors	Line #
hyperth.gif	GIF87a	11399	6.33	360	108	256	13
demo-b.gif	GIF89a	5741	3.19	137	86	256	14
client-m.gif	GIF89a	5731	3.18	137	86	256	14
servic-m.gif	GIF89a	5788	3.22	137	86	256	14
about-m.gif	GIF89a	5711	3.17	137	86	256	14
ie.gif	GIF89a	14942	8.30	88	31	256	23

FIGURE 15-15

The Image Analysis gives you a formatted table with a complete listing of all the information that you need to fix and examine your images in your Web pages.

I can instantly tell that my HYPERTH.GIF and my IE.GIF are on the high end for this page because they are bright red. It gets better. If you want to see what image is hogging all your bandwidth so that you can go and change it later, just click on the image name. Another Netscape Browser session is launched, and when I hop over to the other Browser window, I can see the image (see Figure 15-16).

I can now find the original image on my hard drive, or I can pull this image directly into Netscape Navigator Gold, and then save it and use a graphics program to work on it.

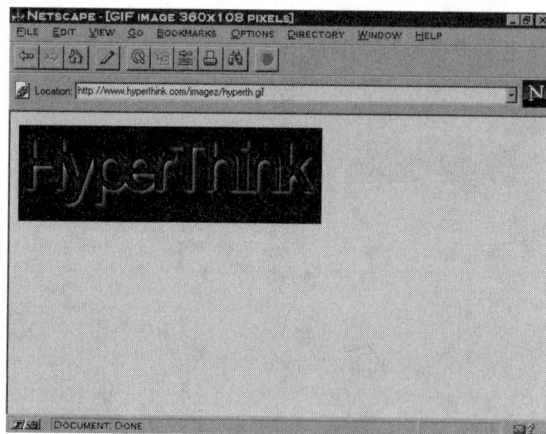

FIGURE 15-16

The HYPERTH.GIF file is a bit over 11K in size.

Figure 15-17 shows my spelling errors. As you can see, Doctor HTML picked out the company name HyperThink, which is okay because it is the name of the Web Development Company. It also grabbed the word *com* (as in dot com). This is also a Web term, so it's okay.

FIGURE 15-17

The spell check feature is a blessing. My editors wish that I used this more often on a daily basis. As you can see, I passed on this page.

Spelling Check		
Unrecognized Word	**Suggested Replacements**	**Line #**
HyperThink	Hyper Think, Hyper-Think	6
com	cam, cm, cod, cog, coma, comb, come, con, coo, cop, cot, cow, coy, Hom, mom, ROM, tom	6

The hyperlink analysis is also a valuable tool. I can see all the hyperlinks in my page. I can see the names of all the hyperlink files, their content type, the size of these files, when I last updated these pages, the line number in my HTML code that has this hyperlink, and a comment section, which, in this example, is telling me that the links that are tagged okay are on my Web site and work fine; and the link to Microsoft's Web site, which is quite a trip away from my Web server, was also found intact. Take a look at this in Figure 15-18. Clicking on the file name launches another browser session, and the link is followed to the corresponding Web page.

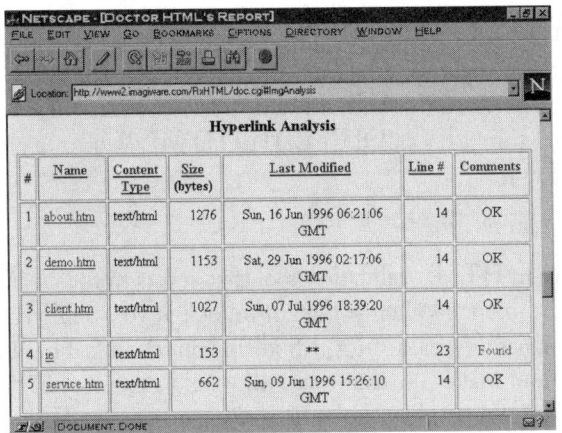

FIGURE 15-18

You can see all of your hyperlinks, and tell instantly whether they are valid. You can also follow links from here to check on pages that might have changed their content.

Your HTML page code is also displayed. So, now you can go into the code itself and edit it. You can make changes and find errors by line number. After you have fixed everything, you can just highlight the text and copy it to NotePad or an HTML editor, and save the file. Here is some of the code from the Web page that I just examined (see Figure 15-19).

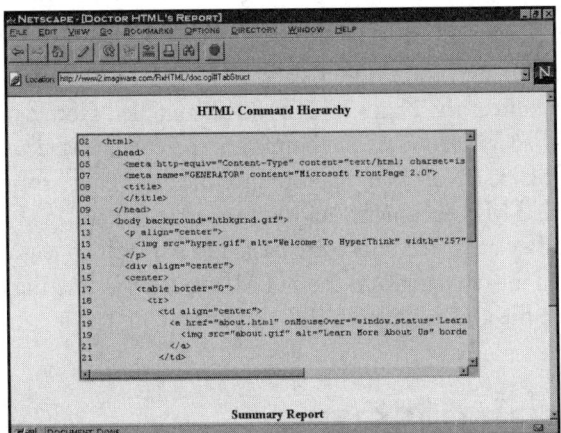

FIGURE 15-19

The HTML code is displayed for you so that you can find your mistakes and fix them right away. You can copy the code to NotePad and save your changes from here.

Be sure to visit the Doctor HTML Web site. You will be able to try out this application for yourself, and you can also get information on registering a copy for your intranet. It's one of the best tools that allows you to do everything you need to do to maintain your intranet pages and to check your work.

I Like the Little Guys

I have to show you this one. It's a simple yet effective tool that also validates your HTML code for you. You can download this and, if you decide to keep it, the cost of registering it is around $15.00, I think. It's called CSE 3310 HTML Validator, and you can check it out and download it at:

```
http://206.54.183.54/htmlvalidator.html
```

CSE 3310 HTML Validator is an HTML validation tool that assists in the creation of syntactically correct HTML documents. When you tell it to look at your HTML document, CSE 3310 will give you a listing of any error it finds in your coding. This allows you to correct your documents and make sure that they will work in a variety of browsers before you place them on your intranet and let the entire organization see a Web page that might not display correctly.

The CSE 3310 HTML Validator includes tools that change HTML tags and attributes to uppercase or lowercase. It also has a tool that strips HTML tags, and a tool that converts different operating system text file formats to other text file formats.

CSE 3310 HTML Validator also runs on both Windows 95 and NT.

After downloading and using the easy to follow install program, I did a little testing of some of my intranet Web pages to see what CSE 3310 HTML Validator would find.

I set up CSE 3310 to use NotePad, and chose File | Validate HTML Document. Then, I chose an intranet page from the directory. That's it. CSE 3310 launched NotePad and placed all my code in the NotePad Window. At the bottom of the code, I have an option set to display the errors that CSE 3310 has found and to give me an overall listing of general information about my HTML document. As you can tell in Figure 15-20, I have 10 errors in my HTML code; they are listed above the basic HTML stats. I can view the errors and suggestions, and then make changes to the HTML code or ignore the errors altogether. I can then resave the file and move onto the next one.

Content Ownership Issues

This differs for each organization, but I mention it because you need to address it in your organization. If you have a small organization with only a few key players, you should not have to worry that much about who owns what and who updates what. When you have a large organization, it is often unclear who owns what information and who has the right to update and change that information. You need to determine this structure up front. What you don't want is to have departments creating and duplicating the same information. This can easily happen in large organizations, because one department might be

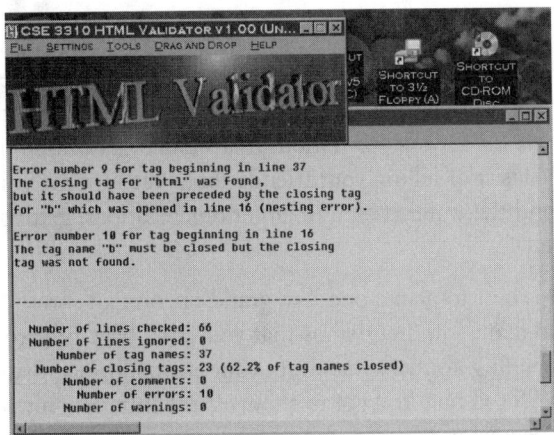

FIGURE 15-20

CSE 3310 HTML Validator is easy to use and set up. Here are some of the errors it found in my intranet page. I made some of the changes and then moved on to check another page.

working on a project in a totally different office that generates the same information that another department has been doing for years. When this duplicate information makes its way to your intranet, then the issues of who actually owns the information arises.

You don't want the same information displayed by two separate areas on your intranet, for several reasons. One, it takes up space, time, and effort. Two, users will not trust the integrity of the information on your intranet if they are look, for example, for prices, and they see one price on one intranet page, and a totally different price for the same item on another intranet page. Just make sure to address these issues so that you will have a plan of action when they arise.

Selling and Marketing

Now I discuss how to market and sell your intranet concept. This includes getting management involved, promotions, and that killer app that will require all the employees to use the intranet to get their daily work done.

In the Beginning

You would not have made it this far if you did not have someone backing you in the organization, so I won't dwell on the importance of having great support. You need grass-root support as well as top-down support. You need both to succeed and get your intranet up and running. After it is running, it will most likely take on a life of its own and take off from there.

Promotions

When you are all done with the beta testing that I discussed earlier, and your super users are all trained on your intranet applications, navigation, and the browser, you can then start to focus on the roll out. This is your big promotion. In a small organization of 10 people, your promotion might consist of telling your friends about the intranet going live while everyone is standing around the water cooler. In larger organizations, getting the word out is more of a challenge.

First, in a large organization, it is best to plan a one-day, grand opening of sorts. Otherwise, you will be giving so many intranet demos that you won't have time to ever turn the thing on. This grand opening also lets you target your efforts for one main event. This is kind of like a Windows 95 roll out. You get to show off the intranet only once to your entire organization, with the goal of generating interest that stirs users to participate and other departments to contribute—so do it right.

It all comes down to basic marketing. There are no rocket-science secrets here that will make your intranet roll out as a whopping success. Just think of creative ways to advertise and generate interest in your intranet. The following sections describe a few.

The Intranet Café

This is original, and I have to give credit to a friend and partner of mine who came up with this idea. Charlie Broschart, who works at Disney, thought of this idea. Internet cafés are popping up in major cities all across the world and are very popular. So, why not lug a few PCs over to the employee cafeteria and set up an intranet café? This way, employees can get a chance to see the intranet up close and personal. They can ask you questions and they can ask the trainers, who are also on hand, about the new intranet. It's a very relaxed setting, and a free cup of coffee helps break the ice for employees who might not show interest in a formal meeting setting.

Trade Show

Trade shows are popular, and large organizations are starting to have their own internal technology trade shows and departmental trade shows to let the rest of the organization know what is happening in various areas. Try to set up an area at one of these events. Grab a data monitor, some flyers, and a computer or two and go generate some interest in your project. If you already have more interest in your project than you can handle, then save these types of events for your grand rollout to the huddled masses.

Flyers, Posters, Paycheck Attachments, and Other Junk Mail

This stuff usually ends up in the employee parking lot or covering the floor of the cafeteria, but it's inexpensive and it works. Make a brochure in a word processing program and hand it out. Make flyers and posters and post them by the time clocks. You might even be able to attach a note to employee paychecks to generate interest in your intranet, or to tell them of the rollout date and what to expect.

Free Stuff

Everyone eats this up. I always come back with a 40-pound bag of mostly junk when I go to Internet/intranet conventions. The trick here is to give your users something useful. Don't give them a pen that looks like a neon straw, or a magnet that they can stick on their PC and watch all their files start to disappear one by one. Try making a mouse pad with all the key intranet functions printed on it. Every time employees sit down at their computer, they will have all the killer app functions and help keys printed out right there in front of them. If you can't afford a mouse pad, then print up a short of quick-reference card that can be placed in a clear pouch on the side of the monitor. Or a small booklet with tips and intranet help listed in it.

The Big Day

If you do a big production to get other departments and users interested in your intranet, make sure that you do something you can handle. Usually, a few hours set aside one day is plenty of time for your intranet open house. This gives people an opportunity to come anytime during the time slot, and you will get a better turn-out than if you schedule a meeting that starts at x time and ends at y time. This creates a more casual atmosphere, and users and managers can gather around and discuss intranet issues and test yours out. The trainers should be available to help answer questions and demonstrate the intranet applications. You can hand out your mouse pads and tell everyone to start budgeting for next year, because now they will all want to upgrade their computers to get intranet access in their department.

Summary

You now have some ideas on how to market your intranet, get some buy-in for your department's budget, and recruit some help. There is a plethora of ways to get users excited about this new technology, and I've discussed some of the ones that have worked for me. I also covered training issues and ways to add online training right to your intranet. I then moved on to tools that allow you to verify your Web pages. You now know how to verify your hyperlinks and check your code to make sure that it passes the standards.

Book Wrap Up!

That's it! You now know it all. Well, at least enough to make informative decisions, create a solid project plan, lay out a design, test your ideas, choose a Web server based on your needs, get the server up and running, and use one of many methods to access information. You also have learned more than the average Joe when it comes to audio and video types, and you even dived into CGI and survived. You can now wow your friends and colleagues with dancing bologna and eye candy (visual effects) in the next business presentation that you do in a Web browser. You know about almost every plug-in available (and you should download some of the ones discussed in Chapter 12, if you haven't already). For a different approach to communicating information, you have seen PointCast's I-Server and know about its new approach to broadcasting information. You've also prepared for the issue of security by reading about certificates and access control methods. And, finally, this book covered implementation and marketing.

Now you can use the appendixes to brush up on your HTML, or learn HTML first hand. Some authoring tools are covered in Appendix C, and there is an HTML reference guide in Appendix D that comes in handy when you need to look up those tags.

I enjoyed touring the endless possibilities that intranets have to offer with you. As intranets keep evolving, I will try to keep up with all of the developments so that I can bring you the latest breaking technologies. Until then, you can e-mail me at:

steveg@gate.net

Best,

Steve

PART V

Appendixes

Appendix | A

Basic HTML

To many people, HTML seems like some sort of arcane and difficult-to-learn foreign language—one that, given a choice, they would really prefer not to mess with. But hey, come on now, is it really all that tough to learn? Well, it probably does take a initial time investment, but after you sit down for a few solid hours with it, you will be surprised how quickly you are cranking out award-winning Web pages and building huge and complex sites. (Stop me if I am starting to sound unbelievable). Speaking of something incredible, I have recently found two pieces of clip art (don't groan) on the Netscape site (see Figures A-1 and A-2) that very succinctly point out exactly why HTML is going to change not only the way you work but also the way you live your life. Take a look and see what you think.

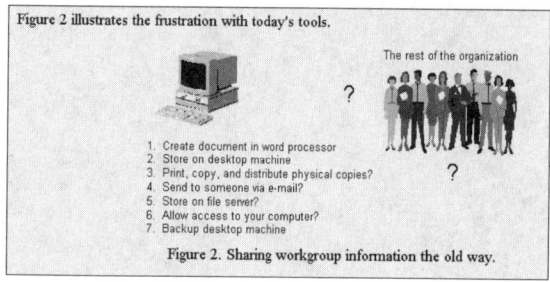

FIGURE A-1

Sharing information the old way.

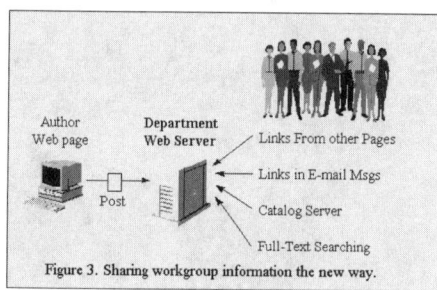

FIGURE A-2

Sharing information the new way.

Wow. Hello. Are you there? Run to the light! This is really what it is all about when you break it down to its essence. It amounts to sharing information in a whole new way, on a one-to-many basis, in a manner in which information is readily accessible to all members of your organization. Your workforce can tap into one of many information "repositories" that will contain the information that all the employees need, when they need it. Workgroups become truly cross-functional and are able to share ideas without regard to time or distance. The individual in an organization becomes truly info-empowered.

You may have heard someone around your office say (usually the person trying to sell a new concept to you) something like this: "Six months? *Six months?* We can't wait six months—do you realize how long six months is in computer years?" Computer years are very much like dog years; that is, each human year is equal to around seven dog years (it has something to do with their metabolism being faster than ours). There is a parallel here to the pace of technology and to the degree that HTML has evolved from a purely "raw coded" development approach to one that employs a bevy of "editors" and "converters."

Raw Coding

In the old days (just over a year ago), Web pages were done by hand—or by what is called "raw coding." Now, the ability to raw code has a certain sort of rough elegance to it. So, it was kind of cool to show people your newly created Web page, while you anxiously hoped that they would ask how you had created it so that you could say, "I raw coded it." Wow, this was great party conversation and something sure to get the spotlight shifted firmly on you for the next hour or so. Raw coding! You had them in the palm of your hand. If you felt like pushing the envelope, you could casually mention that you had just come off an all-nighter of trying to create an animated GIF of a dog running across the screen and wagging its tail (keep this dog and tail image in your mind—I'll bring it up again a bit later).

Those Who Don't Remember the Past...

I want to tell you about how my development partner, Charlie, and I actually got started doing our own raw-coding. We both work at a huge entertainment company whose name we cannot reveal for fear of loss of PC and network access (I am exaggerating a bit; I'm sure that the company would still allow us to write Web pages, but they just wouldn't let us put them on any of our company's servers, or something like that). Anyway, we had this bright idea that our company needed an intranet or a Web site, so we went out and bought a book on HTML. We went over to Charlie's house because he had the latest version of Netscape (1.2!!!) and because, though I don't like to admit it, I still hadn't figured out how to connect to my ISP.

There we were at Charlie's house sitting in front of the PC with our HTML book opened to Day 1 (please note that "days" in computer books are much like "computer years" but are probably actually much longer). We first opened a text editor (in this case, NotePad, though we later switched to WordPad because our Web server didn't seem to like the pages that we had created in NotePad) and made sure to save our file with the .HTM extension.

> **NOTE:** This would be an .HTML extension on a MAC—later versions of Netscape Gold will add the .HTML extension as the default when you try to save files. Also, you must be consistent in using either upper- or lowercase characters; your Webmaster should be able to tell you which one the server will not choke on.

Then we opened up our browser, Netscape Navigator v1.2, in this case (and still the most prevalent browser in most corporate intranets, according to informed sources). We typed the following:

```
<html>
<head><title>This Is Our First WebPage!>title>
<body>
Hello world! How do you like us now!
</body>
</html>
```

The result of this code is shown in Figure A-3.

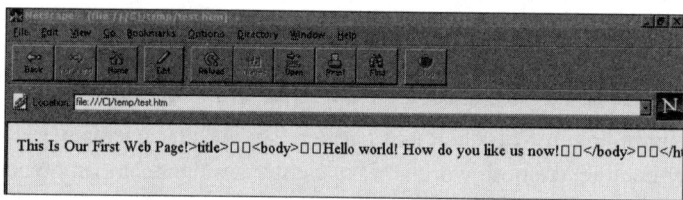

FIGURE A-3

Our first Web page.

Well, well, well. Something was definitely rotten in the state of HTML! But what was it? Please send in your SASE to the following address with your best guess (just kidding). We had obviously made at least a couple of HTML faux paus. In our excitement, we had left out the following very important HTML 2.0 tags (tags that are *not* as critical in the new HTML 3.2 proposed standards—coming soon to a browser near you!):

- ◆ We had forgotten to put a </>, or closing tag, around the title entry
- ◆ We had omitted the </> around the head entry

Here's what we should have typed:

```
<html>
<head><title>This Is Our First Web Page!</title></head>
```

```
<body>
Hello world! How do you like us now!
</body>
</html>
```

Figure A-4 shows what we should have seen.

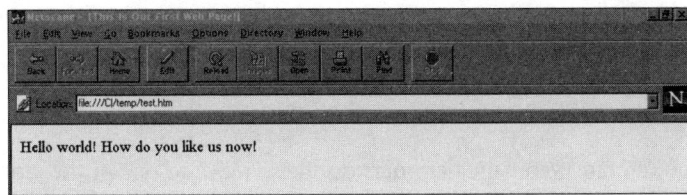

FIGURE A-4

*If at first you don't
succeed . . . .*

Wow! We both looked at each other and said, "We have seen the future, and it is
HTML. World peace is just a closing tag away from becoming a reality in our
lifetime"(or something like that). Seriously, we really did freak a bit when we typed our
text, went over our open browser using Alt-Tab, opened the file, and BAM! We had
become publishers on the new frontier—the World Wide Web. Charlie immediately
wanted to dump some of his ponderous poetry into a Web page, but I quickly blocked
this by changing the preferences on his browser so that he could publish only locally.

After that initial near-Web experience, Charlie and I immersed ourselves in our HTML
book and actually got to Day 8, when we realized that we now knew enough to be dan-
gerous (to ourselves and to our company). Three months later, we had built and put up a
beautiful Web site that created tremors of creativity throughout all areas of our company.
(And to think that it all started with two guys sharing—due to limited resources—the
same HTML book and the same dream: to see our names dancing or spinning across the
screen in an animated GIF!) I would imagine that the point of all this is:

Hey kids, you can try this at home! (And it actually works).

Enough storytelling. It's just about time to get under the hood and see what makes my
Web pages go—the HTML engine. But first, I want to explain briefly why it would be
helpful for you to learn the basics of HTML. I follow that discussion with one about the
ongoing browser wars and how the real winner (no matter what company's browser wins)
will be you. Please refer to Appendix B for a very interesting take on whether there really
is a war between browsers, or a war between competing file formats.

Is All This Really Worth It?

If you have made it to this point, you must truly be interested in weaving the perfect Web—one that will contain fresh and immediate (and, you hope, up-to-date) information that will connect all areas of your company or organization.

At the beginning of this chapter, I referred to the dizzying pace of evolution that HTML and the creation of Web pages and corporate sites has undergone in just the past six months. The "old days" of raw coding pages by hand are still very much with us, but even the more experienced Web designers are opting for one of the many new Web editors that are now available, such as Netscape Gold, Microsoft FrontPage, NetObjects, WebEdit, PageMill, and so on.

Why do these same veteran Web page designers decide to move to one of the aforementioned editors? They do this mainly for reasons of speed and a plethora of added features (tables, forms, image map creation, and so on) that make building a site much faster and efficient than starting with a text editor and building from scratch. This was simply not possible as little as six to eight months ago! Back then, some of these same editors existed, but they had a tendency to blow apart the HTML code that you had so lovingly crafted by hand. Today's editors are for the most part generating what is called "clean" code, or code that may require only a bit of tweaking by the designer in order to make it look the way it was intended.

Even with this added and only occasional tweaking, the sheer speed of these editors makes them well worth a hard look by any company wishing to build a Web site—especially a large-scale company. Please refer to Appendix C for a more detailed exploration of some of the more popular editors available today.

So, why should you even bother to learn the basics of HTML if you can pick up an editor from the Internet and start cranking away? It's the tweaking, silly. Yes, today's editors (and converters) are getting better and better (I must admit that I use one to create all of my pages), but I feel strongly that it is important to at least have a basic or even rudimentary understanding of what is going on behind your Web pages. It is important to have a grasp of raw coding in order to have a deeper understanding of what your editor is actually doing. If you ever get any strange output from your browser, wouldn't it be nice to just open your favorite text editor (which you can do from within most of the existing WYSIWYG Web page editors available today—at least the ones worth their salt) and insert that <CENTER> tag, or even tweak that table over just a tad in order to balance out your overall page design?

There are actually five (5) versions or flavors of HTML currently residing on a Web page near you. They are the following:

- HTML v2.0 (first published around September, 1995)
- HTML v3.0 (March, 1995; not widely implemented and actually no longer supported by W3C working group, which is also called HTML+)
- HTML v3.2 (should be in wide use by the time you read this)
- Netscape Extensions (proprietary tags introduced by Netscape—not initially a part of HTML standards, but many if not all of the features or tags suggested by Netscape have found their way into the newly proposed HTML 3.2 standards
- Microsoft Extensions (Microsoft has also taken the opportunity to introduce its own proprietary tags)

The Browser Wars: Who Really Wins?

It is interesting to note that as the so-called browser wars continue in earnest, any proprietary tags created by Netscape are typically included in subsequent releases of Microsoft Internet Explorer. As Microsoft has been in the catch-up mode (it has increased browser-share from 12 percent to almost 38 percent in only the past six-month period (March 1996–October 1996; source: *WebWeek*, October, 1996), Microsoft has managed to include all of the Netscape tags and have even created a few of its own for good measure (for example, the <MARQUEE> tag). As things stand now, you have a choice between two browsers, Netscape Navigator and Microsoft's Internet Explorer, and both of these companies create HTML standards or tags that are quickly adopted by Web designers across the world in spite of the fact that these same tags and HTML extensions have not been officially adopted by the W3C (World Wide Web Consortium) HTML working group. You may wish to visit the W3C Web site at http://www.w3.org/pub/WWW. Spend some time on that site and you will quickly appreciate the value of having a knowledgeable Webmaster to create and maintain your company's Web site.

Black-and-White versus Color TV

But what if your company is still using Netscape 1.2 as your default (and supported) browser? Will you still be able to take advantage of the new HTML 3.2? Yes and no— and why don't you make that leap of faith and upgrade to at least Netscape v2.02? A friend of mine compared the continued use of Netscape v1.2 as something at least as bad as forcing people to continue watching black-and-white television even though color is widely available. I thought this was a rather clever analogy and very true for those who are still using Netscape v1.2. You're missing all the fun!

Animated GIFs and different font colors are just a couple of the amazing things that your users will miss if you don't upgrade. So, the answer to that question a moment ago concerning HTML 3.2 compatibility is that the 3.2 standard was designed to have backward compatibility with HTML 2.O browsers, which means that you would be covered even if you continued using the Netscape v1.2 browser. You would *not*, of course, have the advantage of the so-called Netscape Extensions. Just upgrade and get it over with.

To Converge or Diverge? That Is the Question

Convergence is probably the concept that will save us all in the end. Divergence, of course, could then be construed as our potential enemy or barrier to standardization or even innovation. For the most part, standards are converging so that a user can be on either Netscape Navigator or Microsoft Internet Explorer and expect a satisfying Web experience. But there is also a smattering of divergence in, for example, Microsoft's introduction of ActiveX as an answer to Netscape's adoption of Java and, as another example, in the introduction (or rather inclusion) of Cascading Style Sheets (CSS) in Microsoft's new browser (4.0). Initially, Netscape decided not to include CSS (a decision that it recently changed). All of this posturing and maneuvering for market share typically only benefits the end users, as they have all these neat tricks at their disposal—features that are ultimately included or adopted by both players in the browser wars (in order to at least hedge or cover their bets).

Probably the biggest advantage to the Webmaster in a corporation is that a given company will typically settle on one of the two major browsers (apologies to those companies that are utilizing the Mosaic browser. Do you really think your users are not busily downloading the latest Netscape Navigator or Microsoft Internet Explorer? I'm kidding—but, on second thought, you'd better go check this out): either Netscape Navigator or Microsoft Internet Explorer. This is good for those two companies and good for you as a Webmaster and Web page designer. When we designed pages for our company, it was always one less worry to know that everyone (within reason) would be seeing the same content on their screens that you had spent so much time designing for them. This is a good thing.

Then, what is the bad thing? The bad thing is having to wait to upgrade all your users to a browser higher than Netscape v1.2. While you had all that bologna dancing across your screen, most of your users were able to see only a single slice just standing there, not moving at all.

Just What Is HTML?

So, the advantage is for the most part in the Webmaster's court. How he or she goes about creating that award-winning site comes down to a choice of tools. What follows is a description of how one of the more important weapons in your Web development arsenal— HTML—actually works.

According to the W3C (World Wide Web Consortium) working group:

> "The HyperText Markup Language (HTML) is a simple markup language used to create hypertext documents that are portable from one platform to another. HTML documents are SGML (Standard Generalized Markup Language) with generic semantics that are appropriate for representing information from a wide range of applications."

This roughly translates to something like the following:

HTML documents are small, making them ideal for transmission over the Net. HTML documents also load very quickly (usually), due to the fact that all formatting and font information is interpreted or accomplished by the client, as opposed to you having to stuff it all into a bandwidth-eating document.

HTML documents are also cross-platform, which means that a document created on a Mac can be easily read by a PC or even a UNIX box. HTML allows the browser to make any formatting decisions.

In its basic form, the intent of HTML is to define a document's structure or content, but *not* the layout or appearance of the document. Therefore, HTML is limited in the kinds of things you can do with the elements of a Web page (for example, placement of images, types of fonts). But, as you probably have guessed by now, this limitation of HTML is undergoing an evolution through the introduction of style sheets and other HTML elements that allow virtually unlimited options for placing images, tables, and a wider selection of font faces. This is good news.

Getting Under the Hood

An HTML document consists of text and tags. These tags are what give the document its aspect of structure. Here are some unique properties of tags that you will want to keep in mind as you begin creating your own Web pages:

- The majority of HTML tags will have a beginning (opening) and an ending (closing) tag that enclose the text that is to be formatted. As you may have guessed, the opening tag turns on text formatting (such as bold, headings, emphasis, and so on), whereas the closing tag turns text formatting off.

Opening tags look like this: <tag name>

Closing tags look like this: </tag name>

◆ Certain HTML tags have only an opening tag

◆ HTML tags are case insensitive, which means that they don't care about letter case (imagine that!). Some people like to write all their tags in uppercase so that they can easily pick out the tags from the text. Charlie prefers to put all of his tags in lowercase because doing so helps remind him to put filenames in lowercase, which was important because our Web server *was* case sensitive.

Forget about putting in extra spaces, nice tabs, and carriage returns in your HTML document. When the browser interprets your document, it will ignore anything not contained within a tag. That is why, when you look at some people's document source code (pull down View and then Document Source in Netscape Navigator—also a good way to learn how to create Web pages), you will see some that line every element up quite neatly, with everything stacked up and easy to read. But you will also sometimes find a considerate individual who has simply strung all his code together in one continuous line of text. Hey, it still works! If you find that you have a lot of time on your hands, then open your text editor and type this wacky code:

```
<html>
<head><title>Careful with that axe, Eugene</title></head>
<body>
<h1>Obscure Song Titles</h1>
<p>I                    can              type my  text just about      anyway
I want to                                    and it will      still
turn out looking just                   fine.</p>
</body>
</html>
```

What good is this trick? A great conversation starter?

Additional spaces placed in your HTML code will not display when opened in your browser.

The Tags

And now, ladies and gentleman, I am proud to present for your Web-weaving pleasure: The tags!

> **NOTE:** The following tags are the majority of, or most widely used, tags found in the HTML 2.0 specifications. I will focus on the HTML 3.2, Netscape, and Microsoft tag extensions in Appendix B.

<HTML>

This is the first tag that you will insert at the beginning of your HTML document. This tag lets the browser know that it is loading an HTML document. A dirty little secret that is passed around at HTML-coding festivals is that, technically, you don't have to use either the <HTML>, <HEAD>, or even the <BODY> tags and your pages will still load. Well, personally, about 10 million Web weavers (myself included) continue using these tags, particularly the <HTML> tag, which was the very first one we ever typed. This tag has both opening and closing attributes. Please note that I have the indicated tag in a bold and larger font size so that it jumps right out at you.

```
<html>

<head><title>Web Development – HyperThink</title></head>

<body>

...your stuff...

</body>

</html>
```

< HEAD >

This tag could also be called the "prologue" tag. Just about the only tag that goes into the <HEAD> tag is the old reliable <TITLE> tag. This tag has both opening and closing attributes. You'll see it in the following code:

```
<html>
<head><title>Real Estate Appraisals</title></head>
<body>
...your stuff...
</body>
</html>
```

< TITLE >

This is a very important tag in that it gives your document a title. Try to think of a title that is very descriptive—not too long, yet not too vague; not too wordy, yet not too pithy (opposite of wordy). The title is also used when you add a bookmark (in Netscape) or create a favorite (in Microsoft Internet Explorer) in your browser. If you are creating Web sites that you would like to have listed in any of the major search engines, you should pay very close attention to how you write your title, or you will find that your pages rarely if ever come up during a search query. This tag has both opening and closing attributes. It's shown in the following code:

```
<html>
<head><title>UFO Sightings - -Confirmed</title></head>
<body>
...your stuff...
</body>
</html>
```

< BODY >

After the <TITLE> tag is inserted, you will typically list the <BODY> tag (or element). Literally everything of any relevance or importance to your Web page will reside between the opening and closing <BODY> tags. You can also insert some very useful tags within the <BODY> tag, which I'll show you a bit later (the background tag is one that comes to mind). The following code shows the use of the <BODY> tag.

```
<html>
<head><title>Brady Bunch--Bios</title></head>
<body>
...anything of importance or relevance...i.e. your document!
</body>
</html>
```

<H1> through <H6> (The Headings Tags)

There are six levels of headings in HTML: <H1>, the largest-sized heading, down through <H6>, which is the smallest. Headings are just that—headings. You utilize them to separate sections within your HTML document. They default to a flush-left setting, but you can add a <CENTER> tag to the heading tag if you would like to center the heading. Don't confuse the heading tag with the <HEAD> tag. This tag has both opening and closing attributes. Want to see the different heading tags all stacked up with no place to go?

```
<html>
<head><title>Fun With Heading Tags <h1> thru <h6>!</title></head>
<body>
<h1>Welcome To The Miracle Toy Co</h1>
<h2>Our Vision</h2>
<h3>A Worldwide Distribution System</h3>
<h4>Employment Opportunities</h4>
<h5>How To Contact Us</h5>
<h6>Complaints</h6>
</body>
</html>
```

Figure A-6 shows the result of the preceding code.

<P> (Paragraph Tag)

The <P> tag encloses the paragraph text in your document. This tag has an opening attribute only, though you can insert a closing </P> tag if you feel the need to do so; doing so is not required. Some Web weavers may use the <P> tag as a way of inserting additional spacing in their document. Doing so is generally okay, but you may occasionally run into problems with older browsers that will ignore your additional <P> tags. If you need some additional space, you can also use the <BR> tag, which I discuss a bit later. There is also a special character in HTML 3.2,   (for nonbreaking space), which could be used as a spacer between lines of text or images when you do not want the affected text or image to "break" (or line up) directly below the line or image preceding (or above) it. (This special character must be in all lowercase).

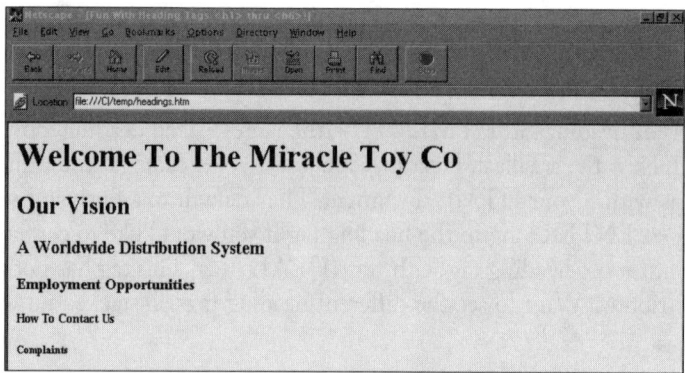

FIGURE A-6

Fun with heading tags <H1> through <H6>.

The following code demonstrates the use of the <P> tag.

```
<html>
<head><title>Miracle Toy Co.—Vision</title></head>
<body>
<p>The Miracle Toy Co. is devoted to making the highest quality toys at the lowest price
➥possible. Gosh darn it, we love making toys, and it shows! We believe in giving back
➥to the community that made us what w are today. Can you believe it? A company that
➥cares about quality more than just making money? We invite you to come and visit us so
➥we can give you the factory tour. Miracle Toys—Toys for tomorrow. . . Today!</p>
</body>
</html>
```

Figure A-7 shows the result of the preceding code.

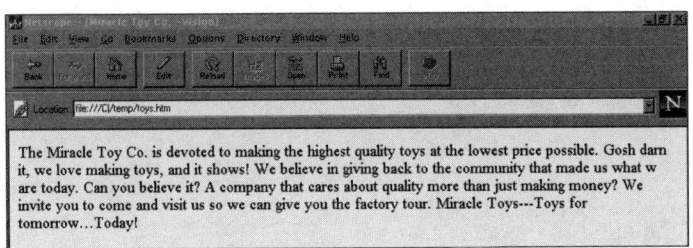

FIGURE A-7

For spacing between lines or defining paragraphs, the <P> tag.

<A> (The Link Tag)

Creating a bunch of Web pages is cool and all that, but the real power of the Web (and your corporate intranet) is the ability to create links or hyperlinks between documents. You have may have noticed when you're surfing the Web that there are words in the document that are a different color than the surrounding text (typically blue). These are the hyperlinks or just plain links to other documents within the same document, within your intranet, or even to documents located on servers halfway around the world. These links represent the true power of the Web.

The <A> or link tag is also referred to as an anchor tag. The <A> link tag is a bit different than your typical HTML tag in that it encloses a bit of information about the document being linked to. This tag has both opening and closing attributes. It also has the following attributes: href (HyperText reference), name (used for anchors), and title. You will most typically be using the href attribute when you create your links. The image in Figure A-8 shows a typical link and its component parts.

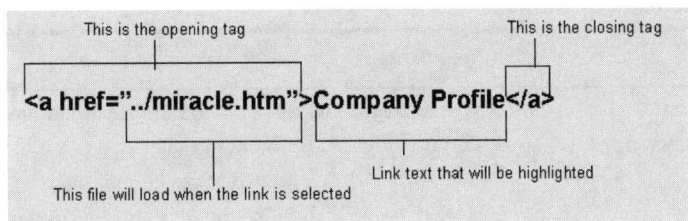

FIGURE A-8

A typical link with its component parts.

The following code shows what a typical link within a document would look like in your browser.

```
<html>
<head><title>The Missing Link?</title></head>
<body>
```

```
<p>Could we have actually found the "missing link"? Scientists at the <a
➥href="../livermore.htm">Livermore Laboratory</a> in East Hanover were up all night
➥trying to determine this very fact.</p>
</body>
</html>
```

Figure A-9 shows the result of the preceding code.

FIGURE A-9

The Missing Link.
This is how you create a
typical hyperlink.

This is, obviously, a very simple example. I strongly encourage you to try some of your own. Keep in mind that what I did here was to link to what is called a local document; I used a relative path name to tell the browser where to find the required file. I might have used something called an absolute path name to accomplish the same thing, but when you're creating links between documents, it is usually best to stay with relative path names. They are more portable than their counterpart, absolute path names. Tables A-1 and A-2 give some examples of what I mean.

Table A-1   Relative Path Names

Path	Meaning
href="miracle.htm"	MIRACLE.HTM can be found in the current directory
href="miracle/toys.htm"	TOYS.HTM can be found in the directory called miracle (and MIRACLE is located in the current directory)
href="../miracle.htm"	MIRACLE.HTM can be found in the directory one level up from the current directory
href="../../miracle/toys.htm"	TOYS.HTM can be found two directory levels up in the MIRACLE directory

Relative path names describe a file location in relation to the current document.

You can usually tell whether you are dealing with an absolute path because it will begin with a forward slash (/).

Table A-2   Absolute Path Names

Path	Meaning
href="/miracle/toys/pricing.htm	PRICING.HTM can be found in the directory /MIRACLE/TOYS
href="/e¦/miracle/toys/pricing.htm	PRICING.HTM can be found on drive E in the directory MIRACLE/TOYS

As I mentioned previously, in terms of your Web site and its directory structure, it is almost always advantageous to utilize relative rather than absolute paths. Again, the reason is the portability of the relative path as opposed to the absolute. If you were to create absolute pointers to your Web files, and then you changed servers or renamed directories on your existing server, your links would break and you would spend a bit of time trying to reconstruct them. Please note that there are a number of excellent site management programs that will take care of this problem for you and will help maintain the integrity of your link structure. Relative versus absolute is a tad confusing until you start creating your pages and setting up your links. Experiment a little and you will soon find the advantage of using relative path names.

<HR> (The Horizontal Rule Tag)

Creates a horizontal line on your page? You guessed it! The <HR> tag is an excellent way of helping to break up huge walls or chunks of text on your Web pages. The rule line is also useful for separating or highlighting images or tables. This tag has only opening attributes. The following code shows the use of this tag.

```
<html>
<head><title>A Rule By Any Other Name</title></head>
<body>
<p>A rule by any other name would still be a rule or something straight and and narrow
➥and with the ability to separate parts of a document. I have never seen a rule so
➥straight as the one that is willing to lay down on it's side and keep my images from
➥fighting with my paragraphs.</p>
<hr>
<img src="bluegran.gif">
<hr>
</body>
</html>
```

Figure A-10 shows the result of the preceding code.

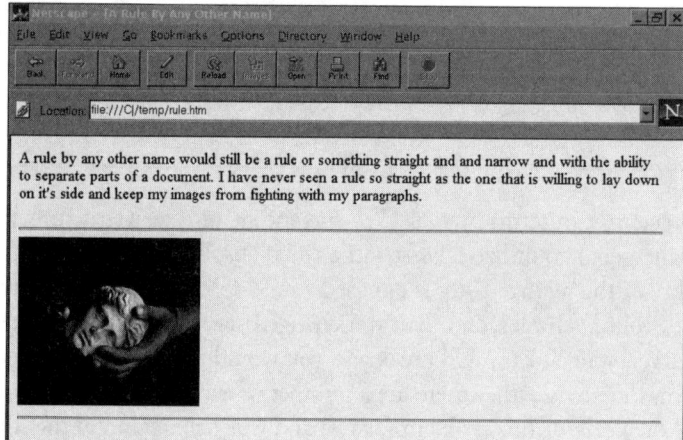

FIGURE A-10

*The <HR> tag is an easy
way to break up your
page content.*

I apologize for putting in the <IMG>, or image tag, that you see in the HTML preceding code. Hey, I thought you might be ready for it. I'll get into the <IMG> tag more as the wonderful world of HTML continues to unfold.

 (The Line Break Tag)

If you are typing away in a document and you would like your next line of text to start exactly where the previous line had started, then put in a <BR>, or line break tag. A good example of where you might use a <BR> tag is when you are writing a poem and want to separate (and line up) each line of the poem. This tag has an opening attribute only. The following code shows an example of using the <BR> tag.

```
<html>
<head><title>What You Will</title></head>
<body> <p>If music be the food of love, play on;<br>
Give me excess of it; that, surfeiting,<br>
The appetite may sicken, and so die. —-<br>
That strain again;—-it had a dying fall:<br>
</p>
</body>
</html>
```

Figure A-11 shows the result of the preceding code.

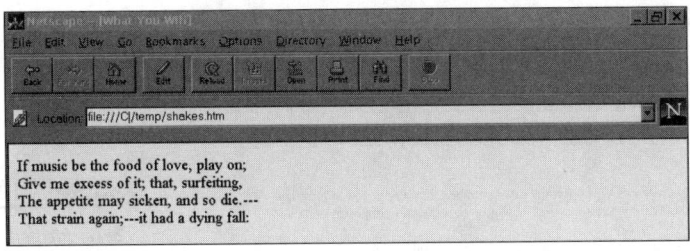

FIGURE A-11

*A bit of Shakespeare
with line breaks!
wraps the text to the next
new line.*

<BLOCKQUOTE> (The Quotation Tag)

Although it's typically used for formatting longer quotations, the <BLOCKQUOTE> tag is also useful for helping to set off chunks of your body text. The <BLOCKQUOTE> tag will take your paragraphs and squeeze them (bring the margins in on either side) a bit so that they will stand out from the regular paragraph formatting. This tag has both opening and closing attributes.

```html
<html>
<head><title>Blockquote--A Clear Choice</title></head>
<body>
<p>I was recently up in northern Pennsylvania, right near Scranton which is very close
➡to the New York state border, visiting my great Aunt. While there I had a pleasant
➡series of revelations and experiences where I discovered much about my family's
➡origins. My great Aunt had a library with books from all the way back to the early
➡1800's most of them being original editions. At random I chose Tolstoy's
Resurrection and then spent the rest of my vacation under a tree unable to put this book
➡down. Here is an excerpt:</p>
<blockquote>The next morning Nekhludoff awoke, conscious that something had happened to
➡him, and even before he had remembered what it was he knew it to be something
➡important and good.<p>
"Kathusa--the trial!" Yes, he must stop lying and tell the whole truth.</blockquote>
➡</p>
</body>
</html>
```

Figure A-12 shows the result of the preceding code.

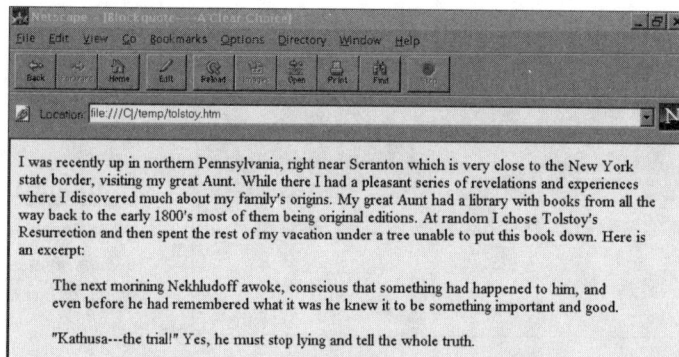

FIGURE A-12

The resurrection of the blockquote.

Logical and Physical Character Styles

Basically, character styles affect how certain parts of a documents text can be made to look different from the surrounding text in that same document. Some examples will give you a clearer picture of what this means.

Logical Style Tags

Logical style tags tell the browser how a piece of text should be used but *not* how it is to be displayed. In other words, different browsers may interpret an <EM> or emphasis tag just slightly differently than another browser. An <EM> tag says, "Here I am, browser; now please give this text some sort of emphasis in order to set it off from the surrounding text." (A browser will typically show <EM> text as italic*).* All of the logical style tags require both opening and closing tags. The logical style tags that you are most likely use are as follows:

- <EM>: Emphasize characters in some fashion
- <STRONG>: Strongly emphasize
- <CITE>: For a short quote

Some others that you might encounter are the following:

- <CODE>: Sample code
- <SAMP>: Sample text
- <KBD>: Text that you want users to type
- <VAR>: A variable
- <DFN>: A definition

The following code shows the use of these tags.

```
<html>
<head><title>It's Very Logical, Captain</title></head>
<body>
<p>The Miracle Toy Company makes the <em>best</em> toys in the whole wide world!</p>
<p>We will <strong>CRUSH</strong> the competition!</p>
<p><code>#4 is "toys.tcl"</code></p>
<p>Check out the Miracle Toys web site at <samp>http://www.toys.com</samp></p>
<p>When you find our site type: <kbd>I want toys!</kbd></p>
<p><code>guest</code> <var>anonymous</var></p>
<p>A high quality low cost toy? <dfn>Miracle Toys! </dfn></p>
<p>There is NO toy like a Miracle Toy <cite>(Martin Miracle, 1996) </cite></p>
</body>
</html>
```

Figure A-13 shows the result of the preceding code.

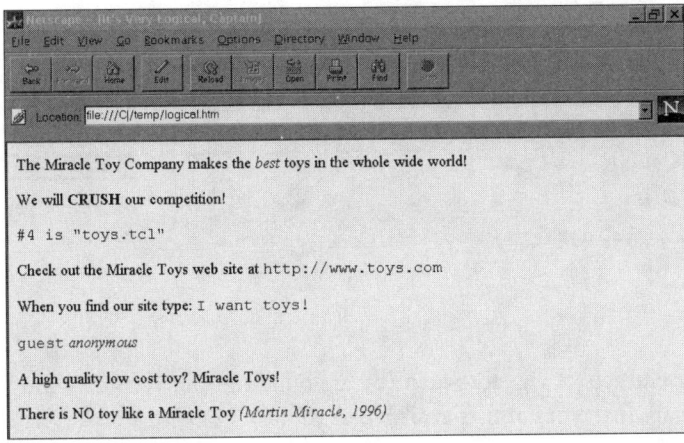

FIGURE A-13

Examples of logical styles.

Physical Styles

Physical style tags actually send information that changes the look of the text, instead of relying on the browser to add its own interpretation. The browser, however, may still choose to substitute a physical style that it considers to be close to what you asked for if it cannot meet your exact requirements. The physical style tags are the following:

- ◆ <B>: The boldface tag
- ◆ <I>: The italic tag
- ◆ <TT>: For a typewriter font

These tags are shown in the code that follows.

```html
<html>
<head><title>Let's Get Physical</title></head> <body>
<p>The title, <I>Our Lady of Television</I>, was originated in 1954 by Bishop Fulton J.
➥Sheen.</p>
<p>The Miracle Toy Company was founded on <b>April 6, 1958</b></p>
<p>For an old-time look for your documents <tt>try the typewriter tag--you'll love
➥it!</tt></p>
</body>
</html>
```

Figure A-14 shows the result of the preceding code.

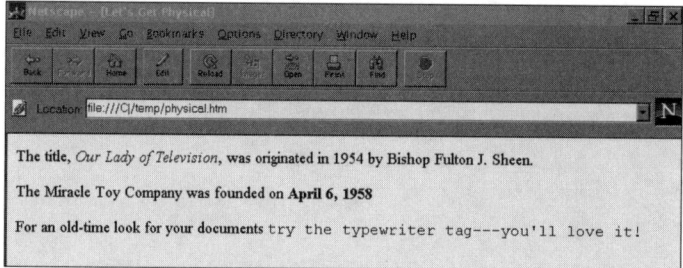

FIGURE A-14

Examples of physical styles.

Lists

One of the more useful sets of tags for when you are building your corporate intranet are the list tags. There are five types of lists available to you:

- ◆ Ordered lists (also called numbered)
- ◆ Unordered lists (also called bulleted)
- ◆ Glossary list
- ◆ Menu list
- ◆ Directory list

Here's a look at the ones that you will use most often, the ordered and unordered list, as well as examples of each.

<OL> (The Ordered List Tag)

Ordered lists are simply lists with numbers. Each list is surrounded by the <OL> opening and </OL> closing tags. Items within the list are designated by the <LI>, or list item, tag (an opening tag); there is no closing tag for the <LI> tag. When you create an ordered or numbered list, you do not need to put numbers in—the browser will do that for you. Lists are great for telling people how to complete some task that requires a series of steps. The following code shows the use of these tags.

```
<html>
<head><title>Miracle Toys--How Do They Do It?</title></head>
<body>
<h2>Making The Best Toys Possible</h2>
<p>How We Do It</p>
<ol>
<li>Extensive market research
<li>Finding the right materials at the right price
<li>A properly organized manufacturing facility
<li>Highly trained workforce
<li>Set-up strong distribution channels
<li>Advertise, advertise, advertise, and then advertise again
<li>Count money
</ol>
</body>
</html>
```

Figure A-15 shows the result of the preceding code.

<UL> (The Unordered List)

The unordered list is also called the bulleted list because it uses bullets rather than numbers to put items in some sort of order. When you create an unordered or bulleted list, the bullet that you typically get will be a black dot, but you can also select a couple of other types of bullets that are a part of the Netscape and the new HTML 3.2 standards (more on these in Appendix B). Just as with ordered lists, the unordered list tags have both opening and

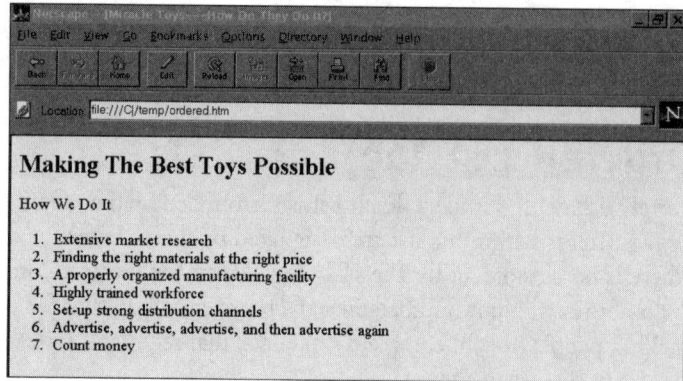

FIGURE A-15

For displaying items in a sequence, an ordered list fits perfectly.

closing attributes. Also like the ordered list, you still use the <LI> tag, which does not require a closing tag. The following code shows the use of an unordered list tag.

```
<html>
<head><title>Favorite Books? Please Spare Us</title></head>
<body>
<p>These aren't my favorite books—-but they could be:</p>
<ul>
<li>Catcher in the Rye by <I>J.D. Salinger</I>
<li>Scoop by <I>Evelyn Waugh</I>
<li>Computer Lib/Dream Machines by <I>Ted Nelson</I>
<li>Resurrection by <I>Leo Tolstoy</I>
</ul>
</body>
</html>
```

Figure A-16 shows the result of the preceding code.

<TABLE> (The Table Tag)

Probably the tag that deserves the most respect is the <TABLE> tag, and it is a very useful one indeed. Through the use of tables, you can gain much more control over the design and layout of your pages. Tables are a bit tricky, and certainly cumbersome to create, but again, I must give credit to the current crop of editors, almost all of which have table-creation capabilities built-in. If you can make a table in Word or Excel, you can surely make one using Netscape Gold or Microsoft FrontPage.

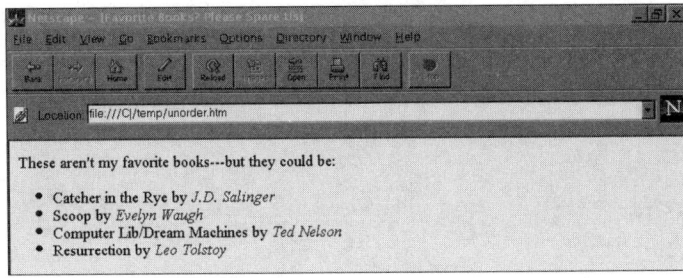

FIGURE A-16

To display items with bullets, use the unordered list.

I recommend using an editor to make your tables. My purpose in this short HTML treatise, though, is to give you some understanding of what one of those editors might be doing as you click on Create Table.

Tables consist of these basic and necessary tags:

♦ <TABLE>: Opens the table element (required)

♦ </TABLE>: Closes the table element (required)

♦ <TR>: Defines a table row

♦ <TD>: The table data, which resides in cells within the rows

♦ <TH>: The table heading, usually in a bolder font (requires a </TH> closing tag)

♦ <CAPTION>: An optional tag that can go at the top or the bottom of the table

If you know and understand these simple tags, you are already part of the way there to understanding HTML. The problem with tables is that they take a lot of typing to create—thus the beauty of a table generator within an editor.

I want to show you how to make a very simple table to get you going. Keep in mind that when you generate tables by hand, you have to have at least one positive personality trait: patience. Be prepared to spend a good amount of time flipping back and forth between your text editor and your browser, anxiously waiting for your page to load so that you can see how your table needs to be tweaked. I think it's kind of fun, though some would consider it a waste of valuable time. You decide.

```
<html>
<head><title>My Very Own Table</title></head>
<body>
<table>
<caption>This Is My Very First Table</caption>
<tr>
```

```
<th>1994</th>
<th>1995</th>
<th>1996</th>
</tr>
<tr>
<td>Sales were flat</td>
<td>Sales were up</td>
<td>Sales were down</td>
</tr>
</table>
</body>
</html>
```

Figure A-17 shows the result of the preceding code.

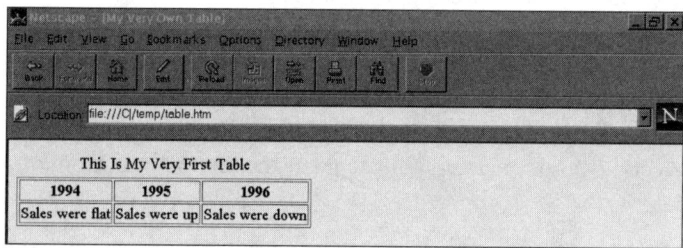

FIGURE A-17

Tables are great for data or to hold your content in place.

I told you it would be real simple, didn't I? You may have noticed that I inserted a border element in the <TABLE> tag. This gives the table a border or otherwise encloses the table data in a frame. If I had left the "border" element out of the <TABLE> tag, I would have had my data correctly set up, but it would have looked like it was hanging there with no support. The example I've shown you is of a very simple table (you could spend a month of Saturdays creating a complex and very beautiful table that might even show a way to balance our federal deficit). Tables allow you to put images where basic HTML just won't let you. There are even things called table workarounds and collapsing columns that give you almost total—or what they are calling pixel-level placement—of your text and images.

In my simple table example, I just had three headings and one word entries in each of my data cells. You have probably seen tables on Web pages that had a whole bunch of text in them (as well as images). What would happen if I wanted to put a longer text entry into my existing data cells? I'll do that with the same simple table that I started with.

```
<html>
<head><title>My Very Own Table</title></head>
<body>
<table border>
<caption>This Is My Very First Table</caption>
<tr>
<th>1994</th>
<th>1995</th>
<th>1996</th>
</tr>
<tr>
<td>Sales were flat due to storms in the Mid-West which delayed shipments of
➥materials.</td>
<td>Sales were up because we sold more, duh!</td>
<td>Sales were down</td>
</tr>
</table>
</body>
</html>
```

Figure A-18 shows the result of the preceding code.

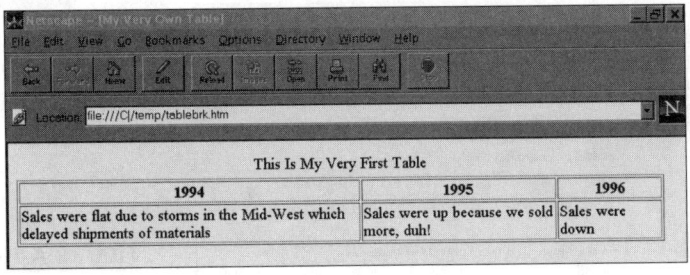

FIGURE A-18

A simple table in which the cell text "breaks."

Notice how the table's cells expanded to accommodate the longer text string. Also notice how the text "wrapped" or "broke" to the next line down (kind of like using a <BR> tag). Tables will default to this wrapped text state unless you tell them not to by inserting the nowrap attribute into the <TD> tag. The following code shows what doing that looks like:

```
<html>
<head><title>My Very Own Table</title></head>
<body>
<table border>
<caption>This Is My Very First Table</caption>
<tr>
<th>1994</th>
<th>1995</th>
<th>1996</th>
</tr>
<tr>
<td nowrap>Sales were flat due to storms in the Mid-West which delayed shipments of
➥materials.</td>
<td>Sales were up because we sold more, duh!</td>
<td>Sales were down</td>
</tr>
</table>
</body>
</html>
```

Figure A-19 shows the result of the preceding code.

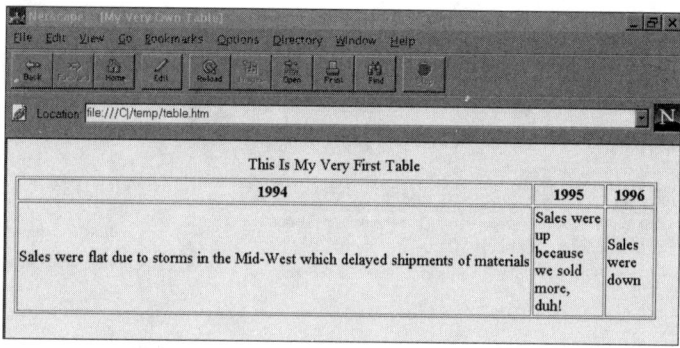

FIGURE A-19

The nowrap *attribute added to a simple table.*

You can also align data within each of your data cells, either horizontally or vertically. Horizontal alignment options for cell data are left, right, center (with the align attribute added). Vertical alignment options are top, bottom, middle (with the valign attribute added). The next simple table shows what this looks like.

```
<html>
<head><title>Alignment Options Uncovered</title></head>
<body>
<table border>
<caption>Horizontal and Vertical Alignment</caption>
<tr>
<th></th>
<th>left</th>
<th>centered</th>
<th>right</th>
</tr>
<tr>
<th>top</th>
<td align=left valign=top><img src="redball.gif"></td>
<td align=center valign=top><img src="redball.gif"></td>
<td align=right valign=top><img src="redball.gif"></td>
</tr>
<tr>
<th>centered</th>
<td  align=left valign=middle><img src="redball.gif"></td>
<td  align=center valign=middle><img src="redball.gif"></td>
<td  align=right valign=middle><img src="redball.gif"></td>
</tr>
<tr>
<th>bottom</th>
<td align=left valign=bottom><img src="redball.gif"></td>
<td align=center valign=bottom><img src="redball.gif"></td>
<td align=right valign=bottom><img src="redball.gif"></td>
</tr>
</table>
</body>
</html>
```

Figure A-20 shows the result of the preceding code.

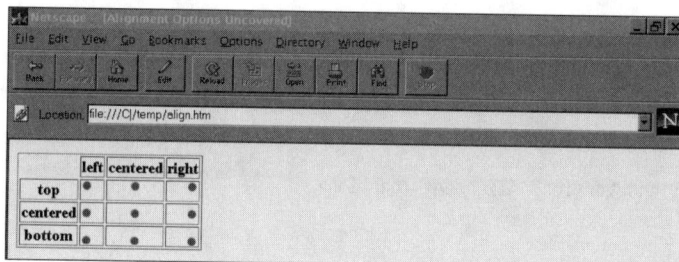

FIGURE A-20

Cell alignment options uncovered.

Well, what do you think? Are you ready to go out and start making your own tables? Truthfully, I've only just scratched the surface in regards to the types of things that you can do with tables in your HTML documents. I hope that this introduction to tables is enough to whet your appetite (or to drive you immediately to the nearest table generator in Netscape Gold or Microsoft FrontPage). When and if you get a chance, you might also want to check out some of the Netscape Extensions (which are included in the new HTML 3.2 standards proposal) to table creation. They are as follows:

♦ width: Can be used with the <TH> or <TD> (as a column width attribute) and to set the size of the table in the <TABLE> tag itself. The width attribute is usually expressed in pixels or as a percent of the entire table width.

♦ border: This attribute defaults at 1, and setting it to border=0 is the same as just using the <TABLE> tag by itself—in other words, there would be no border.

♦ cellspacing: This attribute goes inside the <TABLE> tag and allows you to adjust the amount of space between cells.

♦ cellpadding: This attribute goes inside the <TABLE> tag and allows you to adjust the amount of space between a cell's contents (or data) and the sides or edges of the cell.

In Appendix B, I move on to explore the remaining Netscape extensions, as well as any new features proposed in HTML 3.2. I'll also mention some of the cool tags that Microsoft has introduced in its Internet Explorer 3.0 browser. We live in exciting times, don't you think? This is our revolution, and instead of reading about it in a history book, we are actually helping to make it happen.

Appendix | B

I suppose that there's nothing quite like working backward or starting from the bottom and working your way up so, that's just what I'll do: work backward from Figure B-1, which is yet another interesting proof of the old adage, "a picture is worth a thousand words."

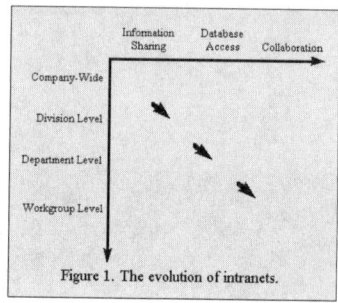

Figure 1. The evolution of intranets.

FIGURE B-1

The evolution of the intranet.

Look at the chart in Figure B-1 and ask yourself, "What is this chart trying to tell me?" Just keep staring at that chart until it becomes imprinted upon your very psyche. This is where *your* intranet is headed.

Netscape recently unveiled Netscape Communicator, which consists of Open E-Mail (Netscape Messenger), Groupware (Netscape Collabra), Netscape Composer (for creating richly-formatted Web pages), Netscape Conference (real-time voice and information collaboration), and the new 4.0 browser. The Communicator Professional Edition also includes Calendar (allows use of a shared calendar) and AutoAdmin (allows central management of Netscape Communicator).

Netscape views the future of the intranet and, actually, the Internet as well, as one in which e-mail will serve as the primary information creation and distribution engine from within your browser. Considering the number of unreadable e-mail messages that I have sent to friends just over the last couple of months, this seems strange to me. I started using Microsoft Exchange (and then stayed when they changed the name to Messaging) and have had a continual problem sending "clean" messages (either text or graphics) to my colleague, Charlie. He is always sending me messages that don't wrap, or that are completely unopenable by any mail client I might have on my PC. If he sends me messages through Netscape, then we never seem to have a problem. Go figure.

My point is that if Netscape wants to drive everything from within e-mail, fine—but I need proof that I can send a simple e-mail without having to call my intended recipients to read them the messages that they can't open. Perhaps I exaggerate. In any case, the October 1996 issue of *The Red Herring* magazine had a debate between browser-god Marc Andreesen, of Netscape Navigator fame, and John Ludwig, Microsoft's Vice

President of Internet Tools and Platforms. This article addressed the very same thing that I was just speaking about: Netscape really is trying to bring the browser and your e-mail window ever closer together so that you will barely see a working difference between the two. As any respectable gearhead knows, e-mail is the killer app that makes the Internet (and probably the intranet) as fun and exciting as it is today. E-mail is the hook that draws new users into the net, and the one they most often use and feel comfortable with (all of my trials and tribulations aside).

The article in *The Red Herring* (also available on the Web site: http://www.herring.com) was inspired by a research report by J. William Gurley. Mr. Gurley is a high-powered analyst (my perception of him) who works for Deutsche Morgan Grenfell Technology Group. Gurley's research report was based on the proposition that which browser "wins" is not important. What matters is which file format wins—HTML or Microsoft's DocObjects—and which would become the universal standard for rich text documents.

The real race is for Netscape Navigator to become a rich text editor before Microsoft Office can become a universal communications tool. The recent release of Netscape's Communicator suite of programs puts Netscape on the road to realizing its rich text dream.

How about Microsoft? In the Herring article, John Ludwig mentioned (and I roughly paraphrase) that Netscape is in favor of a "rip and replace" strategy, whereby Netscape is expecting the millions upon millions of Microsoft Office users to suddenly stop using their seamless suite of office production tools, and replace this proven package with Netscape's content development tools. This is something that Ludwig and Microsoft don't expect a significant number of users to do. Ludwig may be right, because human nature has a way of making people lazy when it comes to making any sort of major (or sometimes even minor) change in the way they accomplish their work. Time will tell.

Now I move on to a description and discussion of HTML 3.2 and the new Netscape and Microsoft tags.

HTML 3.2: An Overview

I would like you to read a recent statement that I found on the Microsoft site at www.microsoft.com that gives you an idea of the approach Microsoft is taking in regards to HTML and its evolution. Microsoft's statement is specifically directed at the introduction of what are called *proprietary tags*.

To date, W3C has been an effective standards body, making significant contributions to the industry and keeping up with the incredible pace of innovation on the Internet. Because of this effectiveness, Microsoft is committed to working with the W3C to further advance the HTML standard. Microsoft will agree to:

- Not ship extensions to HTML without first submitting them to W3C.
- Implement all W3C approved HTML standards.
- Clearly identify any not-yet-approved HTML tags we support as such.
- Publish a Document Type Definition (DTD) for its browser as mandated by SGML.
- Follow the architecture principles of HTML and its parent, SGML, when proposing new extensions.

What is your impression of the preceding statements of intention made by Microsoft? Sounds good, but it seems to me that there are a few loopholes that someone could drive a truckful of tags through. I am sure that both Microsoft and Netscape will continue to include new (and very cool) tags and extensions to HTML without waiting for them to be included in the new HTML standard proposals—but who cares? Not me, for one, as I see myself benefiting from all this one-upsmanship and innovation. Whatever! And finally, if you look at the current HTML 3.2 standards proposal on the W3C site, you'll see that almost every tag that used to be a part of the famed Netscape Extensions is now included on the site.

Netscape took the lead in introducing HTML tags (and attributes) that were supported (for the most part) in only its browser—thus the reason for all the "best viewed with Netscape v.X.X" icons that you saw on Web sites when you first started surfing the Web. It can be argued that Netscape's introduction of these proprietary tags was a shrewd move that played an important part in helping to secure its (at one time) 85-plus percent of browser share. After Microsoft woke up and discovered the Internet and the Web, it quickly incorporated the Netscape Extensions into its Internet Explorer browser. Then, in a tit-for-tat move, Microsoft even brought out a few proprietary tags of its own (such as <MARQUEE> and <BGSOUND>, to name a couple).

Here, then, is an overview of HTML 3.2 proposed standards and related tags. Almost all of the former Netscape Extensions have found their way into HTML 3.2, and since the release of the new standards, Netscape has continued to release new extensions (as has Microsoft). I will attempt to cover some of the more useful new tags from all three sources. You may wish to visit the W3C (World Wide Web Consortium) Web site for more detailed information about the proposed HTML 3.2 standards. (Check back often, because this document is living, breathing, and growing—and even shrinking—as time goes on). The address is as follows:

http://www.W3.org/pub/WWW/TR

Scroll down and look for the "HTML 3.2 Reference Specification" listing.

And now, on to those HTML 3.2 proposed standards and some more of the always popular Netscape Extensions.

<!DOCTYPE> (Declaration Tag)

First, this is not a new tag by any means; you should have been using this in your earlier HTML documents as a signal to the browser about what type of document it was about to try to load. Strangely enough, you can actually forget about having to put the following tags into your HTML pages: <HTML>, <HEAD>, <BODY>. Why? Because if your browser conforms to the new HTML 3.2 standards, then it will know or infer that these tags are indeed a part of the ensuing HTML document. The <!DOCTYPE> declaration tag is the signal to the browser that the document it is now loading *does* conform to the new HTML 3.2 standards, thus the importance of including the <!DOCTYPE> declaration tag in your newly created documents.

Take some time to go to some Web pages and look at the source code; you will most likely see this new tag at the top of the page. You could actually have omitted the <HTML>, <HEAD>, and <BODY> tags in HTML 2.0 as well. I will probably keep putting them in my documents because I am used to doing so, but maybe I will change as time goes on, or as I move toward using an "editor" to generate my pages.

The following listing demonstrates the use of the <!DOCTYPE> tag. The resultant Web page is shown in Figure B-2.

```
<!DOCTYPE HTML PUBLIC "-//W3C//DTD HTML 3.2//EN">
<HTML>
<HEAD>
<TITLE>Punctuation--Friend or Foe?</TITLE>
... other head elements
</HEAD>
<BODY>
... document body
</BODY>
</HTML>
```

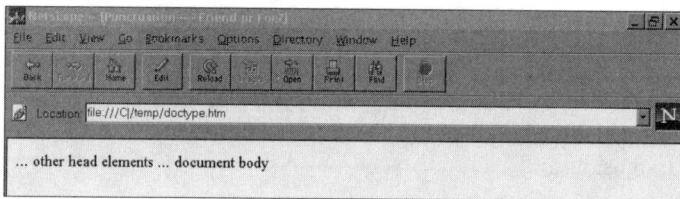

There isn't a whole lot to see here. The important thing was for you to see how the code looks. Notice in the browser view the <TITLE> of the document that appears at the top of the screen. Also notice the text that enclosed in the <HEAD> and <BODY> tags that appears in the browser window. The <!DOCTYPE> declaration tag tells the browser, "This is an HTML 3.2 document."

<APPLET> (Tag and Attributes)

Java! Welcome to the new frontier. Java has literally exploded onto the Web as a means of delivering rich, interactive content (in the forms of "applets") that are executed by an enabled browser on the user's machine (as opposed to having the applet processed by the server and then being sent to the requesting browser). This is an efficient way of delivering multimedia content quickly and without tying up the server more than necessary. Please do some reading about Java; you can hardly avoid seeing something about it in just about every computer magazine available today.

The <APPLET> tag allows you to insert Java applets into your Web pages. A short description of the <APPLET> tag and related attributes follows.

This element is supported by all Java-enabled browsers, which should be what you are, or will soon be, using in your corporate intranet. This tag has both opening and closing attributes. The <APPLET> tag uses the <PARAM> element to pass parameters to the applet. Following the <PARAM> element, text should be used to provide an alternative to the applet for browsers that don't support Java. If your browser is Java compatible, then it will ignore this extra HTML code. You can use it to show a snapshot of the applet running, with text explaining what the applet does. You could also have a link to a page that is more useful for the Java-ignorant browser, or even text that harasses the user for not having a Java-compatible browser. The following code shows what a typical Java <APPLET> tag looks like.

```
<applet code="Bubbles.class" width=500 height=500>
Java applet that draws animated bubbles.
</applet>
```

Here is another example of an applet, this one incorporating the <PARAM> element:

```
<applet code="AudioItem" width=15 height=15>
<param name=snd value="Hello.au¦Welcome.au">
Java applet that plays a welcoming sound.
</applet>
```

The attributes are described next.

codebase = codebaseURL

This attribute specifies where the applet is physically located, such as the directory or folder that contains the applet's code. If this attribute is not specified, then the document's URL is used. This attribute is optional.

code = appletFile

This required attribute gives the name of the file that contains the applet's compiled Applet subclass. This file is relative to the base URL of the applet. It cannot be absolute.

alt = alternateText

This optional attribute specifies any text that should be displayed if the browser understands the <APPLET> tag but can't run Java applets.

name = appletInstanceName

This optional attribute specifies a name for the applet instance, which makes it possible for applets on the same page to find (and communicate with) each other (kind of like an anchor tag).

width = pixels

height = pixels

These required attributes give the initial width and height (in pixels) of the applet display area, not counting any windows or dialogs that the applet brings up.

align = alignment

This required attribute specifies the alignment of the applet. The possible values of this attribute are the same (and have the same effects) as those for the <IMG> tag: left, right, top, texttop, middle, absmiddle, baseline, bottom, absbottom.

```
vspace = pixels

hspace = pixels
```

These optional attributes specify the number of pixels above and below the applet (vspace) and on each side of the applet (hspace). They're treated the same way as the <IMG> tag's vspace and hspace attributes.

There is an additional, though optional, element that you should know about called the <TEXTFLOW> element. This tag has both opening and closing attributes. Previously, I mentioned that you should include alternative text within your <APPLET> tag in order to accommodate those browsers that cannot execute a Java applet. You can use the <TEXTFLOW> element to do the same thing, but it is a bit more powerful because you can insert higher-level markup tags (<IMG>, for example) that would allow you to show users a representation of the Java applet that they cannot see (a still frame, for example). But, having said that, you can still (for the time being, at least) insert similar types of code within the <APPLET> tag and achieve the same effect.

Actually creating Java applets and putting them on your Web pages is a bit more complicated than my description may make it sound. Go to any bookstore and you will find a plethora of books on this worthwhile addition to the Web. (Beware of books that promise that you can learn Java in 14 days; it will take you *at least* 21). Besides, there are many, many sources for Java applets that have already been created and that you can drop into your own pages. Please be very careful, however, to make sure that you have permission to do so, especially in a corporate intranet setting.

Here is a very cool source (probably *the* source on the Web) for Java applets:

```
http://www.gamelan.com
```

If you can't find the applets and information on creating them on this site, then close this book and go over to your PC and turn it off. You should really consider dragging that old typewriter out of the attic and starting over from scratch. (I'm kidding.) Definitely spend some time on this site; the future of the Web may be found in these humble pages.

<SMALL> and <BIG> Tags for Smaller and Bigger Text

The <SMALL> and <BIG> tags tell the browser to draw or insert a smaller or larger font (if available) for that text enclosed by either of these tags. These tags work much like the <FONT> tag with the size attribute(s) added (either +1 (for bigger) or -1 (for smaller)). The following code provides an example. You can see what this looks like in your browser by looking at Figure B-3.

```
<!DOCTYPE HTML PUBLIC "-//W3C//DTD HTML 3.2//EN">
<html>
<head><title>small to BIG</title></head>
<body>
<p>Here are some examples of the possible uses for the "small" and "big" font tags in
➡comparison with the typically used "font" tag with "size" attributes:</p><br><br>
<small>(small tag) size=-1</small><br>
<font size=-1>(font tag) size=-1</font><br>
<small><small>(nested small tag)size=-2?</small><br><br>
<big>(big tag)size=+1</big><br>
<font size=+1>(font tag)size=+1</font><br>
<big><big>(nested big tag)size=+2?</big>
</body>
</html>
```

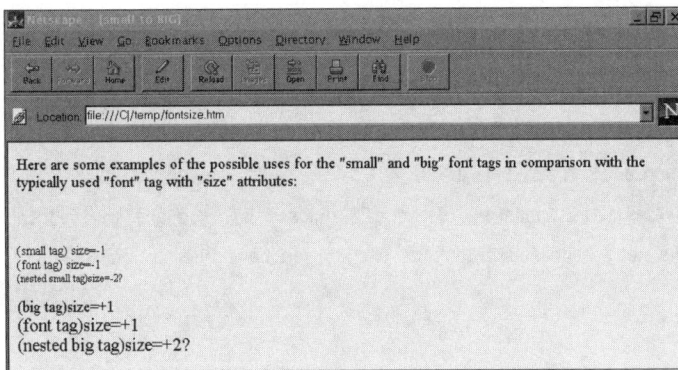

FIGURE B-3

Some neat tricks with the <SMALL> and <BIG> tags.

Take a close look at the code and the resultant Web page. It looks like the browser will typically render the text the same way whether you use the <SMALL> or <FONT SIZE=-1> tags or the <BIG> or <FONT SIZE=+1> tags. And, if you look closer, you can see where I nested or stacked the <SMALL> and <BIG> tags and was able to increase the resultant font size another notch in the bigger or smaller direction. This use of nesting will most likely work, but may be unpredictable, depending on browser.

< BODY >

HTML 3.2 has finally included the following attributes to the <BODY> tag, which were first introduced as Netscape Extensions. They are as follows:

◆ background: Specifies the URL (or location) for an image that is to be used as a tiled background

◆ bgcolor: Indicates the desired background color for the document

◆ text: Specifies the color of the text to be used in the document, especially when you have indicated a background color that may cause your viewer to not see your text (due to contrast problems)

◆ link: Indicates color to be used for text of unvisited links

◆ vlink: Indicates color to be used for text of visited links

◆ alink: Indicates color to be used to highlight link as the user clicks on it

The following code makes use of the background attribute to put some nice clouds on your Web page. You can see what this looks like in Figure B-4.

```
<!DOCTYPE HTML PUBLIC "-//W3C//DTD HTML 3.2//EN">

<html>

<head><title>A Tiled Background, Man!</title></head>

<body background="clouds.jpg">

<h2>The Wonderful World of CLOUDS!!!</h2>

<p>Yes, it's true—-it's the Wonderful World of Clouds! And, you are invited in to
➥sample some of the best representations of clouds you have ever seen. Send in the
➥clouds!</p>

</body>

</html>
```

That is actually not a bad tiled background pattern. Experiment with some yourself and see what you come up with. Beware, however, of the dreaded background that actually looks tiled (although this is an effect that you might sometimes want). Keep in mind that you will want your background patterns to appear seamless. There are many sites on the Web from which you can get cool backgrounds that people will gladly let you use on your very own Web pages. They are very easy to make in programs such as Photoshop or PaintShop Pro.

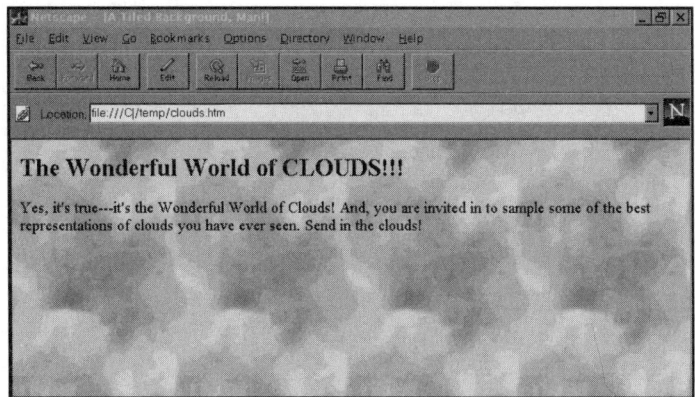

FIGURE B-4

Send in the clouds. With the addition of backgrounds, designers can now add more feeling and a sense of place to different areas on an intranet.

Here is an example of how you might use the bgcolor attribute of the <BODY> tag:

```
<!DOCTYPE HTML PUBLIC "-//W3C//DTD HTML 3.2//EN">

<html>

<head><title>A Colored Background</title></head>

<body bgcolor="#00FFFF">

<h1>Aqua...man!</h1>

<p>Colors are given in RGB (red, green, blue) as hexadecimal numbers (for example
➥bgcolor="#00FFFF") or you can now use one of 16 colors (i.e. just type in the name of
➥the color) from the Windows VGA palette. What are the 16 colors you ask: Black
➥(#000000), Silver (#C0C0C0), Gray (#808080), White (#FFFFFF), Maroon (#800000), Red
➥(#FF0000), Purple (#800080), Fuchsia (#FF00FF), Green (#008000), Lime (#00FF00), Olive
➥(#808000), Yellow (#FFFF00), Navy (#000080), Blue (#0000FF), Teal (#008080), Aqua
➥(#00FFFF).<br><br>

P.S. Don't forget to put the " " or you won't see your colored background!</p>

</body>

</html>
```

The Web also has many places on the Web where you can get RGB-to-hex information and examples. There are sites where you can put in the RGB numbers (which you have pulled from your image program—Photoshop or PaintShop Pro, for example) and then submit them, and the appropriate hex numbers come back at you for easy insertion into your waiting Web page, as shown in the preceding code example. Take a look at Figure B-5 to see the effects of inserting hexadecimal values into your HTML code. Check the following site for a typical RGB-to-hex converter:

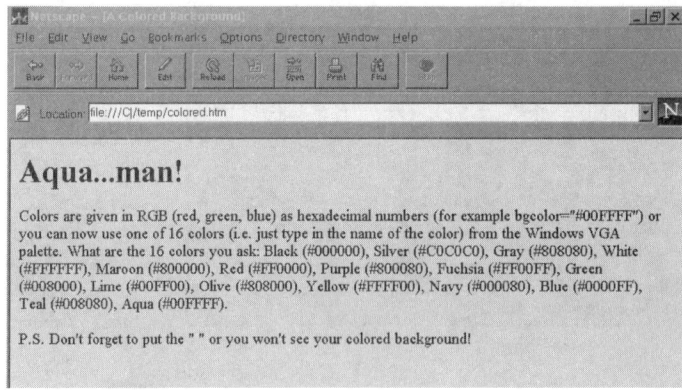

You can change the background color as well as link and text colors by using these hex values in your code.

http://www.univox.com/rgb2hex.html

Here is an address where you can see a chart that a guy named Doug spent a lot of time putting together:

http://www.phoenix.net/~jacobson/rgb.html

This table can be used to help find the correct colors for bgcolor, text, link, vlink, alink, and font html, as described for use with the Netscape (and other) browsers. Very helpful, yes? Yes.

 with Clear Attributes

As you know by now, the <BR>, or break tag, is used to force a line break. The clear attributes are used to move the line break down past floating images on either side of the Web page. The possible attributes are as follows:

- ◆ clear=left: Moves down past floating images on the left margin
- ◆ clear=right: Moves down past floating images on the right margin
- ◆ clear=all: Clears both sides of the Web page

In other words, if that image uses align=left or align=right, the text will flow around it. If you have text that you want below the image, you can do this with <BR clear=left> or clear=right to force scrolling down to a clear left or right margin, respectively.

<TABLE>

I covered tables fairly well in Appendix A, so please refer to that section for a review. Here, I point out a few additions to HTML 3.2 that I did not cover in Appendix A. For the most part, the tags and attributes that have now been included in the HTML 3.2 standards proposal were already implemented by the Netscape Extension to tables.

◆ <CAPTION>: With the `align` attribute, you can put your table caption at the top or bottom of your newly created table. This tag has opening and closing attributes. Your browser will most likely place your caption at the top of your table if you don't tell it where you want it.

◆ <TH> and <TD>: The <TH> (table heading) and the <TD> (table data) tags have opening attributes only. These tags also have the following attributes:

`nowrap`: Disables automatic word wrap within contents of a cell

`rowspan`: Specifies number of rows that a cell will span

`colspan`: Specifies number of columns that a cell will span

`align`: Specifies horizontal alignment of data in a cell

`valign`: Specifies vertical alignment of data in a cell

`width`: Specifies width of a cell in pixels (excluding cell padding)

`height`: Specifies height for a cell in pixels (excluding cell padding)

> **NOTE:** Be careful when specifying width and height of cells. If there is a conflict between height or width of cells (for example, different sizes within a row), then your attribute will be ignored.

◆ <TR>: The <TR>, or table row tag, requires only an opening tag (but I always put a closing tag in order to neaten things up a bit). The <TR> tag has the following attributes:

`align`: Specifies the horizontal alignment of a data in a cell. You can use `left`, `center`, or `right` (case insensitive) to align data elements within a cell.

`valign`: Specifies the vertical alignment of data in a cell. You can use `top`, `middle`, or `bottom` to position data elements within a cell.

At the end of Appendix A, I mentioned the Netscape Extensions to tables, all of which have been adopted by HTML 3.2. Now I show you what some of these extensions look like, and I do that by taking some of my earlier examples and tweaking them a bit.

The Table width Attribute

The width attribute is expressed in either pixels or a percentage of the current screen width. I recommend using the percent because it will size or resize to fit the screen, as opposed to forcing the screen to strictly follow pixel values (which could cause your tables to look very strange). Here is a table that is using the width attribute set at a value of 100 percent. I have also included the original table so that you can see the difference.

Figure B-6 shows the original table that I used to show alignment options in the HTML appendix.

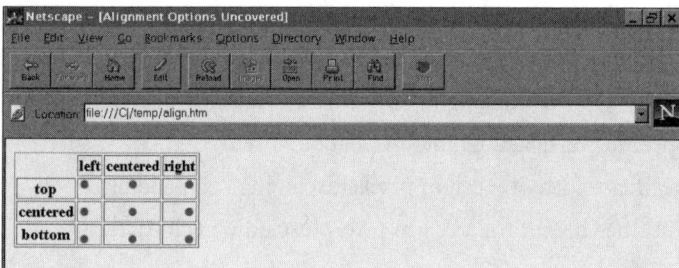

FIGURE B-6

No table width *attribute set.*

Now I use the same table, but I set a width attribute of 100 percent. Figure B-7 shows the result of the following code:

```
<table border width=100%>
```

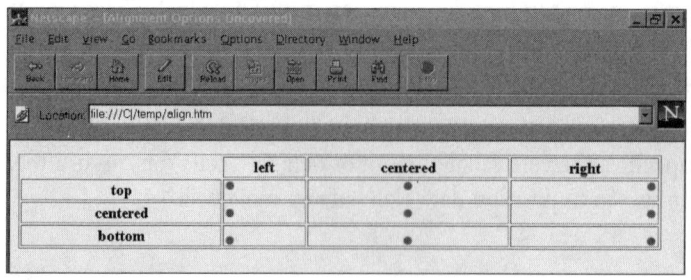

FIGURE B-7

Same table with 100 percent width *attribute.*

The Column width Attribute

You can also use the width attribute on <TD> or <TH>. This is done to indicate the desired width of your columns.

Here is the alignment options table with the column width attribute set:

```
Some of the code——<th width=10%></th>
<th width=30%>left</th>
<th width=30%>centered</th>
<th width=30%>right</th>
```

(I also set the overall table width at 50 percent.) Figure B-8 shows the result.

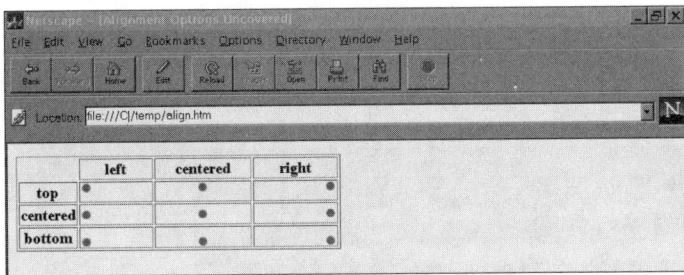

FIGURE B-8

Use of the column width *attribute.*

Table Border Widths

You have probably noticed in the code given for some of my examples that there is usually a border attribute listed inside the <TABLE> tag. If you insert the following code , <TABLE BORDER>, then you will typically get a border width of 1 pixel drawn around your table. What if you use a higher value? (Using nothing, or using border=0, will completely delete any border.) Again, I use the alignment options table to show this. In Figure B-9, shown below, you will see a table with a border width of 15 pixels.

```
<table border=15 width=50%>
```

NOTE: I will go ahead and continue using the 50 percent table width attribute throughout.

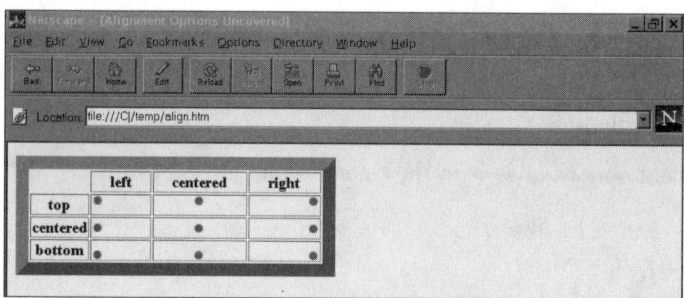

FIGURE B-9

A table border width of 15 pixels.

The `cellspacing` Attribute

This attribute determines the amount of space between cells in a table. Here is an example:

```
<table border=5 cellspacing=10 width=50%>
```

Figure B-10 shows the result.

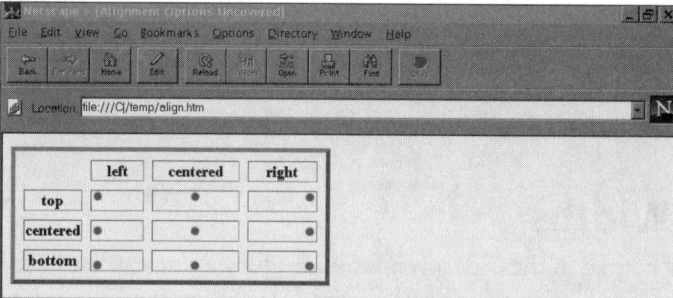

FIGURE B-10

Cellspacing of 10 pixels.

The `cellpadding` Attribute

This is similar to the `cellspacing` attribute, but different in the sense that the `cell-padding` attribute sets the amount of space between the edges of the cells and its data.

Typing the code that follows will result in a table with a cellpadding of 10 pixels, as shown in Figure B-11.

```
<table border=5 cellpadding=10 width=50%>
```

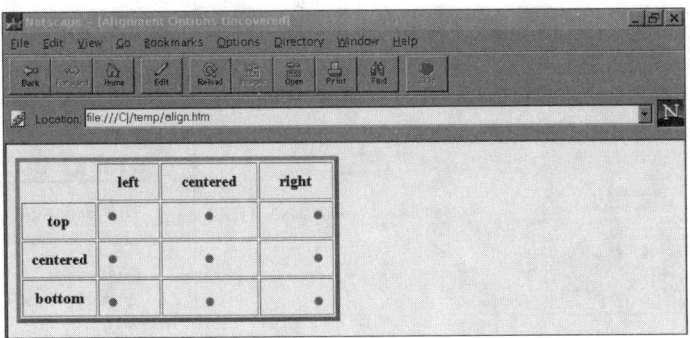

FIGURE B-11

Cellpadding of 10 pixels.

<DIV> (The Division Tag)

The <DIV> tag is included in HTML 3.2 and is designed to allow you to set options for blocks or divisions of a document. In other words, you could insert the <DIV ALIGN=CENTER> tag at the beginning of several blocks of text, and those text blocks would automatically be centered. You might be saying, "But this works just like the <CENTER> tag." If so, you are correct. An interesting thing about the <DIV> tag is that even if you have set it for a block of text, you can still use the alignment attribute somewhere inside your <DIV> block and it will override or ignore the set <DIV> attributes. This is good if you wish to set something off even further than you intended with your original <DIV> tag.

There will probably be much more that you can do with the <DIV> tag in the near future. If the <DIV> tag really bugs you, then just continue using the other alignment attributes. But don't be surprised if your editor puts them in. Now you will at least know what they mean and why they are there.

The <TR> Tag with the bgcolor Attribute

Have you ever awakened in the middle of the night with that urge to put color into your table cells? Well, your sleepless nights are over—just insert the bgcolor attribute (as you would in a <BODY> tag) and away you go:

```
<tr bgcolor="#00FFFF">
<tr bgcolor="#FFFF00">
<tr bgcolor="#000080">
<tr bgcolor="#800080">
```

Figure B-12 shows the result.

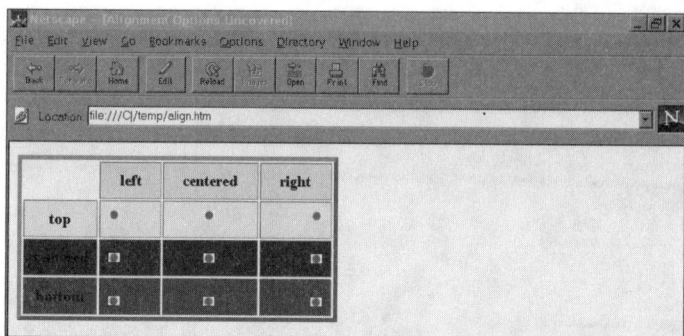

FIGURE B-12

Color my world (and my cells). You can change each table cell background with a solid color or an image file.

<HR> (The Horizontal Rule Tag Attributes)

I discussed the <HR> tag in the HTML appendix. The following former Netscape Extensions have made it into HTML 3.2. I show you some of those here, using a previous <HR> example. Figure B-13 shows what the example originally looked like.

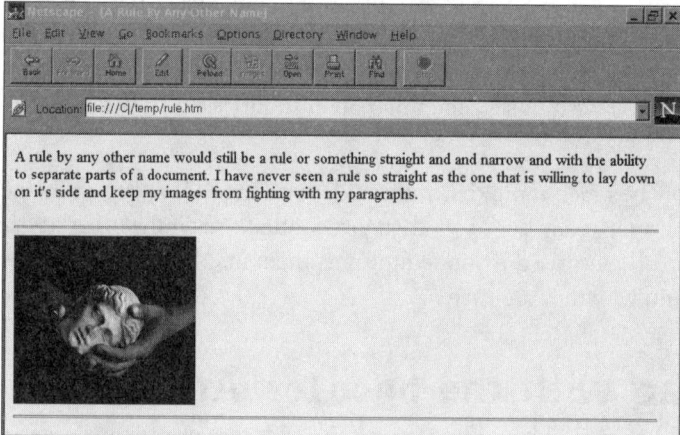

FIGURE B-13

My original <HR> example.

Now I play with some of the attributes of the <HR> tag.

The size Attribute

Take a look at the horizontal rule in the above example. It looks fairly normal, eh? You can vary the thickness of this rule by using the size attribute along with the <HR> tag. Here's what it looks like:

```
<hr size=10>
```

Figure B-14 shows the result of this code.

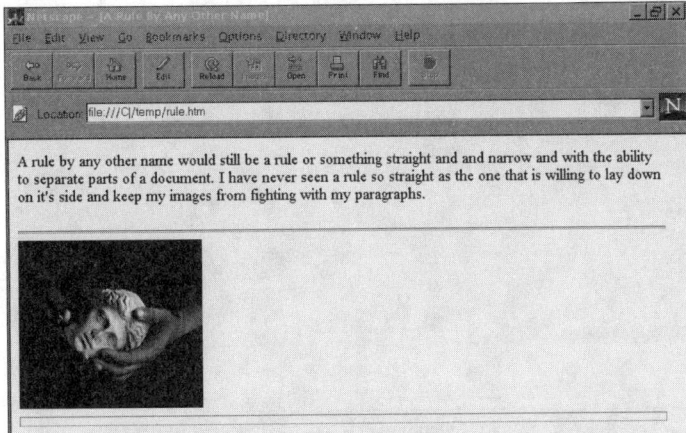

FIGURE B-14

A `size` *attribute of 10 pixels.*

Notice that I only changed the rule at the bottom of the page so that you can see the difference between the two.

The `width` Attribute

The width attribute can be expressed in terms of either pixels or percent of screen size (go with percent to avoid problems).

```
<hr size=10 width=50%>
```

Figure B-15 shows the result of this code.

The `align` Attribute

Here's a neat trick: Using the `align=center` attribute in your <HR> tag and the following code example, you can put various sizes of rules in a stacked fashion, as shown in Figure B-16.

```
<hr size=10 width=20% align=center>
<hr size=7 width=40% align=center>
<hr size=3 width=70% align=center>
```

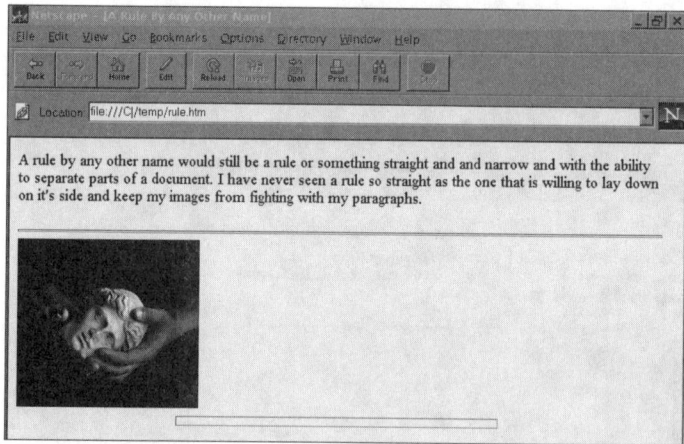

FIGURE B-15

A width *attribute of 50 percent.*

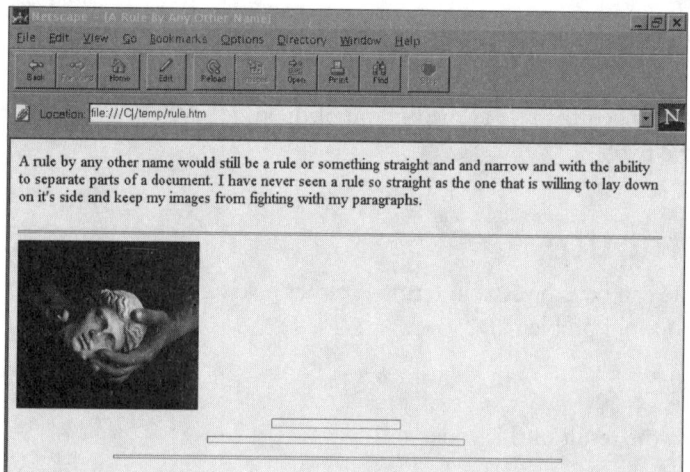

FIGURE B-16

You can stack your <HR> or horizontal rules one on top of each other. You can also use the align=center *attribute to center text and image files.*

You can also align your rules (assuming that you have indicated a width shorter than 100 percent) to either a left, right, or center alignment. Take a look at these rules and their alignments:

```
<hr size=10 width=20% align=right>
<hr size=7 width=40% align=left>
<hr size=3 width=70% align=center>
```

Figure B-17 shows the result of this code.

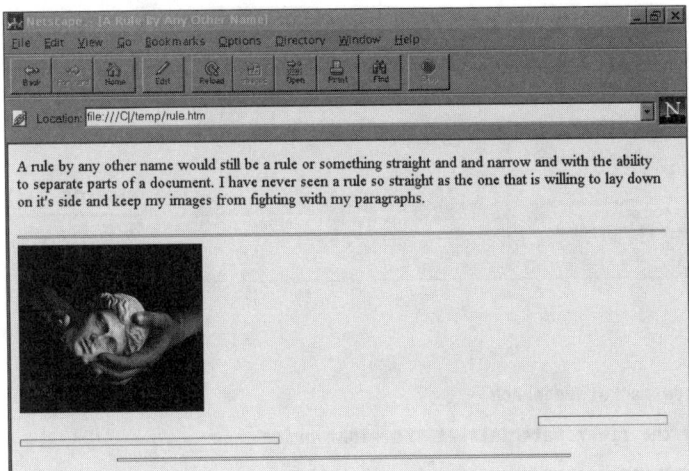

FIGURE B-17

To the right, to the left, in the center: the align *attribute.*

<LI> (The List Item Tag and Its Attributes)

When working with the <UL> unordered list tag and the <OL> ordered list tag, you have the option of choosing what types of bullets that you want to appear in your document. You set these attributes in the <LI>, or list item tag, using the type attribute. Following are some examples.

Unordered List

This is an example from the appendix on HTML.

```
<ul>
<li type=square>Catcher in the Rye by <I>J.D. Salinger
<li type=disc>Scoop by <I>Evelyn Waugh<li type=circle>Computer Lib/Dream Machines by
<I>Ted Nelson
<li type=circle>Resurrection by <I>Leo Tolstoy
</ul>
```

The result is shown in Figure B-18.

Ordered List

There are also bullet options for ordered lists, as shown in the following code and its result, shown in Figure B-19.

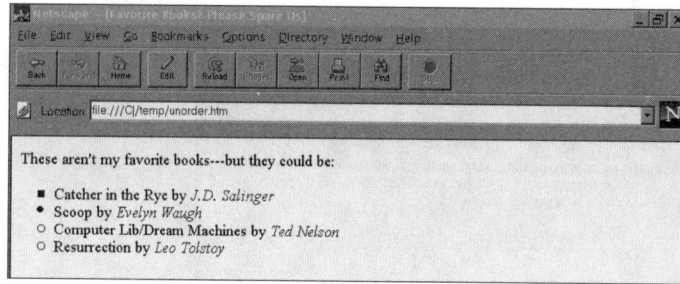

FIGURE B-18

Bullet options for <UL> (unordered lists).

```
<ol>

<li type=1>Extensive market research

<li type=a>Finding the right materials at the right price

<li type=A>A properly organized manufacturing facility

<li type=i>Highly trained workforce

<li type=I>Set-up strong distribution channels

<li>Advertise, advertise, advertise, and then advertise again

<li>Count money

</ol>
```

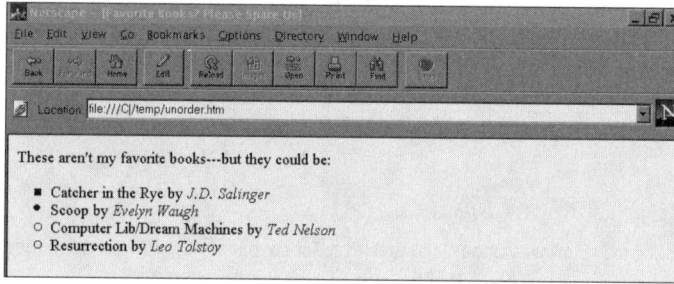

FIGURE B-19

Bullet options for <OL> (ordered lists).

NOTE: Notice how the last two <LI> list items take on the formatting of the one directly above it, thus you need to set the type attribute only at the first <LI> tag.

<STRIKE> (The Strike-Through Text Tag)

Obviously, this affects any text within the confines of the <STRIKE>, or strikethrough, tag. This is useful for indicating that a document has been edited.

<SUB> (The Subscript Tag)

Used mainly for mathematical formulas, any text within the <SUB> or subscript tag is positioned slightly lower than the surrounding text.

<SUP> (The Superscript Tag)

Also useful for mathematical formulas. Any text within the <SUP> tag will be positioned slightly higher than the surrounding text.

<SCRIPT> (The Inline Script Tag)

The <SCRIPT>, or inline script tag, is considered a placeholder for the impending (actually now here) arrival or introduction of client-side scripts and style sheets. The <SCRIPT> tag is already in use through JavaScript on Netscape Navigator and JScript (Microsoft's open implementation of Netscape's JavaScript) through Microsoft Internet Explorer 3.0. Here is an example of a very simple script. If you look closely at the HTML code below, you will see text within the <BODY> tag that will appear in the browser window after this file is loaded. What is new to you at this point is what appears within the <SCRIPT> tags—in this case, the text, "Miracle Toys." This is the JavaScript. After this document is loaded into your JavaScript-enabled browser, you will see the result shown in Figure B-20. The <SCRIPT> tag tells the browser to insert the text, "Miracle Toys."

```
<HTML>
<HEAD>
<SCRIPT LANGUAGE="JavaScript">
document.write("Miracle Toys.")
</SCRIPT>
</HEAD>
<BODY>
The best...and you darn well know it!</BODY>
</HTML>
```

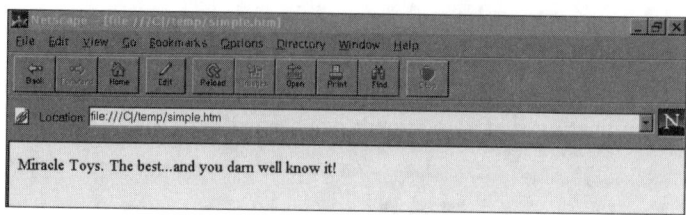

FIGURE B-20

Your very first JavaScript!

You might be thinking that this sure looks a lot like HTML. You're right! It is very much like an advanced form of HTML, which is why it is in some ways a very accessible (and fairly easy to learn) programming language. Start checking the source code on sites such as Netscape's and you will see that most of the coding is now done using JavaScript. Take a look at a JavaScript that is a bit more complicated, but also quite useful as a calculator. The code for this follows, along with its result, shown in Figure B-21.

```
<HEAD>
<SCRIPT LANGUAGE="JavaScript">
function compute(form) {
if (confirm("Are you sure?"))
form.result.value = eval(form.expr.value)
else
alert("Please come back again.")
}
</SCRIPT>
</HEAD>
<BODY>
<FORM>
Enter an expression:
<INPUT TYPE="text" NAME="expr" SIZE=15 >
<INPUT TYPE="button" VALUE="Calculate" ONCLICK="compute(this.form)">
<BR>
Result:
<INPUT TYPE="text" NAME="result" SIZE=15 >
<BR></FORM></BODY>
```

This is just the tip of the iceberg when it comes to what JavaScript can accomplish. If you would like to learn more about how JavaScript can make your Web pages more interactive, please go to the following address:

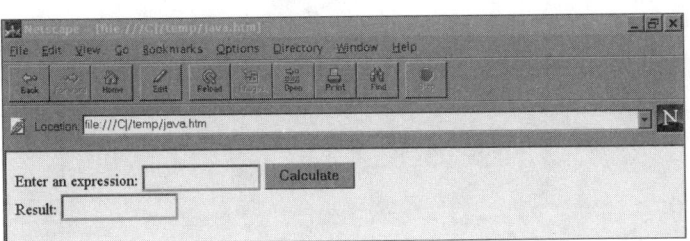

FIGURE B-21

*A neat little
JavaScript calculator.*

```
http://home.netscape.com/comprod/products/navigator/version_3.0/building_blocks/
➡examples/js_example/index.html
```

You will find many, many examples of scripts, applets, and even easy-to-understand tutorials that will get you up and running in no time at all.

<STYLE> (The Style Markup Tag)

The <STYLE> tag encloses information detailing one of the most eagerly awaited new features to hit the Web: style sheets! Microsoft has already included support for Cascading Style Sheets in its Microsoft Internet Explorer 3.0; Netscape had initially indicated that it would not support Cascading Style Sheets, but it recently announced that it will in fact support "some form of style sheets" in its upcoming Netscape Navigator 4.0 (Netscape Communicator) release.

Style sheets are a positive step for Web developers, because style sheets represent a step closer to having nearly total control over page layout and the appearance of HTML documents. A style sheet gives you the ability to attach styles to HTML pages. You can control the margins, line spacing, placement of page elements, colors, font faces, and even font sizes. Style sheets make it easy to index a page or even make global changes because you need make the necessary changes only to the relevant style sheet, and changes will take across the whole document referenced by that particular style sheet.

At this time, style sheets are supported only by Microsoft Internet Explorer 3.0, so take a look at an example of what types of things you might implement through the <STYLE> tag . You can see the result of this code in Figure B-22.

```
<html>
<style>
body {background: aqua; color: black}
h3 {font: 14pt Arial bold}
p {font: 10pt Arial; text-indent: 0.5in}
```

```
a {text-decoration: none; color: blue}
</style>
<body>
<h3>The Miracle Toy Company! In 14-point Arial bold!</h3>
</body>
</html>
```

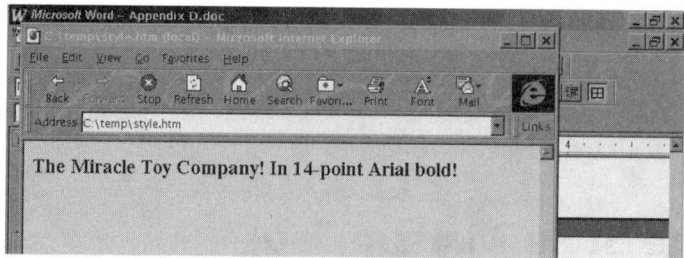

FIGURE B-22

A style sheet in Microsoft Internet Explorer.

Hey, it actually worked! Don't fret, Netscape will soon have this same capability built into its browser. Remember: in the browser wars, we are the real winners. Now I move on to the <IMG>, or image tag.

<IMG> (The Image Tag and Attributes)

Although I did place a couple of images as I wended my way through the HTML labyrinth, I did not go too deeply (if at all) into exactly how you use the <IMG> tag and its related attributes. Without images, we might still have had the explosion that we have witnessed in the growth of the Web—but then again, maybe we wouldn't have had the Web at all. The ability to view graphics and images in Web pages was the hook that encouraged people to start surfing like mad.

Currently, two main image extensions are supported by the two major Web browsers: .GIF and .JPEG. There are others that are floating around from something called PNG (Portable Network Graphic) to something as seemingly esoteric as a fractal image compression method (FIF), but the main problem with any new image compression method or extension is its acceptance by or inclusion in the two major browsers from Netscape and Microsoft. I recently read an article that described each of the new image compression methods (*Boardwatch Magazine*, August 1996). Although the compression methods described were all highly rated, there was one big hitch with using any of them: all required the use of a plug-in to make them viewable on your Web pages. This is obviously a major drawback, because viewability depends on all of your viewees having the right viewer. Time will take care of this problem.

I want to take another of my previous HTML examples and do some experimenting with the <IMG> tag and its attributes. Here are the attributes for the <IMG> tag, as listed in the HTML 3.2 standards (keep in mind that Netscape has its own extensions that are widely supported):

- `align=top`: Aligns the image with the top part of the line
- `align=middle`: Aligns the image with the middle of the line
- `align=bottom`: Aligns the image with the bottom of the line

The following code demonstrates the use of the `align=middle` attribute. The result is shown in Figure B-23.

```
<html>
<head><title>A Rule By Any Other Name</title></head>
<body>
<p>A rule by any other name would still be a rule or something straight and and narrow
➥and with the ability to separate parts of a document. I have never seen a rule so
➥straight as the one that is willing to lay down on it's side and keep my images from
➥fighting with my paragraphs.</p>
With Head In Hands<img src="hands.jpg" width=216 height=191 align=middle>
<p>But where are the fighting paragraphs that you speak of? Well, they are right here my
➥good friend— -and ready to do battle at the drop of a verb or prepositional phrases.
➥Don't let your particple dangle loosely in the winds of time for they are blowing
➥quickly towards an untimely demise. I must remove the horizontal rule in order that
➥the paragraphs can finally know one another and realize that they have much more in
➥common than they ever could have imagined, period.</p>
</body>
</html>
```

Take a good look at where the text is sitting in relation to the image; notice how it hangs at the mid point of the image. Keep in mind, though, that it is the image that is moving, not the text. Also notice the code and see where I typed the text, "With Head In Hands." I typed it in front of the image so that it fell on the left side; I could have typed it on the right side of my <IMG> tag and it would have ended up on the right and in the middle of the image. Play with the other attributes if you get the chance. Now I'll show you something else that you might find interesting.

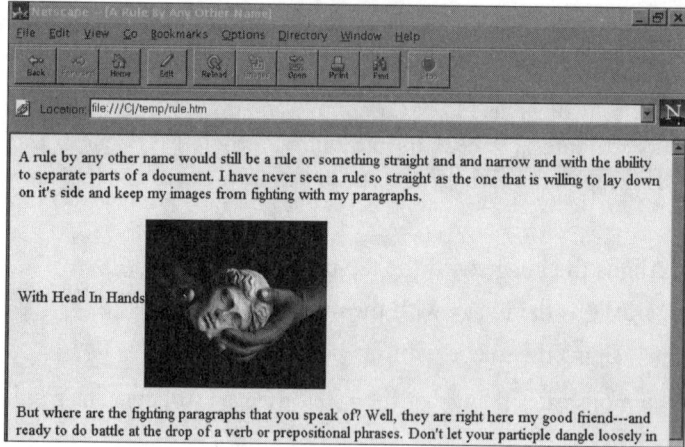

FIGURE B-23

The <IMG> tag with the align=middle *attribute.*

I use the same example, but watch where I place the <IMG> tag this time. Figure B-24 shows a good example of a text-wrapping problem.

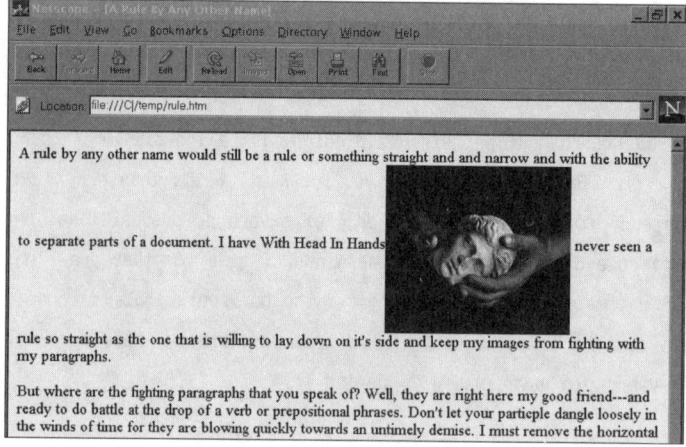

FIGURE B-24

This is in need of some serious wrapping of text.

Oops! This clearly demonstrates one of the problems with placing images and text together in the early days of HTML): you simply could not put more than one line of text next to an image (the remaining lines would not end up where you wanted them on your page). How was this annoying problem solved? By using one of the following tags (which started out as Netscape Extensions that you can find in the HTML 3.2 standards:

- `align=bottom`: The default; aligns the bottom of the image with the baseline.
- `align=left`: Floats the image to the current left margin, temporarily changing this margin so that subsequent text is flowed along the image's right side. The rendering depends on whether there is any left aligned text or images that appear earlier than the current image in the markup. Such text (but not images) generally forces left aligned images to wrap to a new line, with the subsequent text continuing on the former line.
- `align=right`: Floats the image to the current right margin, temporarily changing this margin, so that subsequent text is flowed along the image's left side. The rendering depends on whether there is any right aligned text or images that appear earlier than the current image in the markup. Such text (but not images) generally forces right aligned images to wrap to a new line, with the subsequent text continuing on the former line.

Now I take the preceding example and use the `align=right` attribute to see whether I can make things look a bit better. You can see the result in Figure B-25.

```
<img src="hands.jpg" width=216 height=191 align=right>
```

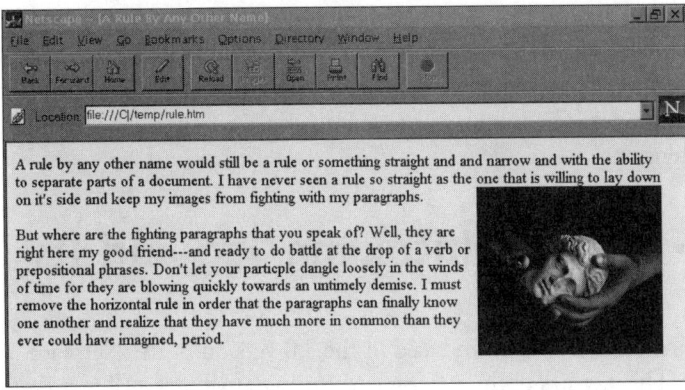

FIGURE B-25

The right *(align, that is) way to do it.*

That looks a bit cleaner. I inserted the `align=right` attribute inside the <IMG> tag, which forced the image to the flush right side of the page, thereby allowing the text to wrap around the left side of the image. Try it yourself. But wait—take another look at the preceding image. Doesn't it look kind of scrunched up against the text above it? You can fix that with the `vspace` attribute (see Figure B-26).

```
<img src="hands.jpg" width=216 height=191 align=right vspace=10>
```

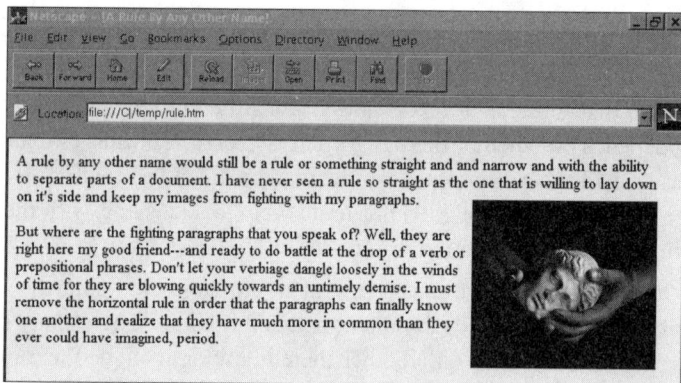

FIGURE B-26

It's a wrap.

Use the vspace attribute to give your images some breathing room. You can also use the hspace attribute to take care of any horizontal claustrophobia that your image might be experiencing.

The New Netscape Extensions

Most of the original Netscape Extensions have been incorporated into the new HTML 3.2 working standards proposal. Microsoft Internet Explorer 3.0 has incorporated literally all of them as well—so much so that you can feel 99.9 percent safe using either browser for your corporate intranet. The following section describes a few of the more interesting new Netscape Extensions.

<MULTICOL> (The Multicolumn Tag and Its Attributes)

This is an interesting tag that was introduced in the 3.0 version of the Netscape Navigator browser. This tag has both opening and closing attributes. All text that appears between the opening and closing tags will be displayed in a multicolumn format. The attributes of this tag are as follows:

- ◆ cols: This is a mandatory tag because it will tell the browser how many columns the text will be split into. You can also use the width attribute with the cols attribute to control how text will spread across columns.

- ◆ gutter: This attribute controls the space between columns; it defaults to a value of 10.

- width: As mentioned previously, the width attribute controls the width of individual columns

The following code uses the <MULTICOL> tag; the result of this code is shown in Figure B-27.

```
<html>
<head><title>A Rule By Any Other Name</title></head>
<body>
<multicol cols=2>
<p>A rule by any other name would still be a rule or something straight and and narrow
➥and with the ability to separate parts of a document. I have <img src="hands.jpg"
➥width=216 height=191 align=right vspace=10>
never seen a rule so straight as the one that is willing to lay down on it's side and
➥keep my images from fighting with my paragraphs.</p>
<p>But where are the fighting paragraphs that you speak of? Well, they are right here my
➥good friend – and ready to do battle at the drop of a verb or prepositional phrases.
➥Don't let your verbiage dangle loosely in the winds of time for they are blowing
➥quickly towards an untimely demise. I must remove the horizontal rule in order that
➥the paragraphs can finally know one another and realize that they have much more in
➥common than they ever could have imagined, period.</multicol></p>
</body>
</html>
```

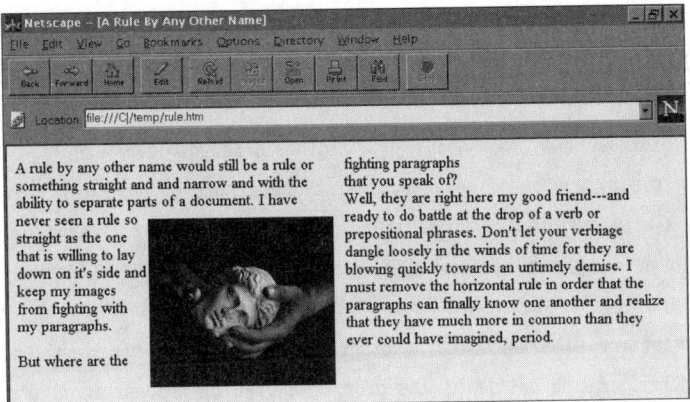

FIGURE B-27

Head in hands with columns.

Did you notice how it still honored the way I had set up my image? It put everything into two columns, put my image in, and then still wrapped my text quite nicely around that same image. You can play with it some yourself to see how the other attributes work out. I wondered whether this works in IE 3.0, so I checked—and it doesn't (not yet, anyway).

<SPACER> (Horizontal and Vertical Spacing Tag)

Another step in the right direction as far as page layout is concerned. This tag sounds like it will do what I usually am amazed at when I use NetObject Fusion: I have total control over where I place images, text, and anything else imaginable. I can open the source code and find comments such as "Netscape table workaround" (or something to that effect). I am betting that this is the general direction that the <SPACER> tag is heading, or could head. Here are the attributes (and values for each) for the <SPACER> tag:

- type: This attribute has three possible values: horizontal, vertical, and block. Here is what each of the 3 values actually will do for you:

  horizontal: Inserts a horizontal space between words. You can control the width of this space through the size attribute.

  vertical: Inserts a vertical space between lines. You can control the height of the space through the size attribute.

  block: This spacer is much like an invisible image. You don't use the size attribute with this tag; instead, you treat it as you would the <IMG>, or image tag, and use the width, height, and align attributes.

The following code shows how the <SPACER> tag works. The result is shown in Figure B-28.

```
<html>
<head><title>A Rule By Any Other Name</title></head>
<body>
<spacer type=block width=90><img src="hands.jpg" width=216 height=191>
<multicol cols=2>A rule by any other name would still be a rule or something straight
and and narrow and with the ability to separate parts of a document. I have never seen
a rule so straight as the one that is willing to lay down on it's side and keep my
images from fighting with my paragraphs.<br>
But where are the fighting paragraphs that you speak of? Well, they are right here my
good friend--and ready to do battle at the drop of a verb or prepositional phrase.
Don't let your verbiage dangle loosely in the winds of time for they are blowing
```

```
➡quickly towards an untimely demise. I must remove the horizontal rule in order that
➡the paragraphs can finally know one another and realize that they have much more in
➡common than they ever could have imagined, period.</multicol>
</body>
</html>
```

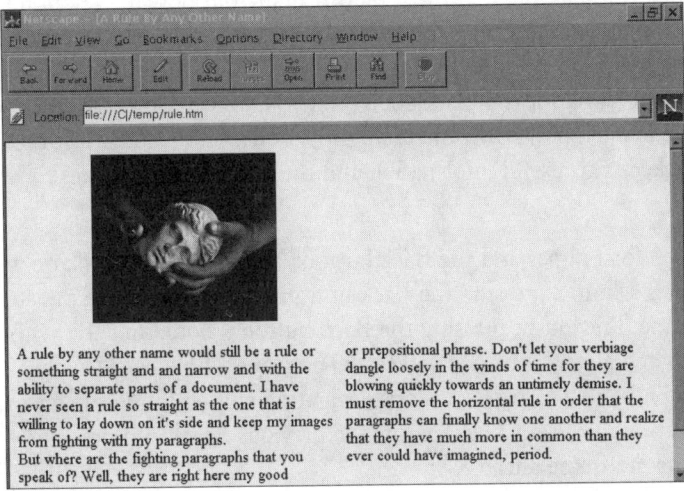

FIGURE B-28

Just a nudge to the right, using the <SPACER> tag.

Take a look at the code for the <SPACER> tag and you will notice the block attribute with a value of 90 pixels inside the tag. This attribute acts as an invisible image that nudges the image over just a bit. You are in control, at last! Play with the <SPACER> tag yourself and plug in all those attributes. Notice also that I kept the <MULTICOL> in just for laughs.

<FONT> (The font face=fontname Tag)

The <font> tag now supports the face attribute (originally rolled out by IE 3.0). With this tag, you can specify which fonts you would like your enclosed text to appear in. You simply select the font face that you would prefer the browser to load—for example, <font face="Arial"> and if the Arial font is resident on the target browser's machine, then Arial will be loaded. You can also list your tag in this way: <font face="Arial, Times, Courier">. Doing so allows your browser to select an alternate font if the first one listed is not available on the target machine.

<FRAMESET> (The Frame Tag and Its Attributes)

The wonderful world of frames. Introduced in Netscape Navigator 2.0, frames have a controversial reputation, to say the least. You either love them or you hate them? No, that's not quite it, but close. It seems that everyone jumped on the framewagon when it first pulled into town, and then, as time went on, articles started appearing about how some companies were backing off from frames for the time being. You may have overheard people at lunch complaining that they couldn't figure out how to "get around" in frames. Then there were complications with the Back button. I'll have Netscape explain it to you (I found this useful information in the Netscape Handbook at home.netscape.com. (At that site, you should look for the Handbook or, if you are working from the Netscape Navigator browser, then just pull down the Help drop-down menu and select the Handbook. It is packed with useful information and the latest Release Notes for each browser upgrade):

> New Navigation for Frames and the Back button: Now, when you click on a link that updates a frame, pressing the Back button returns you to the previous state of the frame. Previously, pressing the Back button ignored updates within a page's frames and always returned you to the previous whole page (further back than you probably wanted). In short, navigating among frames now works on a per frame basis: pressing Back revisits the previous frame and pressing Forward revisits the frame ahead.

So, Netscape fixed the problem with navigation and now, finally, people are starting to realize the power of using frames.

Here is a rather silly example of how a frame is set up.

```
<html>
<head><title>Your Very First Frame(s)</title>
</head>
<frameset rows="55, 300, 100">
<frame src="simple.htm" name="banner" marginwidth=1 marginheight=4 scrolling=no noresize>
<frameset cols="100, 400">
<frame src="menu.htm" name="menu" scrolling=no noresize>
<frame src="rule.htm" name="main_content" scrolling=auto noresize>
</frameset>
<frameset cols="100, 400">
```

```
<frame src="test.htm" name="logo" scrolling=no noresize>
<frame src="ordered.htm" name="details" scrolling=auto noresize>
</frameset>
</frameset>
</html>
```

This is called the frameset document, in which you lay out the design of the frame and specify the frames that you want your links to go to. You should save this document as FRAME_BASE.HTM.

```
<html>
<head><title>Main Menu</title></head>
<body>
<p>
<a href="simple.htm" target="main_content">Our Vision</a><br><br>
<a href="java.htm" target="main_content">Simple Calculator</a><br><br>
<a href="rule.htm" target="main_content">Head In Hands</a><br><br>
<a href="test.htm" target="main_content">A Test</a><br><br>
<a href="ordered.htm" target="main_content">Ordered List</a><br><br>
</body>
</html>
```

This is where you create the menu that you will use to navigate throughout your frameset document. As you can see in the code, the link that you click on is the name of the HTML file that you wish to display in what is called the main content frame, which you designated in your FRAME_BASE.HTM document. Make sure that you are properly referencing or pointing to the correct directories where your linked and targeted files can be found.

Take a look at Figure B-29 to see what your silly frame example will actually look like.

There is an excellent site that will teach you more about frames then you will ever wish to know. Point your browser to http://www.newbie.net/frames/index.html. This is probably the definitive source for frame education.

In this appendix, I wanted you to see some good examples of how HTML 3.2 has evolved, and how it looks. Again, I encourage you to experiment (and find a good HTML editor).

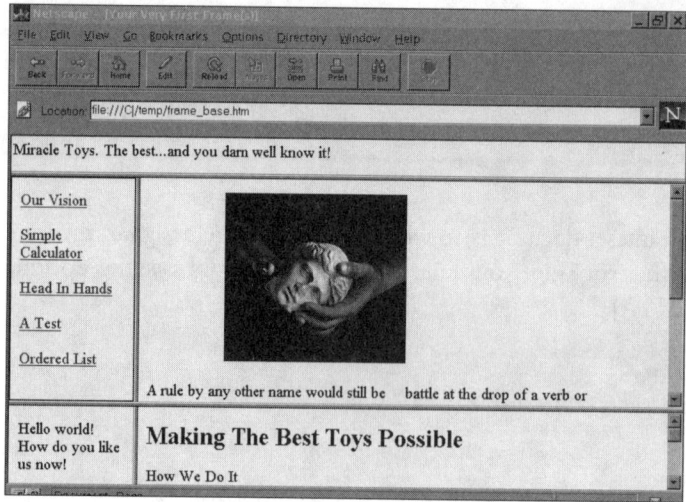

FIGURE B-29

A silly frame example that shows how you can divide up your content into different frames or sections.

Appendix | C

Authoring for Your Intranet

Okay, I put you through the HTML boot camp in the previous appendixes, and you survived. Now that you know the basics for creating intranet Web pages, you can use this to create Web content from an entirely blank screen in Windows NotePad or, better yet, you can use what you have learned as a foundation, and now move to an editor to create your intranet content. Six months ago, editors were a bug fest and tackled only the simplest of tags. Now, editors have caught up, and there are several WYSIWYG editors that you can download off the Internet that will allow you to create Web pages—static and dynamic—quickly for your intranet. I still have not found one that does not lock up from time to time, so remember to save your work often.

Organizations gain significant advantages by creating intranets to make it easier for employees to access and share information. To increase the development and scope of corporate intranets, getting others in the organization involved is necessary. This refers to the employees, management, and the IS department. Increasing interest in the intranet will mean that one person or even a handful of people will not be able to handle the entire corporation's intranet. This is where authoring tools come in, allowing users to take responsibility to develop and maintain their own department's intranet presence. The tools that allow users to develop content quickly, without having to learn a suite of development tools, are the WYSIWYG authoring tools.

Netscape Navigator Gold

I'll start with Netscape Navigator Gold 3.01. Navigator Gold 3.01 is a final release and is pretty stable. In addition to being a great browser, it is also an editor—all in one. Netscape Navigator Gold is perfect for intranet users. It has been designed to allow users to browse the intranet, share ideas, and create their own content. Netscape Navigator Gold packages all the necessary applications, including mail applications, news, Web browsing, and an easy-to-use authoring tool. Because all these applications have been combined into one user-friendly product, Netscape Navigator Gold reduces training time and enables corporations to standardize through one application, instead of having to support multiple mail clients, FTP clients, authoring tools, and browsers.

Editing a Page

With Netscape Navigator Gold, you can create your Web pages with the Navigator Gold Page Wizard, or you can start from scratch with your own layout. You can also select templates that provide predesigned layouts for all types of intranet pages. And, yes, Navigator Gold lets you take advantage of built-in Java and JavaScript editing.

One-Button Publishing

Netscape Navigator Gold not only makes Web page creation easy, but also makes transferring files painless for new users. The one-button publishing feature in Netscape Navigator Gold allows users to place their department's Web pages directly on the intranet Web server. It has password protection so that users can't just randomly edit and update your corporation's Web pages. One-button publishing is very easy to use and eliminates the need for your organization to purchase an FTP client and train users on that separate application as well.

Netscape Navigator Example

Okay, go ahead and fire up Netscape Navigator Gold 3.01. If you do not have a copy of it, you can get it from Netscape's Web site:

```
http://home.netscape.com/comprod/mirror/client_download.html
```

When you have Netscape Navigator Gold installed, you'll want to launch it and get ready to start creating your intranet pages. The first figure is one of Miracle Toy's Intranet pages and was created entirely in Netscape Gold. Check it out in Figure C-1.

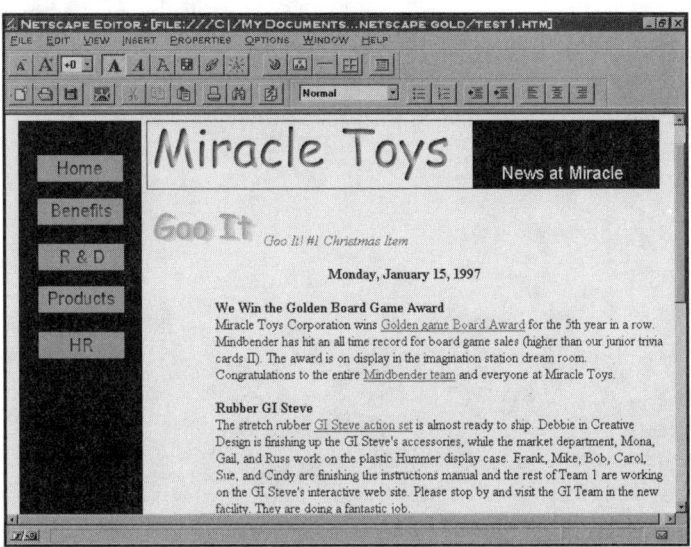

FIGURE C-1

Netscape Navigator Gold lets you browse, share, and create Web content for your intranet.

I'm going to show you how to create several different pages in Netscape Navigator Gold so that you can get the hang of it. You must first create a new document. You can do this by selecting File | New Document from the file menu at the top of the Netscape Navigator Gold window. Or you can clicking on the New Document icon that will display in the edit mode for Netscape Navigator Gold. Figure C-2 shows the start of a new page in Navigator Gold.

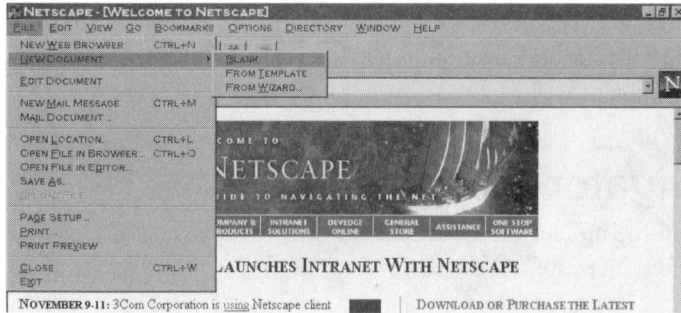

FIGURE C-2

Creating a new document, which places you in edit mode so that you can start on content creation.

If you already have an HTML document open that you want to modify, you can click on the yellow pencil icon on the tool bar. This will allow you to edit the document that you have in your browser window.

You could also have chosen two other options rather than the blank new document. You can get help from the wizard, or you can use existing Netscape templates to help you design your intranet pages. Figure C-3 displays the icons that I have discussed so far. If you place your mouse cursor over an icon and let it rest there for a few seconds, a display will tell you what each icon is.

FIGURE C-3

The New Document icon and the Edit Icon in Netscape.

> **NOTE:** I have two Netscape windows open in Figure C-3. The top window is the regular Netscape Browser window that has the Edit icon. When you click on the Edit icon, you will launch another window, which allows you to edit the document that you were displaying in the browser. In the new window, you will see the New Document icon.

You should have a blank Netscape Gold Editor screen in front of you now. This screen looks very similar to a word processor screen. It has your menu bar, which has different drop-down text menus, and it has your toolbar, which has different icons. Your cursor should be blinking in the top-right corner of the screen in the document area. This large area is your work space where you will to create your Web pages. It is so simple that all you have to do is start typing your information. If you have the information already typed as a text file, you can save some time by cutting and pasting it into Netscape's editor.

I am going to create the Miracle Toys News Page. To do this, I start by typing the top three news stories. You can follow along in Figure C-4.

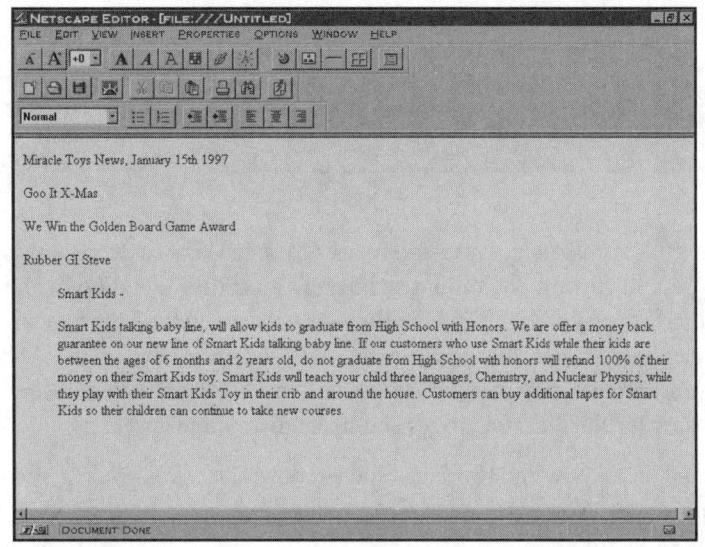

FIGURE C-4

Type your ideas for your corporate news stories. I show you how to dress then up later.

When you type in Netscape Gold's Editor you are creating HTML code but it is all behind the screens. You don't have to code with the normal HTML tags; rather, just type as you would in a word processor. If you want to edit the HTML code, you have that option as well. The cool thing here is that anyone can create a Web page for your intranet with

Netscape Gold, and also post it directly on your intranet and maintain it. After a user creates a Web page, it can be accessible to everyone in your organization with a Web browser.

It takes only seconds to dress up your text in Netscape Navigator Gold. By selecting your text and then choosing one of the many formatting options from the toolbar, you can create Web pages in no time (see Figure C-5). Now I am going to take my regular text and select it to add different formatting options.

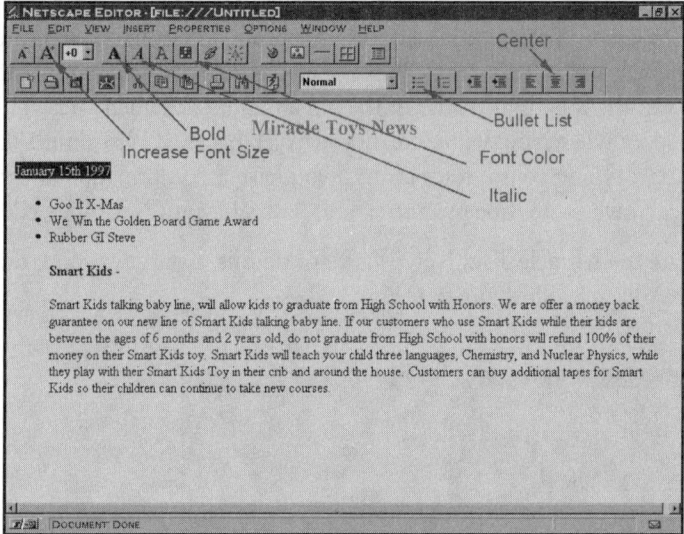

FIGURE C-5

Select your text and then choose a formatting option.

Netscape Navigator Gold makes it easy to add images to your Web pages, such as logos, charts, photographs, and clip art. You can insert images or just drag and drop them into your Web page. If you open another Netscape Browser window and tile the two windows side by side, you can drag images from the browser into your editor. You might also want to make a page on your intranet, consisting of bullets, buttons, logos, and other images so that users can grab images for their intranet pages and make them more appealing.

Look at Figure C-6 to see how the two Netscape windows allow you to drag and drop images into your intranet Web page.

After you have your images in place, you can adjust the images' properties so that text can wrap around your images. You can then adjust spacing. I added several images to my document and left aligned the images to place them on the left side of my screen. I added more information to my text and changed the spacing to allow it to look good with the images I added. The result can be seen in Figure C-7.

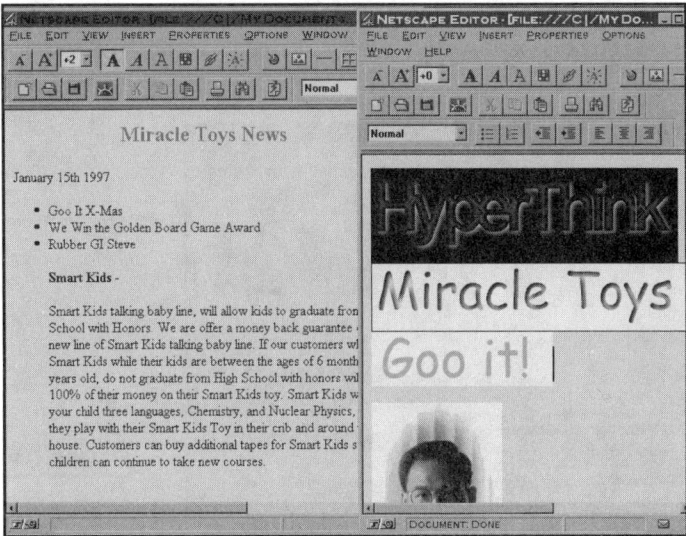

FIGURE C-6

Just drag and drop images from your browser to your new intranet Web page.

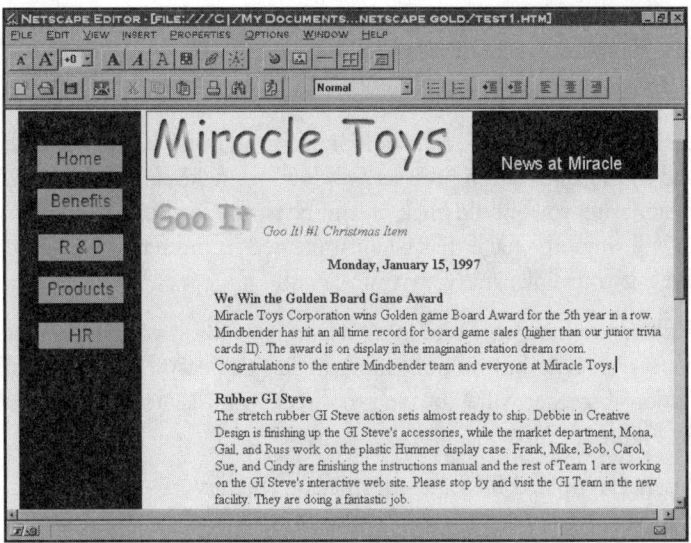

FIGURE C-7

With the images, the page now starts to look like a professional intranet news page.

I have not yet added a very important element: hyperlinks. Hyperlinks allow users to navigate your pages by clicking on images and selected text. Creating hyperlinks in Navigator Gold is simple. Select the image or text that you want to use as your link. After you select your text or image, click on the Make Link icon on the toolbar. This is the icon that looks like a link in a chain. You will see a pop-up menu enabling you point to this hyperlink to a new page that you define. That's it. This is shown in Figure C-8.

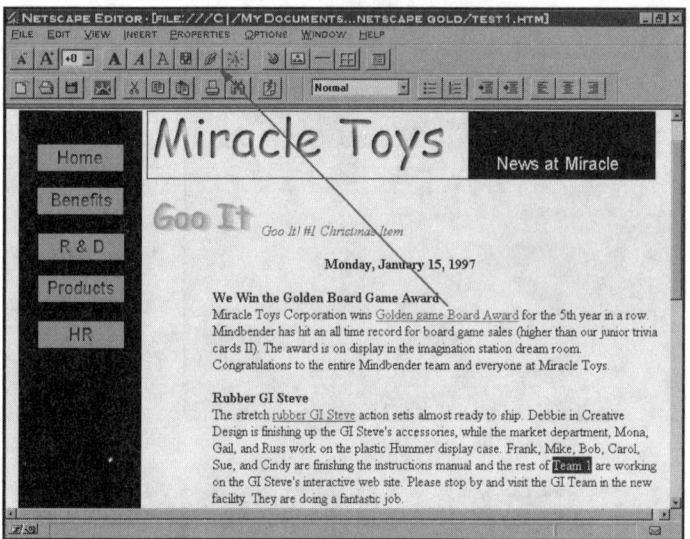

FIGURE C-8

I created a few hyperlinks to allow employees to link to other pages on the intranet and to get more information on top news stories.

What you are creating is WYSIWYG, but sometimes it might be a little bit different when it is displayed in the actual Web browser window. To make sure that you will achieve the look you desire, you should click on the Netscape icon on the toolbar from time to time. This will show the page that you just created in the actual Netscape browser so that you can test out your links and view your layout.

When it all looks okay, you have only one thing left to do: submit your page, images and all, to your intranet server. One-button publishing makes this easy. Press the Publish icon; you will see an Options box that will allow you to direct your files to the Web server. This is demonstrated in Figure C-9.

Only authorized users can upload files and edit files on the server.

NOTE: If you have created separate directories on your Web server for HTML documents, images, and other files, you cannot specify that Netscape Navigator Gold send the image files to one directory and your HTML files to another. Netscape Navigator Gold will place your image files and HTML files all together in the same directory. I believe that the company is working to fix this and allow you to specify different directories for your different files.

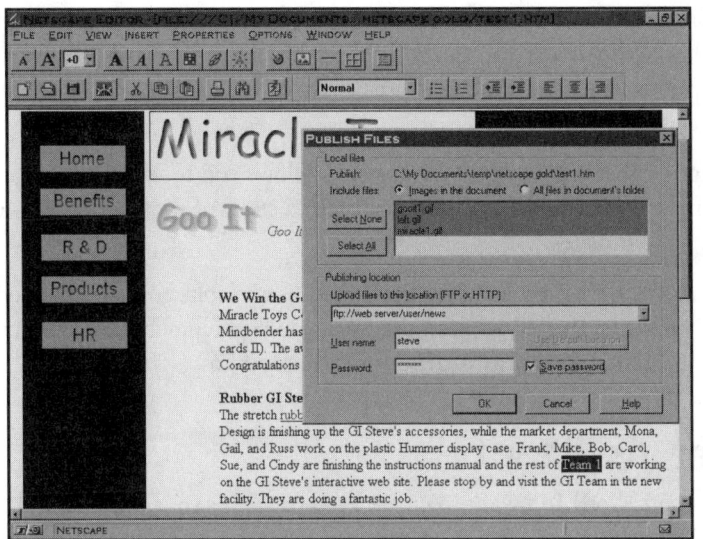

FIGURE C-9

*Press the Open Button
Publishing icon and direct
your Web and image files
to the path of your
directory on your
intranet Web server.*

Other Authoring Tools

Netscape Navigator Gold is not the only authoring tool available. There are many, many others. Some are WYSIWYG; some are code editors that allow work like a text editor but place the HTML tags in for you to make sure that both tags are inserted correctly; and some are converters that take word processing documents and convert them into HTML.

Microsoft FrontPage 97

If your corporation uses Microsoft Office products, you should look at Microsoft's FrontPage 97. It is available at Microsoft's Web site at:

```
http://www.microsoft.com/frontpage
```

You can download FrontPage along with the Bonus Pack and be on your way to creating your intranet content.

The FrontPage Editor is WYSIWYG and you don't need to know HTML except to tweak your code. Drag and drop makes FrontPage easy to use, and the FrontPage Explorer makes this more than just an editor. You can view all of your hyperlinks, and both edit and rename them on the spot. You don't have to worry about broken links anymore—FrontPage Editor will keep all your links intact when you move Web pages around in your intranet directory structure.

FrontPage 97 also comes with WebBots. These are robots that make dynamic pages a snap. Just drop in a WebBot and you can add full-text searching to your site and forms. There are also options to add in JavaScript, Visual Basic, Java applets, and plug-ins, as well as ActiveX controls.

The Image composer that comes in the Bonus Pack allows you to work with images and then import them into your pages. It also comes with a stock of professional photographs that you can use in your pages.

FrontPage 97 with the Bonus Pack is easy to use because it looks and feels so much like all the Office 97 products. In fact, you can use the shared spelling checker, thesaurus, and find and replace in FrontPage just as with your Office products.

Word Internet Assistant

If you have Microsoft Word and want to create Web pages for your intranet and convert existing Word documents over to HTML, then you need to get Word Internet Assistant. It is easy to use and, best of all, it is free. Just install it and it adds on to your existing Microsoft Word. Now you can create HTML documents from within Word. If you are already familiar with Microsoft Word, you will be able to get the hang of creating Web pages very quickly; you use the same commands to create Web pages as you do to create Word documents.

Internet Assistant does more than just create basic HTML. It allows you to add hyperlinks and graphics. You can even test your hyperlink right in Word. You can still export your documents as Word Documents if you like, and have your employees use the Word Viewer plug-in to view regular Word documents directly in their Web browser. The Word Viewer is also available for free at Microsoft's Web site.

NetObjects Fusion

NetObjects Fusion gives you page layout control over your Web creation. If you like total control over design, production, and the ability to update your entire Web site instantly, then NetObjects Fusion is worth a try. You can download an evaluation copy at:

```
http://www.netobjects.com/html/products.html
```

Creating your entire site with NetObjects Fusion is very simple.

First, design your overall site structure with the use of the visual site structure tool. NetObjects Fusion will then automatically create your navigation controls, buttons, banners, and links, and it will even update them as you change the structure of your site.

Rather than design an intranet site a page at a time with other authoring tools, NetObjects Fusion takes an entire-site approach to provide a total solution.

The page layout ability in NetObjects Fusion is also amazing. You can drag and drop images, text fields, and almost any content on your page. It gives a new meaning to *total* layout control.

You can add in all the bells and whistles such as sound files, Java applets, Shockwave, movies, and CGI scripts. You can also get started very quickly with site-wide graphics. These are professionally designed graphics that can be used throughout your site. When you are done, you can submit all of your content directly to your intranet server with the push of a button.

What Should You Use?

I have used all of these tools, and each one has its strong points and its weak ones. Some of the editors have features such as frames; some don't. Certain ones are more powerful than others. Word Internet Assistance is very easy to use but not as powerful as the rest. What to use depends on what you like, and on what you are trying to accomplish. I use all of these editors from time to time.

> **CAUTION:** There is also something that you need to watch out for. When you constantly take documents from editor to editor, make sure that you have saved copies of your documents. You will find that some editors will chew up your code when you import it from another editor.

I like Netscape Gold for doing anchor tags (bookmarks) and I also like the one-button publishing feature. I like the link control that I find with Microsoft FrontPage 97, along with the WebBots for dynamic content creation. NetObject Fusion rules for layout control and the ability to control your site's links and structure. And Word Internet Assistant is great for new users who are accustomed to working in Word. It comes in handy as well when you need to convert existing Word Documents into HTML files for your intranet. So, get them all and try them out.

Appendix | D

The Bare Bones Guide to HTML

Kevin Werbach has graciously allowed us to include his HTML reference guide, "The Bare Bones Guide to HTML" (Version 3.0, July 21, 1996), as an appendix in this book to help you find those HTML tags you always seem to forget. This is a great reference to use when creating or tweaking your pages.

This document is permanently located at <http://werbach.com/barebones/>.

The Bare Bones Guide to HTML lists all the tags that current versions of most browsers are likely to recognize. I have included all the tags in the HTML 3.2 specification, as well as Netscape extensions included in versions of Netscape Navigator up to 3.0b5. The Guide is designed to be as concise as possible, and therefore it doesn't go into any detail about how to use the various tags. There are numerous step-by-step HTML guides on the Web; I have links to many of them at <http://werbach.com/web/wwwhelp.html>.

Comments and suggestions are always welcome; you can reach Kevin Werbach via Email at <barebones@werbach.com>.

The Bare Bones Guide to HTML

by <http://werbach.com/>

Version 3.0 — July 21, 1996

Formatting Of This Document

For clarity, I have separated out different attributes that can be applied to the same tag onto separate lines. Generally, multiple attributes can be combined in the same tag.

Tags are listed in upper case for ease of reading, although most tags are not case sensitive.

Symbols Used

The following symbols are used throughout this document:

URL	URL of an external file (or just file name if in the same directory)
?	Arbitrary number (i.e. <H?> means <H1>, <H2>, <H3>, etc.)
%	Arbitrary percentage (i.e. <HR WIDTH="%"> means <HR WIDTH="50%">, etc.)
***	Arbitrary text (i.e. ALT="***" means fill in with text)
$$$$$$	Arbitrary hex (i.e. BGCOLOR="#$$$$$$" means BGCOLOR="#00FF1C", etc.)

, , ,	Comma-delimited (i.e. COORDS=",,," means COORDS="0,0,50,50", etc.)
¦	Alternatives (i.e. ALIGN=LEFT¦RIGHT¦CENTER means pick one of these)

Compatibility

Remember, HTML is evolving and browser implementations vary.

(no notation)	In the HTML 3.2 spec.; should work on all browsers
N1.0	Netscape extension introduced with Navigator version 1.0
N1.1	Netscape extension introduced with Navigator version 1.1
N2.0	Netscape extension introduced with Navigator version 2.0
N3.0B	Netscape extension introduced with Navigator version 3.0 beta

General

All HTML documents should have these:

Document Type	<HTML></HTML>	(beginning and end of file)
Title	<TITLE></TITLE>	(must be in header)
Header	<HEAD></HEAD>	(descriptive info, such as title)
Body	<BODY></BODY>	(bulk of the page)

Structural Definition

Appearance controlled by the browser's preferences:

Heading	<H?></H?>	(the spec. defines 6 levels)
Align Heading	<H? ALIGN=LEFT¦CENTER¦RIGHT></H?>	
Division	<DIV></DIV>	
Align Division	<DIV ALIGN=LEFT¦RIGHT¦CENTER¦JUSTIFY></DIV>	
Block Quote	<BLOCKQUOTE></BLOCKQUOTE>	(usually indented)
Emphasis	<EM></EM>	(usually displayed as italic)
Strong Emphasis	<STRONG></STRONG>	(usually displayed as bold)
Citation	<CITE></CITE>	(usually italics)
Code	<CODE></CODE>	(for source code listings)
Sample Output	<SAMP></SAMP>	
Keyboard Input	<KBD></KBD>	
Variable	<VAR></VAR>	
Definition	<DFN></DFN>	(not widely implemented)

Author's Address	`<ADDRESS></ADDRESS>`	
Large Font Size	`<BIG></BIG>`	
Small Font Size	`<SMALL></SMALL>`	

Presentation Formatting

Author specifies text appearance:

	Bold	`<B></B>`	
	Italic	`<I></I>`	
N3.0b	Underline	`<U></U>`	(not widely implemented yet)
	Strikeout	`<STRIKE></STRIKE>`	(not widely implemented yet)
N3.0b	Strikeout	`<S></S>`	(not widely implemented yet)
	Subscript	`<SUB></SUB>`	
	Superscript	`<SUP></SUP>`	
	Typewriter	`<TT></TT>`	(displays in a monospaced font)
	Preformatted	`<PRE></PRE>`	(display text spacing as-is)
	Width	`<PRE WIDTH=?></PRE>`	(in characters)
	Center	`<CENTER></CENTER>`	(for both text and images)
N1.0	Blinking	`<BLINK></BLINK>`	(the most derided tag ever)
	Font Size	`<FONT SIZE=?></FONT>`	(ranges from 1-7)
	Change Font Size	`<FONT SIZE="+¦-?"></FONT>`	
N1.0	Base Font Size	`<BASEFONT SIZE=?>`	(from 1-7; default is 3)
	Font Color	`<FONT COLOR="#$$$$$$"></FONT>`	
N3.0b	Select Font	`<FONT FACE="***"></FONT>`	
N3.0b	Multi-Column	`<MULTICOL COLS=?></MULTICOL>`	
N3.0b	Column Gutter	`<MULTICOL GUTTER=?></MULTICOL>`	
N3.0b	Column Width	`<MULTICOL WIDTH=?></MULTICOL>`	
N3.0b	Spacer	`<SPACER>`	
N3.0b	Spacer Type	`<SPACER TYPE=horizontal¦vertical¦block>`	
N3.0b	Size	`<SPACER SIZE=?>`	
N3.0b	Dimensions	`<SPACER WIDTH=? HEIGHT=?>`	
N3.0b	Alignment	`<SPACER ALIGN=left¦right¦center>`	

Links and Graphics

	Link Something	`<A HREF="URL"></A>`	
	Link to Target	`<A HREF="URL#***"></A>`	(if in another document)
		`<A HREF="#***"></A>`	(if in current document)
N2.0	Target Window	`<A HREF="URL" TARGET="***"></A>`	
	Define Target	`<A NAME="***"></A>`	

	Display Image	`<IMG SRC="URL">`	
	Alignment	`<IMG SRC="URL" ALIGN=TOP¦BOTTOM¦MIDDLE¦LEFT¦RIGHT>`	
N1.0	Alignment	`<IMG SRC="URL" ALIGN=TEXTTOP¦ABSMIDDLE¦BASELINE¦ABSBOTTOM>`	
	Alternate	`<IMG SRC="URL" ALT="***">`	(if image not displayed)
	Dimensions	`<IMG SRC="URL" WIDTH=? HEIGHT=?>`	(in pixels)
	Border	`<IMG SRC="URL" BORDER=?>`	(in pixels)
	Runaround Space	`<IMG SRC="URL" HSPACE=? VSPACE=?>`	(in pixels)
N1.0	Low-Res Proxy	`<IMG SRC="URL" LOWSRC="URL">`	
	Imagemap	`<IMG SRC="URL" ISMAP>`	(requires a script)
	Imagemap	`<IMG SRC="URL" USEMAP="URL">`	
	Map	`<MAP NAME="***"></MAP>`	(describes the map)
	Section	`<AREA SHAPE="RECT" COORDS=",,," HREF="URL"¦NOHREF>`	
N1.1	Client Pull	`<META HTTP-EQUIV="Refresh" CONTENT="?; URL=URL">`	
N2.0	Embed Object	`<EMBED SRC="URL">`	(insert object into page)
N2.0	Object Size	`<EMBED SRC="URL" WIDTH=? HEIGHT=?>`	

Dividers

	Paragraph	`<P></P>`	(closing tag often unnecessary)
	Align Text	`<P ALIGN=LEFT¦CENTER¦RIGHT></P>`	
	Line Break	` `	(a single carriage return)
	Clear Textwrap	`<BR CLEAR=LEFT¦RIGHT¦ALL>`	
	Horizontal Rule	`<HR>`	
	Alignment	`<HR ALIGN=LEFT¦RIGHT¦CENTER>`	
	Thickness	`<HR SIZE=?>`	(in pixels)
	Width	`<HR WIDTH=?>`	(in pixels)
	Width Percent	`<HR WIDTH="%">`	(as a percentage of page width)
	Solid Line	`<HR NOSHADE>`	(without the 3D cutout look)
N1.0	No Break	`<NOBR></NOBR>`	(prevents line breaks)
N1.0	Word Break	`<WBR>`	(where to break a line if needed)

Lists

Lists can be nested.

	Unordered List	`<UL><LI></UL>`	(`<LI>` before each list item)
	Compact	`<UL COMPACT></UL>`	
	Bullet Type	`<UL TYPE=DISC¦CIRCLE¦SQUARE>`	(for the whole list)
		`<LI TYPE=DISC¦CIRCLE¦SQUARE>`	(this & subsequent)
	Ordered List	`<OL><LI></OL>`	(`<LI>` before each list item)
	Compact	`<OL COMPACT></OL>`	

Numbering Type	`<OL TYPE=A¦a¦I¦i¦1>`	(for the whole list)
	`<LI TYPE=A¦a¦I¦i¦1>`	(this & subsequent)
Starting Number	`<OL START=?>`	(for the whole list)
	`<LI VALUE=?>`	(this & subsequent)
Definition List	`<DL><DT><DD></DL>`	(`<DT>`=term, `<DD>`=definition)
Compact	`<DL COMPACT></DL>`	
Menu List	`<MENU><LI></MENU>`	(`<LI>` before each list item)
Compact	`<MENU COMPACT></MENU>`	
Directory List	`<DIR><LI></DIR>`	(`<LI>` before each list item)
Compact	`<DIR COMPACT></DIR>`	

Backgrounds and Colors

Tiled Bkground	`<BODY BACKGROUND="URL">`	
Bkground Color	`<BODY BGCOLOR="#$$$$$$">`	(order is red/green/blue)
Text Color	`<BODY TEXT="#$$$$$$">`	
Link Color	`<BODY LINK="#$$$$$$">`	
Visited Link	`<BODY VLINK="#$$$$$$">`	
Active Link	`<BODY ALINK="#$$$$$$">`	

You can find more info at <http://werbach.com/web/wwwhelp.html#color>

Special Characters

These must all be in lower case:

Special Character	`&#?;`	(where ? is the ISO 8859-1 code)
<	`&lt;`	
>	`&gt;`	
&	`&amp;`	
"	`&quot;`	
Registered TM	`&#174;`	
Registered TM	`&reg;`	
Copyright	`&#169;`	
Copyright	`&copy;`	
Non-Breaking Space	` `	

You can find a complete list at

<http://www.uni-passau.de/%7Eramsch/iso8859-1.html>

Forms

These generally require a script on your server:

	Define Form	`<FORM ACTION="URL" METHOD=GET¦POST></FORM>`	
N2.0	File Upload	`<FORM ENCTYPE="multipart/form-data></FORM>`	
	Input Field	`<INPUT TYPE="TEXT¦PASSWORD¦CHECKBOX¦RADIO¦ IMAGE¦HIDDEN¦SUBMIT¦RESET">`	
	Field Name	`<INPUT NAME="***">`	
	Field Value	`<INPUT VALUE="***">`	
	Checked?	`<INPUT CHECKED>`	(checkboxes and radio boxes)
	Field Size	`<INPUT SIZE=?>`	(in characters)
	Max Length	`<INPUT MAXLENGTH=?>`	(in characters)
	Selection List	`<SELECT></SELECT>`	
	Name of List	`<SELECT NAME="***"></SELECT>`	
	# of Options	`<SELECT SIZE=?></SELECT>`	
	Multiple Choice	`<SELECT MULTIPLE>`	(can select more than one)
	Option	`<OPTION>`	(items that can be selected)
	Default Option	`<OPTION SELECTED>`	
	Input Box Size	`<TEXTAREA ROWS=? COLS=?></TEXTAREA>`	
	Name of Box	`<TEXTAREA NAME="***"></TEXTAREA>`	
N2.0	Wrap Text	`<TEXTAREA WRAP=OFF¦VIRTUAL¦PHYSICAL></TEXTAREA>`	

Tables

	Define Table	`<TABLE></TABLE>`	
	Table Border	`<TABLE BORDER></TABLE>`	(either on or off)
	Table Border	`<TABLE BORDER=?></TABLE>`	(you can set the value)
	Cell Spacing	`<TABLE CELLSPACING=?>`	
	Cell Padding	`<TABLE CELLPADDING=?>`	
	Desired Width	`<TABLE WIDTH=?>`	(in pixels)
	Width Percent	`<TABLE WIDTH=%>`	(percentage of page)
	Table Row	`<TR></TR>`	
	Alignment	`<TR ALIGN=LEFT¦RIGHT¦CENTER VALIGN=TOP¦MIDDLE¦BOTTOM>`	
	Table Cell	`<TD></TD>`	(must appear within table rows)
	Alignment	`<TD ALIGN=LEFT¦RIGHT¦CENTER VALIGN=TOP¦MIDDLE¦BOTTOM>`	
	No linebreaks	`<TD NOWRAP>`	
	Columns to Span	`<TD COLSPAN=?>`	
	Rows to Span	`<TD ROWSPAN=?>`	
N1.1	Desired Width	`<TD WIDTH=?>`	(in pixels)
N1.1	Width Percent	`<TD WIDTH="%">`	(percentage of table)

N3.0b	Cell Color	`<TD BGCOLOR="#$$$$$$">`	
	Table Header	`<TH></TH>`	(same as data, except bold centered)
	Alignment	`<TH ALIGN=LEFT¦RIGHT¦CENTER` `VALIGN=TOP¦MIDDLE¦BOTTOM>`	
	No Linebreaks	`<TH NOWRAP>`	
	Columns to Span	`<TH COLSPAN=?>`	
	Rows to Span	`<TH ROWSPAN=?>`	
N1.1	Desired Width	`<TH WIDTH=?>`	(in pixels)
N1.1	Width Percent	`<TH WIDTH="%">`	(percentage of table)
N3.0b	Cell Color	`<TH BGCOLOR="#$$$$$$">`	
	Table Caption	`<CAPTION></CAPTION>`	
	Alignment	`<CAPTION ALIGN=TOP¦BOTTOM>`	(above/below table)

Frames

Define and manipulate specific regions of the screen:

N2.0	Frame Document	`<FRAMESET></FRAMESET>`	(instead of `<BODY>`)
N2.0	Row Heights	`<FRAMESET ROWS=,,,></FRAMESET>`	(pixels or %)
N2.0	Row Heights	`<FRAMESET ROWS=*></FRAMESET>`	(* = relative size)
N2.0	Column Widths	`<FRAMESET COLS=,,,></FRAMESET>`	(pixels or %)
N2.0	Column Widths	`<FRAMESET COLS=*></FRAMESET>`	(* = relative size)
N3.0b	Borders	`<FRAMESET FRAMEBORDER="yes¦no">`	
N3.0b	Border Width	`<FRAMESET BORDER=?>`	
N3.0b	Border Color	`<FRAMESET BORDERCOLOR="#$$$$$$">`	
N2.0	Define Frame	`<FRAME>`	(contents of an individual frame)
N2.0	Display Document	`<FRAME SRC="URL">`	
N2.0	Frame Name	`<FRAME NAME="***"¦_blank¦_self¦_parent¦_top>`	
N2.0	Margin Width	`<FRAME MARGINWIDTH=?>`	(left and right margins)
N2.0	Margin Height	`<FRAME MARGINHEIGHT=?>`	(top and bottom margins)
N2.0	Scrollbar?	`<FRAME SCROLLING="YES¦NO¦AUTO">`	
N2.0	Not Resizable	`<FRAME NORESIZE>`	
N3.0b	Borders	`<FRAME FRAMEBORDER="yes¦no">`	
N3.0b	Border Color	`<FRAME BORDERCOLOR="#$$$$$$">`	
N2.0	Unframed Content	`<NOFRAMES></NOFRAMES>`	(for non-frames browsers)

Java

Applet	`<APPLET></APPLET>`	
File Name	`<APPLET CODE="***">`	
Parameters	`<APPLET PARAM NAME="***">`	
Location	`<APPLET CODEBASE="URL">`	
Identifier	`<APPLET NAME="***">`	(for references)
Alt Text	`<APPLET ALT="***">`	(for non-Java browsers)

Alignment	`<APPLET ALIGN="LEFT¦RIGHT¦CENTER">`	
Size	`<APPLET WIDTH=? HEIGHT=?>`	(in pixels)
Spacing	`<APPLET HSPACE=? VSPACE=?>`	(in pixels)

Miscellaneous

	Comment	`<!— *** —>`	(not displayed by the browser)
	Prologue	`<!DOCTYPE HTML PUBLIC "-//W3C//DTD HTML 3.2//EN">`	
	Searchable	`<ISINDEX>`	(indicates a searchable index)
	Prompt	`<ISINDEX PROMPT="***">`	(text to prompt input)
	Send Search	`<A HREF="URL?***"></a>`	(use a real question mark)
	URL of This File	`<BASE HREF="URL">`	(must be in header)
N2.0	Base Window Name	`<BASE TARGET="***">`	(must be in header)
	Relationship	`<LINK REV="***"`	(must be in header)
		`REL="***" HREF="URL">`	
	Meta Information	`<META>`	(must be in header)
	Style Sheets	`<STYLE></STYLE>`	(not widely supported yet)
	Scripts	`<SCRIPT></SCRIPT>`	(not widely supported yet)

Appendix | E

What's on the CD?

The CD that accompanies this book contains numerous tools and utilities to assist in the development and implementation of corporate intranets. There are servers, Web tools, HTML editors, Windows utilities, and more. Examples and source code from the book are included as well.

Running the CD

To make the CD more user friendly and take up less of your disk space, no installation is required. This means that the only files transferred to your hard disk are the ones you choose to copy.

> **CAUTION:** Significant differences between the various Windows operating systems (Windows 3.1, Windows 95, and Windows NT) sometimes render files that work in one Windows environment inoperable in another. Prima has made every effort to ensure that this problem is minimized. Eliminating it entirely is not possible, however. Therefore, you may find that some files or directories appear to be missing from the CD. Those files are, in reality, on the CD, but remain hidden from the operating system. To confirm this, view the CD using a different Windows operating system.
>
> Note: This problem most often occurs while viewing the CD in Windows 3.1.

Windows 3.1

To run the CD:

1. Insert the CD in the CD-ROM Drive.
2. From File Manager, select File, Run to open the Run window.
3. In the Command Line text box, type **D:\PRIMACD.EXE** (where D:\ is the CD-ROM drive).
4. Select OK.

Windows 95

Because there is no install routine, running the CD in Windows 95 is a breeze, especially if you have autorun enabled. Simply insert the CD in the CD-ROM Drive, close the tray, and wait for the CD to load.

If you have disabled autorun, place the CD in the drive and follow these steps:

1. From the Start menu, select Run.
2. Type **D:\PRIMACD.EXE** (where D:\ is the CD-ROM drive).
3. Select OK.

The Prima User Interface

Prima's user interface is designed to make viewing and using the CD contents quick and easy. It contains five category buttons, five options buttons, a title list, a description text box, a URL box, and Next and Previous buttons. Select a category button to display a list of available titles. Choose a title to see a description and the associated URL. At the title screen, select an option button to perform the desired action.

Category Buttons

Servers. An assortment of NT and UNIX Internet servers.

Intranet Tools. HTML editors, templates, and add-ons to help you create sophisticated Web pages.

Graphics Tools. Graphics viewers, image converters, and drawing tools.

Utilities. File and system utilities to help manage your system and improve its performance.

Book Examples. Examples and source code from the book.

Options Buttons

Explore. Left-clicking on this option in Windows 95 and NT allows you to view the folder containing the program files, using Windows Explorer. Right-clicking in Windows 3.x, 95, or NT brings up the Windows File Manager, from which you can easily explore the CD.

Run. If the selected title contains an executable file that runs without prior installation, left-clicking the Run button launches the program. If the program requires installation, an appropriate message is displayed.

Install. If the selected title contains an install routine, selecting this option begins the installation process. If no installation is available, an appropriate message is displayed.

> **NOTE:** You can install some of the shareware programs that do not have installation routines by copying the program files from the CD to your hard drive and running the executable (.EXE) file.

URL. Left-click to activate the URL associated with the selected title. If a URL is available, it will appear in the URL box at the bottom right of the CD window. In Windows 95 and NT, clicking on the actual URL will launch your browser and take you to the Web site (you must have a compatible browser and an Internet connection).

Exit. When you're finished and ready to move on, select Exit.

Prev. Takes you to the previous screen. Please note: This is not the last screen that you viewed, but the screen that actually precedes the current one.

Next. Takes you to the next screen.

The Software

This section gives you a brief description of some of the software that you'll find on the CD. This is just a sampling. As you browse the CD, you will find much more.

Examples and Source Code. Web pages, HTML examples, and source code used in the book.

Alibaba SSL Web Server. A multithreaded, high-performance WWW server.

Amazing JPEG Screen Saver for Win95/WinNT. A screen saver to display your corporate logos, family pictures, or any of your favorite JPEG images.

Carmel Anti Virus for Windows NT. A sophisticated antivirus program for Windows NT.

db-Connector Database Interface. A database/Web-connector that gives you the power to connect any ODBC database to your Web server.

Designer HTML. An HTML editor that now supports tables, targets, and centering.

Directory Toolkit For Windows 95, NT 4.x (shareware version). An application that provides features missing from Windows 95 and Windows NT 4.0.

Drag And File for Win 95/NT. A handy utility that lets you copy, move, or delete files across multiple directories and drives.

FaxMail Network for NT. A fax/mail management system, integrating FaxModem technologies into computer document generation.

GifWeb. An easy-to-use shareware program that makes the background of your GIF images transparent.

Icon To Bitmap Converter 3.25. Ico2Bmp! converts icons from ICO, EXE, DLL and ICL files into Windows bitmaps (BMP).

WinZip. One of the leading file compression utilities for Windows 95, NT, and Windows 3.1.

Index

Symbols/Numbers

20/20 Software, Net-Install, 360-361
32-bit ODBC drivers, Cold Fusion program, 207
3D and Animation plug-ins, 362-368
404 error, 26, 418-419

A

Access Control Lists, security, 388
access control, servers, 123-124
access logins, servers, 126
access questionnaire form, 56
accessibility, plug-ins, 351-353
ActiveX by Ncompass, 354-357
ActiveX controls, installing, 346
add-ons, 27-28
 Microsoft Excel Viewer, 152-154
 viewers, 152-154
addresses
 See also Web sites
 bind, 120
 resolve IP, 121
 URL, 43
ADO (Active Data Object), 130
Adobe Acrobat program, 156-157
Adobe Acrobat Reader 3.0 Beta, 354
Adobe Acrobat Reader plug-in, 339-341

Adobe Distiller program, 156
advertising, Intranet, 429
aliases, server names, 119
Alibaba server, 89-93
 Cold Fusion support, 206
alignment
 image options, 169-172
 images, 188-189
Altia ProtoPlay, 365
anchor <A HREF> tag, thumbnail image links, 174 -175
anchor <A> and </A> tag, hyperlink <A HREF> references, 190
Andreessen, Marc, 4
animated GIFs, 227, 262-268
animation, 262-268
 animated GIFs, 262-268
 AppletAce program, 264-268
 banners, 264-268
 GIF construction set, 263-264
 vector-based, 343
AppletAce program, 264-268
applications
 Cold Fusion program creation, 210-211
 form, job opportunities Web area, 196
 gateway, firewall security, 386
 helper, 27-28, 323, 334, 337-338, 347-349
ASAP Webshow plug-in, 323-324

ASCII files, 135-137
Astound Web Player program, 324
attributes
  ALIGN, 169-172
  ALT, 167-168
  BACKGROUND, 162
  BGCOLOR, 160-161
  BORDER, 173-174
  cols, 240
  DYNSRC, 261
  form action, 230
  form method, 230
  GET, 230
  HEIGHT, 168-169
  hidden, 231
  HSPACE, 173
  HTML 3.2, 474, 476-491
  LOOP, 261
  LOWERS, 172
  maxlength, 232
  multiple, 239
  name, 231, 240
  password, 233
  POST, 230
  rows, 240
  selected, 238
  size, 231, 239
  SRC, 167, 255
  textarea <TEXTAREA> tag, 240
  type, 231
  VSPACE, 173
  WIDTH, 168-169
AU file format, 253
audience
  defining, 37-38
  plug-in target, 351-353
audio, 253-258
  AU format, 253
  continuous play across Web pages, 256
  embedding, 255-256

  libraries, 262
  MIDI format, 255
  MPEG format, 254
  numbered file approach, 257-258
  RealAudio player, 254
  streaming, 254
  WAV format, 254-255
audio and video plug-ins, 368-371
AUTH_TYPE environment variables, 290
authentication
  digital certificates, 391-392
  password, 125
Authenticode Security Technology,
  described, 345
author, 36
authoring for the intranet, 499-510
authors, local, 24
automated slide shows, 321-322
AVI format, 260

B

background colors
  changing, 413
  user preference setting conflicts, 185
backgrounds
  color hexadecimal codes, 161
  images, 74-77, 162
  tiled images, 162
  transparent, 166, 178 -179
backup files, servers, 127
band width, checking with Doctor HTML, 420
banners, 264-268
bare bones guide, HTML, 511-519
Basic HTML, 433-462
Berners-Lee, Tim, 4-5, 27
beta testing, 406-407
  browser, 408
  TCP/IP stacks, 408
  time frames, 408

bind address, servers, 120
blink <BLINK> tag, 227
Bob's Web Server, 349
body <BODY> tag, 188
  BACKGROUND attribute, 162
  BGCOLOR attribute, 160-162
borders, image, 173-174
brackets, opening/closing < > HTML tags, 75
brainstorming, 39-40
broadcast, described, 374
broken links, 404 error, 26
Broschart, Charles, 428
browser wars, 439-441
browsers
  alternate text-only display, 74
  client-side image map nonsupport, 285
  embed <EMBED> tag nonsupport, 330-332
  GIF format support, 163, 166
  graphics nonsupport, 74
  GUI (Graphical Users Interface), 6
  helper applications, 323
  image format support, 163, 166
  image nonsupport alternate text display, 167
  intranet, 11
  JPEG format support, 163, 166
  Lynx, 6
  Microsoft Internet Explorer, 6-7, 309-310
  NCSA Mosaic, 11-12
  Netscape Navigator, 6-7, 309-310
  Netscape/Internet explorer analogy, 11-12
  NeXT workstation, 4
  opening text files, 135-136
  plug-ins, 323
  presentation advantages, 309
  security, 389-391
  testing, 408
  text only, 6
  wars, 439-441
Bruck, Bill, 313

bullet icons, 177-178
bullets, image, 192-193
business and utility plug-ins, 354-361
business presentations, 308-302
buttons, radio, 233-235

C

caching proxy server, 386
capture hot key (F11), 409-411
capturing screen shots, 409-414
Carbon copy/Net by Microlcom, 356-357
catalogs, versus intranet information
  distribution, 10
CD-ROM
  contents, 521-525
  Netscape Overview, 58
  prima user interface, 523-524
  programs, 524-525running, 522-523
  versus intranet information distribution, 9-11
centralized approach, organizational model,
  30-32
CERN (European Laboratory for Particle
  Physics), 4
certificates, public-key, 395
Certifying Authorities, digital certificates, 392
CFML (Cold Fusion Markup Language), 206
CGI (Common Gateway Interface)
  cgi-bin directory, 230, 285
  Cold Fusion program, 206
  compiled applications, 286
  dynamic intranet pages, 285-286
  interpreted applications, 286
CGI applications
  compiled, 286
  interpreted, 286
  language support, 286
CGI methods, 286-287
  GET, 286-287
  POST, 286-287

CGI (Common Gateway Interface) scripts, 19, 226-230
cgi-bin directory, 230
executable, 230
forms, 19
security, 387
cgi-bin directory, 230, 285
CGI/Perl applications
displaying environment variables, 291-294
form data processing, 300-305
return Web page based on user's browser, 294-296
sending comment form to viewer, 297-300
challenges, security, 392-393
character sets, ISO-Latin-1, 193-194
characters
pound sign (#), 292
slash+n (\n), 293
check boxes, forms, 235-236
CineWeb plug-in, 261
ClearFusion plug-in, 260-261
clickable image maps, 276
client pulls
meta <META> tag, 321-322
presentations, 319, 321-322
client updating, PointCast I-Server, 378-379
client-side image maps, 277
browser nonsupport, 285
clients, GUI, 6
clips, video, 258-259
closing tags, 441-442
Cold Fusion program, 205-221
32-bit ODBC drivers, 207
application creation, 210-211
application features, 205
CFML (Cold Fusion Markup Language), 206
CGI (Common Gateway Interface), 206
Cold Fusion Application Server, 206
Cold Fusion Support Forum, 206

DBML tags, 212
employee database creation, 214-221
form elements, 210
GETSTART.HTM file, 208
Getting Started home page, 208-209
HTTP connection, 208
installation, 208
Intersolv DataDirect ODBC pack, 207
query form, 208-209
RESULTS.DBM file, 212-213
SEARCH.HTML file, 210-211
SETUP.EXE file, 208
system requirements, 206-208
template file creation, 212-214
testing installation, 208-209
Collage Capture program, 163
color values, backgrounds, 75
colors
amount in images, 420
background, 185
default (256 colors) depth, 180
hexadecimal codes, 161
hyperlink text, 162
hyperlinks, 8
palettes, Netscape Navigator, 161-162
project design/layout, 74-77
RGB numeric values, 76
titles, 189
unfollowed hyperlinks, 77
user preference setting conflicts, 185
visited link, 77
combined centralized/decentralized approach, organizational model, 32-33
comment forms, 240-241
sending to viewer, 297-300
comment interpreter, pound sign (#), Perl scripts, 292
comments, Perl scripts, 292
Common Logfile Format, 126

communication media, intranet advantages, 9-11

communications, security, 385-386

company news, PointCast I-Server, 377

compiled applications, CGI, 286

compression, plug-ins, 336

Configure Administration, NES, 122-127
  access control, 123-124
  access logging, 126
  backup files, 127
  configuration change logs, 127
  daemon configuration, 122
  hostnames to allow, 124-125
  passwords, 125
  server port number, 123
  server user, 123
  SSL activation, 123
  user name, 125

content, Web page
  authoring, 24-25
  categorizing, 50-51
  converters, 25
  HTML requirements, 25
  ownership issues, 426-427
  plug-in responsibility, 350
  storage, 26-28
  summary, 191

CONTENT_LENGTH environment variable, 287-288

CONTENT_TYPE environment variable, 290

controls, navigation, 65-66

conventions
  passwords, 388
  usernames, 388

conversions
  Excel format to text files, 152
  GIF/JPEG formats, 166
  images, 166

  PageMaker files to PDF files, 156
  PowerPoint presentations to HTML, 316-317
  text file to HTML table, 154-156
  word processor file format to text files, 137-141

converters, content filters, 25

Cool Talk program, 268-271

copyright symbols, 193-194

criteria, Web server rating, 80-89

crosshairs, 411

cryptography, 393-396
  described, 393-394
  encryption, 395-396
  public-key, 394-395
  public-key certificates, 395
  symmetric-key, 394-395

Crystal Reports program, 129

CSE 3310 HTML Validator, 425

CSM Alibaba server, Cold Fusion support, 206

CSS (Cascading Style Sheets), 440

D

daemon, server configuration, 122

data processing, forms, 300-305

databases
  32-bit ODBC drivers, 207
  Cold Fusion program, 214-221
  employee, 214-221
  Intersolv DataDirect ODBC pack, 207
  queries, 204-205
  record creation, 219-221
  record editing, 214-219

DBML tags, template files, Cold Fusion program, 212

DeBabelizer program, 166

decentralized approach, organizational model, 30

dedicated servers, 387

departments
gatekeepers, 23
intranet value issues, 22
themes, 63
training, 23
descriptive text, adding to screen shot, 414
destination anchor, hyperlinks, 191
diagrams, Web flow, 52-55
Diffie, Whitfield, 394
Digigami, CineWeb plug-in, 260
digital
certificates, security, 391-392, 395
IDs (digital certificates), 395
passports, 395
directories
cgi-bin, 230, 285
root, 121, 211
dividing line, horizontal rules, 189
Doctor HTML 419-425
check bandwidth, 420
find code disasters, 420
hyperlink analysis, 424-425
Image Analysis, 423
spell checker, 419
using, 421-423
document root, servers, 122
documents
background images, 74-77
colors, 74-77
HTML conversions, 25
images, 74
root directory, 122
downloads, virus-checking, 341
drivers
32-bit ODBC, 207
Cold Fusion program, 207
Intersolv DataDirect ODBC pack, 207
drop-down menus, forms, 236-239
dynamic intranet pages, 285-286

E

e-mail, 5, 465-466
forms, 241-243
sending from an HTML form using
CGI/Perl application, 297-305
editors, HTML, 25
embed <EMBED> tag, 255-256
presentation plug-ins, 330-332
SRC attribute, 255
embedded audio, 255-256
employee
database, Cold Fusion program, 214-221
handbook, intranet policies and procedures
manual, 21
identification card update form, 19
Employee Handbook online, 146
employment listings, 146
EMWAC freeware HTTPS server, 93-96
**EMWAC HTTPS server, Cold Fusion
support, 206**
encryption, security, 395-396
**engineering department, manual storage
capability, 17-18**
enterprise data file, Netscape Navigator, 389
entities, character, 193-194
environment variables
AUTH_TYPE, 290
CONTENT_LENGTH, 287-288
CONTENT_TYPE, 290
displaying, 291-294
GATEWAY_INTERFACE, 290
HTTP_REFERER, 289
HTTP_USER_AGENT, 289
PATH_INFO, 291
QUERY_STRING, 286, 288
REMOTE_ADDR, 289
REMOTE_HOST, 289
REMOTE_IDENT, 289

REMOTE_USER, 289
REQUEST_METHOD, 288
SCRIPT_NAME, 291
SERER_SOFTWARE, 290
SERVER_ADMIN, 290
SERVER_NAME, 290
SERVER_PORT, 291
SERVER_PROTOCOL, 291
error codes, 404, 418-419
Excel files, intranet posting, 151-152
executable, CGI script, 230
external
  images, 165
  Web pages, 14-15

F

FAQ (Frequently Asked Questions), 24, 415-418
feedback forms, 240-241
file extensions
  htm, 144
  txt, 135
file formats
  AU, 253
  AVI, 260
  GIF, 27, 163, 166
  GIF87 (CompuServe GIF), 166, 179
  GIF89a, 166, 179
  graphics, 27
  JPEG, 27, 163, 166
  MIDI, 255
  MPEG, 254, 259-260
  Video for Windows (AVI), 260
  WAV, 254-255
files
  ASCII, 135-137
  backup, 127
  enterprise data, 389

FLORIDA.HTM, 278
GETSTART.HTM, 208
GI-BOB.PPT, 315
htm, 42
IMAGE.TPL, 319
INDEX.HTM, 317
MAIN.DBM, Cold Fusion program, 214-217
MAPUSA.GIF, 277
NEW.DBM, Cold Fusion program, 219-221
PDF (Personal Document Format), 156-157
PDF (Portable Document Format), 339
RESULTS.DBM, Cold Fusion program, 212-213
saving to server root directory, 211
SEARCH.HTML, Cold Fusion program, 210-211
self-extracting, 342
SETUP.EXE, 208
SLD001.HTM, 317
spreadsheet, 150-156
text, 135-137
TEXT.TPL, 319
TSLD001.HTM, 317
UPDATE.DBM, Cold Fusion program, 217-219
word processing, 137-150
zipped, 342
fill-in forms, 227-229
filters
  documents, 25
  HTML converters, 25
financial information services, 16
firewalls, 386
  application gateway, 386
  LAN (Local Area Network), 386
  PointCast I-Server, 377-378
  screening router, 386
FLORIDA.HTM file, MapEdit program, 278

flow diagrams, storyboarding, 52-55
font <FONT> and </FONT> tag, font color/sizing, 189
fonts
   presentation size adjustments, 311
   sizing, 189
   titles, 189
foreach loops, Perl scripts, 293
form <FORM> tag, 230
   action attributes, 230
   attributes, 230
   GET attribute, 230
   method attributes, 230
   POST attribute, 230
form elements, Cold Fusion program, 210
formats, Common Logfile, 126
forms, 225-250
   access questionnaire, 56
   CGI scripts, 19
   check boxes, 235-236
   comment (feedback), 240-241, 297-300
   creation, 230-243
   data processing, 300-305
   drop-down menus, 236-239
   e-mail, 241-243
   employee identification card update, 19
   fill-in, 227-229
   form <FORM> tag, 230
   input <INPUT> tag, 231
   job opportunities Web area, 196
   multiple input capability, 239
   option <OPTION> tag, 237-238
   passwords, 233
   personnel file, 196-198
   query, 208-209
   radio buttons, 233-235
   scrolling lists, 236-239
   select <SELECT> tag, 236-239
   simple, 231-232
   text box sizing, 232

   textarea <TEXTAREA> and </TEXTAREA> tag, 240-243
   user base survey, 40-42
Formula Graphics Multimedia System plug-in, 324-325
frames
   continuous audio play across Web pages, 256
   Microsoft Internet Explorer, 66-67
   navigation aids, 66-67
free stuff, advertising Intranet, 429
FrontPage program, 130
FTP (File Transfer Protocol), 5
FTP Software, KeyView, 359-360
FutureWave, FutureSplash Player, 343, 363

G

Gamelan Web site, 355
gatekeepers, 23
GATEWAY_INTERFACE environment variables, 290
GET method, CGI, 286-287
GETSTART.HTM file, Cold Fusion program, 208
Getting Started home page, Cold Fusion program, 208-209
GI-BOB.PPT file, 315
GIF construction set, 263-264
GIF file format, 27
GIF formats
   browser support, 163, 166
   interlaced, 166
   non-interlaced, 166
GIF, animated, 227
GIF87 (CompuServe GIF) format, 166, 179
GIF89a format, 166, 179
global rollout, 406
Gold Disk Inc, Astound Web Player, 324
Gopher, 5
graphic artists, 35-36

graphics
background, 160-162
default (256 colors) depth, 180
external images, 165, 175-177
file formats, 27
GIF, 27
GIF format support, 163, 166
icons, 177-178
inline images, 165-175
JPEG, 27
JPEG format support, 163, 166
project design/layout, 64
pros/cons, 160
GUI (Graphical User Interface), 5-8
browsers, 6
clients, 6
guidelines
Web page approval, 22-24
Web shop, 62

H

handshake, SSL, 398-399
**Harrow Software, Formula Graphics
Multimedia System, 324-325**
heading levels, HTML document, 190
height tags, images, 420
Hellman, Martin, 394
help button, including on Intranet page, 415
help, providing, 415
helper applications, 27-28, 347-349
browsers, 323
described, 334
Netscape Navigator, 337-338
hexadecimal codes
colors, 161
background colors, 75
Hi Jaak program, 163
**hierarchical structure, navigation model,
44-47**

home pages
component ideas, 59
creation, 275-306
described, 42-43
first impression, 59
Getting Started, Cold Fusion program,
208-209
hierarchical structure, 44-47
idea testing, 55-57
image insertion, 280-285
linear structure, 47-48
mixed hierarchical/linear structure, 48-49
navigation, 59-60
horizontal rule <HR> tag, 191, 238
horizontal rules, HTML document, 189
host names
allowable, 124-125
resolving IP addresses, 121
servers, 119
hosts, allowable, 124-125
hot key (F11), 410
hot links, image maps, 277-278
htm file, 42
htm file extension, 144
**HTML (Hypertext Markup Language), 8,
19, 25, 58**
bare bones guide, 511-519
basics, 433-462
description, 441
document converters, 25
editors, 25
layout tag development, 308
opening and closing tags, 441-442
raw coding, 435-439
spell checker, 419
tags, 443-462, 467-492
HTML 3.2
overview, 465-466
specification, 308

HTML code
create FAQ Web page, 416-418
validators, 418-426
HTML code validators, CSE 3310 HTML Validator, 426
HTML documents
body section, 188
copyright symbol, 193-194
formatting, 512-519
heading levels, 190
horizontal rules, 189
htm file extension, 144
hyperlinks, 189-190
image alignment, 188-189
image hot areas, 284
image map size/shape, 284
image references, 188
image/text white space separator, 189
items listing 191
line breaks, 189
meta tags, 283
new paragraphs, 188
problems, finding, 419-425
summary content, 191
text descriptions, 189
titles, 189
unordered list, 191
HTML editors, 25
HTML formatting, word processing files, 141-145
HTML tags, proprietary, 11
HTTP connection, Cold Fusion program GETSTART.HTM file, 208
HTTP_REFERER environment variable, 289
HTTP_USER_AGENT environment variable, 289
human resources
services, 15-16

Web pages, job opportunities, 194-205
word processing files, 137-141
hyperlink reference <A HREF> tag, 190
hyperlinks
analysis, Doctor HTML, 424
audio/video libraries, 262
Click Here avoidance, 54
colors, 8, 162
destination anchor, 191
external images, 175-177
HTML document, 189-190
PowerPoint slides, 314-315
presentations, 311
reference <A HREF> tag, 190
slide objects, 318
thumbnail images, 174-175
underlined text, 8
unfollowed color, 77
visited color, 77
hypermedia, 4, 8-9, 252
animation, 262-268
audio, 253-258
Cool Talk, 268-271
defined, 8
Microsoft NetMeeting, 271-272
PowWow program, 272
video, 258-262
HyperPage program, 326
hypertext, 4-5
defined, 8-9
links, 4

I

Ichat by Ichat, 357-358
icons
bullets, 177-178
thumbnails, 177-178
Web page, 177-178
idea testing, 55-57

ideas, generating, 33
identifiers, server, 121
image <IMG> tag, 167
  ALIGN attribute, 169-172
  alignment options, 169 -172
  ALT attribute, 167-168
  BORDER attribute, 173-174
  DYNSRC attribute, 261
  HEIGHT attribute, 168-169
  HSPACE attribute, 173
  LOOP attribute, 261
  LOWERS attribute, 172
  SRC attribute, 167
  VSPACE attribute, 173
  WIDTH attribute, 168-169
Image Canvas size, changing, 412-413
image maps, 276
  clickable, 276
  client-side, 277
  home page insertion, 280-285
  hot links, 277-278
  sizing/shaping, 284
image sources, HTML document reference, 188
IMAGE.TPL file, presentations, 319
images
  alignment, 188-189
  background, 74-77, 162
  bandwidth used, 420
  capturing, 163-164
  changing size in screen shots, 412-413
  default (256 colors) depth, 180
  external, 175-177
  GIF format support, 163, 166
  home page insertion, 280-285
  hot areas, 284
  icon, 177-178
  inline, 165-175
  JPEG format support, 163, 166
  list bullets, 192-193

  response time, 74
  theme matching, 74
  tiling, 162
  total number of colors, 420
  transparent backgrounds, 178-179
  white space, 189
implementation, super users, 405
implementing, Intranet 405-430
includes, Web servers support criteria, 83-85
Index Server 1.1 program, 129
INDEX.HTM file, presentations, 317
information
  distribution, intranet advantages, 9-11
  just-in-time, 18
  organizational files, 135-158
  ownership, plug-ins, 351
  sharing, broadcasting, 374-380
  spreadsheet files, 150-156
  word processing files, 137-150
information access, 184-222
  human resources Web pages, 194-205
  internal page links, 184-194
  product description Web page, 184-194
inline images, 165-175
  alignment, 169-172
  borders, 173-174
  browser nonsupport alternate text display, 167-168
  conversions, 166
  interlaced, 166
  low-resolution, 172
  non-interlaced, 166
  sizing, 168-169
  text separations, 173
  thumbnail links, 174-175
  white space, 173
input <INPUT> tag
  attributes, 231
  form input, 231
  hidden attribute, 231

maxlength attribute, 232
name attribute, 231
password attribute, 233
size attribute, 231-232
type attribute, 231
installation
Cold Fusion program, 208
plug-ins, 342-347
interactive Web pages, 130, 226-250
interactivity, two-way communications, 18-19
interfaces, text-base versus graphical, 11
interlaced GIF files, 166
internal Web pages, 14-15
Internet
information distribution applications, 5
intranet advantages/differences, 13-20
Internet Explorer, plug-in configuration, 338
Internet Factory
Communications/Commerce Builder, Cold Fusion support, 206
interpreted applications, CGI, 286
Intersolv DataDirect ODBC pack, 207
Intranet Cafe, 428
intranet
alternatives, 20
authoring, 499-510
benefits, 12-13
business-use policy, 21
communication media advantages, 9-11
defined, 12
departmental value issues, 22
engineering department manual storage, 17-18
financial information services, 16
firewalls, 386
gatekeepers, 23-24
helper applications, 347-349
human resource services, 15-16
interactivity, 18-19

issues, 20-25
just-in-time information, 18
local authors, 24
marketing/selling to the boss, 37
mission statement, 20-21
multiplatform support, 9-11
newspaper comparisons, 24
organization selling, 37
organizational models, 30-33
organizational services, 15-16
page approval guidelines, 22-24
planning, 33-36
plug-ins, 347-349
policies and procedures manual, 21
project plan, 36-37
security, 383-404
standard browser interface, 11
storyboarding, 49-55
system requirements, 38-39
task completion advantages, 16-17
telephone policies, 21
user base survey form, 40-42
versus catalog information distribution, 10
versus CD-ROM information distribution, 9-11
versus Internet, 13-20
Webcompare, 118
Webmaster, 23
IP address, servers, 121
IS (Information Services), plug-in technical responsibility, 350
IS (Information Systems) service, intranet advantages, 19-20
ISO-Latin-1 character set, copyright symbols, 193-194
IT (Information Technology), plug-in recommendations, 348
item lists, HTML document, 191
Iterated Systems, ClearFusion, 260

J

JavaScript, 256-258
  numbered file approach, 257-258
Jetform Corporation, Jetform Webfiller, 358-359
job opportunities Web area, 194-205
  application forms, 196
  general inquiries, 196
  job titles listings, 195-196
  personnel file form, 196-198
job titles listings, 195-196
jobs listings, 146
JPEG file format, 27
  browser support, 163, 166
  presentation slide compression, 316-317
just-in-time information, 18

K

KeyView by FTP Software, 359-360
Knowledge Engineering, MacZilla, 368

L

LAN (Local Area Network), firewalls, 386
languages, Perl, 287
launching, Web servers criteria, 81-83
layout tags, development, 308
LCD panel, presentation resolutions, 310
levels, headings, 190
libraries, audio/video, 262
line break <BR> tag, 189
line breaks, HTML document, 189
linear structure, navigation model, 47-48
link checkers, 418-426
link verificaton application/service, Doctor HTML, 419-425
links
  audio/video libraries, 262
  Click Here avoidance, 54

  hypertext, 4
  mailto URL, 297
  PowerPoint slides, 314-315
  slide objects, 318
  subject matter relevancy, 54
  thumbnail images, 174-175
  Web page, 26-27
list item <LI> and </LI> tag, 191
list tags, 454-462
lists
  images as bullets, 192-193
  scrolling, 236-239
  unordered, 191
Live 3D by Netscape, 363-364
LMSOFT, HyperPage plug-in, 326
local authors, 24
logging, Web servers criteria, 81-83
logical style tags, 452-453
logs, server configuration changes, 127
loops, foreach, 293
Lotus ScreenCam program, 320-321
low-resolution images, 172
LView Pro program, 166
Lynx browser, 6
Lynx, VT100 terminal emulation, 6

M

Macintosh, Netscape Navigator plug-in configuration, 337-338
Macromedia
  AppletAce program, 264-268
  Shockwave, 330, 366-367
MacZilla by Knowledge Engineering, 368
mailto URL, 297
MAIN.DBM file, Cold Fusion program, 214-217
manuals
  color or black and white?, 413
  information storage, 17-18

intranet policies and procedures, 21
making, 415
screen shots, 409-414
training, 409-415
MapEdit program, 277-285
FLORIDA.HTM file, 278
home page image, 280-285
hot links, 277-278
image selection, 277
MAPUSA.GIF file, 277
MAPUSA.GIF file, MapEdit program, 277
marketing
beta testing, 406-407
dreamer, 34-35
free stuff with information, 429
Intranet, 405-430
Intranet cafe, 428
Intranet open house, 429
paper advertising, 429
promotion, 428
trade shows, 428
trainers, 409
mastheadings, 72-73
menus, drop-down, 236-239
message integrity, SSL, 398
message privacy, SSL, 398
meta <META> tag
client-pulls, 321-322
HTML documents, 283
methods
CGI, 286-287
GET, 286-287
POST, 286-287
Microcom Carbon Copy/Net, 356-357
Microsoft Active Server Pages, 130
Microsoft ActiveMovie plug-in, 329-330
Microsoft Authenticode Security Technology, 345
Microsoft Excel Viewer add-on, 152-154

Microsoft FrontPage 97, 198, 507-508
Microsoft Internet Assistants, 25
Microsoft Internet Explorer, 6-7, 309-310, 408
Excel file postings, 151-152
frames, 66-67
layout tags, 308
opening text files, 135-136
presentation font size adjustment, 311
proprietary HTML tags, 11
RealAudio Player installation, 343-344
tags, 492-498
versus Netscape Navigator, 440
Microsoft Internet Information Server (IIS), 96-99
Cold Fusion support, 206
Crystal Reports program, 129
features, 129-130
FrontPage program, 130
Index Server 1.1, 129
installation, 128
NetShow, 129
Microsoft NetMeeting, 271-272
Microsoft Office 97, 25
Microsoft PowerPoint, 313-320
Microsoft PowerPoint Animation Player & Publisher, 329, 362-363
Microsoft Web site, 465
Microsoft's Site Builders Workshop, 261
mid files, MIME type, 256
MIDI file format, 255
MIME (Multipurpose Internet Mail Extensions) type, 334-335
described, 334-335
mid files, 256
Netscape Navigator files, 335-336
Miracle Toys, Florida sales office image, 163
Mirage program, 326-327
mission statement, 20-21, 33-34
movies, plug-ins, 336

MPEG file format, 254, 259-260

multiplatform support, World Wide Web, 9-11

multiple input forms, 239

mutual authentication, SSL, 398-399

N

navigation controls, project design/layout, 65-66

navigation models, 44-49
  hierarchical structure, 44-47
  linear structure, 47-48
  mixed hierarchical/linear structure, 48-49

navigation
  frames, 66-67
  Web pages, 59-60

Ncompass ActiveX, 354-357

NCSA Mosaic browser, 11-12

Nelson, Ted, 4

Net Nanny, 404

Net-Install by 20/20 Software Inc., 360-361

Net-Scene, PointPlus, 327, 361-362

NetMeeting program, 271-272

NetObjects Fusion, 508-509

Netscape
  Cool Talk program, 268-271
  Live 3D, 363-364
  SDK (Software Development Kit), 349

Netscape 1.2, upgrade needs, 439

Netscape Administration Kit, 389-390

Netscape Communications/Commerce Server, Cold Fusion support, 206

Netscape Enterprise Server, 99-103, 118-128
  Cold Fusion support, 206
  Configure Administration, 122-127
  Netscape Server Selector, 118-122

Netscape FastTrack Server, 103-106, 206

Netscape Navigator, 6-7, 309-310, 408
  background HTML tag, 74

  color palette, 161-162
  embed <EMBED> tag, 330-332
  enterprise data file, 389
  extensions, 492-498
  future directions, 400-401
  HTML 3.2, 453-498
  Macintosh plug-in configuration, 337-338
  MIME/file-types, 335-336
  Ncompas Labs, 355
  Netscape Administration Kit, 389-390
  opening files, 135-138
  opening image files, 163-164
  plug-in setup, 335-338
  presentation font size adjustment, 312
  proprietary HTML tags, 11
  proxy servers, 390-391
  RealAudio Player installation, 342
  spreadsheet format viewers, 152-154
  versus Microsoft Internet Explorer, 440
  Windows plug-in configuration, 337

Netscape Navigator Gold, 25, 500-507
  WYSIWYG (What You See Is What You Get) interface, 25

Netscape Plug-in Finder page, 355-356

Netscape PowerStart Web site, 243-248

Netscape Server Selector
  Administration Server, 118-122
  bind address, 120
  document root, 122
  resolve IP address, 121
  server identifier, 120-121
  server name, 119
  server port, 120

Netscape SuiteSpot server, security, 401-402

NetShow program, 129

NEW.DBM file, Cold Fusion program, 219-221

newspapers, intranet comparisons, 24

NeXT workstation, browsers, 4

noembed <NOEMBED> tag, presentation plug-ins, 331
non-interlaced GIF files, 166
Norton AntiVirus Scanner, 341
numbers, hexadecimal, 75
NZBs, 63

O

O'Reilly WebSite server, Cold Fusion support, 206
object links, slides, 318
one-step Web creation, PointCast I-Server, 377
online help, 415
online publications, The Red Herring, 465
open house, publicize Intranet, 429
opening tags, HTML basics, 441-442
operating system criteria, Web servers, 80-81
option <OPTION> tag, 237-238
organizational models, 30-33
  combined centralized/decentralized approach, 32-33
  decentralized approach, 30
organizations, information sources, 135-158
output styles, presentations, 316
overhead projectors, 308
Overs, Mark, 63
ownership issues, content, 427

P

PageMaker program, PDF file conversion, 156
pages
  content ownership issues, 426-427
  FAQ, 414-418
  length of time to load, 420
Paint Shop Pro 163, 409-414
  crosshairs, 411
  customizing screen shots, 410

paragraph <P> tag, 188-189
paragraphs, starting new, 188
passwords
  authentication, 125
  forms, 233
  security conventions, 388
patches, security, 388
PATH_INFO environment variables, 291
PCN (PointCast Network), 374-380
  PointCast I-Server, 374-379
PDF (Portable Document Format) files, 339
  Adobe Acrobat, 156-157
Perl language, CGI applications, 287
Perl scripts
  comments, 292
  content type, 293
  displaying environment variables, 291-294
  foreach loops, 293
  Perl interpreter server location, 292
  pound sign (#) character, 292
  print lines, 293
  slash+n (\n) print line characters, 293
personnel file form, job opportunities Web area, 196-198
Photoshop, animated GIFs, 263
physical styles tags, 453-454
pictures, plug-ins, 336
PKUNZIP program, 342
planning
  author, 36
  brainstorming, 39-40
  graphic artist, 35-36
  idea generation, 33
  marketing dreamer, 34-35
  mission statement, 33-34
  programmer, 36
  task definitions, 34
plug-ins, 347-349, 353-372
  3D and animation, 362-368
  accessibility, 351-353

ActiveX, 354-357
ActiveX controls, 346
adding new, 346
Adobe Acrobat Reader, 157, 339-341
Adobe Acrobat Reader 3.0 Beta, 354
ASAP Webshow, 323-324
Astound Web Player, 324
Audio and Video, 368-371
business and utility, 354-361
Carbon Copy/Net, 356-357
CineWeb, 261
ClearFusion, 260-261
compression, 336
content responsibility, 350
described, 323, 334
embed <EMBED> tag, 330-332
embedding in presentations, 330-332
Formula Graphics Multimedia System, 324-325
FutureSplash, 363
HyperPage, 326
Ichat, 357-358
information ownership, 351
installation, 342-347
Internet Explorer configuration, 338
Jetform Webfiller, 358-359
KeyView, 359-360
Live 3D, 363-364
MacZilla, 368
Microsoft ActiveMovie, 329-330
Microsoft PowerPoint Animation Player & Publisher, 329
Mirage, 326-327
Net-Install, 360-361
Netscape Navigator configurations, 337-338
Netscape Navigator setup, 335-338
noembed <NOEMBED> tag, 331
pictures/movies, 336
PointPlus, 327, 361-362
PowerMedia plug-in, 327-328
PowerPoint Animation Player and Publisher, 362-363
PowerPoint for Netscape Navigator viewer, 315
presentations, 361-362
ProtoPlay, 365
RealAudio Player, 341-347
RealSudio, 369
SDK (Software Development Kit), 349
Shockwave, 330, 366-367
sound files, 336
support issues, 348
technical responsibility, 350
VDOLive, 369-370
video, 260-261
Viscape, 367-368
ViVoActive Player, 370-371
Web development process, 348-353
Web sites, 353
PointCast I-Server, 374-379
client updating, 378-379
company news, 377
hardware requirements, 378-379
one-step Web creation, 377
security, 377-378
SmartScreen, 375-377
PointPlus by Net-Scene, 327, 361-362
policies and procedures manual, 21
port number, servers, 123
ports, server, 120
POST method, CGI, 286-287
pound sign (#) character, Perl scripts comment interpreter, 292
PowerMedia plug-in, 327-328
PowerPoint Animation Player and Publisher, 362-363
PowerPoint program
Netscape Navigator viewer, 315
presentation to HTML converter, 316-317
presentations, 313-320
slide object links, 318

PowWow program, 272
presentation methods, Web pages, 43-44
presentations, 308-332
 automatic slide shows, 321-322
 browser advantages, 309
 client pulls, 319, 321-322
 color versus black and white, 413
 creation, 310-313
 display resolutions, 310
 embedding plug-ins, 330-332
 font size adjustments, 311
 GI-BOB.PPT file, 315
 hyperlinks, 311
 IMAGE.TPL file, 319
 INDEX.HTM file, 317
 Lotus ScreenCam program, 320-321
 Microsoft PowerPoint, 313-320
 monitor screen resolutions, 317
 output styles, 316
 overhead projectors, 308
 plug-ins, 3551-362
 projection TV system resolutions, 310-311
 slide object links, 318
 slide shows, 308
 supported slide formats, 316
 TEXT.TPL file, 319
 TSLD001.HTM, 317
print lines, Perl scripts, 293
Process Software Purveyor server, Cold Fusion support, 206
product description Web page, 184-194
programmer, 36
programs
 ActiveX, 354-357
 Adobe Acrobat, 156-157
 Adobe Acrobat Reader, 157, 339-341
 Adobe Acrobat Reader 3.0 Beta, 354
 Adobe Distiller, 156
 ASAP Webshow, 323-324
 Astound Web Player, 324
 Carbon Copy/Net, 356-357
 CineWeb, 261
 ClearFusion, 260-261
 Cold Fusion, 205-211
 Collage Capture, 163
 Cool Talk, 268-271
 Crystal Reports, 129
 DeBabelizer, 166
 Formula Graphics Multimedia System, 324-325
 FrontPage, 130, 198
 Futuresplash, 343, 363
 Hi Jaak, 163
 HyperPage, 326
 Ichat, 357-358
 Index Server 1.1, 129
 Jetform Webfiller, 358-359
 KeyView, 359-360
 Live #D, 363-364
 Lotus ScreenCam, 320-321
 LView Pro, 166
 Macromedia AppletAce, 264-268
 MacZilla, 368
 MapEdit, 275-285
 Microsoft ActiveMovie, 329-330
 Microsoft Excel Viewer, 152-154
 Microsoft FrontPage, 130, 198
 Microsoft Internet Explorer, 408
 Microsoft NetMeeting, 271-272
 Microsoft PowerPoint, 313-320
 Microsoft PowerPoint Animation Player & Publisher, 329, 362-363
 Mirage, 326-327
 Net-Install, 360-361
 Netscape Navigator, 408
 NetShow, 129
 Norton AntiVirus Scanner, 341
 Paint Shop Pro, 163, 409-414
 PKUNZIP, 342
 PointPlus, 327, 361-362

PowerMedia, 327-328
PowWow, 272
ProtoPlay, 365
RealAudio, 341-347, 369
ROOMS 2.2, 357
screen-capture, 163
Shockwave, 330, 366-367
VDOLive, 369-370
Viscape, 367-368
VivoActive Player, 370-371
WinZip, 342
Progressive Networks, RealAudio, 379
project design/layout, 62-78
  alternate text-only display, 74
  background images, 74-77
  colors, 74-77
  departmental relationships, 62
  directional sense, 70-72
  frames navigation, 66-67
  graphics display, 64
  images, 74
  mastheadings, 72-73
  navigation controls, 65-66
  themes, 63
  visitor short attention span, 64-70
  Web shop guidelines, 62
  white space, 68-70
project plan, 36-37
projection TV system, presentation resolutions, 310-311
promotions
  Intranet Cafe, 428
  marketing, 428
proprietary tags, 465
protocol designators, servers, 119
protocols
  SSL (Secure Sockets Layer), 396-400
  TCP/IP, 392-393
  Web servers support criteria, 83-85
ProtoPlay by Altia, 365

prototypes
  development, 57-59
  text-only, 57-59
proxy servers, 390-391
  application gateway, 386
public-key
  certificates, 395
  cryptography, 394-395
publications, Essential Office 97, 313
publicity release, 405
Purveyor WebServer, 107-110

Q

queries, database, 204-205
query form, Cold Fusion program, 208-209
QUERY_STRING environment variable, 286, 288
quick reference cards, 409
quick-loading, Web page optimization, 179-180
QuickTime video player, 260

R

rack rate, 63
radio buttons, forms, 233-235
RadMedia, PowerMedia plug-in, 327-328
rating criteria, Web servers, 80-89
raw coding, 435-439
RealAudio by Progressive Networks, 369
RealAudio Intranet Server, 254
RealAudio player, 254, 341-347
  Microsoft Internet Explorer installation, 343-344
  Netscape Navigator installation, 342
records, 214-221
REMOTE_ADDR environment variable, 289
REMOTE_HOST environment variable, 289

REMOTE_IDENT environment variables, 289

REMOTE_USER environment variable, 289

REQUEST_METHOD environment variable, 288

requirements, system, 38-39

resolutions

monitor screen, 317

presentation display, 310

projection TV system, 310-311

resolve IP address, servers, 121

RESULTS.DBM file, Cold Fusion program, 212-213

RGB numeric values, colors, 76

rich text documents, file format, 465

rollout, planning, 428

root directory

saving files to, 211

servers, 122

routers, screening, 386

S

S/MIME (Secure Multipart Internet Mail Encoding), security, 393

screen captures

customizing, 410

for manuals, 409-414

Paint Shop Pro, 409-414

programs, 163

screen shots

adding text, 411-414

background color 413

changing image size, 412-413

screen-capture programs, 163

screening router, firewall security, 386

SCRIPT_NAME environment variable, 291

scripts, CGI, 19, 226-230

scrolling lists, forms, 236-239

SDK (Software Development Kit), Netscape plug-ins, 349

SEARCH.HTML file, Cold Fusion program, 210-211

security

Access Control Lists, 388

application gateway, 386

browsers, 389-391

CGI scripts, 387

challenges, 392-393

communication, 385-386

compromising, 384-385

cryptography, 393-396

digital certificates, 391-392, 395

firewalls, 386

intranet, 383-404

intranet versus Internet, 384-385

Net Nanny, 404

Netscape Administration Kit, 389-390

Netscape Navigator future directions, 400-401

password conventions, 388

patches, 388

PointCast I-Server firewall, 377-378

proxy servers, 390-391

S/MIME (Secure Multipart Internet Mail Encoding), 393

screening router, 386

server placement, 385

SET (Secure Electronic Transactions), 393

SSL (Secure Sockets Layer), 392, 396-400

TCI/IP protocol, 392-393

username conventions, 388

Web servers criteria, 85-86

select <SELECT> tag

forms drop-down menus, 236-239

multiple attribute, 239

size attribute, 239

separators, text/images, 173 , 189

server identifier, 121

server names, aliases, 119

server port, 120

SERVER_ADMIN, environment variable, 290

SERVER_NAME environment variable, 290

SERVER_PORT environment variable, 291

SERVER_PROTOCOL environment variables, 291

SERVER_SOFTWARE environment variable, 290

servers
access logins, 126
administration user, 123
Alibaba, 206
bind address, 120
Bob's Web Server, 349
caching, 386
cgi-bin directory, 230
configuration change logs, 127
CSM Alibaba, 206
dedicated, 387
EMWAC HTTPS, 206
hostnames to allow, 124-125
identifiers, 121
Internet Factory Communications/
    Commerce Builder, 206
Microsoft IIS, 206
Microsoft Internet Information, 128-130
MID file settings, 256
Netscape Communications/Commerce
    Server, 206
Netscape Enterprise, 206
Netscape FastTrack, 206
Netscape SuiteSpot, 401-402
O'Reilly WebSite, 206
physical security, 385
PointCast I-Server, 374-379
port number, 123
Process Software Purveyor, 206
protocol designators, 119
proxy, 386, 390-391
RealAudio Intranet Server, 254

resolve IP address, 121
Spry Safety Web, 206
SurfWatch ProServer, 402-403
user names, 125

services
financial information, 16
human resources, 15-16
IS (Information Systems), 19-20
organizational, 15-16

SET (Secure Electronic Transactions), security, 393

SETUP.EXE file, Cold Fusion program, 208

Shockwave by Macromedia, 330, 366-367

simple forms, 231-232

slash+n (\n) characters, Perl scripts, 293

SLD001.HTM file, 317

slide shows, 308
self-running, 321-322

slides
client pulls, 319, 321-322
JPEG compression, 316-317
monitor screen resolutions, 317
object links, 318
PowerPoint links, 314-315
supported formats, 316

SmartScreen, PointCast I-Server, 375-377

Software Publishing Corporation, ASAP Webshow, 323

sound files, plug-ins, 336

specifications, HTML 3.2, 308

Spinnaker Web Server, 110-114

spreadsheet files, 150-156
Excel postings, 151-152

Spry Safety Web server, Cold Fusion support, 206

SpyGlass, SurfWatch ProServer, 402-403

SSL (Secure Sockets Layer), 392, 396-400
described, 396
handshake, 398-399
hash functions, 398

message integrity, 398
message privacy, 398
mutual authentication, 398-399
public-key technology, 397-398
server activation, 123
versions, 400
standards, ITU X.509, 395-396
storage, content, 26-28
storyboarding, 49-55
flow diagrams, 52-55
stages, 50-51
Web flow diagrams, 52-55
Strata, Mirage plug-in, 326-327
streaming audio, 254
Strom, David, 118
structure
hierarchical, 44-47
mixed hierarchical/linear/linear, 48-49
styles, presentation output, 316
summary content, HTML document, 191
super users, 406
SuperScape, Viscape, 367-368
support issues, plug-ins, 348
SurfWatch ProServer server, security, 402-403
survey forms, user base, 40-42
symbols, copyright, 193-194
symmetric-key cryptography, 394-395
system requirements, 38-39
Cold Fusion program, 206-208
PointCast I-Server, 378-379

T

tags
alternate text <ALT>, 74
anchor <A HEF>, 174-175
anchor <A> and </A>, 190
background color <BGCOLOR>, 75
blink <BLINK>, 227
body <BODY>, 160-161, 188
embed <EMBED>, 255-256, 330-332

font <FONT>, 189
<FORM>, 230
headings <H2> and </H2>, 190
horizontal rule <HR>, 191, 238
HTML, 443-462, 467-492
HTML 3.2, 457-392
hyperlink reference <A HREF>, 190
image <IMG>, 167
input <INPUT>, 231
layout development, 308
line break <BR>, 189
list, 454-462
list item <LI> and <LI>, 191
logical style, 452-453
meta, 283
meta <META>, 321-322
Microsoft Internet Explorer, 492-498
Netscape Navigator, 492-498
noembed <NOEMBED>, 331
opening/closing < > brackets, 75
option <OPTION>, 237-238
paragraph <P>, 188-189
physical styles, 453-454
proprietary, 465
select <SELECT>, 236-239
textarea <TEXTAREA> and
</TEXTAREA> 240-243
unordered list <UL> and </UL>, 191
target audience, 351-353
tasks, definitions, 34
TCP/IP
protocol, security, 392-393
stacks, 408
TELNET, 5
template files
DBML Cold Fusion program, 212
MAIN.DBM, 214-217
NEW.DBM, Cold Fusion program, 219-221
UPDATE.DBM, Cold Fusion program,
217-219

templates
Cold Fusion program,
212-221
job opportunities Web area, 194-205
presentation files, 319
product description, 187-194
text
add to screen shots, 414
style tags (HTML), 452-454
text boxes
forms, 232
sizing, 232
text files
HTML table conversion, 154-156
opening in browsers, 135-137
word processor file format conversions,
137-141
text separations, images, 173, 189
text-only prototype, 57-59
TEXT.TPL file, presentations, 319
**textarea <TEXTAREA> and
</TEXTAREA> tag, 240-243**
attributes, 240
cols, 240
name, 240
rows, 240
themes
departmental, 63
Web pages, 26
thumbnails
icons, 177 -178
images as links, 174-175
tiled images, backgrounds, 162
time frames, beta testing, 408
titles
colors, 189
font sizing, 189
HTML document, 189
trade shows, internal, 428
trainers, help at open house, 429

training users, 407-409
transparencies, 308
transparent backgrounds, 166
images, 178-179
TSLD001.HTM file, 317
tweaking Web pages, 438
txt file extnsion, 135

U

underlined text, hyperlinks, 8
unfollowed hyperlinks, colors, 77
UNIX, text-only browsers, 6
UNIX-based server criteria, 81
unordered list, 191
unordered list <UL> tag and </UL>, 191
**UPDATE.DBM file, Cold Fusion program,
217-219**
URL (Uniform Resource Locator), 8, 43
URL, mailto, 297
Usenet newsgroups, 5
user base survey, 40-42
user ID, 388
user names
security conventions, 388
server access, 125
users
acquiring, 407-408
beta testing, 408
training, 409

V

VDOLive by VDOnet, 369-370
**vector-based animation, FutureSplash player,
343**
vendors, application security patch, 388
video, 258-262
AVI format, 260
ClearFusion plug-in, 260-261
clips, 258-259

formats, 259-260
libraries, 262
plug-ins, 260-261
QuickTime player, 260
video clips, 258-259
Video for Windows (AVI format), 260
viewers, spreadsheet format, 152-154
viruses, downloads, 341
**Viscape by SuperScape,
367-368**
visited link color, 77
visitors
sense of direction, 70-72
short attention span, 64-70
VivoActive Player by Vivo Software, 370-371
VT100 terminal emulation, 6

W

**W3C (World Wide Web Consortium) Web
site, 439**
WAV file format, 254-255
Web development process, plug-ins, 348-353
Web diagrams, storyboarding, 52-55
Web pages
approval guidelines, 22-24
authoring tools, 500-510
AVI file insertion, 261
described, 42-43
external images, 175-177
hierarchical structure, 44-47
icons, 177-178
idea testing, 55-57
inline images, 165-175
interactive, 130, 226-250
internal versus external, 14-15
linear structure, 47-48
links, 26-27
mailto URL, 297
mixed hierarchical/linear structure, 48-49

presentation methods, 43-44
product description, 184-194
quick set up, 416-418
quick-load optimizing, 179-180
set up FAQ page, 416-418
theme, 26
thumbnail image links, 174-175
tweaking, 438
Web servers
Alibaba, 89-93
choosing, 80-89
EMWAC freeware HTTPS, 93-96
includes criteria, 83-85
launching/logging criteria, 81-83
Microsoft Internet Information Server, 96-99
Netscape Enterprise Server, 99-103, 118-128
Netscape FastTrack Server, 103-106
operating system criteria,
80-81
proprietary features criteria, 86-89
protocol support criteria,
83-85
Purveyor WebServer, 107-110
rating criteria, 80-89
security criteria, 85-86
Spinnaker Web Server,
110-114
UNIX-based criteria, 81
WebSite Professional,
114-117
Windows NT CPUs criteria, 81
Web shop, 62
Web sites
ActiveX by Ncompass, 355, 357
Adobe Acrobat Reader, 157, 339
Alibaba server, 92
Allaire's Cold Fusion program, 205
ASAP Webshow, 323
Astound Web Player, 324
Atlanta Olympic Games, 68-70

Carbon Copy/Net, 357
CERN, 5
CineWeb plug-in, 261
ClearFusion plug-in, 261
Cold Fusion Support Forum, 206
color palette, 76
color schemes palette, 76-77
CSE 3310 HTML Validator, 425
Doctor HTML, 419, 421
EMWAC freeware HTTPS server, 96
Formula Graphics Multimedia System, 324-325
FrontPage 97, 25
FutureSplash, 363
Gamelan, 355
GIF construction set, 263-264
Headspace, 255
HTML editors, 25
HyperPage, 326
HyperThink, 14
Ichat, 358
Java applets, 355
Jetform Webfiller, 359
Keyview, 360
Live 3D, 364
Lotus ScreenCam Player, 320
Lynx (DOS version), 6
MacZilla, 368
Mark Overs sculpture, 63
Matt's Script Archives, 229
mechanical.com, 66-67
Microsoft, 25, 99, 465
Microsoft ActiveMovie, 329-330
Microsoft Authenticode Security Technology, 345
Microsoft Excel Viewer, 152-154
Microsoft FrontPage, 198
Microsoft FrontPage 97, 507-508
Microsoft NetMeeting, 271

Microsoft PowerPoint Animation Player & Publisher, 329
Microsoft PowerPoint for Netscape Navigator viewer, 315
Microsoft's Site Builders Workshop, 261
Mirage, 326-327
Net Nanny, 404
Net-Install, 360
NetObjects Fusion, 508
Netscape, 25, 103, 106
Netscape business templates, 198
Netscape Navigator Gold, 25
Netscape Overview, 309
Netscape PowerStart, 243-248
NWU Computer Learning Lab, 226
Paint Shop Pro, 409-414
Pathfinder, 226
PDF (Portable Document Format) files, 340-341
plug-ins, 323, 353
PointCast, 374
PointPlus program, 327, 362
PowerMedia, 327-328
PowerPoint Animation Player and Publisher, 362-363
PowWow, 272
Prima, 309
ProtoPlay, 365
Purveyor WebServer, 110
QuickTime video player, 260
RealAudio player, 254, 341, 369
Red Herring, The, 465
Shockwave, 330, 366
Spinnaker Web Server, 110-114
SurfWatch ProServer, 403
VDOLive, 369
VeriSign, 392
Viscape, 367
VivoActive, player, 370

W3 (World Wide Web Consortium), 6
W3C, 439
WebSite Professional, 114-117
Webster University, 13-14
Word Internet Assistant, 508
Webmaster, 23
WebSite Professional, 114-117
white space, 68-70
 images/text separations, 173, 189
whiteboarding, 268
whitepaper, 146
width tags, images, 420
Windows NT CPUs server criteria, 81
Windows, Netscape Navigator plug-in configuration, 337
WinZip program, 342
Word Internet Assistant, 508
word processing files, 137-150
 HTML formatting, 141-145
 human resource, 137-141
 saving as text files, 137-141
workstations
 intranet hardware requirements, 38-39
 NeXT, 4

WWW (World Wide Web)
 communication media advantages, 9-11
 development, 4-5
 GUI (Graphical User Interface), 5-8
 HTML (Hypertext Markup Language), 8
 hypertext, 8-9
 least common denominator development, 11
 multiplatform support, 9-11
 Netscape/Internet Explorer analogy, 11-12
 text-based versus graphical interface, 11
 URL (Uniform Resource Locator), 8
WYSIWYG (What You See Is What You Get), 25

X

X.509 ITU standard, digital certificates, 395-396

Z

zipped files, 342

To Order Books

Please send me the following items:

Quantity	Title	Unit Price	Total
_____	_____	$ _____	$ _____
_____	_____	$ _____	$ _____
_____	_____	$ _____	$ _____
_____	_____	$ _____	$ _____
_____	_____	$ _____	$ _____

Subtotal $ _____

Deduct 10% when ordering 3-5 books $ _____

7.25% Sales Tax (CA only) $ _____

8.25% Sales Tax (TN only) $ _____

5.0% Sales Tax (MD and IN only) $ _____

Shipping and Handling* $ _____

Total Order $ _____

Shipping and Handling depend on Subtotal.

Subtotal	Shipping/Handling
$0.00–$14.99	$3.00
$15.00–$29.99	$4.00
$30.00–$49.99	$6.00
$50.00–$99.99	$10.00
$100.00–$199.99	$13.50
$200.00+	Call for Quote

Foreign and all Priority Request orders:
Call Order Entry department
for price quote at 916/632-4400
This chart represents the total retail price of books only
(before applicable discounts are taken).

By Telephone: With MC or Visa, call 800-632-8676, 916-632-4400. Mon-Fri, 8:30-4:30.
WWW {http://www.primapublishing.com}

Orders Placed Via Internet E-mail {sales@primapub.com}
By Mail: Just fill out the information below and send with your remittance to:

Prima Publishing
P.O. Box 1260BK
Rocklin, CA 95677

My name is _____

I live at _____

City_____ State_____ Zip _____

MC/Visa#_____ Exp._____

Check/Money Order enclosed for $_____ Payable to Prima Publishing

Daytime Telephone _____

Signature _____

Other books from Prima Publishing, Computer Products Division

ISBN	Title	Price	Release Date
0-7615-0801-5	ActiveX	$40.00	Available Now
0-7615-0680-2	America Online Complete Handbook and Membership Kit	$24.99	Available Now
0-7615-0915-1	Building Intranets with Internet Information Server and FrontPage	$45.00	Available Now
0-7615-0417-6	CompuServe Complete Handbook and Membership Kit	$24.95	Available Now
0-7615-0849-X	Corporate Intranet Development	$45.00	Available Now
0-7615-0692-6	Create Your First Web Page in a Weekend	$29.99	Available Now
0-7615-0503-2	Discover What's Online!	$24.95	Available Now
0-7615-0693-4	Internet Information Server	$40.00	Available Now
0-7615-0815-5	Introduction to ABAP/4 Programming for SAP	$45.00	Available Now
0-7615-0678-0	Java Applet Powerpack	$30.00	Available Now
0-7615-0685-3	Javascript	$35.00	Available Now
0-7615-0901-1	Leveraging Visual Basic with ActiveX Controls	$45.00	Available Now
0-7615-0755-8	Moving Worlds	$35.00	Available Now
0-7615-0690-X	Netscape Enterprise Server	$40.00	Available Now
0-7615-0691-8	Netscape FastTrack Server	$40.00	Available Now
0-7615-0852-X	Netscape Navigator 3 Complete Handbook	$24.99	Available Now
0-7615-0759-0	Professional Web Design	$40.00	Available Now
0-7615-0773-6	Programming Internet Controls	$45.00	Available Now
0-7615-0780-9	Programming Web Server Applications	$40.00	Available Now
0-7615-0063-4	Researching on the Internet	$29.95	Available Now
0-7615-0686-1	Researching on the World Wide Web	$24.99	Available Now
0-7615-0695-0	The Essential Photoshop Book	$35.00	Available Now
0-7615-0752-3	The Essential Windows NT Book	$27.99	Available Now
0-7615-0689-6	The Microsoft Exchange Productivity Guide	$24.99	Available Now
0-7615-0769-8	VBScript Master's Handbook	$45.00	Available Now
0-7615-0684-5	VBScript Web Page Interactivity	$40.00	Available Now
0-7615-0903-8	Visual FoxPro 5 Enterprise Development	$45.00	Available Now
0-7615-0814-7	Visual J++	$35.00	Available Now
0-7615-0383-8	Web Advertising and Marketing	$34.95	Available Now
0-7615-0726-4	Webmaster's Handbook	$40.00	Available Now
0-7615-0751-5	Windows NT Server 4 Administrator's Guide	$50.00	Available Now